THE
PREACHER'S
OUTLINE & SERMON
BIBLE®

PSALMS II

(PSALMS 42–106)

THE
PREACHER'S
OUTLINE & SERMON
BIBLE®

OLD TESTAMENT

NEW INTERNATIONAL VERSION

Leadership Ministries Worldwide
Chattanooga, TN

Please address all requests for information or permission to:
Leadership Ministries Worldwide
PO Box 21310
Chattanooga, TN 37424-0310
Ph.# (423) 855-2181 FAX (423) 855-8616 E-Mail info@outlinebible.org
http://www.outlinebible.org

Library of Congress Catalog Card Number: 00133499
International Standard Book Number: 978-1-57407-271-6

LEADERSHIP MINISTRIES WORLDWIDE
CHATTANOOGA, TN

Printed in the United States of America

2   3   4   5   6   17   18   19   20   21

DEDICATED

To all the men and women of the world
who preach and teach the Gospel of
our Lord Jesus Christ and
to the Mercy and Grace of God

- Demonstrated to us in Christ Jesus our Lord.

  In him we have redemption through his blood, the forgiveness of sins, in accordance with the riches of God's grace. (Ep.1:7)

- Out of the mercy and grace of God, His Word has flowed. Let every person know that God will have mercy upon him, forgiving and using him to fulfill His glorious plan of salvation.

  For God so loved the world that he gave his one and only Son, that whoever believes in him shall not perish but have eternal life. For God did not send his Son into the world to condemn the world, but to save the world through him. (Jn.3:16-17)

  This is good, and pleases God our Savior, who wants all men to be saved and to come to a knowledge of the truth. (1 Ti.2:3-4)

6/10

The Preacher's Outline & Sermon Bible®

is written for God's servants to use in their study, teaching, and preaching of God's Holy Word...

- to share the Word of God with the world.
- to help believers, both ministers and laypersons, in their understanding, preaching, and teaching of God's Word.
- to do everything we possibly can to lead men, women, boys, and girls to give their hearts and lives to Jesus Christ and to secure the eternal life that He offers.
- to do all we can to minister to the needy of the world.
- to give Jesus Christ His proper place, the place the Word gives Him. Therefore, no work of Leadership Ministries Worldwide—no Outline Bible Resources—will ever be personalized.

ACKNOWLEDGMENTS AND BIBLIOGRAPHY

Every child of God is precious to the Lord and deeply loved. And every child as a servant of the Lord touches the lives of those who come in contact with him or her or the ministry he or she is associated with. The writing ministries of the following servants have touched this work, and we are grateful that God brought their writings our way. We hereby acknowledge their ministry to us, being fully aware that there are many others down through the years whose writings have touched our lives and who deserve mention, but whose names have faded from our memory. May our wonderful Lord continue to bless the ministries of these dear servants—and the ministries of us all—as we diligently labor to reach the world for Christ and to meet the desperate needs of those who suffer so much.

THE REFERENCE WORKS

Archer, Gleason L. *A Survey of Old Testament Introduction.* Chicago, IL: Moody Press, 1994.

Baker, Warren and Eugene Carpenter. *The Complete Word Study Dictionary—Old Testament.* Chattanooga, TN: AMG Publishers, 2003. WORDsearch CROSS e-book.

Baxter, J. Sidlow. *Explore the Book.* Grand Rapids, MI: Zondervan Publishing House, 1960.

Benware, Paul N. *Survey of the Old Testament Revised.* Chicago, IL: Moody Press, 1993.

Bromiley, Geoffrey W., Editor, et. al. *The International Standard Bible Encyclopedia.* Grand Rapids, MI: Eerdmans Publishing Co., 1988.

Brown-Driver-Briggs' Hebrew Definitions. Electronic Edition STEP Files: Parsons Technology, 1999.

Bullock, C. Hassell. *Encountering the Book of Psalms: A Literary and Theological Introduction.* Grand Rapids, MI: Baker Academic, 2001.

Burlingname, Michael. *Lincoln Observed: The Civil War Dispatches of Noah Brooks.* Baltimore, MD: Johns Hopkins University Press, 1998.

Cambron, Mark G. *Bible Doctrines: Beliefs That Matter.* Grand Rapids, MI: Zondervan Publishing House, 1954.

Carpenter, Eugene E. and Philip W. Comfort. *Holman Treasury of Key Bible Words: 200 Greek and 200 Hebrew Words Defined and Explained.* Nashville, TN: B & H Publishing Group, 2000. WORDsearch CROSS e-book.

Criswell, W.A., ed. *The Believer's Study Bible.* Nashville, TN: Thomas Nelson, 1991. Electronic Edition STEP Files, Parsons Technology, 1998.

Davidson, A.B. *Hebrew Syntax.* Edinburgh, Scotland: Morrison and Gibb, 1896.

DeYoung, Donald B. *Astronomy and the Bible: Questions and Answers.* Grand Rapids, MI: Baker Book House, 2000.

Edersheim, Rev. Alfred. *A History of the Jewish Nation After the Destruction of Jerusalem Under Titus. Third Edition ed.* London: Longmans, Green, and Co., 1896. WORDsearch CROSS e-book.

Elwell, Walter A. and Philip W. Comfort. *Tyndale Bible Dictionary.* Wheaton, IL: Tyndale House Publishers, 2001. WORDsearch CROSS e-book.

ESV Study Bible, English Standard Version. Wheaton, IL: Crossway Bibles, 2008.

Futato, Mark D. *Interpreting the Psalms: An Exegetical Handbook.* Grand Rapids, MI: Kregel, 2007.

Geisler, Norman L. *A Popular Survey of the Old Testament.* Grand Rapids, MI: Baker Academic, 1977.

Gilbrant, Thoraf and Gregory A. Lint, eds. *The Complete Biblical Library: The Old Testament Hebrew-English Dictionary.* Springfield, MO: World Library Press Inc, 1998. WORDsearch CROSS e-book.

Green, Jay Patrick, Sr. *The Interlinear Bible.* Peabody, MA: Hendrickson Publishers, Inc., 2005.

Haldeman, I.M. *Bible Expositions, Volume I.* Grand Rapids, MI: Baker Book House, 1964.

Halley, Henry H. *Halley's Bible Handbook.* Grand Rapids, MI: Zondervan Publishing House, 1965.

Harris, R. Laird, Gleason L. Archer, Bruce K. Waltke, eds. *Theological Wordbook of the Old Testament.* Chicago, IL: Moody Press, 1980. WORDsearch CROSS e-book.

HCSB Study Bible. Nashville, TN: B & H Publishing Group, 2010.

History of the Jewish Nation. WORDsearch CROSS e-book.

Hodgkin, A.M. *Christ in All the Scriptures.* London: Pickering & Inglis, 1907.

Holman Bible Dictionary. Nashville, TN: B & H Publishing Group, 1991. WORDsearch CROSS e-book.

Holy Bible, The: The Amplified Bible. La Habra, CA: The Lockman Foundation, 1987.

Holy Bible: The Open Bible Edition. Nashville, TN: Thomas Nelson, 1975.

James, Fleming. *Thirty Psalmists: Personalities of the Psalter.* New York: Seabury Press, 1965.

Jensen, Irving L. *Jensen's Survey of the Old Testament.* Chicago, IL: Moody Press. 1978.

Josephus, Flavius. *The Works of Flavius Josephus.* Translated by William Whiston. Hartford, CN: S. S. Scranton, 1905. WORDsearch CROSS e-book.

Kee, Howard C., ed. *Cambridge Annotated Study Bible.* Great Britain: Cambridge University Press, 1994. Electronic Edition STEP Files: Parsons Technology, 1998.

Kelly, Page H. *Biblical Hebrew: An Introductory Grammar.* Grand Rapids, MI: Eerdmans, 1992.

Longman, Tremper, III. *How To Read the Psalms.* Downers Grove, IL: InterVarsity Press, 1988.

Life Application Study Bible. Grand Rapids, MI: Zondervan Publishing House, 2000.

MacArthur, John. *The MacArthur Study Bible.* Nashville, TN: Thomas Nelson, 1997.

_____. *The Murder of Jesus: A Study of How Jesus Died.* Nashville, TN: Thomas Nelson, 2000.

ACKNOWLEDGMENTS AND BIBLIOGRAPHY

THE REFERENCE WORKS
(continued)

Merrill, Eugene H. *An Historical Survey of the Old Testament Second Edition.* Grand Rapids, MI: Baker Book House, 1991.

Morgan, G. Campbell. *The Unfolding Message of the Bible: The Harmony and Unity of the Scriptures.* Westwood, NJ: Fleming H. Revell, 1961.

Nave, Orville J. *Nave's Topical Bible: A Digest of the Holy Scriptures.* Grand Rapids, MI: Baker Book House, 1984.

Nelson Study Bible, The. Nashville, TN: Thomas Nelson, 1997. Electronic Edition STEP Files: Parsons Technology, 1999.

NLT Parallel Study Bible. Carol Stream, IL: Tyndale House, 2011.

Orr, James, ed. *International Standard Bible Encyclopedia.* Electronic Edition STEP Files, Parsons, Technology, 1998.

Peterson, Eugene H., trans. *The Message: The Bible in Contemporary Language.* Colorado Springs, CO: Nav-Press, 2002. WORDsearch CROSS e-book.

Pratico, Gary D. and Miles V. Van Pelt. *Basics of Biblical Hebrew Grammar: Second Edition.* Grand Rapids, MI: Zondervan Publishing House, 2001.

Renn, Stephen D., ed. *Expository Dictionary of Bible Words.* Peabody, MA: Hendrickson Publishers, Inc., 2005.

Rice, John R. *Christ in the Old Testament.* Murfreesboro, TN: Sword of the Lord, 1969.

Rogers, Adrian. *Adrian Rogers Legacy Bible, The.* Memphis, TN: Love Worth Finding Ministries, 2009.

Ryrie, Charles C. *The Ryrie Study Bible.* Chicago, IL: Moody Press, 1976.

Scofield, C.I., ed. *The Scofield Study Bible.* New York: Oxford University Press, 1945.

Smith, William. *Smith's Bible Dictionary: Comprising Antiquities, Biography, Geography, Natural History, Archaeology and Literature.* Philadelphia, PA: A.J. Holman & Co., 1901. WORDsearch CROSS e-book.

Steidl, Paul M. *The Earth, the Stars, and the Bible.* Grand Rapids, MI: Baker Book House, 1979.

Strauss, Lehman. *In God's Waiting Room: Learning through Suffering,* 1984. Used by permission.

Strong, James. *Strong's Concordance.* Austin, TX: WORDsearch Corp., 2007. WORDsearch CROSS e-book.

_____. *Strong's Exhaustive Concordance.* Electronic Edition STEP Files: Parsons Technology, 1998.

_____. *Strong's Greek Hebrew Dictionary.* WORDsearch CROSS e-book.

Swindoll, Charles R. *Christ's Agony and Ecstasy.* Waco, TX: Word Publishing, 1982.

Thompson, Frank C., ed. *The Thompson Chain-Reference Bible, Second Improved Edition.* Indianapolis, IN: B.B. Kirkbride, 1990.

Unger, Merrill. *The New Unger's Bible Dictionary.* Chicago, IL: Moody Press, 1957. WORDsearch CROSS e-book.

_____. *Unger's Bible Handbook.* Chicago, IL: Moody Press, 1967.

Vine, William E. *Vine's Expository Dictionary of Old Testament and New Testament Words.* Nashville, TN: Thomas Nelson, 1940. WORDsearch CROSS e-book.

Water, Mark, ed. *Encyclopedia of Bible Facts.* Chattanooga, TN: AMG Publishers, 2004. WORDsearch CROSS e-book.

Wigram, George V. *Wigram's Hebrew Verb Parsings*, public domain, n.d.

Willmington, Harold L. *Willmington's Bible Handbook.* Wheaton, IL: Tyndale House, 1997.

_____. *Willmington's Guide to the Bible.* Wheaton, IL: Tyndale House, 1981.

Zodhiates, Spiros. *AMG Complete Word Study Dictionary.* Chattanooga, TN: AMG Publishers, 2003. WORDsearch CROSS e-book.

THE COMMENTARIES

Alden, Robert. *Psalms: Songs of Devotion.* Chicago, IL: Moody Press, 1974.

AMG Concise Bible Commentary. WORDsearch CROSS e-book.

Anders, Max and Steven J. Lawson. *Holman Old Testament Commentary: Psalms 1–75.* Nashville, TN: B & H Publishing Group, 2003.

_____. *Holman Old Testament Commentary: Psalms 76–150.* Nashville, TN: B & H Publishing Group, 2003.

Barnes, Albert. Barnes *Notes on the Old Testament: Psalms, Volume 1.* Grand Rapids, MI: Baker Books, Electronic Edition STEP Files, Parsons Technology, n.d.

Barton, Bruce B.; Grant R. Osborne; and Philip W. Comfort, eds. *The Life Application Bible Commentary.* Carol Stream, IL: Tyndale House Publishers, Inc. WORDsearch CROSS e-book.

Boice, James Montgomery. *An Expositional Commentary–Psalms, Volume 2: Psalms 42–106.* Paperback ed. Grand Rapids, MI: Baker Books, 1994. WORDsearch CROSS e-book.

Broyles, Craig C. *New International Biblical Commentary: Psalms.* Peabody, MA: Hendrickson Publishers, 1999.

Brumfield, J.C. *The Shadow: An Exposition, Interpretation, and Application of the 23rd Psalm.* Los Angeles, CA: World Wide Publishing Co., 1950.

Calvin, John. *Calvin's Commentaries.* WORDsearch CROSS e-book.

Carson, D. A., G. J. Wenham, J. A. Motyer, R. T. France, eds. *New Bible Commentary: 21st century edition.* Leicester, England: Inter-Varsity Press, 1994.

Clarke, Adam. *Adam Clarke's Commentary on the Old Testament.* Electronic Edition STEP Files: Parsons Technology, 1999.

Davis, John J. *The Perfect Shepherd: Studies in the Twenty-Third Psalm.* Grand Rapids, Baker Book House, 1979.

ACKNOWLEDGMENTS AND BIBLIOGRAPHY

THE COMMENTARIES
(continued)

Delitzsch, Franz. *Commentary on the Old Testament—Volume 5: Psalms.* Edinburgh, Scotland: T. & T. Clark, 1891. WORDsearch CROSS e-book.

Dilday, Russell. *Preacher's Commentary on 1, 2 Kings.* Nashville, TN: Word Publishing, 1987, 2003.

Douglas, J.D., ed. *New Commentary on the Whole Bible: Old Testament Volume.* Wheaton, IL: Tyndale House, n.d. Electronic Edition STEP Files, Parsons Technology, 1998.

Exell, Joseph S. The Psalms, Vol.I, "The Biblical Illustrator." Grand Rapids, MI: Baker Book House, 1954.

_____. The Psalms, Vol.II, "The Biblical Illustrator." Grand Rapids, MI: Baker Book House, 1955.

Gaebelein, Arno C. *The Book of Psalms: A Devotional and Prophetic Commentary.* Neptune, NJ: Loizeaux Brothers, 1939.

Gaebelein, Frank E., ed. *The Expositor's Bible Commentary with the New International Version, Vol.5.* Grand Rapids, MI: Zondervan Publishing House, 1991.

Gill, John. *Gill's Exposition of the Entire Bible.* Biblos.com. Psalms. 2011. Web. 14 May 2012. http://gill.bible commenter.com/psalms/13.html

Gray, James M. Christian *Workers' Commentary on the Old and New Testaments.* New York: Fleming H. Revell Co., 1915.

Henderson, George. *The Pearl of Psalms.* Edinburg, Scotland: B. McCall Barbour, n.d.

Henry, Matthew. *Matthew Henry's Commentary on the Whole Bible, Vol. III: Job to Song of Solomon.* Old Tappan, NJ: Fleming H. Revell Co., n.d. WORDsearch CROSS e-book.

House, Paul R. *1, 2 Kings.* "The New American Commentary," Vol.8. Nashville, TN: B & H Publishing Group, 1995.

Ironside, H.A. *H. A. Ironside Commentary – Psalms.* San Diego, CA: Horizon Press, 1908. WORDsearch CROSS e-book.

Jamieson, Robert, A.R. Fausset, and David Brown. *Commentary on the Whole Bible.* Grand Rapids, MI: Zondervan Publishing House, n.d. WORDsearch CROSS e-book.

Kaiser, Walter C., Jr. *The Journey Isn't Over: The Pilgrim Psalms for Life's Challenges and Joys.* Grand Rapids, MI: Baker Book House, 1993.

Kee, Howard C., ed. *Cambridge Annotated Study Bible.* Great Britain: Cambridge University Press, 1994. Electronic Edition STEP Files: Parsons Technology, 1998.

Keil, C.F. and F. Delitzsch. *Commentary on the Old Testament*, WORDsearch CROSS e-book.

Keller, Phillip. *A Shepherd Looks at Psalm 23.* Grand Rapids, MI: Zondervan Publishing House, 1970.

Ketchum, Robert T. *I Shall Not Want: An Exposition of Psalm Twenty-three.* Chicago, IL: Moody Press, 1953.

Kidner, Derek. *Tyndale Old Testament Commentaries: Psalms 1–72.* Downers Grove, IL: InterVarsity Press, 2009.

_____. *Tyndale Old Testament Commentaries: Psalms 73–150.* Downers Grove, IL: InterVarsity Press, 2009.

Kirkpatrick, Alexander Francis. *The Book of Psalms.* Memphis, TN: General Books, 2010.

Knight, George *A.F. Psalms: Volume 1.* Philadelphia, PA: Westminster Press. 1982.

Kretzmann, Paul E. *The Popular Commentary of the Bible*, public domain, 1921. WORDsearch CROSS e-book.

Lane, Eric. *Focus on the Bible Commentary.* Scotland, UK: Christian Focus Publications, 2006. WORDsearch CROSS e-book.

Leupold, H.C. *Exposition of the Psalms.* Grand Rapids, MI: Baker Book House, 1969.

Lewis, C.S. *Reflections on the Psalms.* San Diego, CA: Harcourt Brace & Co., 1986.

Lockyer, Herbert, Sr. *Psalms: A Devotional Commentary.* Grand Rapids, MI: Kregel, 1993.

MacDonald, William. *Believer's Bible Commentary.* Edited by Art Farstad. Nashville, TN: Thomas Nelson, 1995.

Maclaren, Alexander. *Expositions of the Holy Scripture: Psalms I to XLIX.* Grand Rapids, MI: Baker Book House, n.d.

_____. The Psalms, Volume II, Psalms 39–89. "The Expositor's Bible." London: Hodder and Stoughton, nd.

_____. *The Psalms, Volume III, Psalms 90–150.* "The Expositor's Bible." New York: Funk and Wagnalls, 1900.

McGee, J. Vernon. *Thru the Bible with J. Vernon McGee.* Nashville, TN: Thomas Nelson, 1983. WORDsearch CROSS e-book.

Meyer, F.B. *The Shepherd's Psalm.* New York: Fleming H. Revell Co., 1895.

Morgan, G. Campbell. *Notes on the Psalms.* Westwood, NJ: Fleming H. Revell Co., 1947.

Murphy, James G. *A Critical and Exegetical Commentary on the Book of Psalms.* Minneapolis, MN: James Family Publishing, 1977.

Patterson, Richard D. and Hermann J. Austel. *1, 2 Kings.* "The Expositor's Bible Commentary," Vol.4. Grand Rapids, MI: Zondervan Publishing House, 1988.

Perowne, J.J. Stewart. *The Book of Psalms: A New Translation with Introductions and Notes.* London: George Bell and Sons, 1880.

Phillips, John. *Exploring Psalms, Volume 1.* "John Phillips Commentary Series." WORDsearch CROSS e-book.

_____. *Exploring Psalms, Volume 2.* "John Phillips Commentary Series." WORDsearch CROSS e-book.

_____. *Exploring the Scriptures.* Chicago, IL: Moody Press, 1970.

Poole, Matthew. *Matthew Poole's Commentary on the Holy Bible.* Peabody, MA: Hendrickson Publishers, 1985. WORDsearch CROSS e-book.

Robinson, Haddon W. *Psalm Twenty-Three.* Chicago, IL: Moody Press, 1968.

_____. *The Good Shepherd.* Chicago, IL: Moody Press, 1968.

Scroggie, W. Graham, *The Psalms: Psalms I to CL.* Old Tappan, NJ: Fleming H. Revell Co., 1965.

ACKNOWLEDGMENTS AND BIBLIOGRAPHY

THE COMMENTARIES
(continued)

Spence, H. D. M. and Joseph S. Exell. *The Pulpit Commentary*. WORD*search* CROSS e-book.

Spurgeon, Charles. *Treasury of David*. Peabody, MA: Hendrickson Publishers, Inc., 1990.

Waltke, Bruce K. and James M. Houston. *The Psalms as Christian Worship: A Historical Commentary*. Grand Rapids, MI: William B. Eerdmans, 2010.

Walton, John H., Victor H. Matthews, Mark W. Chavalas. *The IVP Bible Background Commentary – Old Testament*. Downers Grove, IL: InterVarsity Press, 2000. WORDsearch CROSS e-book.

Walvoord, John F. and Roy B. Zuck, eds. *The Bible Knowledge Commentary: An Exposition of the Scriptures by Dallas Seminary Faculty*. Colorado Springs, CO: Victor Books, 1985. WORD*search* CROSS e-book.

Wesley, John. *Wesley's Notes on the Bible*. Biblos.com. Psalms. 2004–2011. Web. 4 April 2012. http://wes.biblecommenter.com/psalms/1.html

Wiersbe, Warren W. *Meet Yourself in the Psalms*. Colorado Springs, CO: David C. Cook, 1983.

_____. *The Bible Exposition Commentary – Wisdom and Poetry*. Colorado Springs, CO: David C. Cook, 2004. WORDsearch CROSS e-book.

Williams, Donald. *Psalms 1–72*. "The Preacher's Commentary," Volume 13. Nashville, TN: Thomas Nelson Publishers, 2002. Reprinted by permission. All rights reserved.

_____. *Psalms 73–150*. "The Preacher's Commentary," Volume 14. Nashville, TN: Thomas Nelson Publishers, 2002. Reprinted by permission. All rights reserved.

Wilson, T. Ernest. *The Messianic Psalms*. Port Colborne, Ontario: Gospel Folio Press, 1997

ABBREVIATIONS

&	= and		O.T.	= Old Testament	
Bc.	= because		p./pp.	= page/pages	
Concl.	= conclusion		Pt.	= point	
Cp.	= compare		Quest.	= question	
Ct.	= contrast		Rel.	= religion	
e.g.	= for example		Rgt.	= righteousness	
f.	= following		Thru	= through	
Illust.	= illustration		v./vv.	= verse/verses	
N.T.	= New Testament		vs.	= versus	

THE BOOKS OF THE OLD TESTAMENT

Book	Abbreviation	Chapters	Book	Abbreviation	Chapters
GENESIS	Gen. or Ge.	50	Ecclesiastes	Eccl. or Ec.	12
Exodus	Ex.	40	The Song of Solomon	S. of Sol. or Song	8
Leviticus	Lev. or Le.	27	Isaiah	Is.	66
Numbers	Num. or Nu.	36	Jeremiah	Jer. or Je.	52
Deuteronomy	Dt. or De.	34	Lamentations	Lam.	5
Joshua	Josh. or Jos.	24	Ezekiel	Ezk. or Eze.	48
Judges	Judg. or Jud.	21	Daniel	Dan. or Da.	12
Ruth	Ruth or Ru.	4	Hosea	Hos. or Ho.	14
1 Samuel	1 Sam. or 1 S.	31	Joel	Joel	3
2 Samuel	2 Sam. or 2 S.	24	Amos	Amos or Am.	9
1 Kings	1 Ki. or 1 K.	22	Obadiah	Obad. or Ob.	1
2 Kings	2 Ki. or 2 K.	25	Jonah	Jon. or Jona.	4
1 Chronicles	1 Chron. or 1 Chr.	29	Micah	Mic. or Mi.	7
2 Chronicles	2 Chron. or 2 Chr.	36	Nahum	Nah. or Na.	3
Ezra	Ezra or Ezr.	10	Habakkuk	Hab.	3
Nehemiah	Neh. or Ne.	13	Zephaniah	Zeph. or Zep.	3
Esther	Est.	10	Haggai	Hag.	2
Job	Job or Jb.	42	Zechariah	Zech. or Zec.	14
Psalms	Ps.	150	Malachi	Mal.	4
Proverbs	Pr.	31			

THE BOOKS OF THE NEW TESTAMENT

Book	Abbreviation	Chapters	Book	Abbreviation	Chapters
MATTHEW	Mt.	28	1 Timothy	1 Tim. or 1 Ti.	6
Mark	Mk.	16	2 Timothy	2 Tim. or 2 Ti.	4
Luke	Lk. or Lu.	24	Titus	Tit.	3
John	Jn.	21	Philemon	Phile. or Phm.	1
The Acts	Acts or Ac.	28	Hebrews	Heb. or He.	13
Romans	Ro.	16	James	Jas. or Js.	5
1 Corinthians	1 Cor. or 1 Co.	16	1 Peter	1 Pt. or 1 Pe.	5
2 Corinthians	2 Cor. or 2 Co.	13	2 Peter	2 Pt. or 2 Pe.	3
Galatians	Gal. or Ga.	6	1 John	1 Jn.	5
Ephesians	Eph. or Ep.	6	2 John	2 Jn.	1
Philippians	Ph.	4	3 John	3 Jn.	1
Colossians	Col.	4	Jude	Jude	1
1 Thessalonians	1 Th.	5	Revelation	Rev. or Re.	22
2 Thessalonians	2 Th.	3			

HOW TO USE
The Preacher's Outline & Sermon Bible®

Follow these easy steps to gain maximum benefit from The POSB.

1 SUBJECT HEADING

2 MAJOR POINTS

3 SUBPOINTS
&
SCRIPTURE

4 COMMENTARY

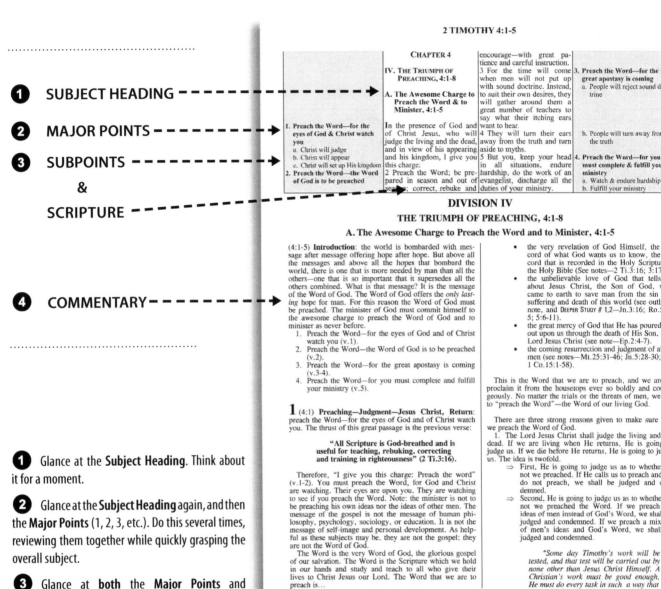

1 Glance at the **Subject Heading**. Think about it for a moment.

2 Glance at the **Subject Heading** again, and then the **Major Points** (1, 2, 3, etc.). Do this several times, reviewing them together while quickly grasping the overall subject.

3 Glance at **both** the **Major Points** and **Subpoints** together while reading the **Scripture**. Do this slower than Step 2. Note how these points sit directly beside the related verse and simply restate what the Scripture is saying—in Outline form.

4 Next read the **Commentary**. Note that the *Major Point Numbers* in the Outline match those in the Commentary. When applicable, a small raised number (**DS1, DS2, etc.**) at the end of a Subject Heading or Outline Point directs you to a related **Deeper Study** in the Commentary (not shown here).

Finally, read the **Thoughts** and **Support Scripture** (not shown).

As you read and re-read, pray that the Holy Spirit will bring to your attention exactly what you should preach and teach. May God bless you richly as you study and teach His Word.

The POSB contains everything you need for sermon preparation:

1. **The Subject Heading** describes the overall theme of the passage and is located directly above the Scripture (keyed *alphabetically*).

2. **Major Points** are keyed with an outline *number* guiding you to related commentary. Note that the Commentary includes *"Thoughts"* (life application) and abundant Supporting Scriptures.

3. **Subpoints** explain and clarify the Scripture as needed.

4. **Commentary** is fully researched and developed for every point.

   • **Thoughts (in bold)** help apply the Scripture to real life.

   • **Deeper Studies** provide in-depth discussions of key words or phrases.

*Woe to me if I do not
preach the gospel!*
(1 Co.9:16)

TABLE OF CONTENTS
PSALMS II
(PSALMS 42–106)

OUR APPROACH TO UNDERSTANDING PSALMS

We at Leadership Ministries Worldwide are excited and deeply grateful to God as we present to you the book of *Psalms*. When it is finished, *The Preacher's Outline and Sermon Bible* will be completed for all sixty-six books of God's Holy Word. Additionally, God's people have been asking for *Psalms* for years; it is the most anticipated book of the commentary series.

Psalms is the most personal and most often read book of the Old Testament, if not the entire Bible. No book of the Bible has meant more to God's people throughout the generations. Truly, it is a "practical theology of vivid human experience."[1] Most of us read the psalms devotionally or to secure God's help in times of personal need. Because of this, we have taken a different approach to outlining *Psalms* than we have taken in any other book of the Bible: the psalms are being outlined to each of us *personally*. That is, the personal pronoun "you" is being used, as though God's Word is speaking directly to *you*. By doing this, God's instructions and help (His presence, guidance, and power) are directly applied to you personally. What you must do to secure God's help is more immediately seen as you face the varied circumstances and situations of life. Just glance at the outline of *Psalms*, chapter by chapter, and you will see how it is directed to you personally.

In the outlines, we have tried to apply the psalms to specific situations of life. These applications are certainly not the only ones that can be made. God's Word is alive, and it is sharp enough to delve into the deepest parts of our souls and spirits, thereby helping us with the deepest needs in our lives (He.4:12). As you study *Psalms,* allow God's Spirit to guide you and speak to *your* heart, making the application to the needs of *your* life.

Jesus and the apostles recognized the power of the psalms in our lives, referring to them more than any other book of Scripture. As we have outlined and explained *Psalms*, our prayer has been that God's Spirit will work through us to make each psalm as easy to understand and apply as possible by you, God's dear child and beloved servant. As you study *Psalms*, we not only pray that your preaching and teaching will be changed, but that your life will be changed, as ours have been in the process of producing this work.

KEYS TO UNDERSTANDING PSALMS

1. *Understand how the psalms are organized. Psalms* is actually a volume consisting of five books. The 150 psalms that are inspired by God's Holy Spirit are grouped into five books:

➢ Book I   1-41
➢ Book II   42-72
➢ Book III   73-89
➢ Book IV   90-106
➢ Book V   107-150

a. The five books of *Psalms* correspond to the five books of the Pentateuch (the first five books of the Bible, the *Torah* or books of the Law, authored by Moses). Jewish tradition states that David intentionally began the organization of the psalms in this fashion in order to give Israel a hymnal that corresponded with the Law of God to His chosen nation.

➢ Book I   Genesis
➢ Book II   Exodus
➢ Book III   Leviticus
➢ Book IV   Numbers
➢ Book V   Deuteronomy

English preacher and author J. Sidlow Baxter explains how these books are connected:

> *The first group, corresponding with Genesis, has much to say about man. The second group, corresponding with Exodus, has much to say about deliverance. The third group, corresponding with Leviticus, has its emphasis in the Asaph psalms, upon the sanctuary. The fourth group, corresponding with Numbers, and beginning with Psalm 90, the prayer of Moses, stresses the time when unrest and wandering will cease in the coming worldwide kingdom when the nations shall bow to God's King. The fifth group, corresponding with Deuteronomy, has much of thanksgiving for the Divine faithfulness, and lays much emphasis upon the word of the Lord, as, for instance, in the longest of all the psalms, which has for its theme the written word of the Lord.*[2]

b. Each of the five books concludes with a doxology—an outburst of praise and glory to God (41:13; 72:18-19; 89:52; 106:48; 150:1-6). Psalm 150 is placed as a conclusion to both the fifth book and the entire psalter.

c. Within each book, certain sections are grouped by author or by theme. Two examples are the psalms of the Sons of Korah (42-49) and the Songs of Degrees or Ascent (120-134), which were sung by the Israelites as they journeyed up to Jerusalem and the temple.

---

[1]   J. Sidlow Baxter. *Explore the Book.* (Grand Rapids, MI: Zondervan, 1960), p.83.

[2]   Ibid., p.87.

2. *Understand the types or categories of the psalms.* Scholars vary as to the categories of psalms and how the specific psalms are assigned to these categories. Many psalms fit into more than one category. Additionally, individual psalms or a small number of psalms may comprise other categories than the ones listed below. However, the great majority of the psalms fit into one of the following six categories:

a. *Praise*—these psalms are hymns composed for the primary purpose of exalting God. The works and character of God are emphasized. Psalms 8, 9, 33, 92, 103, and 145 are examples of praise psalms.

b. *Lament or complaint*—in these psalms, the author presents his—or his nation's—troubles or burdens to God. At times, the author expresses frustration with God Himself. Usually, a cry for God's help is included and confidence in God is expressed. Examples are Psalms 13, 22, 42, 60, and 69.

c. *Kingdom or enthronement*—these are psalms that proclaim and celebrate the truth that the LORD reigns over the earth, its nations, and its people. Psalms 2, 47, 93, and 96 are examples.

d. *Confession or penitential*—most of these psalms were written by David. Though fewer in number than the other categories, psalms of confession are especially significant because of our need to understand how to confess our sins to God. Psalms 32, 38, and 51 are examples.

e. *Imprecatory (cursing) or judgment*—Psalms 5, 11, 35, 69, and 109 are examples of imprecatory psalms. Many people struggle to understand and accept these psalms in which the author prays— sometimes violently and graphically—for the destruction or judgment of his enemies. How can it be right for God's people to pray this way, especially when some of these prayers seem to be contrary to God's law and the teachings of Christ? In reading and understanding the imprecatory psalms, it is important to remember the following:

1) These are prayers for protection. In most cases when David prayed for the destruction of his enemies, they were aggressively seeking his life. In many of these psalms, they were also trying to overthrow Israel.

2) The Israelites were the people of the covenant. The heathen nations that opposed them worshipped idols. Therefore, an attack on Israel was an attack on God and His people and His purpose to send both His son and His Holy Word to the world through Israel.

3) David was God's anointed king for His covenant people. When Saul, Absalom, and others sought to destroy David, they were seeking to thwart God's will.

4) These are prayers for justice, not vengeance. David and others who prayed for the destruction of their enemies were not seeking personal revenge. They desired that justice be served on evildoers. Their prayers are pleas for God to vindicate *Himself* as the Judge of the earth.

5) In offering these prayers, the psalmists were obeying the command of Scripture, that no person should take vengeance against others, but rather commit all judgment to the LORD.

6) The psalms are brutally honest, teaching us that we can pour out our hearts to God. This is one of the reasons the imprecatory psalms are a part of inspired Scripture. They reveal to us the emotions of the human heart against those who do evil toward us and others. Because of our strong emotions, we do not always pray as we ought. The New Testament teaches us that God's Spirit intercedes for us at such times (Ro.8:26-27).

7) The imprecatory psalms emphasize God's holiness and the severity of His judgment against sin. "When one properly understands the nature of a holy and sinless God, he, with the psalmists, must cry out against the iniquity that so terribly offends him. This does not mean that the sinner himself is to be hated, but that sin is despicable and unrepentance unforgivable. To the Old Testament mind, the distinction between the two may not have been as clear as it is this side of the cross."[3]

8) The psalmists lived before the cross and the teachings of Christ. When Jesus came, He taught us a better way to pray for our enemies (Mt.5:44; 23:37; 1 Pe.2:21-23). Still, the New Testament sanctions our praying for God's justice and judgment of evildoers (1 Co.16:22; Ga.1:8-9; 5:12; 2 Ti.4:14; Re.6:10). When we, as New Testament believers, pray for the Lord to protect us and judge evildoers, we should also pray for God to bring them to repentance, and for them to come to Christ and be saved.

9) Many of the imprecatory psalms are prophetic, pointing to the future day when God will judge all unrighteousness and ungodliness in men (Ro.1:18). "There is usually a strong eschatological [end times] sense involved in the imprecatory psalms. That is, the poet is not so much invoking and expecting the immediate judgment of God as he is looking forward to the day of the Lord when all unrepentant sinners must be dealt with according to their impiety toward God."[4]

---

3 Eugene H. Merrill. *An Historical Survey of the Old Testament Second Edition.* (Grand Rapids, MI: Baker Book House, 1991), p.221.

4 Ibid., p.221.

f. *Thanksgiving*—these psalms offer thanks to God for deliverance, answered prayer, or some other blessing. They often include an offering or sacrifice, or the fulfilling of a vow to the LORD. Many scholars group them with the psalms of praise rather than as a distinct group. Examples of thanksgiving psalms are 21, 30, 34, 40, and 66.

3. *Understand the spiritual purpose of the psalms.* The psalms teach us how to pray and relate to God in every circumstance and situation of life. A relationship with God is a two-way relationship: God reveals Himself to us, and we reveal ourselves to Him. The psalms teach us the latter. Some scholars have noted that the categories of psalms mirror the model prayer given to us by Jesus (Mt.6:9-13). Additionally, the psalms illustrate Ph.4:6-7:

Do not be anxious about anything, but in everything, by prayer and petition, with thanksgiving, present your requests to God. And the peace of God, which transcends all understanding, will guard your hearts and your minds in Christ Jesus (Ph.4:6-7).

When we take our problems to God in prayer, His peace will flood our hearts, resulting in our praise to Him.

4. *Understand the titles and headings of the psalms.* While there is much criticism of the authenticity of these notes, they are a part of the text of the Hebrew Bible and are considered to be authoritative by Jesus and the New Testament (Mk.12:35-37; Ac.2:29-35; 13:34-37).[5] Therefore, the *POSB* regards them as authoritative, and the commentary is written in light of them.

5. *Understand the musical terms used in many of the psalms.* These terms give instructions on the performance and purpose of the psalm. They are listed below, along with a brief explanation of each and an example of where it appears. Where deemed to be helpful, terms are discussed in more detail in the commentary.

   a. *To the chief musician*—indicates that it was to be used in temple worship (Ps.4).

   b. *Al-taschith*—literally means *do not destroy*; how it applied to the performance of the song is unknown. The term may have been the name of a popular tune to which the psalm was to be performed (Ps.57).

   c. *Alamoth*—to be sung by female or high-pitched voices (Ps.46).

   d. *Gittith*—literally means *winepresses*; how it applied to the performance of the song is unknown. It may mean that the song was to be performed in the autumn of the year at the Feast of Tabernacles, or it may also have been a stringed instrument (Ps.8).

   e. *Mahalath*—the meaning of this term is unclear. It may refer to a musical instrument, a popular tune to which the psalm was to be performed, or a direction to the way the psalm was to be performed.

   f. *Maschil* or *maskil*—for instruction or teaching (Ps.32).

   g. *Michtam* or *miktam*—meaning unknown; thought to be a meditation worthy of remembrance or a song of atonement (Ps.16).

   h. *Mizmor*—to be accompanied by musical instruments; usually translated as *a psalm* in the headings (Ps.3).

   i. *Neginoth*—to be accompanied by string instruments (Ps.4).

   j. *Nehiloth*—to be accompanied by wind instruments or flutes (Ps.5).

   k. *Selah*—a musical interlude for the purpose of meditation (Ps.3).

   l. *Sheminith*—means *the eighth* and probably refers to the octave in which it was to be performed. It may also refer to an eight-stringed instrument. Some scholars believe it is a term of contrast to *alamoth* and means that the psalm is to be sung by male or low-pitched voices (Ps.6).

   m. *Shiggaion*—to be sung with intense emotion; a song with an irregular rhythm (Ps.7).

   n. *Shir*—common Hebrew word for song; usually translated as *song* (Ps.18:1).

   o. *Shoshannim*—literally means *lilies*; how it applied to the performance of the song is unknown. It may mean that the song was to be performed in the spring of the year at the Feast of Passover (Ps.45).

   p. *Tehillah*—a song of praise; usually translated as *praise* (Ps.145).

   q. *Tephillah*—a prayer; usually translated as *prayer* (Ps.86).

6. *Understand the names of God in the psalms.* One of the ways God has revealed Himself to us is through His names. In *Psalms,* the specific name of God used is significant and emphasizes God's relationship to His people.

   a. *Jehovah* (usually translated as LORD or GOD) is God's covenant name and emphasizes His faithfulness to His covenant with us.

   b. *El* or *Elohim* (usually translated as God) emphasizes God's power to do all things.

   c. *Adonai* (usually translated as Lord) emphasizes God's authority over us as our Master. Accordingly, it also emphasizes God's commitment to care for us and to meet our needs.

---

5   Derek Kidner. *Tyndale Old Testament Commentaries: Psalms 1-72.* (Downers Grove, IL: InterVarsity Press, 2009), p.47.

THE BOOK OF

PSALMS

AUTHOR: unique from every other book of the Bible, the great book of *Psalms* served as the hymnal of ancient Israel. *Psalms* is the most quoted book in the New Testament and is the most personal book in God's inspired Word. Through the ages, God's people have continually turned to it for comfort, hope, and encouragement in times of need. Like our modern day songbooks, it is the compilation of the work of various authors. The authors of 100 of the 150 psalms are identified in the Scripture.

1. David is identified as the author of 73 of the inspired psalms and may have written others. For many years, critics have opposed the Davidic authorship of many of these psalms, but their arguments are weak and have been easily refuted.[1] Some argue that, just because a psalm is attributed to David, it does not mean that he wrote it. It may have been written *for* David, or it may have been a part of David's personal collection of psalms. Others suggest that some of these songs may have been written *in the style of* David. While it is true that the Hebrew preposition translated *of* David may also be rendered as *for* or *to* David, this is by no means sufficient reason to conclude that David did not write the psalms attributed to him. Scripture overwhelmingly supports David as the primary author of the psalms. Therefore, the *POSB* views the psalms of David as written by David, rather than for him, to him, or in his style.

The historical books of the Old Testament indicate that David was a fascinating character, a man of striking contrasts. Although he was small in stature, he stood head and shoulders above the rest on the battlefield. The courage and confidence in God that possessed him when he dared to face Goliath clung to him throughout the rest of his days. An episode near the end of David's life testifies to the fear he evoked in others. In his twilight years, the sons of Goliath set their sights on David, seeking to avenge the death of their father by slaying Israel's celebrated warrior-king (2 S.21:15-22). *Only in his old age* did these bitter cowards dare come against David, waiting over forty years after the young shepherd had slain their beastly father in the name of the LORD.

David's bravery on the battlefield was rooted in his zeal for the LORD. He fought for the honor of God and His chosen nation, Israel. To him, the armies of Israel were "the armies of the living God" (1 S.17:36). Some critics cannot accept the fact that such a fierce warrior was an intensely spiritual man, a man who could write with the passion for God that characterizes the psalms. They are silenced by no less than God Himself, who described David as "a man after my own heart" (Ac.13:22; 1 S.13:14). David was a man of intense emotions, and his relationship with God reflected the depth of his feelings, emotions that he could not contain. On one occasion he celebrated God so enthusiastically that his wife was embarrassed by his behavior (2 S.6:14-23). In many of the psalms, he spoke to God with a boldness that makes many people cringe. The fervor and freeness that characterized both his praise and his prayers were the outgrowth of David's flaming heart for the LORD.

At the same time, David was a man of the arts, a musician and a poet. As an accomplished harpist in his teenage years, David was sometimes called in to soothe the troubled soul of King Saul with the beautiful melodies that flowed from his skilled hands (1 S.16:14-23). David understood the power of music, both in the human soul and in worship.

He personally organized the choirs and orchestras that performed in the sanctuary, and he invented musical instruments that were used in the worship of the LORD (2 Chr.7:6; Amos 6:5). In his last words, David referred to himself as "the "sweet psalmist of Israel" (2 S.23:1).

Most compelling, however, is the testimony of the New Testament to David's authorship of the psalms:

➢ Jesus Himself affirmed David as the author of Psalm 110 (Mt.22:43-45; Mk.12:36; Lk.20:42-44).

➢ In discussing prophecies regarding Judas, Peter attributed Psalms 41, 69, and 109 to David (Ac.1:15-20).

➢ On the Day of Pentecost, Peter verified that David was the author of Psalms 16 and 110 (Ac.2:25-28, 34-35).

➢ The early church sang that God spoke "by the mouth of [His] servant David" in Psalm 2 (Ac.4:25).

➢ Paul affirmed David as the author of Psalm 32 (Ro.4:6-8), Psalm 69 (11:9), and Psalm 72 (Ro.11:12).

➢ The author of Hebrews revealed that David penned Psalm 95 (He.4:7). More significant, however, is the fact that he referred to the book of *Psalms* by the name "David," confirming that both the Jews and the early church regarded David as the primary author of *Psalms*.

2. *Asaph* was one of the three chief musicians and choir directors in David's court (1 Chr.15:16-19; 16:4-7, 37; 25:1-ff.). He wrote twelve of the inspired psalms (50, 73-83). Some of the psalms attributed to him were most likely written by his descendants, an order of temple musicians who were identified by his name (2 Chr.35:15; Ezr.2:41; 3:10).

3. Eleven inspired psalms (42-49, 84–85, 87) were penned by the *Sons of Korah*. Although their forefather perished because of his rebellion against Moses and Aaron (Nu.16, 26:10-11), Korah's descendants were among the most devoted worshippers of God during David's reign (1 Chr.6:22-44).

4. Of the 1,005 songs written by *Solomon*, three were inspired by the Holy Spirit and are preserved in Scripture: *The Song* of *Solomon*, Psalm 72, and Psalm 127 (1 K.4:29-34).

---

[1] Gleason L. Archer provides a clear, concise refutation of the major arguments against Davidic authorship in his excellent work *A Survey of Old Testament Introduction*.

5. Psalm 90 was written by *Moses* during Israel's 40 years of wandering in the wilderness.

6. *Heman,* the second of David's chief musicians, penned Psalm 88 (1 Chr.6:33; 15:17; 2 Chr.5:12). In addition to his musical abilities, Heman was respected for his wisdom and served as one of David's chief spiritual advisors (1 K.4:31; 1 Chr.25:5; 2 Chr.35:15).

7. Like Heman, *Ethan* was an Ezrahite and was noted for his wisdom (1 Ki.4:31). The third of David's chief musicians, he wrote Psalm 89 (1 Chr.15:17-19). He is probably also the musician referred to as Jeduthun (2 Chr.5:12; Ps.39, 62, 77).

DATE WRITTEN: through the identification of the authors, we know that the majority of the inspired psalms were written during the time of 2 Samuel and 1 Kings, a 100 year period from approximately 1030–930 BC.[2] Obviously, Moses' psalm was written during his lifetime, and, next to Job, is believed to be the oldest portion of Scripture. The time of the writing of many of the anonymous psalms cannot be positively established. Some, like Psalm 137, were apparently written during the Babylonian Exile. Others, such as Psalms 126 and 147, appear to have been penned after the Jews were released from Babylon.

We do not know for certain how and when the book of *Psalms*, as we have it today, was compiled. Like many of our hymnals and songbooks, it was revised over time until it was assembled and completed exactly as God's Spirit would have it. The Divine Superintendent of Scripture moved upon men to compose songs He inspired, and He moved upon men to recognize those songs as inspired and include them in the book of *Psalms.*

It is reasonable to conclude that David compiled the psalms written before and during his life. King Hezekiah, who reigned in Judah about 250 years after David's death, sparked a great revival among the nation (2 Chr.29-31). His burning zeal for God's house and God's Word prompted him to appoint a committee of men to restore the Scripture. Along with *Proverbs,* Hezekiah's men likely added to *Psalms* as well (Pr.25:1). "It seems certain that his was, in all the nation's history, the greatest single agency in compiling and adapting the older Davidic Psalms, and in the composition of new ones. Perhaps this union of collecting and creative work in psalmody is referred to in the mention of 'the words of David, and of Asaph the seer' (2 Chron. 29:30). To Hezekiah himself is attributed one 'writing' which is virtually a psalm, Isaiah 38:20."[3]

Some think that young king Josiah, who ushered in another great revival in Israel, may have added to the Psalter (2 Ki.22:1-23:30). Many trustworthy scholars believe that the inspired collection of psalms was completed by Ezra when he and Nehemiah restored worship in Jerusalem after the return from captivity (Neh.8).

TO WHOM WRITTEN:

1. From Moses' psalm to those written after the Babylonian Captivity, the inspired psalms were composed over a span of approximately 1,000 years. The original recipients, therefore, were those of the age in which they were written.

2. *Psalms* was written to the nation of Israel. A number of psalms were penned for specific occasions in Israel's life and history. Guided by the Holy Spirit, those who compiled the book of *Psalms* assembled a collection of praise songs to be used in the worship of their day.

3. *Psalms*—through its divine inspiration and preservation—is written to all people of every nation and generation...

- to give an example and warning to us

  "Now all these things happened unto them for examples: and they are written for our admonition, upon whom the ends of the world are come" (1 Co.10:11).

- to teach us how to live and give us hope

  "And that he was buried, and that he rose again the third day according to the scriptures" (1 Co.15:4).

- to teach us how to praise and pray to God, how to relate to Him in every circumstance of life

PURPOSE:

1. *The Historical Purpose:*
   a. The Book of *Psalms* was compiled for the purpose of providing a hymnal for the Jewish people to use in worship.
   b. The psalms teach the importance of singing in worship as well as in the experience of God's people as they walk through each and every day. Moses wrote songs for the children of Israel as they wandered in the wilderness. David wrote songs for the people as they worshipped in Jerusalem. When Jesus instituted the Lord's Supper, He and the disciples sang a hymn before departing for the Mount of Olives (Mt.26:30). Paul instructed the church to sing "psalms and hymns and spiritual songs" (Ep.5:19). When God's Spirit pulled back the veil that separates this dimension from heaven, John saw God's people singing a new song of praise to the Lamb (Re.5:9; 14:2-3). Additionally, he witnessed the singing of old songs: the song of Moses, one of the oldest recorded in Scripture (Ex.15), and the song of the Lamb, which incorporates parts of Psalms 22 and 92 (Re.15:3).

---

2   Paul N. Benware. *Survey of the Old Testament.* (Chicago, IL: Moody Press, 2001).

3   James Orr, Editor, et. al. *The International Standard Bible Encyclopedia.* (Grand Rapids, MI: Eerdmans Publishing Co., 1988).

2. *The Doctrinal or Spiritual Purpose:*

a. Through the psalms, the Jewish people sang their doctrines. "The psalms take the basic themes of Old Testament theology and turn them into song."[4] Among the great doctrines declared and celebrated in the psalms are the doctrines of...

- *God*—His exclusivity, power, sovereignty, righteousness, justice, mercy, faithfulness, and love
- Creation
- Man
- God's covenant
- Redemption and salvation
- God's Word
- The future

b. The psalms were written and compiled for the spiritual purpose of teaching us to praise God in every circumstance of life. The Hebrew title of the book, *Tehillim*, means praises. *Psalms* teaches us to praise God in every occasion of life: joy and sorrow, victory and defeat, trouble and triumph, burden and blessing. This is reflected in the different types of psalms (see KEYS TO UNDERSTANDING PSALMS).

Additionally, the psalms teach us *how* to pray and praise God in every occasion of life. The psalms are model prayers, examples from which we can learn. Of all that the psalms teach us, two powerful, life-changing lessons rise to the top:

1) *We have the liberty to empty our heavy hearts at the throne of God, holding nothing back.* The psalms are brutally honest. Like blazing lava shooting out of a volcano, they erupt with raw emotion. Every emotion of the human soul is found in *Psalms.*

2) *Problems turn to praise when you pray.* Many of the psalms, especially David's psalms, follow a similar pattern: they begin with a problem, and they end in praise. In a number of these, prayer resulted in the solving of the problem and the changing of circumstances. In many others, however, the praise flowed before victory over the trouble came. *Prayer changes us!* In the midst of problems, troubles, trials, sufferings, and distresses, we can have jubilant spirits that sing praise to the LORD. The message of *Psalms* is that we can cry out to God about anything and everything, and when we do, fear turns to faith, sorrow turns to joy, and worry turns to peace.

3. *The Christological or Christ-Centered Purpose:* after Jesus' resurrection, He opened the understanding of the disciples to the things "which were written...in the psalms, concerning [Him]" (Lk.24:44). *Psalms* abounds with prophecies and information about God's Son. The psalms that refer particularly to Christ are referred to as *Messianic Psalms.* Among other things, the Messiah's deity, life, obedience, betrayal, death, resurrection, ascension, lordship, and reign are prophesied in *Psalms.* These prophecies will be identified and discussed in the commentary.

Key Messianic Psalms are Psalm 2, which speaks of Christ's future kingship and judgment; Psalm 22, which prophesies our Savior's death in startling detail; and Psalm 110, which announces His lordship and priesthood.

SPECIAL FEATURES:

1. *Psalms* is "The Great Book of Praise to God." As previously mentioned, the Hebrew title of the book means *praises.* It teaches how to praise God in every circumstance of life. Every psalm, in some way, offers praise to God, but other psalms are for the exclusive purpose of praising God. Each of the five books that comprise *Psalms* ends with a doxology; that is, a direct expression of praise (41:13; 72:18-19; 89:52; 106:48; 150:1-6).

2. *Psalms* is "The Great Book of Desperate Pleas to God." In many of the psalms, especially those of David, the author cries out to God in desperate need (3:1-8; 4:1-8; 5:1-12; 13:1-6; 22:1-31; 39:1-13; 40:1-17). These cries of distress are honest, blunt, and often unrestrained, teaching us that we can speak to the LORD freely and without fear. In times of trouble, we can—and should—turn to God.

3. *Psalms* is "The Great Book That Teaches Us to Trust—Take Refuge—in the LORD" (5:11-12; 7:1; 11:1-7; 16:1-5; 31:1-24; 36:7; 37:3-6). In every troubling situation of life, we can find shelter, safety, and security in God.

4. *Psalms* is "The Great Book That Reveals the Excruciatingly Painful Consequences of Sin" (31:9-12; 32:1-5; 38:1-22; 41:1-4; 51:8). The broken heart and body of David—broken due to his sin—are seen in several of his psalms. His agony and anguish are displayed to remind us that sin carries a painful price.

5. *Psalms* is "The Great Book That Shows Us How to Approach God in Times of Agonizing Suffering" (22:1-31; 38:1-22). Throughout *Psalms*, we are not only exposed to David's suffering in the various circumstances of life, but also to the future suffering of Christ—in vivid prophetic detail.

6. *Psalms* is "The Great Book That Gives Us Hope in Life's Darkest Hours" (16:9; 31:24; 30:5; 33:22; 38:15; 39:7).

7. *Psalms* is "The Great Book That Teaches Us How To Trust God When Facing Opposition and Enemies" (3:1-8; 5:8-12; 7:1-17; 9:1-20; 17:1-15; 18:1-50; 27:1-14; 35:1-28; 41:1-13).

8. *Psalms* is "The Great Book That Includes the Best-Loved Chapter of the Bible" (23:1-6). Throughout the generations, the Twenty-Third Psalm has been turned to for comfort more than any other portion of God's Word.

9. *Psalms* is "The Great Book Most Frequently Quoted or Referred to by Jesus Christ" (Mt.5:35; 7:23; 13:35; 21:16, 42; 23:39; 27:46; Lk.2:49; 23:46; 24:44; Jn.10:34).

---

4   *The ESV Study Bible.* (Wheaton, IL: Crossway Bibles, 2008), p.937.

AN EXTENSIVE HISTORICAL AND PRACTICAL BACKGROUND TO THE TIMES OF PSALMS

"Blessed is the man who does not walk in the counsel of the wicked or stand in the way of sinners or sit in the seat of mockers. But his delight is in the law of the LORD, and on his law he meditates day and night" (Psalm 1:1-2).

"Let everything that has breath praise the LORD. Praise the LORD" (Psalm 150:6).

An Extensive Historical and Practical Background to the Times of Psalms

OVERVIEW: the most accurate history book in the world is, of course, the Bible. Therefore, to gain a proper understanding of the second, third, and fourth books of *Psalms*, it is important to be aware of the historical background in which these books were written and read. The psalms in *Books II, III,* and *IV* of *Psalms* were written over a period of approximately 600 years. And some of the psalms are about events that occurred during other periods of Israel's history. Obviously, the outlines and commentary for all these events are too lengthy to include in this volume.

To give you an overview of the background, we are including the divisional outlines from *The Preacher's Outline and Sermon Bible* (POSB) that cover the most prominent events in *Books II–IV* of *Psalms*. Scripture references for other relevant events are included in the Introduction to each individual psalm. The complete outlines and commentary can be found in the corresponding volumes of the *POSB*. To help you preach and teach *Psalms* most effectively, we encourage you to study the commentary for these events along with *Psalms*.

BACKGROUND TO PSALMS II
(DIVISION OVERVIEWS)

I. THE STORY OF SAUL AND DAVID (PART 1): THE LORD GIVES ISRAEL A KING "AFTER HIS OWN HEART," 1 SAMUEL 16:1–20:42

II. THE STORY OF SAUL AND DAVID (PART 2): DAVID THE FUGITIVE, 1 SAMUEL 21:1–31:13

III. THE STORY OF DAVID'S PERSONAL WEAKNESSES, FAILURES, AND CRISES: HIS TRAGIC SIN AND GOD'S JUDGMENT, 2 SAMUEL 11:1–20:26

IV. THE UTTER DISINTEGRATION AND FALL OF ISRAEL, THE NORTHERN KINGDOM: A TRAGIC END DUE TO AN UNBROKEN STREAM OF WICKEDNESS AND LAWLESSNESS, 2 KINGS 14:1–17:41

V. THE UTTER DISINTEGRATION AND FALL OF JUDAH, THE SOUTHERN KINGDOM: AN APPALLING DESTRUCTION DUE TO INCONSISTENCY, DISLOYALTY, AND EVER-GROWING WICKEDNESS, 2 KINGS 18:1–25:30

VI. THE FIRST RETURN OF EXILES FROM CAPTIVITY AND THEIR RESETTLEMENT—LED BY ZERUBBABEL, EZRA 1:1–6:22

VII. THE SECOND RETURN OF EXILES FROM CAPTIVITY AND THEIR REFORM—LED BY EZRA, EZRA 7:1–10:44

THE STORY OF SAUL AND DAVID (PART 1): THE LORD GIVES ISRAEL A KING "AFTER HIS OWN HEART," 1 SAMUEL 16:1–20:42

(16:1–20:42) **DIVISION OVERVIEW**: the LORD had given the people just what they wanted, a king "like all the nations" had (8:5). But King Saul had failed miserably and been rejected by the LORD. Now it was time for the LORD to give Israel not the leader they wanted but the leader they needed, a man "after God's own heart" (13:14). Sometime earlier the LORD had predicted that He would raise up a man "after His own heart" (13:14; 16:1). Although Saul was to rule about 15 more years, it was time for the LORD to unfold His plan for raising up the righteous king who was to rule His people after Saul. At the time of Saul's rejection by the LORD, the future ruler was only a small boy whose name was David. Nevertheless, the LORD wanted the young boy *secretly anointed* as the future king so that his preparation could begin and be guided by Samuel himself. A suspenseful picture of high drama took place with the secret anointing of David. This event marked a shift in power within Israel, power secretly transferred from the ruling monarch to a young boy who was destined to become king.

From the very day of David's secret anointing, the LORD began to move events to prepare the young boy for future rule. Soon thereafter, although Saul knew nothing about David's secret anointing, the king brought David into his royal court to serve as the king's very own harpist. As a member of the royal court, David was able to observe and learn about the nation's economic, military, and justice systems, as well as about the morality and character needed by its officials.

A few years later, although still too young to serve in the military (age 20), David demonstrated an unusual courage and fearlessness by defeating the giant Goliath. Because of his stunning victory over Goliath, Saul promoted David and brought him permanently into the king's court and service. Such a brave, courageous man was just the kind of person the king wanted serving him in his royal court. After serving the king faithfully for some time, David was given a command in the army of Israel. As commander, he proved very successful, winning victories over one enemy after another, never losing a single battle. Almost immediately David became a hero in the minds of the people, becoming even more popular than Saul himself. Because of David's popularity, Saul became extremely jealous and convinced that David and others were plotting to overthrow his kingdom. From this moment on, Saul launched a fierce pursuit to kill David, a pursuit that was to consume the rest of Saul's life. The king made attempt after attempt to assassinate the young man whom God had appointed to be the future ruler of His people, the young man "after God's own heart."

THE STORY OF SAUL AND DAVID (PART 1): THE LORD GIVES ISRAEL A KING "AFTER HIS OWN HEART," 1 SAMUEL 16:1–20:42

A. The Story of David's Secret Anointing As King and His Service in Saul's Court: God Judges the Heart, Not the Appearance, of a Person, 16:1-23

B. The Story of David and Goliath: Defeating the Oppressor of God's People, 17:1-58

C. The Story of Saul's Jealous Rage and Attempts to Kill David (Part 1): A Look at the Evil of Jealousy, 18:1-30

D. The Story of Saul's Jealous Rage and Attempts to Kill David (Part 2): A Look at the Evil of Jealousy, 19:1-24

E. The Story of David and Jonathan's Friendship: A Lesson on Loyalty, 20:1-42

THE STORY OF SAUL AND DAVID (PART 2): DAVID THE FUGITIVE, 1 SAMUEL 21:1–31:13

(21:1–31:13) **DIVISION OVERVIEW**: Saul's jealous rage and relentless determination to assassinate David eventually forced David to flee for his life. Most likely David was in his early twenties when he was forced to flee, leaving behind his family, friends, and home. This calculation is based upon the fact that David was younger than the twenty-year old age requirement for military duty when he first began to serve Saul, for he was not yet enlisted in the king's army. And David was thirty years old when he began to reign over Judah right after Saul's death (2 S.5:4-5).

Just imagine! Being no more than twenty-two or twenty-three years old and being forced to leave family, friends, and home, fleeing for one's life and living as a fugitive on the run for seven or eight long years. From this point on to the end of First Samuel, David was to live a life of strain, stress, adversity, and affliction—a life of extreme hardship. Until Saul's death, he was to be fiercely pursued by the king as a fugitive with the charge of a capital crime hanging over his head. He was to live one of the most distressful, tension-filled lives imaginable. But through all the strain and stress, the LORD was preparing David to become the *servant* of the LORD's people. Although he was to be the ruler of the nation, he was first of all to be the servant of the people, empathizing with their needs and seeking to help them in every way he could. In order to empathize and feel for the people, David had to go through the experiences of intense, agonizing suffering during the days of his fugitive years. And because of the suffering he had to bear, David became the great psalmist whose life and writings so clearly point us to the LORD Himself as our great Savior, Deliverer, Provider, and Protector (He.2:18; 4:15-16).

THE STORY OF SAUL AND DAVID (PART 2): DAVID THE FUGITIVE, 1 SAMUEL 21:1–31:13

A. The Immediate, Desperate Flight of David from Saul: A Picture of Desperation and of God's Deliverance, 21:1–22:5

B. The Insane Murder of the Priests by Saul: A Picture of the Terrible Evil of Certain Sins, 22:6-23

C. The Rescue of Keilah by David and the Insane Pursuit of David by Saul: A Picture of the Believer's Deliverance from All Enemies, 23:1-29

D. The Life of Saul Mercifully Spared by David: Lessons on Honoring God's Anointed, 24:1-22

E. The Encounter of David with Nabal and Abigail: Lessons on Dealing with a Harsh, Selfish Man and a Wise, Courageous Woman, 25:1-44

F. The Life of Saul Again Spared by David: Lessons on Reaping What One Sows, 26:1-25

G. The Desperate Flight of David to Philistia, Seeking a Safe Residence: Giving in to Doubt and Unbelief, to Deception and Lies, 27:1-12

H. The Desperation of Saul Seen in His Seeking a Spirit Medium: A Study of the Occult, 28:1-25

I. The Dismissal of David to Keep Him from Fighting against Israel: A Picture of God Working All Things Out for the Believer, 29:1-11

J. The Defeat of the Amalekites by David: A Picture of Christ Setting the Captives (His Loved Ones) Free, 30:1-31

K. The Tragic End of Saul and His Sons, Including Jonathan, David's Closest Friend: The Surety of God's Word and of God's Judgment, 31:1-13

THE STORY OF DAVID'S PERSONAL WEAKNESSES, FAILURES, AND CRISES: HIS TRAGIC SIN AND GOD'S JUDGMENT, 2 SAMUEL 11:1–20:26

(11:1–20:26) **DIVISION OVERVIEW**: since his earliest youth, the day he had reached the age of personal accountability, David had lived a righteous life. He had acknowledged the LORD in all he did, strictly obeying the commandments of God. Because of David's faithfulness, the LORD had fulfilled His promises in David's life and poured out blessings never before seen in Israel.

In God's estimation, David was most definitely "a man after [God's] own heart" (1 S.13:14). David was a person totally committed to the LORD, whose heart was filled with love and compassion and with a deep desire for righteousness, justice, and peace throughout the earth. (See outline and notes—2 S.5:1-10:19, esp. chapters 7-8, for more discussion.)

But suddenly, without any warning, David was confronted with an overwhelmingly seductive temptation. No doubt, David had been tempted many times before in his life, but this time—tragically—he gave in to the temptation and slipped into sin. He committed the terrible sins of adultery and murder as well as the sins of condoning and indulging the wicked behavior of his children. Catastrophic results followed, falling upon him, his family, and the nation. These consequences were the very curses God had warned would fall upon those who disobeyed him, those who broke their covenant or promise that they would follow Him:

➢ There was the curse of losing one's family (De.28:18).
➢ There was the curse of exile (De.28:64-67).[1]

In this division of *Second Samuel*, David is seen bearing these two terrible curses of sin. An example of this is revealed in the rape of Tamar by her half-brother, the Crown Prince Amnon, David's oldest son. In the words of the preacher and commentator Kenneth Chafin:

> For seven chapters Absalom [becomes] the focus of the story, but Absalom's story does not begin with himself but with the rape of his beautiful sister Tamar. While sexual abuse in the family is a familiar story in today's world, the casual reader will probably wonder what a sordid story like this, told in such vivid detail, is doing in the Bible....

> ...this story of sexual violence describes part of the punishment that Nathan had prophesied. He had said that the sword would never depart from David's house (2 Sam. 12:10), and this story tells of one of his sons murdering another. He had prophesied that adversity would rise up in David's own household (2 Sam. 12:11), and this is the incident that creates the original rupture in the relationship between Absalom and David. Nathan had promised that what David had done in secret would be seen by all Israel (2 Sam. 12:12), and David's two sons recreated their father's sins for all to see. Amnon modeled his father's unbridled passion when he [David] took Bathsheba, and Absalom modeled his father's deceit and cunning when he [David] arranged the death of Uriah the Hittite.

> There are many people who think the idea of being punished for our sins is an Old Testament idea that has no relevance for today—but they are wrong. David's story ought to be a reminder that one of the ways in which God punishes us is by allowing our children to copy our sins. It was a painful experience for David to have Nathan hold his sins before him, but it was much worse to see them acted out in the lives of his children....

> ...[This] narrative shows us the historical consequences of what seems to be a purely private act. We live in a day that has tried hard to separate character from performance in the public arena. Some have gone so far as to suggest that to probe into the private morality of a person seeking employment or public office is an invasion of privacy. Yet the scandals that have rocked the nation as leaders in business and government and religion have betrayed their trust ought to remind us that the kind of persons we are will be reflected in what we do. This is why God's first step in a different kind of world is the creation of a different kind of people.[2]

---

1 Robert D. Bergen. *1, 2 Samuel.* "The New American Commentary," Vol.7. (Nashville, TN: B & H Publishing Group, 1996), p.361.

2 Kenneth Chafin. *1, 2 Samuel.* "Mastering the Old Testament," Vol.8. (Dallas, TX: Word Publishing, 1989), pp.312-313.

THE STORY OF DAVID'S PERSONAL WEAKNESSES, FAILURES, AND CRISES: HIS TRAGIC SIN AND GOD'S JUDGMENT, 2 SAMUEL 11:1–20:26

A. The Terrible Sins of David: The Evil of Adultery and Murder, 11:1-27

B. The Rebuke of David and His Confession: A Strong Lesson on God's Chastisement of the Believer, 12:1-31

C. The Consequences of David's Sin Began to Fall upon His House: Rape, Incest, Revenge, and Murder, 13:1-39

D. The Reconciliation of David with Absalom: A Lesson on Balancing Justice with Compassion and Mercy, 14:1-33

E. The National Rebellion Led by Absalom, and David's Flight: Lessons on Rebellion and on Great Trust and Hope in God, 15:1-37

F. The People Encountered by David As He Fled and the Horrible Advice Given to Absalom: Lessons Concerning Gross Evil and God's Hand of Discipline, 16:1-23

G. The Advice of Hushai That Enabled David to Escape: Lessons on God's Sovereign Care and Guidance, 17:1-29

H. The Defeat and Death of Absalom: A Picture of God's Judgment upon an Indulgent, Permissive Parent, 18:1–19:8

I. The Return of David to Jerusalem: A Dramatic Lesson on How to Treat Others, 19:9-43

J. The Troublemaker Sheba: Lessons on the Need for Unity, Peace, and Faithfulness, 20:1-26

THE UTTER DISINTEGRATION AND FALL OF ISRAEL, THE NORTHERN KINGDOM: A TRAGIC END DUE TO AN UNBROKEN STREAM OF WICKEDNESS AND LAWLESSNESS, 2 KINGS 14:1–17:41

(14:1–17:41) **DIVISION OVERVIEW**: for over 150 years, since the division of the kingdom, the Israelites had lived wicked, lawless lives and engaged in false worship, rejecting the LORD. As a result, both the Northern and Southern Kingdoms had deteriorated and were now weak politically, economically, militarily, socially, and spiritually. Because of their divisive spirit and weakened condition, both nations were in constant turmoil. They were in conflict with each other and with the surrounding nations. In addition, both were suffering under the continued oppression of the Syrian Empire. There was little hope for a bright future among the people. Because of their self-centered, indulgent and sinful lifestyles, there was little chance their society and nation could ever again become strong and prosperous. Based upon God's warnings, the future could only be the inevitable hand of utter destruction. For God's patience with the Israelites and their leaders was bound to be running out.

However, in the present division of Scripture the reader witnesses an amazing event. The LORD had mercy upon the Israelites, both the Northern and Southern Kingdoms. Note what the author of *Second Kings* has just said in the former chapter:

> **But the LORD was gracious to them and had compassion and showed concern for them because of his covenant with Abraham, Isaac and Jacob. To this day he has been unwilling to destroy them or banish them from his presence (2 K.13:23).**

Although the leaders and people of Israel had given no indication of interest in the LORD, the LORD took the initiative and gave them one *last chance* to repent. The Northern Kingdom of Israel received one *final opportunity* to turn to the LORD, to turn from their wicked, lawless, and unjust ways.

Once again, the LORD poured out His blessings of success and prosperity upon the people. By giving them an era of success and prosperity, the LORD longed for the people to realize their blessings had come from Him.

And in their realization, there was the hope that they would turn from their unrighteous ways back to Him. This period of success and prosperity came during the reigns of Jeroboam II in Israel and Amaziah, who was also known as Uzziah, in Judah (14:23–15:7). But as the prophets Amos and Hosea pointed out, instead of arousing the people to turn to the LORD, the enormous success and prosperity caused the leaders and people to become proud, boastful, and self-sufficient. They gloried in their own abilities and achievements, ignoring, denying, and rejecting the LORD. The kings and people continued their downward spiral into utter corruption and decadence. Thus the inevitable hand of judgment fell upon the Northern Kingdom of Israel, and they entered a period of severe political disorder soon thereafter (15:8-31). The nation was conquered by the Assyrians, who had some years earlier defeated and replaced the Syrians as the dominant world power.

Samaria, the capital of Israel, was destroyed and the people exiled by the Assyrian King Shalmaneser V in 722 B.C. (17:1-6). In discussing why God executed judgment against the Northern Kingdom, it is interesting to note that God gives an astounding twenty-two reasons for the judgment in Scripture (17:7-23).

Judah lasted longer than Israel because of the good, righteous kings who occasionally ruled the nation. For this reason the LORD delayed their judgment, hoping that the leaders and people would make a permanent commitment to Him. Every generation of Judeans needed to be taught to live consistent, righteous lives and to acknowledge the LORD alone as the only living and true God.

But as has been seen since David, the rulers and generations refused to heed the Word of God and the warnings of the prophets. Thus one of the primary causes for the coming judgment upon Judah is that of *inconsistency*. The generations of Judean people had the major flaw of being half-hearted, double-minded, indecisive, indifferent, neglectful—just *inconsistent*. Consequently, as will be seen in the next division, the inevitable hand of judgment against an immoral, unrighteous nation will also fall upon Judah.

THE UTTER DISINTEGRATION AND FALL OF ISRAEL, THE NORTHERN KINGDOM: A TRAGIC END DUE TO AN UNBROKEN STREAM OF WICKEDNESS AND LAWLESSNESS, 2 KINGS 14:1–17:41

A. The Reign of Amaziah in Judah and His Provoking War with Israel: Losing One's Opportunity to Serve, 14:1-22

B. The Long Reigns of Jeroboam II in Israel and Azariah (Uzziah) in Judah: God's Blessing the People and Giving Them One Last Chance to Repent, 14:23–15:7

C. The Reigns of Five Kings in Israel, Four of Whom Were Assassinated: Political Disorder Due to the People's Continued Wickedness and Rejection of God, 15:8-31

D. The Reigns of Two Kings in Judah, Jotham and Ahaz: A Sharp Contrast Between Righteousness and Wickedness, 15:32–16:20

E. The Tragic Fall of Israel, Its Conquest and Deportation of the People by the Assyrians (722 BC): The End of God's Long-Suffering and the Execution of His Judgment, 17:1-41

The Utter Disintegration and Fall of Judah, the Southern Kingdom: An Appalling Destruction Due to Inconsistency, Disloyalty, and Ever-Growing Wickedness, 2 Kings 18:1–25:30

(18:1–25:30) **DIVISION OVERVIEW**: when the Northern Kingdom of Israel fell to the Assyrians, a strong and godly king named Hezekiah was on the throne in Judah. And he was experienced, for he had already been ruling for about seven years. He was perhaps the strongest king to ever rule the Southern Kingdom of Judah. Once again, the LORD had looked after the Judean people. He had provided a strong, godly and experienced ruler to guide them through the frightening days of upheaval within the Northern Kingdom, which was obviously a threat to their own survival. For Hezekiah and his people were bound to be gripped by fear, the fear that Assyria might attack Judah next. And just as feared, Assyria did invade Judah about seven years later. But Hezekiah led the people to seek the LORD in prayer, and the LORD miraculously delivered Judah from the terrorizing enemy (18:13–19:37).

However, even Hezekiah slipped into sin by giving in to a spirit of pride and boasting. Although he repented, God sent the prophet Isaiah to pronounce the inevitable judgment and utter destruction of Jerusalem that was coming—all due to the sins of the rulers and people down through the centuries.

After the fall of Samaria in 722, Judah was to survive for an additional 135 years. But eventually the trait of being *inconsistent, double-minded*—sometimes hot and sometimes cold to the LORD—was to lead to the fall of Jerusalem.

Because of some serious illness, Hezekiah had to rule as co-regent with his son Manasseh for a decade. After Hezekiah's death, Manasseh rejected the godly example of his father and turned completely away from the LORD. Among all the kings of Judah, Manasseh and his grandfather Ahaz were the most wicked and brutal and did more to bring about the downfall of Judah than any other king. This persecution and slaughter of true believers had been horrifying. (See outline and notes—2 K.16:1-20 for more discussion). Although Manasseh surprisingly repented and turned back to the LORD in the latter years of his life, the damage to the nation had already been done. And the downward spiral into utter destruction had picked up speed.

Upon the death of Manasseh, his evil son Amon succeeded him. However, he ruled for only two years before he was assassinated. But the verdict upon his reign was clearly pronounced by the LORD and the author. Amon was guilty of an evil life and rule. He failed to use the two years of his reign to turn the people back to God. Thus the downward spiral to destruction only picked up more steam.

However, God was not yet done with Judah. One more chance would be given to the people and nation, one more opportunity for them to turn back to the LORD permanently and to pass the torch of righteousness down to succeeding generations. This last chance was given in the ruler of Josiah, the great-grandson of Hezekiah. Of all the kings of Judah, he was apparently the most godly. But keep in mind this surprising, even shocking fact: during the entire 344 years of the divided kingdom—among all the kings of Israel and Judah—there were only four good and godly kings. And all four were from Judah. The Northern Kingdom of Israel never produced a good and righteous king. The four righteous kings in Judah were:

➢ Asa
➢ Jehoshaphat
➢ Hezekiah
➢ Josiah

Among these four, Hezekiah and Josiah are considered to have been the most godly because of the major reforms they carried out. However, the righteous and just reforms of one generation are often not passed down nor carried over into the next generation. And the LORD knew this fact. For the very trait that had so characterized Judah's history had been that of *inconsistency*, being double-minded.

Consequently, the hand of God's judgment fell. The people of Judah had been warned—warned time and again by the prophets—but they were stiff-necked, refusing to heed God's Word. The result: four successive evil kings took the throne of Judah, and each was either conquered or appointed by Egypt or Babylon.

All hope for the rulers and people of Judah was now gone. During the reign of the last ruler, Zedekiah, the final invasion of Judah by Babylon was launched. Soon thereafter the siege of Jerusalem began. After living under the siege for two years and reaching the point of starvation and insanity, the city collapsed. Because of the people's inconsistent lives—their unrighteous and unjust ways and their false worship—Jerusalem fell to the Babylonian army in 586 B.C. and the people were enslaved and exiled to Babylon.

After centuries of possessing the promised land, God's people now live either outside the land as exiles, or as tenants on their own ground. Only one bright spot remains for the author to report. Jehoiachin, exiled in 597 B.C., is elevated to favored status ca. 560 B.C. David's lineage still exists, albeit in Babylonian exile. Hope does remain. Whenever God chooses, the people can return. However he chooses, the Davidic promise and kingdom can emerge. God is not weak, powerless, or in exile. Therefore, all who turn to this sovereign LORD may also look forward to strength, victory, and a home going.

THE UTTER DISINTEGRATION AND FALL OF JUDAH, THE SOUTHERN KINGDOM: AN APPALLING DESTRUCTION DUE TO INCONSISTENCY, DISLOYALTY, AND EVER-GROWING WICKEDNESS, 2 KINGS 18:1–25:30

A. The Righteous Reign of Hezekiah (Part 1)—Assyria's Invasion of Judah: A Man Who Trusted and Held Fast to the LORD, 18:1-37

B. The Righteous Reign of Hezekiah (Part 2)—Judah's Deliverance from Assyria: God's Power to Rescue His People, 19:1-37

C. The Righteous Reign of Hezekiah (Part 3)—His Terminal Illness and Miraculous Healing: The Power of Prayer and the Danger of Pride, 20:11-21

D. The Evil Reigns of Manasseh and Amon: A Look at the Horrible Depths of Wicked Behavior, 21:1-26

E. The Godly Reign of Josiah (Part 1)—His Temple Restoration and Discovery of God's Word: Two Major Concerns of the Believer, 22:1-20

F. The Godly Reign of Josiah (Part 2)—His Spiritual Renewal and Reform: A Need for Conversion, for Trusting the Only Living and True God, 23:1-30

G. The Reigns Controlled by Egypt and Babylon: A Look at Four Critical Failures, 23:31–24:20

H. The Final Siege and Fall of Jerusalem: The Surety of God's Predicted Judgment, 25:1-30

THE FIRST RETURN OF EXILES FROM CAPTIVITY AND THEIR RESETTLEMENT— LED BY ZERUBBABEL, EZRA 1:1–6:22

(1:1–6:22) **DIVISION OVERVIEW**: after many years of captivity in the land of Babylon, the Persian conqueror King Cyrus issued a decree allowing any Jews who wished to return to Jerusalem to do so. There would eventually be three groups to return to the promised land from captivity. But this division of the book of *Ezra* concerns the first return led by Zerubabbel. Obviously, as with any group of freed captives who set out to return home, the exiles were rejoicing from the depths of their hearts. Yet four difficult tasks still lay out before this first group of returnees:

> ➤ They were to reestablish the worship of the only true God, the LORD Himself
> ➤ They were to rebuild the temple
> ➤ They were to resettle the land
> ➤ They were to rebuild the nation

The returnees were not only reestablishing themselves as a nation, but also reestablishing their religion and the proper worship of God. The tasks were hard, so the decision to be diligent had to be even more firm. Zerubbabel would prove a worthy leader and righteous example before the people. He and his brother rose up with zeal to build the altar of the LORD (3:2). From there, Zerubbabel and the priestly leadership continued to lead and inspire the Jews to success.

Ezra, being a scribe, was careful to record the official government documents important to the story. Moreover, Ezra was a priest; therefore, he was also careful to focus his writings on the importance of remaining faithful to the LORD. Each returnee needed relentless determination to complete the awesome task that lay ahead. They were to face fierce opposition. But because of their dedication and strong stand for the LORD, the foundation of the temple was laid (3:11) and the temple itself was finished (6:15). At last, proper worship was restored, beginning with the celebration of the Passover and the Feast of Unleavened Bread. This was a glorious moment, the height of all that the returnees had worked so hard to achieve.

Remember that Ezra was writing primarily to the exiles who had returned from Babylonian captivity and then to the succeeding generations. When the exiles had first returned, they found their nation in ruins. Now that they had rebuilt the temple and the nation, above all else they had to remain faithful to the LORD. If they and the generations to come were faithful, genuinely trusting in the LORD and living righteously, God would continue to guide and protect them. He would also continue to bless them with the richness of the promised land. The Jews had learned a hard lesson: the blessings of the promised land were directly tied to their relationship with God.

As the reader studies the first return of the Jews from captivity under the direction of Zerubbabel, he should keep this fact in mind: the LORD keeps His promises to His people. The Jewish people lived on; the nation flourished again; the lineage of the Messiah was preserved; the Messiah, the Savior of the world, Jesus Christ, did come.

> "Whoever there is among you of all His people, may his God be with him! Let him go up to Jerusalem which is in Judah and rebuild the house of the LORD, the God of Israel; He is the God who is in Jerusalem" (Ezra 1:3).

THE FIRST RETURN OF EXILES FROM CAPTIVITY AND THEIR RESETTLEMENT— LED BY ZERUBBABEL, EZRA 1:1–6:22

A. The Release and Return of the Exiles (After 70 years of Captivity): Hope Fulfilled, Being Freed from Captivity and Returning to the Promised Land, 1:1–2:70
B. The Major Tasks of the Returned Exiles: Becoming Established, Settling Down, Reviving True Worship, and Building the Temple, 3:1-13
C. The Continued Opposition Faced by the Returned Exiles: Being Attacked, Persecuted for One's Faith, 4:1-24
D. The Completion of the Temple by the Returned Exiles: Four Pictures Demonstrating God's Faithfulness, 5:1–6:22

THE SECOND RETURN OF EXILES FROM CAPTIVITY AND THEIR REFORM—LED BY EZRA, EZRA 7:1–10:44

(7:1–10:44) **DIVISION OVERVIEW**: almost sixty years after Zerubbabel led the first Jewish exiles back to the promised land, Ezra came on the scene. After receiving permission from King Artaxerxes, Ezra led the second group back to their homeland. While this second caravan was not as large in number, it was just as important. In the intervening years since the first return, the Jews in Jerusalem had slipped away from the LORD. Thus, Ezra's commission was to take another group of exiles back to Jerusalem. He was to:

> ➢ investigate the situation
> ➢ stir the people to make a renewed commitment to rebuild the nation
> ➢ restore true worship in the temple

Ezra was a priest and a man of strong character. Therefore, he was the right person for God to use to stir genuine revival among the people. Furthermore, he was a godly leader who could arouse the backslidden priests and Levites to return to their duties in the temple.

Remember that Ezra was writing primarily to the exiles who had returned from Babylonian captivity and to the succeeding generations of Jews. As leader of the second group to return, Ezra had to exhort them to continue in their devotion to the LORD. Above all else, they had to remain faithful to the LORD. If they and the generations to come were faithful, genuinely trusting in the LORD and living righteously, He would continue to guide and protect them. He would also continue to bless them with the richness of the promised land. As a newly resettled nation, the Jews must never again risk captivity by giving in to the wicked and faithless idolatry of the nations around them. Most of their ancestors had lived wickedly; all future generations must live righteously. They had to remain strong in their commitment, unwavering in their devotion and worship of the LORD.

As the reader studies the return of the Jews from captivity under Ezra's direction, this fact should be kept in mind: the LORD watches over His people to make sure they remain totally devoted to Him. Total dedication is essential if God's people are to continue to flourish.

> **Though we are slaves, our God has not deserted us in our bondage. He has shown us kindness in the sight of the kings of Persia: He has granted us new life to rebuild the house of our God and repair its ruins, and he has given us a wall of protection in Judah and Jerusalem (Ezra 9:9).**

THE SECOND RETURN OF EXILES FROM CAPTIVITY AND THEIR REFORM—LED BY EZRA, EZRA 7:1–10:44

A. Ezra's Royal Commission to Return to the Promised Land: The Picture of a Strong and Dedicated Leader, 7:1-28

B. Ezra's Preparations and Return to the Promised Land (Almost 60 Years After the Completion of the Temple): A Picture of Preparing for the Promised Land (a Type of Heaven), 8:1-36

C. Ezra's Confrontation with the People Over Their Evil Associations: A Picture of Genuine Revival, 9:1–10:44

Timeline of Kings, Prophets and History*

History

Date BC	Foreign Kings	World Events
1000	**Ashur-Rabi II** (1010–970) *(Assyria)* **Hiram** (1003–966) *(Tyre)* **Tiglath-Pileser II** (960–935) *(Assyria)*	David captures Jerusalem (1004) Foundation for the Temple (966) 22ⁿᵈ Egyptian Dynasty (945)
950		Kingdom Divided (930)
930	**Shishak I** (945–924) *(Egypt)*	Assyria makes peace with Babylon (915)
900	**Ben-Hadad I** (900) *(Syria)* **Eth-Baal** (887–856) *(Sidon)*	Jehoshaphat leads a revival (865) Elijah's contest with prophets of Baal (857) Elijah's mantle passed to Elisha (845)
850	**Hazael** (840) *(Syria)*	Carthage established (814) Joash repairs Temple (812)
800	**Ben-Hadad II** (798) *(Syria)* **Ben-Hadad III** (773) *(Syria)*	23ʳᵈ Egyptian dynasty (800) Olympic games begin (776) Rome founded (753)
750	**Rezin** (750) *(Syria)*	Babylonian and Chinese calendar (750)

The United Kingdom

Bible Ref.	Kings (Years Reigned)	Prophets
1 S.16:1–1 K.2:11; 1 Chr.11:1-30	**David** (40) (1011–971)	**Samuel** (1095–1015) **Gad** (1015–950) **Asaph** (1004) **Nathan** (1003–931) **Heman** (971)
1 K.2:12–11:43; 1 Chr.28:1–2 Chr.9:31	**Solomon** (40) (971–931)	

The Divided Kingdom

Northern Kingdom of Israel

Prophets	Kings (Years Reigned)	Bible Ref.
Ahijah (931–910) **Man from Judah** (930) **Shemaiah** (927)	**Jeroboam I** (22) (931–910)	1 K.12:1-24; 12:25-14:20; 2 Chr.10:1-16
Jehu (886)	**Nadab** (2) (910–909)	1 K.15:25-31
	Baasha (24) (909–886)	1 K.15:16-16:7; 2 Chr.16:1-6
	Elah (2) (886–885)	1 K.16:6-14
Hanani (870)	**Zimri** (7 days) (885)	1 K.16:9-20
	Omri (12) (885–874)	1 K.16:21-28
Elijah (860–845)	**Ahab** (22) (874–853)	1 K.16:28-22:40; 2 Chr.18:1-34
Micaiah (853) **Elisha** (850–795) **Eliezer** (849–48)	**Ahaziah** (2) (853–852) **Joram/Jehoram** (12) (852–841)	1 K.22:49-51; 2 K.1:1-18; 2 Chr.20:35-37; 22:1-11 2 K.1:17; 3:1-8:15
Zechariah (797)	**Jehu** (28) (841–814)	2 K.9:1-10:36; 2 Chr.22:7-9
Jonah (780–765)	**Jehoahaz** (17) (814–798)	2 K.13:1-9
Amos (750)	**Jehoash** (16) (798–782)	2 K.13:9-25; 14:8-16
	Jeroboam II (41) (793–753)	2 K.14:23-29
	Zechariah (6 mos) (753)	2 K.15:8-12
	Shallum (1 mo) (752)	2 K.15:13-15
	Menahem (10) (752–742)	2 K.15:16-22

Southern Kingdom of Judah

Bible Ref.	Kings (Years Reigned)	Prophets
1 K.12:1-24; 14:21-31; 2 Chr.9:31-12:16	**Rehoboam** (17) (931–913)	
1 K.15:1-8; 2 Chr.12:16-14:1	**Abijah** (3) (913–911)	
1 K.15:9-24; 2 Chr.14:1-16:14	**Asa** (3) (911–870)	**Iddo** (910) **Azariah** (896)
1 K.22:41-50; 2 K.3:6-14; 2 Chr.17:1-21:1	**Jehoshaphat** (25) (873–848)	
2 K.8:16-24; 2 Chr.21:1-20	**Jehoram** (8) (853–841)	**Obadiah** (845)
2 K.8:25-29; 9:27-29; 2 Chr.22:1-10	**Ahaziah** (2) (841)	
2 K.11:1-16; 2 Chr.22:10-23:21	**Athaliah** (7) (841–835)	
2 K.11:17-12:21; 2 Chr.22:11-12; 24:1-27	**Joash/Jehoash** (40) (835–796)	**Joel** (830)
2 K.14:1-20; 2 Chr.24:27-25:28	**Amaziah** (29) (796–767)	
2 K.14:21-22; 15:1-7; 2 Chr.26:1-23	**Azariah/Uzziah** (52) (792–740)	**Hosea** (788–723) **Jonah** (780–765)
2 K.15:32-38; 2 Chr.26:23-27:9	**Jotham** (16) (750–731)	

THE DIVIDED KINGDOM

SOUTHERN KINGDOM OF JUDAH			NORTHERN KINGDOM OF ISRAEL			DATE BC	HISTORY	
BIBLE REF.	KINGS (Years Reigned)	PROPHETS	BIBLE REF.	KINGS (Years Reigned)	PROPHETS		FOREIGN KINGS	WORLD EVENTS
			2 K.15:23–26	Pekahiah (2) (742–740)			Tiglath-Pil[n]eser III [or Pul] (745–727) (Assyria)	Assyria takes control of Northern Kingdom (745–627)
		Isaiah (740–690)	2 K.15:27–31	Pekah (20) (752–732) (752–740) (ruled only in Gilead) (740–732) (ruled in Samaria)			Shalmaneser V (727–722) (Assyria)	Assyria invades Northern Israel (732)
2 K.15:38–16:20; 2 Chr.27:9–27; Is.7:1–9:1	Ahaz (16) (735–715)	Micah (735–725) Oded (733)	2 K.17:1–23	Hoshea (9) (732–722)			So (727–716) (Egypt) Sargon II (710–705) (Assyria)	Fall of Northern Kingdom (722)
2 K.18:1–20:21; 2 Chr.28:27–32:33; Pr.25:1; Is.36:1–39:8	Hezekiah (29) (729–686)					700	Sennacherib (705–681) (Assyria) Merodach-Baladan (721–710, 705–704) (Assyria) Tirhakah (690–664) (Egypt)	Sennacherib defeats Egypt (701) Hezekiah's tunnel (701) 185,000 Assyrians killed by God (701) Sennacherib destroys Babylon (689)
2 K.20:21–21:18; 2 Chr.32:33–33:20	Manasseh (55) (696–642)	Nahum (663–612)				650	Esarhaddon (681–669) (Assyria) Nabopolassar (626–605) (Assyria) Neco (610–595) (Egypt)	Josiah's reform (621) Nineveh destroyed (612) Battle of Carchemish (605) 1st group of exiles from Judah taken to Babylon (605)
2 K.21:18–26; 2 Chr.33:20–25	Amon (2) (642–640)	Zephaniah (640–609) Jeremiah (627–562)						
2 K.21:26–23:30; 2 Chr.33:25–35:27	Josiah (31) (640–609)	Habakkuk (615–598)						
2 K.23:31–33; 2 Chr.36:1–4	Jehoaz/Jehoahaz (3 mos) (609)	Daniel (605–535)						
2 K.23:34–24:7; 2 Chr.36:5–8	Jehoiakim (11) (608–598)	Ezekiel (593–571)				600	Nebuchadnezzar II (605–562) (Babylon)	2nd group of exiles from Judah taken to Babylon (597) Fall of Judah—Third group of exiles from Judah taken to Babylon (586)
2 K.24:8–17; 25:27–30; 2 Chr.36:8–10;	Jehoiachin (3 mos) (598–597)							
2 K.24:18–25:21; 2 Chr.36:10–14; Je.21:1–52:11	Zedekiah/Mattaniah (11) (597–586)							
2 K.25:22–26; Je.40:5–41:18	Gedaliah (2 mos) (Appointed by Nebuchadnezzar) (586)					550	Evil-Merodach (562–560) (Babylon) Cyrus II (559–530) (Medo-Persia)	Fall of Babylon to Medo-Persian Empire (539)
		Haggai (520) Zechariah (520–518)				500	Belshazzar (552–539) (Babylon) Darius I (521–486) (Medo-Persia)	Cyrus II decrees that the Jews may return to the Holy Land (538) 1st exiles return to Holy Land with Zerubbabel (537) 1st Temple foundation laid (536) 2nd Temple foundation laid (520) Temple completed (516) Republic of Rome est. (509) 2nd return under Ezra (458)
		Malachi (430)				450	Artaxerxes (465–425) (Persia)	3rd return under Nehemiah (445)

*Some dates are approximate.

The resources used for the Timeline are as follows:
1 The Bible
2 Archer, Gleason L. Encyclopedia of Bible Difficulties (Grand Rapids, Michigan: Zondervan Publishing House), 1982.
3 Freedman, David Noel, ed., et. al. The Anchor Bible Dictionary. (New York: Doubleday), 1992.
4 Grun, Bernard. The Timetables of History. 3rd ed. (New York: Simon & Schuster), 1991.
5 Kaiser, Walter C. A History of Israel. (Nashville, Tennessee: Broadman & Holman Publishers), 1998.
6 Silverman, David P., ed. Ancient Egypt. (New York: Oxford University Press), 1997.

OUTLINE OF PSALMS

THE PREACHER'S OUTLINE AND SERMON BIBLE® is unique. It differs from all other Study Bibles and Sermon Resource Materials in that every Passage and Subject is outlined right beside the Scripture. When you choose any *Subject* below and turn to the reference, you have not only the Scripture but also an outline of the Scripture and Subject *already prepared for you—verse by verse.*

For a quick example, choose one of the subjects below and turn over to the Scripture; you will find this to be a marvelous help for more *organized* and *streamlined* study.

In addition, every point of the Scripture and Subject is *fully developed in a Commentary with supporting Scripture* at the end of each point. Again, this arrangement makes sermon preparation much simpler and more efficient.

Note something else: the Subjects of *Psalms II* have titles that are both Biblical and *practical.* The practical titles are often more appealing to people. This benefit is clearly seen for use on billboards, bulletins, church newsletters, etc.

A suggestion: for the *quickest* overview of how *Psalms* helps us, read *all the major titles* below and note the practical application to the problems and trials we face every day of our lives.

———————————

OUTLINE OF PSALMS

BOOK II
PSALMS 42–72

PSALM 42

When You Are Deeply Discouraged or Depressed in Life, 42:1–43:5

For the director of music. A maskil of the Sons of Korah.

1. **Tell God how deeply you yearn for His presence**

   a. Bc. you feel alienated from Him, cut off from His presence

   b. Bc. your heart is broken by unbelievers taunting & ridiculing you

   c. Bc. you can no longer go to the house of God...
      1) Where you can fellowship with God's people
      2) Where you can praise God among fellow believers, He.10:25

   d. Bc. your soul is downcast, disturbed, deeply troubled

   e. Bc. your hope is still in God: He is *your* God & *your* Savior

2. **Remember God no matter how desperate your situation**

   a. Remember Him even if you are a foreigner exiled to a distant land

   b. Remember Him even when you feel overwhelmed by problems & sense the judgment of God

   c. Remember the LORD's unfailing love: Pray to & praise the God who gives you life

As the deer pants for streams of water, so my soul pants for you, O God. 2 My soul thirsts for God, for the living God. When can I go and meet with God? 3 My tears have been my food day and night, while men say to me all day long, "Where is your God?" 4 These things I remember as I pour out my soul: how I used to go with the multitude, leading the procession to the house of God, with shouts of joy and thanksgiving among the festive throng. 5 Why are you downcast, O my soul? Why so disturbed within me? Put your hope in God, for I will yet praise him, my Savior and 6 My God. My soul is downcast within me; therefore I will remember you from the land of the Jordan, the heights of Hermon— from Mount Mizar. 7 Deep calls to deep in the roar of your waterfalls; all your waves and breakers have swept over me. 8 By day the LORD directs his love, at night his song is with me—a prayer to the

God of my life. 9 I say to God my Rock, "Why have you forgotten me? Why must I go about mourning, oppressed by the enemy?" 10 My bones suffer mortal agony as my foes taunt me, saying to me all day long, "Where is your God?" 11 Why are you downcast, O my soul? Why so disturbed within me? Put your hope in God, for I will yet praise him, my Savior and my God.

PSALM 43

For the director of music.

Vindicate me, O God, and plead my cause against an ungodly nation; rescue me from deceitful and wicked men. 2 You are God my stronghold. Why have you rejected me? Why must I go about mourning, oppressed by the enemy? 3 Send forth your light and your truth, let them guide me; let them bring me to your holy mountain, to the place where you dwell. 4 Then will I go to the altar of God, to God, my joy and my delight. I will praise you with the harp, O God, my God. 5 Why are you downcast, O my soul? Why so disturbed within me? Put your hope in God, for I will yet praise him, my Savior and my God.

d. Remember Him even when you feel He is distant & has forgotten all about you

e. Remember Him even when enemies oppress you...
   1) Causing you great anguish
   2) Scoffing at your faith, questioning where your God is

f. Remember Him even when you are downcast & disturbed within
   1) Put your hope in God
   2) Praise Him: He is *your* Savior & *your* God

3. **Pray for God to defend & deliver you**

   a. Bc. you live in an ungodly nation—among deceitful & wicked people

   b. Bc. God is your strength, your refuge, your haven

   c. Bc. you feel rejected by God— forsaken to suffer oppression

4. **Ask God to restore you**

   a. To give you His light & truth to guide you

   b. To lead you into His presence—the place where He lives

   c. To make way for you to worship & praise Him—God, who is the source of your joy

5. **Encourage yourself in the LORD: Put your hope in God & praise Him, for He is *your* Savior & *your* God**

BOOK II: *PSALMS 42–72*

PSALMS 42-43

When You Are Deeply Discouraged or Depressed in Life, 42:1–43:5

(42:1–43:5) **Introduction:** surely there is no greater tragedy than a person's committing suicide. Every year, thousands of people choose death over life. Many of these suffer from deep depression and can find no hope for the future.

Depression affects nearly all of us at some point in our lives, if only to a minor extent. Indeed, the illness has many causes, and science has proven that physical or chemical factors in our bodies and minds can contribute to depression. As a result, many drugs have been devel-

oped to help with these deficiencies. Doctors, therapists, and counselors are trained to help people cope with depression. In many cases, long-term treatment is required.

Scripture is not silent about depression, discouragement, or despair. In fact, some of God's greatest heroes battled depression. The Bible records that Moses, Elijah, and Jonah suffered through times of discouragement so deep that they desired to end their lives (Nu.11:14-15; 1 K.19:4; Jon.4:8).

The author of Psalms 42 and 43 was battling depression when he penned these psalms. Exiled from home and oppressed by cruel enemies, he cried out to God for help. He confronted his downcast soul in a refrain that establishes the theme of these psalms. He was totally disheartened and recognized that his only hope was in the LORD.

Most scholars agree that Psalms 42 and 43 were originally one song. Three strong signs supporting this opinion are...

- the common theme and continuous flow of both psalms
- the lack of a title or heading to Psalm 43
- the repeated refrain in both psalms (42:5, 11; 43:5)

We do not know why or when the song was divided into two psalms. However, it appears this way in the Septuagint,[1] indicating that the separation occurred sometime in the late Old Testament period.

Psalms 42–49 are attributed to the *sons of Korah* (see *Psalms*, INTRODUCTION). Whether these songs were actually written *by* the sons of Korah or *for* their use in temple worship is unclear. However, most scholars conclude that the psalms were written by the sons of Korah. Some think, though, that David wrote them and instructed the sons of Korah to sing them. Others believe that the sons of Korah wrote the psalms but that they based them on the events of David's life. These psalms are unquestionably written in David's style and reflect his zealous love for God's house.

Some who hold that David is the author believe the occasion for writing was his son Absalom's rebellion against him, which forced King David into exile. The great nineteenth century preacher Charles Spurgeon argues this position passionately:

> *Although David is not mentioned as the author, this Psalm must be the offspring of his pen; it is so Davidic, it smells of the son of Jesse, it bears the marks of his style and experience in every letter. We could sooner doubt the authorship of the second part of Pilgrim's Progress than question David's title to be the composer of this Psalm.*[2]

Another belief is that the author was a Levite worship leader, perhaps a son of Korah who had been exiled to a Gentile nation, maybe as a hostage in time of war. Still others suppose he was one of Korah's sons who accompanied David into exile.

The fact is, we do not know for certain who wrote these songs. But we do know the purpose for Psalms 42 and 43: they are *maskil* psalms, songs of instruction and teaching. Whatever his circumstances, the author was suffering through a period of intense trials, trials so severe that they plunged him into deep depression. Psalms 42 and 43 are inspired by God's Spirit to teach us what to do when we find ourselves in the same pit of despair. This is, *When You Are Deeply Discouraged or Depressed in Life,* 42:1–43:5.

1. Tell God how deeply you yearn for His presence (42:1-5).
2. Remember God no matter how desperate your situation (42:6-11).
3. Pray for God to defend and deliver you (43:1-2).
4. Ask God to restore you (43:3-4).
5. Encourage yourself in the LORD: Put your hope in God and praise Him, for He is *your* Savior and *your* God (43:5).

1 (42:1-5) **Tell God how deeply you yearn for His presence.**

The dejected psalmist used a vivid image to express his intense need for God's touch: Like a parched *deer* or hart searching desperately for water in the wilderness, his soul craved the energizing strength, hope, and joy found only in the LORD. Emotionally and spiritually dehydrated, he cried out to God from the bottom of his heart.

a. Because you feel alienated from God, cut off from His presence (v.2).

The psalmist desperately longed for the LORD to rejuvenate his spirit. But he was far from Jerusalem and the temple where God's presence dwelt. Because of this, he felt unable to connect with God.

Under the old covenant, God's presence dwelled in one specific place: the Holy of Holies in the tabernacle (and, later, the temple). The psalmist felt alienated from God because he was away from this sacred place. Therefore, he asked God how much longer it would be before he would be able to return to Jerusalem to stand before Him.

Under the new covenant, God does not abide in a specific place but in His people. Through His Holy Spirit, the Lord lives within every true believer (Ro.8:9; 2 Co.6:16). Although God's presence is always within us, we may at times feel disconnected from God just as the psalmist did. Any number of factors can cause us to feel far from God, including...

- sin in our lives
- unanswered prayer
- neglecting Bible reading or prayer
- failing to worship
- closely associating with ungodly people
- uncontrolled emotions
- doubting God or worrying
- sickness or extreme pain
- failing to follow God's will
- lack of understanding
- lack of faith
- things not turning out as expected
- being too busy
- being overwhelmed by demands
- fear
- loneliness
- self-pity
- difficult circumstances

---

1 The Septuagint is a Greek translation of the Hebrew Scriptures that was completed approximately 200 years before Christ came.
2 Charles Spurgeon. *Treasury of David.* (Peabody, MA: Hendrickson Publishers, Inc., 1990). WORD*search* CROSS e-book.

b. Because your heart is broken by unbelievers taunting and ridiculing you (v.3).

The psalmist was under enemy oppression (43:2). One way these hostile unbelievers tormented him was by ridiculing his faith in God. As he continually cried out to the LORD, his circumstances remained unchanged. It seemed as though God did not even exist. This provoked the psalmist's foes to taunt him mercilessly. Hence, their jeering multiplied his pain, causing his tears to flow even more.

Where is your God? is a question that the idolatrous Gentile nations commonly asked the Jews (Ps.79:10; 115:2; Joel 2:17; Mi.7:10).[3] When God's chosen people faced trouble, unbelievers mocked their faith in God, just as they do today. We must remember that *the presence of problems in our lives does not indicate the absence of God.* Believers will always face trials and tribulations, but this does not mean that God has forsaken us or that He does not exist. We serve a God who promises to be with us at all times, especially in the midst of trouble. He will strengthen us to endure whatever trials confront us, and He will carry us safely through them.

> **Keep your lives free from the love of money and be content with what you have, because God has said, "Never will I leave you; never will I forsake you." So we say with confidence, "The Lord is my helper; I will not be afraid. What can man do to me?" (He.13:5-6).**
>
> **So do not fear, for I am with you; do not be dismayed, for I am your God. I will strengthen you and help you; I will uphold you with my righteous right hand (Is.41:10).**
>
> **When you pass through the waters, I will be with you; and when you pass through the rivers, they will not sweep over you. When you walk through the fire, you will not be burned; the flames will not set you ablaze (Is.43:2).**

c. Because you can no longer go to the house of God (v.4).

The psalmist's spiritual suffering was compounded because he could do nothing to change his distressing situation. He could not return to Jerusalem to worship with God's people. Memories of better days—past celebrations in God's house—only intensified his craving for the LORD's presence. There had been a time when he was the most excited of worshippers, leading the joyous procession to God's house. Now, lonely and depressed, he yearned to be among the congregation

again as they marched to the temple on the holy days, the days of celebrating the feasts ordained by God under the law. How he ached to be with the people of God, dancing and singing in praise and worship to Him!

d. Because your soul is downcast, disturbed, deeply troubled (v.5ᵃ).

For the first of three times in these psalms, the author addressed himself. He described the troubled state of his *soul* (42:11; 43:5), the seat of his emotions, as both downcast and disturbed. *Downcast* (shachach) literally means bowed down or sunk low. *Disturbed* (hamah) means in an uproar or in turmoil. Simply put, the psalmist was trapped in the mire of depression. Feelings of despair and hopelessness raged within him, keeping him in spiritual and emotional turmoil.

e. Because your hope is still in God: He is your God and your Savior (v.5ᵇ).

Notice how the psalmist sought to take control of his emotions rather than allow his emotions to control him. In an attempt to lift himself out of the depths of depression, he encouraged himself in the LORD (see 1 S.30:6). He exhorted his soul to hope in God. In his darkest hour, the psalmist spoke to himself in faith rather than doubt, reminding us of Paul's testimony in the midst of his fierce trials:

> **We are hard pressed on every side, but not crushed; perplexed, but not in despair; persecuted, but not abandoned; struck down, but not destroyed. We always carry around in our body the death of Jesus, so that the life of Jesus may also be revealed in our body. For we who are alive are always being given over to death for Jesus' sake, so that his life may be revealed in our mortal body. So then, death is at work in us, but life is at work in you. It is written: "I believed; therefore I have spoken." With that same spirit of faith we also believe and therefore speak, because we know that the one who raised the Lord Jesus from the dead will also raise us with Jesus and present us with you in his presence. (2 Co.4:8-14).**

Just as Paul believed that God would deliver him through his trials and spoke accordingly, the psalmist spoke in faith. He believed that God would help him. He praised God from the pit of despair. When he could not go to the place where God's presence dwelled, he believed that God would come to him. He would be helped by God's presence.

The word *hope* in Scripture means something much stronger than what it often means today. When we talk about hope, we are usually speaking of a positive

---

3   Warren W. Wiersbe. *The Bible Exposition Commentary – Wisdom and Poetry.* Colorado Springs, CO: David C. Cook, 2004. WORD*search* CROSS e-book.

attitude toward the future, or a wish or desire, as in, "I hope what I want will happen...." But hope in Scripture is a firm assurance that God will do what He has promised, according to His perfect timing. Hope is the reality of what is yet to come. It rejoices in promises God has not yet fulfilled. This unshakable confidence strengthens us to wait and endure until the Lord performs what He has promised.

Verse 5 is a refrain that declares the great lesson of this song: in times of severe trial, when we find ourselves getting disheartened or discouraged, we need to proclaim our faith in God. We need to encourage ourselves in His faithfulness and find strength in His promises. Lifting up our praises to Him can drown out our cries of despair from within.

Thought 1. When is the last time you yearned for God, when you fervently desired His presence? Too often our prayers are consumed with what we need from God rather than for God's presence. Certainly, there is nothing wrong with asking God for what we need. In fact, Jesus taught us to do so (Mt.6:11). But we must realize that *the greatest need of our lives is for God Himself, His holy presence*. We were created for a relationship with Him. Through Him, we have lasting satisfaction and fulfillment. We have joy, peace, security, and strength.

Imagine how you would feel if your children only talked to you when they wanted something from you! Imagine how you would feel if they never climbed into your lap, or begged you to play with them, or put their arms around your neck and kissed you! Surely the heart of God must break when we, His dear children, desire only what He can give us. Surely He grieves when we do not yearn for *Him* and for His assuring presence!

The great reward for seeking God is finding Him (Je.29:13). But we must seek Him with all of our hearts, as this psalmist did. When we genuinely and wholeheartedly yearn for God, we will find Him. He will hear and respond to us and, in Him, we will find everything that we need.

> **Blessed are those who hunger and thirst for righteousness, for they will be filled (Mt.5:6).**
>
> **On the last and greatest day of the Feast, Jesus stood and said in a loud voice, "If anyone is thirsty, let him come to me and drink (Jn.7:37).**
>
> **O God, you are my God, earnestly I seek you; my soul thirsts for you, my body longs for you, in a dry and weary land where there is no water (Ps.63:1).**
>
> **You will seek me and find me when you seek me with all your heart (Je.29:13).**

Thought 2. Notice how the psalmist longed to worship God with the congregation (v.4). He was truly grieved because he could not be in God's house with God's people. Sadly, many professing believers today do not share his passion for assembling with God's people for worship. To many, church attendance is a dreaded duty rather than an anticipated delight. Tragically, the zeal for corporate worship that David and the early church experienced is missing in many hearts today (Ac.2:46-47, Ps.122:1). Yet God's command regarding assembling with His people remains unchanged:

> **Let us not give up meeting together, as some are in the habit of doing, but let us encourage one another—and all the more as you see the Day approaching (He.10:25).**

Note the clear exhortation of this verse: as we draw nearer to Christ's return and the day of God's judgment, we should assemble with God's people *more*, not less. We need the encouragement of God's people and the preaching of His Word to help us remain faithful to Him during the perilous times in which we live (2 Ti.3:1). We have to resolve to be faithful to God's house and make gathering with God's people a foremost priority in our lives.

> **Every day they continued to meet together in the temple courts. They broke bread in their homes and ate together with glad and sincere hearts, praising God and enjoying the favor of all the people. And the Lord added to their number daily those who were being saved (Ac.2:46-47).**
>
> **And let us consider how we may spur one another on toward love and good deeds. Let us not give up meeting together, as some are in the habit of doing, but let us encourage one another—and all the more as you see the Day approaching (He.10:24-25).**
>
> **I rejoiced with those who said to me, "Let us go to the house of the LORD" (Ps.122:1).**

2 (42:6-11) **Remember God no matter how desperate your situation.**
One of the greatest lessons of *Psalms* is that we, as believers, have the liberty to empty our souls to God. That is, we can express our deepest, innermost feelings and thoughts to Him. After the psalmist encouraged himself with words of hope, he took his burden to the LORD in prayer. When it seemed that God had forgotten him, he remembered God and looked up to Him from the depths of his despair. Remembering God's unfailing love sustained him in his darkest hours.

a. Remember Him even if you are a foreigner exiled to a distant land (v.6).

The psalmist's despair was likely due, in part, to the fact that he was far from home. The three geographic landmarks he mentioned identify his location as being close to...

- the Jordan River
- Mount Hermon
- Mount Mizar

Reaching over 9,000 feet high, Mount Hermon was the tallest peak in a range of mountains where the Jordan River has its source. Its location is at the northeast boundary of Israel. *Mizar* means *little hill* and was apparently a smaller peak in this same mountain range.

The psalmist was approximately 150 miles from Jerusalem, a short distance by today's travel standards. But in Biblical times, it was a journey of five to seven days. It is no wonder that the depressed psalmist felt he was a world away from his home, Jerusalem, and the temple where God's presence resided. Yet from his remote location he resolved to remember the LORD. When he could not go to God, he was determined to bring God near to him by focusing his thoughts on the LORD and His unfailing love.

Many people find themselves far from home due to necessity or circumstances beyond their control. College students, military personnel, and missionaries are examples of some who spend long periods of time away from home. Employment requires others to leave family and friends behind. And, sadly, in our fallen world, refugees and persecuted peoples are often forced from their homelands.

When we are separated from the people and places we love, we are prone to feel separated from God, as if He too were far from us. Loneliness and a longing for home are powerful emotions that can easily distract us from our purpose or mission. When compounded by other trials or troubling circumstances, we can quickly find ourselves drowning in despair. During these times, we need to focus on God's faithfulness and enter into His comforting presence through earnest prayer.

b. Remember Him even when you feel overwhelmed by problems and sense the judgment of God (v.7).

The psalmist felt overwhelmed by the problems crashing in all around him. As he watched water cascade over the boulders of Hermon and into the Jordan, he felt that the waterspouts or waterfalls were violently pouring down on him, as if he were struggling to survive in the turbulent flow.

The phrase "deep calls to deep" pictures one wave of the deep calling out to another wave of the deep to coordinate a conspiracy in their efforts to drown

the psalmist, figuratively speaking....Like a stranded sailor clinging to a piece of driftwood in a raging storm, he was tossed back and forth, taking in water, sinking fast with no hope of rescue.[4]

At times, God's judgment is portrayed as a storm or as crashing waters in Scripture. Some commentators think that the psalmist viewed his extreme trials as God's judgment being poured out upon him. Because we do not know the identity of the psalmist, we cannot know the specific circumstances that prompted this psalm. It is possible that some sinful action brought God's chastening upon him like a flood. But it is also possible that he was being unjustly persecuted, as when Saul jealously pursued David.

c. Remember the LORD's unfailing love: Pray to and praise the God who gives you life (v.8).

Struggling to survive in a raging sea of doubt and despair, the psalmist grabbed hold of this wonderful truth: he was surrounded by God's love. Note that this is the only time in these psalms the author refers to God as *the LORD* (Yahweh, Jehovah), God's covenant name. *Love* (chesed) is God's covenant love for His people, demonstrating His mercy, His steadfast love. During the psalmist's difficult days, the LORD sent His unfailing love sweeping over his dear follower, keeping him afloat in the rushing current of trials. In the dark nights, the LORD comforted him with His song, like a mother singing a calming lullaby to her frightened child. It was God who sustained his life and strengthened him to endure the severe trials.

d. Remember Him even when you feel He is distant and has forgotten all about you (v.9ᵃ).

The psalmist remembered God's unfailing love when his trouble plunged his soul into doubt. God was his Rock, his refuge, the one to whom he tightly clung in his sea of despair. He cried out to God just as we do, asking why God was allowing him to be harassed by his enemies. He felt as if God had deserted him again, just as we often feel when we are in despair. But this was not true. God loved him, just as He loves us. In fact, Scripture says that God cannot forget us, for we are etched upon the palm of His hand (Is.49:14-16).

e. Remember Him when enemies (unbelievers) oppress you (vv.9ᵇ-10).

Again, the author referred to the stabbing taunts of his enemies who mocked his faith in God. Their ridicule was as sharp as a double-edged sword, piercing all the way through him to his *bones* like a mortal wound. Their relentless scoffing may have tempted him to ask the same question they asked: "Where is your God?"

---

4   Steven Lawson and Max Anders. *Holman Old Testament Commentary—Psalms.* (Nashville, TN: B & H Publishing Group, 2004), WORD*search* CROSS e-book.

f. **Remember Him even when you are downcast and disturbed within (v.11).**

As the author again dwelled on his trouble, despair took control of his spirit. Once more, he confronted his raging emotions and admonished himself to put his hope in God. The antidote for his depression would be to *praise* (yadah) God, to lift his hands in worship to Him, to confess what is right about God in praise and thanksgiving.[5] As he offered the sacrifice of praise, God would fill him with inner peace and joy and replace his troubled expression with a smile.

Thought 1. The psalmist refused to give in to his depression, choosing instead to battle it by remembering God. Note three life-changing applications here that can help us when we are bound by despair:

First, the psalmist focused on the truth of God's Word rather than on the lies that tormented his soul. Overwhelmed by his troubles, the psalmist felt that God had forgotten him. *But this was not true!* The truth was, he was surrounded by God's unfailing love even in the midst of his problems.

One of the most effective ways Satan attacks us is through our minds—through our flawed and often foolish thinking. So many of the doubts that plague us are simply not true. They are the imaginations of our minds, thoughts that are contrary to what we know about God. Scripture teaches that we must take these thoughts captive and subject them to the obedience of Christ (2 Co.10:5). We are commanded to focus our minds on the things that are true, pure, and of good report (Ph.4:8).

Second, the psalmist focused on God's unfailing love even in the midst of his trouble. He recognized God's goodness in his life and clung to God's mercy in his sea of discouragement. No matter how bad things may get in our lives, God loves us and He is good to us. Nothing can separate us from His love (Ro.8:35-39).

Third, the psalmist chose to praise the LORD from his pit of depression. Praising God lifted him out of the depths of despair, putting a smile on his face and giving him a song in his heart. Praise is truly powerful. As our praise blesses the LORD, it also changes us.

> **We demolish arguments and every pretension that sets itself up against the knowledge of God, and we take captive every thought to make it obedient to Christ (2 Co.10:5).**
>
> **Finally, brothers, whatever is true, whatever is noble, whatever is right, whatever is pure, whatever is lovely, whatever is admirable—if anything is excellent or praiseworthy—think about such things (Ph.4:8).**

---

5 Spiros Zodhiates. *AMG Complete Word Study Dictionary*. Chattanooga, TN: AMG Publishers, 1992. WORD*search* CROSS e-book.

> The LORD appeared to us in the past, saying: "I have loved you with an everlasting love; I have drawn you with loving-kindness (Je.31:3).

3 (43:1-2) **Pray for God to defend and deliver you.**
After crying out to God about his troubled soul, the psalmist prayed about the critical situation in which he found himself. With boldness and staunch conviction, he asked God to judge or vindicate him, to determine that he was innocent of his enemies' accusations. The psalmist then wanted God to plead his cause and to defend him before the people. God and God alone could deliver him from such oppression!

a. **Because you live in an ungodly nation—among deceitful and wicked people (v.1).**

By describing his oppressors as ungodly, the psalmist was likely saying that they did not know the LORD. Perhaps they were ungodly neighbors, fellow workers, or the people of a heathen nation. Whatever the case, because they were not living by God's holy law, they were deceitful in their attacks upon him and unjust in their judgments.

b. **Because God is your strength, your refuge, your haven (v.2ᵃ).**

The troubled author trusted in God as his *stronghold* (ma'owz)—his strength, fortress, or place of refuge. Because he had lived faithfully under the shelter of God's protection, he could not understand how these horrible events had happened to him. Therefore, he continued to ask God why he was in this situation (42:9).

c. **Because you feel rejected by God—forsaken to suffer oppression (v.2ᵇ).**

The psalmist felt that God had cast him off, that He had forsaken or rejected him. No doubt, the grief his oppressors caused him was agonizing, but even more unbearable was the feeling that he was separated from God. He needed God, and he yearned for fellowship with Him (42:1-2).

Thought 1. At various times in our lives, we find ourselves trapped in situations over which we have no control. Like the psalmist, we may be victims of slander or false judgment by people who want to hurt us. Or, we may be facing grave illness, marital or family problems, financial crises, or the death of a loved one. At some point in time, we will all know the feeling of being powerless to change an extremely grievous situation.

When we reach the end of ourselves and our abilities, we need to remember that God can do what we cannot do. His strength is revealed through our weakness and inability. Thankfully, He invites us to come boldly to His holy throne, seeking grace and mercy to help us in our time of need (He.4:16).

When under the pressure of crushing circumstances, we are prone to question God's love and care for us. It is easy to feel that He has rejected or forsaken us. In such times, we must rest in His promises to never leave or forsake us. He promises to stand by us in the fiery trials of life. We may not always understand *why* God permits us to face grievous situations, but we can be sure that He does not allow us to go through them alone. Consider Shadrach, Meshach, and Abednego in the fiery furnace (see outline and notes—Da.3:1-30). Just as He was with these faithful servants in their time of dire need, He will surely be with us.

> **He has delivered us from such a deadly peril, and he will deliver us. On him we have set our hope that he will continue to deliver us (2 Co.1:10).**
>
> **Keep your lives free from the love of money and be content with what you have, because God has said, "Never will I leave you; never will I forsake you." So we say with confidence, "The Lord is my helper; I will not be afraid. What can man do to me?" (He.13:5-6).**
>
> **He said: "The LORD is my rock, my fortress and my deliverer; my God is my rock, in whom I take refuge, my shield and the horn of my salvation. He is my stronghold, my refuge and my savior— from violent men you save me (2 S.22:2-3).**
>
> **When you pass through the waters, I will be with you; and when you pass through the rivers, they will not sweep over you. When you walk through the fire, you will not be burned; the flames will not set you ablaze (Is.43:2).**
>
> **Even to your old age and gray hairs I am he, I am he who will sustain you. I have made you and I will carry you; I will sustain you and I will rescue you (Is.46:4).**

4 (43:3-4) **Ask God to restore you.**
The psalmist again asked God to deliver him from his pit of despair. He needed God to restore him to a place of joy and peace. For him, this meant a return to the place where God's presence dwelled. He entreated God to bring him back home to Jerusalem, back to the temple where he would once again worship in the LORD's presence. The psalmist reasoned that this restoration could only come after God had vindicated or defended him before his enemies.

a. **To give you His light and truth to guide you (v.3ᵃ).**
The psalmist realized that his own conduct—his words and actions—played a part in his restoration. Therefore, he asked God to lead or guide him by His light and His truth. Just as God had led the Israelites through the wilderness and into the promised land, the psalmist prayed that God would guide him each step of the way back to Jerusalem. He was not asking for geographical direction but for *personal* direction, what he should do and how he should conduct himself.

At times in the psalms, *light* refers to God's presence (4:6; 44:3; 89:15). It also speaks of God's comfort and guidance during the dark times in our lives (78:14; 112:4). On another occasion, it refers to God's Word (119:105).

Truth (emeth) is one of God's attributes, one of His unique, holy characteristics as God. It speaks of God's faithfulness to His holy character, His laws, and His Word. As it is here, it is frequently connected to God's mercy and *love* (chesed, His steadfast, covenant love) in the *Psalms* (25:10; 40:10-11; 86:15; 138:2). It is also mentioned along with God's righteousness (45:4; 85:11; 96:13), His justice (89:14; 111:7), and His peace (85:10; 2 K.20:19; Is.39:8).[6] God's truth is revealed and preserved in His Holy Word (Ps.119:43, 142, 160; Da.10:21).

To summarize, the psalmist called upon God to demonstrate His faithfulness and love by guiding him back to Jerusalem. Through the light and truth of His Word, God would direct what he should say and do.

b. **To lead you into His presence—the place where He lives (v.3ᵇ).**
The psalmist prayed that God's light and truth would bring him back to the LORD's *holy mountain*, which is Mount Zion or Jerusalem. Mount Zion is called a holy hill because it was the location of the LORD's tabernacle, the place on earth where God dwelled among His people.

c. **To make way for you to worship and praise Him— God, who is the source of your joy (v.4).**
From the very beginning of this song, the exiled psalmist emphasized his heart's burning desire to experience God's presence again. Note his "progression of increasing closeness [to God]…"
- the *holy mountain*
- the dwelling place or tabernacle
- the *altar* of *God*
- *God* Himself [7]

---

6   Spiros Zodhiates. *AMG Complete Word Study Dictionary*. WORD-*search* CROSS e-book.
7   Gordon J. Wenham, J. Alec Motyer, Donald A. Carson and R. T. France. *New Bible Commentary*. IVP Academic, 1994. WORD*search* CROSS e-book.

More than deliverance from his enemies and returning to his home, the psalmist yearned to be in God's holy presence once again. He exuberantly confessed that God was his exceeding joy, his greatest joy, more than anyone or anything else. He vowed that the first thing he would do upon entering Jerusalem would be to go to the altar of God and offer sacrifices of thanksgiving to the LORD. Once there, he would offer a song of praise with his harp in the presence of God, my God. [8]

Thought 1. There is no greater joy in life than basking in the presence of God, than spending time in fellowship with Him. Grasp the psalmist's thirst for a *personal* encounter with God as he addresses the LORD as *God, my God.* God was more to him than just *the* God of heaven and earth; the God of heaven and earth was *his* God. He knew God *personally* through a relationship with Him. The circumstances of his life had kept him from the special place where God's presence on earth was revealed, and he longed to be there.

Today, God's presence dwells within us as believers through His Holy Spirit. God's Spirit is the light who guides us into God's truth (Jn.16:13). Therefore, wherever we are, God is with us. Regardless how severe a circumstance or situation may be, it cannot keep us from living in God's presence. When we are feeling depressed, we need to turn to the Lord right away and ask Him to draw us into His presence. We can enter God's presence through prayer. In fact, we can come directly before His throne (He.4:16). When we are able to take our eyes off our own circumstances and place them on the Lord, basking in His presence, He will lift us from depression and restore joy to our souls. Thus, we can know the joy of the Lord in our hearts even in the most difficult circumstances.

It is critical to understand, however, that sin in our lives hinders our fellowship with God and keeps us from enjoying His presence. We have to resist temptation in order to live in unbroken fellowship with God. But when we do sin—and we all do—we should immediately seek to be restored to fellowship with God. Once we confess our sins to the Lord and turn from them, God promises to cleanse us and to restore our fellowship with Him (1 Jn.1:9).

There is no question that sin is pleasurable for a short season (He.11:25). But what a price we pay for those fleeting moments of sin! We forfeit the privilege of living in fellowship with God. God's presence should be the most important thing in our lives, far more important than the temporary pleasures of sin. No matter what our state of mind, we ought to pray for the joy of the Lord always. He should be our greatest joy, far exceeding the joy offered by this world's pleasures, possessions, and people!

---

8 Scholars who believe that David wrote both Psalms 42 and 43 point to the mention of the harp as an evidence of his authorship.

But when he, the Spirit of truth, comes, he will guide you into all truth. He will not speak on his own; he will speak only what he hears, and he will tell you what is yet to come (Jn.16:13).

If we confess our sins, he is faithful and just and will forgive us our sins and purify us from all unrighteousness (1 Jn.1:9).

You have made known to me the path of life; you will fill me with joy in your presence, with eternal pleasures at your right hand (Ps.16:11).

Do not cast me from your presence or take your Holy Spirit from me. Restore to me the joy of your salvation and grant me a willing spirit, to sustain me (Ps.51:11-12).

5 (43:5) **Encourage yourself in the LORD: Put your hope in God and praise Him, for He is your Savior and God.**
This song closes with the now familiar refrain of self-encouragement. Until God delivered him from his oppressors and returned him to Jerusalem, the psalmist determined to live above depression and despair. As he evaluated the reasons why he was so downcast and disturbed, he realized that his hope in God was greater than the circumstances that depressed him. God was *his* Savior and *his* God. Triumphantly, he resolved to praise Him regardless of his circumstances.

Thought 1. This song teaches us what to do when we are deeply discouraged or suffering from depression: we have to encourage ourselves in the LORD and focus on the great hope we have in Him. Without the Lord, life on this sin-cursed earth is difficult at best. It is filled with natural disasters, devastating tragedies, and endless problems beyond our control. Yet God has given us hope to sustain us in these times. This hope is the anchor of our souls (see outline and notes—He.6:16-20 for more discussion). God has promised to give us sufficient grace to carry us through every trial, and He has promised that He will work out every circumstance for our good (2 Co.12:9; Ro.8:28). Our role is to trust Him and to press on with the full assurance of His promises. He assures us that His promises will come to pass, and it is impossible for God to lie (He.6:11-18). Therefore, through faith and perseverance, even when everything seems to be against us, we should praise God, for He is our Savior and our God. Our hope is in Him and Him alone.

For everything that was written in the past was written to teach us, so that through endurance and the

encouragement of the Scriptures we might have hope (Ro.15:4).

We want each of you to show this same diligence to the very end, in order to make your hope sure. We do not want you to become lazy, but to imitate those who through faith and patience inherit what has been promised (He.6:11-12).

David was greatly distressed because the men were talking of stoning him; each one was bitter in spirit because of his sons and daughters. But David found strength in the LORD his God (1 S.30:6).

Be strong and take heart, all you who hope in the LORD (Ps.31:24).

PSALM 44

When You Are Crushed & Feel Rejected by God, 44:1-26

For the director of music. Of the Sons of Korah. A maskil.

1. Remember God's help & deliverance in the past

  a. He defeated all enemies & planted the ancestors of faith in the promised land (a symbol of heaven)

  b. He was the victor who won the promised land
    1) The promised land was not won bc. of the people's power but bc. of God's triumphant power
    2) The promised land was won bc. He loved them

2. Declare your confidence in God
  a. He alone is your King & your God
  b. He alone can give you victory
    1) You can defeat your enemies only by God's power & authority (name), Ep.6:10-13
      • You should not trust in human weapons for victory, Ep.6:12
      • You need to acknowledge that God alone makes you victorious
    2) You are to boast in God alone & constantly praise His name

3. Tell God how you feel: Rejected, shamed, & abandoned by Him

  a. Reason1: Bc. the enemy has defeated you & stolen what is yours

    1) You feel forsaken
      • Offered up to be devoured

We have heard with our ears, O God; our fathers have told us what you did in their days, in days long ago.
2 With your hand you drove out the nations and planted our fathers; you crushed the peoples and made our fathers flourish.
3 It was not by their sword that they won the land, nor did their arm bring them victory; it was your right hand, your arm, and the light of your face, for you loved them.
4 You are my King and my God, who decrees victories for Jacob.
5 Through you we push back our enemies; through your name we trample our foes.
6 I do not trust in my bow, my sword does not bring me victory;
7 But you give us victory over our enemies, you put our adversaries to shame.
8 In God we make our boast all day long, and we will praise your name forever. Selah
9 But now you have rejected and humbled us; you no longer go out with our armies.
10 You made us retreat before the enemy, and our adversaries have plundered us.
11 You gave us up to be devoured like sheep and have

scattered us among the nations.
12 You sold your people for a pittance, gaining nothing from their sale.
13 You have made us a reproach to our neighbors, the scorn and derision of those around us.
14 You have made us a byword among the nations; the peoples shake their heads at us.
15 My disgrace is before me all day long, and my face is covered with shame
16 At the taunts of those who reproach and revile me, because of the enemy, who is bent on revenge.
17 All this happened to us, though we had not forgotten you or been false to your covenant.
18 Our hearts had not turned back; our feet had not strayed from your path.
19 But you crushed us and made us a haunt for jackals and covered us over with deep darkness.
20 If we had forgotten the name of our God or spread out our hands to a foreign god,
21 Would not God have discovered it, since he knows the secrets of the heart?
22 Yet for your sake we face death all day long; we are considered as sheep to be slaughtered.
23 Awake, O Lord! Why do you sleep? Rouse yourself! Do not reject us forever.
24 Why do you hide your face and forget our misery and oppression?
25 We are brought down to the dust; our bodies cling to the ground.
26 Rise up and help us; redeem us because of your unfailing love.

      • Scattered among unbelievers (heathen nations)
    2) You feel God has disposed of you cheaply for enslavement by the enemy
  b. Reason 2: Bc. you are suffering deep personal anguish
    1) The pain of being despised & scorned by neighbors
    2) The pain of being an object of ridicule, rejected by those around you

    3) The pain of being humiliated & overwhelmed with shame
    4) The pain of being criticized & condemned
    5) The fear of being persecuted by vengeful enemies

4. Search your heart for any known sin
  a. Be loyal: Do not forget God nor disobey His Word (covenant)
    1) Do not backslide, turn away from, or stray from God's way
      • Even when broken or crushed
      • Even when facing the darkness of death
    2) Do not worship false gods

      • Bc. God will know it
      • Bc. God knows the secrets of your heart
  b. Be faithful: Bear all suffering for God's sake, for His honor & praise

5. Keep asking God to deliver you
  a. Bc. you need immediate help
    1) You feel rejected by God
    2) You feel God ignores your suffering

    3) You are as low—as desperate—as you can possibly be
  b. Bc. you need Him to redeem (save) you
  c. Bc. you trust His unfailing love

PSALM 44

When You Are Crushed and Feel Rejected by God, 44:1-26

(44:1-26) **Introduction:** *"...the thrill of victory, and the agony of defeat...."* These gripping words became the catchphrase of a popular television sports program that aired in America for nearly forty years. They not only summarize the essence of athletic competitions around the world but also of life in general. In our time on earth, we too will experience the thrill and the agony, the victory and the defeat, the triumphs and the failures, the wins and the losses.

Throughout the Old Testament, Israel often basked in the thrill of victory. As God's chosen nation and the recipient of His covenant, the LORD fought for Israel, displaying His wonder-working power on her behalf. But the Old Testament also records times when the Hebrews tasted the agony of defeat. Psalm 44 was written on one of those occasions.

We do not know the specific failure that prompted the psalm's writing, nor can we be sure of its author. It is identified as one of the psalms *for* or *of the sons of Korah*. Whether these devoted worshippers wrote these psalms or had them assigned to them is unclear. Some scholars feel that the author of Psalm 44 was the reigning king when this defeat was suffered. Similar to Psalm 60, some believe that it too is a psalm of David. Psalm 44 is a national psalm; that is, it speaks for the entire nation of Israel.

As we study the Bible, we learn that when we live faithfully for God and obey His commandments, we can expect to be victorious, successful, and prosperous. Yet God's Word also teaches us that this is not always true. Consider Hebrews 11, the great chapter that exalts the faith of many Old Testament heroes. Hebrews 11:4-31 recalls the glorious and sometimes miraculous feats of Noah, Abraham, Moses, Joshua, and a number of other faith-filled saints. On the other hand, verses 36-38 remind us that other believers who were just as faithful had totally different experiences:

> **Some faced jeers and flogging, while still others were chained and put in prison. They were stoned; they were sawed in two; they were put to death by the sword. They went about in sheepskins and goatskins, destitute, persecuted and mistreated—the world was not worthy of them. They wandered in deserts and mountains, and in caves and holes in the ground (He.11:36-38).**

When we suffer a crushing failure or defeat, it is easy to feel rejected by God. We do not understand why the overwhelming loss occurred or how God could allow it to happen. Psalm 44 is written for these times in our lives. It is a *maskil* psalm, or a psalm of instruction. God's Spirit, the inspirer of Scripture, teaches us what to do *When You Are Crushed and Feel Rejected by God,* 44:1-26.

1. Remember God's help and deliverance in the past (vv.1-3).
2. Declare your confidence in God (vv.4-8).
3. Tell God how you feel: Rejected, shamed, and abandoned by Him (vv.9-16).
4. Search your heart for any known sin (vv.17-22).
5. Keep asking God to deliver you (vv.23-26).

1(44:1-3) **Remember God's help and deliverance in the past.**
The grieving people of Israel began their prayer by recalling the victories of previous generations. In faithful obedience to the LORD's command, their ancestors had preserved the accounts of God's marvelous power

(Ex.12:24-28; 13:8-9; Jos.4:5-9). Thus, they were fully aware of God's miraculous intervention throughout their history.

a. **He defeated all enemies and planted the ancestors of faith in the promised land (a symbol of heaven) (v.2).**
The Jewish people gave God the glory for everything they enjoyed. He, not they, had driven out the unbelieving heathen or Gentile people of Canaan so their ancestors would possess it. They dwelled in the land because of His grace and His promise to Abraham (see outline and notes—Ge.12:1-3; *Numbers,* INTRODUCTION, Special Feature 26 for more discussion).

b. **He was the victor who won the promised land (v.3).**
Israel's forefathers did not possess the land by their own sword, that is, not by their military might, strategy, or strength (De.7:6-8; Jos.24:1-13). God had fought for them, delivering them from Egypt and establishing them in Canaan. They were triumphant because of His...
* *right hand*—a symbol of authority and unlimited power (Ex.15:6, 12: Is.41:10, 13)
* *arm*—a symbol of might and strength in battle (Ex.6:6; De.4:34; Is.63:12; Je.32:17)
* *face*—a symbol of favor and presence (Ex.33:14-17; Ps.4:6; 11:7; 42:5)

God blessed Israel simply because He loved them and chose them as the recipients of His favor. They did not deserve the bountiful gifts God gave them, nor had they done anything to earn them. God delighted in them, and it pleased Him to shower them with His grace.

Thought 1. We must give God the credit for every victory and blessing that comes our way. Although we may fight and labor, it is God who makes us successful. With Him, we can do all things (Ph.4:13). Without Him, we can do nothing (Jn.15:5).

Likewise, we should remember that our inheritance of eternal life and heaven, as represented by the promised land, is not due to anything we have done. It is entirely the gift of God's mercy and grace toward us. We can do nothing to earn it or purchase it. It is ours through the work of Jesus Christ, who secured it for us through His sacrificial death on the cross. Because God loves us, He chose us and bestowed His unmerited favor upon us, making us the heirs of eternal life through faith in His Son (Ro.5:8; Ep.2:8-9; Tit.3:4-7).

> **Every good and perfect gift is from above, coming down from the Father of**

the heavenly lights, who does not change like shifting shadows (Js.1:17).

"I am the vine; you are the branches. If a man remains in me and I in him, he will bear much fruit; apart from me you can do nothing (Jn.15:5).

For who makes you different from anyone else? What do you have that you did not receive? And if you did receive it, why do you boast as though you did not? (1 Co.4:7).

You may say to yourself, "My power and the strength of my hands have produced this wealth for me." But remember the LORD your God, for it is he who gives you the ability to produce wealth, and so confirms his covenant, which he swore to your forefathers, as it is today (De.8:17-18).

2 (44:4-8) **Declare your confidence in God.**
Even though the people of Israel had suffered a devastating defeat at the hands of their enemies, they still confessed their faith in God. Broken and battered, they did not understand why God had permitted them to experience this crushing loss, for they had not wavered in their commitment to the LORD. Nevertheless, they remained steadfast in their allegiance to God, declaring that they continued to trust Him and His power to give them victory.

a. He alone is your King and your God (v.4ᵃ).
Although Israel had a human leader, her people acknowledged God as their king. Notice the use of *my* in this statement and the use of *I, my,* and *me* in verse 6. These singular pronouns stand in clear contrast to the plural pronouns used throughout the rest of this psalm. Some scholars speculate that the nation's reigning king is the author or speaker of this psalm. If this is the case, he openly submitted himself to God, humbly confessing that God—not he—truly ruled over Israel. Another application can be made from these singular pronouns: a nation can collectively acknowledge God as their king, but it is only effective to the extent that He reigns in the hearts and lives of the individuals of that nation.

b. He alone can give you victory (v.4ᵇ-8)
The people of Israel understood that although their armies fought the battles, the LORD gave the victory (v.4ᵇ). For some reason, God had chosen not to make His people victorious in their most recent conflict. As they called on God to command or decree victories for their nation once again, they taught us two vital lessons:

First, we can only defeat our enemies through the power of God's name and His authority (v.5). The name of God that is prominent in this psalm and

throughout the second book of *Psalms* (ch.42–72) is *Elohim,* which means the strong, all-powerful One. The unbelieving nations that rose up against Israel are a picture of the spiritual enemies that we face today as New Testament believers. We do not battle against human foes, but against Satan and his demonic forces. Scripture instructs us to stand against them in God's power and authority:

Finally, be strong in the Lord and in his mighty power. Put on the full armor of God so that you can take your stand against the devil's schemes. For our struggle is not against flesh and blood, but against the rulers, against the authorities, against the powers of this dark world and against the spiritual forces of evil in the heavenly realms. Therefore put on the full armor of God, so that when the day of evil comes, you may be able to stand your ground, and after you have done everything, to stand (Ep.6:10-13).

Just as the Jewish people did not trust in their bows and swords to give them victory over their enemies (v.6), so we must not rely on our own resources in our battle against spiritual enemies. When spiritual powers try to destroy our effectiveness for Christ, we cannot overcome them with carnal or fleshly weapons.

For though we live in the world, we do not wage war as the world does. The weapons we fight with are not the weapons of the world. On the contrary, they have divine power to demolish strongholds (2 Co.10:3-4).

God has equipped us with two spiritual weapons: His mighty Word and prayer (Ep.6:17-18). We have to use these weapons to break the enemy's hold on us and gain the victory. Satan and his demonic forces are far stronger than we are. In our own strength, we are powerless against them. But, praise God, the Holy Spirit who dwells within us is more powerful than they or any other forces are; thus, through Him we can prevail (1 Jn.4:4). It is essential for us to understand that victory comes through God and God alone (v.7).

Second, we are to boast only in God and not in ourselves, never forgetting that our strength is in Him (v.8). We must resist any temptation to take credit for the victories He has won, for it is only through Him that we can be victorious. For all that He does for us, we should continually praise His name!

Thought 1. We all battle spiritual enemies on a daily basis. Giving in to our human weaknesses and sinful nature can cripple us spiritually. It can rob us of the joy of the Lord and render us ineffective for Him. With this is mind, the author of *Hebrews* instructs us to "throw off everything that hinders, and the sin that so easily entangles" (He.12:1). While temptation to sin comes from within (Js.1:15), Satan and his demonic forces work tirelessly against us. Among other things, they seek to influence our thinking and arrange circumstances to draw us into temptation. Their goal is to turn our weaknesses into strongholds that bind and oppress us.

The list of enemies that believers face is endless, for example...

- pride
- selfishness
- stubbornness
- hatred
- bitterness
- lack of forgiveness
- lack of discipline
- laziness
- procrastination
- gluttony
- gossip or unkind speech
- corrupt or foul language
- lying
- dishonesty
- stealing
- greed
- lack of contentment
- covetousness
- anger
- substance abuse/ addiction
- immorality
- lust
- pornography
- sexual perversion
- hopelessness
- doubt and unbelief
- worry
- discouragement
- depression
- negative thinking
- fear
- feelings of inadequacy
- low self-esteem

Add to this list whatever else you struggle with. Satan knows your weakness, and he and his forces seek ways to make you a slave to it. We will never gain victory over our spiritual enemies until we stop trying to fight them in our own power and surrender to the power of the Holy Spirit. We must faithfully rely on our spiritual weapons—God's Word and prayer—in our struggle against the enemy. We may suffer setbacks, and we may lose some battles against temptation. But we must not surrender the war. We have to keep fighting in the power of God. He is able to keep us from falling, and He promises to conform us into the image of Christ (Jude 24; Ph.1:6). Through faith in Him and His power, we can walk in victory.

> **The seventy-two returned with joy and said, "Lord, even the demons submit to us in your name" (Lu.10:17).**
>
> **No, in all these things we are more than conquerors through him who loved us (Ro.8:37).**
>
> **I can do everything through him who gives me strength (Ph.4:13).**
>
> **The Lord will rescue me from every evil attack and will bring me safely to his**

> **heavenly kingdom. To him be glory for ever and ever. Amen (2 Ti.4:18).**
>
> **You, dear children, are from God and have overcome them, because the one who is in you is greater than the one who is in the world (1 Jn.4:4).**
>
> **For everyone born of God overcomes the world. This is the victory that has overcome the world, even our faith (1 Jn.5:4).**
>
> **To him who is able to keep you from falling and to present you before his glorious presence without fault and with great joy (Jude 24).**

3 (44:9-16) **Tell God how you feel: Rejected, shamed, and abandoned by Him.**
The Israelites were totally devastated by their loss. The people felt that God had abandoned them when they needed Him the most, and they did not understand why. They felt that God—not the enemies who defeated the nation—was responsible for the shame they were experiencing. Hurting and humiliated, they poured out their broken hearts to the LORD.

a. **Reason 1: Because the enemy has defeated you and stolen what is yours (vv.10-12).**
   In their distress, the people of Israel could only attribute their disgraceful defeat to God. From their perspective, *He* had caused them to shamefully retreat from their enemies. *He* was responsible for their adversaries' spoiling or plundering them—stealing their possessions (v.10). *He* had allowed them to be devoured and scattered among the heathen or unbelieving nations (v.11). Like a person who sells property for no profit, *He* had given them over to be enslaved by their enemies (v.12).

b. **Reason 2: Because you are suffering deep personal anguish (vv.13-16)**
   Because God had seemingly abandoned them, the Hebrews suffered indescribable agony and humiliation. They bore the reproach of neighboring nations who mocked and disrespected them (v.13). They had become a byword among the heathen; that is, unbelievers made up jokes and amusing sayings about them (v.14ᵃ; De.28:37; 1 K.9:7). Godless people shook their heads in mocking contempt at what had happened to this nation that had faithfully worshipped the LORD (v.14ᵇ).

   The pain of being so severely shamed was more than the people of Israel could bear. They could not escape the confusion or disgrace they felt God was forcing them to endure (v.15). The voices of those who taunted and reviled them were constantly in their ears, and they lived in nagging fear of their vengeful enemies (v.16).

Thought 1. No matter how badly we are hurting, we can freely pour out our hearts to God. Even when we do not understand His ways, we can cry out to Him. He cares for us more than we can ever imagine! Our Lord actually invites us to come to Him freely and boldly, casting all our cares and requests at His feet. But whatever we ask must be with unwavering faith (Js.1:5-7).

> **For we do not have a high priest who is unable to sympathize with our weaknesses, but we have one who has been tempted in every way, just as we are—yet was without sin (He.4:15).**
>
> **If any of you lacks wisdom, he should ask God, who gives generously to all without finding fault, and it will be given to him. But when he asks, he must believe and not doubt, because he who doubts is like a wave of the sea, blown and tossed by the wind. That man should not think he will receive anything from the Lord (Js.1:5-7).**
>
> **Cast all your anxiety on him because he cares for you (1 Pe.5:7).**
>
> **Cast your cares on the LORD and he will sustain you; he will never let the righteous fall (Ps.55:22).**

Thought 2. Were the people of Israel right in what they were feeling about God? Had the LORD unjustly rejected His people, leaving them to suffer a crushing defeat at the hands of their enemy? Insightful commentator Donald M. Williams offers another perspective, one worthy of quoting here in its entirety:

> *If it is true, as the psalm suggests, that Israel has been faithful to God and doesn't deserve defeat for her sins (see vv.17-22), then is it possible that she has gone to fight the wrong war, presuming upon God's presence rather than waiting for his will and then His presence? As we have already seen, Moses demands the presence of God before he moves. Are not Israel and the church, however, quite willing to assume God's blessing and then launch ahead with battles, plans, and programs? Too often we, like the disciples, come up empty-handed. We have to say with Peter that we have fished all night and caught nothing. This report could be inscribed over many a church and many a Christian work. Idealism, pressing need, even scriptural justification are not enough. Has God told us to move? Has He mandated our ministry? If not, He won't "go out with our armies."[1]*

Simply put, Dr. Williams is saying that we should be sure of God's will before attempting any endeavor. When we fail, it may not be because God has forsaken us, but because we did not follow Him. We cannot expect God to bless any undertaking that is not His will. How can we expect Him to go with us when we are not walking in His direction? We are unjust toward God when we blame Him for our failure to follow Him.

While we do not know if a failure to follow God's direction caused Israel's defeat, it is often the cause of our defeats. We should earnestly seek God's will before making any major decisions or taking any significant steps, refusing to make any move until we have His peace (Ph.4:7; Col.3:15). God's will is not difficult to discern. He wants us to live in His will. Scripture teaches that we can clearly know God's will (Col.1:9), fully understand it (Ep.5:17), and even prove it (Ro.12:2). We can only expect God to go with us when we wait on Him. When we get ahead of God, we should not be surprised when we fail.

> **Therefore, I urge you, brothers, in view of God's mercy, to offer your bodies as living sacrifices, holy and pleasing to God—this is your spiritual act of worship. Do not conform any longer to the pattern of this world, but be transformed by the renewing of your mind. Then you will be able to test and approve what God's will is—his good, pleasing and perfect will (Ro.12:1-2).**
>
> **Do not be anxious about anything, but in everything, by prayer and petition, with thanksgiving, present your requests to God. And the peace of God, which transcends all understanding, will guard your hearts and your minds in Christ Jesus (Ph.4:6-7).**
>
> **Let the peace of Christ rule in your hearts, since as members of one body you were called to peace. And be thankful (Col.3:15).**
>
> **Trust in the LORD with all your heart and lean not on your own understanding; in all your ways acknowledge him, and he will make your paths straight (Pr.3:5-6).**

4 (44:17-22) **Search your heart for any known sin.** Upon suffering such a disgraceful defeat, the Israelites examined themselves to discern if they had sinned against the LORD. God had warned the nation that if they strayed from Him and worshipped other gods, He would remove His blessing from them (De.6:14-19; 8:19). Throughout Israel's history, the people's sin had brought God's judgment on their nation (Jos.7; 2 S.21:1-14; 2 S.24).

---

1 Donald Williams. *Psalms 73-150.* "The Preacher's Commentary," Volume 13. (Nashville, TN: Thomas Nelson Publishers, 2002). Reprinted by permission. All rights reserved, p.343.

a. Be loyal: Do not forget God nor disobey His Word (covenant) (vv.17-21).

Even though Israel had been faithful to the LORD, the people suffered a devastating loss in this case. They boldly declared that they had not forgotten God, nor had they violated His holy covenant (v.17; Ex.19:5-6; 24:7-8). They had not turned back from obeying the LORD, and their feet had adhered strictly to God's way or path of righteousness (v.18).

Even when it seemed God had abandoned them, the Israelites remained faithful to God. Crushed, broken, and overshadowed by death, they steadfastly maintained their devotion to the LORD and His commandments (v.19). *A haunt for jackals* describes "a scene of ruin and desolation, a waste, howling wilderness, [inhabited] only by wild beasts" (Is.34:13; 35:7; Je.49:33).[2]

Specifically, the people strongly insisted that they had not worshipped idols; they had not forgotten the name of God (v.20). If they were lying, God would know, for He knows every secret of the heart (v.21). We can hide nothing from Him.

b. Be faithful: Bear all suffering for God's sake, for His honor and praise (v.22).

For some purpose unknown to Israel, God had allowed them to suffer this appalling defeat. Therefore, they concluded that they were suffering *for [His] sake.* The image of *sheep to be slaughtered* is also used of the Lord Jesus Christ, the lamb of God who was led to Calvary to die for our sin (Is.53:7).

The Holy Spirit inspired New Testament authors to shed more light on this subject of suffering for God's sake. Paul cited this verse in discussing the trials and persecutions that believers encounter (Ro.8:35-36). Paul also stated that our persecutions are "for Jesus' sake" (2 Co.4:8-11; 12:10). Peter added that we sometimes suffer "according to God's will" (1 Pe.4:19).

When God's plan for our lives includes suffering, we should bear it for His sake, always bringing honor and praise to Him. He has promised us sufficient grace for every trial (2 Co.12:9). In addition, He has assured us that He is working all things together for our good (Ro.8:28). The Lord even works good from the evil that others do to us (Ge.50:20). As we suffer for His sake, we are sharing in the sufferings of Christ, and we will likewise share in His glory (1 Pe.4:13; 5:1). At the same time, God is transforming us into the image of His Son (Ro.8:29). For these reasons, we should glorify God when we suffer as Christians (1 Pe.4:16).

Thought 1. Sometimes suffering is the direct result of sin. Therefore, like the defeated Israelites, when trouble or affliction invades our lives, we should examine ourselves to see if we are guilty of some sin. If we do not deal with sin in our lives, God will deal with it by disciplining us (1 Co.11:31-32). Because He loves us so much, our Heavenly Father will not allow us to destroy our lives and hurt others by continuing in sin (He.12:5-11).

As we try to discern God's purpose for a trial or suffering, we should begin by searching our hearts for unconfessed sin. If we find that we are living faithfully in obedience to God's commandments, like the Israelites in this psalm, we can move on in seeking to understand God's purpose for our suffering. But if we find that there is sin in our lives, we need to immediately confess it and forsake it through the power of God's Spirit (Ps.32:1-6; Pr.28:13; 1 Jn.1:9).

> **But if we judged ourselves, we would not come under judgment. When we are judged by the Lord, we are being disciplined so that we will not be condemned with the world (1 Co.11:31-32).**
>
> **If we confess our sins, he is faithful and just and will forgive us our sins and purify us from all unrighteousness (1 Jn.1:9).**
>
> **Blessed is he whose transgressions are forgiven, whose sins are covered. Blessed is the man whose sin the LORD does not count against him and in whose spirit is no deceit. When I kept silent, my bones wasted away through my groaning all day long. For day and night your hand was heavy upon me; my strength was sapped as in the heat of summer. Selah Then I acknowledged my sin to you and did not cover up my iniquity. I said, "I will confess my transgressions to the LORD"—and you forgave the guilt of my sin. Selah Therefore let everyone who is godly pray to you while you may be found; surely when the mighty waters rise, they will not reach him (Ps.32:1-6).**
>
> **He who conceals his sins does not prosper, but whoever confesses and renounces them finds mercy (Pr.28:13).**

5 (44:23-26) **Keep asking God to deliver you.**

The people of Israel never gave up hope that God would deliver them out of the depths of disappointment and disgrace. They concluded their prayer with a brash, passionate plea for God to help them. "Nowhere else in the Bible do we find so bold a statement....This is the language of holy boldness; the language of a man who is absolutely sure that God must act or do the impossible—bring His name into disrepute."[3]

---

2 A.F. Kirkpatrick. *The Book of Psalms.* Cambridge: The University Press, 1912, WORD*search* CROSS e-book.

3 John Phillips. *Exploring Psalms, Volume 1.* WORD*search* CROSS e-book.

a. Because you need immediate help (vv.23-25).

Feeling that they could no longer endure the reproach by their enemy, Israel cried out for God to rescue them from their shameful standing before the unbelieving nations. From their perspective, God appeared to be asleep. They pleaded with Him to wake up and to help them, begging Him not to reject them forever (v.23). Notice that they addressed God as *Lord* (Adonai), which means *Master*. He was their Master and they were His servants; as such, He had a responsibility to care for them.

To the shamefaced Hebrews, God appeared to be hiding His face from them—ignoring their affliction and oppression (v.24). Frustrated and desperate, they described how they had sunk as low as they could possibly sink. Emotionally, they were in the dust. Physically, they felt as if they had been trampled into the earth or ground (v.25).

b. Because you need Him to redeem (save) you (v.26ᵃ).

The people needed God to arise and help them by redeeming or delivering them from their enemy's reproach. *Redeem* (pada) is the word used when God delivered the children of Israel from Egyptian slavery (De.9:26; 24:18). Just as the Jews had been enslaved by Pharaoh, they were now bound by the stigma that this defeat had brought upon them. Consequently, they called on God to deliver them just as He had delivered their ancestors from Pharaoh.

c. Because you trust His unfailing love (v.26ᵇ).

The people of Israel had been faithful to the LORD, so they expected Him to be faithful to His covenant and, in His mercy, to deliver them. *Unfailing love* (chesed) speaks of God's steadfast, covenant love toward His people (see outline and notes—Ps.5:7 for more discussion). They believed God, and they trusted Him to be true to Himself. Because He had committed Himself to them through His covenant, the LORD would surely rescue them from the shame of their defeat.

Thought 1. As Psalm 44 ends, the people of Israel have no answers to their questions. They still do not understand *why* God seemingly rejected them by allowing them to suffer a crushing defeat. Yet, they affirmed their faith in Him, calling upon Him to be true to His Word. Herein lies the great lesson of this psalm: when we are faithful to God and suffer a paralyzing loss or failure, we should trust in God to be true to Himself and His Word. In such times, we need to claim the words of the afflicted Job as our own: *"Though He slay me, yet will I hope in Him"* (Jb.13:15).

What about the faithful...

- believer who is not healed of cancer or some other life-threatening disease?
- husband or wife whose spouse leaves and does not repent or return?
- parent whose child is on drugs?
- businessperson whose company fails?
- employee who does his/her best and still loses the job?
- steward whose investments fail?
- Christian who is persecuted for standing up for Christ?
- pastor or missionary who labors with no visible results?
- believer who tragically loses a parent, spouse, or child?

In these and other crushing situations, we must believe that God is true to Himself and His Word, even when it seems He has rejected us. In bold faith, we must insist that He deliver us from the bondage of our affliction, for He has committed His unfailing love to us (Ro.8:35-39).

In the Bible, God loves people who contend with Him. They knock at midnight demanding bread (Luke11:5-8). They refuse to let Him go until He blesses them (Gen.32:22-32). They are brash in prayer (Luke 11:8)....Psalm 44 tells us to be bold in prayer. Don't be afraid to confront God. Don't hide your anger; He knows your heart.[4]

When we feel God has abandoned us, we need to remember His promise to never leave or forsake us (He.13:5). When we are at our lowest point and feel we can never recover, we need to remember that nothing can separate us from His love. Through Him, we are not *merely* conquerors, but *more than conquerors* over every trial we will face:

Who shall separate us from the love of Christ? Shall trouble or hardship or persecution or famine or nakedness or danger or sword? As it is written: "For your sake we face death all day long; we are considered as sheep to be slaughtered." No, in all these things we are more than conquerors through him who loved us. For I am convinced that neither death nor life, neither angels nor demons, neither the present nor the future, nor any powers, neither height nor depth, nor anything else in all creation, will be able to separate us from the love of God that is in Christ Jesus our Lord (Ro.8:35-39).

---

4   Donald Williams. *Psalms 1-72*, p.346.

	PSALM 45 **A Description of the Ideal King: Four Pictures of Christ & His Bride, the Church, 45:1-17** *For the director of music. To the tune of "Lilies." Of the Sons of Korah. A maskil. A wedding song.*	by anointing you with the oil of joy. 8 All your robes are fragrant with myrrh and aloes and cassia; from palaces adorned with ivory the music of the strings makes you glad.	1) God anoints Him with joy & exalts Him above everyone 2) He is clothed with glorious & fragrant robes 3) He lives in ivory palaces filled with beautiful music

1. He is the king, the most ideal man: A picture of Christ, the Son of God
  a. He is a noble theme for an inspired, sacred writer
  b. His speech is gracious: His words are anointed by God with a message of grace
  c. God has blessed Him forever
	My heart is stirred by a noble theme as I recite my verses for the king; my tongue is the pen of a skillful writer.
	2 You are the most excellent of men and your lips have been anointed with grace, since God has blessed you forever.
		9 Daughters of kings are among your honored women; at your right hand is the royal bride in gold of Ophir.
		10 Listen, O daughter, consider and give ear: Forget your people and your father's house.
		11 The king is enthralled by your beauty; honor him, for he is your lord.
			4) He is honored by the royal bride & bridesmaids (virgin companions, v.14) standing at His right hand
			
			4. He is the exalted bridegroom: A picture of Christ & His bride
			  a. The counsel to His bride (church)
			    1) Forget your past
			    2) Honor, respect, & please Him

2. He is the victorious warrior: A picture of Christ, the mighty one, clothed in glory & majesty
 	
  a. He majestically defends truth, humility, & righteousness (justice): He performs mighty deeds
 	
  b. He will conquer all enemies: In every nation every knee will bow before Him, Ph.2:8-11
	3 Gird your sword upon your side, O mighty one; clothe yourself with splendor and majesty.
	4 In your majesty ride forth victoriously in behalf of truth, humility and righteousness; let your right hand display awesome deeds.
	5 Let your sharp arrows pierce the hearts of the king's enemies; let the nations fall beneath your feet.
		12 The Daughter of Tyre will come with a gift, men of wealth will seek your favor.
		13 All glorious is the princess within [her chamber]; her gown is interwoven with gold.
		14 In embroidered garments she is led to the king; her virgin companions follow her and are brought to you.
		15 They are led in with joy and gladness; they enter the palace of the king.
			• Bc. He delights in you
			• Bc. He is your Lord
			  b. The bride's reward
			    1) She will be exalted among the nations
			    2) She will be clothed in beauty & be glorious (righteous) within, Ep.4:24; Ph.3:20-21
			    3) She will be wed—brought to the king (Christ)
			    4) She will be accompanied by morally pure (righteous) companions

3. He is the righteous & just ruler: A picture of Christ, God's Son, ruling over His eternal kingdom, He.1:2-9
  a. The basis of His rule: He loves righteousness & hates wickedness
  b. The results
	6 Your throne, O God, will last for ever and ever; a scepter of justice will be the scepter of your kingdom.
	7 You love righteousness and hate wickedness; therefore God, your God, has set you above your companions
		16 Your sons will take the place of your fathers; you will make them princes throughout the land.
		17 I will perpetuate your memory through all generations; therefore the nations will praise you for ever and ever.
			5) She will be filled with utter joy as she is led into the king's palace
			  c. The king's reward
			    1) He will father many royal sons & make them princes to rule the promised land
			    2) He will be honored & praised forever & ever

PSALM 45

A Description of the Ideal King: Four Pictures of Christ and His Bride, the Church, 45:1-17

(45:1-17) **Introduction:** for centuries, two themes appear to have inspired more songwriters than any other: love and Jesus Christ. Psalm 45 is a song about both. Its heading informs us that it is a love song, and the New Testament declares that it is a song about Christ.

Most commentators agree that Psalm 45 was written for the wedding of one of David's descendants who was or would become king. But even more noteworthy, through the supernatural involvement of the Holy Spirit, it is unmistakably about David's ultimate descendant, the Lord Jesus Christ, who will one day sit on David's throne forever. Through the author of *Hebrews*, God's Spirit confirmed that this is a Messianic psalm, declaring plainly that verses 6 and 7 apply to our coming King:

> **But about the Son he says, "Your throne, O God, will last for ever and ever, and righteousness will be the scepter of your kingdom. You have loved righteousness and hated wickedness; therefore God, your God, has set you above your companions by anointing you with the oil of joy" (He.1:8-9).**

Critics who deny the prophetic nature of this psalm contend that it is nothing more than a royal wedding song. But down through the centuries God's people understood that it pointed to the Messiah. Outstanding Bible teacher and commentator Warren Wiersbe argues, "If this were merely a secular love song, why would it be given to the chief musician to be used in the worship of the Lord at His sanctuary? That would be blasphemy."[1]

The heading of Psalm 45 includes the instruction *to the tune of "Lilies."* Because the lily is a spring flower, a number of scholars believe that this psalm was to be performed at the Feast of Passover, which occurs during the spring season. Some think that, like the psalm it introduces, Lilies points to Christ: "The lily is the emblem of purity and simple gracefulness and charm. It often grows out of the vilest mud without being contaminated by it. It is therefore a type [prophetic symbol] of Him, who is the lily of the valley, the Lord Jesus Christ."[2]

The introduction to Psalm 45 also informs us that it is a *maskil* psalm, that is, a psalm that teaches or instructs. Prophetically, it teaches us about Jesus Christ, our coming King. Practically, it teaches the church about our union with our bridegroom, Jesus Christ. British preacher and Bible scholar G. Campbell Morgan best stated this lesson:

> *"It is as we see the glory of the Lord that we become ready to renounce all our own people and possessions, that we may be wholly to His praise, and so become the instruments through whom the royal race is propagated, and the glory of the King made known among the generations and the peoples."*[3]

This is, *A Description of the Ideal King: Four Pictures of Christ and His Bride, the Church*, 45:1-17.

1. He is the king, the most ideal man: A picture of Christ, the Son of God (vv.1-2).
2. He is the victorious warrior: A picture of Christ, the mighty one, clothed in glory and majesty (vv.3-5).
3. He is the righteous and just ruler: A picture of Christ, God's Son, ruling over His eternal kingdom, He.1:2-9 (vv.6-9).
4. He is the exalted bridegroom: A picture of Christ and His bride (vv.10-17).

1 (45:1-2) **He is the king, the most ideal man: A picture of Christ, the Son of God.**

As the psalmist picked up his pen to compose a special song for the king's wedding, he joyously celebrated the king's outstanding qualities. But, more significantly, through the supernatural influence of God's Spirit, he testified of a future, greater king: the perfect man and God's only begotten Son, Jesus Christ.

a. He is a noble theme for an inspired, sacred writer (v.1)

The psalmist was thrilled to be given the opportunity to write a song about the glorious king. And he was

---

1 Warren W. Wiersbe. *The Bible Exposition Commentary.* WORDsearch CROSS e-book.
2 H.C. Leupold. *Exposition of the Psalms*, p.198.
3 G. Campbell Morgan. *Notes on the Psalms.* (Westwood, NJ: Fleming H. Revell Company, 1947), pp.87-88.

proud of the work he had produced, filled with the satisfaction and joy that come from doing the best work he was capable of. Notice how he described his task:

➤ He wrote from his heart. Writing this song was not a duty for the psalmist but a delight, not just a job but a joy. He invested all his feelings and ability in the composition of this song about his beloved king.

➤ He wrote from a heart that overflowed with love, gratitude, and admiration for his king. In the Hebrew, *stirred* (rachash) means gushing, bubbling over, overflowing.

➤ He wrote about a good matter—the most excellent subject possible. He appreciated the greatness of his king, and he counted it a privilege to testify about him. Never had he written about a nobler theme. Composing this song was the pinnacle of his life as a writer, the most important work he had ever done.

➤ He wrote to the best of his ability, fully employing the skills God had given him. The psalmist humbly acknowledged that he was a highly-skilled (ready) writer (Ez.7:6; Pr.22:29). As he recited the song, he wanted the king and all who heard it to know that he had done his best. He had utilized all of his skills in composing the song.

b. His speech is gracious: His words are anointed by God with a message of grace (v.2ᵃ).

The king was the ideal leader. In every way, he was superior to other men. In saying that the king was *most excellent,* the psalmist was probably referring to the king's splendor and glory on his wedding day, rather than to physical beauty. Moreover, the king was such a wise, encouraging speaker that it appeared God had anointed his lips with grace.

c. God has blessed Him forever (v.2ᵇ).

No man could be as great as this king without God's blessing. His compelling excellence was the result of God's favor on his life. *Forever* may look back to the past, indicating that God had foreordained this man to be king, and He had prepared him by endowing him with such outstanding qualities. But it may also look to the future, predicting that the great king's legacy and glory would continue long after he was gone. His reign and his kingdom would be remembered and blessed forever.

Thought 1. In these verses, we have a wonderful picture of the King of kings, our Lord and Savior Jesus Christ. First, He is the grandest theme to ever proceed forth from the tongues and pens of men. Like the psalmist, our hearts should overflow with excitement in praising Him. We have been chosen to spread the glories of His name to the world. We should embrace this responsibility as a sacred privilege and honor, enthusiastically telling others about the greatness of our loving Savior and coming King.

Second, Jesus is the ideal man, the perfect king. No one compares to Him. To us who know and love Him, He is the fairest of all. But as Isaiah prophesied, there would be nothing especially attractive about Jesus as a man (Is.53:2). In fact, He would be so grotesquely disfigured on the cross that people would turn their faces away from Him (Is.52:14; 53:3). Yet, it is the crucified one who is most beautiful to us. From His bloody cross, the Man of Calvary draws us to Himself (Jn.12:32). When we at last come face to face with Jesus, we will surely bow and kiss the beautiful scars in His hands and feet, where He was "pierced for our transgressions" (Is.53:5).

Third, the lips of Jesus uttered the most gracious words ever spoken. The crowds marveled at "the gracious words that came from his lips" (Lu.4:22). Even the officers sent by the Pharisees to arrest Him returned empty-handed, stating as their only defense, "No one ever spoke the way this man does" (Jn.7:46). As Peter declared, Jesus spoke "the words of eternal life" (Jn.6:68). Consider some of the gracious words of our Lord:

> **"Come to me, all you who are weary and burdened, and I will give you rest. Take my yoke upon you and learn from me, for I am gentle and humble in heart, and you will find rest for your souls. For my yoke is easy and my burden is light"** (Mt.11:28-30).
>
> **Then Jesus said to her, "Your sins are forgiven"** (Lu.7:48).
>
> **Jesus said, "Father, forgive them, for they do not know what they are doing." And they divided up his clothes by casting lots** (Lu.23:34).
>
> **On the last and greatest day of the Feast, Jesus stood and said in a loud voice, "If anyone is thirsty, let him come to me and drink** (Jn.7:37).
>
> **Jesus said to her, "I am the resurrection and the life. He who believes in me will live, even though he dies; and whoever lives and believes in me will never die. Do you believe this?"** (Jn.11:25-26).

Fourth, Jesus is blessed forever (Ro.9:5). He has been highly exalted to the right hand of the Father in heaven, where God has given Him a name that is above every name (Ac.5:31; Ph.2:9). He will reign for ever and ever (Re.11:15).

> **The Word became flesh and made his dwelling among us. We have seen his glory, the glory of the One and Only, who came from the Father, full of grace and truth (Jn.1:14).**
>
> **The Son is the radiance of God's glory and the exact representation of his being, sustaining all things by his powerful word. After he had provided purification for sins, he sat down at the right hand of the Majesty in heaven. So he became as much superior to the angels as the name he has inherited is superior to theirs (He.1:3-4).**
>
> **And, once made perfect, he became the source of eternal salvation for all who obey him (He.5:9).**
>
> **Your eyes will see the king in his beauty and view a land that stretches afar (Is.33:17).**

2 (45:3-5) **He is the victorious warrior: A picture of Christ, the mighty one, clothed in glory and majesty.** The psalmist praised another quality of the great king: he was a mighty warrior who valiantly led his armies into battle. His nation enjoyed peace and prosperity because of the king's courage and skill on the battlefield. The psalmist portrayed him boldly riding off with his sword on his side. As he entered the conflict, he was clothed with something greater than his battle armor: the glory and majesty adorning those who lay down their lives for a greater cause.

a. **He majestically defends truth, humility, and righteousness (justice): He performs mighty deeds (v.4).**
The courageous king did not fight to conquer nations and win their spoils. He warred for truth, meekness, and righteousness or justice. *Humility* (anvah) reveals that he did not fight out of arrogance, greed, or the thirst for power. Rather, he fought humbly, out of the necessity to stand for what was right. Because of this, the psalmist was confident that he would ride prosperously, that is, be victorious in battle. The right hand was a symbol of strength and skill. With it the king would perform terrible things—awe-inspiring, heroic deeds that would strike fear in the hearts of all who considered coming against him and his nation.

b. **He will conquer all enemies: In every nation every knee will bow before Him, Ph.2:8-11 (v.5).**
The king would be successful on the battlefield. His arrows would find their target, sharply piercing the hearts of his foes. By conquering the nations, he would establish truth and justice throughout the land.

Thought 1. One of the earliest appearances of Jesus in Scripture is as a warrior. As Joshua surveyed Jericho, Jesus came to him as the Captain of the LORD's host with His sword in His hand (Jos.5:13-15). When He came to earth the first time, He came to wage war against Satan for the souls of men (Ge.3:15). Through His sacrificial death, He broke sin's power over us (Co.2:13-15). Through His glorious resurrection, He secured victory over death (1 Co.15:20-22, 54-57).

Satan's campaign against God's truth and righteousness is raging across the earth today. As believers, we have been commissioned to fight in the army of our Lord (2 Ti.2:3-4). Our orders are to resist Satan and his forces, standing steadfastly them. We have been equipped with the armor of God to defend us and with the sword of the Spirit—God's Holy Word—as our weapon (Ep.6:10-17). We do not fight *for* the victory, but *from* the victory of Christ on the cross.

In great glory and majesty, Jesus will come to earth again as a mighty warrior. He will crush His enemies with His mighty, double-edged sword, the very Word of God itself:

> **Out of his mouth comes a sharp sword with which to strike down the nations. "He will rule them with an iron scepter." He treads the winepress of the fury of the wrath of God Almighty (Re.19:15).**

After Christ conquers all the nations of the earth, Satan will be bound and Christ will rule the earth in perfect truth and righteousness (Re.20:1-3; Is.11:1-5). Every knee of every nation will bow before Him and confess Him as Lord (Ph.2:8-11).

> **For he must reign until he has put all his enemies under his feet (1 Co.15:25).**
>
> **I saw heaven standing open and there before me was a white horse, whose rider is called Faithful and True. With justice he judges and makes war (Re.19:11).**
>
> **Ask of me, and I will make the nations your inheritance, the ends of the earth your possession. You will rule them with an iron scepter; you will dash them to pieces like pottery" (Ps.2:8-9).**
>
> **The LORD says to my Lord: "Sit at my right hand until I make your enemies a footstool for your feet."...The Lord is at your right hand; he will crush kings on the day of his wrath. He will judge the nations, heaping up the dead and crushing the rulers of the whole earth (Ps.110:1, 5-6).**
>
> **But with righteousness he will judge the needy, with justice he will give decisions for the poor of the earth. He will strike the earth with the rod of his mouth; with the breath of his lips he will slay the wicked. Righteousness will be his belt and faithfulness the sash around his waist (Is.11:4-5).**

3 (45:6-9) **He is the righteous and just ruler: A picture of Christ, God's Son, ruling over His eternal kingdom, He.1:2-9.**

The psalmist exalted the king for being a righteous and just ruler. But he did so in a startling way, addressing the king as *God.* This has prompted much discussion and an assortment of opinions among scholars. However, the solution is quite simple, for the New Testament specifically interprets this verse:

> **But about the Son he says, "Your throne, O God, will last for ever and ever, and righteousness will be the scepter of your kingdom. You have loved righteousness and hated wickedness; therefore God, your God, has set you above your companions by anointing you with the oil of joy" (He.1:8-9).**

The Holy Spirit inspired the psalmist to address the king as God and, through the author of *Hebrews* explained what this means: he was speaking to Israel's *coming* King, God's Son, Jesus Christ. The psalmist wrote prophetically of the righteous and just reign of Christ, who will rule eternally with His beloved bride, the church, at His right hand.

a. The basis of His rule: He loves righteousness and hates wickedness (v.7ᵃ).

The psalmist exalted the perfect character of the Lord Jesus Christ. As God, He is completely and absolutely righteous. His righteousness was tested when He lived on earth as a man for thirty-three years. He proved His love of righteousness and hatred of wickedness by resisting every temptation He faced (Mt.4:1-11; He.4:15; 1 Pe.2:22).

b. The results (v.7ᵇ-9).

Because of His perfect character, His absolute holiness, God has anointed Christ with the oil of gladness above all others (v.7ᵇ). *Your companions* refers to all of humanity, every other human being who ever lives (Ph.2:7-8). The psalmist referred to four special privileges God has bestowed on His beloved Son:

1) God has exalted Christ above all others to rule eternally over the earth. *Anointing with oil* points to the consecration of Israel's king (1 S.10:1; 16:13). The oil represents the Holy Spirit (1 S.10:6; 16:13; Lu.4:17-21). Paul wrote of the exaltation and Lordship of Christ:

> **Therefore God exalted him to the highest place and gave him the name that is above every name, that at the name of Jesus every knee should bow, in heaven and on earth and under the earth, and every tongue confess that Jesus Christ is Lord, to the glory of God the Father (Ph.2:9-11).**

God has also anointed Christ with the oil of gladness above all others. The author of *Hebrews* revealed that our Savior endured the suffering of the cross "for the joy set before Him" (He.12:2). Because He was willing to tread through the greatest depths of sorrow, our precious Lord will justly know the greatest heights of joy. Jesus suffered like no man has ever suffered. While His physical pain on the cross was excruciating, the spiritual agony of being separated from God as the sin-bearer for the whole world was far greater. Therefore, He will know a measure of joy surpassing that experienced by any other person. This joy includes both the joy of being seated in a place of honor and authority at God's right hand and the joy of receiving a beloved bride, as described in this psalm.

2) Because of His perfect character, God has also clothed Christ with glorious and fragrant robes (v.8ᵃ). The myrrh, aloes, and cassia speak of Christ in three marvelous ways:

These spices identify Christ in His sacred office as priest (He.4:14-15; 7:26; 8:1). Myrrh and cassia were the primary ingredients in the special anointing oil that God ordained to be used only for the Tabernacle and its priests (Ex.30:22-33).

The fragrance of myrrh points to Christ as the radiant Bridegroom of the church. In the *Song of Solomon*, the bridegroom is a picture of the Lord Jesus Christ. Throughout the book, He is described as smelling of myrrh (Song 1:13; 3:6; 5:5,13).

The myrrh and aloes point to Christ's death. The Holy Spirit moved John to carefully note the spices used to embalm the body of our crucified Savior:

> **He was accompanied by Nicodemus, the man who earlier had visited Jesus at night. Nicodemus brought a mixture of myrrh and aloes, about seventy-five pounds. Taking Jesus' body, the two of them wrapped it, with the spices, in strips of linen. This was in accordance with Jewish burial customs (Jn.19:39-40).**

3) The holy King lives in palaces embellished with ivory, one of the most elegant and majestic materials (v.8ᵇ; 1 K.10:18; 22:39; Am.3:15). This speaks of heaven, the exquisite city from whence Jesus came to this earth, and from which He will reign for eternity. The beautiful music of heaven cheers our perfect King along with all who reside there with Him.

4) Citing the royal wedding customs of his day, the psalmist prophetically spoke of the Marriage of the Lamb (v.9; Re.19:7-9). Because of His perfect righteousness and obedience to His Father's will, the King is honored with a glorious bride—the church that He purchased with His own blood (Ep.5:25-27; Ac.20:28). She stands at His right hand, the place of

honor, clad in the gold of Ophir—the finest and purest gold in the ancient world (1 K.9:28; 22:48; Jb.28:16; Is.13:12). Among her attendants are the daughters of other kings, which testifies of the privilege of being the bride of such a great King.

Thought 1. Do we truly realize how blessed we are to be the bride of the King of kings, Jesus Christ? Consider what Paul wrote about Christ's relationship with us, His beloved bride, and how it applies to this passage:

> **Husbands, love your wives, just as Christ loved the church and gave himself up for her to make her holy, cleansing her by the washing with water through the word, and to present her to himself as a radiant church, without stain or wrinkle or any other blemish, but holy and blameless (Ep.5:25-27).**

Christ loves us so much that He laid down His life for us. Notice that He bears the fragrance of myrrh and aloes, the spices with which His broken body was buried. He draws us to Himself by His sacrificial, substitutionary death for us; He woos us with the fragrance of His tomb. And on that joyous day when He weds us, we will bask in the familiar aroma of our Savior's love for us. This indescribable love carried Him all the way to the cross, into the tomb, then out of the tomb when He was gloriously raised for our justification, then back to heaven where He intercedes for us at the right hand of the Father (Ro.4:25; He.7:25).

Because Christ loves righteousness and hates wickedness, He produces righteousness in us. As we read, study, and hear His cleansing Word, our Lord washes the stains of sin out of our lives. In fact, God uses everything that happens in our lives to transform us into the image of His Son (Ro.8:28-29). He lovingly chastens us when we disobey Him in order to make us holy (He.12:10-11). When we are presented to Christ in marriage, we will be clothed in sparkling white, fully free of the spots, wrinkles, and blemishes of our sinful nature (Re.19:8).

Additional blessings are promised to Christ's beloved bride. We are joint-heirs with Him, meaning that we will share in His inheritance (Ro.8:17). This inheritance includes His kingdom. We will reign with Him, first for 1,000 years in the millennium, and then throughout eternity in the new heaven and new earth (Re.20:6; 22:5).

Life in this present world is often discouraging, plagued by trials, difficulties, and struggles that never seem to end. But like our Bridegroom, we must set our focus on the joy set before us, the bliss we will know as we live with Him throughout eternity. When we think about the hope we have in Him—all of God's glorious promises to us—we will be strengthened to endure the struggles of this life (He.6:17-20). The Apostle Paul stated it best:

I consider that our present sufferings are not worth comparing with the glory that will be revealed in us (Ro.8:18).

For our light and momentary troubles are achieving for us an eternal glory that far outweighs them all. So we fix our eyes not on what is seen, but on what is unseen. For what is seen is temporary, but what is unseen is eternal (2 Co.4:17-18).

Note also these Scriptures that support the truths of this passage:

Therefore God exalted him to the highest place and gave him the name that is above every name, that at the name of Jesus every knee should bow, in heaven and on earth and under the earth, and every tongue confess that Jesus Christ is Lord, to the glory of God the Father (Ph.2:9-11).

Let us rejoice and be glad and give him glory! For the wedding of the Lamb has come, and his bride has made herself ready. Fine linen, bright and clean, was given her to wear." (Fine linen stands for the righteous acts of the saints.) Then the angel said to me, "Write: 'Blessed are those who are invited to the wedding supper of the Lamb!'" And he added, "These are the true words of God" (Re.19:7-9).

I saw heaven standing open and there before me was a white horse, whose rider is called Faithful and True. With justice he judges and makes war (Re.19:11).

Let them sing before the LORD, for he comes to judge the earth. He will judge the world in righteousness and the peoples with equity (Ps.98:9).

A shoot will come up from the stump of Jesse; from his roots a Branch will bear fruit. The Spirit of the LORD will rest on him—the Spirit of wisdom and of understanding, the Spirit of counsel and of power, the Spirit of knowledge and of the fear of the LORD—and he will delight in the fear of the LORD. He will not judge by what he sees with his eyes, or decide by what he hears with his ears; but with righteousness he will judge the needy, with justice he will give decisions for the poor of the earth. He will strike the earth with the rod of his mouth; with the breath of his lips he will slay the wicked. Righteousness will be his belt and faith-

fulness the sash around his waist (Is.11:1-5).

"The days are coming," declares the LORD, "when I will raise up to David a righteous Branch, a King who will reign wisely and do what is just and right in the land (Je.23:5).

4 (45:10-17) **He is the exalted bridegroom: A picture of Christ and His bride (the church).**
Every privilege comes with responsibilities. The psalmist challenged the privileged bride of the King of kings to fulfill her duties to her exalted Bridegroom (v.10). Because Christ loved us enough to die for us, we should love Him enough to live for Him (Ro.12:1).

a. **The counsel to the bride (the church) (vv.10-11).**
The psalmist counselled the bride to leave everything behind and devote herself totally to her Bridegroom. *Listen* (shama) means more than to merely listen with the ears; it means to heed or obey what is said. This counsel is eternally important. Therefore, the bride of Christ—the blood-bought church—must follow it.

The exhortation to leave her family coincides with Scripture's teaching about marriage. When God instituted marriage in the Garden of Eden, He instructed all future brides and grooms to leave their parents behind and make their spouses the most important persons in their lives:

For this reason a man will leave his father and mother and be united to his wife, and they will become one flesh (Ge.2:24).

Jesus affirmed this vital principle in His teaching (Mt.19:4-5). Building on this foundation, He issued an ultimatum to His followers:

"If anyone comes to me and does not hate his father and mother, his wife and children, his brothers and sisters—yes, even his own life—he cannot be my disciple (Lu.14:26).

In the same way, any of you who does not give up everything he has cannot be my disciple (Lu.14:33).

Scripture teaches that we have a new life when we repent and receive Christ:

Therefore, if anyone is in Christ, he is a new creation; the old has gone, the new has come! (2 Co.5:17).

This verse means that, having been forgiven of all our sins, we are new *persons* in Christ. Our sinful past is behind us, and we have a fresh start in a new life. But it also means that we have a new *priority* and a new *purpose* for living. Our Bridegroom, Jesus Christ, is to be the first priority of our lives. Our purpose for living is to honor and glorify Him. We should live to please Him by wholly following Him and faithfully obeying His will for our lives. We must be willing to forsake everything—sin, selfish ambitions and desires, worldly pleasures and possessions—for the indescribable privilege of knowing Him. Christ demands and deserves first place in our hearts. Paul understood this and humbly testified of his total devotion to Jesus Christ:

> **But whatever was to my profit I now consider loss for the sake of Christ. What is more, I consider everything a loss compared to the surpassing greatness of knowing Christ Jesus my Lord, for whose sake I have lost all things. I consider them rubbish, that I may gain Christ and be found in him, not having a righteousness of my own that comes from the law, but that which is through faith in Christ—the righteousness that comes from God and is by faith. I want to know Christ and the power of his resurrection and the fellowship of sharing in his sufferings, becoming like him in his death (Ph.3:7-10).**

The psalmist offered two compelling truths as the basis for our total devotion to our Bridegroom. First, Christ greatly desires us (v.11ᵃ). It is the desire of a husband for his wife. In the same way that a husband desires intimacy with his wife, our Lord desires that we surrender ourselves completely to Him. Because He loves us so deeply, our Savior demands that we be faithful to Him. He is not willing to share us with anything else. Though it is beyond our understanding, we should seek to comprehend the love of Christ for us so we can be stirred to give ourselves fully to Him.

> **I pray that out of his glorious riches he may strengthen you with power through his Spirit in your inner being, so that Christ may dwell in your hearts through faith. And I pray that you, being rooted and established in love, may have power, together with all the saints, to grasp how wide and long and high and deep is the love of Christ, and to know this love that surpasses knowledge—that you may be filled to the measure of all the fullness of God (Ep.3:16-19).**

Second, we should be totally devoted to Christ because He is our *Lord* (v.11ᵇ). We are to *worship* (honor, NIV) Him by fully submitting to His Lordship over

our lives. As Paul instructed wives to submit to their earthly husbands, he also appealed to our relationship with Christ:

> **Wives, submit to your husbands as to the Lord. For the husband is the head of the wife as Christ is the head of the church, his body, of which he is the Savior. Now as the church submits to Christ, so also wives should submit to their husbands in everything (Ep.5:22-24).**

Our response to our Savior's sacrificial love for us is to submit ourselves fully to Him, acknowledging Him as the Lord of our lives. Again, we should live for Him because He died for us.

Note that the command to the bride to worship (honor, NIV) the King proves that the psalmist was writing about Christ. Throughout Scripture, worshipping anything or anybody other than God is forbidden (Ex.20:3-5; Re.19:10; 22:9).

b. The bride's reward (vv.12-15).

In return for our devotion to Him, the Lord Jesus promises to reward us with bountiful blessings. As the psalmist described the honors the queen would receive from being married to such a great king, he spoke prophetically of the church's reward as Christ's precious bride:

➢ She will be exalted among the nations (v.12). The church will reign with Christ during the millennium and throughout eternity.

➢ She will be dressed in the most perfect and glorious clothing—the righteousness bestowed upon her as she is transformed into the image of Christ (v.13; Ep.4:24; Ph.3:20-21).

➢ She will be presented and wed to the King wearing fine garments (v.14ᵃ; Re.19:7-8).

➢ She will be accompanied by pure, holy companions (v.14ᵇ). Prophetically, these attendants may represent Old Testament believers, holy angels standing by, or the other believers who make up the bride of Christ. Or, it is possible they have no prophetic significance at all. "It must not be expected that all the details of the scene shall have exact equivalents in the spiritual marriage which it represents."[4]

➢ She will know the greatest gladness and joy possible: living in the presence of the King (v.15; Re.22:3).

c. The king's reward (vv.16-17).

After revealing the honors to be bestowed upon the King's bride, the psalmist addressed the King's reward. The use of the masculine gender in the Hebrew text reveals this transition. Because of His submission to

---

4 H.D.M. Spence. *The Pulpit Commentary*. 1909-1919, WORD*search* CROSS e-book.

His Father's will, our Bridegroom will be exalted throughout eternity (Ph.2:5-11). The psalmist mentioned two of His great rewards:

1) The King will father many royal sons (and daughters) who will be princes (and princesses) (v.16). Genuine believers—Christ's bride—are commanded to be fruitful by bearing strong witness to Jesus and fulfilling the Great Commission (Mt.28:19-20; Mk.16:15; Ac.1:8). As additional people throughout the world come to Christ, more spiritual children are born into God's family, bringing many sons and daughters to glory (He.2:10-13). This generation of royal descendants will reign with Christ on this present earth in the millennium and throughout eternity on the new earth (1 Pe.2:9; Re.1:6; 5:10; 20:6)

2) The King will be honored and praised for ever and ever (v.17). His name is above every name. Every knee will one day bow to Jesus Christ and every tongue will confess Him as Lord (Ph.2:10-12). *The nations* is plural in the Hebrew text. It refers to all the people of all the nations of the world. Throughout eternity, Jesus will reign and His name will be glorified by people of every tongue, tribe, and nation (Re.1:5-6; 5:9-13).

Thought 1. Having been redeemed with the precious blood of Christ, we are His beloved bride (1 Co.6:20; 1 Pe.2:18-19). With this glorious privilege come sacred responsibilities:

First and foremost, we should be totally devoted to Christ. He should be the first priority of our lives. We should never be unfaithful to Him by placing other things or other people ahead of Him. Nor should we be unfaithful by slipping back into sin. As we wait to be joined with Christ at His glorious coming, we should keep ourselves pure, as a virgin remains chaste so she will be pure when she presents herself to her husband (2 Co.11:2). James admonished us to keep ourselves "unspotted from the world" (Js.1:27).

Next, we should serve the Lord Jesus by performing good works for His glory (Mt.5:16; 1 Co.7:22-23; Ep.2:10; Co.1:10; Tit.2:14). When we are presented to Christ at the Marriage of the Lamb, our garment of fine linen will represent the good deeds of our righteousness (Re.19:7).

Finally, we should bear fruit for Christ by telling others about His great love and saving power. He has committed to us the ministry of reconciling others to Him (2 Co.5:18-20). He has ordained us and sent us forth into the world to be fruitful for Him (Jn.15:16; 20:21).

As we live faithfully for Jesus, He will richly reward us. At the Judgment Seat of Christ our lives will be evaluated, and we will be presented crowns to lay at His feet (1 Co.3:12-15; 2 Co.5:9-10; Re.4:10-11). We will also be rewarded with an esteemed place of service in the kingdom of Jesus Christ. Jesus revealed that our position in His kingdom would be determined according to our faithfulness in this life (see notes and DEEPER STUDY #1—Mt.19:28; 19:29; 25:23).

> **"His master replied, 'Well done, good and faithful servant! You have been faithful with a few things; I will put you in charge of many things. Come and share your master's happiness!' (Mt.25:23).**

> **But the one who does not know and does things deserving punishment will be beaten with few blows. From everyone who has been given much, much will be demanded; and from the one who has been entrusted with much, much more will be asked (Lu.12:48).**

> **I am jealous for you with a godly jealousy. I promised you to one husband, to Christ, so that I might present you as a pure virgin to him (2 Co.11:2).**

> **To make her holy, cleansing her by the washing with water through the word, and to present her to himself as a radiant church, without stain or wrinkle or any other blemish, but holy and blameless (Ep.5:26-27).**

> **Therefore, since we are surrounded by such a great cloud of witnesses, let us throw off everything that hinders and the sin that so easily entangles, and let us run with perseverance the race marked out for us (He.12:1).**

> **Let us rejoice and be glad and give him glory! For the wedding of the Lamb has come, and his bride has made herself ready (Re.19:7).**

Thought 2. Dear friend, do you know for sure that you are a part of Christ's church, His bride? Have you genuinely repented and trusted Christ for salvation? Why would you not want to receive Him who loved you so much that He laid down His life for you? Why would you not want to spend eternity with Him? Christ loves you, and He invites you to come to Him today.

> **Yet to all who received him, to those who believed in his name, he gave the right to become children of God (Jn.1:12).**

> **"For God so loved the world that he gave his one and only Son, that whoever believes in him shall not perish but have eternal life (Jn.3:16).**

> **But God demonstrates his own love for us in this: While we were still sinners, Christ died for us (Ro.5:8).**

> **Here I am! I stand at the door and knock. If anyone hears my voice and opens the door, I will come in and eat with him, and he with me (Re.3:20).**

		5 God is within her, she will not fall; God will help her at break of day.
		6 Nations are in uproar, kingdoms fall; he lifts his voice, the earth melts.
		7 The LORD Almighty is with us; the God of Jacob is our fortress. Selah
		8 Come and see the works of the LORD, the desolations he has brought on the earth.
		9 He makes wars cease to the ends of the earth; he breaks the bow and shatters the spear, he burns the shields with fire.
		10 "Be still, and know that I am God; I will be exalted among the nations, I will be exalted in the earth."
		11 The LORD Almighty is with us; the God of Jacob is our fortress. Selah
			b. He indwells & protects His city: All who seek refuge with Him
			c. He gives hope for a new day
			d. He brings chaos to nations & causes governments to fall on behalf of His people, Ro.8:28
			e. He—the LORD of hosts (heaven's armies)—is with us: He is our refuge
			
			3. See the works of the LORD: A picture of the last days
			a. He destroys (judges) the nations
			b. He brings peace to the earth
			  1) He causes wars to cease throughout the world
			  2) He destroys & burns the weapons
			
			4. Be still—wait & hope in the LORD—know that the LORD is God
			a. He will be exalted among all nations & in all the earth
			b. He—the LORD Almighty—is with us: He is our refuge (fortress, stronghold)

	PSALM 46 **When Facing Devastating Misfortune or Overwhelming Trouble, 46:1-11** *For the director of music. Of the Sons of Korah. According to alamoth. A song.*		

1. Confess God as your refuge & strength
a. He is always ready to help you in times of trouble
b. He will enable you to conquer fear even in the most catastrophic circumstances
  1) Earthquakes & hurricanes
  2) Tidal waves & volcanic eruptions
 	
2. Rest assured of God's presence & power
a. He gives a river of refreshment & joy to the citizens of His city
	God is our refuge and strength, an ever-present help in trouble.
	2 Therefore we will not fear, though the earth give way and the mountains fall into the heart of the sea,
	3 Though its waters roar and foam and the mountains quake with their surging. Selah
	4 There is a river whose streams make glad the city of God, the holy place where the Most High dwells.		

PSALM 46

When Facing Devastating Misfortune or Overwhelming Trouble, 46:1-11

(46:1-11) **Introduction:** after Job was battered by a series of devastating tragedies, his friends traveled a great distance to be with him. They sat silently with him for seven days and seven nights, staying by his side during his immeasurable grief. Job finally broke the silence, saying, "What I feared has come upon me" (Jb.3:25). With this statement, Job lamented that the worst tragedy he could imagine had come to pass.

Many of us have wondered what we would do if a terrible tragedy occurred in our lives. For some, this would be the death of a spouse or, perhaps even worse, the loss of a child. For others, it would be a diagnosis of cancer or the loss of mental capacity. For yet others it would be a fire or some other catastrophic natural disaster.

Psalm 46 was written during a time of overwhelming turmoil in Jerusalem. Many scholars believe the setting for this psalm, along with Psalms 47 and 48, is the Assyrian invasion of Judah during Hezekiah's reign (2 K.18-19; 2 Chr.32; Is.36-37). Some think Hezekiah himself wrote these psalms.

However, Psalms 42 to 49, along with Psalms 85 and 87, mention the *Sons of Korah* in their headings; thus many scholars feel they actually wrote these psalms (see *Psalms,* INTRODUCTION for more discussion). The Hebrew preposition following "music" in the title can be translated as either *for, by,* or *of.* Therefore, we cannot be sure if the sons of Korah wrote these psalms or if the psalms were merely assigned to them for use in worship. Whatever the case, we know that it was a time of fierce trouble and that God protected and gloriously delivered His people from it.

Psalm 46 was such an important song that it was committed to the care of the *chief musician,* with the instruction *alamoth.* This likely means it was to be performed by high-pitched voices or, more specifically, by young women. However, it could also mean it was to be accompanied by high-pitched stringed instruments (1 Chr.15:20).

At some point in our lives, we will face circumstances we feel are more than we can handle. We will know the hollow, helpless feeling of being able to do nothing to change our situation. The Lord has given us Psalm 46 for these times. This great psalm was the inspiration for Martin Luther's great hymn, "A Mighty Fortress Is Our God." This is, *When Facing Devastating Misfortune or Overwhelming Trouble,* 46:1-11.

1. Confess God as your refuge and strength (vv.1-3).
2. Rest assured of God's presence and power (vv.4-7).
3. See the works of the LORD: a picture of the last days (vv.8-9).
4. Be still—wait and hope in the LORD—the LORD is God (vv.10-11).

1 (46:1-3) **Confess God as your refuge and strength.** As a terrifying crisis approached Jerusalem, the psalmist led God's people to lean fully on the LORD. With the calmness that only faith can give, he confessed that God was their refuge and strength. A *refuge* (machaceh) is a shelter, that is, a place where we can hide for protection. *Strength* speaks of the power that God gives us to endure and overcome adversity.

a. He is always ready to help you in times of trouble (v.1).

The Hebrew word for *trouble* (tsarah) literally means a narrow or tight place where a person is unable to move. It is also used to describe severe pressure. We all face situations beyond our control, but we do not have to face them alone. When trouble strikes, God is present. In fact, He is always there with us, immediately available to help us when trouble arises. The adverb *ever* (mehode) indicates that He is exceedingly or speedily present. Not even a second goes by when we have to face our troubles alone, or in our own strength.

b. He will enable you to conquer fear even in the most catastrophic circumstances (vv.2-3).

The psalmist took great care to assure us that we need not fear when trouble strikes. Disasters that shake the earth to its core cannot shake us when we take refuge in the LORD. Referring to four types of natural disasters, the psalmist described some of the fiercest catastrophes imaginable:

➢ Earthquakes so powerful they alter the face of the earth and cause the ground to completely collapse beneath us (v.2ᵃ)
➢ Hurricanes so strong and long-lasting that even the mountains are immersed in water (v.2ᵇ)
➢ Massive tidal waves or tsunamis repeatedly crashing against the land (v.3ᵃ)
➢ Fiery volcanic eruptions from mountains surging or swelling with lava (v.3ᵇ)

These violent disasters also point to the *day of the Lord* when God's judgment will fall upon the earth, leading up to the return and reign of Christ. Scripture repeatedly warns that God will exercise His power over the forces of nature when He pours out His wrath on a world that has rejected Him and His Son (Is.24:18-23; Nah.1:2-8; Re.6:12-17; 11:13, 18-19).

Thought 1. We should live day by day with the understanding that life in this sin-cursed world is full of trouble (Jb.5:7; 14:1; Ec.2:23). Trouble assumes many forms, including…

- sickness or injury
- the death of a loved one
- marriage problems
- rebellion or disobedience by our children
- loss or unavailability of employment
- problems on the job
- conflicts with other people
- financial distress
- natural disasters
- persecution
- war

When serious problems occur in our lives, our first tendency can be to panic or fear. We might immediately become anxious, fretting over what may happen or what we are going to do. Realizing there is nothing we can do, our panic and fear might even increase.

Instead of fearing and fretting, we should remember that we do not face the situation alone, but with God's presence and help. As believers, God's Spirit lives within us. Therefore, He is always with us. When trouble attacks, we do not have to wait for God to arrive; He is already there.

Instead of attempting to deal with difficulties in our own strength, we need to flee to God for shelter and strength. We should not speak out of doubt or unbelief, but with full faith in God's love and care for us (2 Co.4:13-14; Js.1:6-7). He stands ready to help us through any and all of our trials.

Even if the worst crisis imaginable occurs, we need not fear. Of all the human emotions, fear may be the most crippling. But the one who is greater than all our troubles is with us. He has given us His Spirit to combat the spirit of fear (2 Ti.1:7). He will protect us, strengthen us, and use the challenges of life to mold us into the image of His Son.

> **I can do everything through him who gives me strength (Ph.4:13).**
>
> **For God did not give us a spirit of timidity, but a spirit of power, of love and of self-discipline (2 Ti.1:7).**
>
> **Have I not commanded you? Be strong and courageous. Do not be terrified; do not be discouraged, for the LORD your God will be with you wherever you go" (Jos.1:9).**
>
> **I will say of the LORD, "He is my refuge and my fortress, my God, in whom I trust" (Ps.91:2).**
>
> **Mightier than the thunder of the great waters, mightier than the breakers of the sea—the LORD on high is mighty (Ps.93:4).**
>
> **The LORD is near to all who call on him, to all who call on him in truth (Ps.145:18).**

2 (46:4-7) **Rest assured of God's presence and power.** The people of Jerusalem could feel secure because God was in their midst. They knew that His power was the protection from all threats. Therefore, they had a sense of gladness within their hearts, even when trouble raged all around them.

a. He gives a river of refreshment and joy to the citizens of His city (v.4)

In stark contrast to the roaring waters of trouble (v.3) is God's quiet, gentle river. Excellent commentator Herbert C. Leupold notes that "the original Hebrew places the river more abruptly into the forefront" of this verse, and that it can be translated as "Lo, a river!"[1] This image emphasizes the wonderful truth that God's peace, refreshment, and joy are available to all

---

1 H.C. Leupold. *Exposition of the Psalms*, p.365.

of us in the midst of our overwhelming trouble. We need to take our eyes off of our problems so we can see this precious gift from our loving Lord.

In Scripture, God's presence is often symbolized by refreshing waters (Ps.36:8; 65:9; Is.8:6; Je.2:13). The prophets Ezekiel and Zechariah spoke of waters flowing out of the sanctuary of God (Eze.47:1-12; Zec.14:8-9). The Apostle John saw a crystal river proceeding from God's throne (Re.22:1). And Jesus described the indwelling of His Holy Spirit in believers as rivers of living water flowing out of our inner being (Jn.7:38-39).

God's presence filled the holy place in Jerusalem, and His presence streamed throughout the city like a refreshing river. Even though Jerusalem faced many difficult situations, God's presence made them glad. Likewise, God's constant presence in our lives through His indwelling Spirit gives us indescribable joy and peace, even in the midst of life's fiercest trials (Ph.4:7; 1 Pe.1:8). When we drink of the LORD's presence, we too will be refreshed (Ps.42:1-2).

b. He indwells and protects His city: All who seek refuge with Him (v.5ᵃ).

Jerusalem was secure because of God's presence. Nothing could move the city, for He protected her. *Fall* (vv.2, 5) is the Hebrew word *mowt*. Even if the mountains—a symbol of stability—were jarred off their foundations and swept into the sea, Jerusalem would still stand firm.

c. He gives hope for a new day (v.5ᵇ).

God protected His city around the clock. *At break of day* is literally translated as the turning to or appearance of day. Cities in Old Testament times were often attacked at daybreak because they were especially vulnerable at this time. But God never slumbers nor sleeps (Ps.121:4). Even when Israel's troops were resting, God was on guard.

The break of day here may also represent the moment when God delivers us from trouble. Morning is sometimes depicted in Scripture as a time of hope and renewal. Times of severe trouble are likened to dark nights, and the dawning of a new day marks the end of a long period of suffering (Ex.14:27; Ps.30:5; Lam. 3:22-23). God's promise to help us gives us hope in the darkest times of our lives. He will not allow us to suffer forever. Just as the sun rises every morning, the darkness in our lives will break, and we will rejoice in a new day. This hope anchors our souls and provides strength to press on in trials (He.6:11-20).

d. He brings chaos to nations and causes governments to fall on behalf of His people (Ro.8:28) (v.6).

Just as God's power exceeds the forces of nature (vv.2-4), He also rules over the kingdoms of this world. Israel's history is an ongoing saga of nations rising up against her. In fact, Scripture *foretells* the troubles that

yet await the nation that brought forth His Son (Eze.38-39; Da.11:36-45; Zec.12:2; Re.11:2; 12:13).

But Israel's history also records God's faithfulness to fight for her. As the *heathen* or Gentile nations *raged* against Israel, one by one their kingdoms *fell* (mowt, see vv.2, 5); they were brought down or carried away. God spoke, and they melted at His powerful Word (Jos.2:9, 24).

This is exactly what will happen in the end times when the nations of the world unite against God's people. Christ will return and destroy His and Israel's enemies with the sword of His mouth—His mighty Word (see outline and notes—Re.19:17-21 for more discussion).

As we look back on Israel's history and forward to her future, we must not overlook the times when God removed His hand of protection due to the people's unfaithfulness to Him. Both history and prophecy testify that God's purpose for His chosen nation will surely be accomplished. His promises to Abraham and David will be fulfilled. God will bring about Israel's repentance: she will at last turn to Christ and be saved (see outline and notes—Eze.36:1-38 and Zec.12:1-13:9 for more discussion).

> **And we know that in all things God works for the good of those who love him, who have been called according to his purpose (Ro.8:28).**

e. He—the LORD of hosts (heaven's armies)—is with us: He is our refuge (v.7).

With great confidence, the psalmist reminded the people that the LORD of hosts—the Commander of heaven's armies—is their God (Jos.5:13-15; 1 K.22:19). Note the emphasis on God's covenant with Israel in this verse:

➤ *LORD* (Yahweh, Jehovah) is God's covenant name to His people

➤ *God of Jacob* speaks of God's grace in choosing Jacob and His descendants as the recipients of His covenant[2] (see outline and notes Mal.1:1-5 for more discussion; also see DEEPER STUDY #1, 2—Ro.9:10-13).

Scripture records numerous occasions when angels fought for God's chosen people. Just before the children of Israel marched on Jericho, the Captain of the LORD's host—Jesus Christ, before He became a man—appeared to Joshua (Jos.5:13-15). Also, the night before the Assyrians planned to attack Israel, the LORD sent an angel who slayed 185,000 of Assyria's mightiest men while they slept (2 K.20:34-35; 2 Chr.32:21-22). Furthermore, God revealed to Daniel that, during the Great Tribulation, Michael (one of God's mightiest angels) will stand up and fight for the children of Israel (Da.12:1).

---

2 Derek Kidner. *Psalms 1-72*, p.193.

Because of Israel's relationship with God through His covenant, He was their refuge. God Himself was their stronghold, fortress, high tower, the place where no enemy could reach them. *Fortress* (misgab) here emphasizes that it is a place of safety due to its height.

The allusion is to the fact that in the ancient world, safety to either the one fleeing or to the one at rest was synonymous with reaching and remaining upon some fortified height which would be inaccessible to beast and enemy alike. The Psalmist as well as the prophets saw this to be the precise picture of the believer's security in God.[3]

Thought 1. This passage reveals five great gifts that God gives us in times of overwhelming trouble:
First, God *refreshes* us in the midst of our trouble (v.4). Because of His unfailing love, He offers us cool, rejuvenating waters of peace and joy. But we must drink of these waters by fellowshipping with Him through prayer and meditating on His Word. In Him, we find strength and safety in times of trouble and also peace and joy for the difficult journey of life.

> **On the last and greatest day of the Feast, Jesus stood and said in a loud voice, "If anyone is thirsty, let him come to me and drink. Whoever believes in me, as the Scripture has said, streams of living water will flow from within him." By this he meant the Spirit, whom those who believed in him were later to receive. Up to that time the Spirit had not been given, since Jesus had not yet been glorified (Jn.7:37-39).**

> **"I have told you these things, so that in me you may have peace. In this world you will have trouble. But take heart! I have overcome the world" (Jn.16:33).**

> **Therefore we do not lose heart. Though outwardly we are wasting away, yet inwardly we are being renewed day by day (2 Co.4:16).**

> **You have made known to me the path of life; you will fill me with joy in your presence, with eternal pleasures at your right hand (Ps.16:11).**

> **My comfort in my suffering is this: Your promise preserves my life....Trouble and distress have come upon me, but your commands are my delight (Ps.119:50, 143).**

Second, whatever may happen in our lives, we can rest *securely* because God lives within us (v.5a). In the same way that God's presence literally dwelled in the city of Jerusalem, God resides within believers today through His Holy Spirit (Ro.8:9; 1 Co.6:19; 2 Co.6:16; Ep.1:13-14). In an unstable world, we can feel perfectly stable because of His presence within us.

> **And you also were included in Christ when you heard the word of truth, the gospel of your salvation. Having believed, you were marked in him with a seal, the promised Holy Spirit, who is a deposit guaranteeing our inheritance until the redemption of those who are God's possession—to the praise of his glory (Ep.1:13-14).**

> **Keep your lives free from the love of money and be content with what you have, because God has said, "Never will I leave you; never will I forsake you." So we say with confidence, "The Lord is my helper; I will not be afraid. What can man do to me?" (He.13:5-6).**

God has given us a third great gift to sustain us in times of trouble: the *hope* of a bright tomorrow (v.5b). Our dark night of trial will not last forever. The sun will rise in God's timing, our season of suffering will end, and we will bask in the joy of God's eternal day. What a glorious future awaits the children of God! When this life that is filled with trouble has passed, we will live forever where there is no night—no sorrow, no suffering, no pain, no death (Re.21:4-5; 22:4). This hope, Scripture says, is the anchor of our souls (He.6:18-20).

> **God did this so that, by two unchangeable things in which it is impossible for God to lie, we who have fled to take hold of the hope offered to us may be greatly encouraged. We have this hope as an anchor for the soul, firm and secure. It enters the inner sanctuary behind the curtain, where Jesus, who went before us, has entered on our behalf. He has become a high priest forever, in the order of Melchizedek (He.6:18-20).**

> **He will wipe every tear from their eyes. There will be no more death or mourning or crying or pain, for the old order of things has passed away." He who was seated on the throne said, "I am making everything new!" Then he said, "Write this down, for these words are trustworthy and true" (Re.21:4-5).**

> **For his anger lasts only a moment, but his favor lasts a lifetime; weeping may remain for a night, but rejoicing comes in the morning (Ps.30:5).**

Fourth, God has given us the *record of His past faithfulness* to strengthen us for our present challenges

---

3 R. Laird Harris, ed. *Theological Wordbook of the Old Testament.* WORD*search* CROSS e-book.

(v.6). In His inspired Word, God has preserved the long history of His faithfulness to His people. Each of us can add our experiences of God's power displayed on our behalf. As we recall these victories, God will encourage us and fill us with hope for our present struggles.

> Not only so, but we also rejoice in our sufferings, because we know that suffering produces perseverance; perseverance, character; and character, hope (Ro.5:3-4).
> For everything that was written in the past was written to teach us, so that through endurance and the encouragement of the Scriptures we might have hope (Ro.15:4).
> Yet this I call to mind and therefore I have hope (La.3:21).

Fifth, God will send his *angels* to protect and assist us in times of trouble (v.7). As angels came and ministered to Jesus when He was tempted, God's heavenly hosts are constantly at hand to minister to us (Mt.4:11; He.1:14). Jesus taught that children have guardian angels who stand ready in the presence of God to be instantly dispatched on their behalf (Mt.18:10). The author of *Hebrews* instructed us to always be hospitable to strangers, for we never know when we might be entertaining an angel (He.13:2). Oh, how our Father loves us, that He would utilize His army of angels—heavenly beings far more powerful than we are—to serve us as we travel through this life!

> "See that you do not look down on one of these little ones. For I tell you that their angels in heaven always see the face of my Father in heaven (Mt.18:10).
> Are not all angels ministering spirits sent to serve those who will inherit salvation? (He.1:14).
> Do not forget to entertain strangers, for by so doing some people have entertained angels without knowing it (He.13:2).

3 (46:8-10) **See the works of the LORD: A picture of the last days.**
After assuring the people of their security in God, the psalmist invited them to see the works of the LORD. To *see* (chazah) means to perceive or to have a vision of. Excellent commentator Derek Kidner mentions that the word "is generally used for seeing with the inward eye, as a 'seer' or prophet sees."[4] The psalmist wanted the people to reflect both on God's past faithfulness to their nation and also on His future plans for them. He prophetically directed their attention to the last days when God's plan for the world and His purpose for Israel will ultimately be fulfilled.

---

4 Derek Kidner. *Psalms 1-72*, p.193.

a. He destroys (judges) the nations (v.8).
Before declaring that God will bring peace to the earth, the psalmist revealed that this peace will not come through some treaty or agreement between the nations of the world. It will come as the result of God's judgment on the nations. *Desolations* is also translated as destructions or devastations. It is frequently used in Scripture to describe the devastating results of God's judgment (Is.64:10; Joel 2:3).

b. He brings peace to the earth (v.9).
When peace at last comes to this earth, it will not be because the leaders of the world sought peace but because God Himself forced it upon them. God will make wars to cease by destroying the nations and their weapons—their bows, spears, and chariots (Is.2:4; Ho.2:18; Zec.9:10). All of the nations that rise up against God and His chosen people will be totally crushed when Jesus Christ returns to earth. The peace that He brings will be a bloody peace.

Thought 1. With its constant wars and chaos, our world seems to be reeling out of control. However, we should always remember that God is in control and His purposes will be accomplished. Through the prophecies of His Holy Word, He has revealed how this world will end. It will end when Christ returns to execute devastating judgment upon the nations of the world. Through conquering His enemies, Christ's peace will finally prevail on earth.

Just as God is in control of world affairs, He is also in control of the details of our lives. Overwhelming trouble can send us into a downward spiral, causing us to crash into uncertainty and fear. Even so, God is aware of what is happening. He knows the work He is doing in us, and He will see to it that His will for us is accomplished (Ph.1:6). When others work evil against us, God uses it for good (Ge.50:20). He wisely weaves every thread of our lives into a garment of holiness, gloriously transforming us into the image of His dear Son, Jesus Christ (Ro.8:28-30).

> And we know that in all things God works for the good of those who love him, who have been called according to his purpose. For those God foreknew he also predestined to be conformed to the likeness of his Son, that he might be the firstborn among many brothers (Ro.8:28-29).
> We do, however, speak a message of wisdom among the mature, but not the wisdom of this age or of the rulers of this age, who are coming to nothing. No, we speak of God's secret wisdom, a wisdom that has been hidden and that God destined for our glory before time began (1 Co.2:6-7).

Who has saved us and called us to a holy life—not because of anything we have done but because of his own purpose and grace. This grace was given us in Christ Jesus before the beginning of time (2 Ti.1:9).

For God has put it into their hearts to accomplish his purpose by agreeing to give the beast their power to rule, until God's words are fulfilled (Re.17:17).

The king's heart is in the hand of the LORD; he directs it like a watercourse wherever he pleases (Pr.21:1).

This is the plan determined for the whole world; this is the hand stretched out over all nations. For the LORD Almighty has purposed, and who can thwart him? His hand is stretched out, and who can turn it back? (Is.14:26-27).

For I know the plans I have for you," declares the LORD, "plans to prosper you and not to harm you, plans to give you hope and a future (Je.29:11).

4 (46:10-11) **Be still—wait and hope in the LORD—know that the LORD is God.**
The prospect of God's destroying Israel's enemies brought hope to the people. Although other nations would continually rise up against her, God's chosen nation could rest in His promise that He would one day deliver her for all eternity. The psalmist concluded by instructing God's people to be still, to cease from their fretting and agonizing and know that God is in control of their destiny (Ps.37:8). *Know* (yada) means to know by experience. Because Israel had experienced God's faithfulness in the past, they could trust Him in the present. Interestingly, the Hebrew word for *be still* means to slacken or make loose. Simply put, God is telling His people to relax and wait for Him to do all that He has promised.

a. He will be exalted among all nations and in all the earth (v.10).
God created this world and everyone in it so that He might be glorified (Ps.86:9; Ep.1:11-12; Re.15:4). Throughout the ages multitudes will respond to His love, a love He demonstrated by giving His only begotten Son for our salvation (Ro.5:8). In the end, everyone, even unbelievers, will respond to God's overwhelming power. His purpose *will* be accomplished. He *will* be exalted among all the peoples of the earth.

b. He—the Lord Almighty—is with us: He is our refuge (fortress, stronghold) (v.11).
This encouraging psalm concludes by comforting us with a great truth: the LORD of hosts is with us (v.7). We do not face overwhelming trouble alone (v.1). The God of Jacob, who has chosen us and called us by grace into a covenant with Him, is our refuge. He will protect us when trouble strikes. *Selah*—may we pause to meditate on and thank God for His unfailing presence and power in our lives.

Thought 1. When overwhelming trouble invades our lives, God wants us to *be still*—to release our anxiety and rest in Him (Mt.11:28; Ph.4:6-7). He is with us, and we are safe in His care. We need to trust Him enough to commit our way to Him and to wait on Him to bring His purposes to pass (Ps.37:5-7; Pr.3:5-6).

Remember, God's ultimate purpose in all things is to be glorified. As we patiently endure trouble and find His grace sufficient for every day, He will be exalted through our faithful testimony.

In the same way, let your light shine before men, that they may see your good deeds and praise your Father in heaven (Mt.5:16).

Do not be anxious about anything, but in everything, by prayer and petition, with thanksgiving, present your requests to God. And the peace of God, which transcends all understanding, will guard your hearts and your minds in Christ Jesus (Ph.4:6-7).

With this in mind, we constantly pray for you, that our God may count you worthy of his calling, and that by his power he may fulfill every good purpose of yours and every act prompted by your faith. We pray this so that the name of our Lord Jesus may be glorified in you, and you in him, according to the grace of our God and the Lord Jesus Christ (2 Th.1:11-12).

Commit your way to the LORD; trust in him and he will do this: He will make your righteousness shine like the dawn, the justice of your cause like the noonday sun. Be still before the LORD and wait patiently for him; do not fret when men succeed in their ways, when they carry out their wicked schemes (Ps.37:5-7).

Trust in the LORD with all your heart and lean not on your own understanding; in all your ways acknowledge him, and he will make your paths straight (Pr.3:5-6).

But those who hope in the LORD will renew their strength. They will soar on wings like eagles; they will run and not grow weary, they will walk and not be faint (Is.40:31).

	PSALM 47	Jacob, whom he loved. Selah	inheritance to His people, Ro.8:16-17; 1 Pe.1:3-4; Tit.3:7
	A Call to Acknowledge & Exalt the LORD: A Picture of God's Coming Kingdom, 47:1-9	5 God has ascended amid shouts of joy, the LORD amid the sounding of trumpets.	d. Because He has ascended as the triumphant LORD: A picture of Christ's ascension & exaltation
	For the director of music. Of the Sons of Korah. A psalm.	6 Sing praises to God, sing praises; sing praises to our King, sing praises.	**2. Sing praises to God—sing repeatedly**
1. Clap & shout to God with the voice of triumph	Clap your hands, all you nations; shout to God with cries of joy.	7 For God is the King of all the earth; sing to him a psalm of praise.	a. Because He is *our King* b. Because He is the King of all the earth
a. Because He is awesome... 1) The *LORD Most High* 2) The great King over all	2 How awesome is the LORD Most High, the great King over all the earth!	8 God reigns over the nations; God is seated on his holy throne.	c. Because He is seated on His holy throne & is sovereign: He reigns over all nations
b. Because He subdues nations (unbelievers) under His people (believers)	3 He subdued nations under us, peoples under our feet.	9 The nobles of the nations assemble as the people of the God of Abraham, for the kings of the earth belong to God; he is greatly exalted.	d. Because all rulers assemble to acknowledge the LORD's supremacy, Ph.2:9-11 1) They assemble with God's people
c. Because He gives the promised land (heaven) as an	4 He chose our inheritance for us, the pride of		2) They honor & exalt Him

PSALM 47

A Call to Acknowledge and Exalt the LORD: A Picture of God's Coming Kingdom, 47:1-9

(47:1-9) **Introduction:** worship calls for different moods at different times and for different occasions. Frequently, the appropriate spirit is a quiet, reflective one. At times, we should stand, sit, kneel, or even fall prostrate on our faces in total silence before Him. On other occasions, we should bow before Him in total adoration and submission.

At the opposite end of the spectrum, there are occasions when it is appropriate to worship God loudly and boisterously, offering our most fervent praise to Him. Psalm 47 was written for just such times, times that call for a triumphant celebration of God.

Scripture does not tell us the occasion for the writing of this psalm, and commentators offer various opinions. Some think it was written in conjunction with Psalm 46, supposing that Psalm 46 was written in preparation for a battle and Psalm 47 was the victory song after the battle. A number of them believe that the specific conflict was the battle against Assyria and Sennacherib under Hezekiah (2 K.18-19). Others think it was written to celebrate carrying the Ark of the Covenant from the house of Obed-edom to Mount Zion (2 S.6). For generations, Psalm 47 has been recited by the Jews on Rosh Hashanah, the Jewish New Year's Day; while many churches use it on the day Christians celebrate Christ's ascension.

Whatever the original occasion for its writing, Psalm 47 is a Messianic psalm, a psalm about Christ. It points to that future day when Jesus Christ will reign over all the earth as King of kings and Lord of lords. Like the believers who first clapped their hands and shouted in response to this psalm, we too should rejoice in that coming day, offering our loudest praise to our great God and King, Jesus Christ. This is, *A Call to Acknowledge and Exalt the LORD: A Picture of God's Coming Kingdom,* 47:1-9.

1. Clap and shout to God with the voice of triumph (vv.1-5).
2. Sing praises to God—sing repeatedly (vv.6-9).

1 (47:1-5) **Clap and shout to God with the voice of triumph.**

The psalmist called the people to praise God loudly by clapping their hands and shouting triumphantly. Commentators are divided about whether *people* refers to the congregation of Israel or the people of all the nations. The theme of the psalm is God's kingship over all the earth (vv.7-8). However, verses 3 and 4 indicate that the worshippers are God's covenant people, the Israelites.

The Jews who first sang and responded to this psalm celebrated God's sovereignty in carrying out His purposes for Israel. But it is also a prophetic psalm. From a prophetic standpoint, the call to worship points to that future day when all the nations will praise God (v.9). Therefore, both interpretations of *people* are correct.

a. Because He is awesome (v.2).

God is worthy of our fervent praise because He is the great King over all the earth. *Awesome* (ya-re') is best translated "to be feared." That is, we should recognize who God is, revere Him or hold Him in awe, willfully submit to Him, and obey Him (see outline and notes—Pr.1:7 for more discussion). As LORD most high (Jehovah Elyown), He is the supreme ruler over every other authority, including all heads of nations as well as spiritual powers (angels and demons).

57

b. Because He subdues nations (unbelievers) under His people (believers) (v.3).

We should praise God not only for who He is—the supreme ruler over all the earth—but also for what He does for His people. The psalmist reflected on the many victories God had given Israel over her enemies. Past triumphs gave him unwavering hope for present and future challenges. He was confident that God would continue to faithfully subdue—place or arrange—the other nations beneath His chosen nation.

Subdued (dabar) literally means to speak or declare. Here, it applies to what God promised His people in His covenant with them. The psalmist could confidently lead Israel to praise God for future victories because of His covenant with Abraham and his descendants, the Jewish nation. The promises of this covenant will ultimately be fulfilled when Christ returns and overthrows all of Israel's enemies.

c. Because He gives the promised land (heaven) as an inheritance to His people, Ro.8:16-17; 1 Pe.1:3-4; Tit.3:7 (v.4).

God's victories on Israel's behalf included conquering the Canaanite nations and establishing the Jews in the promised land. The land of Canaan is the inheritance that God ordained for Abraham and His descendants. It is a symbol of heaven, our inheritance as believers and place of eternal rest (see outline and notes—Ge.12:1-3; *Numbers*, INTRODUCTION, Special Feature 26 for more discussion).

The excellency or pride of Jacob refers to this inheritance, the promised land. God deeded this region to Israel because of His great love for her. Jacob, the father of the twelve tribes of Israel, poetically represents the entire nation.

d. Because He has ascended as the triumphant LORD: A picture of Christ's ascension and exaltation (v.5).

The psalmist charged the congregation to praise God because of His ascension to His throne as King over the earth. The coronation of a new king was cause for great celebration in Israel. It included shouts of joy and the jubilant blaring of trumpets (1 S.10:24; 1 Ki.11:12, 14).

This triumphant scene is undoubtedly a picture of the ascension and exaltation of God's beloved Son, Jesus Christ, as King over all the earth. As many commentators note, Christ must *descend* before He can *ascend*. Again and again, Scripture prophetically declares that Christ will come from heaven to earth a second time. When He returns, He will destroy all of His and Israel's enemies and rule over the earth as King of kings and Lord of lords. The Apostle John was given the holy privilege of peering into the future and describing the return and triumph of Jesus Christ:

I saw heaven standing open and there before me was a white horse, whose rider is called Faithful and True. With justice he judges and makes war. His eyes are like blazing fire, and on his head are many crowns. He has a name written on him that no one knows but he himself. He is dressed in a robe dipped in blood, and his name is the Word of God. The armies of heaven were following him, riding on white horses and dressed in fine linen, white and clean. Out of his mouth comes a sharp sword with which to strike down the nations. "He will rule them with an iron scepter." He treads the winepress of the fury of the wrath of God Almighty. On his robe and on his thigh he has this name written: KING OF KINGS AND LORD OF LORDS (Re.19:11-16).

Thought 1. As believers living today, we are the beneficiaries of God's new covenant of grace through the death and resurrection of Jesus Christ. We too should clap and shout praise to God as we consider the blessings of these verses:

➤ Our God is the great King over all the earth (v.2). Although our world is rapidly turning further and further away from Him, God is unalarmed by all that is taking place. His purposes will ultimately be accomplished. We should walk in the fear of the LORD every day of our lives, willfully submitting to Him and obeying His commands.

➤ We can see the day approaching when Jesus Christ will reign as King over the entire earth (v.3). When He returns, He will overthrow all unbelievers, and we will rule with Him over the nations of the world (Re.19:11–20:4).

➤ God has promised us a glorious inheritance in heaven, our eternal home (v.4; Ro.8:16-17; 1 Pe.1:3-4; Tit.3:7).

➤ Christ's ascension to the throne of this earth reminds us of His ascension back to heaven after His resurrection (v.5). Upon ascending to heaven, He sat down at the right hand of God, signifying that the work for our salvation had been completed. Because of Christ's finished work on the cross, we will share His glory during His earthly reign and throughout eternity (Ro.8:17-18; 1 Pe.4:13).

To keep this command without spot or blame until the appearing of our Lord Jesus Christ, which God will bring about in his own time—God, the blessed and only Ruler, the King of kings and Lord of lords (1 Ti.6:14-15).

They will make war against the Lamb, but the Lamb will overcome them because he is Lord of lords and King of kings—and with him will be his called, chosen and faithful followers" (Re.17:14).

Yours, O LORD, is the greatness and the power and the glory and the majesty and the splendor, for everything in heaven and earth is yours. Yours, O LORD, is the kingdom; you are exalted as head over all (1 Chr.29:11).

The LORD reigns, he is robed in majesty; the LORD is robed in majesty and is armed with strength. The world is firmly established; it cannot be moved. Your throne was established long ago; you are from all eternity (Ps.93:1-2).

Ascribe to the LORD, O families of nations, ascribe to the LORD glory and strength. Ascribe to the LORD the glory due his name; bring an offering and come into his courts. Worship the LORD in the splendor of his holiness; tremble before him, all the earth (Ps.96:7-9).

2 (47:6-9) **Sing praises to God—sing repeatedly.** God's awesomeness and greatness as King call for exuberant praise. The psalmist led the people to passionately exalt God, repeating the direction to sing praises four times. With each repetition, the people would praise God more loudly and with greater zeal until a level of fervor truly worthy of God was reached. The psalm concludes with four reasons why God deserves our most spirited praise:

a. Because He is *our King* (v.6).
The psalmist led the congregation of Israel to jubilantly praise God because He had chosen them as His special people. God had made His covenant with them, as opposed to the other nations of the earth. Their personal relationship with the King called for their loudest, most heartfelt praise.

In our age, we who have received God's grace by believing in Jesus Christ for salvation are the children of God's new covenant. Just as Israel had under the Old Covenant, we today have a personal relationship with God. The King of all the earth is *our King*. We know Him, and we have open access to Him through the blood of His Son (He.4:14-16; He.10:19-23).

b. Because He is the King of all the earth (v.7).
Israel's king—and our king—is the one and only true God; He alone rules over the earth. Thus, the psalmist instructed the people of Israel, and us, to sing His praises with full understanding of and appreciation for God's supreme authority and His goodness to His chosen people.

c. Because He is seated on His holy throne and is sovereign (v.8).
Although the leaders of the nations may not acknowledge it, they are all under God's authority, even those who do not believe in God and worship Him. From His throne of holiness, God sovereignly directs them to accomplish His will (see outline and notes—Pr.21:1 for more discussion). God's holiness governs all that He does; every action that proceeds from His throne is just, righteous, and pure.

d. Because all rulers assemble to acknowledge the LORD's supremacy, Ph.2:9-11 (v.9).
The psalmist described a stirring scene: all the princes or rulers of this world gathering together as one group, *the people of the God of Abraham.* This scene never occurred in his day, nor has it occurred since. The psalmist could only have been speaking of that future day when every knee will bow and every tongue will confess "that Jesus Christ is Lord, to the glory of God the father" (Ph.2:9-11). Excellent commentator Derek Kidner explains the significance of the term *the people of the God of Abraham:*

> *The innumerable* princes *and* peoples *are to become one* people, *and they will no longer be outsiders but within the covenant: this is implied in their being called* the people of the God of Abraham. *It is the abundant fulfilment of the promise of Genesis 12:3; it anticipates what Paul expounds of the inclusion of the Gentiles as Abraham's sons (Rom.4:11; Gal.3:7-9).*[1]

The psalmist concludes by announcing that the shields of the earth belong to God. Other Bible versions translate *kings* (magain) as shields and *leaders* or rulers as in Hosea 4:18. If *kings* is the accurate understanding, the statement speaks of all the earth's rulers submitting to Christ and exalting Him. If *shields* (the usual translation of *magain*) is correct, it may speak of the end of war on earth as all the leaders of the world unite under the Lordship of Christ. The shield is a tool of defense, so it may also refer to Christ's serving as the defender of the world during His reign.

Thought 1. What a glorious day it will be when *our King,* Jesus Christ, is worshipped as King of all the earth! Today, the battle against Jesus Christ is raging, growing fiercer and fiercer as the years go by. Fires of persecution blaze out of control in many countries, with embers being kindled in places where Christ has been historically known. Sadly, the freedom of Christ-followers to publicly practice their faith is being increasingly cut off. Believers are being punished for

---

1 Derek Kidner. *Psalms 1-72*, p.196.

standing for Christ and the truth of His Word, even in the United States of America.

All of this is leading to the antichrist's reign over the earth during the tribulation period. But then Jesus will return to destroy his enemies in the bloodiest war this world has ever seen, the battle of Armageddon (see outline and notes—Re.16:12-16 and Re.19:17-21 for more discussion). On that day, what this psalmist and others prophesied in God's infallible Word will come to pass: Jesus Christ will rule the earth and the people of every nation will worship Him!

In a world where the name of Jesus Christ is cursed and reviled and where His followers are increasingly oppressed, we who love Him can take great hope. Christ will return to reign for all eternity, and we will reign with Him! Jesus warned us of the troubles we would face for following Him, saying that, "In the world you will have trouble." But He continued to say, "But take heart! I have overcome the world" (Jn.16:33).

As this psalm instructs, we should *clap our hands* and *shout to God with cries of joy*, offering our loudest praise to the one who will reign for ever and ever!

For he must reign until he has put all his enemies under his feet (1 Co.15:25).

And from Jesus Christ, who is the faithful witness, the firstborn from the dead, and the ruler of the kings of the earth. To him who loves us and has freed us from our sins by his blood (Re.1:5).

The seventh angel sounded his trumpet, and there were loud voices in heaven, which said: "The kingdom of the world has become the kingdom of our Lord and of his Christ, and he will reign for ever and ever" (Re.11:15).

All kings will bow down to him and all nations will serve him (Ps.72:11).

He was given authority, glory and sovereign power; all peoples, nations and men of every language worshiped him. His dominion is an everlasting dominion that will not pass away, and his kingdom is one that will never be destroyed (Da.7:14).

I will take away the chariots from Ephraim and the war-horses from Jerusalem, and the battle bow will be broken. He will proclaim peace to the nations. His rule will extend from sea to sea and from the River to the ends of the earth (Zec.9:10).

PSALM 48

The City of God, Jerusalem: A Picture of the Heavenly City, 48:1-14 (Ga.4:21-31; Ph.3:20-21; He.12:22-24; Re.21:1-21)

A Song. A psalm of the Sons of Korah.

1. Praise the LORD—praise Him for the city of God a. It is holy because of God's presence, 8 b. It is a beautiful city that stirs the earth to rejoice c. It is indwelled by God Himself & He will defend her always: To be fulfilled in the New Jeruslaem 1) God broke the military alliance against His city • He struck fear in the armies & they fled • He struck the armies with pain & anguish—	Great is the LORD, and most worthy of praise, in the city of our God, his holy mountain. 2 It is beautiful in its loftiness, the joy of the whole earth. Like the utmost heights of Zaphon is Mount Zion, the city of the Great King. 3 God is in her citadels; he has shown himself to be her fortress. 4 When the kings joined forces, when they advanced together, 5 They saw [her] and were astounded; they fled in terror. 6 Trembling seized them there, pain like that of a woman in labor. 7 You destroyed them like ships of Tarshish shattered by an east wind. 8 As we have heard, so have we seen in the city of the LORD Almighty, in the city of our God: God makes her secure forever. Selah 9 Within your temple, O God, we meditate on your unfailing love. 10 Like your name, O God, your praise reaches to the ends of the earth; your right hand is filled with righteousness. 11 Mount Zion rejoices, the villages of Judah are glad because of your judgments. 12 Walk about Zion, go around her, count her towers, 13 Consider well her ramparts, view her citadels, that you may tell of them to the next generation. 14 For this God is our God for ever and ever; he will be our guide even to the end.	like a woman in labor 2) God destroyed the opposition—like ships shattered in a typhoon or hurricane 3) God will make the city secure forever: This is the testimony of God's people **2. Meditate on God's unfailing love & worship Him** a. Because His name deserves to be praised to the ends of the earth 1) Due to His righteousness 2) Due to His justice b. Because of His promised protection of Jerusalem 1) Consider the city's towers, ramparts (fortified walls), & citadels (palaces) 2) Bear witness of God's protection to future generations c. Because the LORD is our God forever & ever: He will guide us throughout life—even until death

PSALM 48

The City of God, Jerusalem: A Picture of the Heavenly City, 48:1-14

(48:1-14) **Introduction:** in most countries, one city usually stands out as the grandest and most important. This city is often the nation's capital. Visitors from near and far flock to these cities to view their sites and enjoy their attractions. In ancient Israel, this city was Jerusalem. Even today, millions of people travel from all over the world to visit the Holy City. In Old Testament times, faithful Jews journeyed to Jerusalem to celebrate the feasts, to offer sacrifices, and to worship. We can just imagine their excitement when, after a long journey, the City of God came into view. As they neared the gates, they would often break into song. Psalm 48 was one of the songs they sang.

As with Psalms 46 and 47, we do not know for certain who wrote this psalm, nor do we know the occasion for its writing (see Introduction—Psalm 46 for more discussion). Nevertheless, we do know its dual purpose: to celebrate the Holy City and her God, and to point us to the Heavenly Jerusalem, the city of God's abode and our eternal home. This is, *The City of God, Jerusalem: A Picture of the Heavenly City,* 48:1-14.

1. Praise the LORD—praise Him for the city of God (vv.1-8).
2. Meditate on God's unfailing love and worship Him (vv.9-14).

1 (48:1-8) **Praise the LORD—praise Him for the city of God.**

The hearts of the faithful overflowed with excitement and joy as they marched up to Jerusalem to worship the LORD at the annual festivals. As they neared Zion, the great city of God, they confessed they were not coming to celebrate the gleaming city iteslf but the great God who dwelled there in the most Holy Place of the temple. In spite of her radiant natural beauty, Jerusalem is glorious because the LORD (Yahweh, Jehovah) is her God. The worshippers recognized God's greatness in the loveliness of the exquisite place, and they praised Him for choosing to reside there among them. Because He is such a great God, they declared that the LORD should be greatly—exceedingly, abundantly, mightily—praised.

a. It is holy because of God's presence, 8 (v.1).

God's presence on this mountain made it a special place, a place of holiness. First, Jerusalem was holy because it was a consecrated spot: it was set apart for the presence, purposes, and people of God. But the city was also holy *because* God resided there, and He is altogether holy. The influence of God's uncompromised purity and righteousness flowed out the doors of the temple and into the atmosphere of the great city, especially among those who truly loved and obeyed Him. As the people walked throughout each and every day, He was with them just as He is with us.

b. It is a beautiful city that stirs the earth to rejoice (v.2).

Gracefully cascading across a plateau in the Judean hills, Jerusalem is a lovely sight to behold. Her *loftiness* (noph, meaning height or elevation) exemplifies majestic simplicity. Mount Zion gradually ascends 2500 feet or 760 meters into the sky. But Jerusalem was *the joy of the whole earth* for a more significant reason: God's presence was there. *The Expositor's Bible Commentary* explains:

> "*Only because of God's condescension to dwell on Mount Zion may she be called beautiful in her elevation (NIV: 'loftiness') and the 'joy of the whole earth' (v.2; cf. 50:2; Lam.2:15)....The godly had a special feeling about Jerusalem that is beautifully and sensitively expressed in this psalm. They looked on the city, mountain, and temple as symbols of God's presence with his people. Therefore, the psalmist used the geographical/spatial references to express the joy of God's people with the blessed presence of God.*"[1]

The joy of the whole earth may also look forward to that glad day when Jesus Christ will rule from the throne of David, and Jerusalem will be the headquarters or capital of the world (Is.2:2-4; Zec.14). Sixteenth-century reformer John Calvin noted that the whole earth would rejoice in Jerusalem because salvation would flow from there to the entire world.[2]

Translations and commentators differ in their understanding of *Zaphon* (tsawfone, Is.14:13). Many think it speaks of Mount Zion's northern location or of heaven, the true Zion. The KJV, NKJV, NASB, ESB, and HCSB translate it accordingly. Many others, including the NIV translators, believe it refers to Mount Zaphon, the home of Baal and other gods in pagan mythology. In this interpretation is accurate, its purpose is to identify the LORD as the one true God and Zion, not Zaphon, as His dwelling.

c. It is forever defended by God Himself (vv.3-8).

Because of God's great love for Jerusalem and His covenant with the Jewish people, He personally defends her against attacks. Palaces or citadels were fortified dwellings usually occupied by kings or other high-ranking leaders.[3] However, Jerusalem's palaces were protected by God Himself. He was Israel's refuge, her stronghold or fortress (v.3).

When the kings of the earth united against Jerusalem and saw that she was defended by God, they swiftly retreated in terror (vv.4-5). Panic-stricken, they trembled in anguish like a woman in the throes of childbirth (v.6). In the same way ships are helplessly shattered by a typhoon or hurricane, the LORD destroyed those who rose up against Jerusalem with an east wind (v.7). "An east wind was notorious for its destructiveness and is often used as a symbol for judgment (Job 27:21; Isaiah 27:8; Jeremiah 18:17)."[4]

Tarshish was a celebrated seaport on the coast of Spain. Located some 2500 miles or 4025 kilometers west of Israel, it was the farthest limit of the western world in Old Testament times. Ships of Tarshish were mighty merchant vessels built to withstand the strenuous journey (1 K.10:22; Eze.27:25). Eventually, the term was used to describe all large ships designed for long voyages. The comparison here is clear: just as the largest, strongest ships are no match for a great storm, the most powerful armies of the world cannot stand against Israel's God.

The people of Israel had witnessed God's defense of their beloved capital time and again. Tales of God's power told by previous generations were confirmed by His continued mighty acts on Jerusalem's behalf (v.8). Note how the titles for Jerusalem convey God's relationship to the Holy City:

➤ *The city of the LORD—God* (Elohim), the name that speaks of God's unlimited power, is prominent throughout the second book of *Psalms* (chs. 42–72). Therefore, when *LORD* (Yahweh, Jehovah) is used, it is even more significant than usual. Here it emphasizes God's protection of Jerusalem because of His covenant with Israel.

➤ *The city of the LORD Almighty*—this name identifies the LORD as the Commander of a mighty army of angels. Scripture records occasions when God dispatched His heavenly troops to defend Israel (2 K.6:15-17; 7:5-7). At times, the Angel of the LORD—Jesus Christ appearing before He came to earth as a man—personally fought for God's chosen people (Jos.5:13-15; 2 K.19:35).

➤ *The city of our God*—the city where God resided.

Historically, this passage speaks of the numerous occasions when earth's kings had attempted to overthrow Jerusalem. She was a constant target for ambitious conquerors who coveted her strategic location, infrastructure, and wealth. Prophetically, this passage describes that coming day when a confederation of world leaders will engage their armies against Israel (see outline and notes—Eze.38:1–39:29 for more discussion).

---

1   Frank E. Gaebelein. *Psalms, Proverbs, Ecclesiastes, Song of Songs.* "The Expositor's Bible Commentary with the New International Version," Vol.5. (Grand Rapids, MI: Zondervan, 1991), p.362.

2   John Calvin. *Calvin's Commentaries.* WORDsearch CROSS e-book.

3   R. Laird Harris, ed. *Theological Wordbook of the Old Testament.* WORDsearch CROSS e-book.

4   John Phillips. *Exploring Psalms, Volume 1.* WORDsearch CROSS e-book.

As we study this passage that praises God for defending Jerusalem, we cannot overlook that the city was destroyed by Nebuchadnezzar in 586 B.C. and by the Roman army in A.D. 70. On these occasions, God lifted His hand of protection from Jerusalem and executed judgment upon the Jewish people for rejecting Him and His Son.

Thought 1. The earthly Jerusalem is a picture of the true Jerusalem, which is heaven. Consider how this passage points beyond Israel's capital to that glorious city beyond the stars.

First, it is the *city where God abides*. God is present everywhere. Yet there is one place—an actual spot—where God's presence is centered. Under the old covenant, this place was the mercy seat in the Holy of Holies of Jerusalem's tabernacle, and later the temple. The author of Hebrews explained how this was a figure or symbol of God's true abode in heaven:

> **The point of what we are saying is this: We do have such a high priest, who sat down at the right hand of the throne of the Majesty in heaven, and who serves in the sanctuary, the true tabernacle set up by the Lord, not by man (He.8:1-2).**
>
> **But God found fault with the people and said: "The time is coming, declares the Lord, when I will make a new covenant with the house of Israel and with the house of Judah. It will not be like the covenant I made with their forefathers when I took them by the hand to lead them out of Egypt, because they did not remain faithful to my covenant, and I turned away from them, declares the Lord (He.8:8-9).**
>
> **It was necessary, then, for the copies of the heavenly things to be purified with these sacrifices, but the heavenly things themselves with better sacrifices than these. For Christ did not enter a man-made sanctuary that was only a copy of the true one; he entered heaven itself, now to appear for us in God's presence (He.9:23-24).**

Second, heaven is a *holy city*. God's presence there makes it a sacred, consecrated place. Because of His absolute holiness, God cannot tolerate sin in His presence. In the earthly tabernacle, two golden cherubim stretched their wings over what was called the mercy seat. The cherubim symbolically protected the spot where God's actual presence was centered. In his thrilling vision of God's heavenly throne, Isaiah saw angels guarding the throne and proclaiming the holiness of God. One of these angels made sure that Isaiah's sins were purged before he approached God (Is.6:1-7).

Third, *God's people came to Jerusalem to worship Him*. The author of Hebrews explained how this too was a symbol, stating that we who live under the new covenant enter into the true presence of God:

> **But you have come to Mount Zion, to the heavenly Jerusalem, the city of the living God. You have come to thousands upon thousands of angels in joyful assembly, to the church of the firstborn, whose names are written in heaven. You have come to God, the judge of all men, to the spirits of righteous men made perfect, to Jesus the mediator of a new covenant, and to the sprinkled blood that speaks a better word than the blood of Abel (He.12:22-24).**

Fourth, heaven is a *city of dazzling beauty*. The Apostle John was privileged to be given a vision of the true dwelling place of God, calling it *the holy city, the New Jerusalem* (Re.21:2). Just as the Hebrews thrilled at the sight of Jerusalem, we should overflow with delight when we consider what is revealed to us about this brilliant city, the capital of the new heaven and the new earth. Golden streets, jasper walls, bejeweled foundations, pearly gates, and a crystal river are only the beginning of heaven's glories. Like the earthly Jerusalem, however, the true beauty of heaven is not because of its sparkling sights but because it is the residence of God. These wonders pale in comparison to God's radiant presence (see outline and notes—Re.21:1–22:5 for more discussion).

> **These things may be taken figuratively, for the women represent two covenants. One covenant is from Mount Sinai and bears children who are to be slaves: This is Hagar. Now Hagar stands for Mount Sinai in Arabia and corresponds to the present city of Jerusalem, because she is in slavery with her children. But the Jerusalem that is above is free, and she is our mother (Ga.4:24-26).**
>
> **But our citizenship is in heaven. And we eagerly await a Savior from there, the Lord Jesus Christ, who, by the power that enables him to bring everything under his control, will transform our lowly bodies so that they will be like his glorious body (Ph.3:20-21).**
>
> **And I heard a loud voice from the throne saying, "Now the dwelling of God is with men, and he will live with them. They will be his people, and God himself will be with them and be their God (Re.21:3).**

2(48:9-14) **Meditate on God's unfailing love and worship Him.**

As the worshippers joyfully praised God in the temple, they thought or meditated on God's *unfailing love* (chesed), His covenant love and faithfulness (see outline and notes—Ps.5:7 for more discussion). The city of Jerusalem itself was a "God-given visual aid, encouraging them to imagine and to reflect on the long history of God's involvement with Israel and of the evidences of his 'unfailing love.'"[5] The temple was filled with symbols of God's covenant with the Hebrews, the most compelling being the Ark of the Covenant resting in the Holy of Holies.

a. Because His name deserves to be praised to the ends of the earth (vv.10-11).

The name *God* (Elohim) testifies to His mighty power that exceeds every other power in the universe. God had faithfully exercised this power on behalf of His covenant people. Therefore, the worshippers determined to sing His praises to the ends of the earth, proclaiming His righteousness and rejoicing in His justice (judgments) (v.11).

b. Because of His promised protection of Jerusalem (vv.12-13).

A person could not survey Zion's landscape without noticing that it was a well-fortified city. In fact, the people were encouraged to walk around the city to note the fortifications God had given them for their protection:

➤ *Towers* were the tallest structures in a city and were usually placed at various points around the city walls. From them, watchmen could see for miles and warriors were protected as they repelled approaching forces. The psalmist instructed the people to *tell* (caphar, count or number) Jerusalem's towers; the more towers a city had, the stronger it was (Is.33:18).

➤ *Ramparts* were steep embankments outside the walls of the city. They were usually built from earth or trees (De.20:20). Before invaders could attack a city, they had to get past them and the armed warriors who hid behind them (2 Chr.26:15).

➤ *Citadels* or *palaces* (see verse 3).

The Hebrews were exhorted to mark these reinforcements for an important purpose: that they might bear witness of God's protection to future generations (v.13c). The strongholds of Jerusalem tell a crucial story of God's love for His chosen people. In faithfulness to His covenant with them, He had protected them from every threat.

c. Because the Lord is our God forever and ever: He will guide us throughout life—even until death (v.14).

This joyful psalm ends as it begins: by praising the great God of Zion. As in Psalm 47, the worshippers rejoiced that this all-powerful God was *their* God (Ps.47:6). Of all the peoples of the earth, He had chosen to dwell among them. They were the recipients of His covenant, and they were blessed with His holy presence. Their security was not in the impressive fortifications that surrounded their beloved city, but in *Him*. As He had led them through the wilderness with the cloud by day and the fire by night—symbols of His presence among them—they were confident that He would guide them throughout the rest of their lives.

Thought 1. As we worship God, we too should meditate on His unfailing love for us. We should remember all the times we have experienced God's faithfulness through difficult circumstances, such as...

- grave illness or injury
- death of a loved one
- financial crisis
- accidents
- injustices or wrongs
- devastating natural disasters
- wartime tragedy
- persecution or oppression
- unemployment or inability to work
- physical, mental, or emotional abuse

In all of these as well as in other perils of life, we are sustained by God's unfailing love for us. As believers in His Son, we are His dear children. Nothing can separate us from His love (Ro.8:35-39). As the recipients of His new covenant, we are kept by His power and are safe in His care (1 Pe.1:5; 2 Ti.1:12).

Just as the Hebrews were instructed to do, we should mark God's faithfulness and bear witness to His power. We need to pass along the stories of God's unfailing love to our children, grandchildren, great-grandchildren, and nieces and nephews. Bible teacher Warren Wiersbe noted that

> *The greatest danger a nation faces is not the invading enemy on the outside but the eroding enemy on the inside—a people gradually turning away from the faith of their fathers. Each generation must pass along to the next generation who the Lord is, what He has done, and what they must do in response to His goodness and faithfulness.*[6]

Meditating on God's faithfulness will also give us hope and encourage us in present trouble. After the destruction of Jerusalem by Nebuchadnezzar and during the Babylonian captivity, Jeremiah was sustained by thinking about God's unfailing love. Every day, he

---

5 Frank E. Gaebelein, ed. *The Expositor's Bible Commentary*, p.365.

6 Warren W. Wiersbe. *The Bible Exposition Commentary*. WORDsearch CROSS e-book.

identified new mercies from the Lord, enabling him to say, "Great is thy faithfulness" (Lam.3:21-24).

Who shall separate us from the love of Christ? Shall trouble or hardship or persecution or famine or nakedness or danger or sword? As it is written: "For your sake we face death all day long; we are considered as sheep to be slaughtered." No, in all these things we are more than conquerors through him who loved us. For I am convinced that neither death nor life, neither angels nor demons, neither the present nor the future, nor any powers, neither height nor depth, nor anything else in all creation, will be able to separate us from the love of God that is in Christ Jesus our Lord (Ro.8:35-39).

That is why I am suffering as I am. Yet I am not ashamed, because I know whom I have believed, and am convinced that he is able to guard what I have entrusted to him for that day (2 Ti.1:12).

And the things you have heard me say in the presence of many witnesses entrust to reliable men who will also be qualified to teach others (2 Ti.2:2).

Who through faith are shielded by God's power until the coming of the salvation that is ready to be revealed in the last time (1 Pe.1:5)

We will not hide them from their children; we will tell the next generation the praiseworthy deeds of the Lord, his power, and the wonders he has done (Ps.78:4).

One generation will commend your works to another; they will tell of your mighty acts (Ps.145:4).

PSALM 49

When the Self-sufficient Deceive & Trouble the Righteous, 49:1-20

For the director of music. Of the Sons of Korah. A psalm.

1. Listen closely to this lesson
  a. It is a lesson for everyone in the world
    1) Both low & high
    2) Both rich & poor
  b. It is a lesson of wisdom shared from the psalmist's heart
    1) It will give insight (understanding) to the listener
    2) It will explain one of the riddles (mysteries) of life

2. Do not fear troublesome days when evil deceivers surround you

  a. Bc. their wealth cannot be used as a ransom to save them (anyone) from death
    1) The ransom for a life costs far more than man can pay
    2) The cost to conquer death & to live forever requires the ultimate payment or sacrifice: Pictures our need for Christ to be our ransom (Redeemer)
  b. Bc. we all die—the wise, the foolish, & the senseless
    1) Our wealth is left to others

    2) Our bodies are forever cut off from the fame &

Hear this, all you peoples; listen, all who live in this world,
2 Both low and high, rich and poor alike:
3 My mouth will speak words of wisdom; the utterance from my heart will give understanding.
4 I will turn my ear to a proverb; with the harp I will expound my riddle:
5 Why should I fear when evil days come, when wicked deceivers surround me—
6 Those who trust in their wealth and boast of their great riches?
7 No man can redeem the life of another or give to God a ransom for him—
8 The ransom for a life is costly, no payment is ever enough—
9 That he should live on forever and not see decay.
10 For all can see that wise men die; the foolish and the senseless alike perish and leave their wealth to others.
11 Their tombs will remain their houses forever, their dwellings for endless generations, though they had named lands after themselves.
12 But man, despite his riches, does not endure; he is like the beasts that perish.
13 This is the fate of those who trust in themselves, and of their followers, who approve their sayings. Selah
14 Like sheep they are destined for the grave, and death will feed on them. The upright will rule over them in the morning; their forms will decay in the grave, far from their princely mansions.
15 But God will redeem my life from the grave; he will surely take me to himself. Selah
16 Do not be overawed when a man grows rich, when the splendor of his house increases;
17 For he will take nothing with him when he dies, his splendor will not descend with him.
18 Though while he lived he counted himself blessed—and men praise you when you prosper—
19 He will join the generation of his fathers, who will never see the light [of life].
20 A man who has riches without understanding is like the beasts that perish.

the lands (wealth, estates) we have sought to secure
    3) Our end—despite our wealth & fame—is the same as the beasts that perish: Death

3. Know the fate of the self-sufficient & the destiny of the righteous

  a. The fate of the self-sufficient
    1) Will be led like sheep to the slaughter (death)
    2) Will be ruled over by the righteous
    3) Will rot in their graves—be far removed from their mansions (estates)
  b. The destiny of the righteous
    1) God will redeem you
    2) God will exalt you to rule over the self-sufficient, 14b

4. Be encouraged because you are redeemed: Do not be dismayed over an unbeliever who is rich & self-sufficient
  a. Bc. the self-sufficient will take nothing with him when he dies—neither wealth nor fame (glory)
    1) Despite claiming to be blessed
    2) Despite people praising him
  b. Bc. the self-sufficient will never see the *light* of God
  c. Bc. the self-sufficient does not understand that he must be redeemed: He is like the beasts that perish, 6-10, 15

PSALM 49

When the Self-sufficient Deceive and Trouble the Righteous, 49:1-20

(49:1-20) **Introduction:** on this sin-cursed earth, many things seem unjust and do not make sense to us. One problem that perplexes a number of believers is that so many ungodly people prosper and enjoy a life of ease while the godly struggle. Like Psalms 37 and 73, Psalm 49 addresses the prosperity of the wicked. A wisdom poem, Psalm 49 echoes themes of *Ecclesiastes*—specifically, the certainty of death and the fact that we will leave our possessions behind when we die. These resemblances, along with the references to *parables* or *proverbs* and *dark sayings* (v.4), have led some to speculate that it is one of Solomon's songs (Pr.1:6; 1 K.4:32).

Unlike *Ecclesiastes*, however, this encouraging psalm points to the hope that believers have beyond this life (v.15). "It brings out into the open the assurance of victory over death which Ecclesiastes leaves concealed."[1] In

addition, Psalm 49 reminds us that we cannot purchase eternal life, prophetically pointing us to the sacrificial death of Jesus Christ (vv.7-9).

On those days when our jobs are difficult and unfulfilling, when our expenses are greater than our incomes, when we are struggling just to get by, and when we are tempted to envy the ungodly whose lives seem easier than ours, we should open our Bibles to this psalm. This is, *When the Self-sufficient Deceive and Trouble the Righteous*, 49:1-20.

  1. Listen closely to this lesson (vv.1-4).
  2. Do not fear troublesome days when evil deceivers surround you (vv.5-12).
  3. Know the fate of the self-sufficient and the destiny of the righteous (vv.13-15).
  4. Be encouraged because you are redeemed: Do not be dismayed over an unbeliever who is rich and self-sufficient (vv.16-20).

---

1 Derek Kidner. *Psalms 1-72*, p.199.

1 (49:1-4) **Listen closely to this lesson.**
The wise psalmist began by calling for the undivided attention of all who hear his song. *Hear* (shama) means more than to simply listen with the ears. It means to pay close attention to, to grasp or understand, to heed, and to obey. Because so many fail to embrace this important message, the psalmist pled with his listeners to focus on what he was saying.

a. It is a lesson for everyone in the world (vv.1-2).
The message of this song is vital to every human being, regardless of nationality, age, or financial status. Both low and high and rich *and* poor need to receive the message of Psalm 49. *All who live in this world* signifies that it is not just for the Israelites who know the LORD but for people of unbelieving nations as well. *World* (cheled) is a seldom-used Hebrew word that refers not only to the earth but also to the span of our lives on this earth.[2] It also speaks of how brief and fleeting our time is on this earth (*years,* Ps.39:5; *fleeting life,* Ps.89:47).

b. It is a lesson of wisdom shared from the psalmist's heart (vv.3-4).
Seeking wisdom from God, the psalmist had given much thought to the problem of the prosperity of the wicked. Through this song, he shared the insight God had given him. He wanted all listeners to understand how earthly riches relate to eternity.

The psalmist spoke of two tools that wisdom teachers used in Old Testament times. A *proverb* or *parable* (mashal) was a short, concise saying that conveyed a vital truth in a way that was easy to remember and understand (see outline and notes—Pr.1:1 for more discussion). A *riddle* (chidhah) was an enigma or difficult subject that required deep consideration and contemplation to understand (see outline and notes—Pr.1:6 for more discussion).

Simply put, the psalmist said that this song would open—explain, disclose, express—a difficult riddle that had perplexed people for generations. It would do so in a manner that would make it easy to understand.

Thought 1. We should all be seekers of truth, people who are willing to invest our time and energy to gain life-changing insight about what is important both in this world and in eternity. God commands us to seek wisdom, and He graciously invites us to ask Him for it (Pr.4:5, 7; 16:16; Js.1:5). Many people think that wisdom is out of our reach, assuming that the answers to life's perplexing questions cannot be found. Nothing could be farther from the truth.

God's wisdom is revealed to us in His Word (Jn.17:17; 1 Co.2:9-10). All people—believers and unbelievers alike—will benefit by heeding the wisdom of God's Word. The beginning of wisdom is the fear of the LORD that leads us to salvation (Jb.28:28; Ps. 111:10; 2 Ti.3:15; see outline and notes—Pr.1:7 for more discussion). When we receive God's gift of salvation by repenting and believing in Christ, God gives us His Holy Spirit. The indwelling Spirit of God leads us into the understanding of God's truth as revealed in His Word (Jn.16:13; 1 Co.2:11-16).

Before we can understand God's truth, though, we must commit to reading and studying God's Word (2 Ti.2:15). We also need to listen to or hear God's Word as others teach it to us. For this reason, we should be faithful in attending church, and we should heed God's servants who truly preach and teach His Word (He.10:25; 2:1).

> **We have not received the spirit of the world but the Spirit who is from God, that we may understand what God has freely given us. This is what we speak, not in words taught us by human wisdom but in words taught by the Spirit, expressing spiritual truths in spiritual words (1 Co.2:12-13).**
>
> **And how from infancy you have known the holy Scriptures, which are able to make you wise for salvation through faith in Christ Jesus. All Scripture is God-breathed and is useful for teaching, rebuking, correcting and training in righteousness, so that the man of God may be thoroughly equipped for every good work (2 Ti.3:15-17).**
>
> **We must pay more careful attention, therefore, to what we have heard, so that we do not drift away (He.2:1).**
>
> **But to this day the LORD has not given you a mind that understands or eyes that see or ears that hear (De.29:4).**
>
> **Come near, you nations, and listen; pay attention, you peoples! Let the earth hear, and all that is in it, the world, and all that comes out of it! (Is.34:1).**

2 (49:5-12) **Do not fear troublesome days when evil deceivers surround you.**
The psalmist now addresses two concerns that bear heavily on the minds of many, many people: the uncertainty of the future and the dishonesty of wicked people (v.5). *Evil days* may also be translated as *days of adversity* (NASB) and *times of trouble* (ESV, HCSB). The specific trouble the psalmist faced was that of being cheated by deceitful people. The psalmist's day was no different than ours; greed was the root of all sorts of evil behavior (1 Ti.6:10). Good people have always had to be on guard against money-hungry swindlers who seek to take their money deceitfully and wicked people who prosper at their expense.

---

2 Francis Brown, S. R. Driver, Charles A. Briggs. *Brown Driver Briggs Hebrew Definitions.* 1906. WORD*search* CROSS e-book.

The wise psalmist then widened the focus to a greater problem, one that can plague even honest people, that is, trusting in wealth and boasting in riches (v.6). The real issue that motivates some people to be dishonest is sometimes the same one that causes us to fear being cheated out of our money or not having enough for the future.

People try to cushion themselves by heaping up wealth with the hope that this will continually provide an income and keep one from harm and abandonment. But the response to fear is not found in the fleeting sense of well-being that wealth may provide.[3]

The correct mindset regarding money and wealth is to keep our eyes fixed on what God has provided for us. We assign too much importance to temporal, material things when instead—as the psalmist counseled us—we ought to be focused on eternity. This is the secret to overcoming the fear that deceitful people stir up in us.

a. Because their wealth cannot be used as a ransom to save them (anyone) from death (vv.7-9).

There is nothing sinful about being wealthy in and of itself as long as the wealth is gained honestly. Realistically, the wealthy usually live more comfortable lives than those who have little, and money can certainly provide many advantages in this life, (Pr.10:15). Despite that, money can do nothing about the common enemy every human being faces: death. As the psalmist stated, nobody can redeem or ransom another person from death. Nor is there any amount of money that can persuade God to spare a person from death (v.7).

As Psalm 49 unfolds, it becomes more and more clear that the psalmist is not speaking merely about life on this earth but also about eternal life (v.15). The price required to redeem a soul is precious—extremely costly, beyond the scope of human wealth (v.8). No amount of money can free us from death. No sum can purchase forgiveness of sins and eternal life (v.9). By highlighting this fact—a truth that makes all humans equal, regardless of wealth—the psalmist pointed us to our need of a Redeemer, Jesus Christ. Only the sinless Son of God can satisfy the debt of our sin. Only God's perfect, spotless lamb can purchase eternal life for us. Only through His power can we conquer death and live for ever (v.9).

b. Because all die—the wise, the foolish, and the senseless (vv.10-12)

Death happens to everyone, whether wise, foolish, or brutish. *Brutish* means senseless or unable to reason, like an animal. (v.10a). This unalterable fact tormented Solomon, the world's richest and wisest man. Speaking of death as the great equalizer of all humans, he wrote:

The wise man has eyes in his head, while the fool walks in the darkness; but I came to realize that the same fate overtakes them both. Then I thought in my heart, "The fate of the fool will overtake me also. What then do I gain by being wise?" I said in my heart, "This too is meaningless." For the wise man, like the fool, will not be long remembered; in days to come both will be forgotten. Like the fool, the wise man too must die! So I hated life, because the work that is done under the sun was grievous to me. All of it is meaningless, a chasing after the wind....All share a common destiny—the righteous and the wicked, the good and the bad, the clean and the unclean, those who offer sacrifices and those who do not. As it is with the good man, so with the sinner; as it is with those who take oaths, so with those who are afraid to take them. This is the evil in everything that happens under the sun: The same destiny overtakes all. The hearts of men, moreover, are full of evil and there is madness in their hearts while they live, and afterward they join the dead (Ec.2:14-17; 9:2-3).

Furthermore, when we die, we will leave our wealth to others—every penny of it (v.10b). Money and possessions are useless to us when our appointment with death arrives (Lu.12:16-21; He.9:27). They cannot keep us alive one minute longer and we cannot take them with us. This, too, plagued the wealthy, hard-working Solomon:

I hated all the things I had toiled for under the sun, because I must leave them to the one who comes after me. And who knows whether he will be a wise man or a fool? Yet he will have control over all the work into which I have poured my effort and skill under the sun. This too is meaningless. So my heart began to despair over all my toilsome labor under the sun (Ec.2:18-20).

We can do nothing to change the fact that when we die, we are cut off from everything we possessed in this life. We no longer reside in the houses we occupied in this life, but rather in the tomb or grave (v.11).[4]

---

3 Frank E. Gaebelein, ed. *The Expositor's Bible Commentary*, p.368.

4 Bible versions vary as to the translation of this verse. The KJV, NKJV, and NASB understand the text to say that some people think inwardly that their houses and dwelling places will go on forever as a tribute to their lives. They name lands and other monuments after themselves in an effort to prolong their memory and influence.

Regardless of our wealth or fame, we leave every-thing behind when we die. We are soon forgotten no matter how much money or honor we accumulated while we walked the earth. In this respect, the psalm-ist noted, we are no different from animals (v.12; Ec.3:18-22).

Thought 1. The message of this passage is clear: we should not give too much importance to money and earthly possessions. Rather, we should be focused on eternity. This is the remedy for fear about the uncer-tainties of the future and the possibility of being swindled or robbed by dishonest, deceitful crooks.

This is not to say that money is not important. Nor does it mean that we should not prepare for the future or be good stewards of all that God has entrusted to us. It simply places money and possessions in their proper place, giving us the right perspective on what is *most* important.

Jesus taught us this perspective. He instructed us not to worry about material things, but to make God's kingdom and righteousness the first priority of our lives (Mt.6:31-34). Warning us against covetousness, Jesus reminded us that our lives are not defined by our possessions (Lu.12:15). He also reminded us that wealth cannot prevent death, telling a parable about a wealthy man who secured his future and set himself up for a lifetime of ease (Lu.12:16-21). This same man was prepared for a long, secure life, but he was not prepared for eternity.

Eternity—and being prepared for it by turning to Jesus Christ for salvation—is what matters most. You may not have much in this world, but if you have Christ, you are eternally rich. In contrast, you may have an abundance of everything this world can offer, but if you do not have Christ, you will have absolutely nothing in eternity.

> So do not worry, saying, 'What shall we eat?' or 'What shall we drink?' or 'What shall we wear?' For the pagans run after all these things, and your heavenly Father knows that you need them. But seek first his kingdom and his righteous-ness, and all these things will be given to you as well. Therefore do not worry about tomorrow, for tomorrow will wor-ry about itself. Each day has enough trouble of its own (Mt.6:31-34).

> Then he said to them, "Watch out! Be on your guard against all kinds of greed; a man's life does not consist in the abun-dance of his possessions." And he told them this parable: "The ground of a cer-tain rich man produced a good crop. He thought to himself, 'What shall I do? I have no place to store my crops.' "Then he said, 'This is what I'll do. I will tear

down my barns and build bigger ones, and there I will store all my grain and my goods. And I'll say to myself, "You have plenty of good things laid up for many years. Take life easy; eat, drink and be merry."' "But God said to him, 'You fool! This very night your life will be demand-ed from you. Then who will get what you have prepared for yourself?' "This is how it will be with anyone who stores up things for himself but is not rich toward God" (Lu.12:15-21).

> For we brought nothing into the world, and we can take nothing out of it. But if we have food and clothing, we will be content with that. People who want to get rich fall into temptation and a trap and into many foolish and harmful de-sires that plunge men into ruin and de-struction. For the love of money is a root of all kinds of evil. Some people, eager for money, have wandered from the faith and pierced themselves with many griefs. But you, man of God, flee from all this, and pursue righteousness, godli-ness, faith, love, endurance and gentle-ness (1 Ti.6:7-11).

> Keep your lives free from the love of money and be content with what you have, because God has said, "Never will I leave you; never will I forsake you" (He.13:5).

3 (49:13-15) **Know the fate of the self-sufficient and the destiny of the righteous.**
Keeping the right perspective toward money and posses-sions is of critical importance; therefore, the psalmist di-rects us to the end of both the self-sufficient and the righteous. This present life may be easier for those who have much, but the future is far brighter for those who trust in the LORD rather than in their wealth (Pr.11:4; 16:8). Tragically, many wealthy people never realize this truth. Because they have everything they need, they fail to see their need for God (Lu.18:25). Self-sufficiency is the folly that keeps them from looking beyond this life to eternity. While they may enjoy every possession and pleasure imaginable in this life, they have absolutely no treasure in heaven (Lu.12:16-34). Even more tragic, those who come after them (their posterity) follow in their foolish footsteps. Because of their worldly success, others view the wealthy as wise and approve their teach-ings and philosophies.

a. The fate of the self-sufficient (v.14).
The psalmist emphasized again that money and pos-sessions cannot stop death. Death is portrayed here as a cruel shepherd who leads his sheep to the slaughter

and then feeds on them. Like every other breathing creature, death will greedily devour the self-sufficient and they will be laid in the grave. *Grave* is the Hebrew word *sheol*, which refers to the world or abode of the dead, as contrasted to the realm of the living.

In eternity, the self-sufficient will not enjoy the prestige and authority that marked their earthly lives. In the morning—a reference to the day of resurrection—the upright will have dominion or rule over them. "Their beauty shall consume in the grave" refers to the body's decaying after death. The self-sufficient will rot in their graves, far from the luxurious dwellings they enjoyed while alive.

b. The destiny of the righteous (v.15).

As the *Pulpit Commentary* notes, this verse is the solution of the dark saying and the key to the parable (v.4)[5] The souls of the righteous will be gloriously redeemed or delivered from the power of the grave! Along with *He* (God) *will surely take me to Himself*, the original text paints a vivid picture of the resurrection of the righteous. *The Message* effectively paraphrases this verse:

> *"But me? God snatches me from the clutch of death, he reaches down and grabs me."*

The commentary of the eloquent British preacher Charles Spurgeon (1834-1892) on this verse is thrilling:

> *But God will redeem my soul from the power of the grave. Forth from that temporary resting place we shall come in due time, quickened by divine energy. Like our risen Head we cannot be holden by the bands of the grave; redemption has emancipated us from the slavery of death. No redemption could man find in riches, but God has found it in the blood of his dear Son. Our Elder Brother has given to God a ransom, and we are the redeemed of the Lord: because of this redemption by price we shall assuredly be redeemed by power out of the hand of the last enemy. For he shall receive me. He shall take me out of the tomb, take me up to heaven. If it is not said of me as of Enoch, "He was not, for God took him, "yet shall I reach the same glorious state. My spirit God will receive, and my body shall sleep in Jesus till, being raised in his image, it shall also be received into glory. How infinitely superior is such a hope to anything which our oppressors can boast! Here is something which will bear meditation, and therefore again let us pause, at the bidding of the musician, who inserts a Selah.*[6]

In the end, God will exalt the righteous to have dominion or rule over the self-sufficient (v.14[b]). The meaning of this statement is unclear, as the unrighteous and the righteous will spend eternity in two completely different places, heaven and hell. The best understanding is that the righteous will ultimately prevail over the unrighteous. In this life, righteous people are often oppressed by those who are wealthy and self-sufficient. But when this life is over, the righteous will be victorious and live with God eternally while the unrighteous and self-sufficient people will perish.

Thought 1. Two groups of people with strikingly different destinies are portrayed in this passage:
➢ Self-sufficient people who have nothing beyond this life
➢ People who trust in God and who will be raised to eternal life

Scripture teaches that the *grave* (sheol) is not the final stopping place of the self-sufficient nor of any other unbeliever. After God's plan for this world has been fully carried out, the unrighteous dead will be raised to appear before God at the Great White Throne Judgment. There, they will be judged according to their deeds, and they will be sentenced to the lake of fire for eternity (Jn.5:28-29; Re.20:11-15).

The bodies of the righteous, however, will be gloriously raised when Jesus Christ returns. Scripture teaches that from that point forward, we will forever be with the Lord, ultimately living with Him eternally in the new heaven and the new earth.

The psalmist confidently identified himself with the redeemed righteous, as noted by the pronouns *my* and *me* (v.15). Now, the most important question regarding eternity is, in which group will you be?

> **"There was a rich man who was dressed in purple and fine linen and lived in luxury every day. At his gate was laid a beggar named Lazarus, covered with sores and longing to eat what fell from the rich man's table. Even the dogs came and licked his sores. "The time came when the beggar died and the angels carried him to Abraham's side. The rich man also died and was buried. In hell, where he was in torment, he looked up and saw Abraham far away, with Lazarus by his side (Lu.16:19-23).**
>
> **"Do not be amazed at this, for a time is coming when all who are in their graves will hear his voice and come out— those who have done good will rise to live, and those who have done evil will rise to be condemned (Jn.5:28-29).**

---

5   H.D.M. Spence. *The Pulpit Commentary*. WORD*search* CROSS e-book.
6   Charles Spurgeon. *Treasury of David*. WORD*search* CROSS e-book.

But Christ has indeed been raised from the dead, the firstfruits of those who have fallen asleep. For since death came through a man, the resurrection of the dead comes also through a man. For as in Adam all die, so in Christ all will be made alive. But each in his own turn: Christ, the firstfruits; then, when he comes, those who belong to him (1 Co.15:20-23).

Brothers, we do not want you to be ignorant about those who fall asleep, or to grieve like the rest of men, who have no hope. We believe that Jesus died and rose again and so we believe that God will bring with Jesus those who have fallen asleep in him. According to the Lord's own word, we tell you that we who are still alive, who are left till the coming of the Lord, will certainly not precede those who have fallen asleep. For the Lord himself will come down from heaven, with a loud command, with the voice of the archangel and with the trumpet call of God, and the dead in Christ will rise first. After that, we who are still alive and are left will be caught up together with them in the clouds to meet the Lord in the air. And so we will be with the Lord forever. Therefore encourage each other with these words (1 Th.4:13-18).

Then I saw a great white throne and him who was seated on it. Earth and sky fled from his presence, and there was no place for them. And I saw the dead, great and small, standing before the throne, and books were opened. Another book was opened, which is the book of life. The dead were judged according to what they had done as recorded in the books. The sea gave up the dead that were in it, and death and Hades gave up the dead that were in them, and each person was judged according to what he had done. Then death and Hades were thrown into the lake of fire. The lake of fire is the second death. If anyone's name was not found written in the book of life, he was thrown into the lake of fire (Re.20:11-15).

And after my skin has been destroyed, yet in my flesh I will see God (Jb.19:26).

Multitudes who sleep in the dust of the earth will awake: some to everlasting life, others to shame and everlasting contempt (Da.12:2).

4 (49:16-20) **Be encouraged because you are redeemed: Do not be dismayed over an unbeliever who is rich and self-sufficient.**

After answering the problem of the prosperity of the wicked, the psalmist concluded his song with a word of wise counsel to the righteous. We should not fear wealthy, self-sufficient unbelievers, nor should we be dismayed when they oppress us. Instead, we should be encouraged because we are redeemed.

a. **Because the self-sufficient will take nothing with him when he dies—neither wealth nor fame (glory) (v.17).**

The self-sufficient are rich only in this life. When they die, they can take nothing with them into eternity (Ec. 5:15; 1 Ti.6:7). Their glory—honor, greatness, prestige—lies solely in the fame and fortune they acquired on this earth. When they die, it will not descend with them into eternity. Their fortunes will remain behind for others to enjoy. Their fame will be quickly forgotten by those who come after them.

b. **Because the self-sufficient will never see the *light* of God (vv.18-19).**

The most tragic part of the empty eternity awaiting the self-sufficient is that they will never see the *light* of God. *Light* represents God's glory and presence. Despite material blessings in this life, and despite having praise heaped upon them by others, self-sufficient people will spend eternity utterly separated from the presence of God. For this reason, Scripture described hell as a place of darkness (Ps.88:12; 2 Pe.2:4; Ju.13). In splendid contrast, the righteous will live eternally where there is no night—no darkness whatsoever. Heaven will be brilliantly illuminated by the glory and presence of God and His dear Son, Jesus Christ, who is the Lamb of God (Re.21:23-25; 22:5).

c. **Because the self-sufficient does not understand that he must be redeemed: He is like the beasts that perish, 6-10, 15 (v.20).**

The psalmist closed by driving home the lesson of this song: the self-sufficient and all other unbelievers lack understanding. In this respect, the psalmist repeats, they are no different from animals that have no comprehension of eternity (v.12).

Wealthy, self-sufficient people are often very intelligent and shrewd. Most achieve success because they understand the principles of business, discipline, and hard work. Yet they lack the most important understanding of all, the comprehension of Scriptural truth that determines their destiny. Specifically, what do the self-sufficient not understand (vv.6-10, 15)? They do not understand that...
- their wealth cannot save them from death (v.7)
- their wealth cannot save their souls (v.8)

- they need a Redeemer before they can live eternally (vv.8-9)
- they will have nothing in eternity if they reject Jesus Christ, God's beloved Son (v.10)
- Christ can raise them from the dead to live eternally in God's presence (v.15).

Thought 1. If we feel disheartened or discouraged by the prosperity of the wicked, we need to look beyond this life to eternity. "Notice there is no promise here that he [the wealthy, self-sufficient person] will not have the upper hand: only the reminder that his glory cannot last...There is nothing more."[7]

When we struggle to get by while the ungodly enjoy lives of ease, we need to remember the lesson of this psalm: in eternity, the self-sufficient will have nothing but we will have everything. The truth of this lesson should encourage us in difficult times, and it should free us from the fear of those who might oppress us. It should also drive us to prayer for the souls of those who lack the understanding of Scriptural truth. We should be burdened for them rather than envious or afraid of them. We should fervently pray that their eyes will be opened to the light of the gospel before it is eternally too late (2 Co.4:4).

However, do not rejoice that the spirits submit to you, but rejoice that your names are written in heaven" (Lu.10:20).

Praise be to the God and Father of our Lord Jesus Christ! In his great mercy he has given us new birth into a living hope through the resurrection of Jesus Christ from the dead, and into an inheritance that can never perish, spoil or fade—kept in heaven for you, who through faith are shielded by God's power until the coming of the salvation that is ready to be revealed in the last time. In this you greatly rejoice, though now for a little while you may have had to suffer grief in all kinds of trials (1 Pe.1:3-6).

So that, having been justified by his grace, we might become heirs having the hope of eternal life (Tit.3:7).

Do not fret because of evil men or be envious of those who do wrong (Ps.37:1).

Be still before the LORD and wait patiently for him; do not fret when men succeed in their ways, when they carry out their wicked schemes (Ps.37:7).

---

7 Derek Kidner. *Psalms 1-72*, p.203.

PSALM 50

You Need to Prepare for God's Coming Judgment, 50:1-23

A psalm of Asaph.

1. **Hear God's summons to the whole earth: Prepare for the great judgment to come**
   a. His warning
      1) He will appear in the blazing light of perfection & beauty
      2) He—His holy presence—will come in the consuming fire & raging storm
      3) He will summon both heaven & earth to be His witnesses
   b. His purpose: To gather & judge His people—all who made a covenant (promise) with Him
   c. His standard of judgment: His righteousness
2. **Hear God's warning against empty, ritualistic worship**
   a. His right to judge: He is God—*your* God
   b. His view of worship: God does not condemn you because of the sacrifices & offerings you give to Him
   c. His indictment: Your concept of God is wrong
      1) God is totally self-sufficient: He does not need your sacrifices because He already possesses all the wealth (animals) in the world
      2) God is omniscient: He knows every bird & animal in the world because they are His
      3) God is the *Creator & Sus-*

The Mighty One, God, the LORD, speaks and summons the earth from the rising of the sun to the place where it sets.
2 From Zion, perfect in beauty, God shines forth.
3 Our God comes and will not be silent; a fire devours before him, and around him a tempest rages.
4 He summons the heavens above, and the earth, that he may judge his people:
5 "Gather to me my consecrated ones, who made a covenant with me by sacrifice."
6 And the heavens proclaim his righteousness, for God himself is judge. Selah
7 "Hear, O my people, and I will speak, O Israel, and I will testify against you: I am God, your God.
8 I do not rebuke you for your sacrifices or your burnt offerings, which are ever before me.
9 I have no need of a bull from your stall or of goats from your pens,
10 For every animal of the forest is mine, and the cattle on a thousand hills.
11 I know every bird in the mountains, and the creatures of the field are mine.
12 If I were hungry I would

not tell you, for the world is mine, and all that is in it.
13 Do I eat the flesh of bulls or drink the blood of goats?
14 Sacrifice thank offerings to God, fulfill your vows to the Most High,
15 And call upon me in the day of trouble; I will deliver you, and you will honor me."
16 But to the wicked, God says: "What right have you to recite my laws or take my covenant on your lips?
17 You hate my instruction and cast my words behind you.
18 When you see a thief, you join with him; you throw in your lot with adulterers.
19 You use your mouth for evil and harness your tongue to deceit.
20 You speak continually against your brother and slander your own mother's son.
21 These things you have done and I kept silent; you thought I was altogether like you. But I will rebuke you and accuse you to your face.
22 "Consider this, you who forget God, or I will tear you to pieces, with none to rescue:
23 He who sacrifices thank offerings honors me, and he prepares the way so that I may show him the salvation of God."

tainer of the whole world
   • He is the world's sovereign Owner
   • He is not like humans—dependent beings—who need food
   d. His emphasis: Your offering to God should be a thankful heart & obedience (keeping your vows)
   e. His promise: You can then call on Him in times of trouble & He will deliver you
3. **Hear God's warning against wicked & hypocritical behavior**
   a. His charge
      1) Your religion is empty
      2) You reject God's instruction & disrespect His Word
      3) You associate with & participate in the sins of the wicked
      4) Your speech is evil
         • Foul & profane
         • Deceitful
         • Slanderous
   b. His warning
      1) He will not always be patient (silent)
      2) He will execute judgment in His time
4. **Hear God's appeal to all who forget Him**
   a. Heed these warnings or face God's ferocious wrath
   b. Praise & give thanks to God
      1) Giving thanks honors God
      2) Giving thanks stirs God to reveal His salvation to you

PSALM 50

You Need to Prepare for God's Coming Judgment, 50:1-23

(50:1-23) Introduction: the thought of appearing before a judge strikes fear in most people's hearts. Even a summons to jury duty can make us uneasy. With that in mind, Psalm 50 announces an unsettling truth: one day we will stand in God's holy courtroom, not as witnesses or spectators but as the individuals being judged! This psalm warns us about two areas in which we will be evaluated: our worship and our obedience to God's commands.

Historically, Psalm 50 was addressed to the Hebrew people. God summoned them into His courtroom to judge them for their heartless worship and hypocritical lives. However, the psalm serves as a warning to all of

God's people: we need to prepare for the day when we will stand before the LORD.

Psalm 50 is the first of twelve psalms written by Asaph (also Ps.73–83). Asaph was one of three chief musical directors in David's court who was an outstanding singer and also played the cymbals. (1 Chr.15:16-19; 16:4-7, 37; 25:1ff). The Holy Spirit used him to remind us that God is observing everything we do, and one day we have to answer to Him, the Supreme Judge of the universe (Ec.12:14; He.9:27). This is God's message to all of us: *You Need to Prepare for God's Coming Judgment,* 50:1-23.

1. Hear God's summons to the whole earth: Prepare for the great judgment to come (vv.1-6).

2. Hear God's warning against empty, ritualistic worship (vv.7-15).
3. Hear God's warning against wicked and hypocritical behavior (vv.16-21).
4. Hear God's appeal to all who forget Him (vv.22-23).

1 (50:1-6) Hear God's summons to the whole earth: Prepare for the great judgment to come.

In the same manner that a court official announces the entrance of the judge, Asaph trumpets the coming of God to judge His people throughout the earth. *From the rising of the sun to the place where it sets* is a poetic expression for the whole earth.

Notice the names of God that Asaph used to introduce Him as the Supreme Judge:

• *Mighty One, God* (El Elohim)—a name that places a double emphasis on God's power and authority. *El* means strong, mighty, and powerful. *Elohim* is the all-powerful God.
• LORD (Yahweh, Jehovah)—God's personal, covenant name through which He reveals Himself and relates to His people.

a. His warning (vv.1-4).

Asaph's announcement is a warning from the LORD Himself. He alerts us that a day is coming when each of us must stand before Him (v.1). He will appear from Zion, the place where His presence was once manifested, in the blazing light of perfection and beauty (v.2; Ps.48:2; La.2:15). The perfect beauty of the earthly Zion, Jerusalem, foreshadows the glory of the heavenly Zion where God sits on His holy throne (He.8:1-5; 9:23-24; 12:22). From there He will shine forth in the glorious radiance of His uncompromised holiness.

When God comes forth to judge His people, His presence will not be calm and quiet (v.3). Asaph used two fearful images to describe God's appearance in judgment: a consuming fire and a raging storm (Ex.24:17; He.12:29). Both heavenly and earthly beings will be summoned to witness His judgment (v.4).

b. His purpose: To gather and judge His people—all who made a covenant (promise) with Him (v.5).

Unbelievers will one day stand before God in judgment (Re.20:11-15), but God's summons in this psalm is to His saints—the people who have entered into covenant with Him. Under the old covenant, this was the Jewish people (Ex.24:1-8). Under the new covenant, it is all who genuinely repent and receive Jesus Christ as Savior by faith (He.8:13–9:15). All who know the LORD will be gathered and judged by Him. The order to gather God's people is most likely given to angels, in accordance with the words of Jesus (Mk.13:27).[1]

Notice the phrase *who made a covenant with me by sacrifice.* This statement highlights a major difference in the old and new covenants. Under the old covenant, the people offered the sacrifice of an animal to God. Under the new covenant, God offered His Son as a sacrifice for us.

c. His standard of judgment: His righteousness (v.6).

The heavens, the entire universe, will stand witness to God's right to judge His people and to His righteousness in judgment. His standard for evaluating His people will be His perfect righteousness and holiness, revealed to us in the commandments of His Word.

Thought 1. The application of this psalm to New Testament believers is that "we must all appear before the judgment seat of Christ" (2 Co.5:10). Having been redeemed by the blood of Christ, we will not be condemned for our sins (Ro.8:1). But our lives and service to the Lord will be evaluated by Jesus Christ Himself, who loved us and gave His life for us (Ep.5:25; Re.1:5). Like a roaring fire that blazes through every room of a house, the flaming eyes of our Savior will penetrate every area of our lives. Everything we have done as believers will be inspected and evaluated by Him. If we have been faithful to Him, we will be gloriously rewarded. If we have been unfaithful, we will suffer the devastating loss of the rewards we could have received (1 Co.3:8-15). Empty-handed, we will surely weep in shame and regret if we have nothing to present to Jesus in return for all He has done for us (Re.4:10).

God has spoken to us in His Word, revealing this coming judgment to us. If we are wise, we will prepare for His evaluation of our lives and service by being faithful to Him. If we truly grasp what will occur at the Judgment Seat of Christ, we will…

• walk in holiness, resisting temptation and obeying God's commands (Ro.6:19; 2 Co.7:1; 1 Th.3:13)
• give the Lord first place in our lives above the temporary things of this world (Mt.6:33)
• offer ourselves as living sacrifices to Him, pursuing and following His will rather than our own (He.12:1-2)
• practice discipline and self-control so we might be qualified to be used by the Lord (2 Co.9:24-27)
• patiently and faithfully endure trials, temptations, and tribulations (Js.1:12; Re.2:10)
• labor to bring others to the saving knowledge of Jesus Christ (1 Th.2:19)
• look for the return of Christ (2 Ti.4:8)

> **For the Son of Man is going to come in his Father's glory with his angels, and then he will reward each person according to what he has done (Mt.16:27).**
> **You, then, why do you judge your brother? Or why do you look down on**

---

[1] Donald Williams. *Psalms 1-72,* p.380.

your brother? For we will all stand before God's judgment seat (Ro.14:10).

The man who plants and the man who waters have one purpose, and each will be rewarded according to his own labor. For we are God's fellow workers; you are God's field, God's building. By the grace God has given me, I laid a foundation as an expert builder, and someone else is building on it. But each one should be careful how he builds. For no one can lay any foundation other than the one already laid, which is Jesus Christ. If any man builds on this foundation using gold, silver, costly stones, wood, hay or straw, his work will be shown for what it is, because the Day will bring it to light. It will be revealed with fire, and the fire will test the quality of each man's work. If what he has built survives, he will receive his reward. If it is burned up, he will suffer loss; he himself will be saved, but only as one escaping through the flames (1 Co.3:8-15).

For we must all appear before the judgment seat of Christ, that each one may receive what is due him for the things done while in the body, whether good or bad (2 Co.5:10)

"Behold, I am coming soon! My reward is with me, and I will give to everyone according to what he has done (Re.22:12).

2 (50:7-15) Hear God's warning against empty, ritualistic worship.

The LORD raised His first charge against the people of Israel: He was displeased with their worship. Instead of offering sacrifices out of sincerity and heartfelt gratitude, the people worshipped thoughtlessly and out of routine. They had diminished worship to the observance of rituals rather than the expression of their relationship with God.[2] God's condemnation of their casual attitude in worship should serve as an eye-opening warning to us today.

a. His right to judge: He is God—*your* God (v.7).

Before confronting the Hebrew people with their sin, the LORD established His right to judge them. First, He is *God* (Elohim)—the one and only all-powerful God, the Creator and Ruler of all humans and the universe. All authority is His and His alone.

Second, He is their God, the personal God of Israel. God had selected them as His chosen people. He had established His covenant with them. Over and over again, He displayed His wonder-working power on

their behalf. Because of this, the Hebrews were accountable to Him in a way no other people of the world were accountable. They knew God personally and had a unique relationship with Him.

b. His view of worship: God does not condemn you because of the sacrifices and offerings you give to Him (v. 8).

The LORD wanted the people of Israel to clearly understand what displeased Him so greatly. He approved of their worship itself; He was not judging them because He was offended by their sacrifices and offerings. The sacrifices themselves were offered according to God's laws and were acceptable to Him.

c. His indictment: Your concept of God is wrong (vv.9-13)

God was displeased with the Hebrews because of their attitude in offering their sacrifices. Their entire basis for sacrificing was distorted, and their concept of God was completely wrong. They had lost sight of the purpose of worshipping God, thereby reducing their worship to nothing more than the thoughtless observance of rituals and obligations.

The LORD called the people back to the heart of worship, emphatically reminding them that He did not need their sacrifices (v.9). God is totally self-sufficient. He can take care of Himself without our help or anyone else's. He already possesses the earth and everything in it (v.10; Ps.24:1). Why should He take their bulls and goats when He owns the cattle on a thousand hills? The lesson is clear: God does not command us to give to Him because He needs something from us.

Furthermore, God is omniscient or all-knowing. He knows where every single creature on the face of the earth is at any given time (v.11). He is the Creator and sustainer of the whole world. Do we really think that, if He were hungry, He would need to come to us for help? He is the sovereign owner of the world (v.12). Besides, God is not like us: He is not a human being who needs food to survive. When had the Hebrew people ever seen God eat the flesh of their sacrifices or drink their blood (v.13)?

d. His emphasis: Your offering to God should be a thankful heart and obedience (keeping your vows) (v.14).

Worship is not about giving God something He needs, nor is it about fulfilling rituals and duties that God imposes on us. Worship is about our relationship with God. He created us for a relationship with Him. He has showered His love and grace on us, redeeming us from our sin and giving us the glorious privilege of fellowship with Him (Jn.1:3). He cares for us daily and provides everything we need (Mt.6:30-32). We should offer our sacrifices to Him because we love Him. God wants us to worship Him from thankful hearts that overflow with gratitude for all He has done for us (v.14a).

---

2 Derek Kidner. *Psalms 1-72*, p.205.

In addition, God wants us to worship Him by obeying Him, as represented by *fulfill your vows.* True worship is keeping God's commandments and honoring our commitment to Him. He does not desire our sacrifices; He wants our hearts to be fully devoted to Him, resulting in our obedience to His Word:

> But Samuel replied: "Does the LORD delight in burnt offerings and sacrifices as much as in obeying the voice of the LORD? To obey is better than sacrifice, and to heed is better than the fat of rams (1 S.15:22).
>
> Sacrifice and offering you did not desire, but my ears you have pierced; burnt offerings and sin offerings you did not require. Then I said, "Here I am, I have come—it is written about me in the scroll. I desire to do your will, O my God; your law is within my heart" (Ps. 40:6-8).
>
> My son, give me your heart and let your eyes keep to my ways (Pr.23:26).
>
> "'This is what the LORD Almighty, the God of Israel, says: Go ahead, add your burnt offerings to your other sacrifices and eat the meat yourselves! For when I brought your forefathers out of Egypt and spoke to them, I did not just give them commands about burnt offerings and sacrifices, but I gave them this command: Obey me, and I will be your God and you will be my people. Walk in all the ways I command you, that it may go well with you (Je.7:21-23).

e. **His promise: You can then call on Him in times of trouble and He will deliver you (v.15).**
Worshipping God by obeying Him opens the windows of heaven to us. We should embrace God's promise to true worshippers: when we live in obedience to His commandments, we have the liberty to call for His help. In times of trouble, we can boldly turn to Him and He will deliver us. As a result, we will continue to glorify God, offering Him our sacrifices of thanksgiving and ongoing obedience.

Thought 1. Jesus taught us that God desires our worship, but only if we worship Him in spirit and in truth (Jn.4:23). Surely God's heart breaks when we who were created to give Him glory worship Him insincerely.

We need to diligently guard against allowing our worship to diminish into anything less than God commands it to be. As we attend church and are involved in the Lord's service, it is very easy to fall into a meaningless routine of going through the motions of worship. We can easily sit in worship services, sing along, bow our heads in prayer, listen to the message, and participate in the offering without involving our hearts. We can even teach or preach carelessly and thoughtlessly.

The same is true in our private worship. Many believers read their Bibles and pray out of routine, fully missing the wonderful privilege of spending time alone with God. The Lord rejects all worship that is formal and thoughtless.

Likewise, God rejects worship that is not accompanied by obedience. The real test of our devotion to God is obedience to His commands (Jn.14:15, 23). As the rebellious Saul tragically learned, our sacrifices are meaningless to God apart from our obedience (1 S.15:22). We can offer our praise, our service, and our gifts to the Lord, but what He truly desires is our hearts—hearts that love Him enough to obey Him.

> "If you love me, you will obey what I command....Jesus replied, "If anyone loves me, he will obey my teaching. My Father will love him, and we will come to him and make our home with him (Jn.14:15, 23).
>
> Therefore, I urge you, brothers, in view of God's mercy, to offer your bodies as living sacrifices, holy and pleasing to God--this is your spiritual act of worship (Ro.12:1).
>
> Through Jesus, therefore, let us continually offer to God a sacrifice of praise—the fruit of lips that confess his name. And do not forget to do good and to share with others, for with such sacrifices God is pleased (He.13:15-16).
>
> Now if you obey me fully and keep my covenant, then out of all nations you will be my treasured possession. Although the whole earth is mine, you will be for me a kingdom of priests and a holy nation.' These are the words you are to speak to the Israelites" (Ex.19:5-6).
>
> I will praise God's name in song and glorify him with thanksgiving. This will please the LORD more than an ox, more than a bull with its horns and hoofs (Ps.69:30-31).
>
> With what shall I come before the LORD and bow down before the exalted God? Shall I come before him with burnt offerings, with calves a year old? Will the LORD be pleased with thousands of rams, with ten thousand rivers of oil? Shall I offer my firstborn for my transgression, the fruit of my body for the sin of my soul? He has showed you, O man, what is good. And what does the LORD require of you? To act justly and to love mercy and to walk humbly with your God (Mi.6:6-8).

3 (50:16-21) Hear God's warning against wicked and hypocritical behavior.

The LORD's second charge was raised against those in Israel who were wicked. These sinful people participated in worship but habitually disobeyed God's laws. They were hypocrites, pretending to be religious while leading ungodly lives.

a. His charge (vv.16-20).

Apparently, these disobedient Hebrews were teachers and leaders of worship. They declared God's statutes, publicly reading His law before the people. They even exhorted the congregation of Israel to faithfully embrace God's covenant. Yet while they commanded the people to obey God, they practiced sin in their own lives. For this reason, their religious acts were empty, meaningless, and unacceptable to God (v.16).

These hypocrites demanded that others adhere to God's laws, but they rejected God's instruction and Word as the standard for their own lives (v.17). "Cast my words behind you" vividly portrays these pretenders throwing God's Word in the garbage. They associated with people who intentionally violated God's laws and they even participated in their sins (Ro.1:32). The LORD cited these three specific examples of their hypocritical behavior...

- theft (v.18[a])
- adultery (v.18[b])
- evil speech: foul, profane language; lies, deceit, and slander (vv.19-20)

These examples of their sinfulness were all violations of the Ten Commandments (Ex.20:14-16). The point is this: the wicked did not merely fail to observe some details of God's law. To the contrary, they blatantly broke the Ten Commandments, the foundational statutes upon which the rest of the law was built. While pretending to uphold God's laws, they rebelliously disregarded God's commands. They were hypocrites.

b. His warning (v.21).

The LORD issued a stern warning to these hypocrites: He would not always keep silent or be patient with them while they continued to break His holy laws. The wicked had mistaken God's patience for His approval.[3] When God did not immediately judge these sinners, they assumed He was not seriously offended by their actions. In reality, our merciful God was giving them the opportunity to repent. But that opportunity was quickly expiring. God was rebuking them, warning them that He would execute judgment against them in His time.

Thought 1. Psalm 50 forcefully reminds us that we will one day stand before God to be judged for our deeds and service to Him. But it also reminds us that God is merciful and longsuffering toward us. In this psalm, God confronts the sinful people of Israel and gives them the opportunity to repent before they face His severe judgment.

God extends His mercy and patience to all. He is patient with His children who walk in disobedience to Him. He lovingly corrects us, first by convicting or rebuking us through His Word and the Holy Spirit. If we do not repent, His correction becomes more severe. If we stubbornly persist in sin, He may decide to take us on to heaven. He may end our earthly lives prematurely so we will not continue to hurt ourselves, others, and the testimony of Christ by our sin (He.12:5-12; 1 Co.5:5; 11:30-32;). We should never take advantage of God's patience when we sin, and we should never be deceived into questioning whether He is displeased with us. Instead, we should be grateful for His love and mercy, confess our sin, and turn from it. Remember this: God will not allow His dear children to continue in sin.

God is longsuffering toward the lost because He loves them. Therefore, He extends their time on earth and delays His judgment so they might repent (2 Pe.3:9). Even so, unsaved people are not God's children. Although they suffer the natural consequences of their sins, God does not correct them as He does His children. Because of this, many unsaved people mistakenly think that God is not going to do anything about their sin. Tragically, others question whether there even is a God. Either way, they continue in their sin, plunging toward the terrible day of God's judgment.

No sinner—saved or lost—should ever abuse God's patience. Instead, we should repent while God mercifully gives us the opportunity. When we as believers sin, we ought to immediately confess our sins and turn from them through the power of God's indwelling Spirit. Unsaved people should turn from their sins and turn to Christ, receiving the forgiveness and salvation He freely offers to all.

> **Or do you show contempt for the riches of his kindness, tolerance and patience, not realizing that God's kindness leads you toward repentance? But because of your stubbornness and your unrepentant heart, you are storing up wrath against yourself for the day of God's wrath, when his righteous judgment will be revealed. God "will give to each person according to what he has done" (Ro.2:4-6).**
>
> **Who disobeyed long ago when God waited patiently in the days of Noah while the ark was being built. In it only a**

---

3 John F. Walvoord, ed. *The Bible Knowledge Commentary: An Exposition of the Scriptures by Dallas Seminary Faculty.*

few people, eight in all, were saved through water (1 Pe.3:20).

The Lord is not slow in keeping his promise, as some understand slowness. He is patient with you, not wanting anyone to perish, but everyone to come to repentance (2 Pe.3:9).

If we confess our sins, he is faithful and just and will forgive us our sins and purify us from all unrighteousness (1 Jn.1:9).

For my own name's sake I delay my wrath; for the sake of my praise I hold it back from you, so as not to cut you off (Is.48:9).

Rend your heart and not your garments. Return to the LORD your God, for he is gracious and compassionate, slow to anger and abounding in love, and he relents from sending calamity (Joel 2:13).

4 (50:22-23) **Hear God's appeal to all who forget Him.**

After rebuking the insincere worshippers and hypocrites of Israel who had forgotten Him, the LORD made a final appeal to them. Offering both a fierce warning and a comforting promise, He left them with a choice: they could continue in their sin and face God's judgment or they could repent and be saved from God's wrath.

a. Heed these warnings or face God's ferocious wrath (v.22).

God exhorted the Hebrews to consider or understand the seriousness of what He was telling them and the decision it forced them to make. If they continued to forget God, they would face God's fierce judgment. The ferocious wrath of God described here is reserved for those who know the truth but never repent and receive God's salvation (Ro.1:18). The individuals to whom this warning is addressed were part of the nation with whom God had made His covenant. However, they had apparently never personally received the salvation offered through God's covenant. In our age, we can compare them to church members who have never truly been born again. Their heartless worship and law-breaking revealed their lost condition. If they would not repent, nothing could deliver them from God's judgment.

b. Praise and give thanks to God (v.23).

In contrast to the worthless sacrifices the hypocritical worshippers had previously offered, God presented them with the opportunity to offer heartfelt sacrifices to Him. Their sacrifices offered in genuine praise or thanks to God would glorify or honor Him. Such sacrifices would also reveal the sincerity of their hearts toward God. If they would repent wholeheartedly, God would show or reveal His salvation to them. That is, they would personally receive God's salvation and be spared His wrath.

Thought 1. God appeals to every sinner just as He appealed to the false worshippers and hypocrites of Israel. He offers every unbeliever the opportunity to repent and be forgiven. The choice, however, belongs to us. Just as these Israelites had to choose whether or not to repent, every person must choose whether to turn to Christ or to continue in their sin.

As individuals living on this side of the cross, we do not need to offer any sacrifices in order to be saved. Christ's once-and-for-all sacrifice on the cross fully paid for our sins. Our part is to turn to Christ in repentance and faith, calling upon Him for salvation. When we genuinely believe in Him, His sacrifice is applied or credtied to us, washing away our sins and guilt.

Our works, however, are what will prove the genuineness of our faith, just as the Israelites' sacrifices of praise and thanks would demonstrate the sincerity of their hearts. Our lives will be different when we truly repent and are converted.

It is you who decides whether you will be forgiven or face God's wrath. It is you who decides where you will spend eternity. God offers you the opportunity to repent and be saved, but the choice is yours.

Produce fruit in keeping with repentance (Mt.3:8).

I tell you, no! But unless you repent, you too will all perish (Lu.13:3).

That if you confess with your mouth, "Jesus is Lord," and believe in your heart that God raised him from the dead, you will be saved. For it is with your heart that you believe and are justified, and it is with your mouth that you confess and are saved (Ro.10:9-10).

For, "Everyone who calls on the name of the Lord will be saved" (Ro.10:13).

In the same way, faith by itself, if it is not accompanied by action, is dead. But someone will say, "You have faith; I have deeds." Show me your faith without deeds, and I will show you my faith by what I do (Js.2:17-18).

PSALM 51

When You Are Guilty of Committing Grievous Sin, 51:1-19

For the director of music. A psalm of David. When the prophet Nathan came to him after David had committed adultery with Bathsheba.

1. Cry out for God's mercy & compassion
  a. Bc. your sin is very serious
    1) Ask God to blot out your *transgressions*
    2) Ask God to wash away your *iniquity*
    3) Ask God to cleanse you of *sin*
  b. Bc. you know you are guilty
    1) You have broken God's law
    2) You are haunted by your sin

2. Confess your sin
  a. Confess that your sin is against God & God alone
  b. Confess that you deserve God's judgment & that His judgment is just
  c. Confess that you have a sinful nature & are depraved—far short of God's glory & perfection, Ro.3:23
  d. Confess that God desires truth & wisdom (right decisions) from the depths of your heart
  e. Confess that God alone can truly cleanse you & wash away your sins

3. Pray for restoration & renewal

Have mercy on me, O God, according to your unfailing love; according to your great compassion blot out my transgressions.
2 Wash away all my iniquity and cleanse me from my sin.
3 For I know my transgressions, and my sin is always before me.
4 Against you, you only, have I sinned and done what is evil in your sight, so that you are proved right when you speak and justified when you judge.
5 Surely I was sinful at birth, sinful from the time my mother conceived me.
6 Surely you desire truth in the inner parts; you teach me wisdom in the inmost place.
7 Cleanse me with hyssop, and I will be clean; wash me, and I will be whiter than snow.
8 Let me hear joy and gladness; let the bones you have crushed rejoice.
9 Hide your face from my sins and blot out all my iniquity.
10 Create in me a pure heart, O God, and renew a steadfast spirit within me.
11 Do not cast me from your presence or take your Holy Spirit from me.
12 Restore to me the joy of your salvation and grant me a willing spirit, to sustain me.
13 Then I will teach transgressors your ways, and sinners will turn back to you.
14 Save me from bloodguilt, O God, the God who saves me, and my tongue will sing of your righteousness.
15 O Lord, open my lips, and my mouth will declare your praise.
16 You do not delight in sacrifice, or I would bring it; you do not take pleasure in burnt offerings.
17 The sacrifices of God are a broken spirit; a broken and contrite heart, O God, you will not despise.
18 In your good pleasure make Zion prosper; build up the walls of Jerusalem.
19 Then there will be righteous sacrifices, whole burnt offerings to delight you; then bulls will be offered on your altar.

  a. Ask God to restore your joy
    1) To relieve your brokenness
    2) To no longer look at your sins (condemning you) but to blot them out
  b. Ask God to radically transform your heart & spirit
    1) To stir you to be steadfast
    2) To not reject you or remove His presence (Spirit) from you, Ep.4:30-32
    3) To restore the joy of your salvation & arouse within you a spirit of obedience

4. Make a renewed commitment to God
  a. To witness to those who transgress (disobey) God's law
  b. To declare & sing the praises of God your Savior
    1) Bc. He has forgiven your terrible sin (murder)
    2) Bc. He is righteous
    3) Bc. He empowers you (your lips) to declare His praise, Ac.1:8
  c. To proclaim the importance of a repentant heart
    1) God does not desire sacrifices or offerings
    2) God desires a broken & repentant (contrite) heart

5. Intercede for others, Ep.6:18
  a. The prayer: That their city (Zion/Jerusalem) would prosper
  b. The result: They will please God by worshipping Him (presenting sacrifices & offerings) in the right spirit

PSALM 51

When You Are Guilty of Committing Grievous Sin, 51:1-19

(51:1-19) **Introduction:** nowhere in the Bible is the danger of falling into sin more powerfully portrayed than in the life of David. Relaxing on his balcony when he should have been at war, David caught a glimpse of a beautiful woman as she bathed. Tragically, he surrendered to temptation and committed adultery with her while her husband, Uriah, fought Israel's enemies. This woman, Bathsheba, became pregnant as a result of David's immoral union with her. The panicked king brought her husband home from the battlefront with the expectation that he would be reunited with his wife. However, Uriah was loyal to his men and refused to enjoy his wife's company while his fellow soldiers slept on the battlefield. When all David's attempts to make Uriah appear to be the baby's father failed, David arranged for Uriah to be placed on the front lines of the fiercest battle. As anticipated, he was slain there (2 S. 11).

Adultery and murder...these are the despicable sins of Israel's king, the sweet psalmist of Israel, the man after God's own heart (1 S.13:14; 2 S.23:1; Ac.13:22). David stole the wife of one of his most faithful warriors—a loyal friend who would have gladly died for David—and then arranged for his death.

For nearly a year, David persistently refused to deal with his shameful sin (see Introduction, outline and notes—Psalm 32 for more discussion). Eventually, God sent the prophet Nathan to confront the king, and he finally repented (2 S.12). Psalm 51 is David's heartfelt confession to God.

Of all the psalms, the fifty-first is one of the best known and loved because it is so personal: we are all guilty of grievous sin and in frequent need of God's abundant grace. This deeply intense psalm teaches us several critical lessons about sin and forgiveness:

➤ Even the most godly people can fall into terrible sin.

➤ Sin is serious, causing inescapable consequences. Just one lapse into sin can change our lives and the lives of others forever (1 K.15:5).

➤ We never sin so grievously that we cannot come to God for forgiveness.

➤ When we confess our sin to God sincerely, He will forgive, cleanse, and restore us regardless how appalling the sin is.

As David confessed his terrible sin to the LORD, he made two promises to God. First, he would use his experience to teach others (v.13). Second, he would praise God for His boundless mercy and grace (vv.14-15). Along with Psalm 32, Psalm 51 is David's fulfillment of these vows. In it, he teaches us how to confess our sins, and he exalts the LORD for His faithfulness to forgive and restore us. This is, *When You Are Guilty of Committing Grievous Sin*, 51:1-19.

1. Cry out for God's mercy and compassion (vv.1-3).
2. Confess your sin (vv.4-7).
3. Pray for restoration and renewal (vv.8-12).
4. Make a renewed commitment to God (vv.13-17).
5. Intercede for others, Ep.6:18 (vv.18-19).

1 (51:1-3) **Cry out for God's mercy and compassion.** When David at last faced God with his terrible sin, he offered no excuses. Guilty and utterly broken, he flung himself on the mercy of the LORD, appealing to God's lovingkindness and His multitude of tender mercies. These terms provide tremendous insight into God's attitude toward sinners.

David asked God for His *mercy* (chanan). This word "depicts a heartfelt response by someone who has something to give to one who has a need. It describes an action from a superior to an inferior who has no real claim for gracious treatment."[1] The LORD delights in stooping down to graciously help us when we least deserve it.

Unfailing love (chesed) is God's lovingkindness, His steadfast love. It is one of God's attributes or qualities that reveal His unparalleled character. This trait stirs God to offer His wonderful promises to us and to keep them without fail. By appealing to God's unfailing love, David believed that God would be faithful to His promises (covenant). Even when we fail Him, as David did, the LORD does not fail us (2 Ti.2:13).

Compassion (rachamim) comes from the Hebrew word for womb, signifying the deep, tender love a mother has for her helpless newborn baby (Is.49:15). It is deep compassion, intensely emotional pity and affection felt from the most inward parts of one's being. David referred to God's great compassion, meaning that His heartfelt mercy toward us is so abundant that it cannot be measured (Ge.32:12).

a. Because your sin is very serious (vv.1-2).
David acknowledged the severity of his sin. In contrast, we as sinners are prone to downplay our disobedience and make less of our sin than it actually is. But David made no such attempt, freely admitting that his sin was most serious. He even used every Hebrew word available to describe his sin in his effort to purge himself completely:

Transgression (pesha) is willful rebellion against God that results in disobeying His holy commandments and breaking His laws. David's transgression needed to be blotted out, wiped away, fully erased.

Iniquity (avown) is from a root word meaning bent or twisted and speaks of the perverseness of sin. It describes acts that stem from the depravity of our human nature, which is "warped, bent, and twisted, instead of being straight, perfect, and true."[2] By using this word, David was not speaking of his outward acts of sin but his inward condition that caused him to sin, that is, his corrupt nature. David confessed that he needed to be washed thoroughly from his iniquity—scrubbed until he was completely clean from the inside out (Je.4:14). He fully understood that, unless he was cleansed of his inward lust, he would fall into sin again.

In all but one case in the Old Testament, *wash* (kabas) is used of ceremonial cleansing, the complete washing of the priests and people when they appeared before God.[3] By using this word with iniquity, David revealed that he not only needed to be washed clean of his sinful acts but also of his corrupt nature from which they sprang. Before he could be accepted by God, he knew he needed to be forgiven of his sin *and* his sinfulness—forgiven from being a bent, twisted sinner.

Sin (chata'ah) is an act that, literally, misses the mark, The root verb is used of the left-handed Benjaminites who were able to sling stones with perfect accuracy, not missing their targets (Jud.20:16). Therefore, a sin is a thought, word, or deed that falls short of God's perfect standard of righteousness (Ro.3:23). David needed to be cleansed or purified of his sin. *Cleanse* (taher) is associated with being purified from contamination (Le.12:7-8; 14:4-7; 22:4-7)

b. Because you know you are guilty (v.3).
Just as we are prone to downplay our sin, we are also prone to justify our sin or to cast the blame on others. But David did no such thing. He freely admitted his guilt, fully acknowledging that he had transgressed and rebelled against God's law (Ex.20:13-14). He was constantly haunted by his sin, and his guilt caused him excruciating pain, both spiritually and physically (see outline and notes—Ps.32:3-4 for more discussion).

---

1 R. Laird Harris, ed. *Theological Wordbook of the Old Testament.* WORDsearch CROSS e-book.

2 John Phillips. *Exploring Psalms, Volume 1.* WORDsearch CROSS e-book.

3 R. Laird Harris, ed. *Theological Wordbook of the Old Testament.* WORDsearch CROSS e-book.

Thought 1. Psalm 51 teaches us how to confess our sins, and the first lesson is what our attitude in confession should be. David's demeanor as he approached God demonstrates the attitude of all who are genuinely broken because of their sin:

➢ We realize we do not deserve God's forgiveness.
➢ We cast ourselves on the LORD's mercy.
➢ We make no excuses for what we have done.
➢ We acknowledge the severity of our sin, refusing to soften or downplay its gravity.
➢ We do not attempt to justify our sin.
➢ We do not blame others.
➢ We freely admit our guilt.

When we cry out to God in humility and brokenness, we can know that He will be faithful to His character and His promises. The LORD is merciful, and He loves us with a steadfast, unfailing love. To demonstrate His immeasurable compassion toward us, He makes a precious and reassuring promise:

> If we confess our sins, he is faithful and just and will forgive us our sins and purify us from all unrighteousness (1 Jn.1:9).

Genuine confession is the key to forgiveness. If we confess our sins sincerely and humbly—fully acknowledging what we have done, accepting responsibility for it, and wholeheartedly desiring never to do it again—God will forgive and cleanse us.

> "But the tax collector stood at a distance. He would not even look up to heaven, but beat his breast and said, 'God, have mercy on me, a sinner' (Lu.18:13).
>
> In him we have redemption through his blood, the forgiveness of sins, in accordance with the riches of God's grace (Ep.1:7).
>
> How much more, then, will the blood of Christ, who through the eternal Spirit offered himself unblemished to God, cleanse our consciences from acts that lead to death, so that we may serve the living God! (He.9:14).
>
> My dear children, I write this to you so that you will not sin. But if anybody does sin, we have one who speaks to the Father in our defense—Jesus Christ, the Righteous One. He is the atoning sacrifice for our sins, and not only for ours but also for the sins of the whole world (1 Jn.2:1-2).
>
> Then I acknowledged my sin to you and did not cover up my iniquity. I said, "I will confess my transgressions to the LORD"—and you forgave the guilt of my sin. Selah (Ps.32:5).
>
> He who conceals his sins does not prosper, but whoever confesses and renounces them finds mercy (Pr.28:13).
>
> For our offenses are many in your sight, and our sins testify against us. Our offenses are ever with us, and we acknowledge our iniquities (Is.59:12).

2 (51:4-7) **Confess your sin.**

After hiding his terrible sin for nearly a year, David confessed it to the LORD. The Hebrew word for *confess* (yada) emphasizes acknowledging or declaring our sin to God. The Greek word used in the New Testament (*homologeo*) literally means to say the same thing about, to agree with. Therefore, confessing sin is both admitting our sin to God and agreeing with Him about it.

a. Confess that your sin is against God and God alone (v.4ᵃ).

David began his confession by recognizing that he had first and foremost sinned against God. In saying this, David was neither denying nor diminishing the fact that he had sinned against others, among them...

• Uriah
• Bathsheba
• his own family
• his nation
• Joab, his top military commander, whom he used to arrange Uriah's death
• himself

David was simply acknowledging that he had sinned against God in a greater way than he had sinned against all these people. He had broken *God's* holy laws. "Sin is against God; as such, it is so enormous an offense, so fearful a guilt, that all human dimensions fade into nothing when compared with it."[4]

Godly Joseph understood this serious truth. When his master's wife attempted to seduce him, he acknowledged that committing adultery with her would be a sin against his master, Potiphar (Ge.39:8-9ᵃ), but then proclaimed, "How then could I do such a wicked thing, and sin against God?" (Ge.39-9ᵇ). In the parable of the prodigal son, Jesus also taught us this truth. When the wayward son returned to his father in repentance, he first confessed that he had sinned against heaven (God) and then his against father (Lu.15:21). *Every sin is a sin against God.* Sinning terribly against others is serious, but sinning terribly against God is vastly more serious.

---

4 John Phillips. *Exploring Psalms, Volume 1.* WORDsearch CROSS e-book.

b. Confess that you deserve God's judgment and that His judgment is just (v.4ᵇ).

Realizing that he had done grievous evil in God's sight, David was ready to accept whatever judgment God imposed on him. Adultery and murder are serious offenses. Under God's law for Israel, both were punishable by death (Le.20:10; 24:17; Nu.35:16-21, 31). David acknowledged that he deserved God's judgment, and he confessed that God would be justified—just, right, righteous—in whatever sentence He demanded.

c. Confess that you have a sinful nature and are depraved—far short of God's glory and perfection, Ro.3:23 (v.5).

David understood that his gross sin was the fruit of what he was: a depraved sinner who fell far short of God's glory and perfection (Ro.3:23). Once again, David made no excuses for his horrific deeds. His sinful nature was present from the time his mother conceived him. Even as he grew in her womb, he was a sinner.

Sinful from the time my mother conceived me does not mean that David's conception was the result of a sinful act committed by his parents (sexual immorality). It simply testifies to his sinful nature. When he was conceived, he inherited the sinful nature of Adam, the first human (Ro.5:12, 19).

d. Confess that God desires truth and wisdom (right decisions) from the depths of your heart (v.6).

David also understood that God does not merely want us to conform outwardly to His commands but to obey them from the depths of our hearts. God desires that His truth abide within us. When God's truth, His Holy Word, fills our hearts, it empowers us to be wise and to make the right decisions. Pastor and commentator Donald M. Williams explains,

> *The Hebrew word for "desire" is strong. God is true, and He wants His character to be found in us. Therefore, He "delights in" our truth; He "takes pleasure in" it. This is the truth of our being, not simply in what we say, but in who we are. God looks for trustworthiness in us, in our "inward parts," our "guts."*[5]

David opened himself up to God's work in his sin-stained heart, inviting the LORD to teach him to make wise decisions. He longed to know God's wisdom personally and intimately, in the innermost depths of his being.

e. Confess that God alone can truly cleanse you and wash away your sins (v.7).

Cleanse me with hyssop is a reference to the ceremonial cleansing of lepers under the law (Le.14:1-7). David desired more than forgiveness for his sinful deeds; he longed to be purified from the disease that defiled him, the leprosy of sin. Only God could truly cleanse him. Only God could wash him within and make him whiter than snow.

The New Testament teaches that this inner cleansing is accomplished as we allow God's Word to work in our lives. We are sanctified or made holy through the truth of God's Word (Jn.17:17). The Bible is the water that washes away the tendencies of our sinful nature, cleansing our motives and desires (Ep.5:26-27). As we receive God's Word into our hearts and submit to it, it will cleanse us of our inner filthiness. As a result, we will do what God's Word commands rather than give in to the desires of our sinful nature (Js.1:21-25).

Thought 1. We need to grasp the lessons David taught us about genuine confession of sin in these verses. First, genuine confession acknowledges what we have done to God by sinning (v.4ᵃ). Not only do we commit an offense against God by breaking His laws, but we break the heart of God when we, His dear children, sin. "Notice the immense contrast here to the self-absorbed outlook of *2 Samuel*, where David's only question was, in effect, 'How do I cover my tracks?' Now it is, 'How could I treat God so?'"[6] Genuine confession is accompanied by godly sorrow that grieves over the pain we have caused God (2 Co.7:10).

Second, genuine confession accepts whatever judgment God deems necessary (4ᵇ). Sin has natural consequences, and God often judges us by allowing those consequences to play out in our lives. At other times, God orders us to be disciplined so that others will fear and be less likely to fall into sin (1 Ti.5:20). In His infinite wisdom, God knows what we need to keep us from continuing in sin. In His infinite love for us, He will discipline us as severely as necessary to produce holiness in our lives (He.12:5-11).

Third, genuine confession revolves around repentance, around the deep, heartfelt desire to turn from our sin. David's repentant spirit was evident in his desire to be clean within (vv.5-7). He knew that the root of the problem was his depraved sinful nature. He did not just ask for forgiveness; He pleaded with God to wash him within. He earnestly longed to be changed within so that He would never again commit such hideous sins. Genuine confession is far more than merely apologizing to God for our sin. It is repenting of our sin, which includes seeking God's help not to repeat it (2 Co.7:9-10).

> **Sanctify them by the truth; your word is truth (Jn.17:17).**
>
> **Repent, then, and turn to God, so that your sins may be wiped out, that times of refreshing may come from the Lord (Ac.3:19).**

---

5 Donald Williams. *Psalms 1-72*, p.389.

6 Derek Kidner. *Psalms 1-72*, p.208.

Repent of this wickedness and pray to the Lord. Perhaps he will forgive you for having such a thought in your heart (Ac.8:22).

Yet now I am happy, not because you were made sorry, but because your sorrow led you to repentance. For you became sorrowful as God intended and so were not harmed in any way by us. Godly sorrow brings repentance that leads to salvation and leaves no regret, but worldly sorrow brings death (2 Co.7:9-10).

Our fathers disciplined us for a little while as they thought best; but God disciplines us for our good, that we may share in his holiness. No discipline seems pleasant at the time, but painful. Later on, however, it produces a harvest of righteousness and peace for those who have been trained by it (He.12:10-11).

Therefore, get rid of all moral filth and the evil that is so prevalent and humbly accept the word planted in you, which can save you (Js.1:21).

Then David said to Nathan, "I have sinned against the LORD." Nathan replied, "The LORD has taken away your sin. You are not going to die (2 S.12:13).

3 (51:8-12) Pray for restoration and renewal.

All sin carries a price. The more grievous our sin, the higher the cost is to us and others. David committed two horrendous sins: adultery and murder. Much of what was lost due to his sin could not be restored; David would suffer the consequences of his sin for the rest of his life. But he himself could be restored, and he prayed for God to grant restoration and renewal to his weak, wounded spirit.

a. Ask God to restore your joy (vv.8-9).

For approximately a year, David carried the massive burden of his sin on his own. He was completely crushed—physically, spiritually, and emotionally—beneath its unbearable weight (see outline and notes—Ps.32:3-4 for more discussion). When he opened the door for sin to enter his life, David's joy and gladness vanished (v.8). Day and night, he was tortured by his guilty conscience. In addition, God's heavy hand of discipline had crushed him all the way to his bones (Ps.32:3). David begged God to restore joy to his heart by relieving the excruciating pain of his brokenness.

But even more tormenting than David's guilty conscience and God's discipline was David's loss of communion with the LORD. His sin had robbed him of the joy and gladness that spring from living in fellowship with God. Not only was David's hideous sin always be-

fore him (v.3), but it was also ever present before the face of the LORD, standing like an impassable wall between him and God (v.9). Desperately thirsting for renewed fellowship with God, David humbly asked the LORD to blot out all of his sin, to completely wipe it away so God would no longer look at it. By doing so, the LORD's condemnation would cease and the joy of his relationship with God would be restored.

b. Ask God to radically transform (renew) your heart and spirit (vv.10-12).

David's depraved heart had caused him to do irreversible damage to himself and others. Never again did he want to give in to his sinful desires. Never again did he want to violently assault others the way he had Uriah, Bathsheba, and his family. Never again did he want to experience God's crushing discipline. Therefore, he asked God to radically transform him by creating a clean heart within him, a completely new heart pure of fleshly desires (v.10; Eze.18:31; 36:26). Along with that, he asked God to renew a *steadfast* spirit within him. *Steadfast* comes from a verb which means to make firm or establish. Until this horrible failure, David had stood firm in the face of temptation. Now, he asked God to once again stir him to be steadfast, to renew that same enduring spirit within him.

David also asked God not to reject him, not to remove the presence of His Spirit from him (v.11). Some interpret this verse to mean that David feared the possibility of God's permanently ending His relationship with him; or, as we commonly say, David feared losing his salvation. However, this is not the case. Excellent Bible teacher Warren Wiersbe explains David's request simply and clearly:

> The Lord gave the Holy Spirit to David when Samuel anointed him (1 Sam. 16:13), and David didn't want to lose the blessing and help of the Spirit, as had happened to Saul when he sinned (1 Sam. 16:1, 14; see 2 Sam. 7:15). Today the Spirit abides with believers forever (John 14:15-18), but God's children can lose His effective ministry by grieving the Spirit (Eph. 4:30-32), lying to Him (Acts 5:1-3), and quenching Him by deliberate disobedience (1 Thess. 5:19).[7]

Notice that David did not ask God to restore his salvation, because he knew it had never been lost. Instead, he asked God to restore the joy of his salvation (v.12ᵃ). God's greatest gift to us is His salvation. Nothing can bring greater joy to our lives than knowing that our sins are forgiven, that we are living in victory over sin and basking in God's presence. David's unconfessed sin had choked this joy out of his heart for nearly a year.

---

7   Warren W. Wiersbe. *The Bible Exposition Commentary.* WORD*search* CROSS e-book.

In order to be upheld or sustained when facing future temptations, David asked God for an additional gift: a free or willing spirit (v.12ᵇ). It is possible that David was referring to the Holy Spirit, but it is more likely that he was repeating his request for a steadfast spirit (v.10). He desired a spirit of integrity, one that would always do the right thing and obey God.

Thought 1. When Christ purchased our redemption on the cross, He bought back everything that sin cost us. This does not mean that we will not suffer the natural consequences of sin. We cannot undo the damage we inflict on ourselves and others when we sin—a tragic truth we should seriously consider when we are tempted.

But as this Scripture teaches, we can be restored. God can heal us from the wounds of our sin, and He stands ready to give back what we forfeit when we give in to temptation, such as...

- a clear conscience
- physical and emotional rest
- joy
- gladness
- fellowship with God
- an open door into God's presence
- a pure heart
- a steadfast spirit
- the power of the Holy Spirit
- the joy of salvation

Many believers who commit terrible sin feel that they have no hope, or that things can never be the same as they once were. But God's grace is greater than our sin (Ro.5:20). We *can be* restored to God. We *can be* forgiven and cleansed. God *can* bring peace to our guilty consciences. We *can* know the joy of fellowship with God once again. We *can* enter into God's presence again. We *can* be cleansed within and given the strength to stand against temptation. We *can* know the power of the Spirit in our lives again. However, these things can only take place if we genuinely confess and repent of our sin.

We also need to remember that healing usually takes time. When we sin, we severely wound our souls and spirits. As physical wounds take time to heal, so do spiritual wounds. As we continue to walk in fellowship with God, His love and grace will soothe the pain of our sin. Eventually, the wounds on our spirits will heal, and we will once again enjoy the fullness of joy and the abundant life Christ gives us (Jn.10:10; 15:11).

> "The Spirit of the Lord is on me, because he has anointed me to preach good news to the poor. He has sent me to proclaim freedom for the prisoners and recovery of sight for the blind, to release the oppressed (Lu.4:18).
>
> "The son said to him, 'Father, I have sinned against heaven and against you. I am no longer worthy to be called your son.' "But the father said to his servants,

> 'Quick! Bring the best robe and put it on him. Put a ring on his finger and sandals on his feet (Lu.15:21-22).
>
> When you were dead in your sins and in the uncircumcision of your sinful nature, God made you alive with Christ. He forgave us all our sins, having canceled the written code, with its regulations, that was against us and that stood opposed to us; he took it away, nailing it to the cross (Col.2:13-14).
>
> You turned my wailing into dancing; you removed my sackcloth and clothed me with joy (Ps.30:11).
>
> "Come, let us return to the LORD. He has torn us to pieces but he will heal us; he has injured us but he will bind up our wounds. After two days he will revive us; on the third day he will restore us, that we may live in his presence (Ho.6:1-2).

4 (51:13-17) **Make a renewed commitment to God.** Since the night he had surrendered to his sinful desires, David had been fruitless in his service to God. When he finally confessed the sin he had long covered, the desire to be used again by God welled up within his spirit. He was prompted to renew his commitment to the LORD. Once he was fully restored, David vowed to use his shameful failure to exalt God and help His people.

a. To witness to those who transgress (disobey) God's law (v.13).
David promised God that he would reach out to those who, like him, had tragically fallen into sin. Having experienced God's amazing grace and boundless mercy, David was stirred to bear strong witness to those who rebelliously disobeyed God's laws. In fact, he was confident that men would turn away from their sin and return to God when they heard how God had received and restored him.

b. To declare and sing the praises of God your Savior (vv.14-15).
David promised to spend the rest of his life singing the LORD's praises for forgiving him of his horrible sin. His *bloodguilt* refers to David's wicked shedding of innocent blood, his heartless murder of his loyal servant, Uriah (v.14ª). Such great sin can only be forgiven by a great Savior, and David pledged to spread the glories of the God of his salvation. David also vowed to sing and declare the righteousness of God (v.14ᵇ). When God forgave and restored David, He displayed His righteousness by being faithful to His Word.

By the righteousness of God, which [David] engages to celebrate, we are to understand his goodness; for this attribute, as usually ascribed to God in the Scriptures, does not so much denote the strictness with which he exacts vengeance, as his faithfulness in fulfilling the promises and extending help to all who seek him in the hour of need.[8]

Addressing God as *Lord* (Adonai) or Master, David asked God to empower his lips to serve Him by declaring His praise (v.15). His humble request reminds us that we need the power of God's Spirit to effectively witness for Him (Ac.1:4-5, 8). Without the anointing of the Holy Spirit, our efforts to share God's love with others will be weak and unproductive.

c. **To proclaim the importance of a repentant heart (vv.16-17).**
As David taught others, he promised to emphasize the importance that God places on repentance. Under the Old Testament law, God required animal sacrifices from those who sinned. But David realized that the sacrifices that God truly desires are a broken spirit and a broken and contrite heart (v.17). A contrite heart is one that is totally crushed by the sorrow and guilt of sin. Such deep, utter sorrow leads to genuine repentance (2 Co.7:9-10). Sacrifices and offerings are meaningless to God unless they are offered from a sincere and repentant heart.

Thought 1. When we confess our sins, we should also renew our commitment to serve the Lord. One way we can serve Him is by reaching out to others who have fallen into sin (v.13). God can use our experiences of restoration to encourage others to repent and come back to Him.

Scripture commands us to help others when sin overtakes them (Ga.6:1-2). Too many believers are guilty of shunning those who err rather than reaching out to them in God's love and grace. When we experience God's forgiveness and restoration in our lives, we should always reach out to those who have slipped away or never received Christ as their Savior.

As part of our recommitment to God, we should loudly proclaim the immeasurable riches of His mercy and grace (vv.14-15). We should let others know that He is true to His promises, and that if we confess our sins, He is faithful to forgive us and cleanse us (1 Jn.1:9).

Finally, we need to continually surrender ourselves to God (vv.16-17). Otherwise, we tend to quickly lose the brokenness produced by the painful consequences of our sin. This does not mean that God wants us to walk around in continual sorrow for sin that is forgiven. To the contrary, He wants to restore our joy and gladness. Yet we should regularly offer ourselves as living sacrifices to the Lord; that is, we should die daily to sin and self in order to live holy, godly, and righteously in this world (Ro.12:1-2; Ga.2:20; Ti.2:12). When our hearts are no longer broken and contrite, we are in grave danger of falling back into sin.

Therefore, I urge you, brothers, in view of God's mercy, to offer your bodies as living sacrifices, holy and pleasing to God—this is your spiritual act of worship. Do not conform any longer to the pattern of this world, but be transformed by the renewing of your mind. Then you will be able to test and approve what God's will is—his good, pleasing and perfect will (Ro.12:1-2).

Brothers, if someone is caught in a sin, you who are spiritual should restore him gently. But watch yourself, or you also may be tempted. Carry each other's burdens, and in this way you will fulfill the law of Christ (Ga.6:1-2).

Through Jesus, therefore, let us continually offer to God a sacrifice of praise—the fruit of lips that confess his name. And do not forget to do good and to share with others, for with such sacrifices God is pleased (He.13:15-16).

My brothers, if one of you should wander from the truth and someone should bring him back, remember this: Whoever turns a sinner from the error of his way will save him from death and cover over a multitude of sins (Js.5:19-20).

If we confess our sins, he is faithful and just and will forgive us our sins and purify us from all unrighteousness (1 Jn.1:9).

With what shall I come before the LORD and bow down before the exalted God? Shall I come before him with burnt offerings, with calves a year old? Will the LORD be pleased with thousands of rams, with ten thousand rivers of oil? Shall I offer my firstborn for my transgression, the fruit of my body for the sin of my soul? He has showed you, O man, what is good. And what does the LORD require of you? To act justly and to love mercy and to walk humbly with your God (Mi.6:6-8).

5 (51:18-19) **Intercede for others, Ep.6:18.**
For many months, the sin in David's heart had hindered his prayers (Ps.66:18). Immediately after confessing his sin and renewing his commitment to the LORD, David prayed for his beloved city, Jerusalem. His terrible sin had affected the nation in troubling ways: it had created disappointment and distrust in the people. News of David's appalling sin had even spread beyond Jerusalem to Israel's enemies, threatening the security of the nation (2 S.12:14). With his sin now removed, the restored king's first order of business was to pray for the city he loved and led.

---

8 John Calvin. *Calvin's Commentaries.* WORDsearch CROSS e-book.

a. The prayer: That their city (Zion/Jerusalem) would prosper (v.18).

Knowing that the sins of leaders drastically affect the people and institutions they serve, David now pleaded with the LORD to help Jerusalem prosper. By God's marvelous mercy and grace, the sinful king had been restored to the LORD through confessing his sin. He humbly asked God to show His *good pleasure* (ratsown) or favor toward Israel by restoring His blessings on her as well.

The words "build up the walls of Jerusalem" have led some excellent commentators to conclude that verses 17-18 were later added to Psalm 51 during the events recorded in *Ezra* and *Nehemiah*. However, there is no reason to question whether they are a part of David's original work. Strong walls were the symbol of a strong, well-protected nation. David would have naturally prayed for the strength and defense of Israel. Moreover, Scripture records that Solomon finished building the wall around Jerusalem early in his reign, meaning that David must have begun the work (1 Ki.3:1).[9] Therefore, it is easy to see how David would have made this request.

b. The result: They will please God by worshipping Him (presenting sacrifices and offerings) in the right spirit (v.19).

As David previously noted, our sacrifices are worthless to the LORD unless they are offered in the right spirit (vv.16-17). God's restored blessings on Israel would have resulted in David's offering sacrifices of thanksgiving to the LORD. These sacrifices would please God, unlike those David had presented while harboring sin in his heart. David would now offer them from a broken and contrite spirit. The people of Israel would follow his lead by offering their sacrifices as well, and the LORD would be worshipped throughout the nation.

Thought 1. One of the most important responsibilities believers have is to pray for others. In fact, Scripture states that it is a sin to neglect to do so (1 S.12:23). When we have unconfessed sin in our lives, we are unable to effectively intercede for others. Because our fellowship with God is severed, He does not hear our prayers (Ps.66:18).

In the face of temptation, we need to remember the often forgotten consequence of sin: we forfeit the privilege of prayer. What greater thing can we do for other people than to pray for them? What more can we do for the protection of our children than to cry out to God on their behalf? What more can we do for our lost loved ones than beg God to bring them to salvation? What greater thing can we do for our sick friends than earnestly call on God to heal them?

Christ died so we could have open, direct access to God. Through His precious blood, we are invited to boldly come before His throne for help in our time of need (He.4:16). May God help us to treasure this powerful privilege, refusing to carelessly dispose of it by giving in to temptation!

> **We know that God does not listen to sinners. He listens to the godly man who does his will (Jn.9:31).**
>
> **And pray in the Spirit on all occasions with all kinds of prayers and requests. With this in mind, be alert and always keep on praying for all the saints (Ep.6:18).**
>
> **I urge, then, first of all, that requests, prayers, intercession and thanksgiving be made for everyone (1 Ti.2:1).**
>
> **Therefore confess your sins to each other and pray for each other so that you may be healed. The prayer of a righteous man is powerful and effective (Js.5:16).**
>
> **As for me, far be it from me that I should sin against the LORD by failing to pray for you. And I will teach you the way that is good and right (1 S.12:23).**
>
> **If I had cherished sin in my heart, the Lord would not have listened (Ps.66:18).**

---

[9]   Warren W. Wiersbe. *The Bible Exposition Commentary.* WORD*search* CROSS e-book.

PSALM 52

When the Wicked & the Righteous Face the LORD, 52:1-9

For the director of music. A maskil of David. When Doeg the Edomite had gone to Saul and told him: "David has gone to the house of Ahimelech."

Why do you boast of evil, you mighty man? Why do you boast all day long, you who are a disgrace in the eyes of God?
2 Your tongue plots destruction; it is like a sharpened razor, you who practice deceit.
3 You love evil rather than good, falsehood rather than speaking the truth. Selah
4 You love every harmful word, O you deceitful tongue!
5 Surely God will bring you down to everlasting ruin: He will snatch you up and tear you from your tent; he will uproot you from the land of the living. Selah
6 The righteous will see and fear; they will laugh at him, saying,
7 "Here now is the man who did not make God his stronghold but trusted in his great wealth and grew strong by destroying others!"
8 But I am like an olive tree flourishing in the house of God; I trust in God's unfailing love for ever and ever.
9 I will praise you forever for what you have done; in your name I will hope, for your name is good. I will praise you in the presence of your saints.

1. The wicked (mighty man)
a. He boasts in the evil he does
b. He is a disgrace to God: He does not realize that God's goodness & justice are always at work
c. He misuses his tongue to destroy & deceive people
d. He has a corrupt heart: He loves evil more than good & loves lies more than truth
e. He loves every harmful word—deception, profanity, vulgarity, cursing, lying, gossip, slander
f. He will face God's terrifying wrath
  1) He will be ruined eternally
  2) He will be plucked out of his home
  3) He will be uprooted from the land of the living

2. The righteous
a. They observe God's judgment & fear
b. They are vindicated: They are filled with *triumphant joy* (laughing) over their deliverance & the judgment of their oppressors
c. They are destined to flourish in the house of God: A picture of God's eternal house, Jn.14:2-3
  1) Bc. they trust in God's love
  2) Bc. they commit themselves to praise God forever
  3) Bc. they place their hope in God's good name
  4) Bc. they praise God in the presence of His people

PSALM 52

When the Wicked and the Righteous Face the LORD, 52:1-9

(52:1-9) **Introduction:** after his son was critically wounded in the United States Civil War, American poet Henry Wadsworth Longfellow wrote "Christmas Bells." Today, we sing the lyrics of this poem in the carol, "I Heard the Bells on Christmas Day." In it, Longfellow lamented the triumph of evil in our sin-cursed world:

> *And in despair I bowed my head;*
> *"There is no peace on earth," I said;*
> *"For hate is strong,*
> *And mocks the song*
> *Of peace on earth, good-will to men!"*

Then, Longfellow recalled God's justice as revealed in Scripture:

> *Then pealed the bells more loud and deep:*
> *"God is not dead, nor doth He sleep;*
> *The wrong shall fail,*
> *The right prevail,*
> *With peace on earth, good-will to men."*[1]

In a perfect world, the wrong would always fail and the right would always prevail. But our world is far from ideal, and wicked men often prevail over the righteous. One glaring example of this is the global persecution of Christians. Every year, thousands upon thousands of believers worldwide lay down their lives for Christ.

David wrote Psalm 52 to address the frequent triumph of the wicked over the righteous. As revealed by the heading, the vicious deeds of Doeg the Edomite, one of Saul's servants, provide the setting for this psalm (1 S.21–22). David was running for his life from the jealous King Saul, when he came to Nob, where the tabernacle rested. He approached Ahimelech, the High Priest, requesting food for himself and his men. Thinking that David was on a secret mission for Saul, Ahimelech gave David the consecrated showbread from the tabernacle, which was the only bread that he had. The priest also sent David away with the sword of Goliath that had apparently been preserved in the tabernacle.

Standing there in the shadows while all of this transpired was Doeg the Edomite. The Edomites were the descendants of Esau, and they bitterly hated Jacob's seed, the Jews. Yet, Doeg had somehow won Saul's confidence, and the self-willed king appointed Doeg chief over his shepherds. Doeg reported what he had seen to Saul, who immediately ordered the execution of the 85 priests in Nob. When Saul's soldiers refused to harm God's anointed priests, the ambitious Edomite slaughtered them himself, jumping at the opportunity to gain favor with the evil king.

By inspiration of the Holy Spirit, David composed Psalm 52 in response to Doeg's abominable act. A *maskil* psalm or psalm of instruction, it teaches us about God's justice for the wicked. Although they may succeed in their devious deeds for the present, their triumph will be

---

1 Henry Wadsworth Longfellow. *Christmas Bells,* 1863.

short-lived. Ultimately, the righteous will rejoice and praise the LORD when He strikes the wicked down in judgment. In the end, the righteous *will* prevail. This is, *When the Wicked and the Righteous Face the LORD,* 52:1-9.

1. The wicked (mighty man) (vv.1-5).
2. The righteous (vv.6-9).

1 (52:1-5) The wicked (mighty man).

David began this psalm by addressing the rich and powerful man who uses his money and position to abuse others. *Mighty man* (gibbor) is the Hebrew word for a valiant warrior. Here, David sarcastically applied it to Doeg for his verbal attack on the benevolent priests. His mocking tone made a point: those who flaunt their strength by harming others deserve contempt, not admiration.

As noted by several commentators, David's description of the mighty man also applies to Saul. The vindictive king abused his power by unjustly convicting Ahimelech of conspiring against him when, in fact, the priest was innocent. Saul's jealous pursuit of David was another abuse of his power as king.

a. He boasts in the evil he does (v.1ª)

David continued to scoff at the cruel oppressor. The mighty man smugly boasts of the evil he inflicts on others. He feeds his ego by attacking those who cannot defend themselves, building himself up by tearing them down.

b. He is a disgrace to God: He does not realize that God's goodness and justice are always at work (v.1ᵇ).

The mighty man is ignorant of a fearsome reality: as he brags about his merciless treatment of the defenseless, God is looking on. While the man is mighty in his own eyes, he is a disgrace to God. His consuming pride deceives him into thinking that he will never be brought down. But God's steadfast love and faithfulness never cease. God is the avenger of the oppressed. Though it may not be apparent to us, God's justice is always at work.

c. He misuses his tongue to destroy and deceive people (v.2).

David quickly pointed out the mighty man's most effective weapon of destruction: his razor-sharp tongue. Doeg had effectively wielded his tongue to attack the priests by informing Saul of Ahimelech's encounter with David. Determined to gain favor with the king, the Edomite deceived Saul by withholding a number of important details from him. Doeg neglected to tell Saul that Ahimelech meant no evil against him. David had told Ahimelech that he was on a secret mission for Saul (1 S.21:2). By helping David, the innocent priest actually thought he was helping the king. He knew nothing of Saul's vendetta against David (1 S.22:15). By omitting this crucial information, Doeg wickedly ignited Saul's anger against the priests, causing their destruction.

d. He has a corrupt heart: He loves evil more than good and loves lies more than truth (v.3).

"For out of the overflow of the heart the mouth speaks" (Mt.12:34). This statement by Jesus condemns those who destroy others with their words. The poison in the oppressor's cruel tongue springs forth from his or her corrupt heart, a perverted heart that loves evil more than good. It is the person's heart that prompts him or her to lie about others rather than speak the truth (righteousness).

e. He loves every harmful word—deception, profanity, vulgarity, cursing, lying, gossip, slander (v.4).

In addition to loving evil, abusive people love to devour or swallow others up with their wicked words. They deliberately say vicious things that harm their victims. Poisonous profanities, lies, half-truths, accusations, gossip, and slander spew out of their mouths. Their corrupt hearts revel in destroying others with their words.

f. He will face God's terrifying wrath (v.5).

As mighty as these people think they are, there is one stronger than all those who trample over others. These abusers will not escape the terrifying wrath of *God* ('El: the Strong One). His judgment upon them will be fast, fierce, and final. God will...

• destroy all abusers forever, just as they have destroyed others (v.5ª)
• snatch the abusers out of their dwellings, leaving them homeless (v.5ᵇ)
• pluck the abusers out of the land of the living, the way a vicious tornado uproots a sturdy tree from the earth

Thought 1. David punctuated this passage with two *selahs*—pauses to reflect on what has been said. The first occurs after his description of abusers. They love evil more than good, using their tongues to harm others (vv.2-3).

We, too, ought to pause to examine ourselves for these traits. At times, we are tempted to say things that damage others. Like Doeg, we sometimes report unnecessary information. Or we may not tell the whole story, intentionally leaving out details to our advantage. Or we build ourselves up by tearing someone else down. Or we blatantly lie about or slander another person. Or we criticize and condemn someone else. Or we speak harshly or unkindly of another.

In his epistle, James cautioned us about the deadly power of the tongue (Js.3:1-10). Although it is a relatively small part of our bodies, it has the power to cause great damage. We can know that we have matured as believers, James noted, when we are able to control our tongues. With the Holy Spirit's help, we should continuously strive to guard every word that we say.

David placed his second *selah* after his reminder that God will judge those who use their wealth, position, or power to mistreat others (v.5). In our selfish world, abuse occurs on many levels. Consider these examples:

➤ Cruel, unloving husbands or wives who physically, verbally, or emotionally abuse their spouse
➤ Parents who abuse their children
➤ Criminals or gangs who prey on the unsuspecting and defenseless
➤ Sexual deviants who force themselves on others
➤ Unfair employers, managers, and supervisors who mistreat their employees
➤ Landlords who are unfair to their tenants
➤ Sharp-tongued people who dishearten and discourage with their piercing words
➤ Gossips, liars, and slanderers
➤ Those who constantly criticize and condemn
➤ Law enforcement personnel who abuse their authority
➤ Dictatorial governments that oppress their citizens
➤ Extremists or religious fanatics who persecute others for their faith
➤ People who discriminate because of race, gender, economic status, or any other unjust basis
➤ Pastors who act like harsh, unloving *lords* or *masters* over God's flock (1 Pe.5:3)

The list could go on and on. As believers, we should carefully guard against attitudes, actions, and words that are harmful to others. In all relationships and dealings, we are commanded to be fair, kind, and loving. As Jesus taught, we should always treat others the way we want to be treated (Mt.7:12). We need to be conscious of the fact that God will judge us when we fail to treat others as Christ commands.

Moreover, we have a God-given responsibility to help the victims of abuse or oppression. We cannot simply turn our backs on those who suffer at the cruel hands of others. As believers, we need to extend the love of Christ by rescuing those who are victims of any type of abuse (see outline and notes—Pr.24:11-12 for more discussion).

Brothers, if someone is caught in a sin, you who are spiritual should restore him gently. But watch yourself, or you also may be tempted (Ga.6:1).

Let us not become weary in doing good, for at the proper time we will reap a harvest if we do not give up. Therefore, as we have opportunity, let us do good to
all people, especially to those who belong to the family of believers (Ga.6:9-10).

We all stumble in many ways. If anyone is never at fault in what he says, he is a perfect man, able to keep his whole body in check. When we put bits into the mouths of horses to make them obey us, we can turn the whole animal. Or take ships as an example. Although they are so large and are driven by strong winds, they are steered by a very small rudder wherever the pilot wants to go. Likewise the tongue is a small part of the body, but it makes great boasts. Consider what a great forest is set on fire by a small spark. The tongue also is a fire, a world of evil among the parts of the body. It corrupts the whole person, sets the whole course of his life on fire, and is itself set on fire by hell. All kinds of animals, birds, reptiles and creatures of the sea are being tamed and have been tamed by man, but no man can tame the tongue. It is a restless evil, full of deadly poison. With the tongue we praise our Lord and Father, and with it we curse men, who have been made in God's likeness. Out of the same mouth come praise and cursing. My brothers, this should not be (Js.3:2-10).

But the cowardly, the unbelieving, the vile, the murderers, the sexually immoral, those who practice magic arts, the idolaters and all liars—their place will be in the fiery lake of burning sulfur. This is the second death" (Re.21:8).

Rescue the weak and needy; deliver them from the hand of the wicked (Ps.82:4).

Rescue those being led away to death; hold back those staggering toward slaughter. If you say, "But we knew nothing about this," does not he who weighs the heart perceive it? Does not he who guards your life know it? Will he not repay each person according to what he has done? (Pr.24:11-12).

2 (52:6-9) The righteous.

After rebuking the powerful of this earth who are abusive, David encourages the righteous. He urges all of us who truly follow the LORD to look beyond the injustices of this life to our glorious future. Although we may be mistreated by others here on earth, we will prevail over the ungodly in the end. Oppressors and abusers will suffer eternally under God's judgment, but we will dwell in the house of the LORD forever (Ps.23:6).

a. They observe God's judgment and fear (v.6ª).

David knew that God would one day judge Saul and Doeg just as He does all who use their wealth, positions, and power to abuse others. When that day came, the righteous would witness it and fear the LORD. This simply means that the righteous will stand in awe of God and His righteousness when He brings down the ungodly. Furthermore, when we see God's judgment come upon evildoers in this life, we will be stirred to live righteously, lest God's wrath fall on us as well.

b. They are vindicated: They are filled with *triumphant joy* (laughing) over their deliverance and the judgment of their oppressors (v.6ᵇ-7).

When God vindicates the righteous, they will *laugh*—a symbol of their triumphant joy over being delivered from their oppressors and receiving justice from the LORD. As Scripture clearly states, their laughter is directed *at* the evildoer who so arrogantly boasted of his abusive treatment of others. Instead of trusting in God, he trusted in his own resources. He made himself strong at the expense of others, mistreating and sometimes destroying them.

By emphasizing the laughter of the righteous, David mocked his boastful oppressors, Saul and Doeg, one last time. Angry over what they had done to the innocent priests, as well as at what Saul was doing to him personally, the frustrated young David sneered at the unchecked arrogance of these evil men.

David longed to be delivered from Saul and to see justice served on the crazed king. However, Scripture records an important fact: upon hearing of Saul's death, David did not laugh. Instead, he respectfully mourned Israel's fallen king (2 S.1). The lesson is clear: the righteous may be angry at their oppressors and desire that they be brought to justice, but they should not rejoice when God's judgment falls on them (Pr.24:17-18).

c. They are destined to flourish in the house of God: A picture of God's eternal house, Jn.14:2-3 (vv.8-9).

David confidently proclaimed a wonderful fact: when Saul and Doeg were brought down, he would still be standing. At God's direction, the prophet Samuel had anointed David as Israel's future king (1 S.16:12-13). David was unwavering in his faith that what God had ordained would come to pass.

David's declaration of faith speaks for the destiny of all the righteous. When the wicked are brought down in God's judgment, the righteous will be flourishing in God's eternal house (Jn.14:2-3). David compared the righteous to an olive tree, a symbol of endurance and permanence. Olive trees live for hundreds of years, thriving in the worst of conditions.

The most fruitful trees are the product of bare and rocky ground...The terraced hills of Palestine, where the earth lies never many inches above the limestone rocks, the long rainless summer of unbroken sunshine, and the heavy "dews" of the autumn afford conditions which are extraordinarily favorable to at least the indigenous olive.[2]

Amazingly, some olive trees thriving in Israel today are over 3,000 years old!

The eternal endurance of the righteous is due to their trust in the LORD. In contrast to the mighty men who lean on their own resources, the righteous trust in God's *mercy* or *unfailing love* (chesed). They have entered into a covenant with God, and they are kept by His faithfulness and His wonderful promises. Throughout eternity, they will praise God for His righteousness in judging the wicked. *What you have done* refers to God's execution of justice on the ungodly. Until God acts, the righteous place their hope in God's good name, praising Him in the presence of His people. When the wicked have all passed into a godless eternity, the righteous will still be praising God eternally in the house of the LORD (Jn.14:2-3).

Thought 1. We should not fret or be anxious over the injustices and abuses that occur in our corrupt world. Nor should we seek vengeance against those who cause us harm. Instead, we are to trust in the LORD, believing that He will be true to His character and His Word. Like faithful Abraham, we should confess that the Judge of all the earth will do what is right (Ge.18:25). We should not allow the temporary triumph of evildoers to shake our faith in God. In His good time, He will judge all men for their unrighteousness and ungodliness (Ro.1:18). We need to place our hope in God's name, in His character and attributes, and patiently wait until He fulfills His Word.

In addition, we ought to rejoice in our glorious future. A firm understanding of what God has in store for us in the future will sustain us as we suffer through the trials and tribulations of this life. When the wicked are destroyed in God's judgment, we will be living in the house of the LORD! This glorious hope is the anchor for our souls in this unjust world (He.6:19). Our temporary afflictions, as painful as they might be, cannot compare to the glories we will know in eternity (2 Co.4:17-18).

> **In my Father's house are many rooms; if it were not so, I would have told you. I am going there to prepare a place for you. And if I go and prepare a place for you, I will come back and take you to**

---

2 Geoffrey W. Bromiley. *The International Standard Bible Encyclopedia.* WORD*search* CROSS e-book.

be with me that you also may be where I am (Jn.14:2-3).

Now we know that if the earthly tent we live in is destroyed, we have a building from God, an eternal house in heaven, not built by human hands (2 Co.5:1).

Then I heard the angel in charge of the waters say: "You are just in these judgments, you who are and who were, the Holy One, because you have so judged; for they have shed the blood of your saints and prophets, and you have given them blood to drink as they deserve." And I heard the altar respond: "Yes, Lord God Almighty, true and just are your judgments" (Re.16:5-7).

He is like a tree planted by streams of water, which yields its fruit in season and whose leaf does not wither. Whatever he does prospers (Ps.1:3).

Surely goodness and love will follow me all the days of my life, and I will dwell in the house of the LORD forever (Ps.23:6).

Do not fret because of evil men or be envious of those who do wrong; for like the grass they will soon wither, like green plants they will soon die away. Trust in the LORD and do good; dwell in the land and enjoy safe pasture (Ps.37:1-3).

PSALM 53

God's Appraisal of the Atheist & of the Human Race, 53:1-6

For the director of music. According to mahalath. A maskil of David.

1. God's appraisal of the atheist a. He is a fool b. The reasons 1) He denies God's existence 2) He is corrupt **2. God's appraisal of the human race** a. God looks down on earth to search for any who truly understand & seek Him b. God's conclusion 1) All have turned away	The fool says in his heart, "There is no God." They are corrupt, and their ways are vile; there is no one who does good. 2 God looks down from heaven on the sons of men to see if there are any who understand, any who seek God. 3 Everyone has turned away, they have together become corrupt; there is no one who does good, not even one. 4 Will the evildoers never learn—those who devour my people as men eat bread and who do not call on God? 5 There they were, overwhelmed with dread, where there was nothing to dread. God scattered the bones of those who attacked you; you put them to shame, for God despised them. 6 Oh, that salvation for Israel would come out of Zion! When God restores the fortunes of his people, let Jacob rejoice and Israel be glad!	from God & become corrupt: No one does good, not even one 2) Evildoers never learn • They continually persecute God's people • They do not call on God, Ro.10:13 3) Evildoers are gripped by fear • Bc. God is with you (the righteous) & you put them (the wicked) to shame • Bc. God despises & destroys those who oppress His people **3. God's great hope offered to His people** a. Salvation: It will come out of Zion (the Jews), Jn.4:22 b. Restoration: It will result in great blessings & rejoicing

PSALM 53

God's Appraisal of the Atheist and of the Human Race, 53:1-6

(53:1-6) **Introduction:** most people would agree that repetition is the key to learning. Surely then, Psalm 14 holds critical lessons for humanity, for God saw fit to repeat it in Psalm 53. Parts of it are echoed a third time in Paul's Epistle to the Romans (Ro.3:10-12). Concerning this, pastor and theologian James Montgomery Boice wrote,

> *Anything God says once demands attention. Anything he says twice demands our most intent attention. How then if he says something three times, as he does in this case? This demands our keenest concentration, contemplation, assimilation, and even memorization.[1]*

Minor differences exist between Psalms 14 and 53. First, where God is called *the Lord* (Yahweh, Jehovah) in Psalm 14, He is referred to as *God* (Elohim) in Psalm 53. No clear explanation for this change exists. It may be due to the fact that *Jehovah* is the prominent name of God in the first Book of Psalms (1-41), whereas *Elohim* is prominent in Book II (42-72).

The largest variation between the two psalms is the content of verse 5. Most commentators think that sometime later in Israel's history, the musicians pulled out Psalm 14 for a specific occasion, set it to a different tune (*mahalath*), and adapted it to suit that event. Many scholars believe that occasion was a celebration of God's destruction of the Assyrian army during the reign of Hezekiah (2 K.19; Is.37). The details of verse 5 certainly seem to apply to that miraculous victory (2 K.19:35; Is.37:36). Sennacherib, Assyria's king, blasphemed God. Thus, "the fool" who says that "there is no God" may be properly applied to him (v.1). This may also explain the changing of *Jehovah* to *Elohim*. *Elohim* is the name of God that emphasizes His mighty, unparalleled power. God certainly displayed that power in slaying 185,000 Assyrian soldiers as they slept.

The most crucial truth of Psalms 14 and 53 for all of humanity is the one repeated for a third time in Romans: not a single one of us is good. We are all corrupt sinners in desperate need of God's salvation. This is, *God's Appraisal of the Atheist and of the Human Race*, 53:1-6.

1. God's appraisal of the atheist (v.1).
2. God's appraisal of the human race (vv.2-5).
3. God's great hope offered to his people (v.6).

1 (53:1) **God's appraisal of the atheist.**
What does God think about the person who totally rejects Him and dares say, *"There is no God"*? Psalm 53 begins with God's appraisal of the atheist, which is stated clearly and bluntly.

a. He is a fool (v.1ᵃ).
In God's estimation, the atheist is a *fool* (nabal). Of the three Hebrew words for *fool* in the Old Testament, this is the strongest. The fool is the person who descends to the depths of depravity because he or she totally rejects God's truth.

Atheistic fools appear in all walks of life. Many are highly educated and, from the world's perspective, highly intelligent. Some perform deeds that contribute

---

[1] James Montgomery Boice. *An Expositional Commentary–Psalms, Volume 2: Psalms 42-106.* (Grand Rapids, MI:Baker Books, 1996). WORD*search* CROSS e-book.

to the welfare of humanity. Some are authors, scientists, entertainers, and educators. Some are faithful to their families. Others are totally immoral. Some are law-abiding citizens, while others are criminals. Regardless of their intelligence, morality, education, vocation, or status in society, God classifies all atheists the same way: they are fools.

b. The reasons (v.1ᵇ).

God appraises atheists as fools because they deny His existence. They are fools because they make a deliberate decision in their hearts not to accept God's revealed truth even though God has placed the knowledge of Himself within the heart of every individual (2 Pe.3:5). Simply put, they lie to themselves.

How has God revealed Himself to every human being? Through the world He created. Nature itself triggers our inner awareness of God:

> **Since what may be known about God is plain to them, because God has made it plain to them. For since the creation of the world God's invisible qualities—his eternal power and divine nature—have been clearly seen, being understood from what has been made, so that men are without excuse. For although they knew God, they neither glorified him as God nor gave thanks to him, but their thinking became futile and their foolish hearts were darkened. Although they claimed to be wise, they became fools (Ro.1:19-22).**

Scripture teaches that God has revealed three truths about Himself to every person's heart...
- the truth of His existence (Ro.1:19-22, see above)
- the truth of His judgment (Ro.1:32)

> **Although they know God's righteous decree that those who do such things deserve death, they not only continue to do these very things but also approve of those who practice them (Ro.1:32).**

- the truth of His moral law as summarized by the Ten Commandments (Ro.2:14-15)

> **Indeed, when Gentiles, who do not have the law, do by nature things required by the law, they are a law for themselves, even though they do not have the law, since they show that the requirements of the law are written on their hearts, their consciences also bearing witness, and their thoughts now accusing, now even defending them (Ro.2:14-15).**

Fools reject God's revelation to them and live as if God does not exist. As a result, they are totally corrupt. They break God's moral laws without fear of God's judgment, never considering that they are going to be held accountable for their conduct (Ro.2:18). They live as if God is not watching...but He is.

Corrupt is the word used to describe the wicked world of Noah's day, a world so violent and depraved that God destroyed it (Ge.6:11-13). It is also used to describe Jeremiah's soiled girdle or sash (Je.13:7, *ruined*). God commanded him to bury it and, by the time he dug it up, it had naturally decayed and become worthless. It symbolized how God would destroy the pride of Judah and Jerusalem because they refused to listen to Him and followed their own desires.

Corruption is a rottenness that spoils everything it contacts. Note how the fool manifests it. First, his actions are continually abominable, that is, vile, detestable, evil. He regularly commits those deeds that are most despised by the LORD. Second, he fails to do good, or that which is godly, right, and beneficial. We are as accountable to God for the good that we neglect to do as we are for the sinful acts that we do commit (Js.4:17).

Thought 1. The Bible records the life of a man whose name, Nabal, was actually the word for *fool* (1 S.25). He was a man who truly lived up to his name (1 S.25:25). In every way, he characterizes the person who denies and defies God. Look closely at his character and actions:
➤ He was surly and harsh (1 S.25:3).
➤ He was evil and mean in all his dealings (1 S.25:3).
➤ He was ungrateful (1 S.25:7-11).
➤ He was uncaring (1 S.25:7-11).
➤ He was selfish (1 S.25:7-11).
➤ He was called a Son of Belial—a worthless, wicked scoundrel (1 S.25:17, 25).
➤ He was unapproachable and unreasonable (1 S.25:17).

Nabal was stricken suddenly by the LORD after a night of drunken revelry. He finally died after spending ten days in a coma (1 S.25:36-38). God's judgment will likewise fall upon all fools who deny and defy Him. We need to carefully guard against living as if God does not exist, as if He does not witness our deeds. Never forget that a day of judgment is coming when God will judge everything we have ever said or done (Ec.11:9;12:14).

> **Now the earth was corrupt in God's sight and was full of violence. God saw how corrupt the earth had become, for all the people on earth had corrupted their ways (Ge.6:11-12).**

Rise up, O God, and defend your cause; remember how fools mock you all day long (Ps.74:22).

For the fool speaks folly, his mind is busy with evil: He practices ungodliness and spreads error concerning the LORD; the hungry he leaves empty and from the thirsty he withholds water. The scoundrel's methods are wicked, he makes up evil schemes to destroy the poor with lies, even when the plea of the needy is just (Is.32:6-7).

He said to me, "Son of man, have you seen what the elders of the house of Israel are doing in the darkness, each at the shrine of his own idol? They say, 'The LORD does not see us; the LORD has forsaken the land'" (Eze.8:12).

2 (53:2-5) **God's appraisal of the human race.** David expanded the focus of this psalm beyond atheistic fools to the *sons of men*—the entire human race. Certainly, we do not all plunge to the atheists' level of folly, but every one of us is a sinner in need of God's forgiveness and redemption.

a. God looks down on earth to search for any who truly understand and seek Him (v.2).

God is watching. This is the sobering reality that fools force from their minds. David paints a graphic picture of God's observance of life on earth. He is literally leaning over heaven and peering down at earth. From His vantage point, God sees every detail of all that takes place on the landscape below. However, David mentioned one specific thing for which God examines all people: to see if anyone is wise and seeks Him. Now note the contrast: the fool says, "There is no God," whereas the person of understanding recognizes that there is a God and seeks Him.

God examines every individual born on earth, all the *sons of men.* He does not condemn human beings collectively but individually. He observes each one and establishes in His heavenly records evidence on every person who rejects Him and His righteous commands (Re.20:12). Everyone's guilt is documented in heaven, and no one will be able to offer an excuse when he or she stands before God to be judged (Ro.1:20; 2:1-3; 3:19).

b. God's conclusion (vv.3-5).

Does God find anyone in the human race, any individual at all, who naturally understands and seeks Him? Paul answers the question in his reference to this passage in Romans 3:

As it is written: "There is no one righteous, not even one; there is no one who understands, no one who seeks God. All have turned away, they have together become worthless; there is no one who does good, not even one" (Ro.3:10-12).

This condemning verdict is pronounced over and over against every member of the human race. Bear in mind four important facts:

First, every individual has turned away from God, beginning with Adam and Eve (v.3ᵃ). Scripture speaks of the human race collectively here because there are no exceptions to these statements. All of us have rejected God and His righteous law, and all have turned to walk in a different direction—away from Him and His holy commandments. Consequently, we all stand guilty before Him. All are *filthy* or *corrupt* (alakh). This word, used of milk that is spoiled and soured,[2] pictures man's original condition. Many people assume that God created man with the sin nature. Nothing could be further from the truth! God did not design human beings to sin. And, like milk that is at first sweet and fresh, man was created in innocence. And, like milk that quickly spoils when not properly cooled, man easily yielded to the heat of temptation and became corrupt—spoiled, rotten through and through. Every single one of us who has drawn a breath of air has followed this pattern (Ro.5:12).

What is true of the fool, the vilest of sinners, is true of all people: none of them do good (v.3ᵇ). Note the emphasis that there is no exception to this, " *not even one.*" Does this mean that in our natural, sinful state we never do any good deeds whatsoever, that every single word, thought, or deed is evil? Does it mean that we all live as wickedly as we are capable of, like the fool? Observation of the human race answers this question, and Scripture answers it too. As sinful people, we do many good things (Lu.11:13). The Bible clearly notes that the natural man is capable of righteous works (Is.64:6; Ep.2:8-9; Ti.3:5).

So what does this Scripture mean when it says that *not even one does good*? Romans 3:23 explains it, briefly but fully:

For all have sinned and fall short of the glory of God (Ro.3:23).

Although we as sinful people may perform some good deeds, none of us is *entirely* good. The glory of God lies in His *perfect* holiness: He is entirely without sin, completely free of defilement or even a trace of corruption. Every one of us falls short of this standard. While some of us are not as corrupt as others, we are all corrupt. Not one person is without sin. Not one

---

2 Warren W. Wiersbe. *The Bible Exposition Commentary.* WORD*search* CROSS e-book.

person who has walked the face of the earth throughout its history has ever lived up to God's glorious standard of perfection.

Second, evildoers are shameless in their wickedness and will never learn (v.4). The human sin cycle goes on and on. David reveals in this verse the specific iniquity that prompted him to compose this psalm: it was the continual persecution of God's people by the heathen, those who did not acknowledge or call upon the LORD as their God (Ro.10:13). Sadly, this evil is just as prevalent today as it was in David's day, if not more so. Persecutors eagerly devour God's people the same way they eat their daily bread (Mi.3:1-3). They live to afflict believers and their strength is renewed by their conquests.

> Then I said, "Listen, you leaders of Jacob, you rulers of the house of Israel. Should you not know justice, you who hate good and love evil; who tear the skin from my people and the flesh from their bones; who eat my people's flesh, strip off their skin and break their bones in pieces; who chop them up like meat for the pan, like flesh for the pot?" (Mi.3:1-3).

Third, those who terrorize God's people will themselves be overwhelmed with dread (v.5). This is where Psalm 53 differs from Psalm 14. In Psalm 14, David wrote of a future day when God's judgment will fall on those who oppress God's people. Here in Psalm 53, David speaks of a victory already granted by God. The enemy had fearlessly attacked Israel, but they were suddenly stricken with great fear. The Hebrew literally says, *"Fear, fear"* or double fear—great terror. The word used for *fear* (pachad) emphasizes that it is fear that comes on suddenly and unexpectedly. God appeared and thoroughly destroyed them, scattering their bones across their camp (2 K.19:35; Is.37:36).

The message is clear: the oppressed never suffer alone because the LORD is always in their midst. God is with the righteous, and He despises and destroys those who oppress His people. Though evildoers continue on as if God does not exist, *He is there* nonetheless. What a glorious truth and a precious promise this is to believers who serve the LORD amidst persecution! The ungodly have no fear of the LORD in the present (Ro.3:13-18). But one day this will quickly change. Without warning, the wicked will be stricken with an intense, tormenting fear when God rises up in judgment against them.

Thought 1. The facts are indisputable: we have all sinned and come short of God's glory. Our punishment? Death! Yet, all is not lost; we can be saved (Ro.6:23)! The first step toward salvation is the recognition of our sinfulness, as taught in this passage

(vv.2-3). Sadly, many people never receive God's forgiveness through Christ because they simply will not acknowledge that they are sinners. This does not necessarily mean that they are atheists. Many believe God exists and many even believe the Bible, to a degree. Yet instead of comparing themselves to God, they compare themselves to other people, to the most wicked and vile people. So, because they are not murderers, adulterers, thieves, or violent people, they view themselves as good. They may even perform many noteworthy and commendable deeds.

But before any of us can be saved, we have to understand that God does not compare us to other sinners but to Himself. In comparison to His perfect holiness and righteousness, we all fall short. We may not all break every rule of God's law, and we may not all break His law as frequently as other people do, but we all disobey God. We are all sinners, short of God's perfection and glory—every one of us. For this reason, we cannot be saved until we acknowledge our sinful condition and our need for a Savior.

> For all have sinned and fall short of the glory of God (Ro.3:23).
> Therefore, just as sin entered the world through one man, and death through sin, and in this way death came to all men, because all sinned (Ro.5:12).
> As for you, you were dead in your transgressions and sins, in which you used to live when you followed the ways of this world and of the ruler of the kingdom of the air, the spirit who is now at work in those who are disobedient. All of us also lived among them at one time, gratifying the cravings of our sinful nature and following its desires and thoughts. Like the rest, we were by nature objects of wrath (Ep.2:1-3).
> If we claim to be without sin, we deceive ourselves and the truth is not in us (1 Jn.1:8).
> We all, like sheep, have gone astray, each of us has turned to his own way; and the LORD has laid on him the iniquity of us all (Is.53:6).

Thought 2. The LORD's people have always been, and always will be, persecuted by the heathen, those people and nations who do not worship the LORD, the only true God (v.4). The persecution of God's people will continue, and even worsen, until the Lord Jesus Christ returns to finally conquer all of His enemies.

In this age, the Age of Grace, persecution is directed against the church. The first generation of believers is noted for the faithful martyrs who laid down their lives for the gospel. Today's world is no different: every day faithful followers of Christ are slain for their belief in and proclamation of the gospel. Godless governments and false religions terrorize believers. This too will worsen and reach its peak in the last days of human history (Re.6:9-11; 7:9-17). Pastor and commentator Donald M. Williams offers a great word of encouragement for the persecuted:

God lives with the righteous and provides refuge for the poor. Wherever ideological atheism has sought to extinguish the church, there has been an encounter with the God of the Cross. Jesus stands with His martyred church. Indeed, the blood of the saints is the seed of the church. In [various countries] today the church suffers but also prospers in her trials...God will triumph over blasphemers and vindicate His name.[3]

3 (53:6) God's great hope offered to His people.

The only hope for us—we who are oppressed by the sin nature (every single one of us) is salvation. God promised His salvation through the Messiah, and David spoke prophetically of the Messiah's coming. He wished for God's great promise to be fulfilled without delay.

a. Salvation: It will come out of Zion (the Jews), Jn.4:22 (v.6ᵃ).

From the very conception of the Hebrew nation, God promised that Israel would be redeemed by one of her own, a Jew. God promised Abraham, the father of Israel, that the Messiah would come from his seed (Ge.22:18). As Abraham's grandson Jacob lay dying, he prophesied that the Messiah would descend from the tribe of Judah (Ge.49:10). Later, the LORD promised David that the eternal King of Israel would come from his house and sit on his throne (2 S.7:12-16). The prophets declared that the Savior would come from and to Zion (Ps.2:6; Is.59:20; Mi.5:2; Zec.9:9). Along with the promises and the prophecies, the record of the Messiah's Jewish genealogy is provided by Matthew in his gospel (Mt.1:1-17).

b. Restoration: It will result in great blessing and rejoicing (v.6ᵇ).

David spoke prophetically of the coming of Christ and His deliverance of Israel from her enemies. He stated that the Messiah will bring great joy to Israel by restoring all that God promised her, all that has been lost because of Israel's unfaithfulness to the LORD. With God's completed revelation, we now know that this will occur at the Second Coming of Christ to earth. Commentator Willem A. VanGemeren describes it:

The psalmist anticipates an era when God will vindicate his people and deliver them from the fools who oppress and harass them. In Jesus' coming Jews and Gentiles are further assured of God's concern, vindication, and presence with his people. When the Jews are restored to faith in Jesus the Messiah, they will rejoice and all Christians will join with them in giving praise to God's faithfulness.[4]

Thought 1. With the coming of the Messiah, Jesus Christ, there is the national promise of salvation and restoration to Israel. But there is also the personal promise of salvation from sin—its penalty, power, and ultimately its presence—to all who have trusted in Christ. "The same Saviour who will transform Israel *nationally* then, can save men *individually* now. God has a Saviour for sinners."[5]

What, or who, is the hope for all sinners who have turned from God and are under His condemnation? Jesus, the friend of sinners, who came and died in our place. He who was without sin fully bore our sin and its awful penalty on Calvary's cross. In Him, we who are redeemed can rejoice and be glad!

> **She will give birth to a son, and you are to give him the name Jesus, because he will save his people from their sins"** (Mt.1:21).
>
> For, **"Everyone who calls on the name of the Lord will be saved"** (Ro.10:13).
>
> And so **all Israel will be saved, as it is written: "The deliverer will come from Zion; he will turn godlessness away from Jacob. And this is my covenant with them when I take away their sins"** (Ro.11:26-27).
>
> **And through your offspring all nations on earth will be blessed, because you have obeyed me"** (Ge.22:18).
>
> **"The Redeemer will come to Zion, to those in Jacob who repent of their sins,"** declares the LORD (Is.59:20).
>
> **Rejoice greatly, O Daughter of Zion! Shout, Daughter of Jerusalem! See, your king comes to you, righteous and having salvation, gentle and riding on a donkey, on a colt, the foal of a donkey** (Zec.9:9).

---

3 Donald Williams. *Psalms 1-72*, p.123.

4 Frank E. Gaebelein. *Expositor's Bible Commentary*, p.147.
5 John Phillips. *Exploring Psalms, Volume 1*. WORDsearch CROSS e-book.

	PSALM 54	3 Strangers are attacking me; ruthless men seek my life—men without regard for God. Selah	c. Cry out & tell God why you need help: Strangers—ruthless people who care nothing for God—are attacking you
	When the Situation is Urgent and You Need God's Immediate Help, 54:1-7	4 Surely God is my help; the Lord is the one who sustains me.	**2. Proclaim confidence in God**
			a. Trust Him because He is your helper & sustainer
	For the director of music. With stringed instruments. A maskil of David. When the Ziphites had gone to Saul and said, "Is not David hiding among us?"	5 Let evil recoil on those who slander me; in your faithfulness destroy them.	b. Trust Him because He is just: Ask Him to execute perfect justice—to vindicate you
		6 I will sacrifice a freewill offering to you; I will praise your name, O LORD, for it is good.	**3. Make a strong commitment to God**
1. Cry out for God's help			a. A commitment to worship & praise the LORD
a. Cry out for God to save you & to vindicate your cause	Save me, O God, by your name; vindicate me by your might.		b. A commitment to bear witness to God's power
b. Cry out for God to hear your prayer—to listen to the desperate plea of your heart	2 Hear my prayer, O God; listen to the words of my mouth.	7 For he has delivered me from all my troubles, and my eyes have looked in triumph on my foes.	1) His power to deliver you
			2) His power to give you victory

PSALM 54

When the Situation is Urgent and You Need God's Immediate Help, 54:1-7

(54:1-7) **Introduction:** throughout the centuries, millions of believers have been sustained by God's comforting promise that He works all things together for our good (Ro.8:28). While trudging through deep, dark valleys, however, we cannot always see *how* God is producing good from our devastating circumstances. It is usually at some point much further down the road—long after a painful trial has ended—that we are able to recognize the good work God did in our lives. We are then able to say with the psalmist, "It was good for me to be afflicted" (Ps.119:71).

One of the good works God performs through our trials is bringing us to a place of total dependence on Him. When all is well in our lives, we tend to become self-sufficient, forgetting how desperately we need the Lord. So, at times, it is good for us to reach a point of utter helplessness and total reliance on God. Nothing accomplishes this more effectively than some dire circumstance beyond our control.

Psalm 54 is one of many psalms born out of a situation so severe that only God could help. Possessed by irrational jealousy, King Saul sought David's life. For a period possibly as long as twelve years, the brave young champion of Israel stayed a step ahead of the crazed king. Shortly after Doeg had slain the priests at Nob (see Introduction—Psalm 52 for more discussion), David hid from Saul in the wilderness of Ziph. The Ziphites, like David, were from the tribe of Judah. Yet they betrayed David, informing Saul exactly where he was hiding (1 S.23:13-23; 26:1-5). Psalm 54 is David's urgent cry for God's help.

Like David, we all encounter circumstances where we need God to do what only God can do. During such times, we can turn to this *maschil* psalm for instruction about how to pray. This is, *When the Situation is Urgent and You Need God's Immediate Help*, 54:1-7.

1. Cry out for God's help (vv.1-3).
2. Proclaim confidence in God (vv.4-5).
3. Make a strong commitment to God (vv.6-7).

1 (54:1-3) **Cry out for God's help.**
With Saul and his men quickly approaching, David stood in grave danger. Before long, Saul's soldiers had completely surrounded David and his men and were about to overtake them (1 S.23:26). Knowing that he could not escape unless God intervened, David cried out to the LORD for help.

a. Cry out for God to save you and to vindicate your cause (v.1).
By asking God to *save* (yasha) him, David called on God to literally lift him out of the narrow place in which he was trapped and to set him free out in an open place. But David desired more than just his life: he longed to be cleared of all the charges Saul had levied against him. If he perished at the hand of Saul, Israel would conclude that David was guilty and that God's justice had been served on him. On the other hand, if the LORD delivered him from Saul, it would show Israel that God had judged David as innocent, and David would be vindicated in the sight of the nation.

David cried out for God to save him by His name and by His might. God's name represents all that He is, including His nature, His character, and His covenant (Ex.34:5-7). The LORD had chosen David to be king (1 S.16:12-13). By invoking God's name, David was calling upon Him to be faithful to His promise. *Might* (geburah) here pertains specifically to military might or valor (2 K.18:20; Is.36:5). Saul's army was mighty, but David believed that God was mightier; therefore, he called on the LORD to display His superior strength by overthrowing his foes.

b. Cry out for God to hear your prayer—to listen to the desperate plea of your heart (v.2).

David implored the LORD to hear and give ear to his prayer. This repetition emphasized how desperately David needed God's help. The words of his mouth conveyed the urgency of his heart. By asking God to *hear* (shama) his prayer, David was calling on God to hearken to his voice and to do what he requested.

c. Cry out and tell God why you need help: Strangers—ruthless people who care nothing for God—are attacking you (v.3).

David urgently needed God's help. He was under attack from violent men who totally disregarded God. These strangers and oppressors sought to destroy David. While this was unquestionably true of Saul and his men, David was referring in particular to the Ziphites who betrayed him to the ruthless king. *Strangers* (zarim) often refers to foreigners or Gentiles, but here it speaks of David's relatives who had alienated themselves from him. Excellent Bible teacher and commentator Warren Wiersbe explains:

> *"Strangers" (v. 3) doesn't suggest that [David's] enemies were Gentiles, for the Ziphites belonged to the tribe of Judah, David's own tribe. The word is used in Job 19:13 to describe Job's family and friends, and David used it in a similar way in 69:8. It can describe anybody who has turned his or her back on someone, which the Ziphites certainly did to David....*[1]

God had rejected Saul as king and ordained David to lead Israel (1 S.15:23-28). But the self-willed Ziphites rejected God's plan, stubbornly refusing to set God before them. Or, simply stated, they cared nothing for God and made no place for Him in their lives. Rebellious and brazen, they aligned themselves with those who opposed God's will by seeking to slay David.

Thought 1. From time to time, we too find ourselves trapped by circumstances beyond our control, such as...

- life-threatening illness or injury
- death of a loved one
- financial crisis
- loss of employment
- persecution
- unfaithfulness by a spouse
- divorce
- rebellion by children
- unresolvable conflict with others
- false accusations or slander
- betrayal by a friend
- depression
- anxiety
- fear

These and countless other challenging circumstances can bring us to a place of total despair and helplessness. During such times, we tend to think that we have no place to turn and that our situation is hopeless. But nothing could be further from the truth. God can do what nobody else can do. He is all-powerful, and He delights in showing Himself strong on our behalf. If He loves us so much that He gave His Son for us, why would He not help us when we need Him most (Ro.8:32)? He is faithful to His great name, and He is stronger than any foe we may face. We can always turn to Him with the confidence that He will hear us and help us in our hour of greatest need. This does not mean He will always *remove* the problem, but, at the very least, He will help us *through* the problem.

> **What, then, shall we say in response to this? If God is for us, who can be against us? He who did not spare his own Son, but gave him up for us all—how will he not also, along with him, graciously give us all things? (Ro.8:31-32).**
>
> **Now to him who is able to do immeasurably more than all we ask or imagine, according to his power that is at work within us (Ep.3:20).**
>
> **The Lord will rescue me from every evil attack and will bring me safely to his heavenly kingdom. To him be glory for ever and ever. Amen (2 Ti.4:18).**
>
> **This is the confidence we have in approaching God: that if we ask anything according to his will, he hears us. And if we know that he hears us—whatever we ask—we know that we have what we asked of him (1 Jn.5:14-15).**
>
> **I call to the LORD, who is worthy of praise, and I am saved from my enemies (2 S.22:4).**
>
> **I call on you, O God, for you will answer me; give ear to me and hear my prayer (Ps.17:6).**
>
> **"I am the LORD, the God of all mankind. Is anything too hard for me? (Je.32:27).**

2 (54:4-5) **Proclaim confidence in God.**

Having cried out to God for deliverance, David confessed his confidence in the LORD. He trusted God to come to his aid, so much so that he invited others to behold—to look, watch, and observe—what God would do.

a. Trust Him because He is your helper and sustainer (v.4).

With unwavering faith, David declared that his helper in this dire situation was *God* (Elohim), the all-powerful

---

[1] Warren W. Wiersbe. *The Bible Exposition Commentary.* WORD*search* CROSS e-book.

One. He "felt so thoroughly that his heart was on the Lord's side that he was sure God was on *his* side."[2] Further, David was the servant of the *Lord* (Adonai). His loving Master would not fail in His responsibility to care for His faithful servant.

David boldly declared that the LORD was with him and the men who upheld or sustained his life. A number of versions translate the Hebrew text less literally by simply stating, "The Lord is the sustainer of my life," or something similar. Commentator Derek Kidner presents an excellent case for the more literal translation of the KJV and NKJV:

> In [verse] 4b the ancient versions, followed by most modern ones, seem to have found the Hebrew text too startling, where it numbers God 'among' the upholders of my life. But this is not belittling him; it is seeing his hand behind the human help—the 'six hundred', the 'thirty', the 'three', of 1 Samuel 23:13 and 2 Samuel 23:8ff—whose faithfulness was David's support and delight.[3]

Bible teacher John Phillips agrees:

> It has puzzled some to think that God is just numbered as one of those who would bring help in time of need. What David is doing, of course, is acknowledging the help of human friends. He accounts for their help by the fact of the presence of God among them—God as Adonai—Sovereign Lord, the One who controls all things. God sometimes acts through our friends.[4]

We may appropriately assume that David originally offered this prayer in the presence of the loyal men who accompanied him into the wilderness of Ziph (1 S.23:26). Imagine how encouraged they would have been when David reminded them that God's presence was among them and that His boundless power would strengthen them to protect David's life.

> **But the Lord stood at my side and gave me strength, so that through me the message might be fully proclaimed and all the Gentiles might hear it. And I was delivered from the lion's mouth (2 Ti.4:17).**
>
> **I lie down and sleep; I wake again, because the LORD sustains me (Ps.3:5).**
>
> **So do not fear, for I am with you; do not be dismayed, for I am your God. I will strengthen you and help you; I will uphold you with my righteous right hand (Is.41:10).**

b. Trust Him because He is just: Ask Him to execute perfect justice—to vindicate you (v.5).

David's confidence in the Lord was rooted in his conviction that God would do the right thing. Deep in his heart, David knew he was innocent of any wrongdoing toward Saul. The unstable king's assault on his life was the fruit of the corrupt king's jealousy and stubborn resistance to God's will. With unshakeable faith in God's righteousness, David called on God to vindicate him by executing perfect justice on his enemies.

Thought 1. When we are going through particularly painful situations, we usually do not understand why God is allowing us to be tested or what good purpose our trials will serve. It is during such times of overwhelming trouble that we need to have confidence in the Lord. We need to trust that He knows what is best for us and that He will not fail us. It is during these times that we need to trust God with all our hearts and not lean on our own understanding (Pr.3:5). We need to commit ourselves to Him with unwavering confidence that He is working out His perfect plan for our lives. He knows what He is doing, and He has promised that He will complete the work He has begun in us (Ph.1:6). *God can be trusted*, and in our darkest hours, we can know with certainty that He will sustain us. He will always do what is right, and He will always do what is best for us.

> **And we know that in all things God works for the good of those who love him, who have been called according to his purpose (Ro.8:28).**
>
> **Being confident of this, that he who began a good work in you will carry it on to completion until the day of Christ Jesus (Ph.1:6).**
>
> **That is why I am suffering as I am. Yet I am not ashamed, because I know whom I have believed, and am convinced that he is able to guard what I have entrusted to him for that day (2 Ti.1:12).**
>
> **If any of you lacks wisdom, he should ask God, who gives generously to all without finding fault, and it will be given to him. But when he asks, he must believe and not doubt, because he who doubts is like a wave of the sea, blown and tossed by the wind. That man should not think he will receive anything from the Lord; he is a double-minded man, unstable in all he does (Js.1:5-8).**
>
> **Though he slay me, yet will I hope in him; I will surely defend my ways to his face (Jb.13:15).**
>
> **Trust in the LORD with all your heart and lean not on your own understanding (Pr.3:5).**

---

2 Charles Spurgeon. *Treasury of David*. WORD*search* CROSS e-book.
3 Derek Kidner. *Psalms 1-72*, p.216.
4 John Phillips. *Exploring Psalms, Volume 1*. WORD*search* CROSS e-book.

> For I know the plans I have for you," declares the LORD, "plans to prosper you and not to harm you, plans to give you hope and a future (Je.29:11).

3 (54:6-7) Make a strong commitment to God.

Believing that God would deliver him from his oppressors, David made a strong commitment to the LORD. His vow was not an attempt to bargain with God. Rather, it was the natural outflow of his grateful heart.

a. A commitment to worship and praise the LORD (v.6).
David promised to worship God by offering a voluntary sacrifice to Him. A *freewill offering* is a sacrifice that is not required by the LORD. Freewill offerings were marked by a stirred heart and a willing spirit to give something to God (Ex.35:21-29).[5] They were usually accompanied by a celebration of the victory or blessing from God that prompted the offering (De.12:6-7).

In calling for God's help, David appealed to God's holy name (v.1). This is significant, for this is the only place in this psalm where David referred to God by His covenant name, Yahweh or Jehovah. David would praise God because He is faithful to His covenant—a truth God would demonstrate by delivering David. God will never fail to fulfill His promises to any of us who enter into a relationship with Him.

b. A commitment to bear witness to God's power (v.7).
David also made a commitment to praise the LORD for His power in rescuing him from trouble. In a noble demonstration of faith, David spoke of God's deliverance from his enemies as if it were already done. Through eyes of faith, David saw himself standing in victory over his enemies.

Scripture records that God was indeed faithful to deliver David. Just when Saul and his men were about to attack, a messenger arrived and informed Saul that the Philistines had invaded the land. Saul immediately left to fight the Philistines (1 S.23:26-28).

What a jubilant celebration must have erupted among David and his men! Just when Saul had David surrounded, God distracted the evil king from his pursuit of the godly young man. From that day forward, David bore witness of God's power to deliver him and to give him victory over all enemies.

Thought 1. God's faithfulness should also motivate us to make strong commitments to the LORD. While the offering of animal sacrifices ceased after Jesus sacrificed his life on the cross, the New Testament speaks of spiritual sacrifices that we should offer freely to God (1 Pe.2:5). Among the sacrifices specifically mentioned are...

- praising God from a grateful heart (He.13:15)
- helping and sharing with others (He.13:16)
- living a holy life devoted to God's will (Ro.12:1-2)
- seeking to bring others to Christ through sharing the gospel (Ro.15:16)
- giving to the Lord's work (Ph.4:14)

God's great love for us, a love He demonstrated by offering up His own Son (Ro.5:8), should stir us to live every day in obedience and devotion to Him. But when God does something special for us—answers an urgent prayer, helps us in a difficult situation, grants healing or provision of a great need, blesses us in an unusual way—we ought to show our gratitude by doing something special for Him. This voluntary, spiritual sacrifice can take many forms, including those mentioned above. We may want to recommit our lives to serve the Lord. Or we may go out of our way—get out of our *comfort zone*—to help someone in need. Or we might be led to give a sacrificial gift over and above our regular tithes and offering to the Lord's work. In every case, though, we should offer the sacrifice of praise to the Lord, taking advantage of every opportunity to proclaim His goodness and power to others.

Our God is a loving Father who delights in blessing us, His dear children (Mt.7:11). When He does, our hearts should overflow with love and gratitude that stir us to do more for Him.

> **Therefore, I urge you, brothers, in view of God's mercy, to offer your bodies as living sacrifices, holy and pleasing to God—this is your spiritual act of worship. Do not conform any longer to the pattern of this world, but be transformed by the renewing of your mind. Then you will be able to test and approve what God's will is—his good, pleasing and perfect will (Ro.12:1-2).**
>
> **Yet it was good of you to share in my troubles (Ph.4:14).**
>
> **Through Jesus, therefore, let us continually offer to God a sacrifice of praise—the fruit of lips that confess his name. And do not forget to do good and to share with others, for with such sacrifices God is pleased (He.13:15-16).**
>
> **You also, like living stones, are being built into a spiritual house to be a holy priesthood, offering spiritual sacrifices acceptable to God through Jesus Christ (1 Pe.2:5).**
>
> **Let them sacrifice thank offerings and tell of his works with songs of joy (Ps.107:22).**
>
> **I will sacrifice a thank offering to you and call on the name of the LORD (Ps.116:17).**

---

5 Holman Bible Publishers. *Holman Bible Dictionary.* (Nashville, TN: B & H Publishing Group, 1991). WORD*search* CROSS e-book.

PSALM 55

When Enemies Threaten You & Close Friends Betray You, 55:1-23

For the director of music. With stringed instruments. A maskil of David.

1. Express your anguish to God
  a. Ask God not to ignore or abandon you
    1) Bc. you are deeply troubled & filled with despair
    2) Bc. your enemies abuse you
      • Shout threats at you
      • Stare you down
      • Oppress you
      • Curse you
      • Hate & revile you
    3) Bc. you are in agony, terrorized by threats of an early death
    4) Bc. fear & trembling have overtaken you, filling you with horror
  b. Tell God how you yearn to escape the situation
    1) To flee like a dove
    2) To flee far away to a desolate place
    3) To flee to a place of safety—far from the storm & the turbulence

2. Express your concern for justice
  a. Pray for God to confuse & frustrate the wicked
    1) Bc. they incite strife
    2) Bc. they prowl about day & night causing mischief (evil) & sorrow
    3) Bc. they are a destructive force in society (the city), lying to & threatening people
  b. Tell God about your close friend's treachery or betrayal

Listen to my prayer, O God, do not ignore my plea;
2 Hear me and answer me. My thoughts trouble me and I am distraught
3 At the voice of the enemy, at the stares of the wicked; for they bring down suffering upon me and revile me in their anger.
4 My heart is in anguish within me; the terrors of death assail me.
5 Fear and trembling have beset me; horror has overwhelmed me.
6 I said, "Oh, that I had the wings of a dove! I would fly away and be at rest—
7 I would flee far away and stay in the desert; Selah
8 I would hurry to my place of shelter, far from the tempest and storm."
9 Confuse the wicked, O Lord, confound their speech, for I see violence and strife in the city.
10 Day and night they prowl about on its walls; malice and abuse are within it.
11 Destructive forces are at work in the city; threats and lies never leave its streets.
12 If an enemy were insulting me, I could endure it; if a foe were raising himself against me, I could hide from him.
13 But it is you, a man like myself, my companion, my close friend,
14 With whom I once enjoyed sweet fellowship as we walked with the throng at the house of God.
15 Let death take my enemies by surprise; let them go down alive to the grave, for evil finds lodging among them.
16 But I call to God, and the LORD saves me.
17 Evening, morning and noon I cry out in distress, and he hears my voice.
18 He ransoms me unharmed from the battle waged against me, even though many oppose me.
19 God, who is enthroned forever, will hear them and afflict them—Selah men who never change their ways and have no fear of God.
20 My companion attacks his friends; he violates his covenant.
21 His speech is smooth as butter, yet war is in his heart; his words are more soothing than oil, yet they are drawn swords.
22 Cast your cares on the LORD and he will sustain you; he will never let the righteous fall.
23 But you, O God, will bring down the wicked into the pit of corruption; bloodthirsty and deceitful men will not live out half their days. But as for me, I trust in you.

    1) That you could bear an enemy's insults & oppression
    2) That it is far more difficult to grasp & cope with a close friend's betrayal
      • Bc. of your former fellowship
      • Bc. of the former spiritual union & worship together
  c. Ask God to swiftly execute justice on your enemies
    1) To seize & send them to hell
    2) Bc. they allowed evil to lodge or stay within them

3. Express your confidence in God
  a. Confidence that God saves you
    1) He hears your cry of distress all throughout the day
    2) He delivers (ransoms) you & gives you peace—even when many oppose you
  b. Confidence that God rules forever & is the great Judge: He will humble those who oppose you
    1) Bc. they refuse to repent & do not fear God
    2) Bc. your friend has shamefully betrayed his friends & broken his promise
      • His heart is evil, full of strife, division, & war
      • His words are smooth & charming, but deceptive
  c. Confidence that God will sustain you—if you cast your burdens on Him
    1) He will never let you fall
    2) He will execute justice upon the wicked: Send them into the pit of destruction (hell)

PSALM 55

When Enemies Threaten You and Close Friends Betray You, 55:1-23

(55:1-23) **Introduction:** one of the most traumatizing experiences in life is that of being betrayed by a friend. The pain pierces to the bone. The wound is deep and slow to heal. Betrayal is often referred to as a "stab in the back," because treacherous friends usually strike when we do not see it coming.

David wrote Psalm 55 in response to his own betrayal by a close friend. Scripture does not identify the specific occasion, but many scholars have concluded that the setting was when David's son, Absalom, revolted against him while he was king (2 S.15-18). Ahithophel was David's chief counsellor and trusted friend. Sensing Israel's increased support of the king's rebellious son, Ahithophel switched his allegiance from David to Absalom (2 S.15:12).

Being betrayed by a friend can inflame our emotions like few other experiences. As we read through Psalm 55, we witness the breadth of David's distraught emotions, among them...

- turmoil and despair (v.2)
- pain and anguish (vv.3-4)
- fear (vv.4-5)
- anger (vv.9-15)
- the desire to escape (vv.6-8)
- grief (vv.12-14)

With all these turbulent emotions raging within him, David poured out his heart to God. And as he cast his burden on the LORD (v.22), a sense of trust and peace conquered his troubled spirit (vv.16-23).

Prayer made the difference. It didn't change David's circumstances—Absalom was still attacking him and Ahithophel had still betrayed him—but it changed David.

Psalm 55 is an *imprecatory* psalm, that is, one in which the author prays for the destruction of his enemies (see KEYS TO UNDERSTANDING *PSALMS* for more discussion). It is also a *maskil* (instructive) psalm, reaffirming two of the book's most powerful lessons: first, we have the precious liberty to pour out our hearts to the LORD, to tell Him whatever we are feeling. Second, prayer empowers us to face every trouble and trial of life. It also foreshadows Judas' betrayal of Jesus, reminding us that our Savior experienced every excruciating trial that we face. He knows the stinging pain of betrayal, and He can sustain us when our friends turn against us (He.2:16-18; 4:14-16). This is, *When Enemies Threaten You and Close Friends Betray You,* 55:1-23.

1. Express your anguish to God (vv.1-8).
2. Express your concern for justice (vv.9-15).
3. Express your confidence in God (vv.16-23).

1 (55:1-8) **Express your anguish to God.**
David's wounded heart throbbed with anguish and despair. His son was trying to destroy him and much of his nation had turned against him. Now his dear friend, turned traitor, had joined their ranks. The painful turmoil in his spirit was more than he could bear, and he could no longer contain it. In desperate need of comfort and help, David released his anguish to God.

a. Ask God not to ignore or abandon you (vv.1-5).
David had cried out to God from the moment Absalom began his revolt, but nothing had changed. From David's perspective, God was not listening to his prayers. Frustrated and fearful, he begged God not to ignore or abandon him. In his desperate attempt to get God's attention, David used every Hebrew word he could think of to appeal to God to...

- *listen* (azan) or give ear to his prayer (v.1ª)
- not *ignore* (alam) his supplication or plea for favor (v.1ᵇ)
- *hear* (qashab) him, give him His full attention and do what he requested (v.2ª)
- *answer* (ana) him, give him a response or reply (v.2ᵇ)

David pled with God to notice how deeply troubled he was, saying that he constantly paced the floor mourning in his complaint, deep in thought about his dilemma. To *trouble* (rude) means to cause restlessness. He was so distraught, so consumed with despair, that he could not suppress his grief.

Abuse from his enemies worsened David's pain (v.3). Their oppression or harassment included shouting vile threats at him, staring him down, and cursing him. Absalom's supporters viciously hated David and thought nothing of expressing their wrath toward him, even though he was their king.

David confessed that his heart was in severe agony because of this unbearable situation (v.4ª). *In anguish* (chuwl) literally means twisting or whirling in circles. It speaks of writhing in pain. David was saying that he was completely "torn up on the inside, or tied in knots, figuratively speaking."[1] His enemies' wrath was so fierce that he feared for his life (v.4ᵇ). He was *overwhelmed* (kasa)—covered by or clothed in—fearfulness, trembling, and horror (v.5).

b. Tell God how you yearn to escape the situation (vv.6-8).
Drowning in his anguish and fear, David longed to escape his desperate situation. He wished for wings like a dove so he could fly *away* and find rest, escape his unbearable trouble (v.6). In his younger days, when Saul pursued him, he had been able to find refuge in the wilderness or desert. Once again, he yearned to flee to a desolate place far from Jerusalem, a place of safety where he could find shelter from the uncontrollable storm and tempest that had cruelly swept in upon him (vv.7-8).

Note the *selah* at the end of verse 7. David paused for a moment to think about how wonderful it would be to run away from it all, far from civilization and from his responsibility as king, and far from the fickle, hateful people who sought to destroy him.

Thought 1. In times of severe trial, we should not try to repress our emotions. In fact, we should never allow the pressure of troubling circumstances to continually build up inside us. There are several reasons for this, not the least of which is that it is very unhealthy for us physically and emotionally. Instead we should immediately seek the LORD's face. We should pour out our hearts to God.

Perhaps the greatest lesson of *Psalms* is that we have the liberty to do just that: to pour out our troubled hearts at God's throne. In our times of deepest despair, when we are overwhelmed with fear, dread, or anguish, God is there for us. He will listen when we cry out to Him. He will not ignore or abandon us. He cares so much for us that He gave us His Son. Because of Christ's sacrifice, we have the freedom to come boldly into His presence to find grace for help in our time of need (He.4:14-16).

"Have we trials and temptations? Is there trouble anywhere?...Are we weak and heavy laden, cumbered

---

1 Steven Lawson and Max Anders. *Holman Old Testament Commentary—Psalms.* WORD*search* CROSS e-book.

with a load of care?...Do thy friends despise, forsake thee? Take it to the Lord in prayer."[2]

> **"Come to me, all you who are weary and burdened, and I will give you rest (Mt.11:28).**
>
> **"Now my heart is troubled, and what shall I say? 'Father, save me from this hour'? No, it was for this very reason I came to this hour (Jn.12:27).**
>
> **Therefore, since we have a great high priest who has gone through the heavens, Jesus the Son of God, let us hold firmly to the faith we profess. For we do not have a high priest who is unable to sympathize with our weaknesses, but we have one who has been tempted in every way, just as we are—yet was without sin. Let us then approach the throne of grace with confidence, so that we may receive mercy and find grace to help us in our time of need (He.4:14-16).**
>
> **Cast all your anxiety on him because he cares for you (1 Pe.5:7).**
>
> **Hear my cry, O God; listen to my prayer. From the ends of the earth I call to you, I call as my heart grows faint; lead me to the rock that is higher than I. For you have been my refuge, a strong tower against the foe (Ps.61:1-3).**

Thought 2. Like many of us when we face troubling circumstances, David had a strong desire to escape. Excellent commentator James Montgomery Boice gives some helpful insights when facing such difficult times:

> *We have not seen anything like this before in David's psalms. He has been fearful before. But always he has seemed ready to confront the evil boldly. Nowhere before has he expressed a wish to escape his trouble, to fly away and be at rest. Yet here he does.*
>
> *What is happening? Why do we find this new element? We have here the weariness that comes to a valiant warrior or worker late in life or at least after the passing of youthful battles and triumphs. When we are young we do not expect life to be easy, and if we are energetic we tackle problems with optimism and with our full strength. We achieve certain victories too. But as life goes on we find that the problems we thought we had overcome earlier are still around. The company we work for is still in trouble. Our taxes are still high. The murder and felony rates have not declined. Our children continue to cause trouble. In addition, we are getting older and therefore have*

less energy to cope with problems. We find ourselves thinking how nice it would be merely to fly away and escape them.

...But it is not always possible to escape our problems—David did not have "the wings of a dove"—and God does not always give us leave to leave either, especially if the problems we face involve continuing responsibilities on our part.

At this point the psalm becomes a lesson to us in steady perseverance, particularly perseverance in middle or late age. Perseverance is one of the virtues God looks for in his children.[3]

We will always have to battle the temptation to flee from out problems instead of addressing them. For many of us, the desire to escape begins in childhood, when we express the desire to run away from home. As we grow older and make our own decisions, its influence is more powerful. Consider the following examples:

➢ Students who drop out of school when things get tough.

➢ Spouses who choose divorce to escape difficult marriages.

➢ Spouses or parents who grow weary of their responsibilities and desert their families.

➢ People who jump from job to job when they get restless.

➢ Pastors or ministers who forsake God's call for an easier vocation.

➢ Church members who move from church to church when they become dissatisfied.

➢ Most tragic of all, people who are so overwhelmed by their problems that they choose to take their own lives.

God has not called us to *escape* but to *endure*. When we lean on Him in prayer and saturate ourselves in His empowering Word, we will find the grace and strength to persevere through difficult situations. As Bible teacher Warren Wiersbe said, "We don't need wings like a dove so we can fly away from the storm. We need wings like an eagle so we can fly *above* the storm (Isa.40:30-31)."[4]

> **Let us not become weary in doing good, for at the proper time we will reap a harvest if we do not give up (Ga.6:9).**
>
> **Endure hardship with us like a good soldier of Christ Jesus (2 Ti.2:3).**
>
> **Therefore, since we are surrounded by such a great cloud of witnesses, let us throw off everything that hinders and the sin that so easily entangles, and let us run with perseverance the race marked**

---

2 Joseph M. Scriven. *What a Friend We Have in Jesus,* 1855.

3 James Montgomery Boice. *An Expositional Commentary–Psalms, Volume 2: Psalms 42-106.* WORD*search* CROSS e-book.

4 Warren W. Wiersbe. *The Bible Exposition Commentary.* WORD*search* CROSS e-book.

out for us. Let us fix our eyes on Jesus, the author and perfecter of our faith, who for the joy set before him endured the cross, scorning its shame, and sat down at the right hand of the throne of God. Consider him who endured such opposition from sinful men, so that you will not grow weary and lose heart (He.12:1-3).

In the LORD I take refuge. How then can you say to me: "Flee like a bird to your mountain (Ps.11:1).

2 (55:9-15) **Express your concern for justice.**
Suddenly, David's mood changed, and his righteous anger at his enemies erupted. In addition to their treachery against him, Absalom and Ahithophel were wreaking havoc throughout Jerusalem. David prayed against their efforts and called upon God to bring them to justice.

a. Pray for God to confuse and frustrate the wicked (vv.9-11).
David asked God to rain down confusion on his foes and to prevent their wicked plans from being accomplished (v.9a). *Confound their speech* is a reference to the action God took to thwart the prideful efforts of the builders trying to construct the Tower of Babel (Ge.11:1-9). David prayed that God would take similar action to keep his enemies from succeeding.

If God did not intervene to stop Absalom and Ahithophel, they would destroy the nation. They constantly stirred up violence and strife, prowling about Jerusalem day and night in their evil efforts (vv.9b-10). *Malice* (awven) describes their activities as evil, sinful, and worthless. *Abuse* (amal) is also translated as trouble and sorrow. It refers to causing trouble and creating hardships for others.[5] The men were a destructive force in the city, using lies and dangerous threats to coerce the people into supporting them.

b. Tell God about your close friend's treachery or betrayal (vv.12-14).
As David expressed his indignation to God, his deep grief over his friend's betrayal surfaced. David unleashed the hurt in his heart, conveying how much easier it would have been to stand against an enemy's insults and oppression than a close friend's (v.12). Being betrayed by his trusted advisor—and praying for God to judge him—was more than David could bear. He poured out his pain to the LORD as if he were speaking directly to Ahithophel, addressing his betrayer as his equal, companion, and acquaintance (v.13). The Hebrew word for *companion* (alluph) indicates that they were the closest of companions, the

best of friends (Pr.16:28). *Close friend* (yada) stresses how personally they had come to know each other through the experiences they had shared. Having sought God's will together, David and Ahithophel had also developed a spiritual bond. They had also enjoyed sweet fellowship as they joined their spirits in worshipping God with the congregation of Israel (v.14).

c. Ask God to swiftly execute justice on your enemies (v.15).
David's responsibilities as king prevailed over his aching heart for both his son and his trusted friend. Fulfilling his duty to his nation, he called upon God to swiftly execute justice on those who had made themselves his and Israel's enemies by revolting against God's anointed king. He prayed for death to seize them, to come suddenly and unexpectedly upon them. By praying for them to go down *alive* into *the grave* or *hell* (sheol), David requested that they would immediately go to the place of the dead, as opposed to living out all of their natural days or living to an old age.[6] This statement is a reference to God's judgment on Korah, Dathan, and Abiram, who rose up against Moses in the wilderness (Nu.16:28-33). Like Moses' opponents, David's foes deserved to die prematurely for allowing evil to dwell within them.

Thought 1. Because we are made in God's image, we become angry over the deeds of evildoers and desire to see them brought to justice. However, we must be careful not to allow our anger to cause us to sin (Ep.4:26). Furthermore, we should never take justice into our own hands, nor should we seek vengeance on those who do evil against us (Ro.12:19). When a crime has been committed, we are to turn to civil authorities for justice, as God has delegated this responsibility to them (Ro.13:1-6). Ultimately, we have to trust the Lord to do right in all things, and we need to wait patiently for Him to act in His good time.

We should also remember that Christ has commanded us to live by a higher law: we are to love our enemies, pray for them, and do good for them (Mt.5:44; Lu.6:35). In so doing, we will be imitating our Heavenly Father, and He will richly reward us.

But I tell you: Love your enemies and pray for those who persecute you (Mt.5:44).

But love your enemies, do good to them, and lend to them without expecting to get anything back. Then your reward will be great, and you will be sons of the Most High, because he is kind to the ungrateful and wicked (Lu.6:35).

---

5 Spiros Zodhiates. *AMG Complete Word Study Dictionary*. WORD-search CROSS e-book.

6 Donald Williams. *Psalms 1-72*, p.409.

God "will give to each person according to what he has done" (Ro.2:6).

Do not take revenge, my friends, but leave room for God's wrath, for it is written: "It is mine to avenge; I will repay," says the Lord (Ro.12:19).

Far be it from you to do such a thing—to kill the righteous with the wicked, treating the righteous and the wicked alike. Far be it from you! Will not the Judge of all the earth do right?" (Ge.18:25).

Therefore disaster will overtake him in an instant; he will suddenly be destroyed—without remedy (Pr.6:15).

3 (55:16-23) Express your confidence in God.

Instead of continuing to fret and to fear what his enemies might do to him, David declared that he would call on God. As he prayed, God assured him that He would protect him from the evildoers. David expressed his confidence in God, that He would save and sustain him and deal justly with his foes.

a. Confidence that God saves you (vv.16-18).

David firmly believed that God would deliver him from his enemies (v.16). His heart was so burdened that he called upon God in the evening, in the morning, and at noon—all throughout the day (v.17). He prayed with the confidence that God heard his cries of distress and would answer his prayers. *Hears* (shama) means more than just listening with the ear. It means to hearken, heed, or act in response to what has been said.

As David prayed, he gained assurance that God was at work in his situation (v.18). As a result, the unexplainable peace of God swept over his soul (Ph.4:6-7). In fact, he used a Hebrew perfect verb to express his deliverance from his many enemies, as if it had already been done.[7]

b. Confidence that God rules forever and is the great Judge: He will humble those who oppose you (vv.19-21).

Continuing to speak in faith, David declared that God rules eternally as the great Judge of the earth, and He will always do what is right (v.19). God would hear the lies and the devious plans of David's enemies, and He would justly respond by afflicting or humiliating them. They would, beyond all question, suffer God's judgment—all because they refused to repent and continued to reject Him.

Once again, David emphasized the treachery of his trusted friend. Ahithophel had betrayed David without cause, callously breaking his promise (covenant) of friendship and loyalty (v.20). David recalled the things his two-faced companion had said to him (v.21). His smooth, soft words were flattering and reassuring, but they were deceptive. They masked his evil heart, a heart full of strife and division, set on making war against God's anointed king.

c. Confidence that God will sustain you—if you cast your burdens on Him (vv.22-23).

David concluded with a word of counsel to all who would read this psalm: when you are in deep distress, *cast your cares on the LORD, and He will sustain you* (v.22a). David had learned this valuable lesson through his experience. When he began his prayer, he was carrying the full weight of his trouble on his own shoulders. When he gave it to God, God granted him glorious peace and confidence. Whereas David had previously feared for his life (vv.4-5), he was now sure that God would never let him fall and that God would execute justice against the wicked. In faith, he declared that his bloodthirsty, lying enemies would go to an early grave (vv.22b-23).

David's trust in God was well-placed, and his enemies tragically reaped the corruption they had sown. As Scripture records, God prevented Ahithophel's evil plans from succeeding, and the disgraced advisor took his own life (2 S.17:1-23). God's justice also came upon the king's rebellious son. As Absalom rode in battle against David's men, he was caught and slain when his heavy and flowing hair became entangled in the branches of an oak tree (2 S.18:9-15). He suffered a bizarre and gruesome death.

Thought 1. If we are wise, we will heed David's advice to cast our burdens on the LORD. Interestingly, the Hebrew word for *cast* (shalak) is also used of breaking the chains or ropes that hold a person captive. When we choose to bear our own burdens, they become chains that keep us in bondage to fear, dread, and worry. But when we give our burdens to the LORD, we are set free to live in the realm of peace and faith.

God does not want us to carry the unbearable load of our afflictions. Again and again in Scripture, He invites us to throw them off and allow Him to bear them for us. But we have to trust God enough to commit our trouble to Him. When we fully trust God with our problems, our fears and anxiety will wondrously vanish, and the precious peace of God will reign in their place. Like David, we will be filled with confidence in God and will experience His sustaining and victorious power (2 Co.4:13-14).

"Come to me, all you who are weary and burdened, and I will give you rest. Take my yoke upon you and learn from me, for I am gentle and humble in heart,

---

7 The Hebrew perfect verb conjugation expresses a completed action.

and you will find rest for your souls (Mt.11:28-29).

Do not be anxious about anything, but in everything, by prayer and petition, with thanksgiving, present your requests to God. And the peace of God, which transcends all understanding, will guard your hearts and your minds in Christ Jesus (Ph.4:6-7).

Cast all your anxiety on him because he cares for you (1 Pe.5:7).

And call upon me in the day of trouble; I will deliver you, and you will honor me" (Ps.50:15).

He will call upon me, and I will answer him; I will be with him in trouble, I will deliver him and honor him (Ps.91:15).

PSALM 56

When Unwise Decisions or Actions Create Troubles for You, 56:1-13

For the director of music. To [the tune of] "A Dove on Distant Oaks." Of David. A miktam—When the Philistines had seized him in Gath.

Be merciful to me, O God, for men hotly pursue me; all day long they press their attack.
2 My slanderers pursue me all day long; many are attacking me in their pride.
3 When I am afraid, I will trust in you.
4 In God, whose word I praise, in God I trust; I will not be afraid. What can mortal man do to me?
5 All day long they twist my words; they are always plotting to harm me.
6 They conspire, they lurk, they watch my steps, eager to take my life.
7 On no account let them escape; in your anger, O God, bring down the nations.
8 Record my lament; list my tears on your scroll—are they not in your record?
9 Then my enemies will turn back when I call for help. By this I will know that God is for me.
10 In God, whose word I praise, in the LORD, whose word I praise—
11 In God I trust; I will not be afraid. What can man do to me?
12 I am under vows to you, O God; I will present my thank offerings to you.
13 For you have delivered me from death and my feet from stumbling, that I may walk before God in the light of life.

Outline:

1. **Pour out your heart to God: Cry out for His mercy**
   a. Cry out bc. people harass, slander, & boldly attack you all day long
   b. Cry out bc. people strike fear in you; still, you trust in God
      1) You praise & trust in His Word, His promises
      2) You trust bc. you know that your enemies are mortal
   c. Cry out bc. people twist your words & plot against you
      1) They spy on you
      2) They watch your every step
      3) They seek to destroy you

2. **Ask God to execute justice**
   a. The requests made
      1) That God not let them escape—that He destroy them
      2) That God take your sorrow & tears & keep them ever before Him—record them in His book (scroll)
   b. The confidence expressed
      1) Your enemies will turn back
      2) Your faith will be proven bc. God is on your side

3. **Praise God & give thanks to Him**
   a. Your reaffirmation
      1) You praise His Word (promises)
      2) You trust in Him: You do not fear those who oppose you
      3) You renew your commitments (vows) to God & give thanks to Him
   b. Your reasons for praising Him
      1) He has delivered you
      2) He has kept you from falling
      3) He has given you the light (fullness, wisdom) of life

PSALM 56

When Unwise Decisions or Actions Create Trouble for You, 56:1-13

(56:1-13) Introduction: devastating circumstances can fall on all of us. Consider the major disasters that fell on God's servant Job. Standing before God, he made a statement that, tragically, describes our time on this earth all too well:

"Man born of woman is of few days and full of trouble" (Jb.14:1).

Many of our hardships are the result of *trouble finding us*, as was true with Job. He was the most upright man on earth, yet he suffered soul-crushing losses, losses he did nothing to cause.

At times, however, we encounter affliction because *we find trouble*. To state it plainly, many of our problems are of our own making. This was the case with David when he wrote Psalm 56.

David was in the throes of a perilous situation. Although David was innocent of any wrongdoing toward Israel's king, Saul was viciously seeking his life. However, an unwise decision made David's bad situation even worse. Desperate to escape the murderous Saul, he foolishly fled to Gath, home of Goliath. As if that were not bad enough, he was carrying the sword of the monstrous giant whom he had recently slain!

At first glance, we might wonder what possessed David to do such an ill-advised thing; but he did have a plan in mind:

➢ David thought Saul would never suspect him of fleeing to Gath, a major city of Philistia.
➢ The Philistines were Israel's sworn enemy.
➢ Saul had declared David to be his enemy.
➢ Because he and the Philistines were both Saul's enemies, David hoped that Achish, king of Gath, would embrace him as an ally.

Sadly, David's logic was seriously flawed, and his plan backfired. Achish's advisors were convinced that David was a threat to the Philistines. Suddenly, David was in grave danger (1 S.21:10-12). As the heading to Psalm 56 states, he was captured by the Philistines in Gath. "It is not expressly stated in 1 Samuel that the Philistines forcibly detained him, but the words 'feigned himself mad *in their hands,*' [v.13] together with the mention of his *escape* in ch. 22, seem to imply that he was practically a prisoner."[1]

Under the intense pressure of a threatening situation, David made an unwise decision that placed his life in even greater peril. Psalm 56 is one of two psalms (along with Psalm 34) that were born from this predicament. He prefaced this psalm with the phrase *jonath-elem-rechokim.* Most commentators understand this term to be the name of a song to the tune of which Psalm 56 was to be performed. It is translated as "the silent dove in far

---

1 A.F. Kirkpatrick. *The Book of Psalms.* WORDsearch CROSS e-book.

away places," or "the silent dove on distant oaks," or something similar. Classic commentator Matthew Poole offered a different perspective:

> *Jonath-elem-reehokim is supposed to be the name of a song; but many render it, as the words signify, concerning the dumb dove afar off; all which agrees very well to David in his present circumstances. He calls himself a dove for his innocency, and folly (which is ascribed to the dove, Ho.7:11) in casting himself into this snare.[2]*

In our lives, we will face frightening, sometimes dangerous, situations. We will also encounter painful hardships that leave us feeling helpless and hopeless. Such crises can be draining, filling us with a wide range of emotions from anguish and anxiety to depression and sheer terror. Along with the emotional stress, extreme adversity can cause headaches, heart attacks, high blood pressure, ulcers, and other physical infirmities.

Like David, we might also make some foolish decisions that result in our situation becoming worse instead of better. Thankfully, our Divine Helper, the Holy Spirit, has given us Psalm 56 for just such times. This psalm is so important that David designated it as one of six *miktam* psalms—meditations worthy of remembrance. Bible teacher John Phillips explained: "The word 'miktam' literally means 'to cut' or 'to engrave.' The thought is that this is a permanent writing, that it partakes of the nature of Job's great cry, 'Oh that my words were written with an iron pen and graven in the rock forever.'"[3] As human beings who are prone to create trouble for ourselves, we should engrave it on our own hearts. This is, *When Unwise Decisions or Actions Create Trouble for You, 56:1-13.*

1. Pour out your heart to God: Cry out for His mercy (vv.1-6).
2. Ask God to execute justice (vv.7-9).
3. Praise God and give thanks to Him (vv.10-13).

1 (56:1-6) **Pour out your heart to God: Cry out for His mercy.**

Trouble upon trouble moved David to beg God for mercy. To *be merciful* (chanan) means to bend down to help someone who cannot help himself. It speaks of "an action from a superior to an inferior who has no claim for gracious treatment."[4] Realizing he had gotten himself into this predicament, David cried out for God's mercy and help.

---

2 Matthew Poole. *Matthew Poole's Commentary on the Holy Bible.* Peabody, MA: Hendrickson Publishers, 1985. WORDsearch CROSS e-book.

3 John Phillips. *Exploring Psalms, Volume 1.* WORDsearch CROSS e-book.

4 R. Laird Harris, ed. *Theological Wordbook of the Old Testament.* WORDsearch CROSS e-book.

a. Cry out because people harass, slander, and boldly attack you all day long (vv.1-2).

Saul and his men were relentless in their attacks on David despite his total innocence. Every day, they harassed, slandered, and sought to devour him (Jb.5:15; Is.42:14). David twice mentioned their daily attacks, emphasizing that they never let up in their efforts and he was never able to rest due to their pursuit.

David was also likely referring to the Philistine officials who were misrepresenting him to Achish. Their accusations against him to Gath's king were false. David was there only to find safety from Saul. He intended no harm to Achish or Gath.

Scholars differ in their translation of *in their pride* (marowm, v.2), which literally means height, elevated place, or exaltedness. Some translators, like those of the KJV, understand it as referring to God. *Others*, including the NIV translators, see it as referring to the arrogance of David's enemies in rising up against him. Regardless which translation is accurate, both descriptions are true.

b. Cry out because people strike fear in you; still, you trust in God (vv.3-4).

David had unwisely placed himself in a situation that intensified his fear: not only was Saul seeking his life, but Achish and the officials of Gath were also considering what to do with him. David confronted his fear with unwavering trust in the LORD and by praising the LORD for the reliability of His Word. Years earlier, God had chosen and secretly anointed David to be Israel's future king (see outline and notes—1 S.16:3-13 for more discussion). Now, David was buoyed by the confidence that God would fulfill that which He had promised. Secure in God's sovereign plan for his life, David determined that he would not fear what *mortal man* (basar) could do to him. No human being could overrule God's purpose for his life (Ps.11:6; He.13:6).

c. Cry out because people twist your words and plot against you (vv.5-6).

David's enemies were doing everything possible to destroy him and to thwart God's will for him. They twisted his words and plotted against him (v.5). They constantly spied on him, watching his every step as they waited for the opportunity to take his life (v.6).

Thought 1. When we are facing the difficult consequences of our unwise actions or decisions, we need to turn to the Lord for help. When we cry out to Him, He will hear us and help us, comfort us and lift us up. Because God is gracious and merciful, He delights in assisting us when we least deserve His help.

Consider this: our greatest and most fundamental problem—sin—is of our own making. We sin because we foolishly choose to do so. But think about the great lengths God went to in order to rescue us from our sin. He loves us so much that He gave His Son to save us. As Paul reasoned, *"He who did not spare his own Son, but gave him up for us all—how will he not also, along with him, graciously give us all things?"* (Ro.8:32). If God cared about us enough to sacrifice His only Son, surely He will not withhold His help from us when we cry out to Him. He invites us to boldly request His grace and mercy (He.4:16). He is available when no one else will help us. And He can do what no one else can do. We should never hesitate to call upon Him.

> **The one who calls you is faithful and he will do it (1 Th.5:24).**
>
> **But the Lord is faithful, and he will strengthen and protect you from the evil one (2 Th.3:3).**
>
> **If we are faithless, he will remain faithful, for he cannot disown himself (2 Ti.2:13).**
>
> **Let us then approach the throne of grace with confidence, so that we may receive mercy and find grace to help us in our time of need (He.4:16).**
>
> **Let us hold unswervingly to the hope we profess, for he who promised is faithful (He.10:23).**
>
> **Know therefore that the LORD your God is God; he is the faithful God, keeping his covenant of love to a thousand generations of those who love him and keep his commands (De.7:9).**

Thought 2. Fear is one of the most powerful emotions we face, and it causes people to react in different ways. Fear compels some people to run away or hide. It completely paralyzes others. Still others are provoked to fight when they are afraid.

The Scriptural response to fear, however, is faith. When overcome with fear, we should confess as David confessed, *"In God I trust"* (v.4). God is greater than any force that threatens us. For that reason, we need to confront fear with unwavering faith in the promises of God's Word.

> **What, then, shall we say in response to this? If God is for us, who can be against us?... Who shall separate us from the love of Christ? Shall trouble or hardship or persecution or famine or nakedness or danger or sword? As it is written: "For your sake we face death all day long; we are considered as sheep to be slaughtered." No, in all these things we are more than conquerors through him who loved us. For I am convinced that neither death nor life, neither angels nor de-**
> **mons, neither the present nor the future, nor any powers, neither height nor depth, nor anything else in all creation, will be able to separate us from the love of God that is in Christ Jesus our Lord (Ro.8:31,35-39).**
>
> **Peace I leave with you; my peace I give you. I do not give to you as the world gives. Do not let your hearts be troubled and do not be afraid (Jn.14:27).**
>
> **For God did not give us a spirit of timidity, but a spirit of power, of love and of self-discipline (2 Ti.1:7).**
>
> **So we say with confidence, "The Lord is my helper; I will not be afraid. What can man do to me?" (He.13:6).**

2 (56:7-9) **Ask God to execute justice.**
Having cried out to God for mercy, David now asked the LORD to deal with his enemies. The crimes of Saul and his men against David were serious. In a desperate attempt to escape their relentless pursuit of him, David had unintentionally placed himself in additional danger by fleeing to the nation of Philistia, the archenemy of Israel. Frustrated and exhausted from his stressful ordeal, David called on God to remember his sorrows and to bring his enemies to justice.

a. The requests made (vv.7-8).
The innocent young man made two requests of the LORD. First, David prayed that God would not let his enemies get by with their evil deeds (v.7). Because their iniquity was so great, they should not escape God's judgment. David boldly called on God to kindle His righteous anger against the people who were seeking his life and cast them down or destroy them.

Second, David asked God to keep his sorrow and tears ever before Him, to record them in His book (v.8). To *record* (saphar) means to count or number (Ge.15:5; 1 Ch.21:2; Ps.48:12). David noted that God had kept track of his wanderings while being exiled from home due to Saul's unjust persecution. Israel's wicked king had brought great sorrow to David's life, causing him to shed many, many tears. David asked God to save every single one of those tears as a testimony of the pain Saul had caused him and to keep a record of David's sorrows in His *book.* [5]

b. The confidence expressed (v.9).
David firmly believed that God would heed his desperate cries and come to his aid. He expressed confidence that God would turn his enemies back and that his own faith in God would be proven. Because he was

---

5 Some commentators think *put my tears into thy bottle* is a reference to an ancient custom of collecting tears of grief into a small bottle and placing it at the tomb of one being mourned.

absolutely innocent of wrongdoing toward Saul, he knew that God was on his side.

Thought 1. When others sin against us or hurt us deeply, we can be comforted by the knowledge that God sees our pain and keeps a record of our sorrows. The image of God collecting our tears in a bottle is a precious one to His hurting people (v.8).

A number of God's servants who read this commentary will be facing severe persecution for their faith in Jesus Christ. Others will be dealing with slander or false accusations. Some will be forsaken by friends or rejected by family due to their faith. Some will have endured imprisonment, the loss of employment, or worse for their stand for Christ. Still others will be mourning loved ones who laid down their lives for our Lord. Welsh commentator Matthew Henry (1662-1714) has excellent thoughts on these verses that should soothe the souls of God's hurting people:

> God has a bottle and a book for his people's tears, both those for their sins and those for their afflictions. This intimates,
>
> (1.) That he observes them with compassion and tender concern; he is afflicted in their afflictions, and knows their souls in adversity. As the blood of his saints, and their deaths, are precious in the sight of the Lord, so are their tears, not one of them shall fall to the ground. I have seen thy tears, 2 Kings 20:5. I have heard Ephraim bemoaning himself, Jeremiah 31:18.
>
> (2.) That he will remember them and review them, as we do the accounts we have booked. Paul was mindful of Timothy's tears (2 Timothy 1:4), and God will not forget the sorrows of his people. The tears of God's persecuted people are bottled up and sealed among God's treasures; and, when these books come to be opened, they will be found vials of wrath, which will be poured out upon their persecutors, whom God will surely reckon with for all the tears they have forced from his people's eyes; and they will be breasts of consolation to God's mourners, whose sackcloth will be turned into garments of praise. God will comfort his people according to the time wherein he has afflicted them, and give to those to reap in joy who sowed in tears. What was sown a tear will come up a pearl.[6]

When Jesus saw her weeping, and the Jews who had come along with her also weeping, he was deeply moved in spirit and troubled (Jn.11:33).

Then one of the elders asked me, "These in white robes—who are they, and where did they come from?" I an- swered, **"Sir, you know." And he said, "These are they who have come out of the great tribulation; they have washed their robes and made them white in the blood of the Lamb. Therefore, "they are before the throne of God and serve him day and night in his temple; and he who sits on the throne will spread his tent over them. Never again will they hunger; never again will they thirst. The sun will not beat upon them, nor any scorching heat. For the Lamb at the center of the throne will be their shepherd; he will lead them to springs of living water. And God will wipe away every tear from their eyes." (Re.7:13-17).**

He will wipe every tear from their eyes. There will be no more death or mourning or crying or pain, for the old order of things has passed away" (Re.21:4).

Those who sow in tears will reap with songs of joy. He who goes out weeping, carrying seed to sow, will return with songs of joy, carrying sheaves with him (Ps.126:5-6).

Surely he took up our infirmities and carried our sorrows, yet we considered him stricken by God, smitten by him, and afflicted (Is.53:4).

3 (56:10-13) **Praise God and give thanks to Him.** David concluded this psalm by praising and offering thanks to God for His faithfulness. David's faith had conquered his fears, and he rested in the assurance that God would save him from the imminent danger he faced. Scripture records how God delivered David from the life-threatening situation he had placed himself in at Gath: After David feigned insanity, Achish actually released him (1 S.21:13-22:15)!

a. Your reaffirmation (vv.10-12).
David reaffirmed his faith in God's Word by repeating the declaration of trust he had spoken earlier (vv.4, 10-11). He praised God's promises because they were trustworthy and reliable (Mt.24:35; He.6:18; 2 Pe.1:4). Over and over again, God had proven Himself true to His Word. Note that David addressed God here as the LORD (Yahweh, Jehovah)—the only time in this psalm—to emphasize God's faithfulness to His covenant and His people. Because David trusted in the LORD, he again declared that he was not afraid of those who opposed him.

As David praised God for His faithfulness to His Word, he reaffirmed his vows to God (v.12). *Present* (shalam) is the word used of paying a debt or obligation. David had promised to offer sacrifices to the

---

6 Matthew Henry. *Matthew Henry's Commentary on the Whole Bible.* WORD*search* CROSS e-book.

LORD for rescuing him from his enemies. Thus, he now pledged to fulfill all of these promises as soon as God delivered him.

b. Your reasons for praising Him (v.13).

David was so confident that God would help him that he spoke of his rescue as if it had already taken place. In a demonstration of unwavering faith, he praised God in advance for delivering him from his enemies and keeping him from falling at the hands of his foes. He further praised the LORD for allowing him to continue to walk before Him in the light of the living. "The words, *before God*...point to the difference between the righteous, who make God the great aim of their life, and the wicked, who wander from the right path and turn their back upon God."7 *Light of life* speaks generally of life as contrasted to death, which is characterized by darkness. But it may also refer to the fullness of life that comes from walking according to God's wisdom. David failed to walk wisely when he sought refuge in Gath, but he determined to follow the light of God's leadership in future decisions.

Thought 1. Note three final lessons from this psalm:

➢ Genuine faith is so certain about God's faithfulness that it rejoices *before* He acts. It considers something done although it has not yet been done. Truly, faith is "being sure of what we hope for and certain of what we do not see" (He.11:1).

➢ When we desperately need God's help, we often make vows or commitments to Him. We must be careful to fulfill these promises. Scripture warns us about the seriousness of not following through on promises made to God. It is better not to make a vow at all than not to pay or follow through with what we have vowed (Ec.5:4-6). Such commitments should never be made as an attempt to secure God's assistance. Rather, they should be the expression of our gratitude to Him for His great mercy and grace.

➢ God is faithful to us even when we act foolishly or make unwise decisions. In Psalm 34, David plainly stated that it was the LORD who delivered him from this life-threatening crisis (2 Co.1:10; 2 Ti.4:18). When we walk in the wisdom of God's Word and the leadership of His Spirit, we can avoid the painful consequences of foolish decisions (Ps.119:105; Ro.8:14; Ga.5:16, 25; Ep.5:8, 15, 17). But even when we fail to follow the LORD, He is still faithful to us, and He keeps His promise to help us (1 Co.10:13; 2 Ti.2:13).

> **Always giving thanks to God the Father for everything, in the name of our Lord Jesus Christ (Ep.5:20).**
>
> **Devote yourselves to prayer, being watchful and thankful (Col.4:2).**
>
> **He says, "I will declare your name to my brothers; in the presence of the congregation I will sing your praises" (He.2:12).**
>
> **Through Jesus, therefore, let us continually offer to God a sacrifice of praise—the fruit of lips that confess his name (He.13:15).**
>
> **The LORD is my strength and my shield; my heart trusts in him, and I am helped. My heart leaps for joy and I will give thanks to him in song (Ps.28:7).**
>
> **That my heart may sing to you and not be silent. O LORD my God, I will give you thanks forever (Ps.30:12).**

---

7 John Calvin. *Calvin's Commentaries.* WORD*search* CROSS e-book.

PSALM 57

When You Need Shelter from Life's Threats & Dangers, 57:1-11

For the director of music. (To the tune of) "Do Not Destory." Of David. A miktam. When he had fled from Saul into the cave.

1. Seek God's protection
a. Cry out for God's mercy
b. Take refuge in the shadow of God's wings, under His protective outreach

2. Declare your trust in God
a. He is God Most High
b. He will fulfill His purpose for you
c. He will send help from heaven to save you
  1) Save you from all enemies
  2) Save you by sending His love & faithfulness
  3) Save you from the vicious, those who threaten & endanger you

  4) Save you by exalting Himself & manifesting His glory over all the earth
  5) Save you from the traps your enemies set & from the deep distress you suffer: He causes your enemies to fall into their own trap

3. Be steadfast & worship God faithfully
a. Arise early to worship the LORD

b. Be a strong witness among all the people & nations of the earth
  1) Bc. of God's great love
  2) Bc. of God's faithfulness

c. Exalt the LORD above the heavens (creation): Ask Him to shine forth His glory over all the earth

Have mercy on me, O God, have mercy on me, for in you my soul takes refuge. I will take refuge in the shadow of your wings until the disaster has passed.
2 I cry out to God Most High, to God, who fulfills [his purpose] for me.
3 He sends from heaven and saves me, rebuking those who hotly pursue me; Selah God sends his love and his faithfulness.
4 I am in the midst of lions; I lie among ravenous beasts—men whose teeth are spears and arrows, whose tongues are sharp swords.
5 Be exalted, O God, above the heavens; let your glory be over all the earth.
6 They spread a net for my feet—I was bowed down in distress. They dug a pit in my path—but they have fallen into it themselves. Selah
7 My heart is steadfast, O God, my heart is steadfast; I will sing and make music.
8 Awake, my soul! Awake, harp and lyre! I will awaken the dawn.
9 I will praise you, O Lord, among the nations; I will sing of you among the peoples.
10 For great is your love, reaching to the heavens; your faithfulness reaches to the skies.
11 Be exalted, O God, above the heavens; let your glory be over all the earth.

PSALM 57

When You Need Shelter from Life's Dangers and Threats, 57:1-11

(57:1-11) Introduction: without question, life on earth is filled with dangers, and our natural instinct is to shelter or protect ourselves from these threats. Few modern events have impacted the world like the United States' dropping atomic bombs on Japan in August, 1945. It was the initiation of a new age in human destruction; the threat of nuclear war struck unparalleled fear in people's hearts worldwide. In response, many people built bomb shelters that they hoped would protect them if nuclear war broke out.

In addition to the horrors of war, the destructive forces of nature regularly threaten people's safety throughout the world. There is not a spot on earth that is completely safe from the possibility of some uncontrollable, catastrophic event. Hurricanes, tornados, typhoons, tsunamis, drought, intense heat, volcanic eruptions—these are just a few of the natural disasters that endanger people. In many places, people build underground shelters or have a designated place to flee if a calamity does strike.

Along with the perils of warfare and natural disasters, we face a host of other threats, not the least of which is evil, dangerous people. When David wrote Psalm 57, King Saul was hunting him down like a common animal, seeking to take his life. For a period of seven to twelve years, David was forced to hide from the deranged king. Scripture records two specific episodes when David found shelter in caves: at Adullam (1 S.22:1) and Engedi

(1 S.24:1-ff.). As the heading to Psalm 57 informs us, it was written during one of these occasions.

Psalms 57–59 include an instruction not previously seen in *Psalms*: *do not destroy*. We do not know for certain how this term should be applied to these psalms, but scholars have several opinions. Some believe it is the title of a tune to which these psalms were to be performed. This is a strong possibility, considering that Asaph also used the term in Psalm 75. Others believe it summarized David's prayer, asking God not to allow Saul to destroy him. Several commentators think that along with *miktam* (see Introduction—Psalm 56 for more discussion), it was an additional instruction to carefully preserve these psalms. A few speculate that it is a memorial to David's command to his servants in the cave at Engedi not to destroy Saul (1 S.24:3-7).

Whatever the meaning of these words, they do not distract from the clear objective of Psalm 57. This psalm is a song about shelter from life's dangers and threats. As God's beloved children—people for whom He has a plan and a purpose—we are safe in Him. Because nothing on this earth can protect us like God's great love and faithfulness, we should hide in Him. This is, *When You Need Shelter from Life's Dangers and Threats*, 57:1-11.

1. Seek God's protection (v.1).
2. Declare your trust in God (vv.2-6).
3. Be steadfast and worship God faithfully (vv.7-11).

1 (57:1) Seek God's protection.

"There is only a step between me and death" (1 S.20:3). David was not exaggerating the seriousness of his situation when he made this dramatic statement to Saul's son Jonathan. Jonathan was also David's closest friend. Destroying David had become Saul's first priority, and David knew that Israel's jealous king would not rest until he had succeeded. Desperate for his life, David sought God's protection from his powerful enemy.

a. Cry out for God's mercy (v.1ᵃ).

As in the previous psalm, David began by crying out to God for *mercy* (chanan, see outline and notes—Ps.56:1 for more discussion). His need was great, as Saul was pursuing him relentlessly (v.3). He knew he could not escape the raging king on his own, so he called on God to stoop down in mercy to help him.

b. Take refuge in the shadow of God's wings, under His protective outreach (v.1ᵇ).

While hiding from Saul in the cave, David recognized a glorious truth: the LORD was his true refuge. *Take refuge* (chasah) means to flee to for protection or to trust in. Imagine David resting in this safe haven—either at Adullam or Engedi—and meditating on his situation. As he gazed on the dome of rock that enclosed him, he saw himself covered by something far stronger: he was safe in the shadow of God's sheltering wings. A wave of sweet peace swept over his troubled spirit as God assured David that He would protect him until these calamities had passed.

Thought 1. What a precious image for us in the opening verse of this fifty-seventh psalm! David compares God to a mother bird that hides her young under her wings to protect them from storms, birds of prey, or any other danger.

Many commentators have noted that Psalm 57 carries a different tone from David's previous psalms written while he was a fugitive from Saul.

> *The earlier psalms were mostly uncertain, fearful, even desperate. Psalm 57 is settled, and its prevailing note is praise. What makes the difference? In the earlier psalms David was hiding from his enemies, in Gath or in the wilderness of the Ziphites. Here he is hiding in God.* [1]

The realization of this soothing truth—that we are safe under God's sheltering wings—transformed David's cry for mercy to a song of praise. We too can find peace and comfort in trouble when we engrave this image on our hearts.

Consider some of the hazards and threats people face today, things such as...

- disease
- danger associated with travel
- hurricanes, tornados, and other weather catastrophes
- criminal acts
- fires or floods caused by nature or negligence
- violence and abuse
- oppressive governments
- terrorist acts

God does not want us living in fear of these or any other threats or dangers (2 Ti.1:7). Like David, we need to take refuge in the LORD, fully trusting Him to protect us and to carry out His will in our lives. We need to learn to rest in God—to practice being in His presence—and not to worry about the threats or dangers posed by nature or evildoers (Ps.37:7). We have no control over those things, but God does.

> *Under His wings, oh, what precious enjoyment!*
> *There will I hide till life's trials are o'er;*
> *Sheltered, protected, no evil can harm me,*
> *Resting in Jesus, I'm safe evermore.* [2]

> **"O Jerusalem, Jerusalem, you who kill the prophets and stone those sent to you, how often I have longed to gather your children together, as a hen gathers her chicks under her wings, but you were not willing (Mt.23:37).**
>
> **But the Lord is faithful, and he will strengthen and protect you from the evil one (2 Th.3:3).**
>
> **Who through faith are shielded by God's power until the coming of the salvation that is ready to be revealed in the last time (1 Pe.1:5).**
>
> **Like an eagle that stirs up its nest and hovers over its young, that spreads its wings to catch them and carries them on its pinions. The LORD alone led him; no foreign god was with him (De.32:11-12).**
>
> **May the LORD repay you for what you have done. May you be richly rewarded by the LORD, the God of Israel, under whose wings you have come to take refuge" (Ru.2:12).**
>
> **Keep me as the apple of your eye; hide me in the shadow of your wings (Ps.17:8).**
>
> **He will cover you with his feathers, and under his wings you will find refuge; his faithfulness will be your shield and rampart (Ps.91:4).**

---

[1] James Montgomery Boice. *An Expositional Commentary–Psalms, Volume 2: Psalms 42-106.* WORDsearch CROSS e-book.

[2] William O. Cushing. *Under His Wings*, 1896.

2 (57:2-6) **Declare your trust in God.**
Resting in the peace of God's protection, David gave a strong testimony: he was placing his total trust in God. What he knew about God convinced him that God cared for him and would not let him down. God is faithful, and He would fulfill His purpose for David and all His people.

a. He is God Most High (v.2ᵃ).
David's unwavering trust was rooted in his understanding that God's very name is *God Most High* (Elohim Elyon). This great name emphasizes the LORD's power and authority. *Elohim* is the All-Powerful One, the One who can do anything and everything. It is the name of God used in Creation. *Elyon* is the Supreme One, the Sovereign God who is above all others. Scripture teaches that, as the Most High, JEHOVAH is "over all the earth" (Ps.83:18). The first mention of *Elyon* in Scripture is in Abram's encounter with Melchizedek (Ge.14:18-20). In identifying God as the Most High, the mysterious king of Salem declared that He is the "creator of heaven and earth" (Ge.14:19).

b. He will fulfill His purpose for you (v.2ᵇ).
Excellent commentator Derek Kidner noted that the "two titles for God in this verse show the enrichment which can be given to a prayer by the way in which it addresses God."[3] The Divine name *God Most High* means that God is supreme and cannot be overruled or overpowered. Therefore, God's purpose for David's life would be fulfilled. *Fulfill* (gamar) means to complete or finish, to perfect, to bring to an end. It refers to "how the Lord finishes or accomplishes in the life of his saints all that he undertakes."[4] David believed that God would deliver him from Saul because God had anointed David to be Israel's king, and God would see to it that His purpose was carried out (Ps.138:8; Ro.8:28; Ph.1:6).

c. He will send help from heaven to save you (vv.3-6).
From His throne in heaven where He rules over all the earth, God would hear David's cry and send help to save him from his enemies (v.3ᵃ). Send from heaven implies that David expected God to do something miraculous to save him. Some commentators think it refers to God's sending angel armies to fight against Saul and his men.

David's confidence in God to deliver him rested on his knowledge that God is always true to Himself—His divine character and attributes (2 Ti.2:13). Therefore, God would send forth his love and his faithfulness (v.3ᵇ). *Love* (chesed) is God's unfailing, covenant love (see outline and notes—Ps.5:7 for more discussion). *Faithfulness* (emeth) speaks of God's dependability,

and trustworthiness. God's faithfulness gives us unshakable faith in Him: we can be absolutely certain of what He will do.

David described Saul and his men as hungry lions that were set on fire—burning with an unquenchable appetite to devour him (v.4). But because of God's unfailing love and trustworthiness, David was sure that God would save him from these vicious men who threatened his life.

David was concerned not only for his own welfare but also for God's glory (v.5). Saul's determination to kill David was an arrogant attack on God's will for His chosen nation. God had ordained David to be Israel's king, and Saul was attempting to overrule God's plan. By saving David from Saul, God would be exalted and His glory would be manifest over all the earth. His supreme authority as God Most High would be established, and the earth would witness His righteous judgment of Israel's rebellious king.

Having considered God's supremacy, faithfulness, and glory, David regarded his enemies as already defeated (v.6). He described Saul as a hunter who had set a net and dug a pit to trap him. In addition, Saul had inflicted indescribable pain on David, causing his soul to be bowed down. David firmly believed that God would save him from Saul's traps. God would set him free from his deep distress by causing his enemies to fall into their own traps. David was so sure of it that he spoke of his foes' defeat as if it were already done. This is signified by the use of *have fallen*, a Hebrew perfect verb, indicating an action that has already been completed.

Thought 1. What David knew about God empowered him to rest in His care. Our faith in God is not blind faith. God has revealed Himself to us in His names and in His Word (2 Ti.1:12). When we are threatened or endangered, we need to recall what we know about God:

➤ He is God Most High. He is all-powerful and has all authority.
➤ He *will* accomplish His purpose for our lives.
➤ He is aware of every detail of our lives, and He will help us when we cry out to Him.

Like David, our ultimate concern should be to bring honor and glory to God's name. Consider Paul: while he awaited execution in a Roman prison, he stated that his foremost priority was that Christ be magnified, whether by his life or by his death (Ph.1:20). Whatever our circumstances, God will be glorified before the world when we proclaim our total trust in Him and rest in His care.

If that is how God clothes the grass of the field, which is here today and tomorrow is thrown into the fire, will he

---

3 Derek Kidner. *Psalms 1-72*, p.223.
4 R. Laird Harris, ed. *Theological Wordbook of the Old Testament.* WORD*search* CROSS e-book.

not much more clothe you, O you of little faith? So do not worry, saying, 'What shall we eat?' or 'What shall we drink?' or 'What shall we wear?' For the pagans run after all these things, and your heavenly Father knows that you need them. But seek first his kingdom and his righteousness, and all these things will be given to you as well (Mt.6:30-33).

Without weakening in his faith, he faced the fact that his body was as good as dead—since he was about a hundred years old—and that Sarah's womb was also dead. Yet he did not waver through unbelief regarding the promise of God, but was strengthened in his faith and gave glory to God (Ro.4:19-20).

That is why I am suffering as I am. Yet I am not ashamed, because I know whom I have believed, and am convinced that he is able to guard what I have entrusted to him for that day (2 Ti.1:12).

Commit your way to the LORD; trust in him and he will do this (Ps.37:5).

The LORD will fulfill [his purpose] for me; your love, O LORD, endures forever—do not abandon the works of your hands (Ps.138:8).

Trust in the LORD with all your heart and lean not on your own understanding; in all your ways acknowledge him, and he will make your paths straight (Pr.3:5-6).

3 (57:7-11) **Be steadfast and worship God faithfully.** Taking hold of God's power and faithfulness brought security to David's heavy spirit. He exuberantly proclaimed that his heart was fixed or steadfast. He then repeated the statement to emphasize his commitment to trust God. He chose to no longer live in fear of Saul. Rather, he committed himself to worship God faithfully by singing and giving praise or making music to Him. *Make music* (zamar) speaks of praising God through playing an instrument. In spite of his pressing trouble, David determined to glorify God for His unfailing love and faithfulness.

a. Arise early to worship the LORD (v.8).
David was ready to worship. He poetically called upon his glory and his instruments to offer their praise to the LORD. Some believe glory refers to David's soul or heart, as in Ps.16:9. However, a better explanation is that David is referring to his outstanding musical abilities, which had brought great honor to his life. The command to awake implies that his voice and his instruments had been asleep—he had not been singing God's praise in recent days. But he would no longer let

his circumstances silence his song. He would arise early to worship the LORD, so early that he would wake up the dawn instead of the dawn awaking him.[5]

b. Be a strong witness among all the people and nations of the earth (vv.9-10).
David declared that he would sing God's praises throughout the earth. He would not limit his praise to the congregation of Israel: he wanted to be a strong witness to all people and nations. He wanted everyone to know of God's great love (mercy) and His faithfulness (truth) (v.3). *Nations* (am) and *people* (le'om) are synonyms that speak of various people groups, whether families, tribes, communities, countries, or the entire human race (v.9).

David wanted every human being of every nation, tribe, and tongue to know that God's unfailing love and faithfulness cannot be contained by the boundaries of this planet. They overflow into the heavens and the clouds (v.10).

c. Exalt the LORD above the heavens (creation): Ask Him to shine forth His glory over all the earth (v.11).
David concluded this triumphant song by repeating his heart's desire for God to be glorified in all things (v.5). David prayed for God to be exalted above the entire universe and for His glory to shine forth over the entire earth. God's glory is manifest in many ways; but it is in His unfailing love and faithfulness—as emphasized in Psalm 57—that it is most brilliantly displayed.

Thought 1. Dangerous and difficult circumstances provide an unparalleled opportunity to worship and glorify God. We need to overcome our tendency to doubt and complain by being steadfast in our faith. We should praise God at all times. When danger threatens or trouble surrounds us, we should always display a spirit of faith and trust in the LORD (2 Co.4:8.14).

Praise is always powerful, but it is never more powerful than when it is offered by a suffering believer. Like Paul and Silas in prison, we should sing praises to God in the midnight hour (Ac.16:25). There is no stronger witness of God's great love and faithfulness than a believer who worships Him in the midst of severe trials.

About midnight Paul and Silas were praying and singing hymns to God, and the other prisoners were listening to them (Ac.16:25).

---

5 Warren W. Wiersbe. *The Bible Exposition Commentary.* WORDsearch CROSS e-book.

So that the Gentiles may glorify God for his mercy, as it is written: "Therefore I will praise you among the Gentiles; I will sing hymns to your name" (Ro.15:9).

It is written: "I believed; therefore I have spoken." With that same spirit of faith we also believe and therefore speak, because we know that the one who raised the Lord Jesus from the dead will also raise us with Jesus and present us with you in his presence (2 Co.4:13-14).

Speak to one another with psalms, hymns and spiritual songs. Sing and make music in your heart to the Lord, always giving thanks to God the Father for everything, in the name of our Lord Jesus Christ (Ep.5:19-20).

He will have no fear of bad news; his heart is steadfast, trusting in the LORD (Ps.112:7).

PSALM 58

When Leaders or Authorities Are Unjust & Corrupt, 58:1-11

For the director of music. [To the tune of] "Do Not Destroy." Of David. A miktam.

1. Be aware of their perversion

a. They pervert righteousness, justice
  1) They speak & rule unjustly
  2) They devise wickedness in their hearts: Cause unjust & violent behavior on earth

b. They are perverted by nature
  1) They stray from what is right
  2) They lie, deceive, & twist the rules for self
  3) Their leadership is poisonous—like a snake's venom: Blocks outside influence
  4) They refuse to listen to & follow the most skillful charmer (a picture of the

Do you rulers indeed speak justly? Do you judge uprightly among men?
2 No, in your heart you devise injustice, and your hands mete out violence on the earth.
3 Even from birth the wicked go astray; from the womb they are wayward and speak lies.
4 Their venom is like the venom of a snake, like that of a cobra that has stopped its ears,
5 That will not heed the tune of the charmer, however skillful the enchanter

may be.
6 Break the teeth in their mouths, O God; tear out, O LORD, the fangs of the lions!
7 Let them vanish like water that flows away; when they draw the bow, let their arrows be blunted.
8 Like a slug melting away as it moves along, like a stillborn child, may they not see the sun.
9 Before your pots can feel [the heat of] the thorns—whether they be green or dry—the wicked will be swept away.
10 The righteous will be glad when they are avenged, when they bathe their feet in the blood of the wicked.
11 Then men will say, "Surely the righteous still are rewarded; surely there is a God who judges the earth."

LORD & His instructions)

2. Pray for justice

a. Ask God to stop the unjust
  1) To break their power to oppress & consume people
  2) To remove the unjust & cause them to vanish
  3) To make their weapons useless
    • Like a snail melts away into slime
    • Like a stillborn child who never sees the sun

b. Express confidence in God
  1) That He will carry out swift & absolute justice
  2) That He will sweep away the wicked

3. Know that you—the righteous—will be vindicated & rewarded

a. God will avenge the unjust & corrupt: He will give you the ultimate victory

b. God will reward you for your loyalty, 1 Co.15:58; Js.1:12

c. God will be acknowledged as the judge of all the earth

PSALM 58

When Leaders or Authorities Are Unjust and Corrupt, 58:1-11

(58:1-11) Introduction: *"Power tends to corrupt and absolute power corrupts absolutely."* History testifies to the truth of this statement by English historian, politician, and writer Lord John Acton (1834-1902). While many leaders are fair, honest, and honorable, corrupt officials can be found at every level of government across the face of the earth.

This was certainly true of Israel during David's youth. Israel was led by King Saul, a rebellious, self-willed ruler. David became a victim of Saul's injustices after stepping up to face Goliath, the monstrous Philistine champion. After falsely accusing David of crimes against Israel, the jealous king set out to take his life. As a result, the valiant young warrior was forced to flee his homeland. For a period of seven to twelve years, David was a fugitive, forced to continually maneuver to stay a step ahead of the ruthless king and his army. The men who supported David were also treated unjustly.

David most likely wrote Psalm 58 during his years as a fugitive from Saul. Some commentators think he read or quoted the psalm when he removed the unjust judges of Saul's corrupt administration. He would have done so upon ascending to the throne of Israel. It is an *imprecatory* psalm, with David praying for God's absolute judgment to fall on the evildoers (See KEYS TO UNDERSTANDING PSALMS for more discussion).

Like David, we all long for a perfect, righteous government. But because of our sinful human nature, even

our best efforts to govern justly fall short. Psalm 58 leaves us sighing for the future era when Jesus Christ will rule the earth in perfect righteousness. Until that glorious day, this psalm assures all who are persecuted by ungodly leaders that God will avenge their suffering and judge their oppressors (Ps.76:12; Is.24:21; 40:23; Je.13:18). This is, *When Leaders or Authorities Are Unjust and Corrupt*, 58:1-11.

1. Be aware of their perversion (vv.1-5).
2. Pray for justice (vv.6-9).
3. Know that you—the righteous—will be vindicated and rewarded (vv.10-11).

1 (58:1-5) **Be aware of their perversion.**
David was well aware that Israel's unrighteous rulers were guilty of gross miscarriages of justice. He boldly rebuked them, identifying their unjust deeds and their defiled, sinful nature.

a. They pervert righteousness, justice (vv.1-2).
David fearlessly confronted the ungodly leaders about their perversion of righteousness and justice. He abruptly asked them if they spoke and ruled justly (v.1). To *speak justly* means to declare and uphold God's law.[1] To *judge uprightly* means to be just and fair.

---

1 Donald Williams. *Psalms 1-72*, p.426.

117

Obviously, the implied answer to David's accusing questions is, "No."

David forcefully stated that the officials' perverted judgments and wicked works were the poisonous fruit of their corrupt hearts (Je.17:9). As a result, violence filled the earth because they did not rule justly and in accordance with God's law.

b. They are perverted by nature (vv.3-5).

The hearts of the wicked rulers were corrupted by their sin nature (v.3). Like every human being, they were sinners from the womb, straying from righteousness as soon as they were born (Ps.51:5). Lying came as naturally to them as breathing, and they purposely deceived the people. Even worse, they twisted the laws to accommodate their sin and to accomplish their unrighteous purposes.

David compared them to venomous snakes. They spread their deadly poison with every untruthful word they spoke and every unjust decision they made (v.4). "Like the cobra that has stopped its ears" refers to their arrogant refusal to listen to correction or counsel from others. They had blocked their ears against all outside influences. "That will not heed the tune of the charmer" further expresses their self-willed defiance, specifically referring to their rejection of the LORD and His instructions (v.5).

Thought 1. Government officials have solemn responsibilities, holy duties delegated to them by God Himself. Whether or not leaders know or acknowledge it, God requires much of those who occupy positions of leadership (Ps.2:10-11; 2 S.23:3; Le.19:15; De.1:16; Ro.13:1-4). However, in every segment of society, injustices exist. Ungodly people lead cities, states, nations, businesses, schools, various organizations, and even churches. Most of us, at some point in time, have been victims of injustice, some far more serious than others.

Just as David cried out against Israel's corrupt officials, so we should oppose evildoers whenever and wherever possible. God has commanded us to resist wickedness and to do all we can to stop it. We should always take a stand against evil (Ep.6:13). Likewise, we need to be aware of oppression and do all that we can to rescue victims of unfair and cruel treatment.

Scripture is clear: God will judge us if we ignore the needs of those who are mistreated. But if we stand up for them and attempt to help them, God will bless us (Pr.24:11-12; 28:27).

> **Stop judging by mere appearances, and make a right judgment" (Jn.7:24).**
>
> **Therefore put on the full armor of God, so that when the day of evil comes, you may be able to stand your ground, and after you have done everything, to stand (Ep.6:13).**

> **Defend the cause of the weak and fatherless; maintain the rights of the poor and oppressed (Ps.82:3).**
>
> **He who gives to the poor will lack nothing, but he who closes his eyes to them receives many curses (Pr.28:27).**

2 (58:6-10) Pray for justice.

The only way for justice to be restored to the land was for God to remove Israel's corrupt officials. As commentator Arno C. Gaebelein concluded, "They refuse to listen to divine admonition, they refuse to be controlled by the Spirit of God and there is therefore nothing left but judgment."[2] To that end, David proceeded to call on God to judge them swiftly and completely.

a. Ask God to stop the unjust (vv.6-8).

David prayed and asked God to forcefully stop Israel's wicked leaders, to stop them from continuing their evil injustices. Comparing them to vicious, bloodthirsty lions, he called on God to break their teeth, break their power to oppress and devour the people (v.6). *Waters* that melt away and run continually are referring to water that evaporates or is absorbed into the ground and disappears (v.7ᵃ). In other words, David was asking God to remove the unjust rulers by causing them to vanish. He asked God to make their weapons useless, like arrows that have been *blunted*—literally, cut short; having their tips cut off, leaving them dull. Using two additional graphic comparisons, David asked the LORD to make them like a...

- snail that melts away into slime (v.8ᵃ)
- a stillborn or miscarried baby that never sees the sun (v.8ᵇ)

b. Express confidence in God (v.9).

David knew that God would deal with Israel's unjust judges. Therefore, he expressed his confidence that God would carry out swift and absolute justice, completely sweeping them away. "Before your pots can feel the thorns" describes a cooking pot being carried away in a storm before the heat from the fire beneath it even warms the pot. The Hebrew text here is unclear, so translations of some details of this verse vary among Bible versions. The point of the verse, however, is crystal clear: God will suddenly and thoroughly judge the corrupt officials. He will completely rob them of their power and influence.

Thought 1. In many situations, people are powerless to fight the injustices they face in life. For instance, most employees need their jobs to survive, which means they have to be very careful about speaking out against unfair treatment at work. When a legal resolution is available, the individuals usually cannot afford

---

2 Arno Gabelein. *The Book of Psalms*, p.237.

the costs involved. And many times the costs go far beyond the legal to the point that people fear speaking out at all. In many nations and societies, citizens do not have the freedom to oppose corrupt governments. Where they do, most people can do little to truly bring about change.

When we are helpless to correct the wrongs we encounter, we can pray. Scripture actually commands us to pray for those in authority. Our first prayer for corrupt officials should be for their salvation. Christ died for them and it is God's will for them to repent and be saved (1 Ti.2:1-4). At the same time, we always need to remember that those who persecute and treat others unfairly are a reproach to the LORD (Pr.14:31; 22:22-23).

We should never forget how much God loves the oppressed and cares about them. We not only have a duty to intercede for the abused, but we should also be compelled to call on God to deliver them and to remove the wicked rulers who mistreat them.

Prayer is powerful and effective (Js.5:16). We must never underestimate its importance. While we should persistently ask God to judge evildoers, we need to keep in mind that He will deal with them in His own time and way. Of this we can be confident!

> "Then they will go away to eternal punishment, but the righteous to eternal life" (Mt.25:46).
>
> "Do not be amazed at this, for a time is coming when all who are in their graves will hear his voice and come out—those who have done good will rise to live, and those who have done evil will rise to be condemned (Jn.5:28-29).
>
> To judge everyone, and to convict all the ungodly of all the ungodly acts they have done in the ungodly way, and of all the harsh words ungodly sinners have spoken against him." (Jude 15).
>
> The nations were angry; and your wrath has come. The time has come for judging the dead, and for rewarding your servants the prophets and your saints and those who reverence your name, both small and great—and for destroying those who destroy the earth" (Re.11:18).
>
> And I saw the dead, great and small, standing before the throne, and books were opened. Another book was opened, which is the book of life. The dead were judged according to what they had done as recorded in the books (Re.20:12).
>
> In that day the LORD will punish the powers in the heavens above and the kings on the earth below (Is.24:21).

3 (58:10-11) **Know that you—the righteous—will be vindicated and rewarded.**
David encouraged the righteous who were suffering at the hands of the wicked officials. He reminded them of the day of God's judgment. He promised that they will rejoice when the LORD avenges them of the corrupt crimes committed against them (v.10). "They bathe their feet in the blood of the wicked" compares the vindicated righteous to a victorious army walking through a battlefield after the war. As they march off, their feet become stained with the blood of their defeated foes. In addition, God will reward the righteous for their faithfulness and loyalty to His law, and all men will recognize it (v.11ᵃ; 1 Co.15:58; Js.1:12). They will then praise God for His righteousness. They will acknowledge that He is the judge of all the earth and that He always does what is right (Ge.18:25).

Thought 1. We will all encounter injustices in our lives and witness or hear of people being persecuted. But we should never allow injustices to depress or defeat us. Instead, we should do everything we can to stand against evildoers. Yet, when all is said and done, we have to commit their judgment to the LORD. If we are faithful to Him, He will vindicate us. He will one day cause us to stand in triumph over the wicked. Therefore, we should rest in the LORD, patiently waiting until that day comes when He will judge all ungodliness and unrighteousness in men. He is keeping careful records on everyone, and on His day of judgment, He will do what is right.

> Therefore, my dear brothers, stand firm. Let nothing move you. Always give yourselves fully to the work of the Lord, because you know that your labor in the Lord is not in vain (1 Co.15:58).
>
> Let us not become weary in doing good, for at the proper time we will reap a harvest if we do not give up (Ga.6:9).
>
> Since you know that you will receive an inheritance from the Lord as a reward. It is the Lord Christ you are serving (Col.3:24).
>
> So do not throw away your confidence; it will be richly rewarded (He.10:35).
>
> You will only observe with your eyes and see the punishment of the wicked (Ps.91:8).
>
> If the righteous receive their due on earth, how much more the ungodly and the sinner! (Pr.11:31).
>
> Tell the righteous it will be well with them, for they will enjoy the fruit of their deeds (Is.3:10).

PSALM 59

When You Have Special Need of God's Deliverance, 59:1-17

For the director of music. [To the tune of] "Do Not Destroy." Of David. A miktam. When Saul had sent men to watch David's house in order to kill him.

1. Pray for God to deliver you
a. Whom you need deliverance from
1) All enemies & adversaries
2) All evildoers who seek to harm you

b. Why you need to be delivered
1) Bc. your adversaries are fierce & ready to attack you for no reason
2) Bc. you are innocent
3) Bc. you desperately need God to awaken & be aware of your dire situation
4) Bc. God alone has the power to judge the nations for their wicked betrayal: He is the "LORD God Almighty" (the LORD of hosts)
5) Bc. your adversaries are like vicious dogs
• They prowl about the city
• They plot & spew out malicious curses & lies
• They feel above the law: Think no one hears them

2. Express confidence in God

Deliver me from my enemies, O God; protect me from those who rise up against me.
2 Deliver me from evildoers and save me from bloodthirsty men.
3 See how they lie in wait for me! Fierce men conspire against me for no offense or sin of mine, O LORD.
4 I have done no wrong, yet they are ready to attack me. Arise to help me; look on my plight!
5 O LORD God Almighty, the God of Israel, rouse yourself to punish all the nations; show no mercy to wicked traitors. Selah
6 They return at evening, snarling like dogs, and prowl about the city.
7 See what they spew from their mouths—they spew out swords from their lips, and they say, "Who can hear us?"
8 But you, O LORD, laugh at them; you scoff at all those nations.
9 O my Strength, I watch for you; you, O God, are my fortress,
10 My loving God. God will go before me and will let me gloat over those who slander me.
11 But do not kill them, O Lord our shield, or my people will forget. In your might make them wander about, and bring them down.
12 For the sins of their mouths, for the words of their lips, let them be caught in their pride. For the curses and lies they utter,
13 Consume them in wrath, consume them till they are no more. Then it will be known to the ends of the earth that God rules over Jacob. Selah
14 They return at evening, snarling like dogs, and prowl about the city.
15 They wander about for food and howl if not satisfied.
16 But I will sing of your strength, in the morning I will sing of your love; for you are my fortress, my refuge in times of trouble.
17 O my Strength, I sing praise to you; you, O God, are my fortress, my loving God.

a. Confidence that He will overpower & judge the nations
b. Confidence that He is your strength & fortress: He will defend & rescue you
c. Confidence that His unfailing mercy & love will lead you & make you victorious

3. Ask God to execute justice & judgment gradually
a. Bc. it will help God's people remember His power

b. Bc. the enemy deserves to be entrapped & consumed by their sin
1) Their evil words
2) Their pride
3) Their curses & lies
c. Bc. God's wrath & judgment will be a strong witness to the world

d. Bc. the enemy repeatedly acts like vicious dogs
1) Prowling about the city looking for food (victims)
2) Howling (complaining) if their search is unsuccessful

4. Make a renewed commitment to praise God's power
a. Praise Him bc. of His love & mercy: He is your refuge in times of trouble

b. Praise Him bc. He is your strength: He is your fortress & shows you unfailing love

PSALM 59

When You Have Special Need of God's Deliverance, 59:1-17

(59:1-17) Introduction: from August 5 to October 13, 2010, the world's attention was focused on the South American country of Chile, where thirty-three miners were trapped 2,300 feet (700 meters) beneath the earth's surface. Governments, agencies, and corporations from around the world came together in an all-out effort to rescue these men. After sixty-nine days, more than one billion people watched by television or the internet as all thirty-three men were delivered from the bowels of the earth and safely returned to their families.

For many of us, just the thought of what these men endured for over two months makes us shudder. Our hearts beat faster at the mere mention of the word *trapped.*

When David wrote Psalm 59, he was trapped in his home by Saul's bloodthirsty soldiers. They were watching his house, waiting to slay him when he came out the next morning (1 S.19:11). His situation seemed hopeless, and he cried out for God to deliver him.

Everyday, hosts of people are caught up in situations that seem inescapable. Some are trapped by wicked people, such as abusive spouses or parents, tyrannical governments, crazed religious fanatics who threaten their safety, criminals, and other evildoers. Others feel trapped by traumatic experiences in the past that have left them paralyzed by fear.

Still others feel trapped by circumstances in their lives—sickness or physical impairment, depression, fear, troubled relationships, stressful jobs, poverty, oppression, financial challenges, and an endless list of other hardships.

Untold millions are trapped by sin and the weakness of the flesh. Many are addicted to alcohol, drugs, or other substances. Others are slaves to pornography. Millions of others are bound by the love of money and possessions.

The list of things from which people need deliverance goes on and on. Psalm 59 was specifically written about David's human enemies who had trapped him in his house. However, we can apply it to any sin or circumstance that holds us captive as well. By crying out to God for deliverance and following His directions, we too can be set free. This is, *When You Have Special Need of God's Deliverance,* 59:1-17.

1. Pray for God to deliver you (vv.1-7).
2. Express confidence in God (vv.8-10).
3. Ask God to execute justice and judgment gradually (vv.11-15).
4. Make a renewed commitment to praise God's power (vv.16-17).

1 (59:1-7) Pray for God to deliver you.

With Saul's assassins just outside his door, David cried out for God to deliver him from what appeared to be certain death. He was surrounded with no way of escape in sight. Knowing that only God could save him, David sought refuge in the LORD.

a. Whom you need deliverance from (vv.1-2).

Fearing for his life, David fervently prayed that God would deliver him from his adversaries who had risen up against him (v.1). Specifically, he was referring to Saul and the men whom the raging king had ordered to spy on and then slay him (1 S.19:11). He implored God to protect him from their evil efforts. *Protect* (sagab), as used here, means to set in an inaccessibly high place. David asked God to be like a high tower or wall to him, to protect him so securely that his enemies could not reach him (Ps.18:1; 69:29; Pr.18:10).

David described his foes as workers of inquity and bloody or bloodthirsty men (v.2). He called on God to rescue him from these evildoers and their plan to murder him.

b. Why you need to be delivered (vv.3-7).

As he continued his urgent prayer, David described the undeserved danger in which he found himself. For no justifiable reason, Saul was determined to execute him. The king's strongest and fiercest soldiers were standing by, waiting for the opportunity to take his soul or life (v.3a). David declared that he was innocent of any wrongdoing whatsoever against Saul or the nation of Israel (v.3b-4a; 1 S.20:1; 24:11). He was guilty of no…

- *offense* (pesha)—willful rebellion or revolt
- *sin* (chata'ah)—offense or trespass against the law or the king
- *wrong* (avown)—perversion or corruption in his heart that would prompt him to do wrong toward Saul, no ill will or animosity

It appeared to David that God was unconcerned about this life-threatening crisis. Therefore, he called on God to awaken and be aware of his dire situation (v.4b). David confessed that the LORD is the God of hosts—the Commander of heavenly armies. He alone has the power to visit or judge the *nations* (goy) or heathen of the world (v.5).[1] David called on God to judge wicked transgressors in every nation—including Israel, with whom He had made His covenant. By ruthlessly and unjustly pursuing David, King Saul was sinning against both the God of Israel and the nation itself. He was betraying God by trying to force his will over God's will for the nation: David was God's choice to be Israel's king, and Saul was furiously attempting to prevent this from ever coming to pass. In addition, by directing his armies to focus on pursuing David, the treacherous king was leaving the nation open to enemy attack. "He was so obsessed with destroying David that he neglected his duties as king and made the nation vulnerable."[2]

David proceeded to describe his wicked adversaries, comparing them to vicious, growling dogs that prowled the city at night (v.6). As they rummaged the streets, they polluted the evening air with the foul stench of the slander they belched out. Their weapon against David was their words: they spewed out their malicious curses and lies like swords aimed at David's heart (v.7). Because they were on the king's business, they felt they were above the law. Therefore, they spoke freely, as if nobody—including God—could hear them.

Thought 1. David set an example that we should follow in response to threats and potential dangers. He and his wife, Michal, took action to protect him from Saul; but David realized that, ultimately, the LORD was his protector. Therefore, he called on God to deliver him from his enemies. God answered his prayer by speaking to Michal's heart with a plan for David's escape. She listened to the LORD, followed His leading, and saved her husband's life (1 S.19:11-16). Note two lessons for believers in every generation:

First, we should recognize that our protection lies in the LORD, not in our own resources. We can always call upon God with full assurance that He is listening and is deeply concerned about us. He is with us at all times, and He will dispatch His angels to protect us. He can set us in a place where no evil can touch us. Turning to Him and resting in His perfect love is the secret to overcoming our fears (1 Jn.4:18).

---

1 *Goy* usually refers to the heathen or Gentile nations, those who do not know and worship the LORD. There are occasions, however, when it is used of Israel (De.4:6-7; Ps.83:4). By using it here, it gives the impression that David was grouping Saul with those who do not have a relationship with the LORD.

2 Warren W. Wiersbe. *The Bible Exposition Commentary.* WORD*search* CROSS e-book.

Second, we should avail ourselves of the resources God has given us and use them to protect ourselves and others. In our modern world, we have many resources available for protecting ourselves, and God expects us to use them. He has provided them for our defense. Certainly, God works supernaturally to protect us and care for us. We should never forget that He is at work in ways we cannot see. He is constantly arranging circumstances for our benefit, and angelic activity is always in motion. However, God often works *in* us and *through* us directly, and sometimes He works in our lives through others. This is how he delivered David, by working in and through Michal.

We always need to seek God's guidance when we are facing threats or trouble. When we call on God, we should carefully listen for Him to answer (Je.33:3; Mt.7:7). Then when He speaks to our hearts and gives us direction, we need to follow His leading, just as Michal did.

And pray that we may be delivered from wicked and evil men, for not everyone has faith (2 Th.3:2).

But the Lord stood at my side and gave me strength, so that through me the message might be fully proclaimed and all the Gentiles might hear it. And I was delivered from the lion's mouth. The Lord will rescue me from every evil attack and will bring me safely to his heavenly kingdom. To him be glory for ever and ever. Amen (2 Ti.4:17-18).

For everyone born of God overcomes the world. This is the victory that has overcome the world, even our faith (1 Jn.5:4).

'Call to me and I will answer you and tell you great and unsearchable things you do not know' (Je.33:3).

But let all who take refuge in you be glad; let them ever sing for joy. Spread your protection over them, that those who love your name may rejoice in you (Ps.5:11).

Thought 2. These same principles apply to deliverance from anything that has us trapped, whether it is a sinful habit or addiction, oppression, or any other situation. We must recognize that our deliverance lies in the LORD, not in our own power. At the same time, we need to utilize the resources God has given us; we are to do what we can to help ourselves. Then, we are to seek God's guidance, listen to Him, and obey what He tells us to do.

Everything that holds us in bondage is, on some level, the result of our sinful nature or an effect of living in a sin-cursed world. Christ died to set us free from everything that ensnares us and to restore everything that this sinful world has taken from us. Complete, lasting deliverance can only be found in Him. "If the Son therefore shall make you free, ye shall be free indeed" (Jn.8:36).

"The Spirit of the Lord is on me, because he has anointed me to preach good news to the poor. He has sent me to proclaim freedom for the prisoners and recovery of sight for the blind, to release the oppressed (Lu.4:18).

Then you will know the truth, and the truth will set you free" (Jn.8:32).

But now that you have been set free from sin and have become slaves to God, the benefit you reap leads to holiness, and the result is eternal life (Ro.6:22).

It is for freedom that Christ has set us free. Stand firm, then, and do not let yourselves be burdened again by a yoke of slavery (Ga.5:1).

Those who oppose him he must gently instruct, in the hope that God will grant them repentance leading them to a knowledge of the truth, and that they will come to their senses and escape from the trap of the devil, who has taken them captive to do his will (2 Ti.2:25-26).

2 (59:8-10) **Express confidence in God.**
"But you, O LORD" is the transition point of this psalm. David took his eyes off his imminent danger and focused on God. As in many of his psalms, David's fears vanished when he focused on the LORD. Because he trusted in God's unchanging faithfulness and unfailing love, he was able to express absolute confidence that the LORD would protect and deliver him from his wicked adversaries.

a. Confidence that He will overpower and judge the nations (v.8).
By addressing God as the LORD (Yahweh, Jehovah), David triumphantly declared that God is ever faithful to His covenant. God was not threatened by Saul's attempts to assassinate David. The picture of God's laughter at His enemies shows that He is not shaken by His foes. The picture is for our benefit who trust in Him, giving us assurance that He is in control (see outline and notes—Ps.2:4-5 for more discussion). It gave David solid confidence that the LORD would overpower and judge all the heathen who opposed His plan, including Saul.

b. Confidence that He is your strength and fortress: He will defend and rescue you (v.9).
The LORD was David's *strength* (owz) and his *fortress* (misgab) or defense, his stronghold, refuge, high tower.

Enemies could not touch David (or us) when he was hiding in God. He depended solely on God for His protection; therefore, he would wait and watch for God to come to his rescue.

c. Confidence that His unfailing mercy and love will lead you and make you victorious (v.10).
David's unshakable confidence was rooted in God's *steadfast, unfailing covenant love* (chesed), His mercy (see outline and notes—Ps.5:7 for more discussion). He declared in faith that he would see the fall of his enemies, for God would go before him (*prevent,* qadam) and confront them, making him victorious.

Thought 1. When trouble surrounds us, we need to remember what we know to be true about God:
➤ God can be trusted. He is always true to His Word; it is impossible for God to lie (He.6:18).
➤ God loves us so much that He gave His one and only Son to die for us (Ro.5:8; 8:32).
➤ Nothing can be against us (defeat us) when God is for us, (Ro.8:31).
➤ Nothing is impossible with God (Mt.17:20; Lu.1:37).
➤ God is always with us, and He has promised to never leave us or forsake us (Josh.1:8; Is.43:2; He.13:5-6).
➤ God is our rock and our fortress. We will be safe when we take refuge in Him (Ps.18:2).
➤ We are protected by God's mercy or steadfast love and His faithfulness is great (Lam.3:22-23).
➤ God always causes us to triumph (2 Co.2:14).

Scripture emphasizes the importance of praying with full confidence in God. If we pray with wavering faith, we should not expect to receive answers to our prayers (Js.1:6-7). Jesus taught us about the unlimited power of faith—if we pray and do not doubt, we can move mountains. All things are possible through prayer when we pray with full faith in God. When we are surrounded by trouble, we should heed our Lord's command to, "Have faith in God" (Mk.11:22-24). Likewise, we should never speak from a spirit of doubt but always with full confidence that God will see us through our trials (2 Co.4:8-13).

"'If you can'?" said Jesus. "Everything is possible for him who believes." (Mk.9:23).

"Have faith in God," Jesus answered. "I tell you the truth, if anyone says to this mountain, 'Go, throw yourself into the sea,' and does not doubt in his heart but believes that what he says will happen, it will be done for him (Mk.11:22-23).

In addition to all this, take up the shield of faith, with which you can extin-guish all the flaming arrows of the evil one (Ep.6:16).

I want men everywhere to lift up holy hands in prayer, without anger or disputing (1 Ti.2:8)

But when he asks, he must believe and not doubt, because he who doubts is like a wave of the sea, blown and tossed by the wind. That man should not think he will receive anything from the Lord (Js.1:6-7).

This is the confidence we have in approaching God: that if we ask anything according to his will, he hears us. And if we know that he hears us—whatever we ask—we know that we have what we asked of him (1 Jn.5:14-15).

Commit your way to the LORD; trust in him and he will do this: He will make your righteousness shine like the dawn, the justice of your cause like the noonday sun (Ps.37:5-6).

3 (59:11-15) **Ask God to execute justice and judgment gradually.**
Psalm 59 is different from other psalms in which David prayed for God to judge his enemies. Usually, David asked God to destroy his adversaries swiftly and completely. In this psalm, however, David prayed for God to execute justice gradually.

a. Because it will help God's people remember His power (v.11).
Remarkably, David asked God not to slay his enemies this time. He felt that their gradual judgment would display God's power over the wicked for a longer period of time than if he destroyed Saul and his men swiftly. Instead, David prayed that God would scatter the enemy and cause them to be exiled as homeless fugitives, forced to wander the land. If God slayed them, David reasoned, the people would soon forget their judgment. But as long as they were alive and suffering, they would continue to be an example of God's power to execute justice. David felt that the people of Israel needed this constant reminder of God's authority and judgment, for they too were prone to stray from God's will.

b. Because the enemy deserves to be entrapped and consumed by their sin (v.12).
The sins of Saul and his men against David were severe. Their evil words were like swords, piercing the future king to his very core and causing him great agony (v.7). Their slander robbed him of his good name and credibility before the people God had ordained to follow him. David prayed that Saul would be caught or

123

taken in the pride that moved him to slander David so viciously. Because of their curses and lies about David, the arrogant king and his army deserved to be entrapped and consumed by their sin.

c. Because God's wrath and judgment will be a strong witness to the world (v.13).
David prayed that, after his enemies had suffered the humiliation of being exiled, God would *consume* (kala) them in His wrath. He called on God to then complete His process of judgment by utterly destroying the enemy and removing them from the earth (1 S.15:18; Ps.37:20). God's final judgment on these evildoers would be a strong witness throughout the entire world that God rules in Jacob, that He and He alone is the true King of Israel. Anyone who exalts himself and goes against God's will for His chosen nation stands to be destroyed in God's holy wrath.

d. Because the enemy repeatedly acts like vicious dogs (vv.14-15).
Once again, David reminded the LORD that his foes were like a vicious pack of dogs that prowled about the city at night in search of food (v.14; vv.6-7). They fed on their victims, those they devoured with their malicious lies and slander. If their appetite for evil was not satisfied, they *howl* (luwn) or stayed out all night, growling in angry complaint.

Thought 1. Like David, we have a natural desire to see justice served on those who threaten or endanger us. It is not wrong for us to pray for God to judge our enemies; nor is it wrong, when appropriate, to involve civil authorities, for God has delegated the punishment of evildoers to them (Ro.13:1-4).

We should also remember, though, that our Lord commanded us to love our enemies and to pray for those who sin against us (Mt.5:44). Paul also exhorted us to help our enemies and to overcome their evil with good (Ro.12:20-21). Of course, this is not easy to do. But it is the example left for us by our Savior who, from the cross, prayed for God to forgive those who were crucifying Him (Lu.23:34). Jesus assured us that when we follow His example, we will be the children of our Heavenly Father. We will show that we have inherited His nature and He will greatly reward us (Mt.5:45-46).

> **Do not take revenge, my friends, but leave room for God's wrath, for it is written: "It is mine to avenge; I will repay," says the Lord (Ro.12:19).**
>
> **And that in this matter no one should wrong his brother or take advantage of him. The Lord will punish men for all such sins, as we have already told you and warned you (1 Th.4:6).**

> **For we know him who said, "It is mine to avenge; I will repay," and again, "The Lord will judge his people" (He.10:30).**
>
> **Why should the nations say, "Where is their God?" Before our eyes, make known among the nations that you avenge the outpoured blood of your servants (Ps.79:10).**
>
> **May they ever be ashamed and dismayed; may they perish in disgrace. Let them know that you, whose name is the LORD—that you alone are the Most High over all the earth (Ps.83:17-18).**

4 (59:16-17) **Make a renewed commitment to praise God's power.**
David would not let his bloodthirsty foes rob him of his song, his joy. In spite of the danger that threatened him, he would continue to sing the praises of his faithful LORD. He knew with certainty that the LORD would protect him from the bloodthirsty men who sought his life.

a. Praise Him because of His love and mercy: He is your refuge in times of trouble (v.16).
"In the morning" may appear to be merely poetic words, but it is a highly significant phrase in this psalm. Saul's assassins were camped out at David's house, waiting to slay him *in the morning* (1 S.19:11). In a profound demonstration of faith, David declared that he would be singing the song of deliverance in the morning. He would be proclaiming the mercy or steadfast and unfailing love of God, for the LORD would prove once again to be his defense and refuge in time of trouble!

b. Praise Him because He is your strength: He is your fortress and shows you unfailing love (v.17).
David concluded Psalm 59 by declaring once more that God was his strength (v.9), his defense or fortress (vv.9, 16), and the God of mercy (vv.10, 16). As Saul's men loomed outside his house that dark night, the future king sang God's praises. And he would continue to sing them long after God had delivered him from Saul's evil plan to destroy him.

Thought 1. What David declared in faith gloriously came to pass. God protected and delivered him from Saul's diabolical plot. David's wife, Michal, let him down through a window and tricked Saul's men into thinking he was sick in bed (1 S.19:12-14). Like David, we must not allow the fear of foes to shake our faith and rob us of our song. We have to trust God's faithfulness, for He will deliver us from or through whatever may threaten us. The safest place we can be on this earth is in the center of God's will for our lives.

When we are walking in complete submission and obedience to Him, He will be with us and will protect us. He will bring His purpose for our lives to pass. Therefore, we can praise Him in the midst of our trials, for when the dark night is over, we too will be singing the song of deliverance.

About midnight Paul and Silas were praying and singing hymns to God, and the other prisoners were listening to them (Ac.16:25).

He has delivered us from such a deadly peril, and he will deliver us. On him we have set our hope that he will continue to deliver us (2 Co.1:10).

Now to him who is able to do immeasurably more than all we ask or imagine, according to his power that is at work within us (Ep.3:20).

He said: "The LORD is my rock, my fortress and my deliverer; my God is my rock, in whom I take refuge, my shield and the horn of my salvation. He is my stronghold, my refuge and my savior—from violent men you save me. I call to the LORD, who is worthy of praise, and I am saved from my enemies (2 S.22:2-4).

It is good to praise the LORD and make music to your name, O Most High, to proclaim your love in the morning and your faithfulness at night (Ps.92:1-2).

PSALM 60

When You Suffer a Setback or Defeat & Feel Rejected By God, 60:1-12

For the director of music. To [the tune of] "The Lily of the Covenant." A miktam of David. For teaching. When he fought Aram Naharaim and Aram Zobah, and when Joab returned and struck down twelve thousand Edomites in the Valley of Salt.

You have rejected us, O God, and burst forth upon us; you have been angry—now restore us!
2 You have shaken the land and torn it open; mend its fractures, for it is quaking.
3 You have shown your people desperate times; you have given us wine that makes us stagger.
4 But for those who fear you, you have raised a banner to be unfurled against the bow. Selah
5 Save us and help us with your right hand, that those you love may be delivered.
6 God has spoken from his sanctuary: "In triumph I will parcel out Shechem and measure off the Valley of Succoth.
7 Gilead is mine, and Manasseh is mine; Ephraim is my helmet, Judah my scepter.
8 Moab is my washbasin, upon Edom I toss my sandal; over Philistia I shout in triumph."
9 Who will bring me to the fortified city? Who will lead me to Edom?
10 Is it not you, O God, you who have rejected us and no longer go out with our armies?
11 Give us aid against the enemy, for the help of man is worthless.
12 With God we will gain the victory, and he will trample down our enemies.

1. Ask God to restore you
   a. Bc. you feel God has cast you aside
      1) You sense His displeasure
      2) Your world (the land) has been shaken to the core as though by an earthquake
   b. Bc. you cannot comprehend why God has caused you so much hardship: You stagger at the extent of His wrath
   c. Bc. your hope is still in God: He has raised a banner (His very own presence) over all who fear Him, Ex.17:15

2. Cry out for God to save & receive you by His mighty power
   a. Bc. He loves & *can* deliver you
   b. Bc. He promised to give His people the promised land: A picture of heaven
      1) Shechem & the valley of Succoth
      2) Gilead & Manasseh
      3) Ephraim
      4) Judah
   c. Bc. He promised to make His people victorious over all enemies: He will subject the enemies of this world under Him

3. Express absolute trust in God
   a. God alone can answer your perplexing questions & doubts
      1) He whom you feel has rejected you
      2) He who allowed your adversaries to defeat you
   b. God alone can help you
      1) Human help is useless in defeating the world's enemies
      2) God alone can make you victorious over the enemies of this world, Ep.6:10-18

PSALM 60

When You Suffer a Setback or Defeat and Feel Rejected by God, 60:1-12

(60:1-12) Introduction: *"Three steps forward, two steps back"* is a common American catchphrase dealing with life's realities, that is, that life includes defeats as well as victories. At times, it seems that *two steps forward and three steps back* is more accurate—that we are losing ground rather than gaining it. Setbacks and defeats are a part of life in our relationships, careers, finances, personal growth, and every other area.

One false idea about the Christian life is that, once you believe in Christ, all of your problems will be solved; you will know only victory and not defeat. American pastor and author Charles Swindoll wrote,

We do a great disservice to an unbeliever when we bait him by saying, "Come to Christ and all your problems will be over." The Bible never says that. It promises that we will be new creatures; it assures us that we will have a destiny that is secure; but it does not guarantee a downhill slide once Christ comes into a person's life. In fact, in some instances problems increase and the road gets rougher![1]

David wrote Psalm 60 after Israel suffered a crushing defeat. The heading of the psalm identifies its Scriptural setting as 2 Samuel 8:1-14, 1 Kings 11:15-16, and 1 Chronicles 18:1-13. While David was fighting in the north against *Aram-naharaim* (Mesopotamia) and *Aram-zobah* (Zobah), Edom attacked Israel in the south, inflicting severe damage on Judah. David sent Joab to retaliate against Edom, and he won a great victory in the Valley of Salt (2 S.8:13-14).

The heading to Psalm 60 also states that Joab led the slaughter of 12,000 Edomites, while other Scriptures set the number at 18,000 (2 S.8:13; 1 Chr.18:12). The *Bible Knowledge Commentary* clarifies quite simply what some have falsely deemed a contradiction in Scripture: "This difference is explainable by noting that the entire campaign was under Abishai's direct command, and that Joab was responsible (with the soldiers in his contingency) for killing two thirds of the Edomites."[2]

Psalm 60 is another *miktam* psalm, one worthy of preserving and remembering. It is a national psalm for Israel rather than a personal one for David, as indicated by the plural pronouns used. *Shushan-eduth* means "the lily of the covenant" and was apparently a popular tune to

---

[1] Charles R. Swindoll. *Three Steps Forward Two Steps Back.* (New York: Bantam Books, 1980), p.19.

[2] John F. Walvoord, ed. *The Bible Knowledge Commentary: An Exposition of the Scriptures by Dallas Seminary Faculty.*

which the song was to be performed. The Holy Spirit inspired and preserved Psalm 60 to instruct and encourage us when we lose ground in some area of our lives. This is, *When You Suffer a Setback or Defeat and Feel Rejected by God,* 60:1-12.

1. Ask God to restore you (vv.1-4).
2. Cry out for God to save and receive you by His mighty power (vv.5-8).
3. Express absolute trust in God (vv.9-12).

1 (60:1-4) Ask God to restore you.

Humiliated, brokenhearted, and perplexed, King David cried out to the LORD on behalf of his devastated nation. Israel had been ravaged, and the people could not see their defeat as anything other than God's indignation with them. David interceded for the nation, passionately asking God to restore Israel to favor and fellowship with Him.

a. Because you feel God has cast you aside (vv.1-2).

Having suffered a crushing defeat, Israel felt that God had cast them aside or rejected them (v.1). Sensing that God was displeased or angry with the nation, David prayed for God to bring Israel back to the place where He could bless them. The people felt that God, in His wrath, had judged their nation by bursting forth upon them or breaking down her defenses so the nation could be attacked (1 Chr.15:13; Ps.80:12; 89:40; Is.5:5). The Hebrew word for *burst forth* (parats) means to breach or break.

The Israelites were stunned by the thought that God had turned His back on them. They compared His rejection to an earthquake so strong that it split open the earth or land (v.2). Shaken to their core by what they perceived as God's judgment, they prayed for God to repair the breaches or cracks in their nation. They needed God to heal the damage done by their enemy and to restore them to fellowship with Him.

b. Because you cannot comprehend why God has caused you so much hardship: You stagger at the extent of His wrath (v.3).

Israel was devastated by the defeat they were forced to endure. They could not understand why God would cause them such paralyzing hardship. *Desperate times* (qasheh) comes from a root word used of a yoke or weight too heavy to bear.[3] It refers to acts that are intentionally cruel, harsh, and even fierce. The Israelites were staggering in astonishment at the extent of God's wrath toward them. It was unbearable. David compared it to being forced to drink exceedingly strong wine so intoxicating that it left them reeling in confusion.

c. Because your hope is still in God: He has raised a banner (His very own presence) over all who fear Him, Ex.17:15 (v.4).

By describing the people of Israel as *those who fear the LORD,* David clarified that they were neither angry nor bitter at God. Rather, they were utterly devastated and broken that God had inflicted, as they saw it, such humiliating agony upon them. Yet, they hoped in Him, declaring that He had raised a banner over them—a symbol of His very own presence with them. The LORD was Israel's banner (Ex.17:15). In Him, they found stability and the truth, that is, the certainty of His unfailing love and unchanging purpose for their nation.

Some versions end verse 4 with "because of the truth." *The truth* (qoshet) means that which is certain; it comes from a Hebrew root meaning "to balance, as in a scale."[4] The image is that of the Israelites balancing their feelings of rejection by God with what they knew to be true of God. However, other scholars believe it is a variation of *qeshet,* which is the Hebrew word for the archer's bow. It is therefore translated as *bow* by some Bible versions, as in the NIV. With this understanding, the thought of the verse is that God is a banner for Israel against her foes. When they are attacked, they can flee to God and gather under Him for protection.

Thought 1. When we face a setback, defeat, or other adverse circumstance, we may feel as if God has rejected or forsaken us, just as Israel did. During such times, we need to balance our feelings with the truth of God's Word. Note that this passage ends with a *selah,* an instruction to pause and meditate on what has been said. When we suffer a crushing loss or trial, we should pause for a moment to remember some truths from Scripture that apply to Israel's feelings as expressed in these verses, truths that can help us as well:

(1) Adverse circumstances are not the result of God's forsaking us but may be the consequence of our disobeying or turning away from God. Sin has natural consequences. When we break God's commandments, we will suffer those painful consequences. Furthermore, God will chasten or discipline us when we persist in sin, just as a loving father disciplines his children (He.12:5-11). One way God may chasten us is by lifting His hand of protection from our lives, making us vulnerable to an enemy's attack. He may also withhold His blessing from us. We should search our hearts when we face trials, setbacks, or defeats, repenting of any sin and asking God to restore us to His favor and fellowship (1 Jn.1:9; Ps.51:1-12).

(2) If we are truly God's children through genuine, saving faith in Jesus Christ, He will never reject us

---

3 R. Laird Harris, ed. *Theological Wordbook of the Old Testament.* WORD*search* CROSS e-book.

4 Spiros Zodhiates. *AMG Complete Word Study Dictionary.* WORD*search* CROSS e-book.

or cast us aside. He has promised to never leave us nor forsake us. He is with us at all times through His indwelling Holy Spirit, and nothing can separate us from His love (Mt.28:20; Ro.8:35-39; He.13:5; 1 Jn.4:15). God has specifically promised to be with us in difficult times (Is.43:2).

(3) When we suffer wounds from painful trials, the consequences of our sin, or enemy attack, we should call upon God to heal us (v.2). He is *Jehovah Rapha*, the God who heals (Ex.15:26; Ps.103:3). He can heal us physically, spiritually, and emotionally. He can restore our lives, relationships, homes, careers, and businesses. (Is.57:18; Ho.14:4; Lu.15:22).

(4) God is never harsh or cruel to His dear children. He loves us, and He is full of mercy toward us. He comforts us when we are going through painful tribulations (La.3:22-23; 2 Co.1:3-4). He promises that He will never allow us to suffer more than we are able to bear and that He will always give us grace sufficient for our trials (1 Co.10:13; 2 Co.12:9).

> The law was added so that the trespass might increase. But where sin increased, grace increased all the more (Ro.5:20).
>
> I ask then: Did God reject his people? By no means! I am an Israelite myself, a descendant of Abraham, from the tribe of Benjamin. God did not reject his people, whom he foreknew (Ro.11:1-2ᵃ).
>
> If we confess our sins, he is faithful and just and will forgive us our sins and purify us from all unrighteousness (1 Jn.1:9).
>
> He restores my soul. He guides me in paths of righteousness for his name's sake (Ps.23:3).
>
> For men are not cast off by the Lord forever. Though he brings grief, he will show compassion, so great is his unfailing love (La.3:31-32).

2 (60:5-8) Cry out for God to save and receive you by His mighty power.

The horrible defeat did not shake David's confidence in God's covenant with His people. The damage to Israel was great, but God's faithfulness was greater. Standing firmly on God's promises, David cried out to the LORD to save Israel by His mighty power. This passage is identical to Psalm 108:6-13, another of David's psalms.

a. Because He loves and *can* deliver you (v.5)

Focusing on the truth about God reminded David that the Israelites were His beloved people. Indeed, the LORD loves Israel with an everlasting love (Je.31:3). Even if He had chastened her by allowing her to be defeated by her enemy, it was out of His immeasurable love for her (Pr.3:11-12). Accordingly, David asked God to save Israel with His right hand—a symbol of His unlimited power. He could unquestionably deliver His cherished nation (Ex.15:6; Ps.20:6; 89:13).

b. Because He promised to give His people the promised land: A picture of heaven (vv.6-7).

David reminded the downtrodden Israelites what God had spoken to Abraham many generations earlier: in His holiness, God promised to give him and his descendants the promised land (v.6; Ge.13:14-18). God's holiness emphasizes the fact that He is above sinning. He will keep His promises, for He cannot lie (He.6:18).

Shechem was the first place to which Abraham came in the land of Canaan. It was there that he built his first altar in the promised land (Ge.12:7). Here, it represents all of Israel's promised territory west of the Jordan River. Succoth was in the territory of Gad and represents all of the land God promised to Israel east of the Jordan.[5] The LORD had rejoiced in dividing the promised land among the twelve tribes of Israel (Jos.13-21). Divide and mete out paint a vivid picture of a property owner precisely surveying his land and distributing it to his children as an inheritance.

Specifically mentioning Gilead and Manasseh on the east side of Jordan, and Ephraim and Judah on the west, God reminded David that all the land belonged to Him (v.7). Even though it had been ravaged by the enemy, God was still in control of it.

The LORD declared Ephraim to be "my helmet," Israel's defense or protection. Commentator J.J. Stewart Perowne (1823-1904) described Ephraim as a "strong and warlike tribe" that was to Israel "what the helmet is to the warriors in battle" (De.33:17).[6] It is a symbol here of God's protection and defense of Israel. A blow to the head is a mortal wound (Ge.3:15). Although Israel sometimes suffered loss, her head was always protected; that is, she was never destroyed.

God also described Judah as His lawgiver or scepter, the symbol of His kingship and authority over Israel. Along with David, the promised Messiah would spring up from the tribe of Judah (Ge.49:10; Re.5:5).

The promised land is a picture of heaven, our inheritance as believers and our place of eternal rest (see outline and notes—Ge.12:1-3; *Numbers*, INTRODUCTION, Special Feature 26 for more discussion). It is promised to all who genuinely repent, who turn from sin and the world, and trust Christ for salvation

---

5   John Phillips. *Exploring Psalms, Volume 1.* WORDsearch CROSS e-book.

6   J.J. Stewart Perowne, *The Book of Psalms.* (London: George Bell and Sons, 1880), p.251.

(1 Pe.1:3-5). Believers will forever live with Christ in the promised land, the new heaven and new earth (Re.21:1-7).

c. Because He promised to make His people victorious over all enemies: He will subject the enemies of this world under Him (v.8).

In addition to promising Israel the land, the LORD also promised to make His chosen people victorious over their enemies who occupied the land, including Moab, Edom, and Philistia. In sharp contrast to the honor bestowed on Ephraim and Judah, God declared that Moab was His washpot—the bowl in which he washed His feet. He depicted Edom as the one upon whom He would *toss His sandal*. These comparisons are drawn from a common practice of the day. Upon entering his house, a man would take off his shoes and give them to a servant who would clean them. Then, another servant would wash the man's feet before he proceeded into the house. These tasks were assigned to the lowest-ranking servants in the household.

God also promised that He would give victory over Philistia, Israel's persistent enemy. The words "over Philistia I shout in triumph" is to "acclaim God with shouts of triumph, as would faithful servants of a king."[7] In Psalm 108:9, this statement is "over Philistia will I triumph." The meaning is clear: God would lead His chosen nation to triumph over their greatest enemy. Ultimately, He will subject all the enemies of this world under Him.

Thought 1. As followers of Christ, we can expect to be attacked by His enemies. Remember, the Christian life is a battleground, not a playground. We are at war with Satan and his demonic forces (Ep.6:12; 2 Co.10:3-4). Moreover, we are in a never-ending battle with our sinful nature, referred to in the Bible as the *flesh*. The sinful desires of our old nature are in constant conflict with our new nature, the nature of Christ that is within us (Ro.7:15-8:14; Ga.5:16-25). We also have to deal with a world system that appeals to our flesh—a system controlled by Satan that is in total opposition to God's Word and will (1 Jn.2:15-17; Ep.2:2; Jn.12:31; Js.4:4).

Like Israel, we may suffer some setbacks and defeats along the way. There may be times when Satan gains an advantage over us (2 Co.2:11). Until we are fully and finally transformed into the image of Christ (Ph.3:20-21), we will lose some battles with temptation and give in to the sinful tendencies of our flesh. But just as David was undaunted by Israel's enemies, we, too, should strike back at the enemy, remembering and claiming the promises of God. We should cry out for His help, asking Him to give us victory over Satan and sin by His mighty power. God loves us and has the power to deliver us. He has promised that we can walk in victory now, just as we will walk in eternal victory in the new heaven and new earth. Christ has defeated all of our enemies—the world, the flesh, and the devil—through His death on the cross and resurrection from the grave. He has placed His Word in our hands and His Spirit in our hearts. Through the power of Scripture and the power of His Holy Spirit, we can prevail! We must never give up, and we must never give in. When we are knocked down by the enemy, we need to get up and get back in the fight. We must not accept defeat.

"That's the spirit!" wrote Bible teacher John Phillips. "When the enemy attacks, don't just settle for a renewal of the status quo...Make him pay. Go on the offensive. Take back the territory Satan has attacked in your life and then take some away from him in the very area where he has attacked you."[8]

> Then the end will come, when he hands over the kingdom to God the Father after he has destroyed all dominion, authority and power. For he must reign until he has put all his enemies under his feet. The last enemy to be destroyed is death (1 Co.15:24-26).
>
> But thanks be to God, who always leads us in triumphal procession in Christ and through us spreads everywhere the fragrance of the knowledge of him (2 Co.2:14).
>
> For though we live in the world, we do not wage war as the world does. The weapons we fight with are not the weapons of the world. On the contrary, they have divine power to demolish strongholds. We demolish arguments and every pretension that sets itself up against the knowledge of God, and we take captive every thought to make it obedient to Christ (2 Co.10:3-5).
>
> For our struggle is not against flesh and blood, but against the rulers, against the authorities, against the powers of this dark world and against the spiritual forces of evil in the heavenly realms. Therefore put on the full armor of God, so that when the day of evil comes, you may be able to stand your ground, and after you have done everything, to stand (Ep.6:12-13; see vv.12-18).
>
> Having canceled the written code, with its regulations, that was against us and that stood opposed to us; he took it away, nailing it to the cross (Col.2:14).

---

7 Donald Williams. *Psalms 1-72*, p.443.

8 John Phillips. *Exploring Psalms, Volume 1*. WORDsearch CROSS e-book.

3 (60:9-12) Express absolute trust in God.

David was stouthearted! He resolved to strike back against the enemy who had invaded Israel. But he dared not march into battle without the LORD. David confessed his absolute trust in God, declaring that with the LORD's help, Israel would be victorious .

a. God alone can answer your perplexing questions and doubts (vv.9-10).

Apparently, Edom was the enemy that had invaded and brutally defeated Israel. Inspired by God's promise to make Edom His servant, David resolved to repay the Edomites for their crimes against his nation. But Edom was a force to be reckoned with. The strong or fortified city to which David referred was its capital, Petra, "the impregnable rock-fortress which could be approached only down a narrow [ravine] in the mountains."[9] As eager as David was to serve justice on Israel's enemy, he knew that he could not prevail in his own power. He expressed this feeling by asking two questions (v.9):

> ➤ Who can empower me to penetrate Petra?
> ➤ Who can lead me to victory over Edom?

Acknowledging his dependence on the LORD, David answered his questions: God was Israel's only hope (v.10). Yet from the nation's perspective, God had rejected them, having allowed their adversaries to defeat them.

b. God alone can help you (vv.11-12).

David cried out for God to come to the aid of His chosen people (v.11a). Only God could help Israel prevail against her enemy. *Enemy* (tsar, also translated as trouble in some Bible versions) is the most appropriate word David could have chosen to describe his dilemma. It refers to a narrow or tight place and perfectly conveys the only approach to Petra. David's army had no choice but to pass through the pinched gorge that led to Edom's capital. As they squeezed through the ravine, they would be an easy target for the city's highly-skilled defenders. Unless God went before them, they would surely fall before they ever made it to the city gates.

In appealing to God for help, David declared two important truths that guided him as a man of war (1 S.16:18; 2 S.17:8): First, human help is useless in defeating the world's enemies (v.11b). Second, God alone can make us victorious over the enemies of this world (v.12; Ep.6:10-18).

David concluded Psalm 60 by declaring His faith in God. God would empower Israel to win a great victory over the Edomites. He would trample their brazen enemy.

And trample them He did. Scripture records that God empowered Israel to seize Edom, and the Edomites became David's servants (2 S.8:13-14).

Thought 1. Although David had a valiant army with strong leaders, he did not trust in his own resources for victory over Edom. He knew that he could be victorious only with God's help. As we fight against our spiritual enemies—the world, the flesh, and the devil—we too need to fully trust in God for victory. God's Word teaches us how to battle our spiritual foes:

> **Finally, be strong in the Lord and in his mighty power. Put on the full armor of God so that you can take your stand against the devil's schemes. For our struggle is not against flesh and blood, but against the rulers, against the authorities, against the powers of this dark world and against the spiritual forces of evil in the heavenly realms. Therefore put on the full armor of God, so that when the day of evil comes, you may be able to stand your ground, and after you have done everything, to stand. Stand firm then, with the belt of truth buckled around your waist, with the breastplate of righteousness in place, and with your feet fitted with the readiness that comes from the gospel of peace. In addition to all this, take up the shield of faith, with which you can extinguish all the flaming arrows of the evil one. Take the helmet of salvation and the sword of the Spirit, which is the word of God. And pray in the Spirit on all occasions with all kinds of prayers and requests. With this in mind, be alert and always keep on praying for all the saints (Ep.6:10-18).**

Note three commands in this passage:
(1) Go forth in God's strength and power (v.10).
(2) Clothe yourself in the armor of God (vv.11-17a).
(3) Arm yourself with God's Word and prayer (vv.17b-18).

Through the power of God, you can overcome every enemy that oppresses you, such as...

- fear
- worry
- discouragement
- depression
- substance abuse or addiction
- bitterness
- painful memories
- addiction to pornography
- sexual perversion
- anger
- lack of self-control
- doubt and unbelief
- guilt
- greed
- pride
- love of possessions
- love of pleasure
- lust

---

[9] John Phillips. *Exploring Psalms, Volume 1.* WORD*search* CROSS e-book.

...and whatever else you are battling. Through God, you can do valiantly. He can trample down every enemy in your life (v.12). Never accept defeat. Refuse to live in bondage to the enemy and always believe that there is hope. Do not let setbacks stop you. Keep moving forward and God will give you victory if you fully trust and obey Him. "For nothing is impossible with God" (Lu.1:37).

"I have told you these things, so that in me you may have peace. In this world you will have trouble. But take heart! I have overcome the world" (Jn.16:33).

What, then, shall we say in response to this? If God is for us, who can be against us? (Ro.8:31).

No, in all these things we are more than conquerors through him who loved us (Ro.8:37).

The Lord will rescue me from every evil attack and will bring me safely to his heavenly kingdom. To him be glory for ever and ever. Amen (2 Ti.4:18).

You, dear children, are from God and have overcome them, because the one who is in you is greater than the one who is in the world (1 Jn.4:4).

For everyone born of God overcomes the world. This is the victory that has overcome the world, even our faith. Who is it that overcomes the world? Only he who believes that Jesus is the Son of God (1 Jn.5:4-5).

He rescued me from my powerful enemy, from my foes, who were too strong for me (Ps.18:17).

With flattery he will corrupt those who have violated the covenant, but the people who know their God will firmly resist him (Da.11:32).

| | PSALM 61

**When You Feel Over-
whelmed by Life,
61:1-8**

*For the director of music.
With stringed instru-
ments. Of David.* | 4 I long to dwell in your tent forever and take refuge in the shelter of your wings. Selah
5 For you have heard my vows, O God; you have given me the heritage of those who fear your name.
6 Increase the days of the king's life, his years for many generations.
7 May he be enthroned in God's presence forever; appoint your love and faithfulness to protect him.
8 Then will I ever sing praise to your name and fulfill my vows day after day. | **2. Tell God you long to live with Him forever**
a. Bc. He will shelter you under His wings
b. Bc. He has heard the promises you made to Him
c. Bc. He has promised to give an inheritance to all who fear Him, 1 Pe.1:3-4
3. Approach God boldly in prayer
a. Ask Him to prolong your life & testimony for generations
b. Ask Him to appoint you to live in His presence forever—to keep you by His mercy & love
4. Make a renewed commitment to praise God & to fulfill your promises each & every day |
| **1. Cry out to God: Beg Him to hear your prayer**
a. When you feel lost & far away from God, call on His name
b. When you feel overwhelmed, ask God to lead you to safety
　1) Bc. He is the rock
　2) Bc. He is your refuge & tower of strength—your protection from the enemy | Hear my cry, O God; listen to my prayer.
2 From the ends of the earth I call to you, I call as my heart grows faint; lead me to the rock that is higher than I.
3 For you have been my refuge, a strong tower against the foe. | | |

PSALM 61

When You Feel Overwhelmed by Life, 61:1-8

(61:1-8) Introduction: we cannot escape the demands of day-to-day life. At every stage of our time on earth, pressures exist:

➢ Children and teens face the pressures of learning, completing homework, passing tests, fitting in socially, and obeying parents and other authorities.

➢ Young adults face the pressures of securing employment, supporting themselves, finding a spouse, and making their own way in the world.

➢ Parents deal with the demands of working to provide for a family, training their children and being involved in their activities, meeting their spouse's needs, maintaining a home, assisting or caring for aging parents, being involved in civic and community affairs, and being faithful to church responsibilities.

➢ Senior adults must endure the challenges of declining health, physical limitations, diminishing income, the inability to care for themselves, loss of independence, loss of a spouse, loneliness, and a host of other circumstances that can complicate life for the aging adult.

These are just the demands of everyday life. Additional adversities make life's burdens even heavier: an illness, accident, or medical emergency; unexpected expenses, loss of employment, or decrease in income; conflict with coworkers, marriage problems, or misbehaving children; threats to our safety or national security, and countless other trials that stretch us beyond our limits.

At times, the pressures of life are so strong that we feel we are going to collapse beneath their weight. We feel overwhelmed, helpless, and inadequate to handle all that is happening in our lives. Our loving Lord has given us Psalm 61 for such times.

David wrote this psalm during a time of extreme stress. Scripture does not inform us of its exact setting, but the psalm indicates that David was now king of Israel and, for some reason, he was far from home (vv.2, 6). Many commentators think he wrote it during Absalom's rebellion (2 S.15-18). Because of its placment immediately after Psalm 60, others feel it was written during David's extensive military campaign in the north (2 S.8; 1 Chr.18).

Whatever pressures he was under, David knew he could not endure them in his own strength. "His longing is for restoration to God rather than to circumstances."[1] It is an intensely personal psalm, one we can claim as our own when we feel like we are drowning under life's demands. This is, *When You Feel Overwhelmed By Life*, 61:1-8.

1. Cry out to God: Beg Him to hear your prayer (vv.1-3).
2. Tell God you long to live with Him forever (vv.4-5).
3. Approach God boldly in prayer (vv.6-7).
4. Make a renewed commitment to praise God and to fulfill your promises each and every day (v.8).

1 **(61:1-3) Cry out to God: Beg Him to hear your prayer.** When David felt he could no longer withstand the pressures of life, he cried out to God for help. He desperately sought to get God's attention, begging Him to listen to his urgent prayer.

a. When you feel lost and far away from God, call on His name (v.2ᵃ).

"For any Jew the center of the universe was (and is) Jerusalem, where the ark of God was located."[2] *Ends*

---

1 G. Campbell Morgan. *Notes on the Psalms.* (Westwood, NJ: Fleming H. Revell Company, 1947), p.109.

2 James Montgomery Boice. *An Expositional Commentary–Psalms, Volume 2: Psalms 42-106.* WORDsearch CROSS e-book.

of the earth, which can also be translated *ends of the land*, indicates that David may have been physically far from Jerusalem, far from the place where God's presence resided in a special way. Or, it may have indicated that David felt far away from God spiritually, that he did not sense God's presence. Whatever the case, David felt lost and far from God when he needed Him most, so he called on the Lord for strength and protection.

b. When you feel overwhelmed, ask God to lead you to safety (vv.2ᵇ-3).

David confessed that his heart was completely overwhelmed by his demanding circumstances (v.2ᵇ). He was so totally consumed by affliction that he was about to collapse beneath the heavy load (Ps.107:5; Lam.2:11; Jon.2:7). David was mentally and spiritually exhausted, and he could no longer hold up under the burden he was bearing.

Discouraged and desperate, David prayed for God to lead him to safety. The Lord was David's rock, his strength and security in times of trouble. The image here is of God as a high cliff or stony crevice on the face of a mountain. David recalled that God had always been such a shelter or refuge for him—his strong tower where he had been protected from his enemies (v.3; Pr.18:10). Thus, he prayed that God would lead or guide him out of his despair and draw him to Himself. David knew he would find the strength he so desperately needed through renewed fellowship with God.

Thought 1. When the demands of life overwhelm us, we need to turn to God for strength. Through God's power, we can handle every pressure and circumstance of life. When we are at our weakest point, God's strength takes over (2 Co.12:9). David teaches us to look beyond ourselves and our own strength to the *rock that is higher* than we are. God is our refuge. He will shelter us when the weight of our responsibility threatens to rob us of our peace, joy, and confidence.

We need to realize, as David did, that strength to endure comes from being in God's presence. We enter God's presence by spending time before Him in prayer, in worship, and in His Word. Renewing ourselves inwardly empowers us to face every outward pressure that life flings at us (2 Co.4:16).

Sadly, when under intense pressure, many people tend to neglect both public and private worship. Because they are tired and overwhelmed by demands on their time, some choose not to attend church services. Nor do they set aside time for prayer and meditation in God's Word. Yet it is at these times that we *most* need communion with God. If we are to hold up under life's pressures, time in God's presence must be the most important priority of our lives.

> Therefore we do not lose heart. Though outwardly we are wasting away, yet inwardly we are being renewed day by day (2 Co.4:16).
>
> But he said to me, "My grace is sufficient for you, for my power is made perfect in weakness." Therefore I will boast all the more gladly about my weaknesses, so that Christ's power may rest on me (2 Co.12:9).
>
> Do not be anxious about anything, but in everything, by prayer and petition, with thanksgiving, present your requests to God. And the peace of God, which transcends all understanding, will guard your hearts and your minds in Christ Jesus (Ph.4:6-7).
>
> I can do everything through him who gives me strength (Ph.4:13).
>
> Hear my prayer, O Lord; let my cry for help come to you (Ps.102:1).
>
> Trust in the Lord forever: for the Lord, the Lord, is the Rock eternal (Is.26:4).

2 **(61:4-5) Tell God you long to live with Him forever.**

David expressed his passion for living in God's presence, stating that he longed to live in God's tabernacle forever (Ps.26:8; 27:4). *Tent* refers to the sacred tabernacle of worship in Jerusalem where God dwelled among his people in a special way. David was proclaiming his confidence not only that God would bring him back home to Jerusalem but also, more amazingly, that he would spend eternity with the Lord (Ps.23:6).

a. Because He will shelter you under His wings (v.4).

Hiding under God's wings is one of the most beautiful and intimate images of safety in all of God's Word (Ru.2:12; Ps.17:8; 36:7; 57:1; 91:4; Mt.23:37). Like a mother bird who gathers her young to her breast and covers them with her wings, God desires that we remain close to Him. There, in His bosom, we find safety from all ungodliness and spiritual harm.

Some commentators feel that "the shelter of your wings" refers to the mercy seat of God, which was covered or draped by the outstretched wings of the golden cherubim. This understanding is certainly possible, especially since it is mentioned along with the tabernacle. The mercy seat was the precise spot in the tabernacle where God's presence was manifest. Therefore, whichever understanding is preferred—the image of a mother bird or the mercy seat—the meaning is the same: we find shelter from the dangers and pressures of life when we abide in God's presence.

b. Because He has heard the promises you made to Him (v.5ᵃ).

As David poured out his anxious heart to the Lᴏʀᴅ in prayer, sweet assurance swept over his spirit (Ph.4:6-7). God heard his vows, the commitments he made in his prayer for deliverance. David had perfect peace that God would see him through this crisis and return him to Jerusalem, where he would fulfill the promises he had made to the Lᴏʀᴅ (50:14-15).

c. Because He has promised to give an inheritance to all who fear Him, 1 Pe.1:3-4 (v.5ᵇ).

The Lᴏʀᴅ also assured David that he would receive the heritage or inheritance promised to those who fear God's name. The land of Canaan is the inheritance of the Jewish people (Ps.135:12; 136:21-22). The land is a picture of heaven, the eternal home of all who believe. Scripture promises that a glorious inheritance—one that is eternal and undefiled—is awaiting believers in heaven (1 Pe.1:3-4).

Thought 1. Note two applications from this passage:

(1) When we stay close to the Lᴏʀᴅ, we will be safe in the shelter of His wings. He will protect us from the dangers of this present world and give us strength to overcome life's challenges. Furthermore, we will bask in the unparalleled joy of intimate fellowship with God. He will hear and answer our prayers and will feed us with the milk and meat of His Word (1 Pe.2:1-2).

(2) God has promised us a glorious inheritance, the brightest future imaginable: we are going to live with Him eternally in the new heaven and new earth. Our eternal home in heaven is not made with human hands (2 Co.5:1). Jesus is there now, preparing it for us (Jn.14:2-3). As the children of God, we are joint heirs with Christ (Ro.8:17). All that the Father has promised Him will be ours as well, and the Lord has promised a special reward to all who persevere through trials and temptations (Js.1:12).

> In my Father's house are many rooms; if it were not so, I would have told you. I am going there to prepare a place for you. And if I go and prepare a place for you, I will come back and take you to be with me that you also may be where I am (Jn.14:2-3).

> Now we know that if the earthly tent we live in is destroyed, we have a building from God, an eternal house in heaven, not built by human hands (2 Co.5:1).

> Praise be to the God and Father of our Lord Jesus Christ! In his great mercy he has given us new birth into a living hope through the resurrection of Jesus Christ from the dead, and into an inher-

itance that can never perish, spoil or fade—kept in heaven for you (1 Pe.1:3-4).

> And I heard a loud voice from the throne saying, "Now the dwelling of God is with men, and he will live with them. They will be his people, and God himself will be with them and be their God (Re.21:3).

> Lᴏʀᴅ, you have assigned me my portion and my cup; you have made my lot secure. The boundary lines have fallen for me in pleasant places; surely I have a delightful inheritance (Ps.16:5-6).

> Surely goodness and love will follow me all the days of my life, and I will dwell in the house of the Lᴏʀᴅ forever (Ps.23:6).

3 (61:6-7) **Approach God boldly in prayer.**
Remembering the covenant God had made with him (2 S.7), David boldly approached God in prayer. Far from home and in a perilous situation, David called on God to keep His promise, the promise of an everlasting dynasty in Israel.

a. Ask Him to prolong your life and testimony for generations (v.6).

The Lᴏʀᴅ had also promised David a personal heritage: a throne that would endure forever (2 S.7:16). In faith, David declared that God would prolong his life and testimony for generations to come. In the short term, David believed that God would deliver him and restore him in Jerusalem. This is especially significant if the setting of Psalm 61 is Absalom's rebellion. In the long term, David's life would extend far beyond his days on earth through his royal line. His ultimate descendant would be the Messiah, who will sit on David's throne throughout eternity (Lu.1:32-33).

b. Ask Him to appoint you to live in His presence forever—to keep you by His mercy and love (v.7).

David appealed to God's mercy as he asked God to preserve him forever by His love and faithfulness. *Love* (chesed) is God's unfailing, steadfast love for His people (see outline and notes—Ps.5:7 for more discussion). *Faithfulness* (emeth) is God's faithfulness to His character and the truth of His Word.

Once again, David pointed to his return to Jerusalem when he declared that he would *be enthroned in God's presence forever*. This statement may refer to David's worshipping God in the earthly tabernacle and then eternally in heaven. Or, it may be "a request for special favor with God throughout eternity."³ Many commentators feel David is continuing to ask God to

---

3 Steven Lawson and Max Anders. *Holman Old Testament Commentary—Psalms.* WORDsearch CROSS e-book.

fulfill His covenant promise of preserving his royal dynasty forever through the eternal reign of the Messiah. One of the definitions of *enthroned* (yashab) is to sit, and it is often used in the Old Testament to describe a king sitting on his throne (Ex.11:5; 1 K.35, 46; 2 K.13:13). In addition, some Bible versions translate it as *abide before God forever.*

Thought 1. Like David, we too can pray with great boldness if we take God at His Word. David looked at his situation, considered God's promises, then spoke in faith that God would deliver him and establish his throne eternally. He applied God's promises to his situation and found hope.

Many people struggle with doubt concerning...

- their salvation and the assurance of living with God eternally
- God's provision of their needs
- God's presence in times of trouble
- God's love and care for them as individuals
- God's ability to deliver them from trials, to change their circumstances, or to give them victory in their lives
- the sufficiency of God's strength and grace
- God's will for them
- God's promises

If we are tempted to doubt, or if a situation seems hopeless, we need to remember God's promises and believe that He is faithful to His Word. God can be trusted. For our part, we have to learn to stand firmly on His promises. God cannot lie, and His faithfulness to Himself—His character and holy attributes—is our anchor of hope in troubling times (He.6:18-19). As Jesus encouraged us, we need to simply, "Have faith in God" (Mk.11:22). Prayers offered in doubt are powerless, but prayers lifted up in bold faith have the power to move mountains (Mk.11:23-24; Js.1:6-7).

> **"Have faith in God," Jesus answered. "I tell you the truth, if anyone says to this mountain, 'Go, throw yourself into the sea,' and does not doubt in his heart but believes that what he says will happen, it will be done for him. Therefore I tell you, whatever you ask for in prayer, believe that you have received it, and it will be yours (Mk.11:22-24).**
>
> **If we endure, we will also reign with him. If we disown him, he will also disown us (2 Ti.2:12).**
>
> **Let us then approach the throne of grace with confidence, so that we may receive mercy and find grace to help us in our time of need (He.4:16).**
>
> **God did this so that, by two unchangeable things in which it is impossible for God to lie, we who have fled to take hold of the hope offered to us may be greatly encouraged. We have this hope as an anchor for the soul, firm and secure. It enters the inner sanctuary behind the curtain (He.6:18-19).**
>
> **But when he asks, he must believe and not doubt, because he who doubts is like a wave of the sea, blown and tossed by the wind. That man should not think he will receive anything from the Lord (Js.1:6-7).**

4 (61:8) **Make a renewed commitment to praise God and to fulfill your promises each and every day.** David's confidence in God was unshakeable. He would live to praise the LORD's name for many years and then throughout eternity. God's name represents everything that He is, including His unfailing love and faithfulness.

Equally firm was David's resolve to honor his commitments to God. He looked forward to returning home and showing his gratitude to God by fulfilling his vows. Day after day for the rest of his life he would worship and serve the LORD.

Thought 1. One of Scripture's most comforting phrases is, "It came to pass." When we are overwhelmed by life's pressures, demands, and trials, we need to remember that our current struggles *will come to pass* at some point. Sooner or later, the difficult circumstances we are facing will find their end. Until they do, we need to rely on God's grace and strength to sustain us, and we need to persevere through the power of God's indwelling Holy Spirit.

When in desperate need of God's help, we sometimes promise God things we intend to do out of gratitude for His help or deliverance. There is nothing wrong with this, as long as the vows are genuine and made from a grateful heart, not in an effort to secure God's favor. However, we must be extremely careful to keep these commitments. Sadly, once God has delivered us and our troubling circumstances have passed, many of us tend to forget the promises we made when we so desperately needed the LORD. Scripture offers a stern warning to all who make commitments: do all that you have promised to do. It is better not to make commitments to God than to make promises and not fulfill them:

> **"Again, you have heard that it was said to the people long ago, 'Do not break your oath, but keep the oaths you have made to the Lord.' (Mt.5:33).**
>
> **Then Peter said, "Ananias, how is it that Satan has so filled your heart that you have lied to the Holy Spirit and have**

kept for yourself some of the money you received for the land? Didn't it belong to you before it was sold? And after it was sold, wasn't the money at your disposal? What made you think of doing such a thing? You have not lied to men but to God" (Ac.5:3-4).

When a man makes a vow to the LORD or takes an oath to obligate himself by a pledge, he must not break his word but must do everything he said (Nu.30:2).

If you make a vow to the LORD your God, do not be slow to pay it, for the LORD your God will certainly demand it of you and you will be guilty of sin (De.23:21).

When you make a vow to God, do not delay in fulfilling it. He has no pleasure in fools; fulfill your vow. It is better not to vow than to make a vow and not fulfill it. Do not let your mouth lead you into sin. And do not protest to the [temple] messenger, "My vow was a mistake." Why should God be angry at what you say and destroy the work of your hands? (Ec.5:4-6).

PSALM 62

When Your Faith in God Is Challenged, 62:1-12

For the director of music. For Jeduthun. A psalm of David.

1. Wait quietly on God
   a. He alone is sufficient to help
      1) He is your hope of salvation
      2) He is your rock & your fortress—the one place where you are safe
   b. He alone is able to protect you from all opponents
      1) All who threaten & attack you
      2) All who plot against & lie about you
      3) All who flatter you to your face but curse you in their hearts
   c. He alone can give you genuine rest & security—reemphasized
      1) He is your hope
      2) He is your rock & your

2. Trust in God at all times
   a. Pour out your heart to God: He is your refuge
   b. Do not trust the world's philosophy about wealth & power
      1) Bc. wealth & power carry no weight with God
      2) Bc. trusting in wealth & power will lead to serious sins
         • Extortion
         • Stealing
         • Worshipping wealth

3. Hear the emphasis of God's Word
   a. God is strong & powerful—able to meet your need
   b. God is loving—willing to meet your need
   c. God is sure—faithful to reward all accordingly

salvation—your fortress of protection
   3) He alone gives you glory (victory) & honor
   4) He alone is your rock, your place of refuge

My soul finds rest in God alone; my salvation comes from him.
2 He alone is my rock and my salvation; he is my fortress, I will never be shaken.
3 How long will you assault a man? Would all of you throw him down—this leaning wall, this tottering fence?
4 They fully intend to topple him from his lofty place; they take delight in lies. With their mouths they bless, but in their hearts they curse. Selah
5 Find rest, O my soul, in God alone; my hope comes from him.
6 He alone is my rock and my salvation; he is my fortress, I will not be shaken.
7 My salvation and my honor depend on God; he is my mighty rock, my refuge.
8 Trust in him at all times, O people; pour out your hearts to him, for God is our refuge. Selah
9 Lowborn men are but a breath, the highborn are but a lie; if weighed on a balance, they are nothing; together they are only a breath.
10 Do not trust in extortion or take pride in stolen goods; though your riches increase, do not set your heart on them.
11 One thing God has spoken, two things have I heard: that you, O God, are strong,
12 And that you, O Lord, are loving. Surely you will reward each person according to what he has done.

PSALM 62

When Your Faith in God Is Challenged, 62:1-12

(62:1-12) **Introduction:** *"How can a loving God allow this to happen?"*

Most of us have heard this question asked at one time or another, usually after a senseless tragedy or natural disaster. Many of us have even asked the question ourselves—if not out loud at least in our hearts.

Satan's oldest trick is enticing us to question God and to doubt His love. In the Garden of Eden, Satan tempted Eve by casting doubt on God's motives in forbidding her and Adam to eat of a particular tree (Ge.3:1-5). In doing so, the devil challenged Eve's faith in God's goodness and love for them. Eve's doubts provoked her to yield to temptation, and sin and death entered the world (Ro.5:12).

Generations later, Satan challenged Job's faith in God by taking everything he had—his wealth, his businesses, his means of producing income, his employees, and worst of all, his children—all in a single day. When Job refused to waver in his faith, Satan cruelly attacked his health, inflicting him with a painful and repulsive disease (Job1:6-2:8). Still, Job stood strong in his faith (Jb.3:15).

When David wrote Psalm 62, he was immersed in a situation that challenged his faith in God. While the psalm's heading does not identify the specific setting, we do know that David was facing intense opposition from enemies who were attempting to dethrone him as king

(vv.3-4). Of all the episodes Scripture records regarding David's reign, Absalom's rebellion best fits these circumstances (2 S.15-18). The heading indicates that the psalm was assigned to Jeduthun, a prophet and one of three men appointed to lead worship in the sanctuary (1 Chr.25:1-3; 16:37-42; 2 Chr.5:12; 35:15).

Because life in our sin-cursed world is uncertain, we can be sure that we too will face circumstances that challenge our faith in God and provoke us to question His goodness and love. It may be…

• sickness, disease, or serious accident
• the death of a child, spouse, or other loved one
• the loss of a business, employment, or income
• a vicious assault or attack
• an unjust law or judgment
• the prosperity of the wicked
• the suffering and cruelty that exist in our world

This short list barely begins to list the circumstances Satan can use to tempt us to doubt God. Psalm 62 was lovingly inspired by God's Spirit to guide, comfort, and encourage us in these times. This is, *When Your Faith in God Is Challenged,* 62:1-12.

1. Wait quietly on God (vv.1-7).
2. Trust in God at all times (vv.8-10).
3. Hear the emphasis of God's Word (vv.11-12).

1 (62:1-7) Wait quietly on God.

Even though he was facing a serious challenge, David could honestly say that his soul was resting in God. To *rest* (dumiyyah) means to keep silent, to be still, or to wait. Realizing he could do nothing to change his situation, David waited quietly on God to deliver him. His soul was at peace. God was empowering him to overcome whatever fear, anxiety, and distress his enemies were causing him.

a. He alone is sufficient to help (vv.1-2).

Silently waiting on God was David's only recourse; neither he nor anyone else could change his desperate situation. His only hope for salvation—deliverance, rescue—was the LORD (v.1ᵇ). Only God was sufficient to help. Trusting fully in the LORD to protect him from his fierce enemies, David declared that God and God alone was his rock, his defense or fortress, the one place where he was safe (v.2). Both of these terms speak of an impenetrable stronghold: a high, fortified place where David's foes could not reach him. Because God was his refuge, he would not be moved or shaken.

Salvation (yeshua) points to "the whole process of redemption" through the promises of God's covenant.[1] In the midst of this serious crisis, David could rest calmly because he knew a very important truth: he was in a covenant relationship with God, and he was convinced that God would do all that He had promised.

b. He alone is able to protect you from all opponents (vv.3-4).

David's enemies were many and strong. They continued to threaten and attack him relentlessly (v.3). The word, *assault* (hathath), means to shout fiercely at or attack. The imperiled king knew that only God could protect him, and his confidence that God would stop his wicked opponents was unwavering. After asking how long his enemies would continue to assault him, David answered his own question: his raging foes were about to be brought down. Like a bowing or leaning wall and a tottering fence, they were on the verge of collapse. Soon, God would intervene and they would be *thrown down* in His judgment.

Many Bible versions, including the NIV, take a different view of the second part of this verse. They translate all of verse 3 as referring to the enemies' attempts to take David's life. They understand the verse to say that the enemy was determined to murder him, believing that the king—like a leaning wall or a tottering fence—was vulnerable and on the brink of falling. One strong argument to support this translation is the Hebrew word for *thrown down* (ratsach). Throughout the Old Testament, this word refers to murdering someone or killing another person illegally. It is not used anywhere else for judicial punishment or God's judgment.[2]

Despite his enemies' persistence, David firmly believed that God would protect him from his adversaries' evil plots and slanderous lies (v.4). David's enemies had *fully intended* (ya'ats) or counselled together, deliberated, and planned, to "topple him from his lofty place" or exalted position as king of Israel. They were two-faced and double-tongued. They flattered David to his face but cursed him in their hearts. When the time was right, they revealed themselves as the king's enemies, spreading vicious lies to turn the people against him.

c. He alone can give you genuine rest and security—reemphasized (vv.5-7)

Naming the wicked deeds of his enemies likely stirred anger and anxiety in David's spirit. He quickly brought his feelings under control, commanding his soul to wait silently on God (v.5ᵃ). He reemphasized his firm conviction that only God could give him genuine rest and security. In the midst of the threatening situation he stated once again that God alone was…

- his expectation or hope (v.5ᵇ)
- his rock and salvation, his fortress of protection (v.6)
- the giver of his glory (victory) and honor (v.7ᵃ)
- his rock of strength and place of refuge (v.7ᵇ)

Thought 1. When our faith is challenged, we have to resist our natural tendency to worry, fear, and doubt. Instead, we need to learn to simply wait on the LORD. When we fully trust Him, we will find the rest for our souls that David found. No one else can give us peace in the midst of troubling times. God alone can enable us to rest when the storms of life are raging all around us. Jesus personally invites us to come to Him for rest:

> **"Come to me, all you who are weary and burdened, and I will give you rest. Take my yoke upon you and learn from me, for I am gentle and humble in heart, and you will find rest for your souls (Mt.11:28-29).**
>
> **Peace I leave with you; my peace I give you. I do not give to you as the world gives. Do not let your hearts be troubled and do not be afraid (Jn.14:27).**
>
> **"I have told you these things, so that in me you may have peace. In this world you will have trouble. But take heart! I have overcome the world" (Jn.16:33).**
>
> **I wait for the LORD, my soul waits, and in his word I put my hope (Ps.130:5).**
>
> **But whoever listens to me will live in safety and be at ease, without fear of harm" (Pr.1:33).**

---

1 Frank E. Gaebelein, ed. *The Expositor's Bible Commentary*, p.421.

2 Donald Williams. *Psalms 1-72*, p.452.

> **You will keep in perfect peace him whose mind is steadfast, because he trusts in you (Is.26:3).**

Thought 2. When our faith is challenged, feelings of frustration and helplessness can spill over into words that are not worthy of the Lord. Desperate, unchanging circumstances tend to bring out the worst in us, causing us to become angry at God, to blame Him, or to think He doesn't care about us. During such times, we need to be silent and resist the urge to speak foolishly against the Lord. The Bible records that Job—upon losing all of his livestock, servants, and children in a single day—did not sin by foolishly accusing God (Jb.1:22). Likewise, David waited silently on God, believing and declaring that God would save him. We would all do well to follow their example.

> **It is written: "I believed; therefore I have spoken." With that same spirit of faith we also believe and therefore speak (2 Co.4:13).**
>
> **In all this, Job did not sin by charging God with wrongdoing (Jb.1:22).**
>
> **I said, "I will watch my ways and keep my tongue from sin; I will put a muzzle on my mouth as long as the wicked are in my presence" (Ps.39:1).**

2 (62:8-10) Trust in God at all times.

After sharing how his soul had found rest in the LORD, David instructed all of us how to find this same calmness when our faith is challenged. The key, David wrote, is to give God our burdens and trust Him fully with them. At all times—in every season and circumstance of our lives—we should put our confidence in God.

a. Pour out your heart to God: He is your refuge (v.8).

David exhorted us to fully unburden ourselves by pouring out our hearts to God (v.8). One of the greatest lessons of *Psalms* is that God has given us the precious liberty of emptying our souls—everything we are thinking and feeling—before Him. Literally, we can pour out our hearts to Him, to His *face*. The reason: because He is our refuge, our shelter and security. When we are hiding in Him, we are free from care. Before we can truly take shelter in God, we have to release our burdens to Him. We have to trust Him to sustain us and to handle every circumstance or situation that affects us.

b. Do not trust the world's philosophy about wealth and power (vv. 9-10).

In sharp contrast to trusting God is the danger of self-sufficiency. The world tells us that we need to accumulate wealth and gain power in order to be strong enough to defend ourselves in time of trouble. But Scripture advises us to reject this philosophy for two practical reasons:

First, trusting in wealth and power is utterly worthless, for these things carry no weight with God (v.9). God is neither impressed nor influenced by our possessions and power. Men of low degree and high degree—poor and rich, common and noble, weak and mighty—are all the same in God's sight. We have nothing to offer God that He needs; our very best is nothing more than *a breath* (hebel) to Him—empty, worthless, meaningless, like a vapor that quickly passes away (Is.57:13; Jb.7:16; Ec.2:11).

Second, trusting in wealth and power can lead to serious sin (v.10). Scripture repeatedly warns us that the love of money is the root of all sorts of evil (Pr.28:20; 1 Ti.6:9-10). David mentioned three sins in particular:

➢ Oppression or extortion (Le.6:1-4)
➢ Stealing (Ex.20:15; Le.19:11)
➢ Worshipping wealth; that is, making money or possessions the most important thing in our lives (De.8:13-14; Pr.30:9; Eze.28:5)

Thought 1. When our faith is challenged, one of God's most helpful promises is this:

> **Do not be anxious about anything, but in everything, by prayer and petition, with thanksgiving, present your requests to God. And the peace of God, which transcends all understanding, will guard your hearts and your minds in Christ Jesus (Ph.4:6-7).**

We should not allow anxiety to control us when difficult circumstances come into our lives. Instead, we can be calmed by taking our burden to the LORD in prayer. As we commit our problems to Him, He promises to give us His indescribable peace. Just as God's peace swept over David's troubled spirit, we too can find rest when we pour out our hearts to the LORD. Sixteenth century theologian John Calvin (1509-1564) wrote about the necessity of giving our heavy load to God before we can find relief from its taxing burden:

> *It is always found, that when the heart is pressed under a load of distress, there is no freedom in prayer. Under trying circumstances, we must comfort ourselves by reflecting that God will extend relief, provided we just freely roll them over upon his consideration. What the Psalmist advises is all the more necessary, considering the mischievous tendency which we have naturally to keep our troubles pent up in our breasts till they drive us to despair. Usually, indeed, men show much anxiety and ingenuity in seeking to escape from the troubles which may*

happen to press upon them; but so long as they shun coming into the presence of God, they only involve themselves in a [web] of difficulties...exposing that diseased but deeply-rooted principle in our nature, which leads us to hide our griefs...instead of relieving ourselves at once by pouring out our prayers and complaints before God.[3]

Refusing to release our burdens to God is an act of pride and self-sufficiency. In doing so, we choose to trust in ourselves rather than God. Pastor and commentator James Montgomery Boice (1938-2000) addressed this problem, emphasizing the importance of trusting God and God alone:

The most important thing about Psalm 62 is that the psalmist is making God his only object of trust. He is not trusting something other than God, nor is he trusting God and something else, or God and someone else. His trust is in God only, and that is why he is so confident...

I think this is something Christians in our day especially need to learn. As I see it, our problem is not that we do not trust God, at least in some sense. We have to do that to be Christians. To become a Christian you have to trust God in the matter of salvation at least. It is rather that we do not trust God only, meaning that we always want to add in something else to trust as well...

Christians in our day are far more inclined to trust the world's tools and mechanisms than to trust Jesus Christ wholly. For many of today's believers Jesus really is not sufficient for all things, regardless of what they may profess publicly.[4]

As Dr. Boice emphasized, we need to completely trust God and God alone with every area of our lives. We only find rest for our troubled souls...

- when we pour out our hearts and *give* our burdens to the Lord
- when we *leave* our burdens with the Lord and fully trust Him to take care of us

Such confidence as this is ours through Christ before God. Not that we are competent in ourselves to claim anything for ourselves, but our competence comes from God (2 Co.3:4-5).

Command those who are rich in this present world not to be arrogant nor to put their hope in wealth, which is so uncertain, but to put their hope in God, who richly provides us with everything for our enjoyment (1 Ti.6:17).

So then, those who suffer according to God's will should commit themselves to their faithful Creator and continue to do good (1 Pe.4:19).

Commit your way to the LORD; trust in him and he will do this: He will make your righteousness shine like the dawn, the justice of your cause like the noonday sun. Be still before the LORD and wait patiently for him; do not fret when men succeed in their ways, when they carry out their wicked schemes (Ps.37:5-7).

I cry to you, O LORD; I say, "You are my refuge, my portion in the land of the living." Listen to my cry, for I am in desperate need; rescue me from those who pursue me, for they are too strong for me (Ps.142:5-6).

Trust in the LORD with all your heart and lean not on your own understanding; in all your ways acknowledge him, and he will make your paths straight (Pr.3:5-6).

3 (62:11-12) **Hear the emphasis of God's Word.** God has spoken repeatedly of His ability and desire to help us with our trouble (v.11a). The numerical sequence *"one...two"* is a poetic way of saying that God has said this many times (Jb.33:14; 40:5; Am.1:3). David closed Psalm 62 by urging us to hear the emphasis of God's Word:

➢ God is strong and powerful. He is able to meet our needs (v.11b).
➢ God is loving beyond our comprehension, and He is willing to meet our needs (v.12a). *Loving* (chesed) refers to God's unfailing, covenant love (see outline and notes—Ps.5:7 for more information). We may fail the LORD, but He will never fail us, for He is true to His Word.
➢ God is sure. He is faithful to reward every person according to his or her work (v.12b). When we trust the LORD and obey His commands, He blesses us and helps us. And we can be absolutely sure that He will deal righteously with those who sin against us (v.4). Therefore, we should wait quietly and rest in Him when our faith is challenged (v.1, 5).

Thought 1. When David's faith was challenged, he found rest by recalling God's Word and believing what God said. When he could not see God at work, he chose to trust God and to wait quietly for Him to do all He had promised.

Believing what we cannot see is the very essence of faith (He.11:1). The world often describes the believer's faith as "blind faith;" that is, we foolishly believe something for which we have no basis. However, nothing could be further from the truth. Our faith has

---

3 John Calvin. *Calvin's Commentaries* WORDsearch CROSS e-book.
4 James Montgomery Boice. *An Expositional Commentary–Psalms, Volume 2: Psalms 42-106.* WORDsearch CROSS e-book.

a firm foundation: the inspired, inerrant, infallible Word of the Living God. The promises of God are the basis of our faith. Again and again, God has assured us of His power, His unfailing love, and His justice. When our faith is challenged and we cannot see God at work, we need to take God at His word, believing that He will do—in His time and according to His purpose—all He has promised. This is what it means to wait quietly for the LORD. When we do, we will find rest for our troubled souls, just as David did.

Consequently, faith comes from hearing the message, and the message is heard through the word of Christ (Ro.10:17).

For no matter how many promises God has made, they are "Yes" in Christ. And so through him the "Amen" is spoken by us to the glory of God (2 Co.1:20).

God did this so that, by two unchangeable things in which it is impossible for God to lie, we who have fled to take hold of the hope offered to us may be greatly encouraged (He.6:18).

Now faith is being sure of what we hope for and certain of what we do not see (He.11:1).

But with the precious blood of Christ, a lamb without blemish or defect. He was chosen before the creation of the world, but was revealed in these last times for your sake. Through him you believe in God, who raised him from the dead and glorified him, and so your faith and hope are in God (1 Pe.1:19-21).

The law of the LORD is perfect, reviving the soul. The statutes of the LORD are trustworthy, making wise the simple (Ps.19:7).

PSALM 63

When You Are Stirred to Seek God's Presence & Security, 63:1-11

A psalm of David. When he was in the Desert of Judah.

1. Follow the stirrings of your soul: Express your thirst & longing for God

a. Express yourself thru worship
  1) Bc. you see God's power & glory in focused worship
  2) Bc. you realize that God's love is better than life itself: Glorify Him openly
b. Express yourself thru praise
  1) Make a commitment to praise God as long as you live
  2) Praise God bc. He satisfies

O God, you are my God, earnestly I seek you; my soul thirsts for you, my body longs for you, in a dry and weary land where there is no water.
2 I have seen you in the sanctuary and beheld your power and your glory.
3 Because your love is better than life, my lips will glorify you.
4 I will praise you as long as I live, and in your name I will lift up my hands.
5 My soul will be satisfied as with the richest of foods; with singing lips my mouth will praise you.
6 On my bed I remember you; I think of you through the watches of the night.
7 Because you are my help, I sing in the shadow of your wings.
8 My soul clings to you; your right hand upholds me.
9 They who seek my life will be destroyed; they will go down to the depths of the earth.
10 They will be given over to the sword and become food for jackals.
11 But the king will rejoice in God; all who swear by God's name will praise him, while the mouths of liars will be silenced.

your soul: He abundantly provides for you & meets your need
c. Express yourself by meditating on the LORD throughout the night
  1) Bc. He is your helper
  2) Bc. He is your protector: He keeps you under His wings

2. Follow God & cling to Him
a. Bc. He strengthens & upholds you
b. Bc. He will execute true justice on earth
  1) He will destroy those who oppress & seek to harm you (the righteous)

  2) He will vindicate you: He stirs you to praise Him while He silences the liars, the deceivers of this earth

---

PSALM 63

When You Are Stirred to Seek God's Presence and Security, 63:1-11

(63:1-11) Introduction: when all is well in our lives, it is easy to forget how much we need God's presence. Some of us may become too casual in our devotional lives or even totally neglect prayer and meditation on God's Word. Then some crisis strikes and we are shaken into the reality that we desperately need the LORD. Frantically, we begin to seek God's help, and we turn to His Holy Word for comfort, security, and direction. We long for the LORD's assurance that He hears us and is working things out for us. Fortunately for us, God is faithful all the time. He is always ready to hear and answer our prayers when we come to Him sincerely.

David wrote Psalm 63 at a time when he desperately needed a personal experience with God. He needed time in God's presence. The heading to the psalm does not inform us of its specific occasion, only that David was in the Judean wilderness (desert) when he wrote it. The psalm itself reveals that David was king of Israel at the time, which means it was not written during his flight from Saul (v.11). Most likely, the occasion was Absalom's sinful attempt to overthrow his father.

Old Testament believers were not blessed, as we are, to have God's presence abiding within them. Today, God dwells in His people through His Holy Spirit. In David's day, however, God's presence was manifested in the tabernacle. Exiled from Jerusalem, David felt far away from God when he desperately needed to experience God's presence.

David was a deeply spiritual man. In fact, God called him "a man after His own heart" (1 S.13:14; Ac.13:22). David's passion for God is revealed in this psalm. He shows us how intimate our relationship with God can be. Hebrew professor and commentator Alexander Kirkpatrick (1849–1940) wrote, "Such a Psalm teaches, more effectually than any formal definition, what is meant by a Personal God—a God with Whom the soul can hold converse with the whole force and fervor of a loving devotion."[1]

In this psalm, David shows us what it is like to have a deep love for the LORD. As you study it, do so with a prayer that God will kindle within your soul a passion that is comparable to David's. This is, *When You Are Stirred to Seek God's Presence and Security,* 63:1-11.

1. Follow the stirrings of your soul: Express your thirst and longing for God (vv.1-7).
2. Follow God and cling to Him (vv.8-11).

1 **(63:1-7) Follow the stirrings of your soul: Express your thirst and longing for God.**
David expressed just how desperately he longed for the LORD. *You are my God* emphasizes David's personal relationship with the LORD and is the heartbeat of God's covenant with His people.[2] Because He so passionately loves us, God offers us a way to be reconciled to Him. When we accept God's terms—repentance of sin and faith in Jesus Christ as Savior—we are given the greatest privilege in all the world: a personal, intimate relationship with the one true God. He becomes our Heavenly Father; Christ becomes our Savior and Lord.

---

1 A.F. Kirkpatrick. *The Book of Psalms.* WORD*search* CROSS e-book.
2 Derek Kidner. *Psalms 1-72*, p.242.

David described his intense spiritual need in terms of his physical surroundings. Having fled for his life from Jerusalem, he was stranded in the Judean wilderness or desert, a dry and thirsty land where there was no water. His dust-dried mouth was a symbol of his parched soul: just as his tongue craved a refreshing drink from a cool stream, his soul desperately thirsted for living water—God's presence and fellowship.

a. Express yourself through worship (vv.2-3).

David recalled how his soul was thrilled when he went into the sanctuary, the holy tabernacle where God's grandeur was so splendidly displayed (v.2). Time and again, he had witnessed God's power and glory when God's people focused on Him in worship. How he longed to enter God's courts once again, to bask in the radiant glory of God's holy presence!

As he envisioned the delight of being in the LORD's company, David considered one of the strongest reasons for worshipping God: His love toward us (v.3). This *love* (chesed) is God's covenant love—His mercy, His steadfast love (see outline and notes—Ps.5:7 for more discussion). David judged God's unfailing love as being better than life itself, "or to put it another way, it is to begin to live."[3] Meditating on God's love moved David to praise and glorify God openly and audibly, with his lips. The Hebrew word for *glorify* (shabach) is seldom used in the Old Testament. It speaks of exalting God as well as holding Him in high esteem.[4] Its primary meaning is to be calm or still, and it points to serene, reflective adoration of God as opposed to loud, boisterous praise.

b. Express yourself through praise (vv.4-5).

David understood that inward worship should be accompanied by outward praise. Accordingly, he made a commitment to *praise* (barak) or bless God, to publicly express gratitude and honor for the LORD because of what He has done (v.4). As he gave honor and glory to God, he would lift up his hands in praise of God's great name.

David committed to praise God because God satisfied his soul with the richest of foods, also modernly translated as "fat and rich food" (ESV) and "the richest feast" (NLT) (v.5). David was saying that God satisfied the cravings of his spirit the way a large meal would fill him physically, until he wanted nothing further (Jn.4:13-14; 6:35). More than that, the experience was delightful to the taste, like a feast of the richest, most exquisite foods. David was saying that God abundantly provides for us and meets our deepest needs. He gives us the very best He has to offer—Himself. His presence brightens the darkest times of our lives, giving us a joyful song in the most difficult circumstances.

c. Express yourself by meditating on the LORD throughout the night (vv.6-7).

Sleep did not come easy for David while he was hiding from his rebellious son in the desert. But as he lay awake on his bed, he remembered or thought about God. During the night watches, the troubled king meditated on God. Commentator Warren Wiersbe notes that "the Jews had three night watches, from sunset to ten o'clock, from ten to two o'clock, and from two to sunrise."[5] All throughout the night, whenever David was awake, his restless soul was soothed by dwelling on two great truths about God (v.7):

➢ The LORD was his helper. As David looked back over his life, he saw that God had sustained and assisted him in every crisis.
➢ The LORD was his protector. He kept David under His wings, the way a mother bird draws her young to her bosom and covers them with her wings (Ps.17:8; 36:7; 91:4).

Thought 1. In this world, we are living in a dry and thirsty land, a barren wilderness where there is no spiritual water. But in the midst of this burning desert, there is an oasis, a well of living water. Through His Son, Jesus Christ, God offers us this living water (Jn.7:13-14). We drink that water through worship, entering God's presence and communing with Him in spirit and in truth (Jn.4:23-24). In the New Testament, the Greek word for worship, *proskuneo*, means to kiss, implying passion. When we passionately shower our love on the Lord, our souls are sustained and refreshed. His love is our water in this sin-saturated world. His presence is our oasis. Consider two vital thoughts:

First, many believers do not thirst for a personal experience with God. Instead, they indulge in the desires of the flesh and the things of this world, which stifle their thirst for the Lord. Others are so busy—even in the work of the church—that they neglect spending time at the feet of Jesus (Lu.10:38-42). Of this, powerful preacher Alexander Maclaren (1826-1910) wrote:

> *Blessed are they who know where the fountain is, who know the meaning of the highest unrests in their own souls, and can go on to say with clear and true self-revelation, "My soul thirsteth for God!"... There is a great deal more in Christianity than longing, but there is no Christianity worth the name without it* [the longing].[6]

Second, all around us souls are perishing for lack of water. Tragically, they are turning to the things of the world—drugs, alcohol, sex, money and possessions,

3 Donald Williams. *Psalms 1-72*, p.459.
4 Spiros Zodhiates. *AMG Complete Word Study Dictionary.* WORD-search CROSS e-book.
5 Warren W. Wiersbe. *The Bible Exposition Commentary.* WORDsearch CROSS e-book.
6 Alexander Maclaren. *Expositions of Holy Scripture: Psalms,* 1908. WORDsearch CROSS e-book.

power, careers, pleasure, entertainment—to satisfy their starving souls. We must point them to the well of living water, where they will find eternal life and lasting satisfaction (Jn.6:35; 7:37-38).

> **Blessed are those who hunger and thirst for righteousness, for they will be filled (Mt.5:6).**
>
> **On the last and greatest day of the Feast, Jesus stood and said in a loud voice, "If anyone is thirsty, let him come to me and drink. Whoever believes in me, as the Scripture has said, streams of living water will flow from within him" (Jn.7:37-38).**
>
> **As the deer pants for streams of water, so my soul pants for you, O God. My soul thirsts for God, for the living God. When can I go and meet with God? (Ps.42:1-2).**
>
> **Whom have I in heaven but you? And earth has nothing I desire besides you (Ps.73:25).**
>
> **I spread out my hands to you; my soul thirsts for you like a parched land. Selah (Ps.143:6).**

2 (63:8-11) Follow God and cling to Him.

Upon recalling the LORD's faithfulness in helping him, David declared that he would follow God and cling to Him. To *cling* (dabaq) means to stick to, or to stay with. It is the word used to describe a man's cleaving to his wife (Ge.2:24) and of Ruth's staying with Naomi after her mother-in-law told her to turn back (Ru.1:14). In his time of intense trouble, David reaffirmed his devotion to the LORD.

a. Because He strengthens and upholds you (v.8).

David confessed his dependence on God to strengthen and uphold him with His right hand, a symbol of God's mighty power (Ps.18:35; Is.41:10). The LORD had always sustained him through every crisis and conflict. He dared not claim as his own the victories God had won, and he knew that he would not survive Absalom's revolt without God's help. For this reason, David resolved to stay close to God.

Some commentators have a different view of this statement; they say that David was declaring that he could only cling to God by *God's* power, not by his own efforts. Commentator Derek Kidner writes, "It is God himself who makes [clinging to God] possible, and the firmness of his upholding grasp is implied in the allusion to the *right* hand, the stronger of the two."[7] Certainly, this is true, for it is God's grace that empowers us to be faithful to Him.

b. Because He will execute true justice on earth (vv.9-11).

David had complete confidence in God's righteousness and firmly believed that God would execute justice in his situation. God would destroy those who sinfully oppressed and sought to harm him (v.9). "Shall go down to the depths of the earth" is a reference to death. David predicted that his adversaries would die violently and that their corpses would remain on the battlefield where animals would feed on them (v.10).

Many people struggle with statements like these in *Psalms* where David prays for the violent destruction of his enemies. For insight into this subject, refer to the discussion on *Imprecatory (cursing)* psalms in KEYS TO UNDERSTANDING PSALMS.

David was certain that God would vindicate him, and his certainty stirred him to praise the LORD with great joy (v.11). He concluded this psalm with a strong declaration of faith that God would deliver him. As a result, all who swore by him—who trusted God and had confidence in His Word—would *praise* (halal) or give God glory when He finally silenced those who lied about Israel's king. Likewise, all who are righteous will rejoice when God finally judges all the deceivers and evildoers of this world.

Thought 1. Trouble will either push us away from God or draw us closer to Him. Many people fall away from or stop following the Lord when a painful crisis ravages their lives. Some become angry or bitter toward God. Some blame God. Others cannot accept that God would allow such a thing to happen, that He did not act supernaturally to prevent it.

Imagine how easy it would have been for David to become angry and blame God when his own son tried to destroy him. Instead, David chose to draw nearer to God. We need to follow David's example and cling to God in times of trouble. We need to trust God to strengthen and sustain us. When others lie about us or sin against us, we need to remember that God is righteous and that He will deal with all evildoers in His good time.

Undoubtedly, we will face problems in our lives, sometimes excruciatingly painful problems. But those are the very times we should hold fast to God and draw closer than ever to Him. He loves us and He will sustain us through the dark nights and deep valleys of our lives. God has given us a wonderful promise: if we draw near to Him, He will draw near to us (Js.4:8).

> **Come near to God and he will come near to you. Wash your hands, you sinners, and purify your hearts, you double-minded (Js.4:8)**
>
> **(For the law made nothing perfect), and a better hope is introduced, by which we draw near to God (He.7:19).**

---

7 Derek Kidner. *Psalms 1-72*, p.244.

Let us draw near to God with a sincere heart in full assurance of faith, having our hearts sprinkled to cleanse us from a guilty conscience and having our bodies washed with pure water. Let us hold unswervingly to the hope we profess, for he who promised is faithful (He.10:22-23).

But as for me, it is good to be near God. I have made the Sovereign LORD my refuge; I will tell of all your deeds (Ps.73:28).

The LORD is near to all who call on him, to all who call on him in truth (Ps.145:18).

So do not fear, for I am with you; do not be dismayed, for I am your God. I will strengthen you and help you; I will uphold you with my righteous right hand (Is.41:10).

PSALM 64

When People Verbally Assault & Plot Evil Against You, 64:1-10

For the director of music. A psalm of David.

1. Ask God to protect you from the enemy's threats	Hear me, O God, as I voice my complaint; protect my life from the threat of the enemy.
a. Bc. He alone knows their evil plans & can hide you from the wicked mob	2 Hide me from the conspiracy of the wicked, from that noisy crowd of evildoers.
b. Bc. the wicked use their tongues like deadly weapons	3 They sharpen their tongues like swords and aim their words like deadly arrows.
1) They verbally assault the innocent	
• They lay in wait to suddenly ambush their targets	4 They shoot from ambush at the innocent man; they shoot at him suddenly,
• They fear neither God nor man as they plot	without fear.
2) They encourage & gather	5 They encourage each

other in evil plans, they talk about hiding their snares; they say, "Who will see them?"	strength from each others' conniving behavior
6 They plot injustice and say, "We have devised a perfect plan!" Surely the mind and heart of man are cunning.	• They feel neither God nor man sees their scheming
	• They are prideful & overly confident in their devious plans
	3) They are cunning & evil through & through
7 But God will shoot them with arrows; suddenly they will be struck down.	**2. Trust God to give you the victory**
8 He will turn their own tongues against them and bring them to ruin; all who see them will shake their heads in scorn.	a. He will suddenly strike down the enemy
	1) God will execute perfect justice: The evil & shame the enemy plotted against you will fall back on them
9 All mankind will fear; they will proclaim the works of God and ponder what he has done.	2) God will use justice to stir fear in everyone: They will acknowledge God & proclaim His mighty works
10 Let the righteous rejoice in the LORD and take refuge in him; let all the upright in heart praise him!	b. He will reward you
	1) Give you a spirit of rejoicing
	2) Give you a place of refuge

PSALM 64

When People Verbally Assault and Plot Evil Against You, 64:1-10

(64:1-10) **Introduction:** "Sticks and stones may break my bones, but words will never hurt me." American children often use this catchphrase to reply to bullies who call them names. In fact, some parents teach their children to respond to unkindness with this saying rather than speaking sharply in return.

While it may help to toughen children's feelings about harsh words, this familiar saying is simply not true. Words are extraordinarily powerful! Whether spoken cruelly to us or about us, words can inflict tremendous harm. Evildoers know this, and they mercilessly wield words like a deadly, double-edged sword.

When David wrote Psalm 64, he was the victim of intimidating threats and destructive slander by his enemies. Scripture does not record the specific occasion for this psalm; however, it fits any number of episodes from David's life. In addition to the attacks on David recorded in God's Word, Israel's king surely faced numerous enemy assaults that are not preserved in Scripture. Psalm 64 may have been written during Saul's attack or Absalom's revolt, or it may have been composed during some other incident. The exact setting for this psalm is unimportant. What is important is that we will all face ungodly people in our lives, who will use their poisonous tongues as weapons against us (Js.3:5-8). This is, *When People Verbally Assault and Plot Evil Against You, 64:1-10.*

1. Ask God to protect you from the enemy's threats (vv.1-6).
2. Trust God to give you the victory (vv.7-10).

1 (64:1-6) **Ask God to protect you from the enemy's threats.**

David asked God to hear his prayer for protection from his foes' furious threats. *Hear me* suggests that David was praying aloud as opposed to silently in his heart. *Complaint* (siyach) literally means babbling or talking. It does not necessarily refer to grumbling or griping, but it is an expression about what is troubling a person inwardly, what is weighing heavily on a person's heart and mind. In today's words, David might say, "Hear me, O God, as I talk about what is bothering me."

Notice that David did not ask God to preserve or guard him from his enemies but from the fear or threat of his enemies. He wisely realized that he could not control what his adversaries said or did, but he could control how it affected him.

a. Because He alone knows their evil plans and can hide you from the wicked mob (v.2).

David was aware there was a sizeable conspiracy against him, but he did not know everything his enemies were planning because they met secretly. Noisy *crowd* (regesh) indicates that a large group of people were involved. Although they gathered under a cloak of secrecy and operated in the shadows, David rested in the knowledge that God was fully aware of everything they said and did. Instead of agonizing or attempting to uncover what his enemies were plotting, he asked God to hide him from their evil plans.

b. Because the wicked use their tongues like deadly weapons (vv.3-6).

David's wicked adversaries had launched a verbal attack against him, targeting his reputation with criticism and slanderous lies. He compared their vicious tongues to two deadly weapons (v.3):

➢ Swords that had been whetted or sharpened
➢ Bitter or poison-tipped arrows

David's foes slithered around Jerusalem like deadly vipers, covertly "sowing doubts and discord" along their path (v.4).[1] Their forked tongues poisoned someone else against David every time they struck. All throughout the city, they lay in wait to suddenly ambush David with accusations and grievances dreamed up in their evil minds. They feared neither God nor man as they plotted against an innocent or perfect man. *Innocent* (tam) here means complete, morally innocent, and having integrity.[2] In using this word, David testified before the LORD that he was absolutely innocent of the charges they levied against him.

These brazen evildoers encouraged each other in their assault on David, and they gathered ongoing strength from each other's conniving behavior (v.5). David compared them to cunning hunters who lay carefully-concealed snares or traps to catch their prey. As they met secretly to devise their next round of attacks against David, they boasted of their successes, gloating that they had covered their tracks so carefully that neither God nor man could see them.[3]

Blinded by their pride, David's enemies believed they had concocted the perfect plan to bring him down (v.6). "Devised a perfect plan" is also translated as "perfected a shrewd scheme." (NKJV) As David reflected on the actions of his enemies, he marveled at the depravity of the human heart (Je.17:9). Indeed, his twisted foes were cunning and evil through and through.

Thought 1. In the course of our lives, we will encounter individuals who want to harm us with their words. In childhood, they could be bullies who call us names, make fun of us, or threaten us. In our teen years, they might be jealous rivals who attempt to turn others against us. And, tragically, some ungodly parents verbally abuse their children, tearing them down and destroying their confidence.

As adults, we may face coworkers who lie about us in order to gain an unfair advantage over us. Others may turn against us for no reason and spread gossip or rumors about us. Those in positions of leadership can expect to be talked about, criticized, and maligned. Some will stop at nothing to get their way. In fact, when we as believers take a stand for what is right, we can count on being attacked by those who oppose God's truth. Some reading these very words actually live in places where they face the threat of Christ-hating terrorists or intimidating government officials.

When people verbally attack or plot evil against us, we need to remember several things:

First, our true enemy is Satan. As Paul wrote, we do not battle against flesh and blood, human beings, but against spiritual powers (Ep.6:12). Satan uses people in his efforts to defeat us and destroy our effectiveness for the Lord. Even professing believers do the devil's work when they lie, gossip, or spread rumors about others.

With this in mind, we need to use spiritual weapons to fight back against Satan (2 Co.10:3-4). God has armed us with two weapons: the sword of the Spirit—His Holy Word—and prayer (Ep.6:17-18). Without a doubt, God knows our hearts and hears our silent prayers. But when we pray aloud, as David did, demons also hear our voices and they fear. The same is true with Scripture. When we quote God's Word in our minds, we will be strengthened by it. But when we speak it out loud, we wield it as a weapon against Satan's forces, just as Jesus did against the devil himself (Mt.4:1-11).

Second, we should ask the LORD to protect us from our enemies, to deliver us from the fear of their wicked words and evil plots (v.1). God does not want us living in bondage to fear (2 Ti.1:7). When we live righteously, we can be assured that God is on our side; therefore, we have no reason to fear (Ps.118:6; He.13:6).

Third, we should pray for our enemies and, whenever possible, do good for them. Although this goes against all human logic, it is how Jesus taught us to respond to those who do evil against us (Mt.5:44; Lu.6:35). We can defeat our enemies by showing them kindness and helping them (Pr.25:21-22). And we should never seek vengeance against our foes but instead trust God to repay them (Ro.12:19-21).

> **One night the Lord spoke to Paul in a vision: "Do not be afraid; keep on speaking, do not be silent. For I am with you, and no one is going to attack and harm you, because I have many people in this city" (Ac.18:9-10).**
>
> **Who shall separate us from the love of Christ? Shall trouble or hardship or persecution or famine or nakedness or danger or sword? As it is written: "For your sake we face death all day long; we are considered as sheep to be slaughtered." No, in all these things we are**

---

1 Derek Kidner. *Psalms 1-72*, p.246.
2 Francis Brown, S. R. Driver, Charles A. Briggs. *Brown Driver Briggs Hebrew Definitions*. 1906. WORDsearch CROSS e-book.
3 Derek Kidner. *Psalms 1-72*, p.247.

more than conquerors through him who loved us (Ro.8:35-37).

The Lord will rescue me from every evil attack and will bring me safely to his heavenly kingdom. To him be glory for ever and ever. Amen (2 Ti.4:18).

For I hear the slander of many; there is terror on every side; they conspire against me and plot to take my life. But I trust in you, O LORD; I say, "You are my God." My times are in your hands; deliver me from my enemies and from those who pursue me (Ps.31:13-15).

No weapon forged against you will prevail, and you will refute every tongue that accuses you. This is the heritage of the servants of the LORD, and this is their vindication from me," declares the LORD (Is.54:17).

2 (64:7-10) Trust God to give you the victory.

After discussing his enemies' vicious deeds, David declared his confidence in God. The LORD would turn his adversaries' weapons—their accusing, slanderous tongues—against them, and He would ultimately give the innocent David victory over them.

a. He will suddenly strike down the enemy (vv.7-9).

In all of their haughty scheming and gloating, David's adversaries overlooked a crucial fact: God *does* see everything we do, and He *does* hear every word we say—no matter how carefully we cover our tracks (Pr.15:3). As they fired their poisonous arrows at David, God shot His arrows of righteousness back at them. They would suddenly be struck down by God's judgment (v.7). In His perfect justice, God would see to it that the evil David's enemies had plotted against him would fall back on them (v.8). Their accusations and slander would backfire, and their supporters would flee from them and shake their heads in scorn.

When they witnessed God's righteous judgment on David's arrogant adversaries, all the people would be filled with fear (v.9). They would acknowledge God and proclaim His mighty works throughout the land. Even more important, they would wisely consider what they had seen: God is all-knowing and just. When evildoers rise up against God's will and His people, He will personally bring them down.

b. He will reward you (v.10).

David concluded Psalm 64 with a word of encouragement for the righteous: the LORD will reward us for our faithfulness by delivering us from those who plot evil against us. Believing this gives us a spirit of rejoicing and it moves us to trust and take refuge in God. In the end, we will praise the LORD for His faithfulness to the upright in heart and for His righteous judgment of those who unjustly rise up against us.

Thought 1. As hard as we may try, we cannot stop ungodly people from accusing and plotting against us. Psalm 37 teaches us how to respond to evildoers (see outline and notes—Ps.37:1-26 for more discussion):

➢ Do not fret because of them (v.1).
➢ Trust in the LORD and keep on doing good (v.3).
➢ Delight in the LORD (v.4).
➢ Commit your way to the LORD (v.5).
➢ Rest in the LORD and wait for Him to vindicate you in His time (vv.6-7).
➢ Do not retaliate with evil (v.8).

We can trust God to do what is right. If we continue to live righteously, God will reward us by giving us victory over our enemies. We will ultimately prevail over their lies, rumors, and wicked schemes. In addition, God promises to repay those who do evil against us.

We also need to remember that the truth will one day be declared at the Judgment Seat of Christ. Paul set a worthy example for us to follow: he did not let criticism and condemnation by others affect his faithfulness to the Lord. He knew that Christ Himself would defend him when he stood before the LORD in judgment (1 Co.4:3-5). When we live faithfully in obedience to God's Word, we can be filled with the same confidence as Paul: Christ will reward us when we stand before the LORD in judgment and attempts by others to discredit us will not matter at all.

"Blessed are you when people insult you, persecute you and falsely say all kinds of evil against you because of me. Rejoice and be glad, because great is your reward in heaven, for in the same way they persecuted the prophets who were before you (Mt.5:11-12).

Do not take revenge, my friends, but leave room for God's wrath, for it is written: "It is mine to avenge; I will repay," says the Lord (Ro.12:19).

I care very little if I am judged by you or by any human court; indeed, I do not even judge myself. My conscience is clear, but that does not make me innocent. It is the Lord who judges me. Therefore judge nothing before the appointed time; wait till the Lord comes. He will bring to light what is hidden in darkness and will expose the motives of men's hearts. At that time each will receive his praise from God (1 Co.4:3-5).

For we know him who said, "It is mine to avenge; I will repay," and again, "The Lord will judge his people." It is a dreadful thing to fall into the hands of the living God (He.10:30-31).

He will make your righteousness shine like the dawn, the justice of your cause like the noonday sun....A little while, and the wicked will be no more; though you look for them, they will not be found. But the meek will inherit the land and enjoy great peace. The wicked plot against the righteous and gnash their teeth at them; but the Lord laughs at the wicked, for he knows their day is coming (Ps.37:6, 10-13).

	PSALM 65 **When You Have a Deep Sense of Gratitude for God's Goodness, 65:1-13** *For the director of music. A psalm of David. A song.*	strength, 7 Who stilled the roaring of the seas, the roaring of their waves, and the turmoil of the nations. 8 Those living far away fear your wonders; where morning dawns and even- ing fades you call forth songs of joy.	c. He has demonstrated His power 1) By ruling over the seas & nations: He calms the roaring & turmoil of both 2) By arousing fear & awe in earth's farthest regions: God's wonders inspire joy in people everywhere
1. Praise God & fulfill your com- mitments (vows) to Him a. Bc. He answers prayer: He is available to all who will come to Him b. Bc. He redeems us, forgives our sins, Ep.1:7 c. Bc. He chooses to bless us 1) To live in His presence, Ep.2:4-7 2) To satisfy us with all good things, Ps.107:9; Mt.5:6 **2. Confess that God is your Savior, the hope of every person on earth** a. He answers our prayers by performing awesome deeds b. He is the omnipotent, all- powerful Creator	Praise awaits you, O God, in Zion; to you our vows will be fulfilled. 2 O you who hear pray-er, to you all men will come. 3 When we were over-whelmed by sins, you for-gave our transgressions. 4 Blessed are those you choose and bring near to live in your courts! We are filled with the good things of your house, of your holy temple. 5 You answer us with awesome deeds of righ-teousness, O God our Sav-ior, the hope of all the ends of the earth and of the far-thest seas, 6 Who formed the moun-tains by your power, hav-ing armed yourself with	9 You care for the land and water it; you enrich it abundantly. The streams of God are filled with water to provide the people with grain, for so you have or-dained it. 10 You drench its furrows and level its ridges; you sof-ten it with showers and bless its crops. 11 You crown the year with your bounty, and your carts overflow with abun-dance. 12 The grasslands of the desert overflow; the hills are clothed with gladness. 13 The meadows are cov-ered with flocks and the valleys are mantled with grain; they shout for joy and sing.	3) By establishing the laws of nature to nourish the land & care for human life • Providing water to en-rich the earth & fill the streams: God assures provision for His people • Providing rain to drench & soften the earth for plowing: God prepares the way to bless the crops • Providing a bountiful, overflowing harvest • Providing lush green land & hills for wildlife • Providing rich pas-turelands & grain for livestock

PSALM 65

When You Have a Deep Sense of Gratitude for God's Goodness, 65:1-13

(65:1-13) **Introduction:** in his gospel, Luke records an incident where Christ encountered a group of ten men suffering from leprosy (Lu.17:12-19). As He entered their village, these hopelessly afflicted men cried out to Jesus for help. Filled with compassion, the Lord gracious-ly healed them.

Luke then noted a startling detail: of the ten lepers Je-sus miraculously healed, only one paused to glorify God and express his gratitude to Jesus. The other nine hur-ried on without stopping to praise or thank the Lord for so powerfully changing their lives.

Sadly, we are too often like the nine ungrateful lepers. We cry out to God for help, and when He comes to our aid we fail to properly glorify and thank Him for what He has done for us.

Psalms 65–68 teach us to balance our petitions with praise. In the four previous psalms, David desperately cried out to God at a critical time in his life, most likely during Absalom's revolt against him. Those who ar-ranged the Hebrew hymnal strategically placed four psalms of thanksgiving and praise immediately after these intense pleas, showing us how to express our grati-tude to God for His goodness. "It was meant that Psalms

of pleading and longing should be followed by hymns of praise."[1]

In His teachings, Jesus emphasized the importance of praising God in our prayers. His model prayer for His fol-lowers begins and ends with praise, with petitions in-cluded between (Mt.6:9-13):
- "Hallowed be thy name" (v.9).
- "Thine is...the glory, forever" (v.13).

Psalm 65 is a hymn of thanksgiving praising God for both spiritual and physical blessings. Most commenta-tors believe it was written for one of the Jewish harvest festivals, either the Feast of Unleavened Bread (Le.23:4-14) or the Feast of Tabernacles (Le. 23:33-34). Bible teacher Warren Wiersbe notes that the phrase *crown the year* (v.11) and the mention of atonement for sins (v.3) point to the Feast of Tabernacles, which is held near the beginning of the Jewish year and is immediately preced-ed by the Day of Atonement.[2] The performance of vows (v.1), the answer of prayers (vv.2, 5), and the mention of

1 Charles Spurgeon. *Treasury of David.* WORDsearch CROSS e-book.
2 Warren W. Wiersbe. *The Bible Exposition Commentary.* WORDsearch CROSS e-book.

national turmoil (v.7) suggest Psalm 65 was written after God delivered David and Israel from a threatening crisis.

Like ancient Israel, we today are the recipients of God's rich blessings. He hears and answers our prayers, forgives our sins, and freely allows us into His presence. He meets our daily needs through His marvelous creation. We, like grateful Israel, ought to faithfully offer our sacrifices of praise to Him (He.13:15). This is, *When You Have a Deep Sense of Gratitude for God's Goodness,* 65:1-13.

1. Praise God and fulfill your commitments (vows) to Him (vv.1-4).
2. Confess that God is your Savior, the hope of every person on earth (vv.5-13).

1 (65:1-4) Praise God and fulfill your commitments (vows) to Him.

David announced to God that praise was awaiting Him in Zion. The people were assembling in Jerusalem where they would celebrate the LORD's goodness and fulfill their commitments to Him. The vows that would be performed or paid were sacrifices promised to God in gratitude for His blessing and help (Ps. 50:14; 107:22). In conjunction with the Feast of Tabernacles, many commitments were fulfilled in gratitude to God for a fruitful harvest.

"Praise awaits you, O God, in Zion" also prophetically points to that coming era when the Lord Jesus Christ will rule the earth from David's throne in Jerusalem. Outstanding commentator Arno C. Gaebelein wrote,

> *"The Lord loves mount Zion (Psa.78:68) and in the book of Isaiah it is written concerning the days when nations come to worship and turn their swords into plowshares, and their spears into pruning hooks, that "Out of Zion shall go forth the law, and the Word of the Lord from Jerusalem" (Is.2:1-5)."*[3]

a. Because He answers prayer: He is available to all who will come to Him (v.2).

The people exalted God as the God who hears prayer. There is an implied contrast here between Israel's God and the idols of the pagans, inanimate objects that could not answer prayers. *Hear* (shama) means more than to merely listen or give attention to. It is to hear effectively, to heed a request, to respond to what has been said. The people gathered to fulfill their vows to God because He had answered their prayers.

"To you all men will come" conveys the great truth that God is not available exclusively to the Jews but to all who come to Him (Ac.10:35; Ro.10:12). The statement is significant prophetically: it points to…

- the Gentiles' coming to God for salvation (Is.60:3; Lu.2:32; Ac.26:23)

- the coming kingdom of Christ, when people of all the earth will worship the LORD (Ps.22:27-28; 86:9; Is.45:23; 66:23; Zec.14:16)

b. Because He redeems us, forgives our sins, Ep.1:7 (v.3).

God had answered Israel's prayers in many areas, but these specific petitions are their prayers for forgiveness. Of God's abundant blessings toward us, the greatest, without question, is atonement or forgiveness for our sins. Because of God's immeasurable love for us, He gave His Son as the sacrifice for our sins (Jn.3:16; Ro.5:8). Through the substitutionary death of Jesus Christ, God redeems and forgives us (Ep.1:7).

Forgave (kaphar) is the Hebrew word for atone or to make atonement. It is the covering and taking away of sin through the offering of an acceptable sacrifice to God (see outlines and notes—Lev.16:1-34; 23:26-32 for more discussion). If Psalm 65 is indeed a hymn for the Feast of Tabernacles, the Jews would have sung it immediately after the Day of Atonement. Accordingly, gratitude for God's covering of their sins would be fresh in their hearts. The Hebrew word used here is an imperfect verb, meaning that it speaks of an incomplete action. The atonement for sin would remain incomplete until Jesus Christ offered Himself as the once-and-for-all sacrifice for the transgressions of all mankind (Ro.5:11; He.9:6-26; 10:1-12).

We cannot fully appreciate the greatness of God's atonement until we fully comprehend the depth of our sin. "We were overwhelmed by sins" is literally translated as *words* or *matters of iniquity have prevailed against me*. This statement expresses that we have been completely overcome by our sin and the guilt or consequences of it. We are totally defeated, hopeless and helpless apart from God's grace. Matthew Henry explained what this, along with the incomparable blessing of God's atonement, means to us:

> *Our sins reach to the heavens, iniquities prevail against us, and appear so numerous, so heinous, that when they are set in order before us we are full of confusion and ready to fall into despair. They prevail so against us that we cannot pretend to balance them with any righteousness of our own, so that when we appear before God our own consciences accuse us and we have no reply to make; and yet, as for our transgressions, thou shalt, of thy own free mercy and for the sake of a righteousness of thy own providing, purge them away, so that we shall not come into condemnation for them.*[4]

c. Because He chooses to bless us (v.4).

Out of His boundless love and grace, God chooses to bless those whose sins He has forgiven. We enjoy the

---

3 Arno Gaebelein. *The Book of Psalms,* p.256.

4 Matthew Henry. *Matthew Henry's Commentary on the Whole Bible.* WORD*search* CROSS e-book.

wonderful privilege of living in His presence day by day. David reminded us of how incredibly blessed we are in being allowed to approach or draw near to God. Under the old covenant, God chose Israel as the people whom He would bring near to Him (De.7:6). Under God's new covenant of grace, we (Gentiles and Jews) who have trusted in Christ have been chosen to receive this same privilege (1 Pe.2:9-10; Ep.2:4-7).

In Old Testament times, the Hebrews alone were blessed with permission to dwell in God's courts—the tabernacle and later the temple where God's presence abided. We, however, are more greatly blessed: God has chosen to dwell within believers through His Holy Spirit (Ro.8:9; 1 Co.3:16). *We* are God's house; therefore, we spend every moment of every day in His presence. When this life is over, we will instantly be transported into God's heavenly abode (2 Co.5:8). Later, after God's plan for this earth has been fulfilled, He will make His dwelling place with us in the new heaven and the new earth (Re.21:1-3).

From God's presence—His house, His Holy Temple—all good things flow. He satisfies every longing of our souls, filling us so completely that we no longer thirst for the things of this world (Ps.107:9; Mt.5:6; Jn.4:13-14; 6:35). In His infinite goodness, He meets every need of our hearts. Nothing this world can offer compares to the joy of being in God's presence (Ps.16:11).

Thought 1. Commentator J.J. Stewart Perowne's excellent introduction to this passage applies it simply and effectively to our lives:

> *In Zion God is known, there He is praised and worshipt [sic]. He is the hearer of prayer; that is His very character, and therefore all flesh comes to Him. All who feel their weakness, all who need help and grace, seek it at His hand. It is true that they who thus come, come with the burden of sin upon them: their iniquities rise up in all their strength and might, and would thrust them away from the presence of the Holy One. But He Himself, in the plenitude [abundance] of His mercy, covers those iniquities, will not look upon them, and so suffers sinners to approach Him. And how blessed are they who, reconciled and pardoned, are thus suffered to draw nigh! Of that blessedness may we ourselves be partakers, may we be filled and satisfied therewith.*[5]

> **Through Jesus, therefore, let us continually offer to God a sacrifice of praise—the fruit of lips that confess his name (He.13:15).**

> **You also, like living stones, are being built into a spiritual house to be a holy**

priesthood, offering spiritual sacrifices acceptable to God through Jesus Christ (1 Pe.2:5).

> **Sacrifice thank offerings to God, fulfill your vows to the Most High (Ps.50:14).**

> **Then will I ever sing praise to your name and fulfill my vows day after day (Ps.61:8).**

> **All the nations you have made will come and worship before you, O Lord; they will bring glory to your name (Ps.86:9).**

2 (65:5-13) Confess that God is your Savior, the hope of every person on earth.

Once again, David emphasized the glorious truth that God is not exclusively Israel's God (v.2): He wants people everywhere to come to Him as Savior (Ac.10:34-35). He is the confidence or hope of every person on earth, and He reaches out to all people with His goodness (Mt.5:45; Ro.2:4).

a. He answers our prayers by performing awesome deeds (v.5).

Throughout Israel's history, God had supernaturally answered the people's prayers in ways they could never have imagined. *Awesome deeds* are works that cause us to stand in awe of God—to fear, revere, and serve Him because of His mighty power (De.10:19-21). The miracles God performed in delivering the Hebrews from Egyptian bondage stand as the leading example of God's wonder-working power in behalf of His chosen people (Ps.66:1-7; 106:22; 2 S.7:23). As David previously stated, this same power is available to all who will come to God and call upon Him (v.2).

b. He is the omnipotent, all-powerful Creator (v.6).

Nowhere is God's power demonstrated more clearly than in His magnificent creation. To those dwelling in Jerusalem, the mountains surrounding the city were the most obvious example of an omnipotent or all-powerful creator (Ps.125:2). The mountains are set fast or firmly established; neither the strongest winds nor the most violent earthquakes can move them, for they are held in place by God's strength and girded or clothed with His power.

c. He has demonstrated His power (vv.7-13).

In addition to the majestic mountains so firmly anchored to the earth, the omnipotent God has demonstrated His power in a host of other ways. David mentioned three in this passage:

First, God has shown His power by ruling over the seas and the nations (v.7). The raging seas are under God's command; He stills the surging billows and

---

[5] J.J. Stewart Perowne, *The Book of Psalms*, p.268.

waves (Ps.107:29; 89:9). The roaring waters are a symbol of the people's tumult or the nations' turmoil (Is.17:12-13). Once again, David spoke prophetically of the coming kingdom of Christ. Wars and conflicts never seem to cease, but when Jesus Christ returns, He will calm the storms and the strife among the nations just as He quieted the angry waves of Galilee (Mk.4:35-41). Under His righteous rule, peace will reign on earth at last (Ps.46:9; Is.2:4; Mic.4:3; Zech.9:10).

Second, God displays His power through His many wonders that stir people universally to fear and stand in awe of Him (v.8). Nature is filled with breathtaking marvels that serve as tokens or signs of God's incredible power. Only the fool looks upon these amazing works and fails to recognize the hand of a wise, all-powerful, artistic creator (Ro.1:20-22). In the farthest regions of the earth—everywhere the sun rises in the *morning* and sets in the *evening*—the glories of creation inspire people to *rejoice* in God and worship Him (Ps.19:1).

The Message, a paraphrase of Scripture, effectively captures the spirit of this verse:

> *Far and wide they'll come to a stop, they'll stare in awe, in wonder. Dawn and dusk take turns calling, "Come and worship."*[6]

Third, God has demonstrated His power by establishing the laws of nature to nourish the land and to care for human life (vv.9-13). In conjunction with the harvest festival, David eloquently described how God, in His infinite wisdom, designed the earth to supply life's necessities. God brilliantly and lovingly provides:

➤ Water to enrich the earth and fill the streams, thereby assuring the provision of food for His people (v.9). To *care for* (paqad) means to attend to or provide oversight to. *Streams of God* most likely refers to the rains, which fall from the heavens (De.11:10-11).

➤ Rain to drench and soften the earth for plowing, thereby preparing the way to bless the crops (v.10). "The *ridges* are the lines of earth thrown up by the action of the plough between the *furrows*."[7]

➤ A bountiful, overflowing harvest (v.11). God's gift of an abundant harvest was the crown or high point of the year. "Your carts overflow with abundance" describes the farmers' carts so filled to overflowing that some of the bounty spilled out onto the paths as the harvest was transported to the barns.

➤ Lush green land and hills for wildlife (v.12). God had so blessed the land that even the wilderness

or desert, the uncultivated area, was green with sufficient growth to provide *grasslands* (nawa) or habitations for the creatures who lived in the wild.

➤ Rich pasturelands and grain for livestock (v.13). *Meadows* (kar) are the pastures where livestock graze and are fattened. Nature itself seemed to praise God for His goodness, shouting for joy and singing.

Thought 1. Psalm 65 serves first as a thanksgiving psalm. As Paul taught, we should give thanks to God at all times for all things (Ep.5:20; 1 Th.5:18). However, many nations and cultures dedicate a special day each year to giving thanks to God. For example, Americans celebrate Thanksgiving in November, after the harvest season. Psalm 65 is appropriate for those special days and every other occasion of thanksgiving. We should always remember God's goodness in providing for our salvation as well as for every other need of life.

Second, Psalm 65 is an evangelistic psalm. This present passage emphasizes in particular God's goodness to all people (vv.5-13). He is mankind's only hope. And Jesus Christ died for all of us (Jn.3:16; 2 Co.5:14). Scripture plainly states that God reveals Himself—His existence and His power—to every person on earth through His creation (Ro.1:20). As Psalm 65 teaches, God's creation also reveals His goodness to all people, for He sends His rain on the unjust as well as the just (Mt.5:45). Through His goodness, God seeks to draw people to Himself, leading them to repentance and faith in Christ (Ro.2:4; 1 Ti.2:4; 2 Pe.3:9).

In summary, this psalm should stir us to...

- praise God and serve Him sacrificially
- be more aware of God's goodness every day of our lives
- be more thankful to God and express our gratitude to Him daily
- point others to God's goodness in hopes of bringing them to faith in Christ

That you may be sons of your Father in heaven. He causes his sun to rise on the evil and the good, and sends rain on the righteous and the unrighteous (Mt.5:45).

Or do you show contempt for the riches of his kindness, tolerance and patience, not realizing that God's kindness leads you toward repentance? (Ro.2:4).

Again, it says, "Rejoice, O Gentiles, with his people." And again, "Praise the Lord, all you Gentiles, and sing praises to him, all you peoples." And again, Isaiah says, "The Root of Jesse will spring up, one who will arise to rule over the nations; the Gentiles will hope in him" (Ro.15:10-12).

---

6 Eugene Peterson. *The Message*. Colorado Springs, CO: NavPress Publishing Group, 1993.
7 J.J. Stewart Perowne, *The Book of Psalms*, p.272.

Remember that at that time you were separate from Christ, excluded from citizenship in Israel and foreigners to the covenants of the promise, without hope and without God in the world. But now in Christ Jesus you who once were far away have been brought near through the blood of Christ....For through him we both have access to the Father by one Spirit (Ep.2:12-13, 18).

This is good, and pleases God our Savior, who wants all men to be saved and to come to a knowledge of the truth (1 Ti.2:3-4).

Every good and perfect gift is from above, coming down from the Father of the heavenly lights, who does not change like shifting shadows (Js.1:17).

PSALM 66

When You Receive God's Help & Deliverance, 66:1-20

For the director of music.
A song. A psalm.

1. **Praise God's supremacy**
   a. Everyone should shout with joy
   b. Everyone should honor God's name & tell others how glorious He is
2. **Acknowledge God's awesome power**
   a. Power that causes enemies to cringe & submit before Him
   b. Power that stirs people to worship & praise Him

   c. Power that performs awesome works for people, such as the dividing of the Red Sea, Ex.14:1-31

   d. Power that rules forever over the nations: Watching & warning the defiant not to rebel against Him, Ob.4; Mt.23:12
3. **Rejoice in God's protection**

   a. He faithfully sustains us

Shout with joy to God, all the earth!
2 Sing the glory of his name; make his praise glorious!
3 Say to God, "How awesome are your deeds! So great is your power that your enemies cringe before you.
4 All the earth bows down to you; they sing praise to you, they sing praise to your name." Selah
5 Come and see what God has done, how awesome his works in man's behalf!
6 He turned the sea into dry land, they passed through the waters on foot—come, let us rejoice in him.
7 He rules forever by his power, his eyes watch the nations—let not the rebellious rise up against him. Selah
8 Praise our God, O peoples, let the sound of his praise be heard;
9 He has preserved our lives and kept our feet from slipping.
10 For you, O God, tested us; you refined us like silver.
11 You brought us into prison and laid burdens on our backs.
12 You let men ride over our heads; we went through fire and water, but you brought us to a place of abundance.
13 I will come to your temple with burnt offerings and fulfill my vows to you—
14 Vows my lips promised and my mouth spoke when I was in trouble.
15 I will sacrifice fat animals to you and an offering of rams; I will offer bulls and goats. Selah
16 Come and listen, all you who fear God; let me tell you what he has done for me.
17 I cried out to him with my mouth; his praise was on my tongue.
18 If I had cherished sin in my heart, the Lord would not have listened;
19 But God has surely listened and heard my voice in prayer.
20 Praise be to God, who has not rejected my prayer or withheld his love from me!

b. He keeps us from slipping & losing our way
4. **Remember God's testing & purification**

   a. He purifies us through burdens & afflictions: Just as He did Israel when enslaved to Egypt
   b. He delivers us from intense trials into a life of rich fulfillment: Just as He delivered Israel into the promised land (a land of abundance)
5. **Make a renewed commitment to worship & obey God**
   a. A renewed commitment to fulfill your vows
      1) By keeping your promises

      2) By giving God the very best you have

   b. A renewed commitment to bear a stronger witness for God: Invite all who fear God to listen to your testimony
      1) How you cried out & praised God

      2) How you repented of your sin to ensure that the LORD would listen, Is.59:2
      3) How God heard your cry for help

   c. A renewed commitment to praise God: Bc. He has not ignored your prayer or withdrawn His love from you

PSALM 66

When You Receive God's Help and Deliverance, 66:1-20

(66:1-20) **Introduction:** until this point, most of the psalms are prayers for God's help. We identify with them so willingly because we frequently find ourselves in situations where we urgently need God's strength and deliverance. They serve as compasses that keep us on course through the distresses and challenges of life.

What are we to do, then, after God gives us the victory, after we receive His help and deliverance? Psalm 66 answers the question, guiding us to acknowledge and praise Him, to understand His purpose for trials, and to renew our commitments to Him.

The author and original occasion of Psalm 66 are not specifically revealed. One thing is clear, however: it is a hymn of thanksgiving to celebrate God's deliverance of Israel from a severe crisis (vv.10-12). God had done something so miraculous for His people that they ranked the occasion with the parting of the Red Sea (v.6). Many scholars believe the occasion was God's supernatural deliverance of the nation from Assyria and Sennacherib (2 K.19: Is.36-37). If this is the setting, King Hezekiah would have been the leader of this celebration and the one whose personal testimony concludes the psalm (vv.13-20).

Psalm 66 continues the atmosphere of praise that closes the previous psalm: Psalm 65 ends with nature itself singing God's praises, and Psalm 66 begins with a command for all the earth to exalt God. The sixty-sixth psalm is marked by a clear movement from corporate praise (vv.1-12) to personal praise (vv.13-20). Commentator Derek Kidner captured what was most likely the original setting:

We may picture the scene of public worship...in which the corporate praise gives way to the voice of this single worshipper, who stands with his gifts before the altar, and speaks of the God whose care is

not only world- and nation-wide, but personal: I will tell what he has done for me (16).[1]

Psalm 66 also has a prophetic flavor, sparking thoughts of Christ's (the Messiah's) return to earth to deliver Israel from all of her enemies and to rule over the whole world from David's throne. At that time, the invitation to sing God's glorious praises will be accepted by all the earth (vv.1-2). Then, throughout eternity, we who have truly trusted the Lord will assemble with the redeemed of all the ages to shout God's glory. And we will never tire of sharing with the saints of the new heaven and new earth our personal stories of what the Lord did for us. This is, *When You Receive God's Help and Deliverance,* 66:1-20.

1. Praise God's supremacy (vv.1-2).
2. Acknowledge God's awesome power (vv.3-7).
3. Rejoice in God's protection (vv.8-9).
4. Remember God's testing and purification (vv.10-12).
5. Make a renewed commitment to worship and obey God (vv.13-20).

1 (66:1-2) Praise God's supremacy.

This celebration of the LORD's deliverance begins with a fervent call to praise God. Israel's leader humbly recognized that this victory they were enjoying was not achieved by their own hands. It was the wondrous work of the LORD, the only true and living God who is faithful and omnipotent and who reigns supremely over all.

a. Everyone should shout with joy (v.1).

The worship leader—most likely Israel's king—called upon the people of all the earth to shout joyfully to the LORD. *Shout with joy* (ruah) means to make a loud and victorious noise. Note the following verses where this Hebrew word appears:

> While the morning stars sang together and all the angels shouted for joy? (Jb.38:7).
>
> Clap your hands, all you nations; shout to God with cries of joy (Ps.47:1).
>
> Sing for joy, O heavens, for the LORD has done this; shout aloud, O earth beneath. Burst into song, you mountains, you forests and all your trees, for the LORD has redeemed Jacob, he displays his glory in Israel (Is.44:23).
>
> Rejoice greatly, O Daughter of Zion! Shout, Daughter of Jerusalem! See, your king comes to you, righteous and having salvation, gentle and riding on a donkey, on a colt, the foal of a donkey (Zech.9:9).

b. Everyone should honor God's name and tell others how glorious He is (v.2).

The purpose of praise and worship is to glorify God. The psalmist emphasized this, instructing the people to sing forth the *glory* (*honor*) of God's name and to make His praise glorious. God's name represents everything that He is: His character, His attributes, His greatness, His works, His worthiness. To *make His praise glorious* is…

- to praise God with your entire being, all of your strength
- to give God the full measure of glory that He is due
- to tell others how glorious God is

Thought 1. It is significant that the entire earth, all nations, are called to glorify God for His deliverance of Israel. Why? "Because through Israel, the Lord brought truth and salvation to the Gentiles. 'Salvation is of the Jews' (John 4:22)."[2] All the nations of the earth have been blessed by Israel, for it is through Abraham's seed that the Savior came (Ge.22:18). Therefore, every victory for Israel was a victory for all of humanity.

Nothing in history reveals God's supremacy more than His establishment and preservation of the Hebrew nation. Again and again throughout the Old Testament, God delivered Israel. When she was in bondage, He set her free. When she was attacked, He defended her. When she was unfaithful to Him and forced His hand to chasten her, He restored her. At last, "when the fullness of time was come," the nation of Israel brought forth God's Son (Ga.4:4). God thwarted Satan's every attempt to destroy Israel and to prevent the birth of the Messiah (see outline and notes—Re.12:1-5 for more discussion).

Today, much of the world stands in opposition to Israel. This animosity toward God's chosen nation will only worsen as we grow closer to Jesus Christ's return. When Christ comes back to earth, He will come as the unstoppable Champion of Israel, destroying her enemies and establishing Himself as King of kings from David's throne (Re.19:11-21). God's promises to both Abraham and David will be completely fulfilled, and His supremacy—His dominance, authority, sovereignty—over all the earth will be proclaimed eternally.

Looking back at what God has done for Israel and forward to what God will do for her should stir us to shout joyfully and to sing the glory of God's supremacy over all the earth!

> Now to the King eternal, immortal, invisible, the only God, be honor and glory for ever and ever. Amen (1 Ti.1:17).
> Whenever the living creatures give glory, honor and thanks to him who sits

---

1 Derek Kidner. *Psalms 1-72*, p.251.

2 Warren W. Wiersbe. *The Bible Exposition Commentary.* WORDsearch CROSS e-book.

on the throne and who lives for ever and ever, the twenty-four elders fall down before him who sits on the throne, and worship him who lives for ever and ever. They lay their crowns before the throne and say "You are worthy, our Lord and God, to receive glory and honor and power, for you created all things, and by your will they were created and have their being" (Re.4:9-11).

Saying: "Amen! Praise and glory and wisdom and thanks and honor and power and strength be to our God for ever and ever. Amen!" (Re.7:12).

Sing to the LORD, all the earth; proclaim his salvation day after day. Declare his glory among the nations, his marvelous deeds among all peoples (1 Chr.16:23-24).

Sing to the LORD, praise his name; proclaim his salvation day after day. Declare his glory among the nations, his marvelous deeds among all peoples (Ps.96:2-3).

Let them give glory to the LORD and proclaim his praise in the islands (Is.42:12).

2 (66:3-7) Acknowledge God's awesome power.

Everything is possible with God (Mk.10:27; Lu.1:37). Put another way, nothing is too hard for Him (Ge.18:14; Je.32:27). God is omnipotent (all-powerful), and He can do what others cannot. We should acknowledge God as the source of the wondrous things we see and praise Him for His awesome power.

a. Power that causes enemies to cringe and submit before Him (v.3).

God never withheld His supernatural power when Israel needed His help. When the Assyrians threatened God's chosen nation, He demonstrated His might by sending His angel to slay 185,000 Assyrian soldiers as they slept. As a result, Sennacherib retreated in fear and returned to Ninevah (2 K.19:35-36; Is.37:36-37). This was likely the most recent of God's *awesome deeds* and the occasion for this sixty-sixth psalm. *Awesome* (ya-re') *deeds* are works that cause us to stand in awe of God, that is, to fear, revere, and submit to Him because of His mighty power (De.10:19-21). Israel's history was punctuated with occasions when their enemies—and thereby God's enemies—had cringed before Him after witnessing His astonishing works.

b. Power that stirs people to worship and praise Him (v.4).

It was the demonstration of God's wonder-working power that stirred Israel to come together to worship and praise Him. As the nation's leader conducted this celebration of God's glory, he acknowledged that future day when all the earth will bow down to God and sing praises to His incomparable name.

c. Power that performs awesome works for people, such as the dividing of the Red Sea, Ex.14:1-31 (vv.5-6).

The worship leader invited the congregation to recall with him the awesome things God had done for His people in the past (v.5). In Israel's glorious history, the parting of the Red Sea was chief of these marvelous miracles (v.6; Ex.14:1-31). The nation's fleeing ancestors had rejoiced in God when He divided this intimidating barrier right before their eyes. As they walked across the dry bed of the great sea, they triumphed in the all-surpassing power of their unrivalled God.

d. Power that rules forever over the nations: Watching and warning the defiant not to rebel against Him, Ob.4; Mt.23:12 (v.7).

The psalmist reminded the congregation that God was in control of their destiny, and He was keenly aware of the activity of all their enemies. By His unconquerable power, God rules forever over the nations. Notice the key words of this verse:

➤ *Power* (geburah) refers to military might or valor (2 K.18:20; Is.36:5). It is the root of the Hebrew word translated as *mighty man* (gibbor), referring to a great warrior and military champion (Jos.1:14; 2 S.17:8; 23:8).

➤ *Watch* (tsaphah) "conveys the idea of being fully aware of a situation in order to gain some advantage or keep from being surprised by an enemy."[3] It is used as a noun for the watchmen who were posted on the city wall to keep an eye out for approaching danger (1 S.14:16; 2 K.9:17).

The psalmist proclaimed a word of comfort to Israel but issued a fearful warning to the rest of mankind: God is on patrol throughout the world. He carefully observes the actions of every nation, lest they defiantly exalt themselves or rise up against Him and His chosen people. He is the mightiest of warriors, and He will not be defeated.

Thought 1. The enemies of God and His people should heed the grim truths of this passage. God is aware of the evil things His enemies are doing and planning to do, and He will overpower them in their efforts. Prophecy foretells the assault by the nations of the world against God's people in the last days. Think about it: God already knows—and has always known—the future plans of His people's enemies.

---

3 R. Laird Harris, ed. *Theological Wordbook of the Old Testament.* WORD*search* CROSS e-book.

Prophecy also informs us that God's Son, Jesus Christ, will return to earth as a mighty warrior who delivers His people from those who rebelliously rise up against Him. The entire world will then acknowledge Christ's awesome power, and He will rule over the nations forever.

> **And lead us not into temptation, but deliver us from the evil one' (Mt.6:13).**
>
> **And sang the song of Moses the servant of God and the song of the Lamb: "Great and marvelous are your deeds, Lord God Almighty. Just and true are your ways, King of the ages. Who will not fear you, O Lord, and bring glory to your name? For you alone are holy. All nations will come and worship before you, for your righteous acts have been revealed" (Re.15:3-4).**
>
> **Then I heard what sounded like a great multitude, like the roar of rushing waters and like loud peals of thunder, shouting: "Hallelujah! For our Lord God Almighty reigns (Re.19:6).**
>
> **Clap your hands, all you nations; shout to God with cries of joy. How awesome is the LORD Most High, the great King over all the earth! He subdued nations under us, peoples under our feet (Ps.47:1-3).**
>
> **You who are far away, hear what I have done; you who are near, acknowledge my power! (Is.33:13).**

Thought 2. As individuals, we should also acknowledge God's power and submit to Him. The warning here to the nations is a warning to each of us as well. We are often tempted to think we can get by with sin, that God does not see us or that He will not do anything in response to our disobedience. We must not be deceived by this lie (Ga.6:7-8). God observes everything we do and hears every word we say (Pr.15:3). He will not wink at our defiance of His commands. He promises to bring down all who rebelliously rise up against Him—both nations and individuals (Obad.4). If we are wise, we will humble ourselves before God and submit to His Word (Mt.23:12).

> **For whoever exalts himself will be humbled, and whoever humbles himself will be exalted (Mt.23:12).**
>
> **Do not be deceived: God cannot be mocked. A man reaps what he sows. The one who sows to please his sinful nature, from that nature will reap destruction; the one who sows to please the Spirit, from the Spirit will reap eternal life (Ga.6:7-8).**

> **The pride of your heart has deceived you, you who live in the clefts of the rocks and make your home on the heights, you who say to yourself, 'Who can bring me down to the ground?' Though you soar like the eagle and make your nest among the stars, from there I will bring you down," declares the LORD (Obad.3-4).**

3 (66:8-9) Rejoice in God's protection.

As Israel celebrated God's help and deliverance, they acknowledged God's protection. They had survived a serious threat to their freedom and to their very existence, but only by God's power. They were still alive, still a nation, and still in the land because God was faithful. Appropriately, they praised God for His supernatural protection.

a. He faithfully sustains us (v.9a).

The psalmist reminds us that God faithfully sustains our lives from day to day. Every day is a gift from Him. The root word for *preserved* (siym) means to put, set, place, or appoint. Simply stated, it is God who put us on this earth, and it is He who keeps us here each day.

b. He keeps us from slipping and losing our way (v.9b).

Second, the psalmist reminds us that God keeps us from slipping and losing our way. He "kept our feet from slipping." He protects us from falling and keeps us on the path He has ordained for us.

Thought 1. As we walk through the routines and activities of daily life, it is so easy to forget God's constant protection of our lives. It is He who sustains us, who preserves and protects us from danger. This sin-cursed world is full of hazards: accidents, illnesses, diseases, disasters, and criminal acts to name a few. But God continuously guards us, often deploying His angels to keep charge of us (Ps.91:10-12).

We need to recognize that each day is a gift from God and that He has a purpose for leaving us on this earth. In addition, we should never take our lives for granted or boast in our plans for the future. We will live to see tomorrow *only* if God ordains it and preserves our lives for another day (Js.4:13-15). With this in mind, we ought to live each day for His glory and in His service (1 Co.10:31).

> **'For in him we live and move and have our being.' As some of your own poets have said, 'We are his offspring' (Ac.17:28).**
>
> **If we live, we live to the Lord; and if we die, we die to the Lord. So, whether**

we live or die, we belong to the Lord (Ro.14:8).

Now listen, you who say, "Today or tomorrow we will go to this or that city, spend a year there, carry on business and make money." Why, you do not even know what will happen tomorrow. What is your life? You are a mist that appears for a little while and then vanishes. Instead, you ought to say, "If it is the Lord's will, we will live and do this or that" (Js.4:13-15).

It was the LORD our God himself who brought us and our fathers up out of Egypt, from that land of slavery, and performed those great signs before our eyes. He protected us on our entire journey and among all the nations through which we traveled (Josh.24:17).

You alone are the LORD. You made the heavens, even the highest heavens, and all their starry host, the earth and all that is on it, the seas and all that is in them. You give life to everything, and the multitudes of heaven worship you (Neh.9:6).

You gave me life and showed me kindness, and in your providence watched over my spirit (Jb.10:12).

4 (66:10-12) **Remember God's testing and purification.**

As the congregation praised God for His help and deliverance from a serious crisis, the worship leader reminded them of God's purpose for allowing them to go through trials (v.10). God uses the crises of life to do two things in particular:

➢ To *test* (bachan) or prove us. Precious metals were subjected to the fire in order to test their strength. Likewise, God examines us in order to discern our strength, to see what we will do when put under intense pressure, to see what we are made of, so to speak (Jb.23:10; Pr.17:23).

➢ To *refine* (tsaraph)—or purify—us, as silver is refined. Just as precious metals are melted down to remove their impurities, God puts us through fiery trials to drive us to cry out to Him for mercy and forgiveness of sin. Trials force us to draw closer to God, and when we draw closer, we become more pure and holy (Mal.3:3; 1 Pe.1:7).

a. He purifies us through burdens and afflictions: Just as He did Israel when enslaved to Egypt (v.11).

The psalmist again directed the congregation back to Israel's experience in Egypt. God allowed them to be brought into the net or taken into bondage like an animal captured in a trap. *Laid burdens on* (siym mu'aqah) means to put under intense pressure or to afflict. While enslaved in Egypt, the burden of the Hebrews' affliction was so great that they cried out to the LORD for relief (Ex.1:11-14; 2:23; 3:7).

b. He delivered us from intense trials into a life of rich fulfillment: Just as He delivered Israel into the promised land (a land of abundance) (v.12).

The psalmist continued describing Israel's bondage in Egypt. "Ride over our heads" pictures the brutality of the Egyptians toward the Hebrew slaves. Egyptian taskmasters are compared to a ruthless army that rides over the bodies of soldiers already fallen in battle. The hardships the Hebrews faced were mercilessly severe; they were like a people who had been forced to endure the perils of both fire and water (or flood). But God heard Israel's cries and delivered them from their intense trials. He brought the Hebrews out of the bondage of Egypt and into the promised land, a wealthy place of glorious abundance, overflowing with blessings (Ex.3:8).

Thought 1. God allows, and sometimes ordains, trials in our lives, just as He did with Israel. His purposes are the same for us as they were for them. First, God tries us in order to purify us. The fires of tribulation have a way of purging sin out of our lives. Because we so desperately need God's help, we tend to pray more than usual when we are suffering. As we try to pray, God's Spirit brings our unconfessed sins before us, reminding us that they are hindering our prayers (v.18). Accordingly, we deal with our sins and draw closer and closer to God. In other cases, trials are God's chastening or correction for sins we have committed. We who believe in Christ are God's precious sons and daughters whom He loves ever so much. Because of His love, God does not simply ignore or overlook our sins. If we refuse to repent, He disciplines us to stir us to turn back to Him and become more holy—more pure and set apart to Him (He.12:5-11).

Second, God uses trials to prove us. God permitted Satan to test Job in order to prove the strength of his faith and the sincerity of his love for the LORD (Jb.1:6-12). God also tested Abraham in order to prove his faith and obedience (Ge.22:1-19).

Scripture encourages us to rejoice when we face various trials because they work in our lives to build character and produce patience (Ro.5:3-5; Jas.1:2-4). Scripture also says that Jesus learned obedience through suffering—a fascinating yet mind-boggling truth (He.5:8). If this was true for God's perfect, sinless Son, how much more is it true for us sinners who have a rebellious nature!

We can also rejoice in trials because God bountifully blesses us when we endure them. Scripture records how God blessed both Abraham and Job for their faithfulness throughout their trials (Ge.22:15-18; Jb.42:10-16; Js.5:11). A special crown is promised to those who love the Lord and are faithful when they are severely tried (Js.1:12).

During our time on this earth, we may be required to walk through fire and flood. But remember this: we do not walk through them alone. God has promised His comfort and strength along with His very presence throughout trials (Is.43:2; Josh.1:9). The fires and floods of tribulation will not overtake us (Is.43:2). Commentator Matthew Henry wrote, "They are in fire and water, but they get through them: 'We went through fire and water, and did not perish in the flames or floods.' Whatever the troubles of the saints are, blessed be God, there is a way through them."[4] Like Shadrach, Meshach, and Abednego, we may go into the fiery furnace, but we will surely come out. And while we are there, we will find the glorious presence of God's Son with us (Da.3:21-27).

5 (66:13-20) **Make a renewed commitment to worship and obey God.**

Verse 13 marks a pointed transition from congregational worship to personal worship. The psalmist publicly proclaimed how God's help and deliverance had stirred him to greater service for the LORD. He bore a strong testimony about what God had done for him (v.16).

Pastor and commentator Donald M. Williams said, "It is not enough to know what God has done for Israel. What has God done for you? Witness must become personal."[5] And so must commitment. Churches are made up of individuals, and the church is only as strong as the personal commitment of its members.

Israel's leader, most likely Hezekiah, stood before the people and made a personal commitment to worship and obey the LORD. He set an example for the rest of the congregation to follow. Leaders today should follow his example. We should not just *tell* our people how to live but also *show* them how to live. Paul said, "Follow my example, as I follow the example of Christ." (1 Co.11:1). By modeling a personal commitment to the Lord, we will inspire our people to worship and obey God with all their hearts.

a. A renewed commitment to fulfill your vows (vv.13-15).

During Israel's time of trouble, her leader made vows to God: promises to offer sacrifices to God in gratitude for delivering him and the nation from crisis. As he stood before the people, he committed to keep those promises, declaring that he would sacrifice burnt offerings in God's house, the temple (vv.13-14).

Israel's ruler specified the sacrifices he would offer to God in fulfillment of his vows and as a token of thanksgiving for God's help and deliverance (v.15). He would sacrifice...

- fatlings or fat animals—healthy, robust animals as opposed to thin, weak ones; animals fully fattened out and ready for slaughter
- rams
- bulls
- goats

Notice that all of these sacrifices are plural, indicating that the psalmist intended to offer more than one of each of these animals. Few people in Israel had the ability to present such an extravagant offering, which supports the opinion that Israel's king authored this psalm. The psalmist committed to give the very best he had as a voluntary offering to the LORD (Le.22:17-21). God had miraculously delivered Israel, and the king believed that such great deliverance deserved a great sacrifice.

Thought 1. The psalmist's sacrifices teach us two important truths. First, he specified that his sacrifices would be burnt offerings (v.13). Burnt offerings were distinct from other sacrifices in that the entire animal was consumed on the altar with nothing kept back for the family or the priest to eat (Ex.29:18; Le.1:1-9). This is an illustration of total dedication to God. We, too, should give ourselves fully to the Lord, holding nothing back.

Second, the psalmist offered fatlings, rams, bulls, and goats, in contrast to less valuable animals. This demonstrates that we should give God the very best that we have to offer.

We have received a costly gift—one purchased with nothing less than the precious, incorruptible blood of God's own Son:

> **For you know that it was not with perishable things such as silver or gold that you were redeemed from the empty way of life handed down to you from your forefathers, but with the precious blood of Christ, a lamb without blemish or defect (1 Pe.1:18-19).**

We are the recipients of God's great salvation (He.2:13). Such great deliverance—deliverance from sin's penalty, power, and ultimately, its presence—deserves a great sacrifice. Like the psalmist, Paul understood this truth. He taught us to present ourselves wholly to God, which is our only reasonable service (Ro.12:1).

> **Therefore, I urge you, brothers, in view of God's mercy, to offer your bodies**

---

4   Matthew Henry. *Matthew Henry's Commentary on the Whole Bible.* WORD*search* CROSS e-book.
5   Donald Williams. *Psalms 1-72*, p.480.

as living sacrifices, holy and pleasing to God—this is your spiritual act of worship (Ro.12:1).

I have received full payment and even more; I am amply supplied, now that I have received from Epaphroditus the gifts you sent. They are a fragrant offering, an acceptable sacrifice, pleasing to God (Ph.4:18).

You also, like living stones, are being built into a spiritual house to be a holy priesthood, offering spiritual sacrifices acceptable to God through Jesus Christ (1 Pe.2:5).

And do not forget to do good and to share with others, for with such sacrifices God is pleased (He.13:16).

b. **A renewed commitment to bear a stronger witness for God: Invite all who fear God to listen to your testimony (vv.16-19).**

The grateful psalmist made a second commitment before the people: to bear a strong witness for God. He would share his testimony of God's deliverance with all who would listen. He passionately invited all who feared God, who revered and trusted Him, to lend an ear as he joyously proclaimed what God had done for Him (v.16).

The psalmist testified how he had cried out to God in prayer (v.17). He had extolled or exalted God—a demonstration of his faith in the midst of severe crisis. Scripture records King Hezekiah's prayer when Assyria's wicked king, Sennacherib, threatened Israel and defied God:

> And Hezekiah prayed to the LORD: "O LORD, God of Israel, enthroned between the cherubim, you alone are God over all the kingdoms of the earth. You have made heaven and earth. Give ear, O LORD, and hear; open your eyes, O LORD, and see; listen to the words Sennacherib has sent to insult the living God. "It is true, O LORD, that the Assyrian kings have laid waste these nations and their lands. They have thrown their gods into the fire and destroyed them, for they were not gods but only wood and stone, fashioned by men's hands. Now, O LORD our God, deliver us from his hand, so that all kingdoms on earth may know that you alone, O LORD, are God" (2 K.19:15-19).

The psalmist had also examined his heart for sin (v.18). He knew that if any iniquity stood between him and God, the LORD would not listen to his prayers. He desperately needed God's help. Therefore, he repent-ed of all sin in his life so God would hear and help him in the midst of a kingdom-threatening crisis (Is.59:2; Pr.28:9). *Cherish* means "to be unwilling to confess and forsake known sins."[6] Had the psalmist clung to any sin in his heart, he would not have been able to get through to God in prayer. This is a vibrant testimony of the purifying power of trials (vv.10-12).

Triumphantly, the psalmist concluded his testimony by declaring that God had heard and given His full attention to his prayer (v.19). After Hezekiah cried out to God, the LORD swiftly answered him by sending the prophet Isaiah to give assurance that God Himself would defend Jerusalem (2 K.20-34). Then, that very night, the LORD slew 185,000 Assyrian soldiers and Sennacherib retreated (2 K.19:35-36). The LORD's miraculous power saved His people.

c. **A renewed commitment to praise God: Because He has not ignored your prayer or withdrawn His love from you (v.20).**

The psalmist ended Psalm 66 with a final burst of praise because God had not ignored his urgent prayer, nor had He withdrawn His *steadfast love* (chesed) from him. By crying out for God to be *praised* (blessed be God), the king...

- was committing himself to continue to praise God for hearing and answering His prayer
- was calling upon the people to forever praise God for His help and deliverance

Thought 1. God's faithfulness stirred the psalmist to rededicate himself to the LORD. When we receive God's help and deliverance, we should follow his example. There is no better way for us to express our gratitude to the Lord than by renewing our commitment to Him.

First, we should carefully account for every promise we have made to God and fulfill our promises as quickly as possible (vv.13-15). Scripture is clear: we should not make vows to God in an attempt to gain His favor; however, it is appropriate to make voluntary commitments to God as an expression of our gratitude to Him. At the same time, we must always remember that failing to keep those commitments is a grave sin that brings God's judgment upon us (Ec.5:4-6). Therefore, whenever we make a commitment—one of money, time, or service—we must not neglect to fulfill it.

Second, we should be bold witnesses for God, sharing God's faithfulness with all who will listen to us (vv.16-17). When we share what God has done for us, we glorify His name and often make a powerful impact upon others. A believer who is caught in the midst of a severe trial may be encouraged by our testimony (2 Co.1:3-6). A doubting Christian may be

---

6 Warren W. Wiersbe. *The Bible Exposition Commentary.* WORDsearch CROSS e-book.

stirred to attempt something great for God. An unbeliever may turn to God upon hearing of His goodness (Ro.2:4).

Third, we should be stirred to promptly confess and repent of any sins we commit (v.18). When we cling to sin, we hinder our fellowship with God. Our joy is suppressed, and our prayers become ineffective. We need God's help every day, and others depend on us to intercede for them in prayer. However, there is a greater motivation for us to turn from our sins: because we love God and do not want to grieve Him.

Finally, we should resolve to never forget God's wonderful works in our lives and to praise Him continually for His faithfulness and love (v.20). God deserves our highest praise, and we should exalt Him every day of our lives. His mercies are new every morning, and His faithfulness is demonstrated both in our lives and in the lives of others. Remembering this gives us hope in the midst of whatever may confront us (Lam.3:21-23).

Whoever tries to keep his life will lose it, and whoever loses his life will preserve it (Lu.17:33).

And he died for all, that those who live should no longer live for themselves but for him who died for them and was raised again (2 Co.5:15).

But whatever was to my profit I now consider loss for the sake of Christ. What is more, I consider everything a loss compared to the surpassing greatness of knowing Christ Jesus my Lord, for whose sake I have lost all things. I consider them rubbish, that I may gain Christ (Ph.3:7-8).

As a result, he does not live the rest of his earthly life for evil human desires, but rather for the will of God (1 Pe.4:2).

| 1. Ask God to be gracious, to bless & shine His face (His approval) on all believers
a. That we might be strong witnesses for Him
b. That we might make His ways & saving power known among all nations, Mt.28:19-20 | **PSALM 67**

What Your Hope & Prayer for the World Should Be, 67:1-7

For the director of music. With stringed instruments. A song. A psalm.

May God be gracious to us and bless us and make his face shine upon us, Selah
2 That your ways may be known on earth, your salvation among all nations. | 3 May the peoples praise you, O God; may all the peoples praise you.
4 May the nations be glad and sing for joy, for you rule the peoples justly and guide the nations of the earth. Selah
5 May the peoples praise you, O God; may all the peoples praise you.
6 Then the land will yield its harvest, and God, our God, will bless us.
7 God will bless us, and all the ends of the earth will fear him. | 2. Ask God to stir everyone to accept His salvation & to praise Him: A picture of Christ's coming kingdom
a. That they be filled & sing with joy
  1) Bc. God rules them in perfect righteousness & justice
  2) Bc. God guides them day by day
b. That they might all repeatedly praise Him

c. That God will always provide for His people

d. That we & they will always fear & reverence Him |

PSALM 67

What Your Hope and Prayer for the World Should Be, 67:1-7

(67:1-7) **Introduction:** generally speaking, nonspecific prayers are less powerful than specific prayers. In his epistle, James taught us that effective prayers are clear and fervent. For example, Elijah prayed and asked God in precise terms to withhold rain—and God did—and then to send rain—and God did (Js.5:16-18). In contrast, praying for everybody to get saved or everybody to be healed or for God to bless everybody is not effective, fervent praying.

Psalm 67, however, gives us an exception to this rule. Here, we are taught to pray for the world *as a whole*—for all the people in the world as opposed to individuals. God has a plan for this world and for all of humanity. We should pray regularly for God's plan to come to pass. Furthermore, we should labor to bring His plan to pass by doing our part to win souls to Christ throughout the world. This is the powerful message of the sixty-seventh psalm: we should be passionate about the salvation of souls and the increase of God's glory.

Psalm 67 continues the concluding theme of Psalm 66, which is bearing a strong witness for God. Its unknown author prays for God's people to be infused with grace so they will be stirred to make the LORD known to the world. The psalmist boldly claims the promise God made to Abraham: that he and his descendants would be blessed by God, and that they in turn would be made a blessing to the entire earth (Ge.12:1-3; 22:18). It is a psalm about global missions and world evangelism, a prayer that will ultimately find its fulfillment in the coming kingdom of Jesus Christ. This is, *What Your Hope and Prayer for the World Should Be*, 67:1-7.

1. Ask God to be merciful, to bless and shine His face (His approval) on all believers (vv.1-2).
2. Ask God to stir everyone to accept His salvation and to praise Him: A picture of Christ's coming kingdom (vv.3-7).

1 (67:1-2) **Ask God to be gracious, to bless and shine His face (His approval) on all believers.**

The unnamed psalmist began by praying for God's blessings on *us*—God's people, those who have accepted His covenant. At the time of its writing, this was a prayer for Israel. Today, it is a prayer for all who have accepted God's new covenant of grace through the salvation offered by Jesus Christ.

This plea for God's grace was not motivated by a desire for personal benefits. The psalmist did not petition God for His help to make Israel prosperous or at peace—although there is certainly nothing wrong with praying for these things. The psalmist requested God's favor for the benefit of the entire world as well as for God's glory.

a. **That we might be strong witnesses for Him (v.1).**
First, the psalmist prayed for God's grace so that we, His people, could be strong witnesses for Him. In a prayer that mirrors the High Priest Aaron's blessing on the people (Nu.6:24-26), the psalmist earnestly requested that God...

- be *gracious* or *merciful* to us. *Be gracious* (chanan) means to stoop to help someone who has a need, to offer undeserved help.
- *bless* us
- *make His face shine* upon us—a symbol of God's approval, favor, and empowering presence

Thought 1. We should never attempt to witness for God in our own strength but rather in the power that God gives through His grace. This is the reason Jesus instructed His followers to wait for the coming of the Holy Spirit before taking the gospel to the world (Ac.1:4-5, 8). Likewise, we need God's help to witness for Him. It is He who gives us the boldness to open our

163

mouths to speak to others about Him (Ac.4:31). And it is God's Spirit who makes our witness effective: God, through His Spirit, draws people to Christ, convicting them of sin, righteousness, and coming judgment (Jn.6:44; 16:8).

> **But I tell you the truth: It is for your good that I am going away. Unless I go away, the Counselor will not come to you; but if I go, I will send him to you. When he comes, he will convict the world of guilt in regard to sin and righteousness and judgment (Jn.16:7-8).**
>
> **On one occasion, while he was eating with them, he gave them this command: "Do not leave Jerusalem, but wait for the gift my Father promised, which you have heard me speak about. For John baptized with water, but in a few days you will be baptized with the Holy Spirit"...But you will receive power when the Holy Spirit comes on you; and you will be my witnesses in Jerusalem, and in all Judea and Samaria, and to the ends of the earth" (Ac.1:4-5, 8).**
>
> **After they prayed, the place where they were meeting was shaken. And they were all filled with the Holy Spirit and spoke the word of God boldly (Ac.4:31).**

b. **That we might make His ways and saving power known among all nations, Mt.28:19-20 (v.2).**

The psalmist asked God to stir His people to shine the light of salvation on the world. He prayed that people in all nations would learn of God's way and come into a right relationship with Him. In doing so, they would understand that God's way is the way of righteousness, as revealed in His Holy Word. They would also learn that God's way is not to destroy people for their unrighteousness, but to redeem and restore them through His *saving health—saving power* (ESV) or *salvation.* Sixteenth-century theologian John Calvin best explained God's *way:*

> *By the way of God is meant his covenant, which is the source or spring of salvation, and by which he discovered himself in the character of a Father to his ancient people, and afterwards more clearly under the Gospel, when the Spirit of adoption was shed abroad in greater abundance. Accordingly, we find Christ himself saying, "This is life eternal, that they might know thee the only true God," (John 17:3).*[1]

Thought 1. The psalmist was burdened for those in the world who did not know God, and he understood his responsibility to take God's salvation to the Gentiles. Accordingly, He prayed for God to be merciful and to pour out His favor on all believers, that we might share the gospel with others. The psalmist's passion for souls should prompt us to examine ourselves:

➢ Are we moved by the untold billions around the world—in our families, neighborhoods, cities, and nations—who do not know God, who do not understand His way of salvation?

➢ Are we shaken by the fact that the unsaved are going to spend eternity in hell separated from God unless they believe? And that they cannot believe without hearing? And that they will not hear unless someone shares the gospel with them (Ro.10:12-14)?

➢ Are we willing to go, to be sent by God to take His salvation to others (Ro.10:15; Is.6:8)?

> **Then Jesus came to them and said, "All authority in heaven and on earth has been given to me. Therefore go and make disciples of all nations, baptizing them in the name of the Father and of the Son and of the Holy Spirit, and teaching them to obey everything I have commanded you. And surely I am with you always, to the very end of the age" (Mt.28:18-20).**
>
> **He said to them, "Go into all the world and preach the good news to all creation (Mk.16:15).**
>
> **And repentance and forgiveness of sins will be preached in his name to all nations, beginning at Jerusalem (Lu.24:47).**
>
> **For this is what the Lord has commanded us: "'I have made you a light for the Gentiles, that you may bring salvation to the ends of the earth'" (Ac.13:47).**
>
> **For there is no difference between Jew and Gentile—the same Lord is Lord of all and richly blesses all who call on him, for, "Everyone who calls on the name of the Lord will be saved." How, then, can they call on the one they have not believed in? And how can they believe in the one of whom they have not heard? And how can they hear without someone preaching to them? And how can they preach unless they are sent? As it is written, "How beautiful are the feet of those who bring good news!" (Ro.10:12-15).**

---

1 John Calvin. *Calvin's Commentaries.* WORD*search* CROSS e-book.

2 (67:3-7) **Ask God to stir everyone to accept His salvation and to praise Him: A picture of Christ's coming kingdom.**

The psalmist wanted everyone in all the world to share in the joy and blessing of knowing God. Therefore, he asked God to stir everyone, to arouse them to accept His salvation and praise Him (v.3).

a. That they be filled and sing with joy (v.4).

The psalmist prayed for everyone on earth to be filled with the joy of knowing God and of living in submission to Him. The people of Israel had personally experienced the blessings that come from living under God's authority:

➤ He rules or judges in perfect righteousness and justice.

➤ He *guides* (nachah) or governs His people day by day, leading them to walk in the ways of righteousness, as a shepherd leads his beloved sheep (Ps.23:3).

b. That they might all repeatedly praise Him (v.5).

Once again, the psalmist prayed that all the people on earth would praise the LORD. This repetition—four times altogether—emphasizes the ultimate purpose of salvation: that God would be glorified by people of every nation, tribe, and tongue for His great love for humanity (Re.5:9).

c. That God will always provide for His people (v.6).

Submitting to God's authority brings His blessings upon our lives. The psalmist acknowledged that a bountiful harvest was the result of living in obedience to God. No matter how hard the farmer may work, only God can send the crucial balance of rain and sunshine to make a seed grow and produce abundantly. This principle is true in every area of our lives. Our best efforts are futile without God's blessing, and obeying God is the key to receiving His blessing (Le.26:3-5).

Some commentators feel this mention of the harvest suggests Psalm 67 was written originally for the Feast of Tabernacles. God ordained this festival, held at the end of the fall harvest, to commemorate His supernatural provision for Israel in the wilderness (Ex.23:16; Le.23:33-44; De.16:13-15).

d. That we and they will always fear and reverence Him (v.7).

God's blessings on Israel were an opportunity for evangelism. The Gentile nations—who worshipped idols—would see God's faithful, abundant provision for His people and recognize that the LORD is the only true God. As a result, they would *fear* (ya-re') the LORD:

➤ Acknowledge who God is and revere Him.

➤ Establish a relationship with Him through His covenant.

➤ Live in obedience to God and His Word (see outline and notes—Pr.1:7 for more discussion).

As outstanding Bible teacher and commentator Warren Wiersbe stated, "The application to the church today is obvious: as we obey the Lord, pray and trust Him, He provides what we need, and the unsaved around us see that He cares for us. This gives us opportunity to tell them about Jesus."[2]

Thought 1. The psalmist's prayer in this passage is being answered progressively as the church takes the gospel to the world and more and more people believe in Jesus Christ. Ultimately, though, his prayer will not fully come to pass until Christ returns to earth to establish His glorious kingdom. This passage clearly points us to the coming kingdom of Christ:

(1) Only then will all the people of the earth praise God (vv.3, 5).

(2) Only then will all the people of the earth be filled with the joy of knowing God and living in submission to Him (v.4).

(3) Only then will all the people of the earth enjoy the blessing of living under the perfect leadership of Jesus Christ and His righteous government (v.4; Is.11:4; Mi.4:3).

(4) Only then will all the earth receive the blessings that come from obeying God (v.6).

(5) Only then will all people fear God (v.7)

Until Christ returns, our Lord has commanded us to do two things: to pray for God's kingdom to come and to take the gospel to all the people of the earth (Mt.28:18-20; Mk.16:15; Lu.11:2; Ac.1:8). When we faithfully obey His Great Commission, the worship of God will increase throughout the world, and His kingdom will be established—one soul at a time.

> **Therefore God exalted him to the highest place and gave him the name that is above every name, that at the name of Jesus every knee should bow, in heaven and on earth and under the earth, and every tongue confess that Jesus Christ is Lord, to the glory of God the Father (Ph.2:9-11).**
>
> **Who will not fear you, O Lord, and bring glory to your name? For you alone are holy. All nations will come and worship before you, for your righteous acts have been revealed" (Re.15:4).**
>
> **All the nations you have made will come and worship before you, O Lord; they will bring glory to your name (Ps.86:9).**

---

2 Warren W. Wiersbe. *The Bible Exposition Commentary.* WORDsearch CROSS e-book.

"Turn to me and be saved, all you ends of the earth; for I am God, and there is no other. By myself I have sworn, my mouth has uttered in all integrity a word that will not be revoked: Before me every knee will bow; by me every tongue will swear (Is.45:22-23).

He was given authority, glory and sovereign power; all peoples, nations and men of every language worshiped him. His dominion is an everlasting dominion that will not pass away, and his kingdom is one that will never be destroyed (Da.7:14).

My name will be great among the nations, from the rising to the setting of the sun. In every place incense and pure offerings will be brought to my name, because my name will be great among the nations," says the LORD Almighty (Mal.1:11).

PSALM 68

How to Be Victorious & Triumphant Throughout Life, 68:1-35

For the director of music. Of David. A psalm. A song.

1. Pray for God's coming
a. That He will rise up & overthrow all who oppose Him
  1) Blow them away as wind blows away smoke
  2) Melt them as wax melts in a fire

b. That He will make the righteous victorious
  1) Give them joy & happiness
  2) Give them cause to rejoice
c. That everyone will praise His name
  1) Bc. He is the Mighty Warrior who rides on the clouds
  2) Bc. His name is "the LORD"
  3) Bc. He watches over His people
    • The fatherless & widows
    • The lonely
    • The prisoners
  4) Bc. He executes justice against the rebellious

2. Remember that God marches out before His people & guides them
a. He guided Israel during the Exodus & wilderness wanderings
  1) He gave them His law at Mt. Sinai, Ex.20:1-20

  2) He provided for His people (His inheritance), Ex.16:4; Ps.78:23-25; Mt.6:31-33
b. He settled His people in the promised land
  1) He gave a bountiful harvest & provided for the needy
  2) He spoke & destined Israel to conquer the land

    • Enemy kings & armies fled
    • The victors as well as those who stayed behind divided the plunder

  3) He scattered the wicked kings like a blowing snowstorm

c. He chose Mt. Zion, not Bashan,

May God arise, may his enemies be scattered; may his foes flee before him.
2 As smoke is blown away by the wind, may you blow them away; as wax melts before the fire, may the wicked perish before God.
3 But may the righteous be glad and rejoice before God; may they be happy and joyful.
4 Sing to God, sing praise to his name, extol him who rides on the clouds—his name is the LORD—and rejoice before him.
5 A father to the fatherless, a defender of widows, is God in his holy dwelling.
6 God sets the lonely in families, he leads forth the prisoners with singing; but the rebellious live in a sun-scorched land.
7 When you went out before your people, O God, when you marched through the wasteland, Selah
8 The earth shook, the heavens poured down rain, before God, the One of Sinai, before God, the God of Israel.
9 You gave abundant showers, O God; you refreshed your weary inheritance.
10 Your people settled in it, and from your bounty, O God, you provided for the poor.
11 The Lord announced the word, and great was the company of those who proclaimed it:
12 "Kings and armies flee in haste; in the camps men divide the plunder.
13 Even while you sleep among the campfires, the wings of [my] dove are sheathed with silver, its feathers with shining gold."
14 When the Almighty scattered the kings in the land, it was like snow fallen on Zalmon.
15 The mountains of Ba-

shan are majestic mountains; rugged are the mountains of Bashan.
16 Why gaze in envy, O rugged mountains, at the mountain where God chooses to reign, where the LORD himself will dwell forever?
17 The chariots of God are tens of thousands and thousands of thousands; the Lord [has come] from Sinai into his sanctuary.
18 When you ascended on high, you led captives in your train; you received gifts from men, even from the rebellious—that you, O LORD God, might dwell there.
19 Praise be to the Lord, to God our Savior, who daily bears our burdens. Selah
20 Our God is a God who saves; from the Sovereign LORD comes escape from death.
21 Surely God will crush the heads of his enemies, the hairy crowns of those who go on in their sins.
22 The Lord says, "I will bring them from Bashan; I will bring them from the depths of the sea,
23 That you may plunge your feet in the blood of your foes, while the tongues of your dogs have their share."
24 Your procession has come into view, O God, the procession of my God and King into the sanctuary.
25 In front are the singers, after them the musicians; with them are the maidens playing tambourines.
26 Praise God in the great congregation; praise the LORD in the assembly of Israel.
27 There is the little tribe of Benjamin, leading them, there the great throng of Judah's princes, and there the princes of Zebulun and of Naphtali.
28 Summon your power, O God; show us your strength, O God, as you have done before.
29 Because of your temple at Jerusalem kings will bring you gifts.
30 Rebuke the beast among

as the place for His sanctuary
  1) He did not choose as men would have chosen
    • The majestic Bashan mtns.
    • The mountains that gaze in envy at God's choice
  2) He chooses to reign & dwell in Mt. Zion forever

d. He led the heavenly armies from Mt. Sinai, where he gave the law, to Mt. Zion, where He entered the sanctuary: He went ahead of His people protecting & guiding them, 7-16
  1) He ascended His throne on Mt. Zion after conquering the nations (captives)
  2) He received tribute from the rebellious: A picture of Christ's ascension & coming rule on earth as King

3. Praise the Lord God, our Savior
a. He bears our burdens, Mt.11:28-30
b. He saves us & delivers us from death

c. He will set a day of reckoning & true justice: Vengeance will fall on all who defy Him & continue in their sin
  1) No sinners will escape: God will bring them down from the highest mtns. & up from the depths of the sea
  2) Believers will share in the Lord's victory: We will see all sinners defeated & subjected under the Lord

d. He—our God & King—will come in a great processional

  1) He will be accompanied by a vast array of musicians

  2) He will be praised & worshipped as the great victor by the congregation of believers
  3) The smallest tribe (Benjamin) will lead the way, Lu.9:48
  4) The throngs from the south (Judah & Benjamin) & north (Zebulon & Naphtali)—all believers—will praise God

4. Ask God to demonstrate His power in our behalf, just as He has in the past

a. Bc. rulers are destined to bring Him tribute in Jerusalem

b. Bc. the beasts & bulls (the

	the reeds, the herd of bulls	33 To him who rides the	1) He is the exalted ruler
leading, oppressive nations) among the calves (all other nations) need to be rebuked	among the calves of the nations. Humbled, may it	ancient skies above, who thunders with mighty voice.	over all
c. Bc. those who love war need to be humbled: All nations will submit to God, including Egypt & Cush (Ethiopia)	bring bars of silver. Scatter the nations who delight in war.	34 Proclaim the power of God, whose majesty is over Israel, whose power is in	2) He possesses all power e. Bc. we need to proclaim God's power, tell others about Him
	31 Envoys will come from Egypt; Cush will submit herself to God.	the skies. 35 You are awesome, O	1) His majesty & power over Israel
d. Bc. all kingdoms & peoples should praise the Lord	32 Sing to God, O kingdoms of the earth, sing praise to the Lord, Selah	God, in your sanctuary; the God of Israel gives power and strength to his people. Praise be to God!	2) His awesome majesty & presence in His sanctuary 3) His power & strength so readily given to His people

PSALM 68

How to Be Victorious and Triumphant Throughout Life, 68:1-35

(68:1-35) Introduction: in his introduction to this sixty-eighth psalm, commentator James Montgomery Boice relates how it has been utilized throughout history by political and military leaders who believed they were fighting for righteousness.[1] As the centuries have rolled by, the first verse has been a battle cry for many commanders as they led their troops into conflict: *"May God arise, may His enemies be scattered!"*

We, too, can make this bold declaration as we march into the conflicts of our daily lives. As believers, we are soldiers in a battle. However, we do not fight against human opponents; rather, our fight is against spiritual foes, that is, Satan and his demonic army (Ep.6:10-12; 2 Co.10:3-4). God's enemies are our enemies. They not only oppose God's will and work in the world but also attack us, His redeemed people. Satan and his evil forces possess great power in this world, and they constantly strive to defeat us through temptation, difficult circumstances, and other people who do their bidding.

Not all temptation comes from Satan. Much of the temptation we face comes from within ourselves (Js.1:14). We are involved in a never-ending internal battle: the war against our corrupt human nature, referred to in the Bible as the flesh (Ga:5:19-20; 1 Co.6:9-10). Scripture lists some of the sins produced by our flesh...

- sexual immorality
- moral impurity
- lust
- hatred
- strife
- jealousy
- anger
- selfishness
- divisiveness
- stealing
- greed
- drunkenness
- substance abuse
- verbal abuse
- dishonesty
- pride

Add to these sins the numerous human weaknesses we deal with, such as discouragement, disappointment, unkindness, impatience, laziness, and lack of discipline, to name a few. On top of that, life in general is difficult.

The point is clear: we constantly wrestle against enemies seeking to defeat us—spiritually, physically, and emotionally. Some of these hold the potential to destroy us and others as well. But all of them can keep us from being everything God wants us to be and accomplishing all that He wants us to do. They can bar us from the abundant life Christ came to give us (Jn.10:10). They can rob us of our joy, peace, confidence, effectiveness, and eternal rewards.

Nevertheless, God's Word tells us that we can triumph over these enemies. We do not have to live in defeat. God's power is greater than all our sins and circumstances. Through His Spirit and His Word, we can be victorious (Ps.44:5; Ro.8:37; 2 Co.2:14; 2 Co.10:4; 1 Jn.4:4; 1 Jn.5:4).

Psalm 68 is one of many passages of Scripture that teach us how to be victorious and triumphant in life. The heading to the psalm identifies David as its author, but the occasion for its writing is not stated. Among the many views about its origin, the most accepted is that David wrote it for the moving of the ark of the covenant to Jerusalem (2 S.6). This came on the heels of another great victory: the taking of Jerusalem for Israel's capital (2 K.5:6-7). Yet even as David celebrated these glorious triumphs, he knew that more battles lay ahead of him and the nation. He recalled and praised God for His help in the past, and He prayed for God's continued power for the future.

The transporting of the ark was an illustration of Israel's, and our, great need for God. The ark represented God's presence among His people. It was carried in front of the procession to Jerusalem, and the people followed behind. This order symbolizes our need for God to march ahead of us as we proceed through life.

As David emphasized in this psalm, God had marched ahead of Israel throughout her challenging but glorious history. From Mount Sinai to the wilderness to the promised land to Jerusalem, God had led them all the way. Commentator John Phillips described Psalm 68 as "a tremendous orchestration of history and prophecy."[2] As

---

1 James Montgomery Boice. *An Expositional Commentary–Psalms, Volume 2: Psalms 42-106.* WORDsearch CROSS e-book.

2 John Phillips. *Exploring Psalms, Volume 1.* WORDsearch CROSS e-book.

David led the people to ponder the past, he also pointed them to the future: the entire world will one day worship God at Zion. Israel and the world's greatest victory is yet to come.

Just as God will lead Israel to His ultimate purpose for her, we may rejoice in the confidence that God will march ahead of us as we persevere through the conflicts of life. God will rise up in our behalf and scatter our enemies. His will for us and His work in us will be performed (Ph.1:6). As we follow Him, we will prevail over the challenges of life. This is, *How to Be Victorious and Triumphant Throughout Life,* 68:1-35.

1. Pray for God's coming (vv.1-6).
2. Remember that God marches out before His people and guides them (vv.7-18).
3. Praise the Lord God, our Savior (vv.19-27).
4. Ask God to demonstrate His power in our behalf, just as He has in the past (vv.28-35).

1 (68:1-6) Pray for God's coming.

As the procession to transport the ark to Jerusalem began, David prayed for God to come and to march ahead of the faithful Jews who followed the ark to Zion. The ark symbolized God's presence among His people, and the call for God to arise was a call for Him to lead His people to victory over their foes.

a. That He will rise up and overthrow all who oppose Him (vv.1-2).

David prayed for God to rise up like a mighty, fearless warrior and overthrow all who opposed Him (v.1). His bold cry echoed Moses' prayer when the ark of the covenant moved ahead of the Hebrews in the wilderness (Nu.10:35). David prayed that God's victory over His foes would be swift and complete, like...

- smoke blown away by the wind (v.2a)
- wax melted in the fire (v.2b)

b. That He will make the righteous victorious (v.3).

The righteous are inseparably linked with God. Through their trust in God and their compassionate behavior, they represent God on earth. They seek to do God's work, and He works through them. Their enemies are actually God's enemies, for they are His chosen people. God fights in their behalf; therefore, a victory for God is a victory for the righteous. Thus, David prayed that God would make the righteous victorious, bringing joy and happiness to their hearts and giving them cause to rejoice.

c. That everyone will praise His name (vv.4-6).

As the people followed the ark to Jerusalem, David instructed them to praise God's name (v.4a). Israel's triumphant king offered four reasons for the people to exalt God:

First, God is the mighty warrior who rides on the heavens or clouds (v.4b). This "poetic description of God's exalted majesty"[3] is significant because the pagans gave this exact title to Baal. David's statement is a direct contradiction of their claim. As God led Israel to victory over her idolatrous foes, He would prove that He—not Baal—is superior to all things.

Second, God's name is the LORD (v.4c). *JAH* is a shortened form of Jehovah or Yahweh, God's sacred name by which He identified Himself to His people. Usually translated as the LORD, it is the name by which God makes and keeps His covenant. David instructed the people to praise God by this name because JAH—not Baal—is the one true God, and He will make His people victorious out of faithfulness to His covenant with them.

Third, God watches over His people, especially those who cannot help themselves (v.5-6a). He is the *father to the fatherless,* and the *defender* (dayyan)—advocate, judge, protector—of widows (Ps.10:14; Je.49:11). He cares for the solitary or lonely, placing people in their lives who will love and look after them. Some scholars understand this statement to be referring to the homeless, noting that *families* (bayith) is usually translated as house. Commentator Albert Barnes stated, "He is the friend of the cast out—the wandering—the homeless; He provides for them a home."[4] He also cares for the prisoners, those unjustly bound or oppressed, leading them out of bondage and into joy (v.6b).

Fourth, God executes justice on all who rebel against Him (v.6c). In contrast to the Jews, who dwelled in a land flowing with milk and honey, the rebellious live in a dry land—a parched, sun-scorched, barren land. This image is of a land void of God's blessing, and it symbolizes His judgment on those who defy Him. It teaches an important lesson: not only do those who rebel against God face eternity separated from Him, but they also forfeit the bountiful blessings of God in this life.

Thought 1. Every day, as we march into battle against the world, the flesh, and the devil, we need to ask God to go before us. We can expect to encounter temptations, challenges, and even dangers. But if we follow Him closely, God will lead us through them.

God is greater than any challenges we may face. He is bigger than our problems, needs, weaknesses, and circumstances. We need not fear anything that lies before us, even death, for He is with us (Ps.23:4; Is.43:2). He promises to guide us each step of the way (Ps.32:8). He has fully equipped us for battle, but we must clothe ourselves in His armor and arm ourselves

---

3 John F. Walvoord, ed. *The Bible Knowledge Commentary: An Exposition of the Scriptures by Dallas Seminary Faculty.*

4 Albert Barnes. *Barnes Notes on the Old Testament.* WORDsearch CROSS e-book.

with His Word. We must also devote much time to prayer. Through God's presence and power, we can be strong, and we can stand fast against our enemies. If we follow the Lord and walk in the power of *His* might, He will make us victorious (Ep.6:10-18).

> No, in all these things we are more than conquerors through him who loved us (Ro.8:37).
> But thanks be to God, who always leads us in triumphal procession in Christ and through us spreads everywhere the fragrance of the knowledge of him (2 Co.2:14).
> Finally, be strong in the Lord and in his mighty power. Put on the full armor of God so that you can take your stand against the devil's schemes. For our struggle is not against flesh and blood, but against the rulers, against the authorities, against the powers of this dark world and against the spiritual forces of evil in the heavenly realms. Therefore put on the full armor of God, so that when the day of evil comes, you may be able to stand your ground, and after you have done everything, to stand. Stand firm then, with the belt of truth buckled around your waist, with the breastplate of righteousness in place, and with your feet fitted with the readiness that comes from the gospel of peace. In addition to all this, take up the shield of faith, with which you can extinguish all the flaming arrows of the evil one. Take the helmet of salvation and the sword of the Spirit, which is the word of God. And pray in the Spirit on all occasions with all kinds of prayers and requests. With this in mind, be alert and always keep on praying for all the saints (Ep.6:10-18).
> Who saves me from my enemies. You exalted me above my foes; from violent men you rescued me (Ps.18:48).
> Even though I walk through the valley of the shadow of death, I will fear no evil, for you are with me; your rod and your staff, they comfort me (Ps.23:4).

Thought 2. David's prayer in these verses will ultimately be fulfilled when Jesus Christ returns. He will return to earth as a mighty warrior, completely destroying His enemies—all the evil and rebellious oppressors on the face of the earth. The image of God riding on the heavens points to Jesus' coming back to earth in the clouds (v.4; Re.1:7; 19:11). We need to

pray for Christ to come and for God's will for this earth to be accomplished.

> Your kingdom come, your will be done on earth as it is in heaven (Mt.6:10).
> Therefore, prepare your minds for action; be self-controlled; set your hope fully on the grace to be given you when Jesus Christ is revealed (1 Pe.1:13).
> He who testifies to these things says, "Yes, I am coming soon." Amen. Come, Lord Jesus (Re.22:20).

2 (68:7-18) **Remember that God marches out before His people and guides them.**

As the Hebrews accompanied the ark to the Holy City, David looked back on Israel's glorious history. God had a wonderful plan for the seed of Abraham: to bring them out of the bondage of Egypt and into their own land, a bountiful region where they would dwell with His blessing. In order to assure that they reached their destiny, God personally marched ahead of them on their exhausting journey. He guided them each step of the way.

a. He guided Israel during the Exodus and wilderness wanderings (vv.7-9).

God Himself guided the Israelites out of Egypt and through their wilderness wanderings. The Lord went before them, leading them with the pillar of cloud by day and the fire by night (Ex.13:21-22; 40:38; De.1:33). Even though their forty-year delay in the wilderness was God's discipline for their faithlessness, He never gave up on Jacob's descendants. He was with them each long day of their journey, protecting and providing for them. He was with them even when they were rebellious—a comforting thought!

As the people marched toward Mount Zion, David reminded them of another mountain, Mt. Sinai, where the Lord had given His holy law to the people (v.8; Ex.20:1-20). There, the Israelites had witnessed the glory of God as the earth quaked when the Lord's majestic presence descended upon it (Ex.19:18). Many commentators recognize verse 8 as a quotation from the Song of Deborah (Jud.5:4). They interpret *the heavens poured down rain* as a torrential downpour of rain. Some, however, see a reference to the giving of the law in this statement. Commentator Matthew Henry stated that "the divine doctrine dropped as the rain (De.32:2)."[5]

The Lord graciously provided for His people on the journey to the promised land (v.9). The *abundant showers* represents all that God did to refresh His weary people along the way. He provided water when they were thirsty, manna when they were hungry, and

---

5 Matthew Henry. *Matthew Henry's Commentary on the Whole Bible.* WORD*search* CROSS e-book.

even meat when they were dissatisfied with the manna. In fact, Scripture states that God rained bread and flesh, or meat, upon them (Ex.16:4; Ps.78:24-27). The people of Israel were God's inheritance—His heritage, His "own unique possession" (De.4:20; Ps.28:9).[6] He confirmed His relationship with them by providing for their needs in spite of their faithless murmuring.

b. He settled His people in the promised land (vv.10-14).

God sustained the Israelites through forty backbreaking years in the wilderness and, in His time, settled them in the promised land (v.10). David recalled how God provided for His people and established them in Canaan. Out of His goodness or bounty, He gave them an abundant harvest that provided for the poor. *The poor* does not describe just the neediest of the Hebrews but the Israelites as a whole, all "who had been afflicted in Egypt."[7]

In addition, God fulfilled Israel's destiny to conquer the land (vv.11-13). The *Lord* (Adonai) gave the word, He spoke the promise or decree, that His people would possess Canaan (Josh.1:2-6). This decree empowered a great company or mighty army who bore the joyful news as they fearlessly charged forth to conquer. As enemy kings and armies fled, Israel prevailed; and the victors, as well as those who stayed behind, divided the spoil or plunder. God gave the Israelites—these poor refugees who escaped Egypt with next to nothing—the silver and gold of those who occupied Canaan (vv.12-13).[8]

To assure Israel's security in the land, the *Almighty* (Shaddai) scattered the wicked kings like a blowing snowstorm in Salmon (v.14). *Zalmon* or *Salmon* was a mountain near Shechem (Judg.9:48-49). Scholars have offered many opinions about the meaning of this statement, but most likely the psalmist was saying poetically that "the kings were scattered like snowflakes in the wind on Mt. Zalmon."[9]

c. He chose Mt. Zion, not Bashan, as the place for His sanctuary (vv.15-16).

As David remarked, Mount Bashan was impressive with its many peaks towering majestically over the earth (v.15). In comparison to it, Zion was merely a common hill. From the human perspective, Bashan would seem the more fitting place for God to make His dwelling. But God does not think as men think, nor does He choose as men would choose. God selected Mount Zion, not Bashan, as the place for His sanctu-

ary. "It is the kind of paradox [contradiction, enigma] that God delights in, like the choice of David himself [as king]...and of little Bethlehem [as the birthplace of the Messiah]."[10]

Again speaking poetically, David described the high hills of Bashan as leaping or looking enviously at Mount Zion, where God had chosen to reign and dwell forever (v.16). David may have intended the peaks of Bashan to serve as a picture of the other nations of the world that were jealous of God's favor on Israel.

d. He led the heavenly armies from Mt. Sinai, where He gave the law, to Mt. Zion, where He entered the sanctuary: He went ahead of His people protecting and guiding them, 7-16 (vv.17-18).

As the ark neared its resting place at Zion, David described it as being accompanied by tens of thousands of unseen chariots filled with angels (v.17). These angels are God's heavenly armies, sent by God to protect both the ark and the people throughout their journey to the promised land (De.33:2; 2 K.6:17). David noted that the Lord Himself was among them. He led the hosts of heaven from Mt. Sinai, where He gave the law, to Mt. Zion, where He entered the sanctuary. God had marched ahead of His people every step of the way from Egypt to Jerusalem, guiding and protecting them.

David proceeded to describe God's ascent to His throne on Mount Zion after conquering the nations (v.18). Using another line from the Song of Deborah, David portrayed God as marching up to His exalted seat with a train of captives following behind Him (Jud.5:12). The captives represent the nations He had conquered in Israel's behalf.[11] Completing the image of a conqueror, David depicted God as receiving gifts or tribute from these rebellious peoples—an act acknowledging God as king.

Nearly 1,000 years later, Paul used this verse to describe Christ's ascension into heaven after conquering death, hell, and the grave (Ep.4:8). Instead of receiving gifts, however, the Lord Jesus gave gifts to His people. "Here is grace abounding as Jesus' triumph spills back upon His church. Every gift He gives is a former enemy now taken captive by Him and radically transformed for His service (see Eph.4:7-16)."[12]

Thought 1. As we journey through life with all of its perils and pitfalls, the Lord is marching ahead of us. Note the encouraging applications from this passage:

First, God will guide us each step of the way (vv.7-8). We do not walk blindly through life. God has promised to guide us with His eye (Ps.32:8). He orders or establishes our steps (Ps.37:23). When we trust in the

---

6 John F. Walvoord, ed. *The Bible Knowledge Commentary: An Exposition of the Scriptures by Dallas Seminary Faculty.*

7 Frank E. Gaebelein, ed. *The Expositor's Bible Commentary*, p.447.

8 The Hebrew text for vv.12-13 is very difficult to translate. Hence, Bible versions and interpretations vary.

9 Geoffrey W. Bromiley. *The International Standard Bible Encyclopedia.* WORD*search* CROSS e-book.

10 Derek Kidner. *Psalms 1-72*, p.260.

11 Some scholars understand the captives to be the children of Israel whom God had led out of the bondage of Egypt and into the glorious freedom of the promised land.

12 Donald Williams. *Psalms 1-72*, p.491.

Lord and lean fully on Him, He has promised to direct our path, that is, to remove obstacles in our way and make our path straight (Pr.3:5-6). He has given us His Word to light our way and His Spirit to lead us (Ps.119:105; Ro.8:14).

Second, God will provide everything we need (v.9). Just as God fed Israel on their journey to the promised land, He has promised to supply all of our needs (Ph.4:19). Jesus taught us not to worry about what we will eat, drink, or wear. Instead, Jesus said, we should seek God's kingdom and righteousness. When we make God our first priority, He will meet our needs (Mt.6:31-33).

Third, God will fulfill His purpose for our lives (vv.10-14). God went ahead of the children of Israel until He established them in the promised land of Canaan. The land is a picture of heaven, our eternal home, as well as the abundant life we now have in Christ. God has promised to complete the work He began in us (Ph.1:6). He has also promised to work out everything in our lives for good and for the fulfillment of His purpose for us: that we might be conformed to the image of Christ (Ro.8:28-29). We are kept by God's power, and He will protect and preserve us until we reach His heavenly kingdom (2 Ti.4:18; 1 Pe.1:5).

Fourth, God will lead us to victory over our enemies (vv.11-14). Through the power of the Holy Spirit, we must fight boldly against the world, the flesh, and the devil.

Fifth, God is always with us, for He dwells in us by His Holy Spirit (vv.15-16). Just as God chose Zion for His sanctuary, He has chosen to abide in us (Ro.8:9). He will never leave us or forsake us but will be with us until He takes us home to heaven to be with Him (Mt.28:20; He.13:5). We can be sure of His presence, His guidance, and His power at all times.

> **To shine on those living in darkness and in the shadow of death, to guide our feet into the path of peace" (Lk.1:79).**
>
> **When he has brought out all his own, he goes on ahead of them, and his sheep follow him because they know his voice (Jn.10:4).**
>
> **But when he, the Spirit of truth, comes, he will guide you into all truth. He will not speak on his own; he will speak only what he hears, and he will tell you what is yet to come (Jn.16:13).**
>
> **He restores my soul. He guides me in paths of righteousness for his name's sake (Ps.23:3).**
>
> **I will instruct you and teach you in the way you should go; I will counsel you and watch over you (Ps.32:8).**
>
> **Teach me to do your will, for you are my God; may your good Spirit lead me on level ground (Ps.143:10).**

3 (68:19-27) Praise the Lord God, our Savior.

As the procession to Mount Zion continued, David led the congregation to praise God. He reminded the worshippers not only of God's deliverance in the past but also of His faithful care in the present. He pointed to that glorious day when Jesus Christ will return to Zion as King of kings and Lord of lords.

a. He bears our burdens, Mt.11:28-30 (v.19).

David praised God for His daily care in our lives. *Load* (amas) can mean either to carry a load or to place a load upon. The literal translation of "who daily bears our burdens" is either a picture of God's continually carrying our load of burdens or of God's continually loading us up with benefit after benefit. Most translators, including the NIV, understand it to mean that God carries our load or bears our burdens. Both are true and emphasize how much God cares for us: God provides abundantly for us every day, continually bestowing upon us the gifts of His grace; and He graciously bears our heavy burdens for us (Mt.11:28-30; 1 Pe.5:7).

b. He saves and delivers us from death (v.20).

David emphasized the greatness of our God over the false gods of the heathen. In doing so, he used three different names for God:

➤ *God* (Elohim)—the strong, powerful One
➤ *GOD* (Yahweh, Jehovah)—His personal name to His people, the name by which He makes and keeps His covenant
➤ *Lord* (Adonai)—master

The use of these three names paints a complete picture of God. It also emphasizes the great truth that there is only one God and He is everything to His people (De.6:4). *Elohim* proclaims that He is the Almighty and the Creator of all things. *Jehovah* declares that He desires a relationship with us and provides for our salvation. *Adonai* teaches that He is Lord and Master of our lives.

Our God is to be praised because He alone saves and delivers His people from death. *Saves* (moshah'ah) means delivers and refers to God's saving acts. It is plural in the Hebrew, speaking of the many times in their history that God had delivered the Israelites from death. He has authority over death, and He has the power to save us from it.

c. He will set a day of reckoning and true justice: Vengeance will fall on all who defy Him and continue in their sin (vv.21-23).

God should be praised because He will retaliate against His people's enemies (v.21). Israel's enemies are His enemies, for they oppose God's plans, His purposes, and His chosen people. He has ordained a day of reckoning and true justice: God's vengeance will fall on all who defy Him and continue in their sins. *Crush* (machats) means to smash or scatter, to wound so severely that one cannot rise again (2 S.22:39; Ps.18:38; De.33:11). When God's judgment finally falls on His enemies, it will be fierce and final. No sinners will escape (v.22). God will bring all foes down from the highest mountains—as represented by Bashan—and up from the depths of the sea to be judged (Am.9:1-3; Re.20:13). Using graphic images, David foretold that believers will share in the Lord's victory: we will see all foes defeated and brought into subjection to God (v.23; Re.19:15-21).

d. He—our God and King—will come in a great processional (vv.24-27).

As David described the triumphant march to the sanctuary with the ark of the covenant, he also spoke prophetically of Israel's future rejoicing at the return of Jesus Christ (v.24). The procession to Mount Zion was an impressive and exceedingly jubilant one, with a vast array of singers, musicians, and young women dancing with timbrels or tambourines in the front (v.25). They all led the congregation of believers to praise and worship God, their great victor (v.26). The smallest of Israel's twelve tribes, Benjamin, led representatives of the other eleven tribes (v.27ᵃ; Lu.9:48). The believing throngs from the south (the tribes of Benjamin and Judah) and the north (Zebulun and Naphtali) all praised God as they marched to Mount Zion (v.27ᵇ).

Thought 1. David reminded us of some important blessings for which we should praise God:

First, we do not have to bear our burdens alone; God will bear them for us (v.19). God is aware of our burdens, and He cares for us so much that He invites us to cast our burdens on Him (Ps.55:22; 1 Pe.5:7). The arms of Jesus are open wide, inviting us to come to Him for rest when we are weighed down with a heavy load (Mt.11:28-30).

Second, God protects us each and every day (v.20). We awaken to breathe another day only because God wills it (Js.4:14-15). From time to time, we may have a close call or a brush with death: a serious illness, a near-fatal accident, or some other threatening situation that, by God's grace, we escaped. At these times, we likely recognize God's protecting hand and acknowledge Him. But on how many other occasions do we narrowly escape death and not even know it? God uses delays, changes of plans, unexpected obstacles, and other often frustrating circumstances to protect us from some imminent danger that only He, in His omniscience, sees. His angels work on our behalf continuously, protecting us from the dangers that can so quickly snatch away our lives (Ps.91:10-12).

Then, God promises to bring justice on those who sin against us as well as upon all evildoers (vv.21-23).

He does not want us agonizing over evildoers nor taking matters into our own hands. Instead, He invites us to rest in Him and wait for Him to bring justice to pass (Ps.37:1-20; Ro.12:19).

Lastly, we have the great hope of Christ's return (vv.24-27). The glorious procession of the ark—the symbol of God's presence—points us to that coming day when Christ will return to earth, march up to Zion, and take His place on David's throne as King of kings and Lord of lords. It will be a magnificent procession with Christ leading the way on a majestic white horse and His heavenly army—clothed in sparkling white linen—following behind (Re.19:11-14).

> **When he came near the place where the road goes down the Mount of Olives, the whole crowd of disciples began joyfully to praise God in loud voices for all the miracles they had seen (Lu.19:37).**
>
> **And they stayed continually at the temple, praising God (Lu.24:53).**
>
> **Every day they continued to meet together in the temple courts. They broke bread in their homes and ate together with glad and sincere hearts, praising God and enjoying the favor of all the people. And the Lord added to their number daily those who were being saved (Ac.2:46-47).**
>
> **When the builders laid the foundation of the temple of the LORD, the priests in their vestments and with trumpets, and the Levites (the sons of Asaph) with cymbals, took their places to praise the LORD, as prescribed by David king of Israel (Ezr.3:10).**
>
> **I will praise you, O LORD, with all my heart; I will tell of all your wonders (Ps.9:1).**

4 (68:28-35) **Ask God to demonstrate His power in our behalf, just as He has in the past.**
The earnest desire of David's heart was that all nations come to God and give glory to Him. Accordingly, he prayed for God to continue His work in the world through Israel, demonstrating His awesome power in behalf of any person or nation of people who truly trusted and followed Him.

a. Because rulers are destined to bring Him tribute in Jerusalem (v.29).

David prayed with a clear understanding of God's purpose for the nations: that He be glorified by people of every kindred, tribe, and tongue (Re.5:9). Through eyes of faith, he saw rulers from across the globe coming to Jerusalem to bring gifts to God at His temple.

Critics deny David's authorship of Psalm 68 based on the use of the word *temple* (hekal) in this verse, arguing that the psalm must have been written much later in Israel's history. However, this is a weak argument, as the word is clearly used in the Old Testament of the tabernacle as well (1 S.1:9; 3:3).

b. Because the beasts and bulls (the leading, oppressive nations) among the calves (all other nations) need to be rebuked (v.30).

David prayed for God to rebuke the nations that rise up against Him and Israel, His chosen nation (v.30a). The animals in this verse represent Israel's enemies. Many scholars believe the beast among the reeds refers to Egypt and her ruler, the pharaoh. Sobek, the ancient Egyptian god who was said to endow the pharaohs with power, was depicted as a crocodile (a reed-dwelling creature) or a human with the head of a crocodile. The bulls represent the leading oppressive nations and their rulers, while the calves symbolize the other nations of the world. David prayed that God would force these countries to submit to Him and offer pieces of silver—tribute, a symbol of their subjection—to God as their King.

c. Because those who love war need to be humbled: All nations will submit to God, including Egypt and Cush (Ethiopia) (vv.30-31).

For the sake of Israel's security, these war-loving nations needed to be humbled. With that in mind, David prayed that God would scatter them, stripping them of their collective power (v.30b). Speaking in faith regarding the present and prophetically regarding the future, David declared that nations from near and far would bow down to God (v.31). Egypt, Israel's neighbor to the south, would send her leaders to Zion to give tribute to God. Ethiopia or Cush, a "remote and distant nation known only by reputation"[13] to Israel, would *submit herself to God*.

d. Because all kingdoms and peoples should praise the Lord (vv.32-33).

David drew Psalm 68 to a close by ordering all kingdoms and peoples of the earth, not just Israel, to sing praise to the Lord (v.32). The use of *Lord* (Adonai) as God's name emphasizes that they should acknowledge God as Master and King. By looking to the skies, the pagan nations could realize that God is the exalted ruler over all and that He possesses all power (19:1-6). He...

- rides upon the *ancient skies*—the ancient heavens (v.33a)
- sends out His mighty voice (v.33b)
- reveals His awesome power or strength in the skies (v.34c)

e. Because we need to proclaim God's power, tell others about Him (vv.34-35).

Lastly, all the earth should ascribe or give credit to God for *His* strength, that is, acknowledge *Him*, proclaim *His* power, and tell others about *Him* (v.34a). David clearly identified this one living and true God: He is the God whose excellency or majesty watches over Israel (v.34b). His awesome majesty is seen in His sanctuary, where His presence is manifested in a very special way (v.35a). Over and over again, God has readily given His power and strength to His people. He has demonstrated His might through His miraculous works on Israel's behalf (v.35b).

Praise be to God, the source of all of Israel's victories, and ours as well!

Thought 1. The God of ancient Israel is our God today. His power is beyond our comprehension, and He can work wonders for us just as He did for His people of old. The Old Testament accounts of God's mighty deeds are inspired by the Holy Spirit and included in Scripture to encourage us and give us hope (Ro.15:4). Against fierce satanic opposition, God brought His purpose for Israel to pass. Nothing could stop Him from using Israel to bring His Son, the Messiah, into the world. In the same way, He will bring His purpose for our lives to pass through His mighty power (Is.14:24; Je.29:11; 2 Ti.1:9). God is greater than our challenges and obstacles. He is mightier than our enemies. He is waiting to help and to lead us to victory over every foe we face—if we will simply call on Him (Ps.50:15; Je.33:3; Mt.7:7).

Furthermore, God will bring His purposes for the world to pass. Although it often seems that evil is prevailing, the final victory will belong to the Lord. He will overpower all the rebellious nations of the world (Re.19:11-21). They will one day submit to Him and acknowledge that "Jesus Christ is Lord, to the glory of God the Father" (Ph.2:11). Until then, we need to continue to call on Him, trust Him, walk in His power, and proclaim His greatness to others.

> **Being fully persuaded that God had power to do what he had promised (Ro.4:21).**
>
> **Now to him who is able to do immeasurably more than all we ask or imagine, according to his power that is at work within us, to him be glory in the church and in Christ Jesus throughout all generations, for ever and ever! Amen (Ep.3:20-21).**
>
> **Who, by the power that enables him to bring everything under his control, will transform our lowly bodies so that they will be like his glorious body (Ph.3:21).**

---

13 John Phillips. *Exploring Psalms, Volume 1.* WORDsearch CROSS e-book.

The LORD is my light and my salvation—whom shall I fear? The LORD is the stronghold of my life—of whom shall I be afraid? (Ps.27:1).

Trust in the LORD forever, for the LORD, the LORD, is the Rock eternal (Is.26:4).

'Call to me and I will answer you and tell you great and unsearchable things you do not know' (Je.33:3).

PSALM 69

When Suffering Persecution or Facing a Desperate Situation, 69:1-36

For the director of music. To [the tune of] "Lilies." Of David.

1. Cry out for God to save or deliver you

a. Bc. your adversity is overwhelming

1) You are sinking in the deep mire of discouragement & drowning in the floodwaters of distress

2) You are utterly exhausted from crying out for help

b. Bc. many hate & falsely accuse you

1) Just as many hated David & tried to destroy him with lies

2) Just as many accused David of stealing & demanded he pay it all back

2. Confess your foolish & sinful behavior

a. Bc. God knows your sin & guilt

b. Bc. you do not want to be a stumbling block to others

3. Recognize that you are suffering because of your faith

a. David's own family turned against him

b. David's zeal for God & for God's house was ridiculed

c. David's prayer life & fasting were mocked

d. David's community—even the drunkards—mocked him

4. Cast yourself on God's mercy & unfailing love: Keep on praying

a. Pray for His sure salvation—a deliverance that is absolutely certain

b. Pray that He rescue you from those who hate you & cause you trouble

1) Rescue you from the depths of anguish & despair

2) Rescue you from being engulfed—swallowed up

Save me, O God, for the waters have come up to my neck.
2 I sink in the miry depths, where there is no foothold. I have come into the deep waters; the floods engulf me.
3 I am worn out calling for help; my throat is parched. My eyes fail, looking for my God.
4 Those who hate me without reason outnumber the hairs of my head; many are my enemies without cause, those who seek to destroy me. I am forced to restore what I did not steal.
5 You know my folly, O God; my guilt is not hidden from you.
6 May those who hope in you not be disgraced because of me, O Lord, the LORD Almighty; may those who seek you not be put to shame because of me, O God of Israel.
7 For I endure scorn for your sake, and shame covers my face.
8 I am a stranger to my brothers, an alien to my own mother's sons;
9 For zeal for your house consumes me, and the insults of those who insult you fall on me.
10 When I weep and fast, I must endure scorn;
11 When I put on sackcloth, people make sport of me.
12 Those who sit at the gate mock me, and I am the song of the drunkards.
13 But I pray to you, O LORD, in the time of your favor; in your great love, O God, answer me with your sure salvation.
14 Rescue me from the mire, do not let me sink; deliver me from those who hate me, from the deep waters.
15 Do not let the floodwaters engulf me or the depths swallow me up or the pit close its mouth over me.
16 Answer me, O LORD, out of the goodness of your love; in your great mercy turn to me.
17 Do not hide your face from your servant; answer me quickly, for I am in trouble.
18 Come near and rescue me; redeem me because of my foes.
19 You know how I am scorned, disgraced and shamed; all my enemies are before you.
20 Scorn has broken my heart and has left me helpless; I looked for sympathy, but there was none, for comforters, but I found none.
21 They put gall in my food and gave me vinegar for my thirst.
22 May the table set before them become a snare; may it become retribution and a trap.
23 May their eyes be darkened so they cannot see, and their backs be bent forever.
24 Pour out your wrath on them; let your fierce anger overtake them.
25 May their place be deserted; let there be no one to dwell in their tents.
26 For they persecute those you wound and talk about the pain of those you hurt.
27 Charge them with crime upon crime; do not let them share in your salvation.
28 May they be blotted out of the book of life and not be listed with the righteous.
29 I am in pain and distress; may your salvation, O God, protect me.
30 I will praise God's name in song and glorify him with thanksgiving.
31 This will please the LORD more than an ox, more than a bull with its horns and hoofs.
32 The poor will see and be glad—you who seek God, may your hearts live!
33 The LORD hears the needy and does not despise his captive people.
34 Let heaven and earth praise him, the seas and all that move in them,

---

c. Pray that God answer you out of the goodness of His love & mercy

1) That He not hide His face from you
2) That He answer you quickly

5. Ask God to redeem you, to set you free from your enemies

a. They persecute you
1) Scorn, disgrace, & shame you

2) Break your heart, leaving you helpless & dejected
3) Fail to offer sympathy & comfort

4) Mistreat you by deliberately adding to your trouble (add gall & vinegar to your meals)

b. They deserve God's justice & judgment, His retribution
1) Deserve to be snared in the trap they set for you
2) Deserve to go blind & lose their strength (have bent backs) so they cannot continue to do evil
3) Deserve to receive God's wrath

4) Deserve to have no future (to be homeless & childless): Bc. they persecute those who suffer adversity & are being disciplined by God

5) Deserve to be charged (to suffer for their crimes)
• To have no hope of salvation
• To be blotted out of the Book of Life

6. Praise God's name

a. Tell God about your suffering: Ask Him to protect you
b. Look ahead to the day of victory & praise God's name

1) Bc. this will please God more than sacrifices & offerings

2) Bc. the humble—all who truly seek God—will see God's victory & be encouraged

3) Bc. the LORD hears the cries of His people, both the needy & the oppressed

4) Bc. God deserves the praise of all that is in heaven, earth, & the seas

5) Bc. God will build the promised land & settle His people there: A picture of heaven	35 For God will save Zion and rebuild the cities of Judah. Then people will settle there and possess it;	36 The children of his servants will inherit it, and those who love his name will dwell there.	• All believing descendants will inherit the promised land • All who love God's name will live there

PSALM 69

When Suffering Persecution or Facing a Desperate Situation, 69:1-36

(69:1-36) **Introduction:** during our time on earth, we will all encounter trials and tests. James warned that we will "face trials of many kinds" (Js.1:2). A variety of things cause our adversities and afflictions. Satan is behind some of them. Others are the natural consequence of living in a sin-cursed world. At times we cause our own trouble: some difficulties are the direct result of our unwise decisions, sinful deeds, or foolish behavior.

For believers, however, some hardships have a different cause. If we are totally devoted to Jesus Christ and live in faithful obedience to God's Word, we can expect to suffer persecution. Jesus warned that we would be hated, persecuted, and slandered (Mt.5:10-12). Paul plainly stated that "everyone who wants to live a godly life in Christ Jesus will be persecuted" (2 Ti.3:12). Peter wrote extensively about suffering for righteousness' sake because we are Christians (1 Pe.3:14-4:19).

Psalm 69 is a prayer in response to persecution (v.7). According to its heading, David is the author. The specific occasion that prompted its writing is not identified. The mistreatment David was experiencing had gone on so long and was so intense that he felt he could bear it no longer (v.17). Therefore, he cried out to God.

The personal suffering David endured was prophetic of the sufferings of Jesus Christ. In this sense, Psalm 69 is a Messianic psalm, one that is frequently quoted in the New Testament. In fact, next to Psalms 22 and 110, Psalm 69 is the most-referenced psalm in the New Testament.

Today, untold numbers of believers around the world are paying a painful price for their devotion to Jesus Christ. As you study this psalm, please keep them in mind and pray for them. As we draw ever closer to the coming of Christ, more and more of His followers will be afflicted for His sake, many to the point of death. Thankfully, for those who suffer for righteousness' sake, Scripture gives us promise after promise of His presence, His strength, and living eternally with Him. This is, *When Suffering Persecution or Facing a Desperate Situation*, 69:1-36.

1. Cry out for God to save or deliver you (vv.1-4).
2. Confess your foolish and sinful behavior (vv.5-6).
3. Recognize that you are suffering because of your faith (vv.7-12).
4. Cast yourself on God's mercy and unfailing love: Keep on praying (vv.13-17).
5. Ask God to redeem you, to set you free from your enemies (vv.18-28).
6. Praise God's name (vv.29-36).

1 (69:1-4) **Cry out for God to save or deliver you.** David was trapped in a helpless situation that was destroying him from the inside out. Cruel enemies had unjustly attacked him and were spreading lies about him. Having reached the point where he could no longer endure their vicious persecution, he desperately cried out for God to deliver him.

a. **Because your adversity is overwhelming (vv.1-3).** Utterly overwhelmed by his adversity, David described himself as a drowning man. He had been cast into such deep waters of affliction that he questioned whether he could survive (v.1). His difficulties were intensified by the discouragement that had set into his troubled soul. He was stuck in its thick mire, and the floodwaters of distress were rapidly overtaking him (v.2). Desperate, he feared he would sink so deep into depression that he would never escape. He struggled for a foothold (standing), but could fine none.

David was also totally exhausted, which worsened his situation (v.3). He had cried out to God for help until his throat was parched and he could cry no more. He waited and waited for God to answer his desperate cries, but no answer came (v.17). He described his futile pursuit of God in physical terms: he had looked for God so long that his vision had failed. With his strength completely spent, he felt he could hold on no longer.

b. **Because many hate and falsely accuse you (v.4).** David proceeded to describe the circumstances that so fiercely oppressed him: many people hated him without cause and were making false accusations against him. Speaking poetically, David said that the number of his enemies exceeded the number of hairs on his head. For no just reason, they sought to destroy him by spreading vicious lies. In an attempt to resolve the situation, David apparently made amends for something he had not done. He made restitution for items he had not stolen. Whether he had actually been accused of stealing or if this was simply a comparison to what had occurred is unclear.

Thought 1. Psalm 69 begins with a familiar lesson: when we are facing overwhelming adversity, we need to cry out for God's help. Perhaps the reason this lesson is so frequently repeated in *Psalms* is that we are too slow to apply it. We tend to take matters into our

177

own hands and rely on our own resources. Only after exhausting our resources and ourselves do we turn to God and cast our burden on Him. Whether our trouble is similar to David's or something entirely different...

- conflicts with others
- discouragement
- fear
- abuse or mistreatment by others
- false accusations
- great personal loss
- financial pressures
- health issues
- overwhelming responsibilities
- grueling deadlines
- depression
- despair

...any number of challenges can cause us to feel as if we are sinking. But like David, we must learn to call on the LORD and to believe the great promises of His Holy Word:

> **And will not God bring about justice for his chosen ones, who cry out to him day and night? Will he keep putting them off? (Lu.18:7).**
>
> **In that day you will no longer ask me anything. I tell you the truth, my Father will give you whatever you ask in my name (Jn.16:23).**
>
> **And the prayer offered in faith will make the sick person well; the Lord will raise him up. If he has sinned, he will be forgiven (Js.5:15).**
>
> **'Call to me and I will answer you and tell you great and unsearchable things you do not know' (Je.33:3).**
>
> **He will call upon me, and I will answer him; I will be with him in trouble, I will deliver him and honor him (Ps.91:15).**
>
> **Before they call I will answer; while they are still speaking I will hear (Is.65:24).**

2 (69:5-6) **Confess your foolish and sinful behavior.** As David prayed earnestly about his distressing situation, he knew he was not perfect and was capable of making mistakes. He was willing to acknowledge any behavior on his part that had contributed to his trouble. For this reason, he confessed his foolish and sinful tendencies to God.

a. Because God knows your sin and guilt (v.5).
God knew David's weaknesses. The king was fully capable of foolish behavior. Like all of us, he was prone to sin. He did not always act wisely, nor did he always obey God's laws. But he was wise enough to know that he could not hide his sin from God. If he was guilty of some trespass that had caused his current trouble, God was fully aware of it. Hence, it would be useless for David to claim innocence before God.

b. Because you do not want to be a stumbling block to others (v.6).
David also knew that many people believe everything they hear without discerning whether it is true. With this in mind, he was greatly concerned that the accusations against him might be a stumbling block to others. Moreover, he feared that his situation might bring reproach on those who genuinely followed the LORD. He prayed earnestly that those who wait on or hope in God would not be *disgraced* because of him. He also prayed that those who *seek* the LORD would not be confounded, that is, that they would not be embarrassed, humiliated, or ashamed.

Thought 1. We need to realize a simple truth: sometimes we cause our own problems. Sometimes our trouble is the result of our own sinful or unwise behavior. The difficulties we then face may be due to God's discipline because of our sin. Occasionally, our conflicts with others are rooted in something we said or did—often without realizing or intending it.

What we have to remember is that we cannot deceive God: He is always aware of everything we say and do. We cannot hide our sins from Him. Therefore, when we pray for His help, we should confess our foolish and sinful behavior to Him. In addition, we should ask Him to thoroughly search our hearts and reveal our failures to us. We will not receive His mercy until we confess our sins (Pr.28:13). And we cannot be reconciled to others until we acknowledge our contribution to the conflict. Refusing to deal with our sins and mistakes will only intensify our difficulties. If we are wise, we will recognize that and confess them to the Lord.

> **Repent of this wickedness and pray to the Lord. Perhaps he will forgive you for having such a thought in your heart (Ac.8:22).**
>
> **If we confess our sins, he is faithful and just and will forgive us our sins and purify us from all unrighteousness (1 Jn.1:9).**
>
> **Search me, O God, and know my heart; test me and know my anxious thoughts. See if there is any offensive way in me, and lead me in the way everlasting (Ps.139:23-24).**
>
> **He who conceals his sins does not prosper, but whoever confesses and renounces them finds mercy (Pr.28:13).**

3 (69:7-12) **Recognize that you are suffering because of your faith.**
As David opened his heart and laid himself bare before God, he realized that the root of his trouble was his

fervent faith in the LORD. He was under attack by people who scorned his devotion to God. To state it simply, David was suffering persecution: "endure scorn for *your* sake [emphasis ours]" (v.7).

a. David's own family turned against him (v.8).

David lamented that his own family had turned against him. His brothers treated him like a *stranger* (zur) and an *alien* (nokri)—one who was unknown and foreign to them, a person who was not a member of their family (De.25:5). By using the term *my mother's sons*, David clarified what he meant by *brothers*: he was referring to his siblings, his brothers by blood, rather than his fellow Israelites. This alienation by his brothers points to the rejection of Jesus by his family (Jn.7:3-5).

b. David's zeal for God and for God's house was ridiculed (v.9).

As a young man, David burst onto the scene in Israel because of his irrepressible zeal for God—a burning passion that he could not contain. His fervor for God would not allow him to stand idly by while blasphemous Goliath mocked his God (1 S.17:23-45).

This same zeal for God marked his later life. As king, he loved to worship and longed to build a house that was worthy of God (2 S.7:1-2). He danced exuberantly before the LORD when the ark of the covenant was brought up to Zion (2 S.6:14). As David often expressed in his songs, he rejoiced in every opportunity to go to the temple for worship (Ps.26:8; 27:4; 65:4; 122:1). He was truly passionate about worshipping God. And his zeal—this passion he freely, publicly, and lavishly displayed—was the true reason he was under attack. He now grasped the reality that the reproaches or insults he was being forced to bear were not so much directed at him as they were at God, whom he shamelessly worshipped.

In this verse as well, David foreshadowed his divine descendant, Jesus Christ. Both parts of verse 9 are prophetic of God's glorious Son, as revealed in the New Testament:

> **His disciples remembered that it is written: "Zeal for your house will consume me" (Jn.2:17).**
>
> **For even Christ did not please himself but, as it is written: "The insults of those who insult you have fallen on me" (Ro.15:3).**

c. David's prayer life and fasting were mocked (vv.10-11).

As David poured out his aching heart to God, he shared that he was mocked for practicing the spiritual disciplines of prayer and fasting. David regularly humbled himself before the LORD through weeping, fasting, and wearing sackcloth (vv.10-11). These practices were expressions of mourning, repentance, and seeking the LORD (Jud.20:26; 2 S.12:16; Ps.35:13; Neh.1:4; 9:1; Da.9:3). David's devotion to God had brought reproach upon him from the ungodly people of his nation (v.10). "Became a proverb to them" means that they made fun of David, that he was the object of their jokes (v.11).

d. David's community—even the drunkards—mocked him (v.12).

David was ridiculed by ungodly people at all levels of society. "Those who sit at the gate" are the respected leaders of the nation—judges, officials, and business leaders. At the other extreme, the drunkards were among the most despised of the community. They too mocked David for his devotion to God.

Here again, David's experience prophetically portrays the rejection of Christ (Is.53:3; Mk.15:3; Lu.4:28-29; 9:22;19:14; 23:18; Ac.4:26). Bible teacher John Phillips wrote,

> *Even the most cursory reading of the Gospels shows how soon and how often Jewish officialdom spoke against Jesus...Think of it!...In yonder glory land angels had crowded around His throne to awaken the echoes of the everlasting hills with their ceaseless chant: "Holy! Holy! Holy!" Now, in the public houses, with drink slopping down their beards, they lifted their tipsy voices in ribald song, mocking Him. And He loved them, died for them; died, indeed, as them.*[1]

Thought 1. May God help us to be like David, so in love with God and aflame with passion for Him that we do not care what others think. We should unashamedly identify ourselves with Jesus Christ and openly profess our love for Him. If we are ashamed of Him, Jesus said, He will be ashamed of us at His coming (Lu.9:26).

But know this: if you openly worship the Lord and stand for Him, you will pay a price. You may be rejected by your family and friends (Lu.14:26). You may be passed over for advancement at work. You may be mocked and ridiculed by ungodly people. In some parts of the world, you may be imprisoned or even put to death.

Scripture offers encouraging promises for the persecuted. First, we will have a great reward in heaven (Mt.5:12). We will also have a closer relationship with Christ. When we are afflicted for Jesus' sake, we enter into a glorious intimacy with Him, an intimacy unlike any other. Through personal experience, we participate in, the "fellowship of sharing in His sufferings" (Ph.3:8-10). We also qualify ourselves to share in

---

[1] John Phillips. *Exploring Psalms, Volume 1*. WORDsearch CROSS e-book.

Christ's coming glory (Ro.8:17). When His glory is revealed, we who shared in His sufferings will have a measure of joy that exceeds that of those who did not suffer for His sake, a joy that is greater than any we have ever known (1 Pe.4:13). Scripture says the sufferings we endure on earth cannot begin to compare to the glory we will receive on that day (Ro.8:18). For these reasons and more, Jesus said, "Blessed are those who are persecuted because of righteousness..." (Mt.5:10).

> Blessed are those who are persecuted because of righteousness, for theirs is the kingdom of heaven. "Blessed are you when people insult you, persecute you and falsely say all kinds of evil against you because of me. Rejoice and be glad, because great is your reward in heaven, for in the same way they persecuted the prophets who were before you (Mt.5:10-12).
>
> "If the world hates you, keep in mind that it hated me first. If you belonged to the world, it would love you as its own. As it is, you do not belong to the world, but I have chosen you out of the world. That is why the world hates you. Remember the words I spoke to you: 'No servant is greater than his master.' If they persecuted me, they will persecute you also. If they obeyed my teaching, they will obey yours also. They will treat you this way because of my name, for they do not know the One who sent me (Jn.15:18-21).
>
> Now if we are children, then we are heirs—heirs of God and co-heirs with Christ, if indeed we share in his sufferings in order that we may also share in his glory. I consider that our present sufferings are not worth comparing with the glory that will be revealed in us (Ro.8:17-18).
>
> If we endure, we will also reign with him. If we disown him, he will also disown us (2 Ti.2:12).
>
> But rejoice that you participate in the sufferings of Christ, so that you may be overjoyed when his glory is revealed. If you are insulted because of the name of Christ, you are blessed, for the Spirit of glory and of God rests on you (1 Pe.4:13-14).
>
> Do not be surprised, my brothers, if the world hates you. We know that we have passed from death to life, because we love our brothers. Anyone who does not love remains in death (1 Jn.3:13-14).

4 **(69:13-17) Cast yourself on God's mercy and unfailing love: Keep on praying.**
David responded to his persecution with a stronger commitment to prayer (v.13). While the ungodly mocked him, he would cast himself on God's *unfailing love* (chesed), His mercy. By calling God the LORD (Yahweh, Jehovah), David emphasized that he was praying to the One who is faithful to His covenant. *In the time of your favor* may be a request for God's favor, or it may mean that the LORD would answer David in the time of His choosing rather than according to David's schedule.[2]

a. **Pray for His sure salvation—a deliverance that is absolutely certain (v.13).**
David prayed for God to hear him—to pay attention to and answer his request—according to His sure salvation. *Sure* (emeth) refers to God's faithfulness to His own character, His Word, His covenant, and His people. By using this word, David declared that his salvation from his situation, his deliverance, was absolutely certain. God would prove Himself true: He would not allow David to be defeated by his ungodly enemies.

b. **Pray that He rescue you from those who hate you and cause you trouble (vv.14-15).**
David returned to the image with which he began this psalm, the illustration of a drowning man (vv.1-2). Notice the terms...
* sinking in mire (v.14)
* deep waters (v.14, 15)
* waterflood or floodwaters (v.15)
* the pit (v.15)

This threatening situation included both the cause and the effect of his trouble: the cause was the people who hated him; the effect was the deep discouragement and depression that held his soul in bondage. David begged God to rescue him from the depths of anguish and despair, to keep him from being completely swallowed up by his distress.

c. **Pray that God answer you out of the goodness of His love and mercy (vv.16-17).**
As David cried out to God, he found a foothold in the miry pit in which he was sinking (v.2): it was the love and mercy of God (v.16). *Love* (chesed) is God's unfailing, steadfast love. It is one of God's attributes or qualities that reveal His unparalleled character. This trait stirs God to offer His covenant to us and to keep it without fail. By claiming God's lovingkindness, David believed God would be faithful to His covenant.

---

2 Donald Williams. *Psalms 1-72*, p.503.

Great mercy (rachamim) comes from the Hebrew word for womb, signifying the deep, tender love a mother has for her helpless newborn baby (Is.49:15). It is deep compassion, intensely emotional pity and affection felt from the most inward parts of one's being. David referred to God's multitude of tender mercies, meaning that His heartfelt compassion toward us is so abundant that it cannot be measured (Ge.32:12).

Standing firmly on God's unfailing love and unlimited compassion, David boldly called on the LORD to no longer hide His face from him (v.17). He prayed that God would answer him quickly, for he was sinking deeper and deeper in despair with every passing day.

Thought 1. Ongoing trouble requires that we persist in prayer. When our prayers are not quickly answered, we often become discouraged, feeling that it is useless to pray. Or we may think that God is not listening or that He does not care about us.

Yet Jesus taught us to be persistent in prayer, to never grow discouraged or quit praying (Lu.18:1). When Jesus commanded us to ask, seek, and knock, He used present tense verbs, meaning we are to continuously do these things (Lu.11:9). Literally, He said, "Keep on asking, keep on seeking, keep on knocking." To illustrate the point, Jesus told of a man who needed his neighbor's help at midnight. At first, his neighbor refused due to the lateness of the hour, but the man persisted until his neighbor gave him what he needed (Lu.11:5-8).

We need to stand on God's promises when we do not receive immediate answers to our prayer, just as David did. God's love for us is unfailing and unconditional. Nothing can separate us from His love (Ro. 8:35-39). He will answer our prayer and freely give us all that we need (Lu.11:10-13; Ro.8:32). Knowing that, we can commit our lives to Him and trust Him to take care of us (1 Pe.4:19; 2 Ti.1:12).

Do not doubt God, suffering believer. Do not give up. Do not quit praying.

> **Then Jesus told his disciples a parable to show them that they should always pray and not give up (Lu.18:1).**
>
> **I tell you, though he will not get up and give him the bread because he is his friend, yet because of the man's boldness he will get up and give him as much as he needs. "So I say to you: Ask and it will be given to you; seek and you will find; knock and the door will be opened to you. For everyone who asks receives; he who seeks finds; and to him who knocks, the door will be opened. "Which of you fathers, if your son asks for a fish, will give him a snake instead? Or if he asks for an egg, will give him a scorpion? If**

> **you then, though you are evil, know how to give good gifts to your children, how much more will your Father in heaven give the Holy Spirit to those who ask him!" (Lu.11:8-13).**
>
> **And being in anguish, he prayed more earnestly, and his sweat was like drops of blood falling to the ground (Lu.22:44).**
>
> **Therefore confess your sins to each other and pray for each other so that you may be healed. The prayer of a righteous man is powerful and effective (Js.5:16).**

5 (69:18-29) **Ask God to redeem you, to set you free from your enemies.**
David was desperate, and God was his only hope. He begged God to come close to him and to redeem or ransom his life by setting him free from his enemies (v.18). Once again, he described the unjust persecution he was living through, boldly appealing to God to judge his foes severely for their cruelty.

a. They persecute you (vv.19-21).
David found relief in the fact that the LORD knew about the reproach he was being forced to bear—scorn, disgrace, and shame. Every act of his adversaries was before the LORD (v.19). This merciless humiliation had broken David's heart, leaving him feeling helpless and dejected. He looked for someone to take pity on him, to comfort or encourage him, but no one cared enough to reach out to him in his distress (v.20).

David's lament paints a clear picture of Jesus on the cross. Notice the prophecies pointing to Christ in David's painful cry:
➤ The *broken* or burst heart—when the soldier pierced our Savior's side, a mixture of water and blood gushed out, indicating that his heart had ruptured (Jn.19:34).
➤ The *heaviness* of his burden—as our Lord prayed in the Garden, His sorrow was so great that He thought He would die (Mt.26:37-38).
➤ The complete rejection by others—the people of His own nation called for Jesus' death, and most of His disciples failed to stand by Him. Even His Father turned away from Jesus as He bore the full weight of our sin (Is.53:3; Mt.26:69-75; 27:46).

The most amazing of David's prophecies, though, is his statement about being served gall, a poisonous substance, and vinegar (v.21). Unless he was a prisoner, it is highly unlikely that David's meals consisted of these bitter elements. Most commentators feel David intended them to be symbolic of the deliberate mistreatment he was suffering at the hands of his enemies. Most likely, they were a picture of his foes doing everything possible to add to his distress.

However, by inspiration of the Holy Spirit, David spoke in precise detail of the abuse Jesus would experience at Calvary. Matthew wrote about the mixture of gall and vinegar that was cruelly offered to Jesus as He suffered on the cross (Mt.27:34). All four gospel authors noted that He was offered vinegar (Mt.27:48; Mk.15:36; Lu.23:36; Jn.19:29). John recorded that, in order to fulfill this specific prophecy, Jesus complained of thirst just before He died (Jn.19:28-30).

b. They deserve God's justice and judgment, His retribution (vv.22-28).

Enraged by the injustice he was suffering, David prayed for God's judgment to fall on his vicious foes. This prayer classifies Psalm 69 as an *imprecatory* psalm—one in which he implores God in graphic terms to pour out His retribution on His enemies (see KEYS TO UNDERSTANDING PSALMS for more discussion).

David presented the case for the merciless judgment of his enemies. He argued, first, that they deserved to be snared in the trap they had set for him (v.22). *The table* refers to their cruel treatment of David, as represented by their serving him gall and vinegar (v.21).

Second, David asserted that they deserved to go blind and lose their strength so they could not continue to do evil (v.23). *Backs* (mothnayim) refers to the lower part of the back, the center of a man's strength. Some scholars say it more specifically describes the "strong musculature linking the upper part of the body with the lower part."[3]

Third, they deserved to receive God's unrestrained wrath, the full measure of His righteous anger (v.24).

Fourth, they deserved to have no future or posterity, that is, to be homeless and childless (v.25). This was the harshest earthly judgment David could fathom. They warranted such unmerciful treatment because they persecuted those who were being afflicted by God (v.26). Nowhere else in this psalm does David even suggest that he was suffering at God's hand. This statement is surely prophetic of the persecution of Christ, whom Scripture says was "smitten by him, and afflicted" (Is.53:4).

Fifth, David called on God to charge them with crime upon crime (v.27-28). They deserved to be doubly charged, to suffer double punishment for their crimes (v.27ᵃ). This double punishment would consist of God's judgment resting on them throughout their earthly lives and then following them into eternity. Specifically, David prayed that God would not allow them to *share in your salvation*—that they would have

no hope of salvation and be blotted out of the Book of Life (vv.27-28).

Thought 1. As discussed, David prophetically portrayed the sufferings of Christ in this psalm. Note the following lessons from this passage:

First, we should ask God to redeem us and set us free from our enemies (v.18). Jesus did exactly this when He prayed in the Garden of Gethsemane, "My Father, if it is possible, may this cup [of suffering] be taken from me" (Mt.26:39). Still, the cup of suffering did not pass from Jesus because it was the Father's will for Him to go to the cross. We too may suffer when we do the Father's will (1 Pe.4:19). In fact, if we are faithful to the Lord, we can expect to suffer reproach from others.

Second, our sufferings reflect Christ's sufferings (vv.19-21). As previously mentioned, we become partakers of Christ's sufferings when we are afflicted for His sake. In return, we will experience a deeper level of intimacy with Him and will know a measure of joy exceeding any we have ever known (Ph.3:10; 1 Pe.4:12-14).

Third, David prayed for God to judge his enemies harshly (vv.22-28). In the New Testament, however, Jesus taught us a better way to pray for our enemies. Instead of praying for their destruction, Jesus taught us to pray for God to have mercy on our persecutors. He modeled this from the cross, saying, "Father, forgive them, for they do not know what they are doing" (Lu.23:34). When Stephen was executed for preaching Christ, he followed our dying Savior's example, saying, "Lord, do not hold this sin against them" (Ac.7:60). We too should follow the command and example of Christ by blessing those who curse us, doing good to those who hate us, and praying for those who persecute us (Mt.5:44; Lu.6:35; 1 Co.4:12; 1 Th.5:14; 1 Pe.3:9).

> **"Praise be to the Lord, the God of Israel, because he has come and has redeemed his people. He has raised up a horn of salvation for us in the house of his servant David (as he said through his holy prophets of long ago), salvation from our enemies and from the hand of all who hate us—to show mercy to our fathers and to remember his holy covenant (Lu.1:68-72).**
>
> **He has delivered us from such a deadly peril, and he will deliver us. On him we have set our hope that he will continue to deliver us (2 Co.1:10).**
>
> **For he has rescued us from the dominion of darkness and brought us into the kingdom of the Son he loves (Col.1:13).**

---

3 R. Laird Harris, ed. *Theological Wordbook of the Old Testament.* WORD*search* CROSS e-book.

The Lord will rescue me from every evil attack and will bring me safely to his heavenly kingdom. To him be glory for ever and ever. Amen (2 Ti.4:18).

If this is so, then the Lord knows how to rescue godly men from trials and to hold the unrighteous for the day of judgment, while continuing their punishment (2 Pe.2:9).

Do not turn me over to the desire of my foes, for false witnesses rise up against me, breathing out violence (Ps.27:12).

6 (69:29-36) Praise God's name.

After pouring out his heart to the LORD and casting his heavy burden on Him, David determined to change his outlook on his situation. Remembering God's unfailing love, compassion, and justice gave him hope. He chose to no longer wallow in self-pity, depression, and defeat. Instead, he would sing the praises of God, showing his gratitude for the LORD's faithfulness by magnifying His great name.

a. Tell God about your suffering: Ask Him to protect you (v.29).

David shared his suffering with the LORD, readily confessing that he was in pain and distress. *Distress* (ani) means afflicted or suffering severe poverty and oppression. David humbly asked God to *protect him* (sagab), to put him in a high, secure place where he would be protected from his enemies.

b. Look ahead to the day of victory and praise God's name (vv.30-36).

Looking ahead to the day God would give him victory over his adversaries, David resolved to praise God's glorious name (v.30). Instead of vowing to offer thanksgiving sacrifices when God answered his prayer, David decided to offer God "a sacrifice of praise—the fruit of [his] lips that confess his name" (He.13:15). This, David realized, would please the LORD more than animal sacrifices (v.31).

When those who were humble saw David praising God for the victory He had given, they would be encouraged (v.32). *Poor* (anav) is from the same Hebrew root as distress (v.29). It too refers to a person who is afflicted or oppressed, one who has been made meek because of severe suffering. It describes people who truly seek God in their affliction. When these humbled people learned of what God had done for David, they would be filled with hope. Their broken hearts would live again and be revived because they would see that the LORD hears the cries of His needy people (v.33). He does not despise His prisoners, those held captive by the bonds of oppression.

David concluded this sixty-ninth psalm with a joyous call to worship (v.34). He proclaimed that God deserves the praise of all creation, including...

- the praise of heaven
- the praise of the earth
- the praise of the seas
- the praise of every living creature

David then declared that God is worthy of universal praise because of His great love for Israel. Speaking prophetically, David pronounced that the LORD would save Zion or Jerusalem and build the cities of Judah (v.35). God's chosen people would face devastating hardships in the centuries to follow, but the LORD would keep His covenant with them. He would build and rebuild the promised land and settle His people there, ultimately through the Messiah.

Of course, the promised land is a picture of heaven. All of Abraham's spiritual seed—true believers, Jew and Gentile alike—will inherit the land (v.36). All who love God's name will live forever in a new heaven and new earth, with the New Jerusalem as its capital:

For, "Whoever would love life and see good days must keep his tongue from evil and his lips from deceitful speech. He must turn from evil and do good; he must seek peace and pursue it. For the eyes of the Lord are on the righteous and his ears are attentive to their prayer, but the face of the Lord is against those who do evil." Who is going to harm you if you are eager to do good? (1 Pe.3:10-13).

Then I saw a new heaven and a new earth, for the first heaven and the first earth had passed away, and there was no longer any sea. I saw the Holy City, the new Jerusalem, coming down out of heaven from God, prepared as a bride beautifully dressed for her husband. And I heard a loud voice from the throne saying, "Now the dwelling of God is with men, and he will live with them. They will be his people, and God himself will be with them and be their God. He will wipe every tear from their eyes. There will be no more death or mourning or crying or pain, for the old order of things has passed away." He who was seated on the throne said, "I am making everything new!" Then he said, "Write this down, for these words are trustworthy and true." He said to me: "It is done. I am the Alpha and the Omega, the Beginning and the End. To him who is thirsty I will give to drink without cost from the spring of the water of life. He who overcomes will

inherit all this, and I will be his God and he will be my son (Re.21:1-7).

Thought 1. The power of praise sets the captive soul free. Even when we are suffering, we should magnify the name of the Lord. As David noted, God is pleased when we offer Him the sacrifice of praise. And others who are suffering will be encouraged when they observe us praising Him.

The great message of this sixty-ninth psalm is the same as many others: when we are troubled, we need to cry out to God. As we pour our hearts out to Him, He will lift our burden from us, remind us of His steadfast love for us, and empower us to praise Him—even while we are yet suffering. This is true in every difficult circumstance of life. In Psalm 69, it is shown to be true for those who must walk through the deep waters of persecution.

All this is for your benefit, so that the grace that is reaching more and more people may cause thanksgiving to overflow to the glory of God (2 Co.4:15).

Always giving thanks to God the Father for everything, in the name of our Lord Jesus Christ (Ep.5:20).

Give thanks in all circumstances, for this is God's will for you in Christ Jesus (1 Th.5:18).

Keep your lives free from the love of money and be content with what you have, because God has said, "Never will I leave you; never will I forsake you" (He.13:5).

Then my head will be exalted above the enemies who surround me; at his tabernacle will I sacrifice with shouts of joy; I will sing and make music to the Lord (Ps.27:6).

The sounds of joy and gladness, the voices of bride and bridegroom, and the voices of those who bring thank offerings to the house of the Lord, saying, "Give thanks to the Lord Almighty, for the Lord is good; his love endures forever." For I will restore the fortunes of the land as they were before,' says the Lord (Je.33:11).

	PSALM 70	in disgrace.	
	When You Need God's Immediate Help, 70:1-5	3 May those who say to me, "Aha! Aha!" turn back because of their shame.	b. By executing judgment against them—perfect retribution: That they reap the horrible shame they seek to sow
	For the director of music. Of David. A petition.	4 But may all who seek you rejoice and be glad in you; may those who love your salvation always say, "Let God be exalted!"	**2. Ask God to bless His people** a. To fill all who seek Him with joy & gladness b. To stir all who love His salvation to praise & exalt Him
1. Pray for God to save you quickly, to give you help without delay a. By shaming & confusing those who seek to harm you: That they be turned back	Hasten, O God, to save me; O LORD, come quickly to help me. 2 May those who seek my life be put to shame and confusion; may all who desire my ruin be turned back	5 Yet I am poor and needy; come quickly to me, O God. You are my help and my deliverer; O LORD, do not delay.	**3. Confess your helplessness before God & ask for His immediate help** a. Bc. you are poor & needy b. Bc. He is your helper & deliverer

PSALM 70

When You Need God's Immediate Help, 70:1-5

(70:1-5) Introduction: the urgency of some situations does not always allow time for lengthy prayers. One of the most effective prayers in the gospels contains only three words: "Lord, save me" (Mt.14:30). When Peter uttered this prayer, he began to sink while walking on water. Psalm 70 is such a prayer. Under attack by adversaries, David suddenly found himself in danger. He needed God's help and he needed it immediately.

With only a few minor differences, Psalm 70 is identical to Psalm 40:13-17. The one notable variation is that the name *God* (Elohim) is used (vv.1, 4) as opposed to *LORD* (Yahweh, Jehovah) in Psalm 40 (vv.13, 16). This is in accordance with the emphasis on God's power in *Book II* of *Psalms*: *Elohim*—the strong, powerful One—is the prominent name in Psalms 42–72.

We can safely conclude that this excerpt from the fortieth psalm is repeated here, with some small changes, for a specific purpose in the life and worship of Israel. Pastor and seminary professor Donald M. Williams offers an excellent comment about this:

> *What we learn from this...is that these prayers are "living word" in Israel's life. As they were used in worship they were modified under the inspiration of the Holy Spirit to fit their times and liturgical purposes. This also helps us to understand further modifications in New Testament quotations of the psalms that may come as paraphrases, citations from the Hebrew text, or from the Septuagint [a Greek translation of the Hebrew Scriptures completed about two centuries before Christ came].*[1]

Trying to live righteously in a increasingly corrupt world can be difficult even for mature believers. Whether we are facing fierce troubles, as David did, or everyday trials, such as...

- a strong temptation to sin
- an urge to gossip or speak unkindly
- the impulse to lose our temper
- the need for a quick decision
- having immoral or impure thoughts
- the threat of sudden danger
- a demonic attack or oppression

...we often find ourselves needing God's immediate help. When we confront these and other circumstances, we need to call on God at once. Psalm 70 teaches us how to pray in these times. This is, *When You Need God's Immediate Help,* 70:1-5.

1. Pray for God to save you quickly, to give you help without delay (vv.1-3).
2. Ask God to bless His people (v.4).
3. Confess your helplessness before God and ask for His immediate help (v.5).

1 (70:1-3) **Pray for God to save you quickly, to give you help without delay.**

David was under enemy attack and desperately needed God's protection from those who sought his life. Because he faced immediate peril, he urgently called out to the LORD to rescue him from his adversaries. And he needed the LORD to act quickly. If the LORD delayed at all, David feared it would be too late.

a. By shaming and confusing those who seek to harm you: That they be turned back (v.2).

David called upon God to confuse his enemies, thwart their plans, and drive them back in disgrace. *Shame* (boosh) and *confusion* (caphare) are frequently used together in the Old Testament. Both speak of humiliation, embarrassment, and dismay. *Disgrace* (kalam) is a third word with the same meaning. In fact, it is

---

[1] Donald Williams. *Psalms 1-72*, p.510.

185

usually translated in the Old Testament as ashamed or confused.

b. By executing judgment against them—perfect retribution: That they reap the horrible shame they seek to sow (v.3).

David asked God to bring perfect retribution on his adversaries. He prayed that they be rewarded with justice and reap exactly what they had sown: the horrible shame they meant for him.

Thought 1. When we need God's immediate help, we should pray urgently and briefly. David's request was short and simple: he needed God to help him quickly, and he told God exactly what he needed Him to do.

Our prayers do not have to be long and flowery, nor do they have to be formal. Every prayer does not have to begin with, "Our Heavenly Father" and end with, "Amen." As Jesus taught us, we should certainly set aside time for more lengthy conversations with God. We should regularly get away from everything else and devote ourselves to prayer. But urgent circumstances usually call for quick prayers. God already knows our need, even before we express it (Mt.6:32). He is always near, waiting for us to call upon Him for help.

> "So I say to you: Ask and it will be given to you; seek and you will find; knock and the door will be opened to you. For everyone who asks receives; he who seeks finds; and to him who knocks, the door will be opened (Lu.11:9-10).
>
> Be joyful in hope, patient in affliction, faithful in prayer (Ro.12:12).
>
> Is any one of you in trouble? He should pray. Is anyone happy? Let him sing songs of praise (Js.5:13).
>
> Let us then approach the throne of grace with confidence, so that we may receive mercy and find grace to help us in our time of need (He.4:16).

2 (70:4) **Ask God to bless His people.**

David prayed that God would bring good from the evil his enemies intended (Ge.50:20). If God would overthrow those who sought David's life, the righteous people of Israel would be blessed, and God would be magnified.

a. To fill all who seek Him with joy and gladness (v.4ª).

By rising up against God's anointed king, David's enemies also rose up against Israel's wellbeing. Therefore, David prayed that God would reward all who sincerely sought Him with an abundance of joy and gladness in contrast to their present disappointment and disgrace.

b. To stir all who love His salvation to praise and exalt Him (v.4ᵇ).

By God's answering His people's prayers and delivering David from his adversaries, the righteous would be stirred to praise and exalt the LORD. They would rejoice in His salvation and magnify the mighty name of *God* (Elohim), the strong, powerful One.

Thought 1. When enemies oppose us, we should pray that God would bring good from their evil. One way He can do this is through using our experience to be a blessing to others. When we are tested and tried, God helps us. As he helps us, He equips us to help others who are walking through a similar experience. As a result, others are filled with joy and God is exalted.

> Praise be to the God and Father of our Lord Jesus Christ, the Father of compassion and the God of all comfort, who comforts us in all our troubles, so that we can comfort those in any trouble with the comfort we ourselves have received from God. For just as the sufferings of Christ flow over into our lives, so also through Christ our comfort overflows. If we are distressed, it is for your comfort and salvation; if we are comforted, it is for your comfort, which produces in you patient endurance of the same sufferings we suffer (2 Co.1:3-6).
>
> Therefore encourage one another and build each other up, just as in fact you are doing (1 Th.5:11).
>
> You intended to harm me, but God intended it for good to accomplish what is now being done, the saving of many lives (Ge.50:20).
>
> May those who delight in my vindication shout for joy and gladness; may they always say, "The LORD be exalted, who delights in the well-being of his servant" (Ps.35:27).
>
> But may all who seek you rejoice and be glad in you; may those who love your salvation always say, "The LORD be exalted!" (Ps.40:16).

3 (70:5) **Confess your helplessness before God and ask for His immediate help.**

Only God could rescue David from his vicious enemies. Admitting that he was poor (afflicted) and needy, David confessed his total helplessness to the LORD. He was totally dependent on God to be his help and deliverer. For that reason, David concluded his prayer as he began it: by urgently asking God to rescue him from his very determined enemies. He again emphasized that time was of the essence, pleading with God to make haste and not tarry or delay. If God did not intervene quickly, it would be too late.

Thought 1. What an encouragement to know the LORD cares about us despite our being poor and needy! Recognizing our own helplessness is the first step toward receiving God's help. Scripture tells us that Paul learned to glory in his infirmities, because it was through his weakness that he came to truly know God's strength (2 Co.12:9-10).

Because God cares for us so deeply, we should never hesitate to bring our requests to Him, whether great or small. And we should never fear to confess our sins to Him, for He is merciful and compassionate. God is our helper and deliverer. When we find ourselves in trouble or in a pit of despair, we need to call on Him. He loves us and is always faithful to us. Knowing that, we can be certain He will help when we call upon His name.

> Cast all your anxiety on him because he cares for you (1 Pe.5:7).

> Do not be anxious about anything, but in everything, by prayer and petition, with thanksgiving, present your requests to God. And the peace of God, which transcends all understanding, will guard your hearts and your minds in Christ Jesus (Ph.4:6-7).

> Let us then approach the throne of grace with confidence, so that we may receive mercy and find grace to help us in our time of need (He.4:16).

> So we say with confidence, "The Lord is my helper; I will not be afraid. What can man do to me?" (He.13:6).

> Because the Sovereign LORD helps me, I will not be disgraced. Therefore have I set my face like flint, and I know I will not be put to shame. He who vindicates me is near. Who then will bring charges against me? Let us face each other! Who is my accuser? Let him confront me! It is the Sovereign LORD who helps me. Who is he that will condemn me? They will all wear out like a garment; the moths will eat them up (Is.50:7-9).

PSALM 71

When Facing the Challenges of Growing Older, 71:1-24

1. Trust in God & cry out to Him
   a. Ask that you never be put to shame, Ph.1:20; 1 Jn.2:28
   b. Ask that God deliver you
      1) By His righteousness—doing what is right in all things
      2) By listening to your prayer
      3) By being your rock of safety
      4) By giving the command to save you: Bc. you acknowledge Him as your rock & fortress
      5) By rescuing you from the wicked & from cruel oppressors

2. Reaffirm your confidence in God
   a. Bc. He has been your hope since conversion (the days of youth)
   b. Bc. you have been dependent on God from birth (whether or not you recognize it): It is He who created you & cared for you, Js.1:17
   c. Bc. your life has become an example for others, the fact that God is a strong refuge
   d. Bc. you are filled with praise for all He has done, declaring His honor & glory all day long

3. Pray that God not set you aside, not forsake you
   a. Bc. your strength declines & fails as you age
   b. Bc. your enemies continue to slander you
      1) They continue to plot against your life
      2) They continue to feel & claim that you are helpless, that God has forsaken you
      3) They need to be disproved
         • By God's coming quickly to help you
         • By God's executing judgment on them: Vindicat-

In you, O LORD, I have taken refuge; let me never be put to shame.
2 Rescue me and deliver me in your righteousness; turn your ear to me and save me.
3 Be my rock of refuge, to which I can always go; give the command to save me, for you are my rock and my fortress.
4 Deliver me, O my God, from the hand of the wicked, from the grasp of evil and cruel men.
5 For you have been my hope, O Sovereign LORD, my confidence since my youth.
6 From birth I have relied on you; you brought me forth from my mother's womb. I will ever praise you.
7 I have become like a portent to many, but you are my strong refuge.
8 My mouth is filled with your praise, declaring your splendor all day long.
9 Do not cast me away when I am old; do not forsake me when my strength is gone.
10 For my enemies speak against me; those who wait to kill me conspire together.
11 They say, "God has forsaken him; pursue him and seize him, for no one will rescue him."
12 Be not far from me, O God; come quickly, O my God, to help me.
13 May my accusers perish in shame; may those who

want to harm me be covered with scorn and disgrace.
14 But as for me, I will always have hope; I will praise you more and more.
15 My mouth will tell of your righteousness, of your salvation all day long, though I know not its measure.
16 I will come and proclaim your mighty acts, O Sovereign LORD; I will proclaim your righteousness, yours alone.
17 Since my youth, O God, you have taught me, and to this day I declare your marvelous deeds.
18 Even when I am old and gray, do not forsake me, O God, till I declare your power to the next generation, your might to all who are to come.
19 Your righteousness reaches to the skies, O God, you who have done great things. Who, O God, is like you?
20 Though you have made me see troubles, many and bitter, you will restore my life again; from the depths of the earth you will again bring me up.
21 You will increase my honor and comfort me once again.
22 I will praise you with the harp for your faithfulness, O my God; I will sing praise to you with the lyre, O Holy One of Israel.
23 My lips will shout for joy when I sing praise to you—I, whom you have redeemed.
24 My tongue will tell of your righteous acts all day long, for those who wanted to harm me have been put to shame and confusion.

ing you & bringing retribution—equal punishment—on them
   c. Bc. you will always place your hope in God & praise Him more & more

4. Be a strong witness for God
   a. Tell everyone about God's righteousness & saving power

      1) That He has performed mighty & miraculous acts throughout human history
      2) That He alone is righteous & perfectly just
   b. Share your personal testimony
      1) What God has taught you since your conversion
      2) What His deeds are
   c. Ask God not to forsake or take you until you bear witness to the next generation
      1) Proclaiming His power

      2) Proclaiming His righteousness that rules all throughout the universe
      3) Proclaiming the wonderful things He has done
      4) Proclaiming your own testimony of God's restoration
         • Thru the hardships of life
         • From the earth's depths: A picture of the resurrection, 16:9-11; 17:15; 49:15
         • By restoring you to a greater honor & comfort (a picture of heaven)

5. Praise God all day long
   a. Praise Him by playing instruments: Bc. He is faithful
   b. Praise Him by singing: Bc. He is the Holy One of Israel
   c. Praise Him by shouting for joy: Bc. He has redeemed you

   d. Praise His righteous acts: Bc. He has made you victorious over your enemies (a picture of both human & spiritual enemies, Ep.6:12-18)

PSALM 71

When Facing the Challenges of Growing Older, 71:1-24

(71:1-24) **Introduction:** every stage of life is taxing, but growing old holds challenges all of its own. For example, Solomon, the world's wisest and wealthiest man, wrote bluntly about the burdens of old age (see outline and notes—Ec.12:1-5 for more discussion). Physical deterioration, memory loss, loneliness, illness, loss of independ-ence, limited finances—these are just some of the challenges growing old can present.

Psalm 71 was written by an elderly man, a man in life's twilight years. Scripture does not identify him, but this seventy-first psalm closely resembles the psalms of David. In fact, the author incorporated portions of many of David's psalms into this prayer—Psalms 22, 31, 35, 38, 40, and 109 to list a few. Bible teacher John Phillips noted, "In this one psalm of two dozen verses we have some fifty quotations from or allusions to other psalms."[1]

Some scholars feel confident that Jeremiah composed Psalm 71. Solid arguments exist for this opinion. Jeremiah knew God's Word thoroughly and could have drawn upon it as the author did. Commentator J. Stewart Perowne pointed out that Jeremiah regularly borrowed from earlier poets in his writings.[2] The author's life circumstances are in perfect agreement with Jeremiah's. His statement about God's hand upon him *from my mother's womb* corresponds with what the LORD told Jeremiah when He called him to be a prophet (Je.1:5).

Whoever the author was, we know that he...

- was facing the challenges of old age (vv.9, 18)
- came to know God at an early age and had served Him all of his life (vv.5-6)
- had experienced God's faithfulness through many trials and difficulties (v.7)
- still dealt with adversaries (vv.4, 10, 13)
- still longed to do something great for God (vv.18)

The psalmist's prayer is one that uniquely appeals to those in their advanced years, but it also instructs people in all stages of life who are struggling with challenges. This is, *When Facing the Challenges of Growing Older*, 71:1-24.

1. Trust in God and cry out to Him (vv.1-4).
2. Reaffirm your confidence in God (vv.5-8).
3. Pray that God not set you aside, not forsake you (vv.9-14).
4. Be a strong witness for God (vv.15-21).
5. Praise God all day long (vv.22-24).

1 (71:1-4) **Trust in God and cry out to Him.**

The psalmist declares his trust in God and cries out for deliverance from his enemies. His lifelong experience with God gave him the confidence to call on Him without reservation. He fully expected God to set him free from his adversaries' grasp.

Note that these verses closely correspond to Psalm 31:1-3. The psalmist took this portion of David's prayer and claimed it as his own, showing us the importance of knowing God's Word and making it apply personally to our circumstances.

a. **Ask that you never be put to shame, Ph.1:20; 1 Jn.2:28 (v.1).**

The aging psalmist asked the LORD to protect him from being put to confusion or shame. Specifically, he was speaking of the shame of being defeated by his enemies. Such disgrace would bring reproach on

God's testimony because he had placed his complete trust in the LORD. He wanted his life to be an enduring example of his faithfulness to God and God's faithfulness to him.

b. **Ask that God deliver you (vv.2-4).**

The psalmist prayed that God would deliver him from any failures that would cause him to be humiliated. *Rescue* (natsal) literally means "to snatch away."[3] It describes "the power of one entity overcoming the power of another."[4] The psalmist's enemies were strong, but He believed unwaveringly that God was stronger, that He could rescue him from his adversaries' powerful grasp.

In seeking God's deliverance, the psalmist appealed to His righteousness (v.2a). Righteousness is one of God's attributes, one of the unique qualities that make Him God. God always does what is right, and He always keeps His word. When He enters into a covenant, He never fails to do all that He promised. Because the psalmist was in a covenant relationship with God, he boldly called on Him to listen to his prayer and save him, to set him free from his enemies' clutches (v.2b).

The psalmist also asked God to be his rock of refuge (v.3a). *Rock* (tsur) is a Hebrew noun that in this context, refers to a rocky cliff or recess in a mountain like the one in which God placed Moses when His glory passed by (Ex.33:22).[5] God was the psalmist's rock and fortress. Accordingly, the psalmist asked God to command that he be saved (v.3b). Armed with his confidence in God, the psalmist boldly called on Him for rescue from the grasp of his oppressors, men who were wicked, unrighteous, and cruel (v.4).

Thought 1. No matter how old we get, we will never outlive our adversaries. That is, we will always have to deal with spiritual enemies:

➤ Satan and his demonic army, who seek to devour us (Lu.22:31; 1 Pe.5:8; Ep.6:11-12)
➤ A world system that is under Satan's authority (Ep.2:2; Jn.12:31)
➤ Our sinful nature, the flesh (Ga.5:16-17)

Giving in to temptation brings shame on us, our families, our churches, and the cause of Christ. As Jesus warned Peter, Satan desires us, wanting to sift through our lives and destroy everything that is good (Lu.22:31). Like the psalmist, we need to cry out to God daily to protect us from the disgrace of falling into the clutches of our spiritual enemies. Paul prayed

---

1 John Phillips. *Exploring Psalms, Volume 1.* WORD*search* CROSS e-book.
2 J.J. Stewart Perowne, *The Book of Psalms*, p.309.

3 James Strong. *Strong's Exhaustive Concordance.*
4 Spiros Zodhiates. *AMG Complete Word Study Dictionary.* WORD*search* CROSS e-book.
5 William E. Vine. *Vine's Expository Dictionary of Old Testament and New Testament Words.* Nashville, TN: Thomas Nelson, 1940. WORD*search* CROSS e-book.

that God would help him live in such a way that he would never be ashamed (Ph.1:20). John exhorted us to abide in Christ so we can stand before Him in confidence and not be ashamed (1 Jn.2:28).

We always need to be conscious of the fact that we cannot overcome temptation, pressures, and the weaknesses of our corrupt nature in our own strength. We need the power of God's Spirit, who leads us to victory. Every day we must take refuge in the Lord, calling on Him to protect and deliver us.

> **And lead us not into temptation, but deliver us from the evil one' (Mt.6:13).**
>
> **No temptation has seized you except what is common to man. And God is faithful; he will not let you be tempted beyond what you can bear. But when you are tempted, he will also provide a way out so that you can stand up under it. (1 Co.10:13).**
>
> **Who gave himself for our sins to rescue us from the present evil age, according to the will of our God and Father (Ga.1:4).**
>
> **If this is so, then the Lord knows how to rescue godly men from trials and to hold the unrigh-teous for the day of judgment, while continuing their punishment (2 Pe.2:9).**
>
> **Guard my life and rescue me; let me not be put to shame, for I take refuge in you (Ps.25:20).**

2 (71:5-8) Reaffirm your confidence in God.

As he faced ongoing battles in his latter years, the psalmist looked back on his lifelong experience with God. God had done a number of miraculous things for him through the years. Remembering God's power and faithfulness reaffirmed his confidence in God for his present and future struggles.

a. Because He has been your hope since conversion (the days of youth) (v.5).

The psalmist tenderly reminisced on his decades-long walk with *GOD* (Yahovih, a form of Yahweh or Jehovah). He had personally placed his hope and trust in the LORD since his conversion during his youth. Throughout the Old Testament, *youth* is broadly used of the various stages of development, from early childhood to young adulthood. Its context here indicates that the psalmist was speaking of his childhood; he believed in the LORD at a very young age (2 Ti.3:15).

b. Because you have been dependent on God from birth (whether or not you recognize it): It is He who created you and cared for you, Js.1:17 (v.6).

The psalmist could not remember a time in his life when he did not trust in God. From his perspective, he had been dependent on God since his birth. Even before he was old enough to recognize it, he had relied on God's protection. From the moment he was conceived in his mother's womb, his Creator had cared for him. Now, as he neared the end of his lifetime, still trusting in the LORD, the grateful psalmist vowed to continue to praise Him.

c. Because your life has become an example for others, the fact that God is a strong refuge (v.7).

Because of God's faithfulness throughout the psalmist's many afflictions, his life had become a positive example for others. God had been his strong refuge. He referred to himself as a *portent* (mopheth). This Hebrew word has both positive and negative meanings. In a positive sense, it refers to wonders or miracles that display God's phenomenal power. Negatively, it speaks of supernatural signs of God's judgment. The psalmist had suffered many trials throughout his life (v.20). Exactly what he meant by *portent*, however, is unclear. Either "his entire life was a wonder, a testimony to others of the goodness and faithfulness of the Lord,"[6] or he was known as "a sign of trouble, chastisement, and divine retribution."[7] Other statements in Psalm 71 point to the latter as the better understanding of this term (v.11). In either case, one thing is clear: throughout his many challenges, the psalmist had taken refuge in the LORD and God had proved Himself strong on the psalmist's behalf.

d. Because you are filled with praise for all He has done, declaring His honor and glory all day long (v.8).

A lifetime of God's faithfulness filled this older man's mouth with praise to God for all He had done for him. All day long, he declared God's honor and glory.

Thought 1. At its best, life is uncertain (Pr.27:1; Js.4:14). But we can be sure of two things: first, we *will* suffer trials and difficulties in this life. And for reasons known only to God, some of us may suffer a great deal of afflictions. Like Job, Jeremiah, Paul, and this psalmist, our trials may be so many and so severe that people assume God has either forsaken or is judging us. Yet regardless of the frequency or fierceness of our trials, God never forsakes or gives up on us.

Second, we can be certain that God will see us through all trials, no matter how many nor how severe they may be. This psalmist's life had been

---

6 Warren W. Wiersbe. *The Bible Exposition Commentary.* WORD*search* CROSS e-book.

7 Frank E. Gaebelein, ed. *The Expositor's Bible Commentary*, p.465.

marked by the intense troubles he had encountered. Still, God had been his refuge through all of them. Just as God promises, He had made His dear follower victorious, carrying him through every dark valley and putting a song of praise in his mouth. Now, as he faced a new struggle, the psalmist reaffirmed his confidence in God, praising God for His faithfulness to him throughout his life.

For every challenge we encounter, we need to remember that God is able and God is faithful. We can take refuge in Him, trusting in His mighty power to deliver us. And we can do so without fear, knowing that God will not forsake us or let us down. The very fact that we are alive to face today's challenges testifies to God's faithfulness in our lives. If we will recall His help in times past, rest in His promises, and claim His Word, we can face our fears, our foes, and our afflictions with full confidence in Him!

> **May the God of hope fill you with all joy and peace as you trust in him, so that you may overflow with hope by the power of the Holy Spirit (Ro.15:13).**

> **We do not want you to be uninformed, brothers, about the hardships we suffered in the province of Asia. We were under great pressure, far beyond our ability to endure, so that we despaired even of life. Indeed, in our hearts we felt the sentence of death. But this happened that we might not rely on ourselves but on God, who raises the dead. He has delivered us from such a deadly peril, and he will deliver us. On him we have set our hope that he will continue to deliver us (2 Co.1:8-10).**

> **We are hard pressed on every side, but not crushed; perplexed, but not in despair; persecuted, but not abandoned; struck down, but not destroyed. We always carry around in our body the death of Jesus, so that the life of Jesus may also be revealed in our body. For we who are alive are always being given over to death for Jesus' sake, so that his life may be revealed in our mortal body. So then, death is at work in us, but life is at work in you. It is written: "I believed; therefore I have spoken." With that same spirit of faith we also believe and therefore speak, because we know that the one who raised the Lord Jesus from the dead will also raise us with Jesus and present us with you in his presence (2 Co.4:8-14).**

> **Though he slay me, yet will I hope in him; I will surely defend my ways to his face (Jb.13:15).**

> **Blessed is he whose help is the God of Jacob, whose hope is in the LORD his God (Ps.146:5).**

> **"But blessed is the man who trusts in the LORD, whose confidence is in him (Je.17:7).**

3 (71:9-14) **Pray that God not set you aside, not forsake you.**
As age increasingly robbed the psalmist of his physical strength, he pleaded with God to stand by him in these years. God had been with him throughout his troubled life, and he prayed that the LORD would not cast him off, not set him aside or forsake him when he needed Him most.

a. Because your strength declines and fails as you age (v.9).
Old age was now settling into the psalmist's once-vigorous body (Ec.12:3-5). Physically speaking, his strength was failing. He could no longer fight as he had once fought. His tired bones could no longer endure the blows they had always been able to absorb.

b. Because your enemies continue to slander you (vv.10-13).
While the psalmist's stamina was dwindling, his adversaries' determination remained strong. They continued to assault him with their full strength, slandering him and plotting against his life (v.10). Because of his age, they believed he was more vulnerable than ever. His physical problems prompted them to conclude God had forsaken him. As a result, they felt now was the time to strike, that he was utterly helpless (v.11).

Age may have been weakening his body, but the psalmist's spirit was as strong as ever. Unable to accept his enemies' gloating over him, he was determined to disprove their claims. With great fervor, he prayed for God to come quickly, to rush to his side to help him without delay (v.12). He asked God to execute judgment on his foes and, in doing so, to vindicate him (v.13). He also called on God to inflict them with the same punishment they were seeking for him, that they be covered with scorn and disgrace.

c. Because you will always place your hope in God and praise Him more and more (v.14).
The psalmist declared that his enemies' threats would not sway his confidence in God. He vowed to continue to place his hope in God and to respond to his adversaries' assaults by praising God more and more.

Thought 1. We need not fear that God will abandon us, for He has promised to never leave us or forsake us (He.13:5-6). He lives within believers through His Holy Spirit. The Holy Spirit will stay with us until our bodies are redeemed and we are fully transformed into the glorious image of Jesus Christ (Ep.1:13-14). We may grieve the Spirit or quench the Spirit, but He will never leave us. As long as we live, God's Holy Spirit will be with us. We are never alone.

Grievous trials may cause us to feel that God has forsaken us. Delayed answers to prayers may make us think that He does not care. But we should not rely on our feelings. Instead, we need to believe what God has promised in His Word: *He will never leave us.* When fighting temptation, we are not alone. When facing life's most painful moments, such as the death of a spouse, parent, or other loved one, we are not alone. Our health may leave us, our strength may leave us, our memory or mental capacities may leave us, other people may leave us, but the Lord will not. When we need Him most, He will be there.

> **God, who has called you into fellowship with his Son Jesus Christ our Lord, is faithful (1 Co.1:9).**
>
> **Keep your lives free from the love of money and be content with what you have, because God has said, "Never will I leave you; never will I forsake you." So we say with confidence, "The Lord is my helper; I will not be afraid. What can man do to me?" (He.13:5-6).**
>
> **If anyone acknowledges that Jesus is the Son of God, God lives in him and he in God (1 Jn.4:15).**
>
> **Be strong and courageous. Do not be afraid or terrified because of them, for the LORD your God goes with you; he will never leave you nor forsake you" (De.31:6).**
>
> **Even to your old age and gray hairs I am he, I am he who will sustain you. I have made you and I will carry you; I will sustain you and I will rescue you (Is.46:4).**

4 (71:15-21) **Be a strong witness for God.** Throughout his long life, the psalmist had been the recipient of God's faithfulness and power. And although the psalmist had crossed through fire and flood, the LORD had done many wondrous works on his behalf. His fervent desire was to live many more years so he might be a strong witness for God to those who were coming behind him.

a. Tell everyone about God's righteousness and saving power (vv.15-16).
The psalmist could not number the times God had vindicated and delivered him. He committed to spend the rest of his days telling everyone he could about God's righteousness and saving power (v.15). Salvation, here, does not refer to God's redemption but to

His help and deliverance in the daily struggles of life. God had been faithful to His promises and done what was right in each of the psalmist's trials.

Throughout history, God has performed mighty and miraculous acts, just as He did in the psalmist's life. The use of *mighty acts* (geburah) may refer either to God's mighty deeds or to His strength. For this reason, Bible versions vary in the translation of this statement. When the word is in the plural form, as it is here, it usually means mighty deeds.[8] The psalmist pledged to bear witness to God's power along with the great truth that the LORD alone is righteous and perfectly just (v.16).

b. Share your personal testimony (v.17).
The psalmist proceeded to share his personal testimony of God's power in his life. The LORD had taught him of His awesome deeds and faithfulness to His people from the time of his conversion as a youth. As a child, he learned of Israel's glorious history, and as he proceeded through life, he experienced God's wondrous works for himself.

c. Ask God not to forsake or take you until you bear witness to the next generation (vv.18-21).
Aflame with passion for God, the psalmist was convinced that, even though he was growing old, his work was not yet done. Therefore, he prayed that God would not forsake him or take him in death until he had borne witness to the next generation (v.18). He longed to proclaim God's...
* *power* and *might* (v.18)
* *righteousness* that rules all throughout the universe (v.19ᵃ)
* wonderful works—the *great things* He had done (v.19ᵇ)

In addition, the psalmist longed to proclaim his own testimony of God's restoration (vv.20-21). God had allowed him to suffer many severe hardships in his life. The Hebrew text is very definite here: his troubles were great, abundant, and sore. In every case, God had powerfully sustained him. With all that he had experienced, the mere fact that he was alive was a testimony to God's mighty power. God's past faithfulness enabled him to confidently declare that God would quicken him again and keep him alive through his present struggles (v.20). Note that he specifically said "from the depths of the earth" God would "again bring him up." In this statement, the psalmist not only spoke of his present life-threatening situation but also of the future resurrection of the righteous dead (17:15; 49:15). Prophetically, he spoke of the resurrection of Jesus Christ (16:9-11).

---

8 Thoraf Gilbrant and Gregory A. Lint, eds. *The Complete Biblical Library: The Old Testament Hebrew-English Dictionary.* (Springfield, MO: World Library Press Inc, 1998). WORD*search* CROSS e-book.

By delivering the psalmist from his trouble, God would restore him to a level of greatness he had never before known (v.21). God would surround him with comfort—a picture of the eternal rest we will enjoy in heaven throughout eternity. All of these things stirred the psalmist to exclaim, "Who, O God, is like you?" (v.19).

Thought 1. Experienced saints have much to share about the faithfulness of God. As we tell others who are going through severe trials—our children, grandchildren, anybody who will listen—what God has done for us, they will be encouraged to place their trust in the Lord.

When the Israelites crossed over Jordan into the promised land, God commanded them to take twelve stones out of the river bed, one for each tribe of Israel, and to build a memorial to the miracle God performed there. Why? So their children would ask the meaning of the stones, and the parents would have the opportunity to witness regarding God's faithfulness and wonder-working power (Josh.4:1-9).

For the same reason, God would have us keep a record of His faithfulness and testify to His mighty acts in our lives. Scripture commands us to encourage those who are going through the same trials we have gone through (2 Co.1:4). Those coming behind us will also walk through fiery trials, just as we have. By telling them what God has done for us, they will be strengthened to walk victoriously through their difficulties. We have a sacred duty to speak to them about the grace, faithfulness, and unlimited power of God.

An old man going a lone highway,
Came, at the evening cold and gray,
To a chasm vast and deep and wide.
Through which was flowing a sullen tide
The old man crossed in the twilight dim,
The sullen stream had no fear for him;
But he turned when safe on the other side
And built a bridge to span the tide.

"Old man," said a fellow pilgrim near,
"You are wasting your strength with building here;
Your journey will end with the ending day,
You never again will pass this way;
You've crossed the chasm, deep and wide,
Why build this bridge at evening tide?"

The builder lifted his old gray head;
"Good friend, in the path I have come," he said,
"There followed after me to-day
A youth whose feet must pass this way.
This chasm that has been as naught to me
To that fair-haired youth may a pitfall be;
He, too, must cross in the twilight dim;
Good friend, I am building this bridge for him!"[9]

---

[9] Will Allen Dromgoole. *The Bridge Builder*, 1931.

We can leave no greater gift to our children, grandchildren, and others who will follow us than a legacy of faith in God. As we bear witness to God's faithfulness, we are building a bridge over which they can cross the dark valleys of their lives. Every account, every story of God's grace, shores up the bridge of faith that will span life's fiercest trials. God has a work for each of us in our twilight years: He wants us to prepare the way for those coming behind us by passing along our story of His faithfulness and mighty power.

> **So the man went away and began to tell in the Decapolis how much Jesus had done for him. And all the people were amazed (Mk.5:20).**
> **Many of the Samaritans from that town believed in him because of the woman's testimony, "He told me everything I ever did" (Jn.4:39).**
> **For we cannot help speaking about what we have seen and heard" (Ac.4:20).**
> **They will proclaim his righteousness to a people yet unborn—for he has done it (Ps.22:31).**
> **We will not hide them from their children; we will tell the next generation the praiseworthy deeds of the LORD, his power, and the wonders he has done (Ps.78:4).**
> **Then those who feared the LORD talked with each other, and the LORD listened and heard. A scroll of remembrance was written in his presence concerning those who feared the LORD and honored his name (Mal.3:16).**

5 (71:22-24) **Praise God all day long.**
In gratitude for God's lifelong goodness to him, the psalmist declared that he would praise God continually—all the day long (v.24). He would use all of his talents, vocal and instrumental, to exalt the LORD. With the *harp*—lute, a bottle-shaped harp—he would extol God's *faithfulness* (emeth) (v.22ᵃ). He would sing praises to the Holy One of Israel while playing his lyre (v.22ᵇ).

Not only had God *redeemed* the psalmist's sinful soul, but on many occasions He had also delivered him from death. Thus, he pledged to celebrate God's redemption by greatly rejoicing or loudly shouting for joy (v.23). God, in his righteousness, had repeatedly made the psalmist triumphant over his enemies. Consequently, the psalmist vowed to spend the rest of his life sharing his testimony regarding God's righteous acts (v.24).

Thought 1. Far too often we are so focused on our struggles that we forget God's goodness. Although the psalmist faced seemingly endless problems, he continually praised God.

The aging psalmist had lived a hard life and had endured an unusual number of severe trials (vv.7, 11). But in his latter years, he did not complain about all he had gone through or all the burdens he had been forced to bear. Instead, he proclaimed that God...

- had been faithful to him (v.22)
- had redeemed him (v.23)
- had displayed His righteousness by making him victorious over his enemies (v.24)

We should follow the psalmist's example. Our mouths should be continually filled with praises to God. He is always faithful to us. He has redeemed us. He has helped us triumph over our enemies. He has equipped us with His armor and His Word so we can stand against all who oppose us—both human and spiritual foes—in His strength (Ep.6:12-18). Every day of our lives, we should praise God for all He has done for us!

And again, "Praise the Lord, all you Gentiles, and sing praises to him, all you peoples" (Ro.15:11).

Through Jesus, therefore, let us continually offer to God a sacrifice of praise—the fruit of lips that confess his name (He.13:15).

But you are a chosen people, a royal priesthood, a holy nation, a people belonging to God, that you may declare the praises of him who called you out of darkness into his wonderful light (1 Pe.2:9).

The LORD is my strength and my shield; my heart trusts in him, and I am helped. My heart leaps for joy and I will give thanks to him in song (Ps.28:7).

I will extol the LORD at all times; his praise will always be on my lips (Ps.34:1).

I delight greatly in the LORD; my soul rejoices in my God. For he has clothed me with garments of salvation and arrayed me in a robe of righteousness, as a bridegroom adorns his head like a priest, and as a bride adorns herself with her jewels (Is.61:10).

PSALM 72

The Benefits That Flow from God's Ruler: A Picture of the Coming Messiah (2 S.7:10-17), 72:1-20

Of Solomon.

1. A just & righteous ruler
a. He will be given divine justice & righteousness bc. people pray
b. He will judge people righteously—fairly & impartially, Is.9:6-7; 11:4-5
c. He will bring peace & prosperity—a full & fruitful life—to the people, Je.23:5-6

d. He will protect & provide security for the people
1) He will rescue the needy
2) He will crush the people's oppressors
3) He will stir fear down through the generations

e. He will refresh the nation

1) The righteous will flourish
2) The nations will prosper

2. A universal ruler, Ps.2:8; Lu.1:33
a. He will rule over the earth, its seas, rivers, & land, Zec. 9:9-10
b. He will be acknowledged as the sovereign ruler over all
1) All rulers, including his enemies, will submit & pay tribute to him

Endow the king with your justice, O God, the royal son with your righteousness.
2 He will judge your people in righteousness, your afflicted ones with justice.
3 The mountains will bring prosperity to the people, the hills the fruit of righteousness.
4 He will defend the afflicted among the people and save the children of the needy; he will crush the oppressor.
5 He will endure as long as the sun, as long as the moon, through all generations.
6 He will be like rain falling on a mown field, like showers watering the earth.
7 In his days the righteous will flourish; prosperity will abound till the moon is no more.
8 He will rule from sea to sea and from the River to the ends of the earth.
9 The desert tribes will bow before him and his enemies will lick the dust.
10 The kings of Tarshish and of distant shores will bring tribute to him; the kings of Sheba and Seba will present him gifts.
11 All kings will bow down to him and all nations will serve him.
12 For he will deliver the needy who cry out, the afflicted who have no one to help.
13 He will take pity on the weak and the needy and save the needy from death.
14 He will rescue them from oppression and violence, for precious is their blood in his sight.
15 Long may he live! May gold from Sheba be given him. May people ever pray for him and bless him all day long.
16 Let grain abound throughout the land; on the tops of the hills may it sway. Let its fruit flourish like Lebanon; let it thrive like the grass of the field.
17 May his name endure forever; may it continue as long as the sun. All nations will be blessed through him, and they will call him blessed.
18 Praise be to the LORD God, the God of Israel, who alone does marvelous deeds.
19 Praise be to his glorious name forever; may the whole earth be filled with his glory. Amen and Amen.
20 This concludes the prayers of David son of Jesse.

2) All rulers will bow before him & serve him, Ph.2:6-11

3. A compassionate ruler, Ps.78:70-72
a. He will deliver all who cry out to him: The needy, poor, oppressed, & helpless
b. He will have pity & save them from death: He will take away the suffering & pain of death, 1 Co.15:52-57
c. He will rescue (save) them from their adversaries: Bc. their lives are precious to him

4. A beloved & prosperous ruler
a. His rule is honored & cherished
1) That he live a long time
2) That homage, tribute, prayer, & praise be given him
b. His land (the entire earth) will flourish: A picture of the new heavens & earth, 2 Pe.3:10-13; see Is. chs.35; 60-62; Je. chs.40-48

c. His name (character & influence) will endure forever
1) All nations will be blessed through Him
2) All nations will praise Him

d. His person & rule should stir you to praise the LORD God, the God of Israel
1) Bc. of His wonderful works
2) Bc. of His glorious name
3) Bc. the whole earth is to be filled with His glory
4) Bc. of King David's example (seen in these prayers & Psalms)

PSALM 72

The Benefits That Flow from God's Ruler: A Picture of the Coming Messiah (2 S.7:10-17), 72:1-20

(72:1-20) **Introduction:** a notable event in the life of any nation is the peaceful transfer of power from one leader to another. In nations where citizens elect their leaders, an inauguration ceremony and celebration are usually held. Where power is held by a king or queen, a coronation ceremony is customary.

Psalm 72 marks the transfer of power in Israel from King David to his son Solomon (1 K.1–2). The heading in the NIV states it is a psalm *of*, or about, Solomon. However, it may also be translated as *for* Solomon, as it is in David's psalms. Therefore, the identity of the author is unclear. Three possibilities exist:

➤ Solomon wrote it about himself.

➤ David wrote it about Solomon.

➤ Another person wrote it about Solomon.

The content of the psalm, though, is clear: it is the written record of David's prayer for Solomon as Solomon took over Israel's throne (v.20). Regardless of who actually put the words on paper, it is unquestionably David's prayer for his son.

In interceding for his son the king, however, David spoke prophetically of another king. Solomon would fulfill this psalm in many ways, but he would also fail to fulfill it in many ways. In fact, "none of Israel's kings could come near the praise and expectations offered here."[1] Only Jesus—the one greater than Solomon—fulfills it perfectly (Mt.12:42). While the New Testament never quotes Psalm 72 when speaking about Jesus, there is no question that it points to Him. Excellent commentator Derek Kidner wrote that it is "so close to the prophecies of Isaiah 11:1-5 and Isaiah 60–62 that if those passages are Messianic, so is this."[2]

Psalm 72 closes *Book II* of *Psalms* (Ps.42–72). It also concludes the prominence of David's psalms in the Hebrew hymnbook (v.20). While *Books III, IV,* and *V* (Ps.72–150) contain some of David's psalms, the great majority were written by other individuals. Of Psalms 1–72, most were written by David.

This seventy-second psalm is David's last prayer (v.20). How fitting that Israel's first *great* king bows off the stage of Israel, and Scripture, by speaking of Israel's last and *greatest* King, Jesus Christ! Clearly, David's final thoughts were of the one who would ultimately fulfill God's covenant with him (2 S.7:8-16; Lu.1:31-33; Ac.2:29-30). As you study Psalm 72, it is crucial that you see not only Solomon, the historic king *for* whom it was written, but also Jesus, the future and eternal King *about* whom it was written. This is, *The Benefits That Flow from God's Ruler: A Picture of the Coming Messiah (2 S.7:10-17),* 72:1-20.

1. A just and righteous ruler (vv.1-7).
2. A universal ruler, Ps.2:8; Lu.1:33 (vv.8-11).
3. A compassionate ruler, Ps.78:70-72 (vv.12-14).
4. A beloved and prosperous ruler (vv.15-20).

1 (72:1-7) A just and righteous ruler.

Israel's dying King David began his prayer for his son by asking God to make him a just and righteous ruler. David obviously loved Solomon, and he dearly loved the people of his nation. If Solomon would govern according to God's laws, the LORD would abundantly bless both him and the God-fearing people of Israel.

a. He will be given divine justice and righteousness because people pray (v.1).

One of the king's most important duties was to judge disputes and then administer justice appropriately. Therefore, David prayed that God would grant Solomon His divine justice, His judgments and righteousness. *Justice* (mishpat) sometimes refers to God's laws, commandments, and ordinances (De.12:1, Ps.119:7, 102, 106). More often, it describes legal cases and the judgments rendered in those cases. David prayed that God would give Solomon His wisdom so he might render rulings according to God's laws and His righteousness. Shortly after taking the throne, Solomon made this same request of the LORD. Above everything else, he asked God for understanding so he could make righteous judgments (1 K.3:9).

b. He will judge people righteously—fairly and impartially, Is.9:6-7, 11:4-5 (v.2).

If God would grant the king His divine wisdom, Solomon would judge the people righteously—fairly and impartially. Notice that David referred to the people as *God's* people—not his or Solomon's. The people of Israel belonged to God, and David prayed that God would grant the king the wisdom necessary to do what was right for *His* people. The poor were those who were afflicted and oppressed. Most of the poor in Israel were not that way because they were lazy or would not work; they were poor because they were somehow afflicted and unable to work. As a result, they were powerless to defend themselves and were often taken advantage of by greedy, wicked people. God, the champion of the poor, delegated their defense to the king (Pr.22:23).

c. He will bring peace and prosperity—a full and fruitful life—to the people, Je.23:5-6 (v.3).

David prayed that peace and prosperity would flow throughout the land under Solomon's leadership, from the mountains to the little hills. *Prosperity* and *peace* are translations of the familiar Hebrew word *shalom.* It is difficult to express the full meaning of *shalom* in one word. Note the following definitions:

➢ *Shalom* is living "happy, untroubled, and with a sense of fulfillment. It would include contentment, prosperity, freedom from oppression by others and a sense of completion....One common meaning is the 'absence of conflict and strife.'...A related, common idea of peace is the absence of fear of the threat of harm and thus a 'sense of security.'...*Shalom* is used of harmony with God in which all a person's needs are met and the person experiences wholeness."[3]

➢ "*Shalom* and its related words...are among the most important theological words in the Old Testament....The true concept of *shalom* [is] completeness, wholeness, harmony, fulfillment... unimpaired relationships with others and fulfillment in one's undertakings."[4]

The name *Solomon* is a derivative of *shalom* and means man of peace. The LORD Himself gave Solomon this name in a special message to David:

> **But you will have a son who will be a man of peace and rest, and I will give him rest from all his enemies on every side. His name will be Solomon, and I will grant Israel peace and quiet during his reign (1 Chr.22:9).**

---

1 Donald Williams. *Psalms 1-72*, p.520.
2 Derek Kidner. *Psalms 1-72*, p.273.

3 Thoraf Gilbrant and Gregory A. Lint, eds. *The Complete Biblical Library: The Old Testament Hebrew-English Dictionary.* WORD*search* CROSS e-book.
4 R. Laird Harris, ed. *Theological Wordbook of the Old Testament.* WORD*search* CROSS e-book.

As Scripture records, what God promised to David fully came to pass:

> During Solomon's lifetime Judah and Israel, from Dan to Beersheba, lived in safety, each man under his own vine and fig tree (1 K.4:25).

d. He will protect and provide security for the people (vv.4-5).

David prayed that Solomon would fulfill his God-given duty to protect and provide security for the people. Specifically, David prayed that his son would rescue the needy, the poor or afflicted and their children, from those who took advantage of them. Because abuse of the needy is such a vile sin, David prayed that Solomon would crush all who cruelly oppressed them (v.4). Dealing swiftly and severely with oppressors would strike the fear of God in those who might mistreat the needy in the future. In addition, it would set a standard for dealing with abusers that would endure throughout future generations in Israel (v.5).

e. He will refresh the nation (vv.6-7).

If Solomon would righteously judge the people and protect them from evildoers, his leadership over Israel would refresh the nation like a summer rain (v.6; 2 S.23:4). If he led according to God's laws, the righteous people of the nation would flourish under his administration. There would be an abundance of *prosperity* (shalom)—wholeness, harmony, fulfillment, peace, freedom—throughout the land. Long after he was gone, as long as the moon endures, the nation would continue to prosper as a result of his godly leadership.

Thought 1. What David requested for Solomon will be true of Christ: David prayed for his son to govern Israel the way God's Son will one day rule the world. When Jesus returns to earth and sits on David's throne, He will govern the entire earth in absolute justice and righteousness. He who is perfect will judge perfectly, and He who is righteous through and through will enforce righteousness to the four corners of the earth (Is.9:6-7; 11:4-5).

Because of Christ's untainted leadership, peace and prosperity will flow throughout the earth. The people of Christ's kingdom will enjoy lives that are full, productive, and free of fear and oppression (Is.14:3, 7; 32:17; Mi.4:4). And, for the first time in history, Israel will exist in unthreatened safety (Je.23:5-6). The reign of Christ will be like a refreshing rain on a world parched by thousands of years of satanic influence and man's corrupt nature. Truly, showers of blessings will fall upon the earth (Eze.34:26).

> But about the Son he says, "Your throne, O God, will last for ever and ever, and righteousness will be the scepter of your kingdom. You have loved righteousness and hated wickedness; therefore God, your God, has set you above your companions by anointing you with the oil of joy" (He.1:8-9).

> I saw heaven standing open and there before me was a white horse, whose rider is called Faithful and True. With justice he judges and makes war (Re.19:11).

> For to us a child is born, to us a son is given, and the government will be on his shoulders. And he will be called Wonderful Counselor, Mighty God, Everlasting Father, Prince of Peace. Of the increase of his government and peace there will be no end. He will reign on David's throne and over his kingdom, establishing and upholding it with justice and righteousness from that time on and forever. The zeal of the LORD Almighty will accomplish this (Is.9:6-7).

> But with righteousness he will judge the needy, with justice he will give decisions for the poor of the earth. He will strike the earth with the rod of his mouth; with the breath of his lips he will slay the wicked. Righteousness will be his belt and faithfulness the sash around his waist (Is.11:4-5).

> Justice will dwell in the desert and righteousness live in the fertile field. The fruit of righteousness will be peace; the effect of righteousness will be quietness and confidence forever (Is. 32:16-17).

> "The days are coming," declares the LORD, "when I will raise up to David a righteous Branch, a King who will reign wisely and do what is just and right in the land. In his days Judah will be saved and Israel will live in safety. This is the name by which he will be called: The LORD Our Righteousness (Je.23:5-6).

> "'In those days and at that time I will make a righteous Branch sprout from David's line; he will do what is just and right in the land (Je.33:15).

2 (72:8-11) **A universal ruler,** Ps.2:8; Lu.1:33.

Along with making Solomon a just and righteous king, David prayed that God would expand his influence. He asked the LORD to make him a universal ruler, one whom all kings would submit to and all nations would serve.

a. **He will rule over the earth, its seas, rivers, and land, Zec.9:9-10 (v.8).**

David asked God to give Solomon dominion or authority over all the earth. "He will rule" can also be translated *may he rule*. From sea to sea means from the Red Sea to the Mediterranean Sea (Ex.23:31). The river referred to is the Euphrates. In mentioning this river, David prayed that God would fulfill His promise to Abraham through Solomon's reign (Ge.15:18).

b. **He will be acknowledged as the sovereign ruler over all (vv.9-11).**

David also prayed that Solomon would be recognized as the world's leader, the sovereign ruler over all the earth. He asked God to cause all rulers, including his enemies, to submit and pay tribute to him (vv.9-10). The places referred to in these verses "...speak of all lands, the Euphrates being the farthest point the writer could think of to the east, Tarshish the farthest city to the west, and Sheba and Seba the farthest kingdoms to the south. In fact, so extensive is this kingdom that, according to the psalmist, even 'the desert tribes [they that dwell in the wilderness] will bow before him and his enemies will lick the dust.'"[5] Along with this, David prayed that all rulers would bow before him, a gesture of submission to his leadership, and serve him (v.11).

Thought 1. As David prayed for his son, he prophesied of God's Son, Jesus Christ. Solomon established an extensive kingdom, earning the respect of many nations and their leaders. As Scripture records, Solomon reigned over his region of the earth and many rulers paid tribute to him (1 K.4:21; 2 Chr.9:23-26). Even so, he did not rule to the ends of the earth, that is, over the entire earth (v.8). He was not the King of all kings (v.11). Only David's Greater Son, Jesus Christ, will fully answer David's prayer. He will reign forever over all the earth (Zec.9:9-10; Ps.2:8; Lu.1:33; Re.11:15). Every knee will bow to Him, including the most powerful leaders of the earth. And every tongue will confess that He is Lord (Ph.2:6-11).

> **That at the name of Jesus every knee should bow, in heaven and on earth and under the earth, and every tongue confess that Jesus Christ is Lord, to the glory of God the Father (Ph.2:10-11)**
>
> **Which God will bring about in his own time—God, the blessed and only Ruler, the King of kings and Lord of lords, who alone is immortal and who lives in unapproachable light, whom no one has seen or can see. To him be honor and might forever. Amen (1 Ti.6:15-16).**

> The seventh angel sounded his trumpet, and there were loud voices in heaven, which said: "The kingdom of the world has become the kingdom of our Lord and of his Christ, and he will reign for ever and ever" (Re.11:15).
>
> On his robe and on his thigh he has this name written: KING OF KINGS AND LORD OF LORDS (Re.19:16).
>
> "I have installed my King on Zion, my holy hill." I will proclaim the decree of the LORD: He said to me, "You are my Son; today I have become your Father. Ask of me, and I will make the nations your inheritance, the ends of the earth your possession (Ps.2:6-8).
>
> He was given authority, glory and sovereign power; all peoples, nations and men of every language worshiped him. His dominion is an everlasting dominion that will not pass away, and his kingdom is one that will never be destroyed (Da.7:14).
>
> Rejoice greatly, O Daughter of Zion! Shout, Daughter of Jerusalem! See, your king comes to you, righteous and having salvation, gentle and riding on a donkey, on a colt, the foal of a donkey. I will take away the chariots from Ephraim and the war-horses from Jerusalem, and the battle bow will be broken. He will proclaim peace to the nations. His rule will extend from sea to sea and from the River to the ends of the earth (Zec.9:9-10).

3 (72:12-14) **A compassionate ruler, Ps.78:70-72.** After asking God to make Solomon a leader whom the world would follow, David called on his son to be compassionate toward the people. This trait, more than any other, would endear him to their hearts and create a desire within them to willingly submit to him.

As outstanding Bible teacher Warren Wiersbe notes, "The king of Israel was looked upon as God's shepherd who lovingly cared for God's flock."[6] Scripture records that David had been a faithful shepherd to the LORD's sheep during his time as Israel's king (Ps.78:70-72). He now charged Solomon to follow his example of sympathetically tending to the needs of God's people.

a. **He will deliver all who cry out to him: The needy, poor, oppressed, and helpless (v.12).**

Israel's king could not overlook nor callously dismiss the pleas of those who cried out to him for help. The needy, the poor or afflicted, and those who had no one

---

5   James Montgomery Boice. *An Expositional Commentary–Psalms, Volume 2: Psalms 42-106.* WORD*search* CROSS e-book.

6   Warren W. Wiersbe. *The Bible Exposition Commentary.* WORD*search* CROSS e-book.

to help them would come to him for relief. It was his responsibility to deliver them from their oppressors, those who were abusing or taking advantage of them. He was to demonstrate loving care for all who could not defend themselves, assuring that they were being treated fairly and their needs were being met.

b. He will have pity and save them from death: He will take away the suffering and pain of death, 1 Co.15:52-57 (v.13).

To spare the poor and needy means to have pity or compassion on them, to take their concerns to heart.[7] As noted previously, most of Israel's poor suffered due to circumstances beyond their control. The conditions in which they were sometimes forced to live—inadequate food, shelter, and care—could lead to their deaths. They were also easy prey for those who would mistreat or oppress them. Still, some suffered because of their bad decisions and foolish actions. As a result, they often lived under cruel, vengeful masters who abused them, at times to the point of death. A godly king would look on all of them with compassion and save their souls or lives from a painful, premature death.

c. He will rescue (save) them from their adversaries: Because their lives are precious to him (v.14).

The king should rescue or save the needy from their adversaries, those who deceive or defraud them and use violence against them. *Rescue* (ga'al) is the word for redeem and means to ransom or deliver from bondage. It usually involved the paying of a price. The price here is "the king's strength and energy" which he exercises on behalf of the oppressed.[8] An unrighteous leader would view the needy with contempt, seeing them as a burden and worthless to society. But a righteous king would personally intervene and advocate for the oppressed in his kingdom because their lives were precious to him.

Thought 1. The redemptive work of Jesus Christ is clearly presented in this passage. As David described the kind of heart Israel's king should have toward the needy, he perfectly portrayed the compassionate, sacrificial heart of our dear Savior toward us.

➤ Christ delivers us when we cry out to Him (v.12). As sinners, we are needy, afflicted, and helpless. There is absolutely nothing we can do to save ourselves. Even though our sin is against *Him*, He will not despise us or turn us away. He loves us and saves us from our sin.

➤ Christ has compassion on us, for we are helpless sinners doomed and destined for death (v.13). He saves our souls from spiritual death—eternal separation from God in hell. The application of

this verse can be extended to the redemption of our bodies as well. Christ will take away the suffering and pain of death, and when He comes again, He will resurrect our dead bodies and transform them into incorruptible, immortal bodies (1 Co.15:52-57; Jn.11:25). Even better news is the proclamation that believers who are alive at His return will never experience or taste death (1 Co.15:51; Jn.11:26)!

➤ Christ has rescued us from our oppressive enemies—Satan, sin, and death (v.14). He reaches down to us at our point of greatest need and sets us free from the bondage of sin. He rescues us from the power of the devil and ransoms us from death (v.14). The price: His precious, incorruptible blood (1 Pe.1:18-19). We are so precious to Him that He offered His blood for ours, His life for ours.

> **When he saw the crowds, he had compassion on them, because they were harassed and helpless, like sheep without a shepherd (Mt.9:36).**
>
> **Jesus had compassion on them and touched their eyes. Immediately they received their sight and followed him (Mt.20:34).**
>
> **When Jesus landed and saw a large crowd, he had compassion on them, because they were like sheep without a shepherd. So he began teaching them many things (Mk.6:34).**
>
> **When the Lord saw her, his heart went out to her and he said, "Don't cry" (Lu.7:13).**
>
> **Greater love has no one than this, that he lay down his life for his friends (Jn.15:13).**
>
> **For we do not have a high priest who is unable to sympathize with our weaknesses, but we have one who has been tempted in every way, just as we are—yet was without sin (He.4:15).**
>
> **A bruised reed he will not break, and a smoldering wick he will not snuff out. In faithfulness he will bring forth justice (Is.42:3).**

4 (72:15-20) **A beloved and prosperous ruler.**
Lastly, David prayed that his son would be a beloved and prosperous ruler. He asked God to use Solomon in such a way that people would honor him long after he was gone. More importantly, David prayed that the people would glorify God for the bountiful blessings brought to them through Solomon's reign.

---

7 Frank E. Gaebelein, ed. *The Expositor's Bible Commentary,* p.473.
8 Donald Williams. *Psalms 1-72*, p.524.

a. His rule is honored and cherished (v.15).

David prayed that Solomon would be a king who is long honored and cherished by the people. "Long may he live" can also be translated as *and he shall live*. This statement requests not only that Solomon be given a long life, but also that he be remembered and held in high esteem long after his death. Once again, David prayed that his son would be honored by the leaders of other nations who paid him tribute, as represented by the gold of Sheba. Among the rulers who would bring Solomon gifts was the queen of Sheba, who presented Israel's great king with 120 talents of gold, approximately 10,000 pounds (1 K.10:10). Then, David requested that people honor Solomon by praying for him continually and by praising him daily. What greater benefit could any parent ask for a child than for continuous prayer? David was a man of prayer Himself; thus, he knew the great importance of it for his son, especially in his role as king.

b. His land (the entire earth) will flourish: A picture of the new heavens and earth, 2 Pe.3:10-13; see Is. chs.35; 60–62; Je. chs.40–48 (v.16).

David went on to pray that God would prosper the nation under his son's leadership. He asked that even the top of the mountains—the thin-soiled, unproductive areas of the land—would be fruitful. Lebanon was an exceptionally fertile region known for its agricultural industry and its mighty cedar trees. So David asked that Israel's fruit trees and vines would shake with an abundance of fruit like those of Lebanon. Further, he prayed that the nation and its people would flourish or thrive like the grass of the fields.

c. His name (character and influence) will endure forever (v.17).

A person's name represents his or her character and influence. David prayed that Solomon's name would endure forever, that it would be remembered as long as the sun continues to shine. Together with that, David asked God to use Solomon to bless people throughout the earth, so much so that he would be called blessed by all nations.

d. His person and rule should stir you to praise the LORD God, the God of Israel (vv.18-20).

Over and above Solomon's blessing the nations and the nations' blessing him, David prayed that Solomon's reign would cause the LORD to be exalted throughout the earth. David's hope was that the heathen nations would recognize the LORD God, the God of Israel as the one truly responsible for the wondrous things that would be accomplished through Israel's king (v.18). God's glorious name is worthy of eternal praise; therefore, David prayed that the whole earth would be filled with the glory of the LORD because of Solomon's leadership (v.19).

On this high note of praise, Scripture records that this is the last of David's prayers (v.20). It also marks the end of *Book II* of *Psalms* (Ps.42–72). David's life was a sterling example of living and serving for the glory of God. As a young man, he valiantly burst onto the scene of Israel because of his great zeal and jealousy for God's glory. Approximately fifty years later, he graciously exited for eternity declaring that the glorious name of the LORD should be praised forever. To this day, he is remembered as Israel's greatest worshipper.

Thought 1. Once again, David's prayer for Solomon forecasts the eternal kingship of Jesus Christ. Certainly, history and Scripture have preserved the glories of Solomon. But in many ways, Solomon fell far short of David's prayer for the ideal, compassionate king. Only one king, God's perfect Son, will be all that David prayed for in Psalm 72. Note how this passage describes the eternal glory of Christ:

➤ Having risen triumphantly from the dead, King Jesus is alive forevermore (v.15a; Re.1:18). He rules by "the power of an indesctructible life" (He.7:16).

➤ Every day, the name of Jesus is praised throughout the earth (v.15b). Certainly, untold millions do not worship Jesus as Lord—one day they will. But in every land, there are believers who bless the wonderful name of Jesus.

➤ The entire earth will flourish under the leadership of King Jesus, first during His earthly reign, and then throughout eternity as a new heaven and new earth (v.16; 2 Pe.3:10-13; see Is. chs.35, 60-62; Je. chs.40–48).

➤ The name of Jesus will endure forever (v.17). Every knee will bow to Him and every tongue will confess Him as Lord (Ph.2:9-11). He will reign in righteousness forever (He.1:8; Re.11:15). There will be no need of the sun in the New Jerusalem, for He will be the light of the celestial city (Re.21:23-24; 22:5). Because of Him, God the Father will be glorified. Through Him, the earth will be filled with the glory of the LORD forever (v.19; Ph.2:11; Re.1:6; Ep.3:21).

> **To him be glory in the church and in Christ Jesus throughout all generations, for ever and ever! Amen (Ep.3:21).**
>
> **Therefore God exalted him to the highest place and gave him the name that is above every name, that at the name of Jesus every knee should bow, in heaven and on earth and under the earth, and every tongue confess that Jesus Christ is Lord, to the glory of God the Father (Ph.2:9-11).**

And again, when God brings his firstborn into the world, he says, "Let all God's angels worship him" (He.1:6).

No longer will a man teach his neighbor, or a man his brother, saying, 'Know the Lord,' because they will all know me, from the least of them to the greatest (He.8:11).

Then the angel said to me, "Write: 'Blessed are those who are invited to the wedding supper of the Lamb!'" And he added, "These are the true words of God" (Re.19:9).

Thought 2. While Psalm 72 is historic with reference to Solomon and prophetic with reference to Christ, it also holds lessons for us. First, we should honor our leaders and not speak evil of them (Ex.22:28; Ro.13:1-7; 1 Pe.2:17).

Second, God has commanded us to pray for our leaders. We should pray for the salvation of their souls as well as for them to rule righteously and according to God's will (1 Ti.2:1-4). As David prayed for Solomon, we too should ask God to make our leaders Christlike in their leadership.

Finally, we should point people to Christ's return and coming kingdom, following Peter's strong example in Acts:

Repent, then, and turn to God, so that your sins may be wiped out, that times of refreshing may come from the Lord, and that he may send the Christ, who has been appointed for you—even Jesus. He must remain in heaven until the time comes for God to restore everything, as he promised long ago through his holy prophets (Ac.3:19-21).

Everyone must submit himself to the governing authorities, for there is no authority except that which God has established. The authorities that exist have been established by God (Ro.13:1).

I urge, then, first of all, that requests, prayers, intercession and thanksgiving be made for everyone—for kings and all those in authority, that we may live peaceful and quiet lives in all godliness and holiness. This is good, and pleases God our Savior, who wants all men to be saved and to come to a knowledge of the truth (1 Ti.2:1-4).

Show proper respect to everyone: Love the brotherhood of believers, fear God, honor the king (1 Pe.2:17).

"Do not blaspheme God or curse the ruler of your people (Ex.22:28).

Outline	Scripture	Scripture	Outline

1. Stand on God's Word
a. God is good to His people
b. God is good to the pure in heart
2. Confess your struggle & lack of understanding to God, 16
a. Confess that you are tempted to slip back: Bc. you envy the prosperity (pleasures & possessions) of the wicked
  1) They seem to be exempt from the struggles of life & death
  • Seem healthy & strong
  • Seem free from ordinary burdens & problems
  • Seem immune to hardship
  2) They exalt themselves & take pride in their wickedness: Show little restraint
  3) They have hard hearts & evil minds that know no limits: They scheme to get what they want
  4) They use their tongues for evil
  • Scoff, speak maliciously, & threaten others
  • Curse & speak against God
  • Boast & intimidate, strutting around as if they were untouchable
  • Entice people to *swallow* (believe) their false promises: People follow blindly
  5) They revile & even deny God: Deny that He knows of their evil & that He exists
  6) They are always at ease—carefree & increasing in prosperity
b. Confess the intense turmoil you are experiencing
	BOOK III
	PSALMS 73–89
	
	PSALM 73
	
	When You See the Righteous Suffer & the Wicked Prosper, 73:1-28
	
	A psalm of Asaph.
	
	Surely God is good to Israel, to those who are pure in heart.
	2 But as for me, my feet had almost slipped; I had nearly lost my foothold.
	3 For I envied the arrogant when I saw the prosperity of the wicked.
	4 They have no struggles; their bodies are healthy and strong.
	5 They are free from the burdens common to man; they are not plagued by human ills.
	6 Therefore pride is their necklace; they clothe themselves with violence.
	7 From their callous hearts comes iniquity; the evil conceits of their minds know no limits.
	8 They scoff, and speak with malice; in their arrogance they threaten oppression.
	9 Their mouths lay claim to heaven, and their tongues take possession of the earth.
	10 Therefore their people turn to them and drink up waters in abundance.
	11 They say, "How can God know? Does the Most High have knowledge?"
	12 This is what the wicked are like—always carefree, they increase in wealth.
	13 Surely in vain have I kept my heart pure; in vain
		have I washed my hands in innocence.
		14 All day long I have been plagued; I have been punished every morning.
		15 If I had said, "I will speak thus," I would have betrayed your children.
		16 When I tried to understand all this, it was oppressive to me
		17 Till I entered the sanctuary of God; then I understood their final destiny.
		18 Surely you place them on slippery ground; you cast them down to ruin.
		19 How suddenly are they destroyed, completely swept away by terrors!
		20 As a dream when one awakes, so when you arise, O Lord, you will despise them as fantasies.
		21 When my heart was grieved and my spirit embittered,
		22 I was senseless and ignorant; I was a brute beast before you.
		23 Yet I am always with you; you hold me by my right hand.
		24 You guide me with your counsel, and afterward you will take me into glory.
		25 Whom have I in heaven but you? And earth has nothing I desire besides you.
		26 My flesh and my heart may fail, but God is the strength of my heart and my portion forever.
		27 Those who are far from you will perish; you destroy all who are unfaithful to you.
		28 But as for me, it is good to be near God. I have made the Sovereign LORD my refuge; I will tell of all your deeds.
			1) That you wonder & question if living for God is useless
			2) That you are plagued daily with trials & trouble with mental & emotional stress
			3) That you know you will betray God's people if you say what you are really feeling
			4) That you are in turmoil trying to understand why God allows the wicked to prosper
			3. Enter the presence (sanctuary) of God & listen to Him (His Holy Word)
			a. You will understand the destiny of the wicked
			  1) They are on a slippery path to destruction
			  2) They will be suddenly destroyed—swept away—utterly terrified
			  3) They will be destroyed by the LORD Himself: Their lives & ideas will pass away as quickly as a dream
			b. You will learn how wrong you are
			  1) That your envy of the wicked's prosperity is wrong
			  2) That you are foolish & ignorant before God, nothing more than a senseless beast
			c. You will learn that you belong to God
			  1) He holds your right hand
			  2) He guides you with His counsel (Holy Word)
			  3) He will take you into glory
			d. You will learn that God is enough, all you need in heaven & on earth
			
			  1) Bc. He is the strength of your life
			  • When your health fails
			  • When your spirit weakens
			  2) Bc. He will destroy all who turn away from Him
			
			4. Bear strong witness for God
			a. He is the Lord GOD, the Sovereign LORD
			b. He is your refuge

BOOK III: *PSALMS 73–89*

PSALM 73

When You See the Righteous Suffer and the Wicked Prosper, 73:1-28

(73:1-28) **Introduction:** Why do the righteous suffer and the wicked prosper? It is impossible to understand. Perhaps more than any one single factor, it jolts the faith of people across the globe. It just does not seem right.

The Bible teaches that God blesses the righteous and judges the wicked. Yet, it so often appears that the ungodly prosper more and suffer less than the godly. From good people who seem to have more than their share of troubles to faithful believers who are attacked by criminals to Christians who are persecuted and martyred for their faith, the suffering of the righteous does not make sense to us.

It was exactly this dilemma that prompted the writing of Psalm 73. The first of *Book III* of *Psalms,* Psalm 73 is also the first of a section of eleven psalms attributed to Asaph, one of three chief musical directors in David's court. An outstanding singer and percussionist, he also authored Psalm 50 (1 Chr.15:16-19; 16:4-7, 37; 25:1ff).

Psalm 73 is the last of three psalms that address the suffering of the righteous and the prosperity of the wicked (Ps.37, 49). Without question, the counsel of the previous psalms is immeasurably profitable. However, what God teaches us through Asaph lends a sense of closure to the subject: the understanding of life's perplexing dilemmas is found only in the presence of God (v.17). When our faith is shaken by the wicked things occuring in this world, we need to draw near to Him (v.28). This is, *When You See the Righteous Suffer and the Wicked Prosper,* 73:1-28.

1. Stand on God's Word (v.1).
2. Confess your struggle and lack of understanding to God, 16 (vv.2-16).
3. Enter the presence (sanctuary) of God and listen to Him (His Holy Word) (vv.17-27).
4. Bear strong witness for God (v.28).

1 (73:1) **Stand on God's word.**
Although Asaph was struggling with the suffering of the righteous and the prosperity of the wicked, he determined to stand on the clear teaching of God's Holy Word: God is good to His people. Surely, He is good to all who are of a clean heart (Ps.24:4). *Surely* is the most important word in this first verse. It emphasizes that, in spite of how things may appear, God *is* good to His people. Commentator Derek Kidner also notes that "the phrase, *pure* [clean] *in heart,* is more significant than it may seem…. *Pure* means more than clean-minded… basically, it is being totally committed to God."[1]

Thought 1. The truth of God's Word is not determined by our experiences and observations. God's Word is true regardless of how things appear. Satan's oldest trick is to cast doubt on God's Word. This is exactly what he did with Eve in the Garden of Eden. He twisted God's command to abstain from eating of the tree of knowledge, leading Eve to question God's goodness (Ge.3:1-5). In the same fashion, he uses the injustices of this world to tempt us to question God's Word and character. Like Jesus when He was tempted, we must stand firm on God's Word, using it to resist Satan (Mt.4:1-10; Ep.6:17). God's Word is absolute truth. Whatever happens, it will stand, and it will en-

dure forever. We must never allow ourselves to be moved from or to doubt what it says, regardless of our experiences or feelings. God is good to His people, to all who are pure in heart!

> **Heaven and earth will pass away, but my words will never pass away (Lu.21:33).**
>
> **And we also thank God continually because, when you received the word of God, which you heard from us, you accepted it not as the word of men, but as it actually is, the word of God, which is at work in you who believe (1 Th.2:13).**
>
> **For you have been born again, not of perishable seed, but of imperishable, through the living and enduring word of God. For, "All men are like grass, and all their glory is like the flowers of the field; the grass withers and the flowers fall, but the word of the Lord stands forever." And this is the word that was preached to you (1 Pe.1:23-25).**
>
> **And the words of the LORD are flawless, like silver refined in a furnace of clay, purified seven times (Ps.12:6).**
>
> **The law of the LORD is perfect, reviving the soul. The statutes of the LORD are trustworthy, making wise the simple. The precepts of the LORD are right, giving joy to the heart. The commands of the LORD are radiant, giving light to the eyes (Ps.19:7-8).**
>
> **The grass withers and the flowers fall, but the word of our God stands forever" (Is.40:8).**

2 (73:2-16) **Confess your struggle and lack of understanding to God, v.16.**
Asaph was struggling with a serious dilemma: he could not understand why he, a righteous man, suffered every day while the wicked prospered. The injustice of this had shaken his faith to the core. He had kept his feelings bottled up for so long that he was now at the breaking point. Feeling unable to speak to anyone else about his questions, he confessed his struggle and lack of understanding to God.

a. Confess that you are tempted to slip back: Because you envy the prosperity (pleasures and possessions) of the wicked (vv.2-12).
What Asaph could not understand—the prosperity of the wicked—seriously threatened his faith. He openly confessed that he was strongly tempted to slip back from following the LORD. He had stood firm in his confidence in God and His goodness, but the prosperity of

---

1 Derek Kidner. *Tyndale Old Testament Commentaries: Psalms 73-150.* (Downers Grove, IL: InterVarsity Press, 2009), p.288.

the wicked troubled him so grievously that he nearly slipped from the right path (v.2). He became envious of the foolish, the proud, arrogant people who exalt themselves and their selfish desires over God's righteous commands (v.3).

As Asaph observed their easy lives, it seemed that the ungodly were exempt from the struggles of life and the bands of death (v.4). *Struggles* (chartsubbah) means fetters or chains (Is.58:6). The wicked somehow appeared to avoid the bondage and pain of affliction that the righteous suffer, even in their deaths. They were well-fed, and their bodies were healthy and strong. They lived free of life's ordinary burdens and problems. From his perspective, they were immune to hardship (v.5).

Even more unjust to Asaph was this fact: the easy lives of the wicked spawned more pride in their sinful hearts (v.6). They wore their rebellion against God's commands like a medal of honor around their necks. Showing little restraint, they clothed themselves with violence, with cruel, criminal acts against others. In spite of this, they seemed to have everything their hearts could desire (v.7).

Asaph continued to describe the despicable behavior of the corrupt. They used their tongues for evil. They scoffed, spoke maliciously, and threatened others (v.8). They even cursed and spoke against God Himself. Asaph painted a graphic picture of their boastful speaking, depicting their arrogant tongues fearlessly strutting across the face of the earth. As they proudly paraded their wickedness, they openly intimidated everybody they encountered as if they were untouchable (v.9).

As the wicked spread their verbal poison throughout the land, many people foolishly believed their false promises (v.10). Enticed by the deceivers' prosperous lives, the people blindly followed them. "Drink up waters in adundance" portrays senseless, simpleminded people heartily drinking up the toxic waters that abundantly spewed out of the evildoers' vile mouths.

With minds totally corrupted, these rebellious people reviled God, going so far as to question His existence and power (v.11). Note their questions: *How does God know? Does the Most High even have the knowledge He claims to have?* Apparently, since they suffered no penalty for their misbehavior and injustice, they assumed that one of three things must be true:

➤ God did not see or know what they did.
➤ God was not powerful enough to stop them or punish them.
➤ God does not exist at all.

This is what the wicked are like, Asaph concluded (v.12). In spite of their fiendish behavior, their blatant flaunting of God's holy law, they are always at ease. They lead carefree lives, and all the while their prosperity continues to increase.

b. Confess the intense turmoil you are experiencing (vv.13-16).

Asaph was brutally honest with God: the prosperity of the wicked had thrust him into intense turmoil. He had begun to question the very foundations of his faith, wondering if living for God was useless (v.13). Day by day, he made every effort to walk righteously. He had turned away from the bright lights, pleasures, and perversions of this world. Was it all in vain? Had he kept his heart clean for nothing? Did he "wash his hands in innocence," carefully guarding his behavior to be innocent of wrongdoing, to no avail?

In spite of his best efforts to live a godly life, Asaph was plagued with trials and troubles (v.14). *Plagued* (nagah) and *punished* indicate that he had been struck by what he felt was God's judgment (Ge.12:17; Is.53:4). *All the day long* and *every morning* suggest that he had been touched by a physical affliction, perhaps an ongoing, incurable disease (2 K.15:5; 2 Chr.26:20).

For some time, Asaph had kept his feelings bottled up within, causing severe mental and emotional stress. As a chief worship leader in Israel, he carefully considered his influence on others. If he talked about what he was feeling, he knew that he would offend God's people. He felt that he would betray the faith that had bound Israel throughout the generations, even to the current generation of children (v.15). At the same time, however, trying to know or understand this—why God allowed the wicked to prosper while he suffered—kept him reeling in utter turmoil (v.16).

Thought 1. Personal suffering can seriously challenge our faith, just as it did Asaph's. This godly man suffered every day with a serious affliction, some severe trial that he felt was God's discipline in his life. At the same time, he watched the wicked go about their vile business untouched by trouble.

Notice, first, that Scripture does not condemn Asaph for having these feelings. One of the greatest lessons of *Psalms* is that *we have the liberty to empty our hurting hearts at God's throne.* That same lesson is taught again here at the beginning of *Book III*: God is not weak or overly sensitive. Rather, He is powerful and understanding. He can handle our burdens, and He can deal with our questions, even when they are about Him. When we do not understand God's ways—when we lack wisdom about our trials—we can ask for God's help (Js.1:2-5).

Second, note Asaph's concern for God's people. As a leader, he did not speak of his struggles to other people, lest he betray their faith. Pastors and other leaders know what it is like to be unable to talk to others when their own faith is challenged. If the individuals they lead learn of their questions and doubts, then they might lose confidence in their pastor or leader, or, they too might be tempted to slip in their faith. At the same time, like Asaph, none of us should keep our feelings bottled up within us indefinitely. When we struggle with questions or feelings that we cannot express to any other person, we can always tell them to Jesus. He knows and understands our conflicts. He became one of us in order to intercede for us. From the cross, He cried out to God, questioning why the Father had forsaken Him (Mt.27:46). Having suffered every trial and temptation that we might face, Jesus is able to help us when we are tried (He.2:17-18). He was "touched with the feeling of our infirmities," and He invites us to come to Him for help in our time of need (He.4:14-16).

> I keep asking that the God of our Lord Jesus Christ, the glorious Father, may give you the Spirit of wisdom and revelation, so that you may know him better (Ep.1:17).
>
> Therefore, since we have a great high priest who has gone through the heavens, Jesus the Son of God, let us hold firmly to the faith we profess. For we do not have a high priest who is unable to sympathize with our weaknesses, but we have one who has been tempted in every way, just as we are—yet was without sin. Let us then approach the throne of grace with confidence, so that we may receive mercy and find grace to help us in our time of need (He.4:14-16).
>
> If any of you lacks wisdom, he should ask God, who gives generously to all without finding fault, and it will be given to him (Js.1:5).
>
> Unless the LORD had given me help, I would soon have dwelt in the silence of death. When I said, "My foot is slipping," your love, O LORD, supported me (Ps.94:17-18).
>
> For the LORD gives wisdom, and from his mouth come knowledge and understanding (Pr.2:6).

3 (73:17-27) **Enter the presence (sanctuary) of God and listen to Him (His Holy Word).**
With his spirit in bondage to his negative feelings, Asaph went to the sanctuary of God—the place where His presence dwelled in a special way. Entering God's presence set Asaph free from the envy and bitterness that gripped his soul. As he bowed before the LORD, God spoke to his heart from His Holy Word. By listening to God, Asaph

learned four invaluable lessons that changed his perspective and his life.

a. You will understand the destiny of the wicked (vv.17-20).
When Asaph entered God's holy presence, the Lord lifted him above the injustices of this present world in order for him to see the destiny of the wicked (v.17). That is to say, God gave him a clear understanding of the end of the ungodly:

➤ They are on a slippery path to destruction (v.18).

➤ They will be suddenly destroyed, utterly consumed or swept away by "instantaneous, unexpected terrors" (v.19).[2] Picture the wicked recklessly going about their ungodly lives, thinking that God does not see them. Then, all of a sudden, some terrifying calamity—God's judgment—rips them out of this world and forcefully thrusts them into eternal condemnation.

➤ They will be destroyed by the Lord Himself (v.20). Like a quickly-forgotten dream, their lives will suddenly pass away, never to be seen again. The picture here is of God awakening in judgment and totally wiping the wicked off the face of the earth. They will be like an image, a fantasy or illusion that never really existed.

b. You will learn how wrong you are (vv.21-22).
Like Isaiah the prophet's experience, Asaph's entering the Lord's holy presence caused him to see himself in a different light (Is.6:1-5). He recognized how wrong he was in allowing himself to be overcome by negative thinking. By saying his heart was grieved, Asaph was confessing that he had become bitter toward God (v.21). *Was grieved* (chamets) means became fermented or sour. Plainly stated, Asaph humbly admitted that his attitude toward God had become rotten. When he said "my spirit [was] embittered," he meant he had allowed his envy of the wicked and his bitterness toward God to pierce through or corrupt his entire life, all the way to his innermost being. Convicted and ashamed, Asaph bluntly stated that he was both foolish and ignorant before God, like a senseless animal (v.22).

c. You will learn that you belong to God (vv.23-24).
Asaph now realized a glorious truth: even though he had slipped away from God, God had never left him (v.23). He belonged to God. At his lowest moment, when he was bitter toward God, the Lord never let go of him. He held tightly onto Asaph's right hand—a picture of God's protection and direction.

God also guided him with His counsel, His Holy Word (v.24). When Asaph strayed from the truth, God's Word led him back, enlightening him to his own

---

2 Spiros Zodhiates. *AMG Complete Word Study Dictionary*. WORD-search CROSS e-book.

foolishness and illuminating God's goodness and righteousness (Ps.19:7; 119:105). With his faith joyously renewed, Asaph declared that God's counsel would continue to guide him through the rest of his life. Then, God would receive him to glory, that is, lead him into His holy presence, Asaph's glorious destiny.

d. You will learn that God is enough, all you need in heaven and on earth (vv.25-27).

Asaph saved his most precious lesson for last: being in God's presence overshadows all the trials and injustices of life. Even as Asaph pondered the glories of heaven, he declared that all he longed for there was God (v.25). To him, "heaven is heaven because God is there."[3] In addition, entering God's presence had now brought complete satisfaction to his life. He was able to say in all honesty that the only thing he desired on earth was God. God is enough. He is all that matters. He is all we need.

In God's presence, Asaph found strength for his difficult life (v.26). He declared that though his flesh and heart, his health and spirit, might *fail* (kalah), God would sustain him through his afflictions. Death held no power over him, for God was his portion forever. *Portion* (cheleq) means a share of an inheritance. Asaph proclaimed that the LORD was his inheritance (Ps.16:5). When he died, he would live eternally in God's glorious presence.

Focusing on his magnificent future enabled Asaph to accept the present reality—the prosperity of the wicked. Although he suffered affliction in this life, he had the splendid hope of living with God forever. In contrast, the ungodly have no hope whatsoever, for God will destroy all who turn away from Him (v.27).

Thought 1. At times, we all struggle with questions about God and why He allows things to happen as they do, both in our own lives and the lives of others around the world. There are many things we simply cannot understand, for instance...

- the many injustices of evil governments
- the suffering of innocent children and the weak
- atrocious acts by criminals, terrorists, dictators, and gangs
- crippling illnesses and disease
- widespread famine and poverty
- natural disasters such as floods, hurricanes, earthquakes, and cyclones
- the tragic death of children and young adults

These and a multitude of other horrible things can leave us reeling physically, mentally, and emotionally and cause us to question God's goodness and love. When this is our state of mind, only one thing can help us: entering God's presence. When we bow before the Lord, He will reveal His goodness to us, and He will speak to our hearts. As His Word and Spirit comfort us, He will teach us about Himself. We will learn that He is all we need and that His strength will empower us to deal with whatever difficulties come into our lives. He will lead us to the realization that His presence in our lives is enough. He will guide us back to the right path.

Like Asaph, we must look beyond the evils and injustices of this world and focus on the future. God is absolutely righteous. He will judge the wicked; and the righteous—as difficult as our lives may be in the present—will spend eternity in His glorious presence. "The glory of God affects one's whole way of life as one lives in the joy of God's love, mercy, patience, grace, and forgiveness. But hope extends beyond this life to the future, when God takes care of all his children's needs."[4] The inheritance of the wicked is everlasting destruction and desolation. But God is our portion, our share, our inheritance. We will live with Him forever!

> **Do not be anxious about anything, but in everything, by prayer and petition, with thanksgiving, present your requests to God. And the peace of God, which transcends all understanding, will guard your hearts and your minds in Christ Jesus. Finally, brothers, whatever is true, whatever is noble, whatever is right, whatever is pure, whatever is lovely, whatever is admirable—if anything is excellent or praiseworthy—think about such things. Whatever you have learned or received or heard from me, or seen in me—put it into practice. And the God of peace will be with you (Ph.4:6-9).**

> **Cast all your anxiety on him because he cares for you (1 Pe.5:7).**

> **You have made known to me the path of life; you will fill me with joy in your presence, with eternal pleasures at your right hand (Ps.16:11).**

> **O God, you are my God, earnestly I seek you; my soul thirsts for you, my body longs for you, in a dry and weary land where there is no water. I have seen you in the sanctuary and beheld your power and your glory (Ps.63:1-2).**

> **Your ways, O God, are holy. What god is so great as our God? (Ps.77:13).**

4 (73:28) Bear strong witness for God.

Realizing that others struggled with the same issue he did, Asaph determined to bear strong witness regarding

---

3   Donald Williams. *Psalms 73-150.* "The Preacher's Commentary," Volume 14. (Nashville, TN: Thomas Nelson Publishers, 2002), p.21.

4   Frank E. Gaebelein, ed. *The Expositor's Bible Commentary*, p.482.

what God had done in his life. Drawing near to God gave Asaph the right perspective on the prosperity of the wicked and the suffering of the righteous. By entering God's presence, he had learned to trust God.

a. He is the Lord GOD, the Sovereign LORD (v.28ᵃ).

Asaph first had to gain the right perspective on who God is. He is the Lord GOD or the *Sovereign Lord* (Adonai Yahovih, a form of Yahweh or Jehovah). This title emphasizes that our covenant-keeping God is the Master of all things. He is ultimately in control of everything that takes place in our lives and in this world.

b. He is your refuge (v.28ᵇ).

Gaining the right perspective on God gave Asaph the right perspective on the injustices of life. Realizing that God is in control enabled him to put his trust in God , to take refuge in Him. Instead of struggling with the question of why he was suffering while the wicked prospered, he decided to rest in God, fully trusting the Lord to take care of him and to do what was right. As a result, Asaph was able to say wholeheartedly that, in spite of how things may appear sometimes, God is truly good to His people (v.1).

Thought 1. Asaph's testimony is the great lesson of Psalm 73: when we are wrestling with the injustices of this world, we need to recognize who God is and trust Him to do what is right. He is our LORD, our personal God with whom we have an eternal relationship through His covenant. As His children through faith in Jesus Christ, He will take care of us (Ga.3:26; Mt.6:31-33). When we draw near to Him and trust Him, we gain the right perspective on the problems of life. Like Asaph, we will then have a testimony we can share with others. We can declare the work God has done in our lives and help others who are struggling to realize that God is always in control and can be trusted in all things.

> **It is written: "I believed; therefore I have spoken." With that same spirit of faith we also believe and therefore speak (2 Co.4:13).**
>
> **We proclaim to you what we have seen and heard, so that you also may have fellowship with us. And our fellowship is with the Father and with his Son, Jesus Christ (1 Jn.1:3).**
>
> **Come and listen, all you who fear God; let me tell you what he has done for me (Ps.66:16).**
>
> **I will meditate on all your works and consider all your mighty deeds (Ps.77:12).**

PSALM 74

When You Feel Abandoned by God & Defeated by the Enemy, 74:1-23

A maskil of Asaph.

1. Share your despair with God

a. God seems to be rejecting you & His people
   1) He seems angry with you
   2) He seems to have forgotten you, His redeemed, & failed to work in your behalf

b. God has allowed the enemy to ruin so much: In Israel's case, an enemy had destroyed the capital city
   1) They shouted their battle cry & set up their banners in God's temple in a show of victory & control
   2) They destroyed the temple
      • Wielded axes like woodcutters in a forest
      • Smashed the carved paneling, 1 K.6:15-18
      • Burned the temple—the place that bore God's name—to the ground
   3) They were determined to destroy & burn down evey worship center in Israel

c. God has not yet delivered His people
   1) He has given no signs or leaders (prophets) to guide them
   2) He continues to let the enemy mock & revile His holy name
   3) He has not yet executed judgment against the en-

Why have you rejected us forever, O God? Why does your anger smolder against the sheep of your pasture?
2 Remember the people you purchased of old, the tribe of your inheritance, whom you redeemed—Mount Zion, where you dwelt.
3 Turn your steps toward these everlasting ruins, all this destruction the enemy has brought on the sanctuary.
4 Your foes roared in the place where you met with us; they set up their standards as signs.
5 They behaved like men wielding axes to cut through a thicket of trees.
6 They smashed all the carved paneling with their axes and hatchets.
7 They burned your sanctuary to the ground; they defiled the dwelling place of your Name.
8 They said in their hearts, "We will crush them completely!" They burned every place where God was worshiped in the land.
9 We are given no miraculous signs; no prophets are left, and none of us knows how long this will be.
10 How long will the enemy mock you, O God? Will the foe revile your name forever?
11 Why do you hold back your hand, your right hand?

Take it from the folds of your garment and destroy them!
12 But you, O God, are my king from of old; you bring salvation upon the earth.
13 It was you who split open the sea by your power; you broke the heads of the monster in the waters.
14 It was you who crushed the heads of Leviathan and gave him as food to the creatures of the desert.
15 It was you who opened up springs and streams; you dried up the ever flowing rivers.
16 The day is yours, and yours also the night; you established the sun and moon.
17 It was you who set all the boundaries of the earth; you made both summer and winter.
18 Remember how the enemy has mocked you, O LORD, how foolish people have reviled your name.
19 Do not hand over the life of your dove to wild beasts; do not forget the lives of your afflicted people forever.
20 Have regard for your covenant, because haunts of violence fill the dark places of the land.
21 Do not let the oppressed retreat in disgrace; may the poor and needy praise your name.
22 Rise up, O God, and defend your cause; remember how fools mock you all day long.
23 Do not ignore the clamor of your adversaries, the uproar of your enemies, which rises continually.

emy nor destroyed them

2. Declare your faith in God

a. He is your eternal King
b. He brings salvation to the earth
c. He has delivered His people in the past: Several examples
   1) He split the Red Sea (the exodus)
   2) He defeated Egypt (the sea monster—Leviathan): Gave up the Egyptians as food to the beasts of the desert, Eze.29:3-5
   3) He provided water in the desert & dried up the Jordan River so His people could enter the promised land
d. He created the universe
   1) Rules over day & night, the sun & moon
   2) Set the boundaries of the earth
   3) Made both summer & winter

3. Express concern for God's name & for His people

a. Ask God to remember how the enemy (foolish people) mocked His name
b. Ask God not to turn His people over to the enemy—not permanently
   1) Not to forget their afflictions
   2) Not to forget His covenant promise: Bc. the land is filled with darkness & violence
   3) Not to let His oppressed people be humiliated but rather be filled with praise: Bc. of His deliverance
c. Ask God to rise up & defend His cause
   1) To remember how fools mock Him continually
   2) To bear in mind the boastful claims & constant uproar of His enemies

PSALM 74

When You Feel Abandoned by God and Defeated by the Enemy, 74:1-23

(74:1-23) **Introduction:** at one time or another, most of us have been devastated by events that shook us to our very core: the death of a loved one, betrayal by a spouse or dear friend, rebellion by a child, loss of employment, the failure of a business, a severe financial crisis, divorce, and so on. These and a host of other crushing circumstances can cause us to feel totally defeated. They can even cause us to feel that God no longer cares about us and has abandoned us.

Psalm 74 was written during a season of humiliating defeat in Israel, a time when the nation felt God had cast them off or abandoned them (v.1). Most commentators agree that the details of the psalm point toward one of two occasions in Israel's history: the destruction of Jerusalem by the Babylonians in 586 B.C. or the defilement of the temple by Antiochus Ephiphanes during the Maccabean Age (approximately 170 B.C.).

Overall, the specifics of the psalm seem to favor the Babylonian invasion as its setting. However, those who lean toward the blasphemous acts of Antiochus point to the statement "no prophets are left" as their convicting factor (v.9). Commentator J.J. Stewart Perowne wrote,

> *It is difficult to understand how such a complaint could have been uttered when Jeremiah and Ezekiel were both living; or with what truth it could be added, "Neither is there any among us who knoweth how long," when Jeremiah had distinctly foretold that the duration of the Captivity should be seventy years (Jer.25:11; 29:10).*[1]

On the other hand, theologian John Calvin noted that Scripture records the prophets being "silent for a time" during the Babylonian Captivity (Lam.2:9).[2] He added, "When it is said a little before [in Ps.74:5-7] that the sanctuaries were burnt to ashes, the carved works destroyed, and that nothing remained entire, these statements do not apply to the cruelty and tyranny of Antiochus."[3]

Either view creates a dilemma with regard to the psalm's heading, which names Asaph as its author. Asaph lived and served during David's time, long before either of the above-mentioned invasions occurred. The best explanation for this is that the psalm was written by Asaph's descendants, an order of temple musicians known by his name (2 Chr.35:15; Ezra 2:41; 3:10). Another possibility is that this is a prophetic psalm actually written by Asaph, pointing to the future invasions of Israel and, ultimately, to the atrocities of the antichrist during the tribulation period.

While we cannot be certain of this seventy-fourth psalm's history and author, we can be sure of its purpose: it is a *maskil*, a psalm of instruction. "The psalm teaches us how to pray when calamity strikes, when it seems as though God is blind and deaf to what is going on."[4] This is, *When You Feel Abandoned by God and Defeated by the Enemy*, 74:1-23.

1. Share your despair with God (vv.1-11).
2. Declare your faith in God (vv.12-17).
3. Express concern for God's name and for His people (vv.18-23).

1 (74:1-11) Share your despair with God.

Israel was living through a horrible time in her history, experiencing a fate the people had never truly believed would happen. An enemy nation had invaded Jerusalem, raiding the temple and taking the people captive. Over-whelmed with despair, the psalmist cried out to God in behalf of his shattered nation.

a. God seems to be rejecting you and His people (vv.1-2).

The devastating events that had occurred led the psalmist to conclude that God had rejected His people (v.1). The continuously-rising smoke from the smoldering city of Jerusalem was a constant picture of God's seething anger toward them. Asaph described the relationship between the Israelites and God by referring to the people as the sheep of His pasture (Ps.23:1; 100:3). Helpless, dumb, and prone to wander, they were totally dependent on the LORD.

Now, it appeared that God had forgotten them. Because He had not worked in their behalf, or so it seemed, the enemy stormed the city and brought about their disastrous fall. Therefore, the psalmist begged God to *remember* (zakhar) the nation of Israel—to keep her people before Him and to act in their behalf (v.2). Desperate for God's help, he reminded God of His commitment to Israel. The LORD had...

- purchased them out of Egyptian bondage (Ex.20:2)
- chosen them as the rod or tribe of His inheritance (De.4:20; 32:9; Je.10:16)
- redeemed them (Ex.15:13; Ps.77:15)
- selected Mount Zion to be His dwelling (Ps.87:2; 132:13-14)

b. God has allowed the enemy to ruin so much: In Israel's case, an enemy had destroyed the capital city (vv.3-8).

The damage inflicted on Israel was nothing less than shocking. God had allowed the enemy to ruin so much of what set them apart from other nations. Jerusalem, their capital city, had been ruthlessly destroyed (v.3). From the people's perspective, things would never be the same. *Everlasting ruins* expresses the sentiment that the city would never recover from this horrific attack. The awful ruins of the sanctuary—the holy place where God dwelled among His people in a special way—would bear eternal witness to their rejection by God.

As if relating a terrifying nightmare, the psalmist described what had taken place in Jerusalem. Their enemies had roared right into the midst of the congregation, shouting out their battle cry (v.4). This statement implies that the conquerors had stormed the temple while the people were worshipping and offering sacrifices. In a display of shameless irreverence, they had set up their ensigns or banners as a sign of their victory and control of God's house.

These unholy intruders had savagely destroyed the temple, wildly wielding their axes like woodcutters in a dense forest (v.5). As they charged through the sanctuary barbarically, they smashed the elegantly-carved cedar paneling that covered the walls and floors of

---

1 J.J. Stewart Perowne, *The Book of Psalms*. WORD*search* CROSS e-book.
2 John Calvin. *Calvin's Commentaries*. WORD*search* CROSS e-book.
3 Ibid.
4 John Phillips. *Exploring Psalms, Volume 1*. WORD*search* CROSS e-book.

God's house (v.6; 1 K.6:15-18). Even then they were not satisfied. Just vandalizing the Holy Place that bore God's name was not enough, so they burned it to the ground, likely igniting the temple's rich linens with their torches and flaming arrows (v.7). Bolstered by demonic determination, these brutes would not rest until they had destroyed every place in Israel where people assembled to worship God (v.8).

c. God has not yet delivered His people (vv.9-11).

At the time the psalmist wrote Psalm 74, God had not yet delivered His people from these oppressors. In fact, the afflicted Israelites were suffering under God's painful silence. He had not given any miraculous signs to guide them, nor had He raised up a prophet to reveal His will to them. With no communication whatsoever from the LORD, the Israelites had no idea how long their persecution would last (v.9).

In the meantime, God continued to allow the enemy to mock and revile His holy name. The grieved psalmist cried out to God, asking how long He was going to let the adversary reproach or scoff at Him (v.10). He also inquired as to why God withheld His judgment from the enemy (v.11). Then, he called on God to take His right hand—a symbol of His righteousness, authority, and power—out of His bosom and to utterly destroy them.

Thought 1. Along with the entire nation, the psalmist was suffering through an excruciatingly difficult situation, one for which there was no end in sight. Understandably, he was totally devastated. He felt...

• that God had rejected him (v.1)
• that things would never change (v.1, 10-11)
• that God was angry at him (v.1)
• that God had forgotten about him and no longer cared (v.2)
• that horrible memories of what had occurred would always haunt him (vv.4-8)
• that he could never regain what had been lost (vv.4-8)
• that God was not speaking to him or guiding him, not comforting him or giving him direction (v.9)
• that he could not understand why God was allowing this to happen to His people nor why God did not do something about it (vv.10-11)

When going through severe trials, we too may experience some of these feelings. Remember, this is a psalm of instruction: when you feel hopelessly rejected by God, when you have suffered a great loss, when you feel God does not care, the first step toward overcoming your despair is to share it with God. Tell Him how you feel. Pastor and commentator James Montgomery Boice wrote,

This is a fierce complaint, bordering just possibly on impropriety as an address to God. But we should not miss the fact that it is at least addressed to God. When we complain it is more often the case that we just complain, either to ourselves or to other people. It is better to complain to God.[5]

We should never be irreverent toward God, nor should we forget who He is when we are speaking to Him. At the same time, we need to remember that He is our Father. As Jesus poured out His heart to God, His Father, so can we. The Lord Jesus Christ—who was touched by every feeling we experience—is always interceding for us, and He invites us to come boldly to God's throne. This invitation is issued along with a comforting promise: we will receive mercy—not judgment—and grace to sustain us in our time of need (He.4:14-16).

> **Do not be anxious about anything, but in everything, by prayer and petition, with thanksgiving, present your requests to God. And the peace of God, which transcends all understanding, will guard your hearts and your minds in Christ Jesus (Ph.4:6-7).**
>
> **Therefore, since we have a great high priest who has gone through the heavens, Jesus the Son of God, let us hold firmly to the faith we profess. For we do not have a high priest who is unable to sympathize with our weaknesses, but we have one who has been tempted in every way, just as we are—yet was without sin. Let us then approach the throne of grace with confidence, so that we may receive mercy and find grace to help us in our time of need (He.4:14-16).**
>
> **Is any one of you in trouble? He should pray. Is anyone happy? Let him sing songs of praise (Js.5:13).**
>
> **Trust in him at all times, O people; pour out your hearts to him, for God is our refuge. Selah (Ps.62:8).**
>
> **Let us lift up our hearts and our hands to God in heaven, and say (Lam.3:41).**

2 (74:12-17) Declare your faith in God.

Suddenly, the psalmist's demeanor changed from fear to faith, from heartache to hope, from panic to peace. "He lifted his eyes by faith from the burning ruins to the holy throne of God in the heavens and received a new

---

5 James Montgomery Boice. *An Expositional Commentary–Psalms, Volume 2: Psalms 42-106.* WORDsearch CROSS e-book.

perspective on the situation."[6] With his spirit renewed by a glimpse of the LORD's faithfulness and power, the psalmist declared his faith in God.

a. He is your eternal King (v.12ᵃ).

The psalmist saw that God is still on His throne. The enemy may have destroyed the earthly structure where God met with His people, but they did not—and could not—shake His holy seat of authority over the universe. God is the *King from of old*—the King from antiquity or ages past, the eternal King.

b. He brings salvation to the earth. (v.12ᵇ).

The psalmist also remembered that the God of heaven brings salvation to the earth. Salvation does not refer here to God's work of redeeming us from sin. It is "physical, rather than spiritual" in nature.[7] The Hebrew word is plural and may be more precisely translated as saving acts (HCSB) or deeds of deliverance (NASB). It means to rescue from danger, to "move from distress to safety."[8]

c. He has delivered His people in the past: Several examples (vv.13-15).

Reflecting on Israel's history, the psalmist cited several examples of God's delivering His people. First, He split the Red Sea by His supernatural strength, making a way for Israel to escape Egyptian bondage (v.13ᵃ; Ex.14:1-22).

Second, God defeated Egypt on Israel's behalf (v.13ᵇ-14). God had overcome the monster in the water and leviathan. These terms are rooted in pagan mythology. The Canaanites believed that their so-called god (Baal) had conquered these sea monsters. Therefore, in their minds, Baal ruled over the seas and rivers. "The point here is that what Baal had claimed in the realm of myth, God had done in the realm of history—and done for His people, *working salvation.*"[9] Here, the monster stands for Pharaoh, Egypt's king (v.13ᵇ; Eze.29:3; Is.51:9-10). The seven-headed leviathan represents Egypt and her vast, highly-organized military forces (v.14ᵃ). Scripture records how God overthrew Egypt's armies in the midst of the sea and their bodies washed up on the shore (Ex.14:26-30). There, the bodies became meat to the living creatures of the wilderness or desert (v.14ᵇ; Eze.29:4-5; 23:2-4).

Third, God provided water for His people in the wilderness and dried up the Jordan River so they could enter the promised land (v.15). "You...opened up springs and streams" refers to God's miraculous provision of water through the smitten rock (Ex. 17:1-7).

d. He created the universe (vv.16-17).

Finally, the psalmist's faith in God was reinforced by remembering that God created the universe. It is He who rules over the day and night as well as the sun and the moon that light them (v.16; Ge.1:14-18). Likewise, God set the boundaries of the earth and the rotation of seasons (v.17; Pr.8:29; Ge.8:22). God's diligent governance of the world and its natural functions reminded the psalmist that God is also in control of every detail that affects His people.

Thought 1. When we feel overwhelmed by trouble and despair, it is easy to forget what we know about God. We need to look up, to take our eyes off of our circumstances and get a glimpse of God. He is still on His throne, and He is powerful enough to deliver us from every defeat, every enemy, and every concern that holds us captive. Furthermore, we need to look back and remember what God has done for us in the past. Focusing on His faithfulness to us through our dark valleys can buoy us with hope for our present struggles.

We also need to remember that we cannot trust our emotions. We have to reject the lies that our feelings tell us...

* that God has forsaken us
* that God does not love us
* that God does not care
* that things will never get any better
* that we cannot have victory
* that we have no hope

Remember that our spiritual enemy, Satan, attacks us through our minds. We need to obey Scripture's command to cast down every thought that goes against what we know about God and bring our thoughts into obedience to Christ (2 Co.10:5-6; Ph.4:8). At the same time, we need to declare in faith what we know to be true about God (2 Co.4:13). By standing on the promises of God's Word and believing what He tells us, we are resisting the devil's influence, and *he* will eventually flee from us (Js.4:7; Mt.4:11).

> **We are hard pressed on every side, but not crushed; perplexed, but not in despair; persecuted, but not abandoned; struck down, but not destroyed. We always carry around in our body the death of Jesus, so that the life of Jesus may also be revealed in our body. For we who are alive are always being given over to death for Jesus' sake, so that his life may be revealed in our mortal body. So then, death is at work in us, but life is at work**

6 Warren W. Wiersbe. *The Bible Exposition Commentary*. WORD*search* CROSS e-book.

7 Thoraf Gilbrant and Gregory A. Lint, eds. *The Complete Biblical Library: The Old Testament Hebrew-English Dictionary*. WORD*search* CROSS e-book.

8 R. Laird Harris, ed. *Theological Wordbook of the Old Testament*. WORD*search* CROSS e-book.

9 Derek Kidner. *Psalms 73-150*, p.297.

in you. It is written: "I believed; therefore I have spoken." With that same spirit of faith we also believe and therefore speak (2 Co.4:8-13).

We live by faith, not by sight (2 Co.5:7).

For everyone born of God overcomes the world. This is the victory that has overcome the world, even our faith (1 Jn.5:4).

I believed; therefore I said, "I am greatly afflicted" (Ps.116:10).

I will tell of the kindnesses of the LORD, the deeds for which he is to be praised, according to all the LORD has done for us—yes, the many good things he has done for the house of Israel, according to his compassion and many kindnesses (Is.63:7).

3 (74:18-23) **Express concern for God's name and for His people.**

Without question, the basis for the psalmist's prayer was his burden for his beloved nation and its people who were suffering at the hands of their enemy. But he was also motivated by another concern: the mocking of God's holy name by Israel's oppressors. He concluded his prayer by expressing his concern for God's name and for His people.

a. Ask God to remember how the enemy (foolish people) mocked His name (v.18).

The psalmist was jealous for the LORD and could not bear to hear the enemy reproach or scoff at God. These foolish people actually blasphemed the LORD's holy name (Yahweh, Jehovah), the name by which He made His covenant with Israel. Having raided God's house and captured His people, they then mocked His power and faithfulness to the Israelites. The psalmist brought this to God's attention, asking Him to remember how these fools mocked His holy name. By calling on God to remember, he was not only asking God to keep it before Him but also to do something about it (v.2).

b. Ask God not to turn His people over to the enemy—not permanently (vv.19-21).

The psalmist pleaded with the LORD not to turn His beloved people, His dove, over to their blasphemous enemy for ever, not to deliver their souls "to *wild beasts*" (v.19ᵃ). *Dove* is a term of endearment. *Wild beasts* (chayyah) means "living things, but its most common translation is animals or beasts."[10] Most reliable translations render it as beasts or wild beasts. The image is that of a small, helpless dove being viciously devoured by a wild beast.

In asking God to deliver His oppressed people, the psalmist made three specific requests:
➤ That God would not forget the lives of the afflicted (v.19ᵇ). *Afflicted* (ani) describes those suffering from some kind of painful distress.
➤ That God would not forget His covenant with Israel (v.20). In a time when the land was filled with darkness and cruelty, or violence, the psalmist called on God to stand by His promises to His chosen people. The great British preacher Charles Spurgeon describes this as the "master key" of Asaph's prayer. "Heaven's gate must open to this. God is not a man that he should lie; his covenant he will not break, nor alter the thing that hath gone forth out of his lips."[11]
➤ That God would not allow His oppressed people to be disgraced or humiliated (v.21). Instead, the psalmist prayed that they would be filled with praise to God for delivering them.

c. Ask God to rise up and defend His cause (vv.22-23).

The heartbroken psalmist concluded by asking God to rise up and to overthrow the enemy for His own sake. "Defend your cause"—defend Yourself and Your holy name—was the psalmist's prayer (v.22). Once again, he implored God to remember and to do something about the fools who continually mocked Him. He begged God not to forget the boastful claims and constant uproar of His enemies against Him (v.23). *Ignore* (shakakh) "generally denotes...a willful choice to ignore something that a person knows he is to do."[12] In other words, the psalmist called on God not to ignore them but to turn His wrath upon His foes for the glory and honor of *His* holy name.

Thought 1. Our prayers and our lives should revolve around a fervent passion for the glory of God's name. God's name is holy, and it represents everything that He is—His character, faithfulness, and power. Certainly, our needs and the needs of others should stir us to pray. Jesus taught us to ask boldly and persistently for whatever we desire. But He also taught us to pray, "Yours is the kingdom, and the power, and the glory, for ever" (Mt.6:13, NKJV, HCSB). We should view everything that happens in our lives, our communities, our churches, our nations, and our world in light of God's glory. Above all else, we should pray for God to act according to what will most glorify and honor His holy name.

He said to them, "When you pray, say: "'Father, hallowed be your name, your kingdom come (Lu.11:2).

---

10 Spiros Zodhiates. *AMG Complete Word Study Dictionary*. WORDsearch CROSS e-book.

11 Charles Spurgeon. *Treasury of David*. WORDsearch CROSS e-book.
12 Thoraf Gilbrant and Gregory A. Lint, eds. *The Complete Biblical Library: The Old Testament Hebrew-English Dictionary*. WORDsearch CROSS e-book.

Are they not the ones who are slandering the noble name of him to whom you belong? (Js.2:7).

"You shall not misuse the name of the LORD your God, for the LORD will not hold anyone guiltless who misuses his name (Ex.20:7).

Let them praise your great and awesome name—he is holy (Ps.99:3).

Let them praise the name of the LORD, for his name alone is exalted; his splendor is above the earth and the heavens (Ps.148:13).

For my own sake, for my own sake, I do this. How can I let myself be defamed? I will not yield my glory to another (Is.48:11).

	PSALM 75 **What Your Focus & Goal Should Be in Light of God's Coming Judgment, 75:1-10** *For the director of music. [To the tune of] "Do Not Destroy." A psalm of Asaph. A song.*	5 Do not lift your horns against heaven; do not speak with outstretched neck.'" 6 No one from the east or the west or from the desert can exalt a man. 7 But it is God who judges: He brings one down, he exalts another.	2) Stop being defiant, stubborn, stiffnecked
1. Give thanks to God a. Because He is near b. Because He has done so many wonderful deeds **2. Pay attention to God's Word** a. Because He alone will choose the time to bring justice to all b. Because He alone brings stability when trouble & turmoil strike **3. Heed God's warning** a. He warns both the arrogant & the wicked 1) Stop boasting & rebelling	**W**e give thanks to you, O God, we give thanks, for your Name is near; men tell of your wonderful deeds. 2 You say, "I choose the appointed time; it is I who judge uprightly. 3 When the earth and all its people quake, it is I who hold its pillars firm. Selah 4 To the arrogant I say, 'Boast no more,' and to the wicked, 'Do not lift up your horns.	8 In the hand of the LORD is a cup full of foaming wine mixed with spices; he pours it out, and all the wicked of the earth drink it down to its very dregs. 9 As for me, I will declare this forever; I will sing praise to the God of Jacob. 10 I will cut off the horns of all the wicked, but the horns of the righteous will be lifted up.	b. He warns all people 1) God alone exalts a person • He alone is the Judge • He alone decides whom He will exalt or put down 2) God is the one who punishes the wicked: They must drink the cup of God's wrath **4. Bear strong witness about God's coming judgment** a. Declare His judgment continually & sing praise to God b. Declare exactly what God says 1) He will cut off the strength (horn) of the wicked 2) He will exalt the righteous

PSALM 75

What Your Focus and Goal Should Be in Light of God's Coming Judgment, 75:1-10

(75:1-10) **Introduction:** many popular books and movies spawn sequels, subsequent works that continue or build upon the theme of the preceding work. In a sense, Psalm 75 is a sequel to Psalm 73. In the seventy-third psalm, Asaph was deeply troubled over the prosperity of the wicked. By the time he wrote Psalm 75, he had witnessed God's judgment come upon the wicked. As he led the people to give thanks to God, he shared what he had learned.

Some commentators think the occasion for Psalm 75 was God's miraculous destruction of the Assyrian army when Sennacherib threatened Israel (2 K.18-19). They believe that like Psalm 74, this psalm was written by the descendants of Asaph who bore his name. However, any number of events that transpired in Israel during Asaph's lifetime could be its background. There is no reason to think that it was not written by Asaph himself.

The heading includes the instruction, "Do Not Destroy." It may be an instruction to sing the psalm to the tune of a familiar song by this name. Or, it may be a directive to carefully preserve the psalm (see Introduction—Psalm 57 for more discussion).

Psalm 75 is a congregational song in which the people give thanks to God for His justice. It serves as a warning to the wicked and a comforting reminder to the righteous that God will, in His good time, judge all ungodly evildoers. This is, *What Your Focus and Goal Should Be in Light of God's Coming Judgment*, 75:1-10.

1. Give thanks to God (v.1).
2. Pay attention to God's word (vv.2-3).
3. Heed God's warning (vv.4-8).
4. Bear strong witness about God's coming judgment (vv.9-10).

1 (75:1) **Give thanks to God.**
Having seen God at work in an amazing way, the psalmist led the congregation to give thanks to Him. God had done great things for them, and they were grateful. The repetition of *we give thanks* emphasizes the depth of their gratitude.

a. Because He is near (v.1).
Seeing God at work assured the psalmist that God was near His people. He had heard their cries, and He had answered their prayers. God's *name* usually represents all that He is, His character and attributes. Here, it is a symbol of His presence. The congregation gave thanks to God because He had proven He was among them, ready to act in their behalf (De.4:7; Je.23:23).

b. Because He has done so many wonderful deeds (v.1).
God's presence among His people was demonstrated by the wondrous works He had performed. Israel's history was marked by God's supernatural deeds, beginning with the parting of the Red Sea. But the miracle for which the people thanked God here was a recent one. He had somehow intervened in a current crisis and done what only He could do for His chosen people. Most likely, He had defeated an enemy that rose up against Israel.

Thought 1. We should always be careful to give thanks to God for all that He does for us. Ingratitude is a shameful sin. In fact, Paul names it as one of the traits that will characterize the ungodly people of the perilous last days. It is listed alongside some of the worst sins imaginable (2 Ti.3:1-4).

We need to cultivate grateful hearts. This we can do by staying alert and by observing every good thing God does for us. The psalmist gave thanks for God's presence with His people and for God's wonderful works in their behalf. On any given day, we have much to be thankful for: life, water, food, air, rain, sunshine, God's presence, care, guidance, strength, salvation, and a host of other daily blessings. We should express our gratitude to God daily by offering the "sacrifice of praise—the fruit of lips that confess his name" (He.13:15).

> **Always giving thanks to God the Father for everything, in the name of our Lord Jesus Christ (Ep.5:20).**
>
> **Do not be anxious about anything, but in everything, by prayer and petition, with thanksgiving, present your requests to God (Ph.4:6).**
>
> **Give thanks in all circumstances, for this is God's will for you in Christ Jesus (1 Th.5:18).**
>
> **When you have eaten and are satisfied, praise the LORD your God for the good land he has given you (De.8:10).**
>
> **Enter his gates with thanksgiving and his courts with praise; give thanks to him and praise his name (Ps.100:4).**

2 (75:2-3) Pay attention to God's Word.

Psalm 75 starts out with the people speaking to God but quickly changes to God speaking to the people. In the midst of a serious crisis, God assured His people that He had everything under control. The people were not only grateful for God's works, but also for His Word. Paying attention to what He said brought peace in the midst of turmoil.

a. Because He alone will choose the time to bring justice to all (v.2).

God spoke and revealed a significant fact to His people: in the time of His own choosing, He will bring justice to all. God reminded the people of two great truths concerning His execution of justice. First, He is upright, just and fair. Second, *He* is in control; we are not. God said that He will righteously judge all people, but He will do it at the time He appoints, according to *His* schedule.

b. Because He alone brings stability when trouble and turmoil strike (v.3).

It appeared to God's people that the world was falling apart and the very foundations of society were *quak-*

ing (mugh), that is, shaking, melting away, crumbling. But God comforted their troubled spirits, assuring them once again of His control. He bears up the pillars of this world. He holds everything together, in spite of the best efforts of the wicked to tear the world apart (1 S.2:8; Co.1:17; He.1:3).

Thought 1. God's Word is sufficient for every issue of life. Instead of worrying and fretting, we need to pay attention to what God has already told us in His Word. The evil and turmoil in our sinful world will only worsen as we grow closer to the return of Jesus Christ (2 Ti.3:13). In fact, we will always have trials that challenge our security and faith. Nevertheless, God's Word is filled with examples, principles, and promises that will give us peace in the midst of our turmoil. Knowing that, it is up to us to pay attention to them and to believe them.

> **For everything that was written in the past was written to teach us, so that through endurance and the encouragement of the Scriptures we might have hope (Ro.15:4).**
>
> **These things happened to them as examples and were written down as warnings for us, on whom the fulfillment of the ages has come (1 Co.10:11).**
>
> **And we also thank God continually because, when you received the word of God, which you heard from us, you accepted it not as the word of men, but as it actually is, the word of God, which is at work in you who believe (1 Th.2:13).**
>
> **And we have the word of the prophets made more certain, and you will do well to pay attention to it, as to a light shining in a dark place, until the day dawns and the morning star rises in your hearts (2 Pe.1:19).**

3 (75:4-8) Heed God's warning.

God also addressed the evildoers who were troubling Israel. He said He will bring down all who arrogantly rise up against Him and His people. They will face the full force of His fierce judgment.

a. He warns both the arrogant and the wicked (vv.4-5).

Referring to them as fools, God issued a grim warning to the arrogant and the wicked. Notice the terms used in these verses. Fools are those who proudly exalt themselves over God. "Boast no more" is a warning not to rise up in rebellion against God's commands and purposes. "Do not lift up your horn" depicts an animal that refuses to be controlled by its master, "holding its head high so a yoke [can] not be put on it."[1] Like people who are stiff-necked, it is a picture of rebellion. Simply stated, God warned the ungodly to stop boasting and rebelling and to stop being defiant, stubborn, and stiff-necked toward Him.

b. He warns all people (vv.6-8).

God released a warning that all people should heed: He alone is in control. He alone exalts a person (v.6). Promotion does not come from this world, as represented by the east, west, and south. Promotion comes from the one direction not mentioned here: the north, where God resides. He alone is the Judge (v.7). He alone decides whom He will lift up and whom He will bring down.

More importantly, God is the one who punishes the wicked (v.8). God's wrath is pictured here as a cup of wine that He holds in His hand. The wine is red, indicating that it has not been diluted to weaken its intoxicating powers. It is full-strength, fermented wine (Pr.23:31). Furthermore, it is full of mixture—spices and other substances (drugs) that have been added to make it even more intoxicating.

When thoroughly understood, this picture is terrifying. God will pour out His full, undiluted wrath upon the wicked, and they will have to drink it—all of it, even the dregs. The *dregs* (shemer) are the particles that settle at the bottom of the wine bottle. These bitter bits were usually filtered out as it was being poured from the bottle to the cup. Here, they illustrate the fact that God's judgment will not be filtered or reduced in any way.

Thought 1. Again and again, God warns us of His coming judgment. Many have the idea that there is only one general judgment at which all people will stand. However, Scripture teaches that there are different judgments for different groups of people.

As believers, we are free of condemnation for our sins, having been washed in the blood of Christ. Yet we are not free from God's correction for our sins. God warns us that He will chasten or discipline us—His beloved sons and daughters—if we continue in sin (1 Co.11:31-32; He.12:5-11). We will always have to face the consequences of our sins here on earth.

God also warns us repeatedly that we must stand before Christ to give an account of our works and service for Him. If we have been faithful, we will receive a reward. If we have been unfaithful, we will suffer the painful loss of rewards we could have received (1 Co.3:11-15; 2 Co.5:9-10).

Along with these warnings are the many warnings of God's Word against sinful and destructive behavior. For example, God's Word warns that pride leads to destruction, and that the desire for wealth brings

many temptations and traps that result in great sorrow (Pr.16:18; 1 Ti.6:9-10).

In light of God's coming judgment, we need to heed every warning in God's Word. One of the great lies of Satan is that we will not reap what we have sown, that God will not follow through with the judgment He has promised (Ge.3:3-4; Ga.6:7-8). But God will not be mocked. He means what He says, and He will do exactly what He says He will do.

> **So then, each of us will give an account of himself to God (Ro.14:12).**
>
> **His work will be shown for what it is, because the Day will bring it to light. It will be revealed with fire, and the fire will test the quality of each man's work. If what he has built survives, he will receive his reward. If it is burned up, he will suffer loss; he himself will be saved, but only as one escaping through the flames (1 Co.3:13-15).**
>
> **But if we judged ourselves, we would not come under judgment. When we are judged by the Lord, we are being disciplined so that we will not be condemned with the world (1 Co.11:31-32).**
>
> **For we must all appear before the judgment seat of Christ, that each one may receive what is due him for the things done while in the body, whether good or bad (2 Co.5:10).**
>
> **I thought in my heart, "God will bring to judgment both the righteous and the wicked, for there will be a time for every activity, a time for every deed" (Ec.3:17).**
>
> **For God will bring every deed into judgment, including every hidden thing, whether it is good or evil (Ec.12:14).**

4 (75:9-10) **Bear strong witness about God's coming judgment.**

The psalmist concluded by making a firm resolution. He determined to bear strong witness about God's coming judgment to others.

a. Declare His judgment continually and sing praise to God (v.9).

Asaph made a commitment to declare what He had learned from God: that God will judge the wicked. In addition, he committed to praise God for His justice and His protection of the people.

b. Declare exactly what God says (v.10).

The psalmist pledged to declare exactly what God had said, just as He had said it. God will cut off the horns of the wicked, and He will exalt the horns of the

---

1 Steven Lawson and Max Anders. *Holman Old Testament Commentary—Psalms.* WORD*search* CROSS e-book.

216

righteous. The *horn* is a symbol of strength. God was saying that He would make the wicked powerless against Him and His people. And he would lift up the strength of the righteous over their oppressors.

Thought 1. We have a sacred responsibility to bear witness about God's judgment to those who do not know Him. We are watchmen over the souls of men, having been charged to warn the wicked to repent and turn to God (Eze.3:18; 33:7-10). Christ has entrusted us with the ministry of reconciling others to God (2 Co.5:18-21). Paul was fully aware of his responsibility to warn others about God's coming judgment. Because he understood the "fear of the Lord," he persuaded men to be reconciled to God (2 Co.5:11).

The most frightening scene in all of Scripture is the Great White Throne Judgment. There, all the unsaved of all the ages will stand before the Lord, be judged for their sinful deeds, and then be cast into the lake of fire for all eternity (Re.20:11-15). We know that this dreadful day is coming. With God's coming judgment in mind, we need to focus on warning the wicked that this will be their eternal fate if they do not repent and receive Christ.

> But you will receive power when the Holy Spirit comes on you; and you will be my witnesses in Jerusalem, and in all Judea and Samaria, and to the ends of the earth" (Ac.1:8).
>
> Therefore, I declare to you today that I am innocent of the blood of all men. For I have not hesitated to proclaim to you the whole will of God (Ac.20:26-27).
>
> As Paul discoursed on righteousness, self-control and the judgment to come, Felix was afraid and said, "That's enough for now! You may leave. When I find it convenient, I will send for you" (Ac.24:25).
>
> The wrath of God is being revealed from heaven against all the godlessness and wickedness of men who suppress the truth by their wickedness (Ro.1:18).
>
> Since, then, we know what it is to fear the Lord, we try to persuade men. What we are is plain to God, and I hope it is also plain to your conscience (2 Co.5:11).
>
> "Son of man, I have made you a watchman for the house of Israel; so hear the word I speak and give them warning from me. When I say to the wicked, 'O wicked man, you will surely die,' and you do not speak out to dissuade him from his ways, that wicked man will die for his sin, and I will hold you accountable for his blood. But if you do warn the wicked man to turn from his ways and he does not do so, he will die for his sin, but you will have saved yourself. "Son of man, say to the house of Israel, 'This is what you are saying: "Our offenses and sins weigh us down, and we are wasting away because of them. How then can we live?"' (Eze.33:7-10).

	PSALM 76 **When God Gives You Victory Over the Enemy, 76:1-12** *For the director of music. With stringed instruments. A psalm of Asaph. A song.*	6 At your rebuke, O God of Jacob, both horse and chariot lie still. 7 You alone are to be feared. Who can stand before you when you are angry? 8 From heaven you pronounced judgment, and the land feared and was quiet— 9 When you, O God, rose up to judge, to save all the afflicted of the land. Selah	2) It is His rebuke that destroys the political & military power of nations **2. Fear God alone—the one true God**

1. Praise the only living & true God
a. He dwells among His people (Judah) & is known by them
  1) His presence fills the worship center
  2) He triumphs over His people's enemies: A picture of Christ's victory on the cross, He.2:14-18
b. He is perfect in glory (holiness & power): More majestic than the mountains
  1) It is His holy presence that dooms the rebellious: They lose all they have when they sink into their final sleep
	In Judah is God known: his name is great in Israel.
	2 His tent is in Salem, his dwelling place in Zion.
	3 There he broke the flashing arrows, the shields and the swords, the weapons of war. Selah
	4 You are resplendent with light, more majestic than mountains rich with game.
	5 Valiant men lie plundered, they sleep their last sleep; not one of the warriors can lift his hands.
		10 Surely your wrath against men brings you praise, and the survivors of your wrath are restrained.
		11 Make vows to the LORD your God and fulfill them; let all the neighboring lands bring gifts to the One to be feared.
		12 He breaks the spirit of rulers; he is feared by the kings of the earth.
			a. Bc. no one can stand before His anger when He pronounces judgment
			  1) People can only fear
			  2) People can only be silent
			b. Bc. He arises in judgment for three very specific purposes
			  1) To save the oppressed
			  2) To stir people to praise Him as the victor over evil
			  3) To restrain the survivors of His wrath (from evil)
			3. Recommit your life & service to the LORD & fulfill your vows
			a. He is the One to be feared: He stirs people to submit & to bring Him tribute
			b. Bc. He breaks the spirit of rulers & arouses them to fear Him

PSALM 76

When God Gives You Victory Over the Enemy, 76:1-12

(76:1-12) Introduction: twentieth Century American General Douglas MacArthur was also a renowned statesman. One of his most famous quotes is, "In war there is no substitute for victory."

The New Testament repeatedly reminds us that, as believers, we are soldiers fighting in a war. It is not a war against flesh and blood but against spiritual enemies (Ep.6:12). This war is being fought on many fronts, from our individual lives to our churches, our communities, our nations, and all across the world. In our personal lives, we face three primary enemies:

➤ Satan and his demonic forces

➤ A world system ruled by Satan

➤ Our sinful nature, referred to in the Bible as the flesh

In our spiritual battles, as in war, there is no substitute for victory. Christ died to give us victory over sin, Satan, and death. Through Him, we can be victorious. Still, we have to fight. And we have to pray for the Lord's strength as we strive to discipline ourselves, avoid temptation, and resist the enemy. Victories are glorious experiences, and when God gives us victory, we should respond appropriately.

Psalm 76 was written on the heels of a great victory in Israel. As in the previous psalm, many scholars believe that the victory given Israel was God's destruction of the Assyrian army (2 K.18-19; Is.37-38). The Septuagint (an early Greek translation of the Hebrew Scriptures) includes a note stating that Psalm 76 was composed for this occasion. Specific statements in the psalm certainly seem to favor this opinion (v.5).

Psalm 76 is designated as one of Asaph's psalms. If the Assyrian invasion was its setting, Asaph's descendants—a group of temple musicians known by his name—would have written it. However, as in Psalm 75, one of Israel's victories during Asaph's life could have prompted its writing.

It is thrilling when God gives us victory over an enemy, be it temptation, a sinful habit, a personal weakness, or some other circumstance in our lives. But we should never presume upon God's goodness, never take God's power or anything else that God does for us for granted. Rather, we should always respond to the grace and victory He gives us with praise and thanksgiving. This is, *When God Gives You Victory Over the Enemy,* 76:1-12.

1. Praise the only living and true God (vv.1-6).
2. Fear God alone—the one true God (vv.7-10).
3. Recommit your life and service to the LORD and fulfill your vows (vv.11-12).

1 (76:1-6) **Praise the only living and true God.**
The psalmist began this triumphant song by exalting the source of Israel's victory, the only living and true God. God was with His people, and He had demonstrated His powerful presence. He had delivered them from their attackers.

a. He dwells among His people (Judah) and is known by them (vv.1-3).

Asaph expressed gratitude and praise because God had made Himself known to His people, the Israelites (v.1). Throughout the entire land, the name of God was great—magnified, honored, proven worthy of the highest esteem and praise. Judah, Israel, Salem, and Zion all identify this place where God had so uniquely manifested His power and glory:

➤ *Judah* is the region of Israel where Jerusalem is located.

➤ *Israel*, of course, is the nation.

➤ *Salem* is the ancient name of Jerusalem (Ge.14:18).

➤ *Zion* may also refer to Jerusalem or, more specifically, to the precise location of the temple.

God had made Himself known, first, through His glorious presence that filled the worship center in Jerusalem (v.2). God is present everywhere, but He dwelled among His people in a unique way in the tabernacle, and later in the temple built by Solomon in the Holy City.

Interestingly, *tent* (sokh) is not the Hebrew word normally used of the tent where God's presence dwelled with His people. It is the word used of a lion's den, the place where the ferocious beast lies in wait to attack (Ps.10:9; Je.25:38). Therefore, God is praised here as Israel's fierce defender. He lay in wait in the tabernacle—His *dwelling place in Zion*—ready to pounce on anyone who threatened His beloved people. *Dwelling place* (me'onah) is also used primarily in the Old Testament of lions' dens (Jb.38:40; Ps.104:22; Song 4:8).

Second, God made Himself known through His mighty power. In a show of unparalleled strength, He had triumphed over His people's enemies (v.3). There, in Zion, He annihilated those who rose up against Israel, destroying them and their weapons.

b. He is perfect in glory (holiness and power): More majestic than the mountains (vv.4-6).

The psalmist also praised God because He is *resplendent with light* (or). Truly, God's holiness and power had shone forth like the flaming sun as He crushed Israel's foes.

The psalmist declared that God is more excellent or majestic than the mountains of prey. The meaning of this term varies widely among scholars. Insightful commentator J.J. Stewart Perowne offered an explanation consistent with the image of the lion's den (v.2). The mountains are the mountains of Jerusalem, where God's presence dwells among His people. Those who dare invade His territory in hopes of preying on His people quickly become His prey.[1] The citizens of Jeru- salem celebrated the splendor of their city's mountains. Yet the psalmist declared that their grandeur did not compare to the majesty of God, who diligently defended His people in those mountains.

The army that dared rise up against Israel was filled with valiant men (v.5). It may mean that they were determined, courageous warriors, or it may mean that they were hardhearted and rebellious toward God (Is.46:12). Regardless, they were doomed by God's holy presence. Under His mighty power, they slept their last sleep. Simply stated, they died in their sleep. *Slept* is in the Hebrew perfect tense, suggesting that they fell asleep, never to awaken again (Jer.51:39, 57).[2] Apparently, this statement points to God's slaying of the Assyrian soldiers as they slept (2 K.19:35). "None of the warriors can life his hands" means that these dead warriors could not use their hands to wield their weapons against Israel. When they sank into their final sleep, they lost their power to fight.

The psalmist declared a significant fact: God's rebuke can destroy any political or military power that rises up against His chosen people (v.6). The chariot and horse represent the military power of nations. Chariot may refer to the vehicle itself or to the driver of the chariot. "Lie still" may correspond to the language of the previous verse, or, it may convey information not reported in the historical accounts of the slaying of the Assyrian army, that God destroyed Sennacherib's chariots and horses along with his warriors (2 K.19:35; Is.37:26).

Thought 1. When we win a victory over an enemy, we need to recognize God as the source of that victory and offer praise to Him. Remember, Scripture identifies our enemies as the world, the flesh, and the devil. Satan and his evil forces are far more powerful than we are, so we cannot overcome them in our own strength. We can only be victorious through "His mighty power" and by clothing ourselves with the spiritual armor that God has furnished (Ep.6:10-18). Furthermore, we cannot overcome our flesh, our sinful nature, except through the power of His indwelling Spirit (Ga.5:16-17; Ro.7:14-8:13). We gain victory over the world only through our faith in Jesus Christ (1 Jn.5:4-5).

Our victories are *God's* victories. We must never take the glory for what God has done. Rather, we must always be careful to give all praise and honor to Him.

> **No, in all these things we are more than conquerors through him who loved us (Ro.8:37).**
> **But thanks be to God! He gives us the victory through our Lord Jesus Christ (1 Co.15:57).**

---

1 J.J. Stewart Perowne, *The Book of Psalms*, p.355.

2 Franz Delitzsch. *Commentary on the Old Testament.* WORD*search* CROSS e-book.

But thanks be to God, who always leads us in triumphal procession in Christ and through us spreads everywhere the fragrance of the knowledge of him (2 Co.2:14).

The weapons we fight with are not the weapons of the world. On the contrary, they have divine power to demolish strongholds (2 Co.10:4).

For everyone born of God overcomes the world. This is the victory that has overcome the world, even our faith. Who is it that overcomes the world? Only he who believes that Jesus is the Son of God (1 Jn.5:4-5).

Through you we push back our enemies; through your name we trample our foes (Ps.44:5).

Thought 2. This passage praising God for His presence and power among His people is prophetic of the Messiah, Jesus Christ. Note the following points of comparison:

➤ God has made Himself known through His Son (v.1; Jn.1:18; 12:45; 14:9; Co.1:15; He.1:3).

➤ Christ came out of the tribe of Judah, was born in Bethlehem, which is in Judah (v.1; Mt.1:2; Lu.3:33; He.7:4; Mic.5:2).

➤ *Salem* (shalem) means peaceful (v.2). Jesus Christ is the Prince of Peace. He made peace for us through His cross. When He comes again and reigns from David's throne, peace will extend throughout the entire earth (Is.9:6; Mic.5:5; Ac.10:36; Ep.2:14-17; Co.1:20).

➤ *Salem* was the name by which Jerusalem was known in ancient times. Its use here links our Savior to Melchisedec, king and High Priest of Salem of old, and a clear type of Christ (Ge.14:18; He.5:6; 7:1-6, 14:17).

➤ God's victories over His people's enemies point to Christ's victory on the cross (v.3; Ge.3:15; Co.2:14-15; He.2:14-18).

➤ The destruction of weapons points to the reign of Christ, when peace will cover the earth and weapons will be converted to useful tools (Is.2:4; Mic.4:3; Zech.9:9-10).

He is the image of the invisible God, the firstborn over all creation (Col.1:15).

Having canceled the written code, with its regulations, that was against us and that stood opposed to us; he took it away, nailing it to the cross. And having disarmed the powers and authorities, he made a public spectacle of them, triumphing over them by the cross (Col.2:14-15).

The Son is the radiance of God's glory and the exact representation of his being, sustaining all things by his powerful word. After he had provided purification for sins, he sat down at the right hand of the Majesty in heaven (He.1:3).

Since the children have flesh and blood, he too shared in their humanity so that by his death he might destroy him who holds the power of death—that is, the devil (He.2:14).

For to us a child is born, to us a son is given, and the government will be on his shoulders. And he will be called Wonderful Counselor, Mighty God, Everlasting Father, Prince of Peace (Is.9:6).

2 (76:7-10) **Fear God alone—the one true God.** Having seen the deadly results of God's judgment, the psalmist declared that God alone should be feared by all people. He is the Divine Warrior, armed with His fierce wrath. He stands ever ready to destroy all who dare rise up against Him, His purposes, and His people. Nobody can prevail against Him.

a. Because no one can stand before His anger when He pronounces judgment (vv.7-8).
The field of fresh corpses proclaimed a critical warning to the entire world: no one can stand before God's anger when He pronounces judgment (v.7). Commentator Donald M. Williams aptly notes that God's anger "is not simply an emotional outburst. It is a manifestation of His *'judgment'* which is [supreme] and absolute."[3] When God wiped out the Assyrian army, the world heard from heaven (v.8). The silent execution of Sennacherib's soldiers preached the power and judgment of God. In response to this supernatural demonstration of furious wrath, people could only fear and be still or silent.

b. Because He arises in judgment for three very specific purposes (vv.9-10).
As the psalmist reflected on the slaughter of the Assyrian forces, the Holy Spirit revealed three specific purposes for which God arises in judgment:

First, God arises in judgment to save the meek or oppressed of the earth (v.9). God is the defender of those who cannot defend themselves. When wicked men cruelly afflict God's people, they can expect to be confronted by God's wrath.

Second, God arises in judgment to stir people to praise Him (v.10a). Asaph declared that God's execution of His wrath would bring Him praise. When God judges the wicked, people glorify Him, for He has shown Himself to be the victor over evil.

---

3 Donald Williams. *Psalms 73-150*, p.41.

Third, God arises in judgment to restrain those who witness His wrath, restrain them from committing evil (v.10[b]). The meaning of "the survivors of your wrath are restrained" is also unclear. The Hebrew text is difficult to translate, and scholars vary both in its translation and its meaning. The probable setting for this psalm, God's judgment on the Assyrian army, provides the best explanation. When those who survived God's wrath arose the next morning to find 185,000 corpses scattered across the Assyrian camp, they retreated in terror (2 K.19:35-36). Witnessing God's wrath restrained them from following through with the evil they had planned against Israel.

However, this statement may have another meaning. The most literal translation of the remark is "the remainder or remnant of wrath You will gird Yourself with." This is reflected in the NKJV, NASB, and ESV. *Restrain* (chagar), here, means to gird up. It is the word used of a soldier girding or fastening his sword, wearing it on a belt around his waist (De.1:41; 1 S.17:39; 25:13; 2 S.21:16). God is pictured here as girding Himself with His fierce wrath, ready to draw and wield it against any who dare rise up against Him. If this is the meaning, then the statement is a strong warning: God has not used up all of His wrath. He has more remaining, and He stands ready to use it against other evildoers.

Either understanding of the text supports the same point: God's wrath is a deterrent to evildoers. Seeing God's wrath keeps some people from following through with their wicked intentions.

Thought 1. Sadly, but truly, we live in a world in which "there is no fear of God" (Ro.3:18)." God has revealed His wrath against all of humanity's ungodliness and unrighteousness (Ro.1:18). We know "the terror of the Lord," and, like Paul, we need to persuade people to repent and be reconciled to God before it is too late (2 Co.5:11, 14-20). Too many preachers and teachers proclaim God's love while neglecting to declare God's wrath. Certainly, we should never fail to emphasize God's unfathomable love for all sinners. At the same time, though, we cannot fail to emphasize that God's fierce judgment awaits all who reject Him. It is our duty—not an option—to sound the alarm, warning people of God's wrath and passionately urging them to fear God and repent.

> **Do not be afraid of those who kill the body but cannot kill the soul. Rather, be afraid of the One who can destroy both soul and body in hell (Mt.10:28).**
>
> **But accepts men from every nation who fear him and do what is right (Ac.10:35).**
>
> **He said in a loud voice, "Fear God and give him glory, because the hour of his judgment has come. Worship him who made the heavens, the earth, the sea and the springs of water" (Re.14:7).**
>
> **Do not be wise in your own eyes; fear the LORD and shun evil (Pr.3:7).**
>
> **Now all has been heard; here is the conclusion of the matter: Fear God and keep his commandments, for this is the whole [duty] of man. For God will bring every deed into judgment, including every hidden thing, whether it is good or evil (Ec.12:13-14).**
>
> **The LORD Almighty is the one you are to regard as holy, he is the one you are to fear, he is the one you are to dread (Is.8:13).**

3 (76:11-12) **Recommit your life and service to the LORD and fulfill your vows.**
Psalm 76 closes with a challenge to God's people and a warning to the rulers of other nations. *The fear of God* is the theme of both admonitions. God's people should recommit themselves to His service and fulfill their vows. The rulers of the earth should beware of rising up against God and His people.

a. He is the One to be feared: He stirs people to submit and to bring Him tribute (v.11).
The psalmist called on the victorious people of Israel to recommit themselves to the fear of God, that is, to obeying, serving, and submitting to Him. As part of that recommitment, they should pay their vows to the LORD and fulfill all the promises they had made to God when they sought His deliverance. The psalmist also called on the people of the surrounding nations to submit to God. They should bring Him presents or tribute as a statement of their fear of Him.

b. Because He breaks the spirit of rulers and arouses them to fear Him (v.12)
Finally, the psalmist warned other rulers: the LORD is God and King. Even Sennacherib, the mightiest king of his day, suddenly retreated from the bloody battlefield out of fear of God. His escape displayed that God had broken his spirit and humbled Assyria's arrogant king. Thus, all the princes and kings of the earth should strongly heed this warning.

A prophetic message is also evident here: the day will come when the princes and kings of the earth will either bow down to Jesus Christ or be destroyed by Him in judgment (Ps.2:6-12; Re.19:11-16).

Thought 1. Every victory that God grants should compel us to rededicate ourselves to Him. The sacrifices of thanksgiving include not only the praise of our lips but also the service of our hands. We are not to neglect doing good out of grateful hearts. God is pleased only when our words of praise are accompanied by our works of righteousness (He.13:15-16).

Of course, the greatest victory we will ever experience is the victory Christ won for us on the cross. And His sacrifice of mercy—His own life—deserves the greatest sacrifice we can offer: the presentation of our lives for His service (Ro.12:1).

Therefore, I urge you, brothers, in view of God's mercy, to offer your bodies as living sacrifices, holy and pleasing to God—this is your spiritual act of worship. Do not conform any longer to the pattern of this world, but be transformed by the renewing of your mind. Then you will be able to test and approve what God's will is—his good, pleasing and perfect will (Ro.12:1-2).

And he died for all, that those who live should no longer live for themselves but for him who died for them and was raised again (2 Co.5:15).

Through Jesus, therefore, let us continually offer to God a sacrifice of praise—the fruit of lips that confess his name. And do not forget to do good and to share with others, for with such sacrifices God is pleased (He.13:15-16).

This is how we know what love is: Jesus Christ laid down his life for us. And we ought to lay down our lives for our brothers (1 Jn.3:16).

All these now join their brothers the nobles, and bind themselves with a curse and an oath to follow the Law of God given through Moses the servant of God and to obey carefully all the commands, regulations and decrees of the LORD our Lord (Ne.10:29).

	PSALM 77 **When You Sink into the Darkness of Despair, 77:1-20** *For the director of music. For Jeduthun. Of Asaph. A psalm.*	the right hand of the Most High." 11 I will remember the deeds of the LORD; yes, I will remember your miracles of long ago. 12 I will meditate on all your works and consider all your mighty deeds.	a. Remember God's wonderful deeds & miracles in behalf of His people down through the ages b. Meditate on all of God's mighty works (in all of life & creation)
1. Cry out for God's help	I cried out to God for help; I cried out to God to hear me.	13 Your ways, O God, are holy. What god is so great as our God?	**3. Trust God to redeem (deliver) you**
a. Seek the LORD in the midst of your trouble 1) Cry out during the day 2) Cry out through the night 3) Cry until you are comforted	2 When I was in distress, I sought the Lord; at night I stretched out untiring hands and my soul refused to be comforted.	14 You are the God who performs miracles; you display your power among the peoples.	a. Bc. His ways are holy & perfect: He is beyond compare b. Bc. He is the true & living God who performs miracles & demonstrates His power
b. Share the depth of your anguish 1) How desperately you long for God's presence & help	3 I remembered you, O God, and I groaned; I mused, and my spirit grew faint. Selah	15 With your mighty arm you redeemed your people, the descendants of Jacob and Joseph. Selah	c. Bc. He redeems & saves His people: He delivered Israel
2) How you cannot sleep 3) How you are so troubled that you cannot speak 4) How you remember the former days of joy & song—days that you no longer experience	4 You kept my eyes from closing; I was too troubled to speak. 5 I thought about the former days, the years of long ago; 6 I remembered my songs in the night. My heart mused and my spirit inquired:	16 The waters saw you, O God, the waters saw you and writhed; the very depths were convulsed. 17 The clouds poured down water, the skies resounded with thunder; your arrows flashed back and forth.	1) He caused the waters of the Red Sea to shrink back & quake, as though fearful of His awesome presence 2) He caused the clouds to pour down rain, the thunder to rumble, & the lightning to flash
5) How you now question God • Will He reject you forever—never again show favor? • Have His mercy & unfailing love ceased? • Have His promises failed? • Has He forgotten to be gracious? • Has His anger against sin ended His compassion?	7 "Will the Lord reject forever? Will he never show his favor again? 8 Has his unfailing love vanished forever? Has his promise failed for all time? 9 Has God forgotten to be merciful? Has he in anger withheld his compassion?" Selah	18 Your thunder was heard in the whirlwind, your lightning lit up the world; the earth trembled and quaked. 19 Your path led through the sea, your way through the mighty waters, though your footprints were not seen.	3) He roared from the whirlwind & lit up the world with lightning: The earth shook from an earthquake 4) He opened up a path through the Red Sea
2. Draw hope from God's power	10 Then I thought, "To this I will appeal: the years of	20 You led your people like a flock by the hand of Moses and Aaron.	5) He led His people by appointing two men as their shepherds, Moses & Aaron

PSALM 77

When You Sink into the Darkness of Despair, 77:1-20

(77:1-20) **Introduction:** despair is a sly creature. Sometimes it comes over us gradually, slowly surrounding us until we are caught in its dark web. Whether an ongoing trial, an unresolved conflict, or a lingering illness—these and countless other issues can enable despair to slowly take hold of us.

At other times, despair swoops in unexpectedly, seizing us in its vice-like grip. A sudden death, the loss of a job, or any other devastating loss can push us instantly into despair's smothering depths.

When Asaph wrote Psalm 77, he was trapped in the darkness of despair. Scripture gives no indication of the specific circumstances that kept him in bondage. However, the use of singular pronouns throughout indicates a personal crisis as opposed to a national one. Psalm 77 seems to be consistent with Psalm 73, which reflects a

personal struggle for Asaph, whereas Psalms 74–76 clearly involve Israel.

The message of Psalm 77 is similar to that of many other psalms: God can lift our distressed spirits when we cry out to Him. By remembering God's past faithfulness, we can find the strength to walk through any present trouble. Even so, excellent commentator Herbert C. Leupold cautioned us to be careful to avoid two extremes as we study this psalm:

> *One is to regard the material offered in the psalm as though it presented a complete solution* [to Asaph's despair], *ready and final in all its parts, as though before the end of the psalm is reached the poet had fully recovered his balance. Such an approach is scarcely warranted.*

The other extreme is to insist that the tension described in the first half of the psalm is still present in [total] force by the time the end of the psalm is reached...[however,] we regard the writer as being well along on the road to recovery by the time the end of the psalm is reached. He has discovered a remedy; he has applied it; it has begun to work; a sure bit of solid ground has been recovered; from this vantage point the writer will be able presently to rehabilitate himself spiritually.[1]

Dr. Leupold's lesson is a valuable one: most depression is not instantly resolved. We do not suddenly jump up and out of the pit of despair. Rather, we climb out, one upward step at a time. As we remember God's past faithfulness, He gives us the strength we need to climb. The promises of God are what we hold on to as we pull ourselves out of depression. However, we should also remember that on some occasions, God does reach down and instantly rescue us, but always according to His will and purpose. He alone knows what we need in every situation to make us stronger and to conform us more and more into the image of Christ.

Psalm 77 reveals a man like the rest of us: a physical, emotional, spiritual human being who has ups and downs, highs and lows, good days and bad days. At this point in time, his emotions are raw and his words are unfiltered. And God's Spirit uses such a man to help lead us out of the pit of depression when we are lost in its darkness. This is, *When You Sink into the Darkness of Despair,* 77:1-20.

1. Cry out for God's help (vv.1-9).
2. Draw hope from God's power (vv.10-12).
3. Trust God to redeem (deliver) you (vv.13-20).

1 (77:1-9) Cry out for God's help.

Drowning in the depths of despair, Asaph cried out to God. "Cried out" reveals that he cried audibly or out loud, not just in his spirit. The repetition of *cried out* conveys the intense agony of his situation. His inner pain was so sharp that he could contain it no longer, finally giving way to heart-rending wails. He was clearly in need of God's help.

a. Seek the Lord in the midst of your trouble (v.2)

By saying "I stretched out untiring hands," Asaph was restating the fact that he earnestly sought the Lord in the midst of his trouble. All during the day and all through the night he reached out to God for comfort, but he could find no solace for his anguished soul. Feeling crushed by his heavy load, he continuously cried out for the Lord's help.

b. Share the depth of your anguish (vv.3-9).

Asaph also shared the extreme depth of his anguish. He desperately longed for God's presence and help, but remembering God brought him no relief (v.3). As he *mused* (siach) or meditated on his situation, going over it in his mind again and again, his spirit was overwhelmed. He was totally consumed by darkness and despair. *Grew faint* is an imperfect Hebrew verb, indicating that he continued to plunge deeper and deeper into hopelessness.

During the quiet of the night, Asaph's problems roared louder in his heart, making it impossible for him to sleep (v.4a). He was so troubled that he could not even speak reasonably about his situation (v.4b). His grieving mind was stuck in the past; he could not help but dwell on former days of joy and song (vv.5-6). The memory of these better times—days he no longer experienced—only added to the weight of his despair. Feeling hopeless and utterly forsaken, he fired off a series of questions aimed at God:

➢ Will He reject me forever—never again show me any favor (v.7)?
➢ Has His *unfailing love* (chesed)— His covenant love, His mercy—ceased forever (v.8a)?
➢ Have His promises failed (v.8b)?
➢ Has He forgotten to be merciful (v.9a)?
➢ Has His anger against sin ended His *compassion* (rachamim; see outline and notes—Ps.51:1-3 for more discussion)?

Thought 1. When we feel overwhelmed by trouble, no matter what it may be, we need to cry out to God for help. Sometimes our trials are so severe that it seems like our prayers are not helping. This is how Asaph felt. And like him, we must continue to cry out to God. Even when we think He is not listening, He hears us (v.1). Remember, we have a great High Priest who has experienced every one of our heartaches. He is touched with the feeling of our infirmities, and He helps us with our afflictions (He.4:14-16). Continue to seek the Lord when you are drowning in despair. He has promised His presence and help when we seek Him with all our hearts (Je.29:13).

> **For we do not have a high priest who is unable to sympathize with our weaknesses, but we have one who has been tempted in every way, just as we are— yet was without sin. Let us then approach the throne of grace with confidence, so that we may receive mercy and find grace to help us in our time of need (He.4:15-16).**
>
> **During the days of Jesus' life on earth, he offered up prayers and petitions with loud cries and tears to the one who could save him from death, and he was heard because of his reverent submission (He.5:7).**

---

1 H.C. Leupold. *Exposition of the Psalms,* p.554.

So we say with confidence, "The Lord is my helper; I will not be afraid. What can man do to me?" (He.13:6).

Then they cried to the LORD in their trouble, and he saved them from their distress (Ps.107:19).

I call on the LORD in my distress, and he answers me (Ps.120:1).

2 (77:10-12) Draw hope from God's power.

As Asaph sought the Lord, he found a way to deal with his grief: he drew hope from the mighty deeds God had performed in the past, the years when God had exercised His right hand, a symbol of His power. Note that translations and interpretations of verse 10 vary among Bible versions. Commentator Derek Kidner best resolves the confusion, explaining that "since two of its key words [*make appeal* and *years*] are open to various interpretations, the translation of the verse must ultimately be controlled by its compatibility with the passage it introduces. That passage (10-20) is an exultant act of worship, recalling the miracles of salvation."[2]

a. Remember God's wonderful deeds and miracles in behalf of His people down through the ages (v.11)
Asaph seized control of his mind and focused his thoughts on God's faithfulness and goodness. He then recalled the glorious deeds God had performed in the past, in behalf of His people. With all of this in mind, the psalmist could begin to feel his spirits lifting.

b. Meditate on all of God's mighty works (in all of life and creation) (v.12).
The depressed psalmist declared that he was going to *meditate* (hagah; see outline and notes—Ps.1:2-3 for more discussion) on all of God's mighty works and consider His doings or exploits. Note that the Hebrew word for consider is the same as that for *mused* (v.3). Instead of complaining about the circumstances that so troubled him, Asaph determined to think of the great things God had done.

Thought 1. Without question, strength for the present can sometimes be found in the past. When we are overwhelmed with despair, we need to pause to remember the mighty works God has performed for His people through the ages. These accounts are recorded in Scripture for a specific reason: that we might be encouraged by and through them (Ro.15:4). We also need to recall God's faithfulness in our own lives. Remembering past victories gives us hope for our present struggles.

Be joyful in hope, patient in affliction, faithful in prayer (Ro.12:12).

For everything that was written in the past was written to teach us, so that through endurance and the encouragement of the Scriptures we might have hope (Ro.15:4).

Give thanks in all circumstances, for this is God's will for you in Christ Jesus (1 Th.5:18).

God did this so that, by two unchangeable things in which it is impossible for God to lie, we who have fled to take hold of the hope offered to us may be greatly encouraged. We have this hope as an anchor for the soul, firm and secure. It enters the inner sanctuary behind the curtain (He.6:18-19).

My comfort in my suffering is this: Your promise preserves my life (Ps. 119:50).

3 (77:13-20) Trust God to redeem (deliver) you.

As Asaph recalled how God delivered His people out of Egypt and into the promised land of Canaan, he found hope for his difficult situation. He trusted God to deliver him out of his despair and through the rough waters of his troubled life (Is.43:1[b]-2).

a. Because His ways are holy and perfect: He is beyond compare (v.13).
Asaph declared that God's ways are holy and perfect. *Holy* (qodesh) may either refer to the holy place of God's presence or to God's holiness itself. Either way the emphasis is on the truth that God's ways are "absolutely perfect and morally pure, without the slightest hint of error in His decisions and ways toward mankind."[3] Note the psalmist's question, *What god is so great as our God?* The answer is, no one! Our God is beyond compare. No one is perfect and holy as He is, and certainly no one is worthy of being called *great* in His presence.

b. Because He is the true and living God who performs miracles and demonstrates His power (v.14).
The LORD's miracles prove indisputably that He alone is the true and living God. Again and again, He has declared His strength or demonstrated His power among the people—openly and visibly. *Peoples* is plural in the Hebrew. This is significant because it proclaims that God did not perform His miracles exclusively in front of the Jews but before the people of heathen nations as well. No so-called heathen god had ever performed wonders like God had.

---

2 Derek Kidner. *Psalms 73-150*, p.308.

3 Steven Lawson and Max Anders. *Holman Old Testament Commentary—Psalms*. WORDsearch CROSS e-book.

c. Because He redeems and saves His people: He delivered Israel (vv.15-20).

Finally, Asaph recalled God's most amazing work of all: the redemption of His people (singular in the Hebrew) with His arm, another symbol of His wonder-working power (v.15). Asaph was referring specifically to God's deliverance of Israel from Egyptian bondage. God's greatest work is the redemption and salvation of His people.

Asaph related how the Red Sea shrank back at the mighty power of God (v.16). He depicted the waters as trembling or being afraid of God's mighty presence. *Writhed* (chuwl) means trembling and shaking in travail. *Convulsed* (raghaz) means quaking or trembling. Asaph painted a vivid image: when the waters of the Red Sea *saw* God, they leapt back in fear, leaving a path through which the fleeing Israelites could cross.

As he continued to rehearse God's mighty works in delivering His people, Asaph moved from the Red Sea to Mount Sinai (v.17). There, God caused the clouds to pour down rain. The booming thunder and brilliant flashes of lightning announced God's holy presence in the mount in an awesome way (Ex.19:16; 20:18).

As God led His people out of Egypt and into full possession of the promised land, He repeatedly reminded them of His power. He roared from the whirlwind and lit up the world with lightning. At times, the land itself shook from earthquakes (Ex.19:18; Ps.68:7-9).

Remembering how God delivered His people taught Asaph a valuable lesson for his own troubled life: God usually leads His people *through* the waters, not around them (v.19). His *way* is *in* or *through the sea.* His *path* is *in* or *through the great waters.* Although His *footprints were not seen*—we cannot see them—He is with us, and He guides us. He opened up a path through the Red Sea for Israel, and He will make a way for us out of the raging billows of despair.

Asaph then recalled that God appointed Moses and Aaron to shepherd His people through the wilderness (v.20). "Just as he called Moses and Aaron (Nu.33:1) and David (Ps.78:70-72) to lead His flock, so He would appoint other shepherds in the years to come. One day, the Good Shepherd would come and give His life for the sheep (John 10)."[4] In doing so, our dear Savior defeated every spiritual enemy we will ever face, including despair and depression. In Him, we have victory. If we will trust and follow Him, He will lead us out of the darkness of despair.

Thought 1. God is greater than our trouble, no matter how severe. Often, it seems there is no solution for our problem, no way through stormy waters, no hope of things getting better. During such times, we need to place our trust in the Lord. He will make a way for us. We never have to walk through our trials alone. We need to hear and believe God's Word and claim the promise below as our own. Although it was spoken to Israel, it is also for each one of us. We need only replace *Jacob* and *Israel* with our own name.

> **But now, this is what the LORD says— he who created you, O Jacob, he who formed you, O Israel: "Fear not, for I have redeemed you; I have summoned you by name; you are mine. When you pass through the waters, I will be with you; and when you pass through the rivers, they will not sweep over you. When you walk through the fire, you will not be burned; the flames will not set you ablaze (Is.43:1-2).**

God loves you so much that He gave His Son for *you.* And if He "who did not spare his own Son, but gave him up for us all—how will he not also, along with him, graciously give us all things (Ro.8:32)?" He will lead you out of your despair. He will guide you through your trouble, and to the victory He has promised in Jesus Christ our Lord.

> **When he has brought out all his own, he goes on ahead of them, and his sheep follow him because they know his voice (Jn.10:4).**
>
> **He has delivered us from such a deadly peril, and he will deliver us. On him we have set our hope that he will continue to deliver us (2 Co.1:10).**
>
> **The Lord will rescue me from every evil attack and will bring me safely to his heavenly kingdom. To him be glory for ever and ever. Amen (2 Ti.4:18).**
>
> **And free those who all their lives were held in slavery by their fear of death (He.2:15).**
>
> **When Pharaoh stubbornly refused to let us go, the LORD killed every firstborn in Egypt, both man and animal. This is why I sacrifice to the LORD the first male offspring of every womb and redeem each of my firstborn sons' (Ex.13:15).**
>
> **If I rise on the wings of the dawn, if I settle on the far side of the sea, even there your hand will guide me, your right hand will hold me fast (Ps.139:9-10).**
>
> **He rescues and he saves; he performs signs and wonders in the heavens and on the earth. He has rescued Daniel from the power of the lions" (Da.6:27).**

---

4   Warren W. Wiersbe. *The Bible Exposition Commentary.* WORD*search* CROSS e-book.

PSALM 78

The Truths You Should Learn from History & Pass On to Others, 78:1-72

A maskil of Asaph.

1. Pay attention to the lessons of the past
  a. Heed the parables & instructions
    1) What you have heard & known
    2) What your ancestors have handed down to you
  b. Teach these lessons to your children: Show how God is & has been at work throughout history—His deeds, power, & miracles

2. Teach the truth of God's Word
  a. God decreed (issued) His Word, its laws & instructions
  b. God commands us to teach His Word to our children & to each succeeding generation

    1) So they will trust & obey God

    2) So they will never follow in the footsteps of the stubborn & rebellious

  c. God warns us about the bad example Ephraim set, 2 Ti.2:3-4
    1) They were well-equipped to fight for God, but refused
    2) They disobeyed God's covenant & rejected His law
    3) They forgot about God's works & miracles

3. Guard against fickleness, against an inconsistent, disobedient life: Israel's failure
  a. God's deliverance from Egypt
    1) He led them through the Red Sea

    2) He guided them in the daytime by a cloud & at night by a pillar of fire
    3) He provided water for them

O my people, hear my teaching; listen to the words of my mouth.
2 I will open my mouth in parables, I will utter hidden things, things from of old—
3 What we have heard and known, what our fathers have told us.
4 We will not hide them from their children; we will tell the next generation the praiseworthy deeds of the LORD, his power, and the wonders he has done.
5 He decreed statutes for Jacob and established the law in Israel, which he commanded our forefathers to teach their children,
6 So the next generation would know them, even the children yet to be born, and they in turn would tell their children.
7 Then they would put their trust in God and would not forget his deeds but would keep his commands.
8 They would not be like their forefathers—a stubborn and rebellious generation, whose hearts were not loyal to God, whose spirits were not faithful to him.
9 The men of Ephraim, though armed with bows, turned back on the day of battle;
10 They did not keep God's covenant and refused to live by his law.
11 They forgot what he had done, the wonders he had shown them.
12 He did miracles in the sight of their fathers in the land of Egypt, in the region of Zoan.
13 He divided the sea and led them through; he made the water stand firm like a wall.
14 He guided them with the cloud by day and with light from the fire all night.
15 He split the rocks in the desert and gave them water

as abundant as the seas;
16 He brought streams out of a rocky crag and made water flow down like rivers.
17 But they continued to sin against him, rebelling in the desert against the Most High.
18 They willfully put God to the test by demanding the food they craved.
19 They spoke against God, saying, "Can God spread a table in the desert?
20 When he struck the rock, water gushed out, and streams flowed abundantly. But can he also give us food? Can he supply meat for his people?"
21 When the LORD heard them, he was very angry; his fire broke out against Jacob, and his wrath rose against Israel,
22 For they did not believe in God or trust in his deliverance.
23 Yet he gave a command to the skies above and opened the doors of the heavens;
24 He rained down manna for the people to eat, he gave them the grain of heaven.
25 Men ate the bread of angels; he sent them all the food they could eat.
26 He let loose the east wind from the heavens and led forth the south wind by his power.
27 He rained meat down on them like dust, flying birds like sand on the seashore.
28 He made them come down inside their camp, all around their tents.
29 They ate till they had more than enough, for he had given them what they craved.
30 But before they turned from the food they craved, even while it was still in their mouths,
31 God's anger rose against them; he put to death the sturdiest among them, cutting down the young men of Israel.
32 In spite of all this, they kept on sinning; in spite of his wonders, they did not believe.

• He split the rocks
• He caused water to gush forth & to flow down like a river
  b. Israel's sin & rebellion in the desert wanderings

    1) They were lustful, craving the food & comforts Egypt once provided, Nu.11:4
    2) They were grumblers: They murmured against God & their circumstances
    3) They were skeptical
      • They acknowledged God's former provision (water)
      • They did not trust God enough to meet their need for bread & meat
  c. God's judgment
    1) Bc. the people aroused His anger: He sent a fiery plague among them, Nu.11:1-35, esp.33
    2) Bc. the people did not believe in God nor trust Him to deliver & care for them
  d. God's mercy & goodness: He continued to provide for the people & gave them what they wanted
    1) He rained down manna for them to eat
      • It was the grain of heaven, the bread of angels
      • It gave them all they could eat

    2) He provided cool winds in the desert for them

    3) He provided meat for them—birds driven inland by the wind, Nu.11:31
      • He caused the birds to land within their camp—all around their tents
      • He gave the people exactly what they craved, Nu.17–18; Ro.1:24, 26, 28
  e. God's repeated judgment, 21, 31, 49-50, 58-59, 62; Ro.1:24-32
    1) He struck the people with a severe plague while they gorged themselves
      • Bc. of their frenzied craving, 17-18, 29; Nu. 11:33-34; 1 Co.10:3-5

      • Bc. they kept on sinning: Despite His care, they refused to trust God, 22

2) He ended the people's lives in fear & failure: They never entered the promised land

f. Israel's cycle of unfaithfulness—inconsistent, fickle behavior

1) God's judgment would stir the people to repent
- To honor God as their Rock
- To acknowledge that God is the Most High, their Redeemer

2) The people would hypocritically profess & flatter God, but...
- They lied to Him
- They were disloyal to Him
- They disobeyed His Word, did not keep His covenant

3) God was still faithful to the people: He mercifully forgave their sins
- He held back His full anger & judgment: He did not totally destroy them
- He remembered their mortality: They were only flesh that passes away as quickly as a breeze

4) The people repeatedly rebelled against God:
- They grieved Him

- They tested His patience time & again
- They provoked Him, the Holy One of Israel

4. Never forget God's power & the day He redeemed (saved) you: Israel forgot

a. The Israelites forgot God's power—the miraculous plagues He cast upon Egypt

1) God turned the rivers to blood: Contaminated their water, Ex.7:17-20; Ps.105:29

2) God sent swarms of disease-carrying flies & frogs: Pestered & devastated the people, Ex.7:25–8:32

3) God sent a horde of caterpillars & locusts: Ruined their crops & produce, Ex.10:1-20

4) God sent hail, sleet, & lightning storms
- Destroyed their fruit vines & their trees
- Destroyed their livestock, Ex.9:1-7

5) God unleashed His anger & judgment on them through a band of destroying angels (messengers)
- He did not spare them from death

33 So he ended their days in futility and their years in terror.
34 Whenever God slew them, they would seek him; they eagerly turned to him again.
35 They remembered that God was their Rock, that God Most High was their Redeemer.
36 But then they would flatter him with their mouths, lying to him with their tongues;
37 Their hearts were not loyal to him, they were not faithful to his covenant.
38 Yet he was merciful; he forgave their iniquities and did not destroy them. Time after time he restrained his anger and did not stir up his full wrath.
39 He remembered that they were but flesh, a passing breeze that does not return.
40 How often they rebelled against him in the desert and grieved him in the wasteland!
41 Again and again they put God to the test; they vexed the Holy One of Israel.
42 They did not remember his power—the day he redeemed them from the oppressor,
43 The day he displayed his miraculous signs in Egypt, his wonders in the region of Zoan.
44 He turned their rivers to blood; they could not drink from their streams.
45 He sent swarms of flies that devoured them, and frogs that devastated them.
46 He gave their crops to the grasshopper, their produce to the locust.
47 He destroyed their vines with hail and their sycamore-figs with sleet.
48 He gave over their cattle to the hail, their livestock to bolts of lightning.
49 He unleashed against them his hot anger, his wrath, indignation and hostility—a band of destroying angels.
50 He prepared a path for his anger; he did not spare them from death but gave

them over to the plague.
51 He struck down all the firstborn of Egypt, the firstfruits of manhood in the tents of Ham.
52 But he brought his people out like a flock; he led them like sheep through the desert.
53 He guided them safely, so they were unafraid; but the sea engulfed their enemies.
54 Thus he brought them to the border of his holy land, to the hill country his right hand had taken.
55 He drove out nations before them and allotted their lands to them as an inheritance; he settled the tribes of Israel in their homes.
56 But they put God to the test and rebelled against the Most High; they did not keep his statutes.
57 Like their fathers they were disloyal and faithless, as unreliable as a faulty bow.
58 They angered him with their high places; they aroused his jealousy with their idols.
59 When God heard them, he was very angry; he rejected Israel completely.
60 He abandoned the tabernacle of Shiloh, the tent he had set up among men.
61 He sent [the ark of] his might into captivity, his splendor into the hands of the enemy.
62 He gave his people over to the sword; he was very angry with his inheritance.
63 Fire consumed their young men, and their maidens had no wedding songs;
64 Their priests were put to the sword, and their widows could not weep.
65 Then the Lord awoke as from sleep, as a man wakes from the stupor of wine.
66 He beat back his enemies; he put them to everlasting shame.
67 Then he rejected the tents of Joseph, he did not choose the tribe of Ephraim;
68 But he chose the tribe of Judah, Mount Zion, which he loved.

- He struck down the firstborn son of every Egyptian family, Ex.11:1–12:36

b. The Israelites forgot God's power—their miraculous deliverance from Egypt & through the desert wanderings

1) They forgot how God had led them safely through the Red Sea

2) They forgot how He had brought them up to the border of the promised land

5. Do not turn back from nor be unfaithful to God: Israel's continued failure

a. God gave the Israelites their inheritance: A picture of the promised land of heaven

b. The Israelites continued their cycle of rebellion & disobedience

1) They followed in the steps of their parents: Were disloyal & untrustworthy to God

2) They turned to idolatry—false gods, false teaching, & false worship

c. The Israelites aroused God's judgment again: He rejected them completely & gave them up to their enemies

1) He allowed the worship center at Shiloh to be destroyed

2) He allowed the capture of the ark, the very symbol of His power & glorious presence

3) He allowed His people to suffer great adversity
- Many died due to war
- Young men were burned by fire & women never had a chance to marry
- Priests were executed
- Widows were so traumatized they could not weep

6. Hear the *good news*—God awoke & chose David to be His servant & shepherd: A picture of Christ

a. God defeated His enemies & sent them to eternal shame

b. God rejected the people of Israel (Ephraim, the northern tribes, vv.9-11) & chose Judah to be the people through whom He would bring salvation to the world, Mt.1:1; Jn.4:22

c. God built His sanctuary or center of worship on Mount Zion in Judah	69 He built his sanctuary like the heights, like the earth that he established forever.	he brought him to be the shepherd of his people Jacob, of Israel his inheritance.	servant 2) He chose him to be the shepherd of His people, His very own inheritance
d. God chose David from the tribe of Judah: A picture of Christ 1) He chose him to be His	70 He chose David his servant and took him from the sheep pens; 71 From tending the sheep	72 And David shepherded them with integrity of heart; with skillful hands he led them.	3) He chose a man who proved faithful: David cared for God's people with integrity of heart & led them with skill

PSALM 78

The Truths You Should Learn from History and Pass On to Others, 78:1-72

(78:1-72) **Introduction:** "Those who cannot remember the past are condemned to repeat it." This quotation from American philosopher George Santayana (1863-1952) accurately summarizes the seventy-eighth psalm. In it, Asaph reminded his people of the repeated failures of their ancestors. He wanted them to learn some essential lessons from Israel's history so they would not commit the same errors.

Psalm 78 is the first of seven that are classified as *historical psalms* (Ps.105, 106, 107, 114, 135, 136). These psalms delve into God's great works in Israel's past for the purpose of either praise or instruction.

As we study Psalm 78, we are reminded how quickly people and nations fall away from righteousness. Thankfully, we also see the comforting truth of God's faithfulness in spite of our unfaithfulness. Asaph's charge to his people then is the same as it is for us today. As Paul pointed out, the things that happened to Israel serve as an example to us. By inspiration of the Holy Spirit, they appear in Scripture as a warning to all who hear or read or study God's Word (1 Co.10:11). This is, *The Truths You Should Learn from History and Pass On to Others*, 78: 1-72.

1. Pay attention to the lessons of the past (vv.1-4).
2. Teach the truth of God's Word (vv.5-11).
3. Guard against fickleness, against an inconsistent, disobedient life: Israel's failure (vv.12-41).
4. Never forget God's power and the day He redeemed (saved) you: Israel forgot (vv.42-54).
5. Do not turn back from nor be unfaithful to God: Israel's continued failure (vv.55-64).
6. Hear the *good news*—God awoke and chose David to be His servant and shepherd: A picture of Christ (vv.65-72).

1 (78:1-4) **Pay attention to the lessons of the past.** With an urgent message burning in his heart, Asaph called for the people's full attention. He was about to take his audience on a journey through Israel's past, emphasizing crucial lessons they needed to learn. He commanded the people to listen carefully to the lessons because they were critical to Israel's future.

a. Heed the parables and instructions (vv.1-3).
Asaph called on his people, Israel, to give their full attention to his *teaching* (torah). Many scholars, including those who translated the NIV, feel that the use of *torah*

here refers to Asaph's instruction. But the word *torah* usually speaks of God's law—the Scripture (v.5). Regardless of which word was intended, Asaph was saying that the people needed to listen attentively. What he was about to say was from Scripture, God's Holy Word. Therefore, it was of extreme importance (2 Ti.3:16-17).

Asaph informed the people that he was going to relate parables (v.2ª). A *parable* (mashal) is a story that sheds light on a truth by way of comparison. By telling the story of Israel's past, Asaph would give the people vital instruction for the present and future.

Further, he announced that he was going to speak *hidden things of old* (v.2ᵇ). A *hidden thing* (chidhah) was an enigma or difficult subject that required deep consideration and contemplation to understand (see outline and notes—Pr.1:6 for more discussion). Here, Asaph declared that he was going to teach the people hidden lessons from their history. That is, he was going to dig deep into Israel's past and explain things that many people did not readily see. The truths that he would share were not new; they had been heard and known, having been handed down from generation to generation by the people's ancestors (v.3).

b. Teach these lessons to your children: Show how God is and has been at work throughout history— His deeds, power, and miracles (v.4).
Asaph stressed the importance of these lessons, insisting that parents teach them faithfully to their children. Without exception, the coming generations had to understand how God had been at work throughout Israel's history. They needed to know of the deeds and miracles He had performed so powerfully in their behalf. The lessons of the past were crucial to the future survival of both Israel and all other nations.

Thought 1. God has done a wonderful thing for us by preserving the history of His people, including their failures. In His Holy Word He has recorded Israel's sins as a nation as well as those of individuals within that nation. The Holy Spirit selected every story for a specific purpose: to teach us valuable life lessons. With that in mind, we ought to heed these lessons closely, being careful not to commit the same sins our ancestors committed.

For everything that was written in the past was written to teach us, so that through endurance and the encouragement of the Scriptures we might have hope (Ro.15:4).

Now these things occurred as examples to keep us from setting our hearts on evil things as they did. Do not be idolaters, as some of them were; as it is written: "The people sat down to eat and drink and got up to indulge in pagan revelry." We should not commit sexual immorality, as some of them did—and in one day twenty-three thousand of them died. We should not test the Lord, as some of them did—and were killed by snakes. And do not grumble, as some of them did—and were killed by the destroying angel. These things happened to them as examples and were written down as warnings for us, on whom the fulfillment of the ages has come (1 Co.10:6-11).

And how from infancy you have known the holy Scriptures, which are able to make you wise for salvation through faith in Christ Jesus. All Scripture is God-breathed and is useful for teaching, rebuking, correcting and training in righteousness, so that the man of God may be thoroughly equipped for every good work (2 Ti.3:15-17).

My dear children, I write this to you so that you will not sin. But if anybody does sin, we have one who speaks to the Father in our defense—Jesus Christ, the Righteous One. He is the atoning sacrifice for our sins, and not only for ours but also for the sins of the whole world (1 Jn.2:1-2).

I have hidden your word in my heart that I might not sin against you (Ps.119:11).

2 (78:5-11) Teach the truth of God's Word.

Asaph's first lesson to his people was that they must teach the truth of God's Word. They needed to pass God's law down to each generation because Israel's future depended on her faithfulness to God. The people must not follow in the footsteps of those who disobeyed God due to their unbelief.

a. God decreed (issued) His Word, its laws and instructions (v.5ᵃ)

Asaph began his lesson by reminding the people who gave the law and what its purpose was (Ex.20:1ff.). From His fiery presence on Mount Sinai, God had issued His Holy Word with its laws and instructions.

The law was a testimony or witness of God's relationship with Israel through His covenant. The people of Israel were God's special people. As long as they obeyed His holy commands, He promised to protect their nation and prosper them in the land (De.6:1-4).

b. God commands us to teach His Word to our children and to each succeeding generation (vv.5ᵇ-8).

Upon establishing His law with His people, God gave them a critical command: they were to teach His Word to their children and to each succeeding generation (De.6:6-9). The truth of God's Word was to be meticulously protected and preserved. As parents proclaimed God's Word to their children, they were to instruct the children to do the same (vv.5ᵇ-6).

The reasons for this emphatic command were clear. First, God's Word was to be passed down so the next generation of God's people would place their hope, their trust or confidence, in God (v.7). In addition, God's wondrous works for His people would be preserved, and future generations would be stirred to obey His commandments.

Second, God's Word was to be passed down faithfully and consistently so the next generation would not follow in the footsteps of their stubborn and rebellious forefathers who did not trust God (v.8). Asaph was referring to the faithless generation that perished in the wilderness, men and women whose "hearts were not loyal" to God. *Loyal* (kuhn) means firmly established or settled. Their hearts were not fixed on God; their spirits were not steadfast, not firm or true toward Him. As a result, they did not believe God enough to obey Him, and they never entered the promised land.

c. God warns us about the bad example Ephraim set, 2 Ti.2:3-4 (vv.9-11).

The children of Ephraim were another example of those who failed to obey God (v.9) Historically, the descendants of Ephraim, who was Joseph's second son, were hot-tempered, aggressive warriors (Jud.8:1-3; 12:1-6). Yet Asaph referred to an occasion when they were well-equipped for battle but refused to fight for God. Scripture does not provide a record of this event, so we do not know exactly when or where this incident occurred. However, what is most important are the reasons they retreated in battle:

➢ They disobeyed God's covenant and rejected His law (v.10).
➢ They had forgotten the wondrous works and miracles God had performed for His chosen people (v.11).

In response to their unfaithfulness, God chose the tribe of Judah over that of Ephraim to bring forth David—Israel's godly king—and ultimately, the Messiah (vv.67-70).

Thought 1. As believers, we have a responsibility not only to heed God's truth but also to teach it to others. Within the church, pastors and teachers have a holy calling to declare the whole counsel of God, warning every person and teaching every person the wisdom of God (Col.1:28). Within the home, parents have the God-given responsibility to teach the truth of God's Word to their children (De.6:6-9). While taking children to Sunday school and church is an important aspect of fulfilling that responsibility, it does not replace the parents' duty within the home. Parents must personally train their children in the truths of God, both in principle and by example.

Pastors, teachers, and parents will all give an account to God for how they fulfilled their sacred duty to teach God's Word. We need to be faithful to our responsibility to tend to the souls of others by sowing the seed of God's Word in their hearts.

> **You know that I have not hesitated to preach anything that would be helpful to you but have taught you publicly and from house to house (Ac.20:20).**
>
> **Fathers, do not exasperate your children; instead, bring them up in the training and instruction of the Lord (Ep.6:4).**
>
> **We proclaim him, admonishing and teaching everyone with all wisdom, so that we may present everyone perfect in Christ (Col.1:28).**
>
> **And the things you have heard me say in the presence of many witnesses entrust to reliable men who will also be qualified to teach others (2 Ti.2:2).**
>
> **These commandments that I give you today are to be upon your hearts. Impress them on your children. Talk about them when you sit at home and when you walk along the road, when you lie down and when you get up. Tie them as symbols on your hands and bind them on your foreheads. Write them on the doorframes of your houses and on your gates (De.6:6-9).**
>
> **Train a child in the way he should go, and when he is old he will not turn from it (Pr.22:6).**

3 (78:12-41) **Guard against fickleness, against an inconsistent, disobedient life: Israel's failure.** Asaph's second crucial lesson was the importance of obeying God. Throughout their history, the people of Israel had walked inconsistently with God. Their up and down behavior—repeatedly going back and forth from obedience to disobedience—grieved God's heart and left Him with no choice but to judge them. Asaph exhorted his people to do better, to sincerely turn from their sin and to be consistently faithful to God's holy commands.

a. **God's deliverance from Egypt (vv.12-16).**
Asaph led his audience through Israel's history—the shameful as well as the glorious—pointing out the people's failures along the way. He recounted the marvelous things God did for their forefathers in delivering them from Egypt and the field of Zoan (v.12). Zoan was an Egyptian city later known as Tanis. Located along a branch of the Nile, it had been built by the forced labor of the oppressed Israelites.[1]

God's wonders accompanied Israel all along their journey from Egypt. He led them through the Red Sea, miraculously parting the waters to allow them to escape Pharaoh's bondage (v.13). He supernaturally guided them along their way. During the day He led them with a cloud. At night He lit their path with a pillar of fire (v.14). As they traveled on, God provided life-sustaining water in the desert in an amazing way. Splitting the rocks, He caused water to gush forth from them and flow down like a river (vv.15-16).

b. **Israel's sin and rebellion in the desert wanderings (vv.17-20).**
In spite of all these astonishing feats—demonstrations of God's mighty power and unfailing care for His people—the Israelites rebelled against Him in the wilderness. By persisting in willful sin, they tempted or tested God. They challenged His righteousness by putting Him in a position where He had to either judge them or else be unrighteous (vv.17-18). They were lustful, with uncontrollable cravings for food, comfort, and the pleasures they had enjoyed in Egypt (Nu.11:4). In essence, they were ungrateful grumblers. Instead of thanking God for delivering them, they murmured against Him and the difficult circumstances of their journey. Their unbelieving, distrustful hearts knew neither fear nor shame. Although they acknowledged that God had miraculously provided water for them, they skeptically questioned whether He could meet their present need for bread and meat (vv.19-20).

c. **God's judgment (vv.21-22).**
The Israelites' sin and rebellion furiously ignited God's anger against them (v.21). He responded by sending judgment in the form of a fiery plague that claimed many lives (Nu.11:33-34). Why? Because the people did not believe in God, nor did they trust Him to care for them (v.21). The mighty miracles He had performed were not enough to convince them of His ability to provide everything they needed.

d. **God's mercy and goodness: He continued to provide for the people and gave them what they wanted (vv.23-29).**
God showered His mercy and goodness upon the faithless people by continuing to provide for them and

---

1 Merrill F. Unger, R.K. Harrison, ed. *The New Unger's Bible Dictionary.* Chicago, IL: The Moody Bible Institute of Chicago, 1957.

give them what they wanted (v.23). He rained down manna for them to eat: the grain of heaven, the bread of angels—as much as they could eat (vv.24-25). He provided a cool wind in the desert to refresh them in the oppressing heat (v.26).

Yet, they were not content with what God gave them. When they became dissatisfied with the manna, He provided meat for them by sending a strong wind that drove birds in from the sea (v.26; Nu.11:31). He caused these birds to land within their camp, all around their habitations or tents (v.28). He gave the ungrateful people exactly what they repeatedly craved: He allowed them to indulge their fleshly desires, leading to their judgment (vv.29-30).

Thought 1. Note a significant fact: God sometimes allows sinful people to do exactly what they want, turning them over to their fleshly desires. He gives the rebellious up to their sinful lusts. This is exactly what Scripture says:

> **Therefore God gave them over in the sinful desires of their hearts to sexual impurity for the degrading of their bodies with one another....Because of this, God gave them over to shameful lusts. Even their women exchanged natural relations for unnatural ones....Furthermore, since they did not think it worthwhile to retain the knowledge of God, he gave them over to a depraved mind, to do what ought not to be done (Ro.1:24, 26, 28).**

e. **God's repeated judgment, 21, 31, 49-50, 58-59, 62; Ro.1:24-32 (vv.30-33).**
Throughout this long lesson, Asaph emphasized to his listeners the truth of God's repeated judgment on the murmuring, rebellious Israelites. In this incident, the people were stricken with a severe plague while gorging themselves on the meat they had demanded (v.31). Still, they craved the things they had enjoyed while slaves in Egypt (vv.17-18, 29; Nu.11:33-34; 1 Co.10:3-5). In spite of God's miraculous care for them, they refused to trust Him and kept on sinning (v.32). Tragically, their lives ended in failure: they never entered the promised land (v.33). The rest of their days were consumed in vanity. That is, their precious time on earth was wasted or spent worthlessly. From then on, futility and fear of what trouble lay ahead marked the rest of their lives.

f. **Israel's cycle of unfaithfulness—inconsistent, fickle behavior (vv.34-41).**
Israel's history revealed a cycle of unfaithfulness, of erratic, up and down behavior. Over and over again, God's judgment would stir the people to repent of

their rebellious ways. But they would only seek the LORD when they were desperate to be set free from His deadly judgment (v.35). Only then did they honor Him as their rock. Only then did they remember that the Most High God was their redeemer.

Even then, their repentance was insincere (v.36). The people were hypocritical and deceptive. When they professed the LORD, they were merely flattering Him. As Asaph bluntly stated, they lied to God. Although the people repented with their lips, their hearts were not right with Him (v.37). They were not loyal to God, did not keep His covenant or obey His Holy Word. "Theirs was a bogus belief, a pseudo [phony] repentance that caused them to return to their unfaithfulness when tested."[2]

Nevertheless, God remained faithful to His people. He was full of compassion and mercy and He forgave their sins (v.38). Again and again, God held back His full anger and judgment. He did not "stir up His full wrath;" that is, totally destroy them. He remembered that they were merely flesh—weak, mortal humans that pass away as quickly as a breeze (v.39).

Still, in spite of God's unfailing mercy, the people repeatedly provoked or rebelled against Him (v.40). Eventually, the Israelites returned to sin, grieving and breaking the heart of God. Time and again, they tempted the LORD—tested His patience, holiness, and righteousness (v.41a).

As Asaph said, the people's recurring sin "vexed the Holy One of Israel" (v.41b). *Vexed* (tavah) appears only here in the Old Testament, making its meaning difficult to determine. Most scholars think it means that Israel either pained God, or they provoked Him to wrath.

Thought 1. We all need to walk consistently with the Lord, obeying Him in all things. At the same time, we have to realize that we will and do come short of God's glory every day. Due to this sinful world and our fleshly cravings, even the strongest of us fall short at times. We fail to do what God commands and fail to be all God wants us to be. Yet, we cannot use that as an excuse to sin. Rather, we need to guard against falling into a pattern of sin. We cannot allow sin to become a habit in our lives. Becoming more and more conformed to the image of Christ should be our desire and our goal.

We can protect ourselves from falling into sin by dealing promptly with the sins we commit. As soon as we sin, we should confess our sin and turn from it. Staying close to God through reading and meditating on His Word and spending time in prayer will help us overcome the desires of our flesh. Separating ourselves from worldly things and activities will help us avoid temptation. By walking in the power of God's Spirit, we can be victorious over sin (Ga.5:16).

---

2 Steven Lawson and Max Anders. *Holman Old Testament Commentary—Psalms.* WORD*search* CROSS e-book.

Just as God judged the disobedient Israelites, He also chastens us when we sin. Do not be deceived into thinking you can get by with sinning. You cannot—not if you are genuinely a child of God, not if you have truly been born again. Scripture is very clear: God disciplines His children when they continue in sin. If you are not chastened by God when you are disobedient, you are not one of His sons or daughters:

Because the Lord disciplines those he loves, and he punishes everyone he accepts as a son." Endure hardship as discipline; God is treating you as sons. For what son is not disciplined by his father? If you are not disciplined (and everyone undergoes discipline), then you are illegitimate children and not true sons (He.12:6-8).

I put this in human terms because you are weak in your natural selves. Just as you used to offer the parts of your body in slavery to impurity and to ever-increasing wickedness, so now offer them in slavery to righteousness leading to holiness (Ro.6:19).

Therefore, I urge you, brothers, in view of God's mercy, to offer your bodies as living sacrifices, holy and pleasing to God—this is your spiritual act of worship. Do not conform any longer to the pattern of this world, but be transformed by the renewing of your mind. Then you will be able to test and approve what God's will is—his good, pleasing and perfect will (Ro.12:1-2).

Since we have these promises, dear friends, let us purify ourselves from everything that contaminates body and spirit, perfecting holiness out of reverence for God (2 Co.7:1).

No one who is born of God will continue to sin, because God's seed remains in him; he cannot go on sinning, because he has been born of God (1 Jn.3:9).

We know that anyone born of God does not continue to sin; the one who was born of God keeps him safe, and the evil one cannot harm him (1 Jn.5:18).

4 (78:42-54) **Never forget God's power and the day He redeemed (saved) you: Israel forgot.**
As Asaph recounted the sad history of his people's ancestors, he targeted a key reason for their recurring failures: they forgot all that God had done for them. This is the third vital lesson for God's beloved people to learn: never forgot God's power and the day He redeemed you.

a. The Israelites forgot God's power—the miraculous plagues He cast upon Egypt (vv.42-51).
The Israelites did not remember God's power (v.42). They tragically forgot the glorious day when God delivered them from Egyptian slavery. Specifically, they lost sight of the wonders they had witnessed, the miraculous plagues God cast on Egypt to convince Pharaoh to let God's people go:

➢ God turned the rivers of Egypt blood red, contaminating the water and making it undrinkable (v.44; Ex.7:17-20; Ps.105:29).

➢ God sent swarms of disease-carrying flies and frogs that pestered and devastated the Egyptians (v.45; Ex.7:25-8:32).

➢ God sent a horde of grasshoppers and locusts that ruined their crops and produce (v.46; Ex.10:1-20).

➢ God sent hail, sleet, and lightning storms. Afterward, their fruit-bearing vines and trees along with their livestock were destroyed (Ex.9:1-7).

➢ God unleashed the fierceness of His anger—the full measure of His unrestrained wrath—in judgment on them. A band of destroying angels, God's messengers, released destruction throughout the land (v.49). *Destroying,* as used here, does not mean that the angels were wicked or demonic. It simply means that they were agents of dreadful circumstances. Through them, God carried out His wrath on Egypt, not sparing them from death (v.50). His final act of judgment was striking down the firstborn child of every Egyptian family (v.51; Ex.11:1-12:36).

b. The Israelites forgot God's power—their miraculous deliverance from Egypt and through the desert wanderings (vv.52-54).
Shockingly, the Israelites even forgot God's mighty power in bringing them out of Egypt and through the wilderness wanderings. They overlooked how God had personally led them the same way a caring shepherd leads his sheep (v.52). He went before them, clearing the way for them to journey safely to the promised land. Somehow, they disregarded one of the greatest wonders in world history: God's parting of the Red Sea. After they had crossed safely and without fear, God's mighty hand merged the waters again, engulfing their enemy who tenaciously pursued them (v.53).

They also forgot how God had brought them up to the border of the sanctuary or promised land (v.54). Here, sanctuary refers to the land of Canaan, the holy territory God had promised to Abraham's descendants. Note Exodus 15:17:

You will bring them in and plant them on the mountain of your inheritance—the place, O Lord, you made for

your dwelling, the sanctuary, O Lord, your hands established (Ex.15:17).

They dwelled in this bountiful place because God's right hand had purchased it. It was obtained by His unstoppable power.

Thought 1. The Israelites fell into sin because they forgot what God had done for them. God's deliverance of Israel from Egypt is a picture of our salvation. Just as God miraculously worked to set Israel free from Egyptian bondage, God supernaturally acted to set us free from the bondage of sin and condemnation.

We must never lose sight of the great price of our salvation. It has been said that, while our salvation costs us nothing, it cost God everything. Indeed, we have been bought with a tremendous price: the precious, incorruptible blood of Jesus Christ. When we willfully sin, we show a lack of gratitude for the blood of Christ.

Jesus suffered on the cross so we could be forgiven our sin. He defeated Satan and sin so we could be set free from its power over us. We should never take lightly the fact that God has brought us salvation by His grace. Nor should we ever stray from the purpose of that work: to give us victory over sin so we can live eternally in fellowship with Him.

You were bought at a price. Therefore honor God with your body (1 Co.6:20).
We must pay more careful attention, therefore, to what we have heard, so that we do not drift away (He.2:1).
But if anyone does not have them, he is nearsighted and blind, and has forgotten that he has been cleansed from his past sins (2 Pe.1:9).
They forgot the God who saved them, who had done great things in Egypt (Ps.106:21).

5 (78:55-63) **Do not turn back from nor be unfaithful to God: Israel's continued failure.**
Out of His marvelous mercy and grace, the LORD continued to bless Israel. He proceeded with His plan for His people, settling them in the promised land. Astoundingly, they lapsed again into unbelief and disobedience.

a. God gave the Israelites their inheritance: A picture of the promised land of heaven (v.55).
After their faithless ancestors perished in the wilderness, God brought the new generation into the promised land. He drove out the heathen nations that occupied Canaan and gave Israel the inheritance He had promised to Abraham. The LORD carefully measured the land by line, assuring the people that He had divided it fairly among the twelve tribes of Israel.

The promised land is a picture of heaven, the inheritance of the redeemed (see outlines and notes—Ge.12:1-3; *Numbers*, INTRODUCTION, Special Feature 26 for more discussion). Through the shed blood of Jesus Christ, the blood of the new covenant, all who place their trust in Him will receive heaven as their eternal home.

b. The Israelites continued their cycle of rebellion and disobedience (vv.56-58).
Once again, the highly blessed Israelites turned away from the LORD. History repeated itself when they failed to keep God's testimonies, His laws and commands as recorded in His Word (v.56). They were faithless, following in the footsteps of their faithless fathers, and continuing the cycle of rebellion and disobedience (v.57a). *Faithless* (bagad) is the Hebrew word used of a husband or wife treacherously breaking the marriage covenant by committing adultery (Je.3:20; Mal.2:14).

Asaph compared the rebellious Israelites to a faulty bow—one that has warped and does not shoot where the archer aims it (v.57b). This was an accurate image of the Israelites: God had intended them to be a holy people who would be His special witness to the world (Is.43:10), but they were warped by their unbelief and persistently refused to follow the course God planned for them.

The treachery they were about to be guilty of was unfathomable. As the Israelites basked in the bounty of Canaan, they forsook God and turned to idolatry (v.58). How could they strike a deeper wound into the heart of a *jealous* God than by turning to false gods, false teaching, and false worship?

c. The Israelites aroused God's judgment again: He rejected them completely and gave them up to their enemies (vv.59-64).
Once again, the Israelites' unfaithfulness provoked God to wrath. Scripture actually says that He greatly abhorred Israel; He utterly rejected her people and gave them up to their enemies (v.59). First, He allowed the worship center at Shiloh to be destroyed (v.60). He even abandoned the tabernacle—the hallowed place where He dwelled among His people in a unique way.

Second, God allowed the ark, the very symbol of His power and presence among His beloved people to be captured (v.61). His *might* refers to the ark of the covenant, which originally struck fear in the hearts of the Philistines. But when God abandoned Israel, the Philistines slaughtered 30,000 of Israel's best soldiers and captured the ark (1 S.4:4-11).

Third, God allowed His people to suffer great adversity. Many died due to war (v.62). Young men and women were burned by fire and never had a chance to marry (v.63). Priests were executed, and widows were so traumatized they could not even weep (v.64).

Thought 1. No matter how mature we are as believers, we must never think we are above sinning. Paul spoke about Israel's unfaithfulness and then offered this warning for all believers:

> **So, if you think you are standing firm, be careful that you don't fall! (1 Co.10:12).**

When we begin to think we are not affected by worldly things, not subject to temptation, not prone to caving into the sinful desires of our flesh, we need to be extremely careful. Satan is constantly pursuing us, seeking to devour our joy, our testimony, and our effectiveness for Christ (1 Pe.5:8). Any one of us is only one temptation away—at just the right time, under just the right circumstances, with just the right enticement—from falling into sin's deadly clutches. We must never turn away from nor be unfaithful to God. To the contrary, we need to stay close to Christ, constantly watching and praying lest we give in to the weaknesses of our sinful nature (Mt.26:41).

> **Peter replied, "Even if all fall away on account of you, I never will." (Mt.26:33).**
> **"Watch and pray so that you will not fall into temptation. The spirit is willing, but the body is weak" (Mt.26:41).**
> **No temptation has seized you except what is common to man. And God is faithful; he will not let you be tempted beyond what you can bear. But when you are tempted, he will also provide a way out so that you can stand up under it (1 Co.10:13).**
> **Be self-controlled and alert. Your enemy the devil prowls around like a roaring lion looking for someone to devour. Resist him, standing firm in the faith, because you know that your brothers throughout the world are undergoing the same kind of sufferings (1 Pe.5:8-9).**
> **Therefore, dear friends, since you already know this, be on your guard so that you may not be carried away by the error of lawless men and fall from your secure position (2 Pe.3:17).**
> **He who trusts in himself is a fool, but he who walks in wisdom is kept safe (Pr.28:26).**

6 (78:65-72) **Hear the *good news*—God awoke and chose David to be His servant and shepherd: A picture of Christ.**
Asaph closed Psalm 78 with good news: in spite of the people's continued failures, God refused to give up on Is-

rael. Suddenly, the LORD sprang to action, like a man startled out of a deep sleep (v.65). He charged forth with such great fervor that Asaph compared Him to a *man* or *mighty man* (gibbor), a heroic warrior who knows no fear. Energized by His unfailing love for the people and His plan for humanity's redemption, God went to work on Israel's behalf.

a. God defeated His enemies and sent them to eternal shame (v.66).
Israel's enemies were God enemies, for the Jews were the people through whom He chose to carry out His plan for the human race. In order to accomplish His will, God fiercely defeated His enemies, sending them to everlasting reproach or shame (De.32:39-43).

b. God rejected the people of Israel (Ephraim, the northern tribes, vv.9-11) and chose Judah to be the people through whom He would bring salvation to the world, Mt.1:1; Jn.4:22 (vv.67-68ª).
God advanced His plan to bring salvation to the world. He selected the tribe of Judah to be the one through whom His deliverance would come, and He chose the land of Judah to be the place where His presence would be centered among His people. He rejected the tents of Joseph, the worship center at Shiloh where the ark had formerly been (v.60). He also rejected the powerful tribe of Ephraim, which represents the ten northern tribes of Israel, choosing Judah instead as the people through whom He would bring salvation to the world.

c. God built His sanctuary or center of worship on Mount Zion in Judah (vv.68ᵇ-69).
Judah was the place God chose to build His sanctuary. Asaph noted that the LORD loved Judah's *Mount Zion* and selected it to be His people's center of worship (Ps.87:2). Mount Zion is a high place, as is God's dwelling place in heaven, after which the tabernacle and temple were patterned (He.9:23-24).

d. God chose David from the tribe of Judah: A picture of Christ (vv.70-72).
God also called David, whom He chose to be His servant, from the tribe of Judah (v.70). David was a simple shepherd, and the LORD lifted him out of this lowly, obscure occupation to be the shepherd of His people, God's very own inheritance (v.71).

Of all the men of Israel, God selected David because he had proved to be faithful. As God observed the way David tended his father's sheep, He saw a man whose heart was like His own (1 S.13:14; Ac.13:22). David cared for God's people with integrity of heart and led them with great skill (v.72). Through David's leadership, God preserved and prospered His chosen nation.

Thought 1. God's selection of David as king was not the pinnacle of Judah's glory. Judah would be favored by God in a way that exceeded all previous blessings: out of Judah would come David's Greater Son, the Messiah, Jesus Christ. God's swift action in rising up in Israel's behalf and appointing David as shepherd of His people pictures the salvation of the sinful human race through Christ. Consider these images of Christ in this passage:

➢ Christ defeated Satan, the enemy of God and man (v.66; Ge.3:15; Lu.11:22; Co.2:15; He.2:14; 1 Jn.3:8).

➢ God dwelled with humanity in the person of Jesus Christ (vv.68-69; Jn.1:1, 14; 12:45; Co.1:15; He.1:3).

➢ Jesus came as the servant of God (v.70; Is.42:1; Mt.12:18; Mk.10:45; Ph.2:7).

➢ Jesus is the shepherd of God's people (v.71; Is.40:11; Zec.13:7; Jn.10:11; He.13:20; 1 Pe.2:25; 5:4).

➢ Jesus is a man of perfect integrity: He is totally without sin (v.72; 1 Jn.3:5; 2 Co.5:21; 1 Pe.2:22; He.4:15; 7:26).

God proved His love for Israel and demonstrated His grace by giving them David to be their king. One thousand years later, He proved His love for humanity and again demonstrated His grace by sending His Son, the Lord Jesus Christ, to be our Savior, Lord, and King.

In the beginning was the Word, and the Word was with God, and the Word was God....The Word became flesh and made his dwelling among us. We have seen his glory, the glory of the One and Only, who came from the Father, full of grace and truth (Jn.1:1, 14).

God made him who had no sin to be sin for us, so that in him we might become the righteousness of God (2 Co.5:21).

But made himself nothing, taking the very nature of a servant, being made in human likeness (Ph.2:7).

Since the children have flesh and blood, he too shared in their humanity so that by his death he might destroy him who holds the power of death—that is, the devil (He.2:14).

He who does what is sinful is of the devil, because the devil has been sinning from the beginning. The reason the Son of God appeared was to destroy the devil's work (1 Jn.3:8).

PSALM 79

When Your Nation Suffers the Ravages of War, 79:1-13

A Psalm of Asaph.

1. Share the pain of your suffering: The psalmist described...
  a. His nation's devastation
    1) The temple was desecrated
    2) The capital was destroyed
    3) The people—especially God's people—were slaughtered

      • The slaughter was savage: Blood flowed like water...
      • The extermination was thorough: No one was left...
    4) The survivors were mocked & scorned

  b. God's seemingly endless anger—His judgment & discipline: He burned with jealousy due to their sin
2. Ask God to defend you who trust in Him: The psalmist prayed...
  a. That God execute judgment on the abusive enemies
    1) Bc. they did not live for God

O God, the nations have invaded your inheritance; they have defiled your holy temple, they have reduced Jerusalem to rubble.
2 They have given the dead bodies of your servants as food to the birds of the air, the flesh of your saints to the beasts of the earth.
3 They have poured out blood like water all around Jerusalem, and there is no one to bury the dead.
4 We are objects of reproach to our neighbors, of scorn and derision to those around us.
5 How long, O LORD? Will you be angry forever? How long will your jealousy burn like fire?
6 Pour out your wrath on the nations that do not acknowledge you, on the kingdoms that do not call on your name;

7 for they have devoured Jacob and destroyed his homeland.
8 Do not hold against us the sins of the fathers; may your mercy come quickly to meet us, for we are in desperate need.
9 Help us, O God our Savior, for the glory of your name; deliver us and forgive our sins for your name's sake.
10 Why should the nations say, "Where is their God?" Before our eyes, make known among the nations that you avenge the outpoured blood of your servants.
11 May the groans of the prisoners come before you; by the strength of your arm preserve those condemned to die.
12 Pay back into the laps of our neighbors seven times the reproach they have hurled at you, O Lord.
13 Then we your people, the sheep of your pasture, will praise you forever; from generation to generation we will recount your praise.

  2) Bc. they slaughtered God's people & destroyed the land
  b. That God not charge His people with the sins & guilt of former generations
  c. That God be merciful & quick: Bc. their plight was desperate
3. Cry out passionately for God's help: The psalmist pleaded...
  a. For God his Savior to help, for the honor & glory of His name
  b. For God to deliver & forgive
  c. For God to deal justly with the abusive nations
    1) That God no longer tolerate their taunts & denial of Him
    2) That God avenge the slaughter of His dear people

  d. For God to demonstrate His power by saving His people—especially the imprisoned & those condemned to die

  e. For God to pay back or execute full retribution on all people (neighbors, nations) who scorn & deny the Lord
4. Reaffirm that you are one of God's followers, Tit.2:11-12: The psalmist vowed that God's people...
  a. Would praise & worship Him
  b. Would bear witness for Him

PSALM 79

When Your Nation Suffers the Ravages of War, 79:1-13

(79:1-13) **Introduction:** September 1, 2001, is considered by many Americans to be the darkest day in their nation's history. On that day, terrorists hijacked passenger jets and rammed them into some of the United States' most prominent buildings, killing nearly 3,000 innocent citizens. It was an act of war against the United States of America.

Psalm 79 was written in response to a similar occasion in Israel. That act of aggression was probably the Babylonian invasion of 586 B.C. (2 K.25:1-21). A song of grief, this seventy-ninth psalm is a companion to Psalm 74. Its heading states that it is a psalm of Asaph, but it describes an event that occurred long after his death. The best explanation is that it was written by Asaph's descendants, an order of temple musicians identified by his name (2 Chr.35:15; Ezr.2:41; 3:10).

Is there a nation that has not suffered the ravages of war? Jesus warned that, as we grow ever closer to His return, wars and rumors of wars will abound (Mt.24:6-7). Sadly, Psalm 79 will continue to be relevant in our world until the Prince of Peace finally reigns in righteousness.

Although its setting is a national tragedy, Psalm 79 is helpful for all nations and indivduals who have experienced deep personal loss. In it, the Israelites pleaded for understanding as well as for God's help. This is, *When Your Nation Suffers the Ravages of War,* 79:1-13.

1. Share the pain of your suffering: The psalmist described... (vv.1-5).
2. Ask God to defend you who trust in Him: The psalmist prayed... (vv.6-8).
3. Cry out passionately for God's help: The psalmist pleaded... (vv.9-12).
4. Reaffirm by your life that you are God's own, Tit.2:11-12: The psalmist vowed that God's people... (v.13).

1 (79:1-5) **Share the pain of your suffering.**
The people of Israel were suffering intensely after the Babylonian attack. Asaph expressed their grief to God, describing the pain of what they had endured.

Notice how Asaph referred to what had been lost:
➢ God's *inheritance* (v.1)
➢ God's *holy temple* (v.1)
➢ God's *servants* (v.2)
➢ God's *saints* (v.2)

Asaph was concerned not only about the suffering of his people but also for God's honor and the glory of His name. His appeal declares the terrible price of unfaithfulness to God. Our sin always brings reproach on God's holy name in addition to whatever discipline we have to endure.

a. The psalmist described his nation's devastation (vv.1-4).

Asaph described the utter devastation that crushed his nation. The temple, the holy place where God's presence was manifest in a special way, had been desecrated (v.1). The beautiful city of Jerusalem, lauded as "the joy of the whole earth" (Ps.48:2), had been altogether destroyed. The stones of the city's buildings and walls lay in heaps upon one another (2 K.25:1-21; 2 Chr.36:17-20; Je.39:8-10).

Most excruciating to the Israelites was the vicious slaughter of God's people. Asaph described a gruesome scene. The corpses of the Jews lay rotting in the hot sun as birds and wild animals feasted on their flesh (v.2). The massacre was savage: Asaph compared the spilled blood of the saints to a stream of water flowing throughout the city (v.3). In fact, no one was left in Jerusalem to bury the bodies of Israel's dead. Those who were not slain were taken captive and dragged away to Babylon. Leaving their dead unburied was the supreme humiliation to the Jews (De.28:26; Je.8:22; 22:18-19).[1]

The survivors of the invasion were scorned by Israel's neighboring nations (v.4). As the pagan soldiers marched the captives through Ammon and Edom en route to Babylonia, Israel's enemies jeered in delight, mocking their faith as well as their God (Ps.44:13; De.28:37).

b. The psalmist described God's seemingly endless anger—His judgment and discipline: He burned with jealousy due to their sin (v.5).

Desperate for relief, Asaph cried out to God, asking Him how long He would remain angry at His people. God's judgment and discipline on the unfaithful Israelites seemed to be lasting forever. His jealousy due to their sin burned like a scorching fire.

Thought 1. The ravages of war can only be fully understood by those who have personally experienced them. The destruction of homes and communities is painfully devastating, but it pales in comparison to the grief caused by the loss of human life. Throughout the world, untold millions of families grieve for loved ones whose lives were taken in war.

When sorrow strikes, we can share our pain with God. He understands. He gave His Son in the war against Satan and sin: Christ died that we might be free from sin's power and penalty. Scripture says that He bore our griefs and carried our sorrows (Is.53:4). Having been touched with the feeling of our infirmities, Christ invites us to come to Him for mercy and grace (He.4:15-16). Hear the gentle voice of our loving Lord:

> **"Come to me, all you who are weary and burdened, and I will give you rest. Take my yoke upon you and learn from me, for I am gentle and humble in heart, and you will find rest for your souls. For my yoke is easy and my burden is light" (Mt.11:28-30).**
>
> **For we do not have a high priest who is unable to sympathize with our weaknesses, but we have one who has been tempted in every way, just as we are—yet was without sin. Let us then approach the throne of grace with confidence, so that we may receive mercy and find grace to help us in our time of need (He.4:15-16).**
>
> **Cast your cares on the LORD and he will sustain you; he will never let the righteous fall (Ps.55:22).**
>
> **So do not fear, for I am with you; do not be dismayed, for I am your God. I will strengthen you and help you; I will uphold you with my righteous right hand (Is.41:10).**
>
> **Surely he took up our infirmities and carried our sorrows, yet we considered him stricken by God, smitten by him, and afflicted (Is.53:4).**

2 (79:6-8) Ask God to defend you who trust in Him.

Asaph did not deny that the people had sinned against God. But it seemed that their sin was not nearly as grievous as the sin of their pagan enemies who did not even acknowledge God. It also seemed that the current generation was being judged for their ancestors' sin. For these reasons, the psalmist appealed to God's justice and mercy, asking Him to vindicate those who trusted in Him.

a. The psalmist prayed that God would execute judgment on the abusive enemies (vv.6-7).

Asaph prayed for God to judge Israel's enemies, calling on Him to pour out His wrath on their attackers (v.6ᵃ). *Pour out* (shaphak) is the same Hebrew word as used in verse 3 about the slaughtered Israelites. Clearly, the psalmist was praying for equal justice, for God's wrath to gush forth in the same measure as the Israelites' blood had been spilled throughout Jerusalem.

---

[1] Eric Lane. *Focus on the Bible, Psalms: 1-89. God Saves.* Scotland, UK: Christian Focus Publications, 2006. WORD*search* CROSS e-book.

The psalmist wanted the Babylonians to be judged first, because they were God's enemies. They did not know God, did not acknowledge, worship or live for Him (v.6ᵇ). God had no obligation to them, because they did not call upon His name. Second, they had ruthlessly slaughtered God's people and laid waste—totally destroyed and left desolate—the city and temple that were His dwelling place (v.7).

b. The psalmist prayed that God would not charge His people with the sins and guilt of former generations (v.8ᵃ).

God's wrath had been building against His unfaithful people for decades. Brief periods of revival could not stop the rising tide of idolatry and unbelief among God's people. Asaph prayed that God would not judge the current generation for former iniquities, the sins of their ancestors.

c. The psalmist prayed that God would be merciful and quick: Because their plight was desperate (v.8ᵇ).

The psalmist begged God to shower His mercies or compassion upon His suffering people. *Mercies* (rachamim) comes from the Hebrew word for womb, describing the compassion a mother has on her helpless baby. Asaph said that the Hebrews had been brought very low. This term expressed that the people were in desperate need and felt that they could not go on much longer. He implored God to take pity on them and to quickly prevent or meet them with His mercy.

Thought 1. Asaph's appeal to God was based on the people's relationship with Him through His covenant. Al-though they had been unfaithful, they trusted in Him. In contrast, their enemies did not even acknowledge God.

If we have repented of our sin and trusted Christ for salvation, we too are in a covenant relationship with God. We have an open door to call on God because of our relationship with Him. Even when we are unfaithful to Him, He remains faithful to us (2 Ti.2:13). When we confess our sins, He promises to forgive us and cleanse us (1 Jn.1:9). He will have mercy on us when we genuinely repent.

However, we must remember that God is also faithful to His role as our Father. When we persist in sin, as Israel did, He will discipline us. He loves us, and He is jealous for us. He will not allow us to continue in sin, not if we truly belong to Him.

> **But the Lord is faithful, and he will strengthen and protect you from the evil one (2 Th.3:3).**
>
> **If we are faithless, he will remain faithful, for he cannot disown himself (2 Ti.2:13).**

> **So then, those who suffer according to God's will should commit themselves to their faithful Creator and continue to do good (1 Pe.4:19).**
>
> **The LORD helps them and delivers them; he delivers them from the wicked and saves them, because they take refuge in him (Ps.37:40).**
>
> **The LORD is good, a refuge in times of trouble. He cares for those who trust in him (Nah.1:7).**

3 (79:9-12) Cry out passionately for God's help.

The psalmist cried out urgently to God. His people were suffering and needed His help immediately.

a. The psalmist pleaded for God his Savior to help, for the honor and glory of His name (v.9ᵃ).

Israel's enemies not only mocked them but also blasphemed God's holy name (Ps.74:10, 18). Recognizing God as their only hope of salvation, Asaph appealed to Him to help for the glory of His own name. If for no other reason, he needed God to forgive Israel's unfaithfulness in order to vindicate His great and holy name before their oppressors.

b. The psalmist pleaded for God to deliver and forgive (v.9ᵇ).

The psalmist then asked God to deliver His people from their suffering and to forgive, or purge away their sins. *Forgive* (kaphar) is usually translated as atone or make atonement. Atonement was traditionally made through the offering of a sacrifice (Le.5:6-16; 16:18; 19:22). Obviously, the captive Jews had no sacrifices to offer. Therefore, Asaph called on God to make atonement for them. This points to our atonement through God's offering of His Son as a sacrifice. Once again, Asaph appealed to God for His name's sake. "If God were to deliver Israel and reverse His judgment, God's mercy would vividly display God's glory."[2]

c. The psalmist pleaded for God to deal justly with the abusive nations (v.10).

Next, the psalmist pleaded with God to deal justly with the nations that had abused them. The heathen had been mocking God for allowing His people to suffer such a devastating fate. Knowing that, Asaph asked God to no longer tolerate their taunts and denial of Him. He called on God to avenge the slaughter of His dear people in their (His people's) sight or before their eyes. They wanted to see God judge their ruthless oppressors for so violently spilling the blood of their fellow Israelites. In doing so, He would also

---

2 Steven Lawson and Max Anders. *Holman Old Testament Commentary—Psalms.* WORD*search* CROSS e-book.

defend His name, proving that all the blasphemous statements made against Him were baseless lies.

d. The psalmist pleaded for God to demonstrate His power by saving His people—especially the imprisoned and those condemned to die (v.11).

Asaph entreated God to listen to the sighing or groans of His people who were *prisoners* of the cruel Babylonians. Some were appointed, or condemned, to die. He called on God to demonstrate the greatness or magnitude of His power by saving His people, especially those who were awaiting execution.

e. The psalmist pleaded for God to pay back or execute full retribution on all people (neighbors, nations) who scorn and deny the Lord (v.12).

Finally, the psalmist prayed for God to judge all those who reproached Him, all who scorned and denied the Lord. Specifically, he prayed for God to enforce justice on their neighbors—the nations surrounding Israel that had delighted in Jerusalem's destruction. He called on God to pay them back seven times for their mocking. Seven times represents full and complete retribution, the entire measure of God's judgment (Re.6, 8, 9, 15, 16). Long before this event, God had warned Israel that if they departed from Him, He would punish them sevenfold (Le.26:18, 21, 24, 28). Now, Asaph called on God to issue no lesser punishment to their godless oppressors.

Thought 1. God is our ever-present help in time of need. Even when we are suffering because of sin, as Israel was, we can call on Him. Yet, our first priority at such times should be to ask God to help us by forgiving our sin. This is the help Asaph requested, that God would make atonement for the sin of his nation and cleanse them of their sin.

Praise God, our sins have been atoned for by the work of Jesus Christ on the cross (Ro.5:11)! Presently, He sits at the right hand of God the Father making intercession for us (He.7:25). When we sin, He is our advocate. He represents us before the Father on the basis of His payment for our sin (1 Jn.2:1-2). When we confess our sins, the blood of Christ continues to cleanse us, and God forgives us (1 Jn.1:7, 9). As our Great High Priest, Christ was tempted in every way that we are tempted. And through Him, God's Word promises grace and mercy when we come to His throne for help, including the essential help of forgiveness (He.4:14-16).

Forgiveness of sin precedes deliverance from trouble. Classic commentator Matthew Henry wrote:

Deliverances from trouble are granted in love, and are mercies indeed, when they are grounded upon the pardon of sin and flow from that; we should therefore be more earnest with God in prayer for the removal of our sins than for the removal of our af-

flictions, and the pardon of them is the foundation and sweetness of our deliverances.[3]

Let us then approach the throne of grace with confidence, so that we may receive mercy and find grace to help us in our time of need (He.4:16)

So we say with confidence, "The Lord is my helper; I will not be afraid. What can man do to me?" (He.13:6).

If we confess our sins, he is faithful and just and will forgive us our sins and purify us from all unrighteousness (1 Jn.1:9).

My dear children, I write this to you so that you will not sin. But if anybody does sin, we have one who speaks to the Father in our defense—Jesus Christ, the Righteous One. He is the atoning sacrifice for our sins, and not only for ours but also for the sins of the whole world (1 Jn.2:1-2).

Be not far from me, O God; come quickly, O my God, to help me (Ps.71:12).

The LORD protects the simplehearted; when I was in great need, he saved me (Ps.116:6).

"You are destroyed, O Israel, because you are against me, against your helper (Ho.13:9).

4 (79:13) **Reaffirm that you are one of God's followers, Tit.2:11-12.**

The psalmist finished this psalm by reminding God that His people were the sheep of His pasture. This term speaks not only of the Israelites' helplessness and need for God but also of their relationship with Him (Ps.23; 100:3). They were *His* people; they were *His* sheep. With His rod and staff of discipline, Israel's Shepherd had pulled them back to Himself (see outline and notes—Ps.23:4 for more discussion). In return for having mercy on them and delivering them from their oppressors, the psalmist pledged that God's people would give Him thanks—praise and worship Him—forever. Furthermore, they would bear witness of His mercy and unfailing love to future generations.

Thought 1. God's grace teaches us to deny ungodliness and worldly lusts in order to live holy and godly lives (Tit.2:11-13). One way God helps us to accomplish this is through His chastening or discipline (He.12:10-11). Allowing the Babylonians to overthrow Israel and take the Jews captive was God's discipline on the nation for their unfaithfulness to Him.

---

3   Matthew Henry. *Matthew Henry's Commentary on the Whole Bible.* WORD*search* CROSS e-book.

This chastening assured the psalmist that they were truly His people, the sheep of His pasture, for God only chastens His true sons and daughters. God's discipline in our lives gives us this same assurance. As His sons and daughters, none of us are exempt from chastening (He.12:6-8). If we persist in sin, He will discipline us.

God's chastening can take many forms. His first course of discipline is to convict us of our sin through His Holy Spirit who dwells within us. If we do not turn from our sin, His discipline can become more severe. Sometimes, a genuine believer who persists in sin may experience illness, and if he or she still refuses to repent, premature death can occur (1 Co.11:30-32). Whatever form God's discipline takes, however, we must never presume to know why someone else is suffering. For instance, we should not assume that a believer who is ill or who dies prematurely is being chastened by God.

Whenever you encounter a trial in your life, you should first seek to determine if it is due to God's discipline. Simply ask God to give you clear insight and to search your heart for sin (Ps.139:23-24). If God reveals unconfessed sin in your life, confess it immediately and seek His forgiveness. As one of His true sons or daughters, you will be forgiven and cleansed completely.

That is why many among you are weak and sick, and a number of you have fallen asleep. But if we judged ourselves, we would not come under judgment. When we are judged by the Lord, we are being disciplined so that we will not be condemned with the world (1 Co.11:30-32).

For the grace of God that brings salvation has appeared to all men. It teaches us to say "No" to ungodliness and worldly passions, and to live self-controlled, upright and godly lives in this present age (Tit.2:11-12).

Because the Lord disciplines those he loves, and he punishes everyone he accepts as a son." Endure hardship as discipline; God is treating you as sons. For what son is not disciplined by his father? If you are not disciplined (and everyone undergoes discipline), then you are illegitimate children and not true sons (He.12:6-8).

He restores my soul. He guides me in paths of righteousness for his name's sake. Even though I walk through the valley of the shadow of death, I will fear no evil, for you are with me; your rod and your staff, they comfort me (Ps.23:3-4).

Know that the LORD is God. It is he who made us, and we are his; we are his people, the sheep of his pasture (Ps.100:3).

PSALM 80

When God's People Need Revival, 80:1-19

For the director of music. To [the tune of] "The Lilies of the Covenant." Of Asaph. A psalm.

1. **Appeal to God as your Shepherd, the Shepherd of His people**
   a. Bc. He leads & cares for His people like a flock
   b. Bc. you need God's presence...
      1) His glory to shine on you
      2) His mighty power to be stirred & to save you
2. **Ask God to turn you back to Him**
   a. Bc. you need His face to shine on you, to accept & save you
   b. Bc. His hand of discipline has fallen on you: Due to your sin & your selfish, insincere prayers, Js. 4:1-3
      1) He has allowed you to suffer the consequences of your sinful desires & selfish prayers—to the point of tears
      2) He has allowed you to suffer oppression & ridicule by neighbors & enemies
3. **Beg God to restore you—make His face shine on you & save you—lest you be condemned: Seen in the example of Israel**
   a. God brought Israel out of Egypt as if she were a tender vine
      1) He cast out pagan nations

Hear us, O Shepherd of Israel, you who lead Joseph like a flock; you who sit enthroned between the cherubim, shine forth
2 Before Ephraim, Benjamin and Manasseh. Awaken your might; come and save us.
3 Restore us, O God; make your face shine upon us, that we may be saved.
4 O LORD God Almighty, how long will your anger smolder against the prayers of your people?
5 You have fed them with the bread of tears; you have made them drink tears by the bowlful.
6 You have made us a source of contention to our neighbors, and our enemies mock us.
7 Restore us, O God Almighty; make your face shine upon us, that we may be saved.
8 You brought a vine out of Egypt; you drove out the nations and planted it.

9 You cleared the ground for it, and it took root and filled the land.
10 The mountains were covered with its shade, the mighty cedars with its branches.
11 It sent out its boughs to the Sea, its shoots as far as the River.
12 Why have you broken down its walls so that all who pass by pick its grapes?
13 Boars from the forest ravage it and the creatures of the field feed on it.
14 Return to us, O God Almighty! Look down from heaven and see! Watch over this vine,
15 The root your right hand has planted, the son you have raised up for yourself.
16 Your vine is cut down, it is burned with fire; at your rebuke your people perish.
17 Let your hand rest on the man at your right hand, the son of man you have raised up for yourself.
18 Then we will not turn away from you; revive us, and we will call on your name.
19 Restore us, O LORD God Almighty; make your face shine upon us, that we may be saved.

from the promised land & planted the vine
   2) He blessed the vine so it filled the land: Its shade (protection & prosperity) reached out & covered the mountains
      • Westward to the Mediterranean
      • Eastward to the Euphrates
b. God executed judgment on Israel (the vine): Bc. of her sin
   1) He tore down her walls: Left her open to assault
   2) He allowed fierce enemy nations to ravage & take over Israel (His vineyard)
c. Israel was desperate: The people needed God to return to them at once—to watch over & take care of them
   1) Bc. He had planted & raised them up for Himself

   2) Bc. His discipline & judgment were destroying them (His vineyard)
4. **Ask God to revive you through the Savior—the Davidic King: A picture of Christ, Ps.110:1; Da.7:13-14; Ep.1:20; He.1:13**
   a. So you will not turn away but be revived & call on His name

   b. So He will turn you back to Himself & grant His presence: Then you will be saved

---

PSALM 80

When God's People Need Revival, 80:1-19

(80:1-19) **Introduction:** when many people hear the word *revival*, they think of a series of special services with an evangelistic emphasis. By definition, however, revival is something different. It is the reviving of *God's people*: a renewal of spiritual life and fervor for the Lord. When a believer is genuinely revived, he or she will sincerely repent of sin, rededicate him- or herself to the Lord, strive for holiness, and walk more closely with Him than ever before.

Psalm 80 is a fervent prayer for revival. Shortly after Solomon's death, the nation of Israel divided into two kingdoms (see outline and notes—1 K.12:1-24 and 2 Chr. 10:1-19 for more discussion). The ten northern tribes banded together and were known as Israel or the Northern Kingdom. The Southern Kingdom, referred to as Judah, was made up of Judah and Benjamin. The Southern Kingdom fell to Babylonia in 586 B.C., and this was the subject of Psalm 79 (2 K.25:1-21). Approximately 135

years earlier, the Northern Kingdom had been overtaken by Assyria (2 K.17:1-23). Psalm 80 was written in response to this tragic event.

The heading for Psalm 80 attributes the psalm to Asaph. Like other psalms bearing his name that were written years after his death, it was presumably composed by his descendants. The sons of Asaph were an order of temple musicians called by his name (2 Chr.35:15; Ezra 2:41; 3:10).

The heading also includes the instruction, To the tune of "The Lilies of the Covenant" (see Introduction—Psalm 45 for more discussion). This was probably the title of a popular song, one whose tune Asaph chose to go with the lyrics of Psalm 80.

Psalm 80 revolves around a refrain or repeated phrase in which the psalmist pleaded with God to turn His face back toward His people in order to save them from their suffering (vv.3, 7, 19). Throughout the prayer,

Asaph addressed the LORD as the *God Almighty*—the commander of heaven's armies (vv.4, 7, 14, 19). In verse 4, he implied that God had not sent angels to protect the nation when Assyria attacked. In the succeeding verses in which he called God by this name, Asaph was indirectly praying for God to send an angel army to liberate His people from their captors. He realized, however, that before God would deliver His people, they would first have to repent and turn back to Him. Therefore, he prayed for God to revive His sinful, rebellious people. He asked God to do a radical work in their hearts, a work so powerful that they would never again turn from Him.

Many churches today are cold, lifeless, and filled with indifference. Others have accepted or even endorsed sin within their ranks, totally ignoring the doctrines of Scriptural separation and holiness. Few souls are saved in these environments; the waters of baptism are seldom stirred; and few individuals are wholehearted followers of Jesus Christ. A form of godliness exists, but the power of God is tragically missing (2 Ti.3:5). Such churches would do well to adopt Psalm 80 as their own, praying for God to reignite their cold hearts and turn His people back to Him. This is, *When God's People Need Revival*, 80:1-19.

1. Appeal to God as your Shepherd, the Shepherd of His people (vv.1-2).
2. Ask God to turn you back to Him (vv.3-6).
3. Beg God to restore you—make His face shine on you and save you—lest you be condemned: Seen in the example of Israel (vv.7-16).
4. Ask God to revive you through the Savior—the Davidic King: A picture of Christ, Ps.110:1, Da.7:13-14, Ep.1:20; He.1:13 (vv.17-19).

1 (80:1-2) **Appeal to God as your Shepherd, the Shepherd of His people.**
Addressing God as the *Shepherd of Israel*, the psalmist called on God to listen attentively to his prayer. The image of God as Shepherd is a tender and precious one to His people. It emphasizes our total dependence on God as well as our foolish tendency to stray from Him. Asaph appealed to God on this basis, reminding God how desperately His sheep need His guidance and help.

a. Because He leads and cares for His people like a flock (v.1ᵃ).
The psalmist gave God praise because He had always led His people like a shepherd leads his flock, even when they turned away from Him. In Asaph's previous psalms, he noted that God had led His rebellious people like a flock of sheep in the wilderness (Ps.77:20; 78:52). Here, he called on God to guide them through this crisis just as He did then.[1] Even when He was

forced to judge them for their unfaithfulness, God faithfully cared for His dear people.

Asaph addressed God as "you who lead Joseph." Joseph may represent the entire Northern Kingdom, as his descendants were a part of this faction or group that had split off from the southern tribes. Or, the psalmist may have been asking God to deliver his descendants for faithful Joseph's sake.

b. Because you need God's presence (vv.1ᵇ-2).
Asaph also praised God for His presence among His people. The cherubim referred to are the angels whose wings covered the ark of the covenant, where God's presence dwelled in a special way. Just as God's glory had shone when His presence filled the tabernacle and later the temple, the psalmist prayed for the glory of God's presence to shine on Israel (v.1ᵇ; Ex.40:35; 2 Chr.7:1-2).

Asaph then asked God to awaken His mighty power and to save His oppressed people (v.2). Notice the mention of Ephraim and Benjamin and Manasseh. The tribes of Ephraim and Manasseh, Joseph's sons, were part of the Northern Kingdom. And, as stated above, the tribes of Judah and Benjamin made up the Southern Kingdom. By mentioning Ephraim, Benjamin, and Manasseh together, the psalmist was undoubtedly praying that God would deliver the Northern Kingdom before all of Israel—both kingdoms. He may have been requesting for this crisis to reunite the LORD's chosen nation. The mention of these specific tribes as representatives of the two kingdoms is significant because Joseph and Benjamin were Rachel's two sons.[2] Note that Asaph mentioned Benjamin *between* Ephraim and Manasseh—an unusual arrangement under the circumstances of the divided kingdom. Asaph's request appears to be for the family to come back together. He may even have been praying that the southern tribes would rise to their brother Joseph's defense—that God would save Israel, the Northern Kingdom, by showing His mighty power through Judah, the Southern Kingdom.

Thought 1. Assyria's capture of the Northern Kingdom was God's discipline upon them for their unfaithfulness. Praise God that He is a faithful Shepherd; He does not just let us, His sheep, go when we stray from Him. He leads us along the path of righteousness, and when we wander from that path, He pulls us back to Him with His staff—a symbol of His correction (Ps.23:2-4). What a comfort to know that God will bring us back to Him even when we turn away (see Ps.23:2-3, Thought 3 for further discussion)!

The image of God as our Shepherd finds its ultimate fulfillment in Jesus Christ, the Good Shepherd

---

1 Warren W. Wiersbe. *The Bible Exposition Commentary*. WORDsearch CROSS e-book.

2 John F. Walvoord, ed. *The Bible Knowledge Commentary: An Exposition of the Scriptures by Dallas Seminary Faculty.*

who gave His life for His sheep (Jn.10:11). One of the most touching stories in Scripture is Jesus' parable of the lost sheep (Lu.15:4-6). In it, Jesus described a shepherd who had one hundred sheep going after one lone sheep that was lost. When he found it, he carried it safely home on his shoulders and rejoiced. The shepherd of whom Jesus spoke was Himself. He will not allow one of His sheep to be lost. When we—His beloved sheep for whom He died—stray from Him, He will do whatever He must to bring us back to the fold. We are secure as believers, but not because we are faithful, because we are not. We are secure because our Shepherd is faithful. He loves us so much that He will find us, bring us back to Him, and discipline us to teach us not to stray. Truly, He is "that great Shepherd of the sheep" (He.13:20).

> "Suppose one of you has a hundred sheep and loses one of them. Does he not leave the ninety-nine in the open country and go after the lost sheep until he finds it? And when he finds it, he joyfully puts it on his shoulders and goes home. Then he calls his friends and neighbors together and says, 'Rejoice with me; I have found my lost sheep' (Lu.15:4-6).

> "I am the good shepherd. The good shepherd lays down his life for the sheep (Jn.10:11).

> For you were like sheep going astray, but now you have returned to the Shepherd and Overseer of your souls (1 Pe.2:25).

> He tends his flock like a shepherd: He gathers the lambs in his arms and carries them close to his heart; he gently leads those that have young (Is.40:11).

> "Hear the word of the LORD, O nations; proclaim it in distant coastlands: 'He who scattered Israel will gather them and will watch over his flock like a shepherd' (Je.31:10).

> As a shepherd looks after his scattered flock when he is with them, so will I look after my sheep. I will rescue them from all the places where they were scattered on a day of clouds and darkness (Eze.34:12).

2 (80:3-6) **Ask God to turn you back to Him.**
Asaph interceded in behalf of Israel's rebellious people. God's painful discipline had brought His sinful people to their knees. Now, God's servant asked God to turn them back to Him, that He might once again view them with favor and deliver them from their suffering.

a. **Because you need His face to shine on you, to accept and save you (v.3).**
The psalmist asked God to make His face shine on Israel. This request is repeated two other times in the psalm (vv.7, 19). "Make your face shine" echoes the ancient blessing that Aaron pronounced over God's people (Nu.6:25). It is a request for God's favor, blessing, and help.

Asaph understood an important spiritual truth: before God could shine His favor on Israel, they had to repent. Accordingly, he first asked God to *restore us* (shub), to revive His people so they would return to Him (see outline and notes—Ps.23:3 for more discussion). More than anything else, Israel needed to be restored spiritually. When they returned to God, God would accept them and save them from their enemies.

b. **Because His hand of discipline has fallen on you: Due to your sin and your selfish, insincere prayers, Js.4:1-3 (vv.4-6).**
Asaph acknowledged that the Assyrian captivity was God's hand of discipline on His wayward people. Because of their atrocious sins and selfish, insincere prayers, Israel had ignited God's wrath (v.4; Js.4:1-3). "Anger smolder against the prayers of your people" may also mean that, because of His anger toward them, God would not hear His people's cries for help (Jer.7:16; 11:14). *Anger* (ashan) is the word used of the smoke that rises from a smoldering fire. It pictures God's continued fury toward His unfaithful people (Ps.74:1; Is.65:15). Asaph asked how long the fire of His wrath toward Israel would continue to burn.

Because of God's painful discipline, the people of Israel wept continually (v.5). God had allowed His disobedient people to suffer the consequences of their sinful desires and selfish prayers. The language Asaph used to describe their grief looks back on God's provision for Israel in their wilderness wanderings. Then, He fed them with manna and gave them water to drink, even when they provoked Him to anger (Ps.78:15-24). Now, an abundance of tears was their food and drink.

God disciplined His unfaithful people by allowing them to suffer oppression at the hands of their enemies. Their humiliating defeat gave their neighbors—the enemy nations that adjoined the land of Israel—reason to mock (v.6). As Israel's adversaries laughed among themselves, their ridicule multiplied the excruciating shame of God's rebellious people.

Thought 1. Revival begins with repentance. Any sincere prayer for revival will begin with a call for repentance. Accordingly, Asaph prayed for God to turn Israel back to Him. Again and again in Scripture, turning back or returning to God is directly connected to turning away from sin (De.30:2; Is.59:20; 1 K.8:33; Je.4:1).

True revival will never come until we are willing to give up our sin. Nor will it come to a church until most are ready to turn away from their sin. God only restores our fellowship with Him when we genuinely repent. Until then, as individual believers, we will continue to live under His painful discipline, and churches will continue to be powerless. Not only that but, like disgraced Israel, we will also continue to be scorned and ridiculed by the world.

> **Remember the height from which you have fallen! Repent and do the things you did at first. If you do not repent, I will come to you and remove your lampstand from its place (Re.2:5).**
>
> **Those whom I love I rebuke and discipline. So be earnest, and repent (Re.3:19).**
>
> **"When your people Israel have been defeated by an enemy because they have sinned against you, and when they turn back to you and confess your name, praying and making supplication to you in this temple (1 K.8:33).**
>
> **If my people, who are called by my name, will humble themselves and pray and seek my face and turn from their wicked ways, then will I hear from heaven and will forgive their sin and will heal their land (2 Chr.7:14).**
>
> **"If you will return, O Israel, return to me," declares the LORD. "If you put your detestable idols out of my sight and no longer go astray (Je.4:1).**

3 (80:7-16) **Beg God to restore you—make His face shine on you and save you—lest you be condemned: Seen in the example of Israel.**

For the second time, the psalmist spoke for the oppressed people of Israel, begging God to restore them to fellowship with Him (v.3). He asked God to make His face shine on them and save them from the shame of their repeated failures. His condemnation had brought them low. Their only hope was for God to revive them.

a. God brought Israel out of Egypt as if she were a tender vine (vv.8-11).

The psalmist appealed to God on the basis of His special love for Israel and all He had done for the nation. God had brought Israel out of Egypt as though she were a vine He had purchased—a vine that was to serve a very distinct purpose (v.8ª). The image of Israel as God's vine was first used by Jacob and is a prominent image in the Old Testament. As Jacob blessed his sons shortly before he died, he declared that Joseph would be a fruitful bough or vine with extensive branches (Ge.49:22). Generations later, the prophets frequently described Israel as God's vine (Is.5:1-7; 27:2-6; Je.2:21; 8:13; Eze.15:1-8; 19:10; Ho.10:1).

The LORD gave Israel the richest region on earth to grow and bear fruit for Him. He drove the heathen nations out of the promised land and planted His vine there (v.8ᵇ). He prepared room before it, clearing the ground so it could take deep root and grow. Then, He blessed the vine so it filled the land (v.9). It grew so great that its shadow or shade—a symbol of its prosperity—covered the mountains, and its branches towered over the mighty cedar trees (v.10).

Notice how the psalmist went to the extreme to convey the extent of God's blessings on Israel. To the ancient Hebrews, the mountains surrounding Israel and the cedars of Lebanon were the most celebrated examples of God's majestic creation. Imagine a grape vine so huge that it shaded the highest mountains in the land. Imagine its branches overreaching the cedars of Lebanon, which were said to be 150 feet tall. This was how profusely God had blessed Israel.

Along with this soaring image, Asaph described the breadth of God's blessings, telling how God expanded Israel's territory (vv.10-11). The mountains and the cedars represent Israel's southern and northern boundaries. God grew her branches out to the sea and to the river—westward to the Mediterranean and eastward to the Euphrates.

b. God executed judgment on Israel (the vine): Because of her sin (vv.12-13).

In spite of God's repeated warnings through the prophets, Israel persisted in disobedience to the LORD. Therefore, God executed judgment on His people, the vine, because of their sin. Hedges or walls around a vineyard protected it from thieves and destructive animals, but God broke down His vineyard's walls, allowing its fruit to be stolen by intruders (v.12). Likewise, He permitted wild beasts to ravage and take over His vineyard (v.13).

The symbolism of these images is clear: God had removed His divine protection from Israel due to her ongoing sin. As a result, Assyria invaded the country and stole those things God had used to bless His special people. Like wild beasts, the enemy nation ravaged the land and overtook Israel.

c. Israel was desperate: The people needed God to return to them at once—to watch over and take care of them (vv.14-16).

Having been plundered and captured by the enemy, Israel's situation was desperate. The people needed God's immediate help. The psalmist pled with God to return to His vine—to look down from heaven and observe how His people were suffering. He humbly asked God to visit them, to watch over and take care of them once again.

Asaph reminded God of His special relationship with the people of Israel, His beloved vineyard. He had planted them with His right hand, a symbol of His favor and power (v.15). He had raised up from among them a son for Himself. Above all the people of the earth, they were God's unique treasure (Ex.19:5; Ps.135:4). Now, His rebuke or discipline was destroying them (v.16). His vineyard had been burned and cut down.

Thought 1. Israel's experience serves as an example for us today (1 Co.10:6-11). God raised up Israel and abundantly blessed the people so they could bear fruit for Him as well as worship and glorify His name. Similarly, we have been redeemed and greatly blessed so that we can worship the Lord and bear fruit for Him (Jn.15:8; 1 Co.6:20). Like Israel before us, we will be judged by God when we turn to sin and live in disobedience to Him.

The image of the vine is continued in the New Testament with Jesus as the vine and believers as branches of the vine (Jn.15:1-8, 15). Jesus taught clearly that the Father will judge all who do not bear fruit for Him (Jn.15:6).

God paid the ultimate price for us—the blood of His own Son (1 Pe.1:18-19). He has blessed us with all spiritual blessings in Christ. Why? So that we will strive to live holy lives before Him (Ep.1:3-4). We have a sacred responsibility to fulfill the purpose for which God redeemed us. When we turn to sin and disobedience, we cease to glorify God's name and to worship Him effectively. At that moment, as soon as the Holy Spirit convicts us, we need to repent and beg God to restore us, lest—like Israel—we suffer the painful discipline of God.

> "I am the true vine, and my Father is the gardener. He cuts off every branch in me that bears no fruit, while every branch that does bear fruit he prunes so that it will be even more fruitful. You are already clean because of the word I have spoken to you. Remain in me, and I will remain in you. No branch can bear fruit by itself; it must remain in the vine. Neither can you bear fruit unless you remain in me. "I am the vine; you are the branches. If a man remains in me and I in him, he will bear much fruit; apart from me you can do nothing. If anyone does not remain in me, he is like a branch that is thrown away and withers; such branches are picked up, thrown into the fire and burned (Jn.15:1-6).

> He himself bore our sins in his body on the tree, so that we might die to sins and live for righteousness; by his wounds you have been healed (1 Pe.2:24).

> Restore to me the joy of your salvation and grant me a willing spirit, to sustain me (Ps.51:12).

> Will you not revive us again, that your people may rejoice in you? (Ps.85:6).

> "Return, faithless people; I will cure you of backsliding." "Yes, we will come to you, for you are the LORD our God (Je.3:22).

4 (80:17-19) **Ask God to revive you through the Savior—the Davidic King: A picture of Christ, Ps.110:1; Da.7:13-14; Ep.1:20; He.1:13.**
Psalm 80 draws to a close with a third plea for God to revive the disobedient people of Israel. The psalmist asked God to place His hand of blessing on "the man at your right hand" (v.17). To whom does this refer?
 ➤ Some commentators say it is a reference to Benjamin, which means *son of the right hand.*
 ➤ Others think it speaks of Israel, "God's firstborn and right-hand man among humanity" (Ho.11:1).[3] Israel was identified with God's right hand earlier in the psalm (v.15).
 ➤ Still others believe it points to Israel's king.

However, further identification of "the man at your right hand" as the son of man points prophetically to the Savior, Jesus Christ. Famous British preacher Charles Spurgeon wrote, "There is no doubt here an outlook to the Messiah, for whom believing Jews had learned to look as the Savior in time of trouble....These striking expressions apply in the fullest and most perfect sense to Christ."[4]

Repeatedly in Scripture, God's Son is said to be at God's right hand:

> The LORD says to my Lord: "Sit at my right hand until I make your enemies a footstool for your feet" (Ps.110:1).

> Which he exerted in Christ when he raised him from the dead and seated him at his right hand in the heavenly realms (Ep.1:20).

> To which of the angels did God ever say, "Sit at my right hand until I make your enemies a footstool for your feet"? (He.1:13).

In the Bible, Jesus is often referred to as the Son of Man. Spurgeon noted that "it is one of Christ's most definite titles, given to Him in Scripture no less than seventy-one times."[5] This is the title by which Jesus most often

---

3 Derek Kidner. *Psalms 73-150*, p.323.
4 Charles Spurgeon. *Treasury of David.* WORDsearch CROSS e-book.
5 Ibid.

referred to Himself. In the Old Testament, Daniel called Christ by this name as well:

> **"In my vision at night I looked, and there before me was one like a son of man, coming with the clouds of heaven. He approached the Ancient of Days and was led into his presence. He was given authority, glory and sovereign power; all peoples, nations and men of every language worshiped him. His dominion is an everlasting dominion that will not pass away, and his kingdom is one that will never be destroyed (Da.7:13-14).**

Note the repetition here of "raised up for yourself" (v.15). The son that grew out of the vineyard of Israel is identified here as the son of man—the Davidic King, Jesus Christ. Israel's only hope for salvation was, and is, Jesus Christ.

a. **So you will not turn away but be revived and call on His name (v.18).**
The psalmist truly believed that if God would revive His people, they would call on His name and never again turn away from Him. Sadly, that was not to be the case; nevertheless, this statement is prophetic of Israel's salvation in the end times.

b. **So He will turn you back to Him and grant His presence: Then you will be saved (v.19).**
For the third time, the psalmist prayed that God would restore His people to Himself and make His face shine on them. This will also come to pass in the end times. "Then they will be saved....The prayer will find its answer in the day when Christ comes back to earth again."[6]

Thought 1. Israel sought salvation in the Messiah, but when He came, they rejected Him (Jn.1:11). When Jesus comes again, however, Israel will receive Him and be saved (Je.23:5-6; Ro.11:26-27).

We too can be saved only through faith in Jesus Christ (Ac.4:12). And when we backslide and turn away from Him, we can be restored only through Christ. He is our advocate with the Father (1 Jn.2:1).

His blood continues to wash away our sin (1 Jn.1:7). God made this wonderful promise: if we confess our sins, He will cleanse us and cause His face to shine on us once again (1 Jn.1:9). If our hearts no longer burn for the Lord and we drift away from Him, we need to repent at once and return to Christ (Re.2:4-5). When we do, we have God's Word, His assurance, that He will revive and restore us to Him.

> **Salvation is found in no one else, for there is no other name under heaven given to men by which we must be saved" (Ac.4:12).**
> **And so all Israel will be saved, as it is written: "The deliverer will come from Zion; he will turn godlessness away from Jacob. And this is my covenant with them when I take away their sins" (Ro.11:26-27).**
> **But if we walk in the light, as he is in the light, we have fellowship with one another, and the blood of Jesus, his Son, purifies us from all sin. If we claim to be without sin, we deceive ourselves and the truth is not in us. If we confess our sins, he is faithful and just and will forgive us our sins and purify us from all unrighteousness. If we claim we have not sinned, we make him out to be a liar and his word has no place in our lives. My dear children, I write this to you so that you will not sin. But if anybody does sin, we have one who speaks to the Father in our defense—Jesus Christ, the Righteous One. He is the atoning sacrifice for our sins, and not only for ours but also for the sins of the whole world (1 Jn.1:7-2:2).**
> **"The days are coming," declares the LORD, "when I will raise up to David a righteous Branch, a King who will reign wisely and do what is just and right in the land. In his days Judah will be saved and Israel will live in safety. This is the name by which he will be called: The LORD Our Righteousness (Je.23:5-6).**

---

6   Arno Gabelein. *The Book of Psalms*, p.313.

PSALM 81

What Your Duty Is Regarding True Worship, 81:1-16

For the director of music. According to gittith. Of Asaph.

1. Join God's people in worship
a. Praise God, our strength
  1) Sing for joy
  2) Play your musical instruments

b. Worship God faithfully at scheduled times & festivals

  1) Bc. this is God's decree for His people, He.10:25

  2) Bc. God made it a law when He delivered His people from Egypt

2. Hear God's promise & warning
a. God will remove the burden of your enslavement (to sin)—even as He did for Israel
  1) He hears your cry of distress
  2) He will save you
b. God will deliver you through all the trials of life—even as

Sing for joy to God our strength; shout aloud to the God of Jacob!
2 Begin the music, strike the tambourine, play the melodious harp and lyre.
3 Sound the ram's horn at the New Moon, and when the moon is full, on the day of our Feast;
4 This is a decree for Israel, an ordinance of the God of Jacob.
5 He established it as a statute for Joseph when he went out against Egypt, where we heard a language we did not understand.
6 He says, "I removed the burden from their shoulders; their hands were set free from the basket.
7 In your distress you called and I rescued you, I answered you out of a thundercloud; I tested you

at the waters of Meribah. Selah
8 "Hear, O my people, and I will warn you—if you would but listen to me, O Israel!
9 You shall have no foreign god among you; you shall not bow down to an alien god.
10 I am the LORD your God, who brought you up out of Egypt. Open wide your mouth and I will fill it.
11 "But my people would not listen to me; Israel would not submit to me.
12 So I gave them over to their stubborn hearts to follow their own devices.
13 "If my people would but listen to me, if Israel would follow my ways,
14 How quickly would I subdue their enemies and turn my hand against their foes!
15 Those who hate the LORD would cringe before him, and their punishment would last forever.
16 But you would be fed with the finest of wheat; with honey from the rock I would satisfy you."

He did Israel at Meribah, Ex.17:1-7; Nu.20:1-13
c. God issues a stern warning to you
  1) You must listen & be faithful to Him
  2) You must never acknowledge or worship a false god, De.5:7

d. God alone can save you from bondage & meet your every need: He wants to fill you with every good thing, Ph.4:19
e. God will judge the disobedient & rebellious—even as He did Israel: Bc. of their stubbornness, God gave them over to their shameful desires, Ro.1:24-32

3. Listen to what God says: Obey His Word & live for Him

a. Then He will protect you
  1) Will subdue your enemies & turn against your foes
  2) Will cause those who hate Him to cringe in submission
  3) Will doom the rebellious to eternal punishment
b. Then He will give you the necessities of life: You will be fully & permanently satisfied, Mt.6:25-35

PSALM 81

What Your Duty Is Regarding True Worship, 81:1-16

(81:1-16) **Introduction:** sadly, a high percentage of professing believers do not regularly attend church services. Of this number, some excuse their failure to gather with God's people by claiming they worship privately and do not need to go to church. Others say they praise God every day and not on one specific day of the week. Certainly, private worship is important and ought to be a crucial part of our daily lives. We can praise God at any time and in any place. But God has also commanded us to worship with other believers. It is His will that we regularly assemble to praise and worship Him (He.10:25). This is true for the church under the new covenant, and it was true for the congregation of Israel under the old covenant.

God has ordained or instituted corporate or congregational worship. As commentator Matthew Henry wisely explained, "No time is amiss for praising God...but some are times appointed, not for God to meet us (He is always ready), but for us to meet one another, that we may join together in praising God."[1] Henry preceded this statement by saying, "[w]e should join many together in this work; the more the better; it is the more like heaven."[2]

Asaph wrote Psalm 81 for an occasion of public worship. Most scholars agree that the occasion was the Feast of Tabernacles (v.3). Like many psalms, it was committed to the chief musician, the director of music in the temple. This call to worship was to be performed on the *gittith*, a harp-like instrument from the region of Gath. Some scholars believe *gittith* was an instruction for a psalm to be performed at the Feast of Tabernacles. This is, *What Your Duty Is Regarding True Worship*, 81:1-16.

1. Join God's people in worship (vv.1-5).
2. Hear God's promise and warning (vv.6-12).
3. Listen to what God says: Obey His Word and live for Him (vv.13-16).

1 (81:1-5) **Join God's people in worship.**
The music director called the people to join together in worshipping the LORD. While some worship is appropriately calm and reflective, this was a time for joyful, exuberant praise. The people were celebrating their powerful God and His mighty works in their behalf.

a. Praise God, our strength (vv.1-2).
The worship leader directed the people to sing to God with joy (v.1). *Shout aloud* (ruah) means to make a

---

1 Matthew Henry. *Matthew Henry's Commentary on the Whole Bible.* WORD*search* CROSS e-book.
2 Ibid.

loud noise and is more clearly translated as *shout for joy*. Interestingly, this verb "always takes a plural or collective subject."[3] In whatever setting it is used, it is an action by a group of people as opposed to an individual. Here, it is a direction to the congregation to shout to the LORD collectively. The object of their triumphant praise was *God our strength,* the *God of Jacob.*

Next, the worship leader directed the musicians to play a psalm or song to the glory of God. He mentioned three instruments in particular:

➢ The *tambourine* or timbrel
➢ The *harp:* pleasant to the ear, delightful, melodious, and sweet-sounding
➢ The *lyre*: either a twelve-stringed instrument or a wind instrument made from animal skins (see outline and notes—Ps.32:2-3 for more discussion)

b. Worship God faithfully at scheduled times and festivals (vv.3-5).

The worship leader announced the occasion for this celebration: it was the scheduled time for the Feast of Booths or Feast of Tabernacles (v.3). The blowing of the ram's horn (shophar) announced the beginning of the festival season (Le.23:24). The new moon refers to the first day of the seventh month of the Jewish religious year, the month in which the Day of Atonement was observed (Le.23:23-32). The time appointed refers to the time of the full moon, which was when the LORD ordered the Feast of Tabernacles to be celebrated. Specifically, it was the fifteenth to twenty-second days of the month (Lev.23:33-34).

God had decreed this special time for His people to come together to praise and worship Him (v.4). He had instituted this statute or law when He delivered His people from Egypt as a testimony to their dwelling in booths after the Exodus (v.5a; Le.23:43). As the first of Jacob's descendants in Egypt, Joseph represents the entire nation. God's deliverance of His people was also a testimony to Joseph's faith. On his deathbed, Joseph prophesied that God would bring them out of Egypt and into the promised land. He proceeded to instruct the people to carry his bones with them when that glorious day came (Ge.50:24-25; He.11:22).

The words "where we heard a language we did not understand" are unclear in the Hebrew text (v.5b). If they belong with the preceding statement, they refer to the Egyptian language. However, some scholars believe the phrase belongs with the verses that follow it (vv.6-12). They note that it can also be translated as, "'We heard a voice we had not known', referring to the message God sent" to the people.[4]

---

3 Thoraf Gilbrant and Gregory A. Lint, eds. *The Complete Biblical Library: The Old Testament Hebrew-English Dictionary.* WORDsearch CROSS e-book.

4 Warren W. Wiersbe. *The Bible Exposition Commentary.* WORDsearch CROSS e-book.

Thought 1. God has commanded us to assemble to worship Him just as He did the people of Israel. They gathered to praise Him for their deliverance from Egypt, a clear picture of our salvation, our deliverance from the world. From the very beginning of the church, which was born on the Day of Pentecost, believers gathered together for worship, fellowship, and teaching. They eventually selected Sunday as their primary day of worship because this was the day of the week Christ rose from the dead. Appropriately it was, and still is, called the Lord's Day (Re.1:10).

The early believers established a pattern for assembling that we should still follow. This pattern was confirmed by a direct command that declares we should not forsake the assembling of ourselves together—not stop going to church (He.10:25). The believer who does not attend church services regularly is living in open disobedience to this command. Naturally, there are legitimate reasons some people cannot attend church services regularly or possibly not at all. Being ill or bedridden are just a few of them. Still, as believers, we are to do everything we can to join God's people in worship.

> **He went to Nazareth, where he had been brought up, and on the Sabbath day he went into the synagogue, as was his custom. And he stood up to read (Lu.4:16).**
>
> **Then they worshiped him and returned to Jerusalem with great joy. And they stayed continually at the temple, praising God (Lu.24:52-53).**
>
> **Every day they continued to meet together in the temple courts. They broke bread in their homes and ate together with glad and sincere hearts (Ac.2:46).**
>
> **And let us consider how we may spur one another on toward love and good deeds. Let us not give up meeting together, as some are in the habit of doing, but let us encourage one another—and all the more as you see the Day approaching (He.10:24-25).**
>
> **Blessed are those who dwell in your house; they are ever praising you. Selah (Ps.84:4).**

2 (81:6-12) Hear God's promise and warning.

Beginning in verse 6, God is the speaker. He had an important message for His people while they were gathered to praise Him. Thus, He commanded the worshippers to hear what He had to say (v.8).

a. God will remove the burden of your enslavement (to sin)—even as He did for Israel (vv.6-7a).

God reminded His people that, by delivering them from Egypt, He had removed the burden of their enslavement (v.6). While in Egypt, the Hebrews were forced to labor in the scorching sun to build Pharaoh's magnificent cities (Ex.1:11-14). Cruelly oppressed, they cried out to the LORD. God heard them in their distress and saved them from their taskmasters (v.7ᵃ; Ex.2:23-25).

b. God will deliver you through all the trials of life—even as He did Israel at Meribah, Ex.17:1-7; Nu.20:1-13 (v.7ᵇ).

God then reminded His people that He had delivered them through all their trials as they journeyed to the promised land. He brought up *Meribah*, where the Israelites had tested God's faithfulness. Thirsty and without water, they had questioned whether God was really with them. In response to their complaining, God miraculously brought forth water out of a rock (Ex.17:1-7; Nu.20:1-13).

c. God issues a stern warning to you (vv.8-9).

God had given Himself fully to His people, and He expected the same measure of devotion from them. For that reason, He issued a stern warning: His people were to listen to His Word and faithfully do everything He commanded (v.8). Furthermore, they must never acknowledge or worship any false god (v.9; De.5:7). This included not having any images of other *so-called* gods, not praying to them, and not allowing for the possibility that they might exist.

d. God alone can save you from bondage and meet your every need: He wants to fill you with every good thing, Ph.4:19 (v.10).

God further reminded His people of His special relationship with them. He was the LORD (Yahweh, Jehovah)—the God who had made a covenant with them and kept His covenant (v.11). He alone had saved them from the bondage of Egypt. He had loved them and met their every need along the way (De.29:5-6). Now, He longed to continue caring for His beloved people and providing for their every need. In all of their history, the Israelites had only begun to see the bountiful blessings God desired to bestow on them. With that in mind, He issued a gracious invitation to them: "Open wide your mouth," He said, "and I will fill it." Out of His steadfast love for His people, the LORD promised to fill them with every good thing (Ph.4:19).

e. God will judge the disobedient and rebellious—even as He did Israel: Because of their stubbornness, God gave them over to their shameful desires, Ro.1:24-32 (vv.11-12).

Finally, God reminded His people that He judges those who are disobedient and rebellious. Their ancestors were the most glaring example of this sobering truth (v.11). In spite of all God had done for them, the Israelites refused to hearken to God, to listen to and obey Him. "Would not submit to me" means that they were not willing to follow God; they would not consent to His will.

Therefore, God gave the people over to the sinful desires of their stubborn hearts (v.12). He allowed them to walk in their own counsels, their own purposes and plans. Simply stated, God let His rebellious people do as they pleased (Ro.1:24-32; Je.7:24).

Thought 1. What God said to the people of Israel is what He says to the church today. First, we need to remember what God has done for us in giving us salvation (v.6). Through the sacrifice of Jesus Christ, God has set us free from our enslavement to sin. No longer do we have to live in bondage. We are free from its *power* over us (Ro.6:14-22; Jn.8:34-3). In addition, we have been set free from sin's *penalty*. No longer do we have to fear death, for He has given us eternal life through Jesus Christ our Lord (Ro.6:23; 8:1-2). One day, praise God, we will be free from sin's very *presence*. We will live eternally with the Lord in a new heaven and a new earth (Re.21:1-27).

Second, God will help us through all the trials of life (v.7). We can call on Him in times of trouble, and He will help us. He promises that His grace will be sufficient for every need (2 Co.12:9; He.4:16). We never have to face our trials alone, for He has promised to be with us always (He.13:5-6).

Third, God will meet our needs (v.10). He wants to fill us with every good thing (Ph.4:19). Jesus taught us not to worry about our needs in this life but to focus on God and His righteousness. When we do, the Father will take care of us. He will provide everything we need (Mt.6:31-33).

God wants to bless us in ways we can never begin to imagine. But it is essential for us to listen to Him and obey Him (v.8). We need to hear God's Word and submit to His will for our lives (v.11). He will judge us if we are disobedient to Him. He will discipline us, just as a loving father disciplines his children (He.12:6-11). If we stubbornly persist in rebellion against Him, He will give us up to our own sinful desires (v.12; Ro.1:24-32). Listen to this stark reality: "The greatest judgment God can send is to let people have their own way."[5] Self-indulgence leads to self-destruction—premature death because of our selfish sin (1 Co.5:5; 11:30-32).

> **Do not merely listen to the word, and so deceive yourselves. Do what it says. Anyone who listens to the word but does not do what it says is like a man who looks at his face in a mirror and, after looking at himself, goes away and immediately forgets what he looks like. But the man who looks intently into the perfect law that gives freedom, and continues to do this, not forgetting what he has heard, but doing it—he will be blessed in what he does (Js.1:22-25).**

---

5 Warren W. Wiersbe. *The Bible Exposition Commentary.* WORDsearch CROSS e-book.

But if anyone obeys his word, God's love is truly made complete in him. This is how we know we are in him (1 Jn.2:5).

And receive from him anything we ask, because we obey his commands and do what pleases him (1 Jn.3:22).

Hear now, O Israel, the decrees and laws I am about to teach you. Follow them so that you may live and may go in and take possession of the land that the LORD, the God of your fathers, is giving you (De.4:1).

If you pay attention to these laws and are careful to follow them, then the LORD your God will keep his covenant of love with you, as he swore to your forefathers. He will love you and bless you and increase your numbers. He will bless the fruit of your womb, the crops of your land—your grain, new wine and oil—the calves of your herds and the lambs of your flocks in the land that he swore to your forefathers to give you (De.7:12-13).

3 (81:13-16) **Listen to what God says: Obey His Word and live for Him.**

God had a compelling message for His people: He urged them to obey and follow His Word. As He looked back on Israel's history, the LORD grieved because they stubbornly refused to live for Him. If they had only listened and walked in His ways, the LORD would have showered His abundant blessings on them. Instead they had to bear His painful judgment.

a. Then He will protect you (vv.14-15).

If Israel had obeyed God, He would have protected His people from their adversaries. But when they stubbornly turned away from Him, God lifted His hand of protection and allowed their foes to conquer them. If they had only stayed true to Him, God would have subdued their enemies and struck them down with His mighty hand, just as He had promised (v.14; De.6:16-24). Remember those who opposed Israel opposed God; therefore, God would have caused the enemy to cringe in fearful submission to Him. He would have doomed them to eternal punishment (v.15). Sadly, though, Israel did not obey God and thus brought about her own defeat.

b. Then He will give you the necessities of life: You will be fully and permanently satisfied, Mt.6:25-35 (v.16).

If the people had obeyed and lived for God, He would have given them the very best He could offer—the finest wheat and honey out of the rock (De.32:13). He would have provided for their necessities in marvelous ways (Mt.6:25-35). They would have enjoyed a life of complete satisfaction. *Satisfy* (sabea) means

filled to the point of desiring nothing more. This is the abundant life God offers those who love and obey Him; they will be fully and permanently satisfied (Mt. 5:6; Jn.4:14; Jn.6:35).

Thought 1. Psalm 81 highlights three elements that ought to be a part of our worship services. When we gather together, we should...

- exalt God in worship and praise (vv.1-5)
- hear what God has to say to us from His Word (vv.6-12)
- respond to what God says to us (vv.13-16)

Presenting ourselves to God—committing to live for Him—is the essence of true worship. Scripture calls this our reasonable service (Ro.12:1). God desires our obedience more than anything else (1 S.15:22). When the LORD speaks to us through His Word, we have to make a decision: we either obey God and follow His Word, or else we disregard God's commands. God wants us to obey Him because He loves us so much. He always desires what is best for us. His commandments are not grievous; that is, they are not intended to bind or restrict us (1 Jn.5:3). They are for our welfare: when we obey God's Word, we are spared the painful consequences of sin. God also longs to bless us richly—His dear sons and daughters for whom He gave His only begotten Son. Obedience brings God's blessing. If we obey and follow His Word, He will reward us with His very best. However, if we refuse to obey Him, we forfeit God's blessings and protection.

"If you love me, you will obey what I command (Jn.14:15).

Therefore, I urge you, brothers, in view of God's mercy, to offer your bodies as living sacrifices, holy and pleasing to God—this is your spiritual act of worship (Ro.12:1).

And receive from him anything we ask, because we obey his commands and do what pleases him (1 Jn.3:22).

Now if you obey me fully and keep my covenant, then out of all nations you will be my treasured possession. Although the whole earth is mine (Ex.19:5).

The LORD heard you when you spoke to me and the LORD said to me, "I have heard what this people said to you. Everything they said was good (De.5:28).

But Samuel replied: "Does the LORD delight in burnt offerings and sacrifices as much as in obeying the voice of the LORD? To obey is better than sacrifice, and to heed is better than the fat of rams (1 S.15:22).

"Now then, my sons, listen to me; blessed are those who keep my ways (Pr.8:32).

	PSALM 82 **What the World's Judges Should Know, 82:1-8** *A Psalm of Asaph.*	4 Rescue the weak and needy; deliver them from the hand of the wicked.	b. You must rescue the vulnerable & needy from the wicked

1. God is the supreme Chief Justice
  a. He presides over heaven's court
  b. He executes justice on all judges
2. God charges all unjust judges
  a. They rule unfairly, unethically
  b. They show bias against the upright & favor the wicked
3. God commands all judges
  a. You must defend & uphold the rights of all—especially the helpless & oppressed
	God presides in the great assembly; he gives judgment among the "gods":
	2 "How long will you defend the unjust and show partiality to the wicked? Selah
	3 Defend the cause of the weak and fatherless; maintain the rights of the poor and oppressed.
		5 "They know nothing, they understand nothing. They walk about in darkness; all the foundations of the earth are shaken.
		6 "I said, 'You are "gods"; you are all sons of the Most High.'
		7 But you will die like mere men; you will fall like every other ruler."
		8 Rise up, O God, judge the earth, for all the nations are your inheritance
			4. God condemns all evil judges
			  a. You are ignorant of the truth, its importance & strength
			  b. You walk in darkness & your unjust rulings shake society
			  c. You are God's representatives of justice but you abuse the office
			  d. You will die like all other mortals & fall like all rulers
			
			  e. You will face God's judgment & lose God's inheritance—the new earth, 2 Pe.3:10-13

PSALM 82

What the World's Judges Should Know, 82:1-8

(82:1-8) Introduction: our God—the only true and living God—is a God of perfect justice. Therefore, when He created us and made us in His image, He also implanted within us an instinctive need, even a hunger, for justice. In nearly every society, some legal system of justice exists. But as with all human works, some systems are better than others, and each is flawed to a certain degree. In oppressive nations and societies, little true justice exists. Other societies strive diligently to provide justice for all.

Many authorities take their responsibility to execute justice seriously. Some, however, abuse the power that has been entrusted to them. Injustice is a universal problem, one that will continue until Jesus Christ returns to earth and establishes a perfect government.

Psalm 82 was written by Asaph to confront Israel's unjust judges. He is the speaker at the psalm's beginning and ending (vv.1, 8). In between, God is the speaker (vv.2-7). God charges Israel's crooked magistrates with judging unjustly, commands them to protect the helpless, and condemns them for their arrogant perversion of His laws. What God said to these corrupt officials applies to those in every age and every place who have been ordained by Him to administer, interpret, and enforce His righteous laws. This is, *What the World's Judges Should Know, 82:1-8.*

1. God is the supreme Chief Justice (v.1).
2. God charges all unjust judges (v.2).
3. God commands all judges (vv.3-4).
4. God condemns all evil judges (vv.5-8).

1 **(82:1) God is the supreme Chief Justice.**
God is the Supreme Judge of the entire universe. He gave the basic laws that are always to govern human societies (Is.33:22). These laws are based on His perfect righteousness and justice, and He has delegated their administration and enforcement to human rulers (De.16:18-20;

Ro.13:1-6). Law enforcement personnel and judges are God's representatives here on earth. As His ordained authorities, they must answer to Him for their execution of justice according to His laws.

a. He presides over heaven's court (v.1a).
The psalmist begins by reminding us of a very significant fact: there is a greater court than our earthly halls of justice. The "great assembly" is heaven's court. It is God's courtroom where all people will be judged by Him. This includes all earthly authorities as well. God will assemble them there to be judged for how they carried out the power that He delegated to them.

b. He executes justice on all judges (v.1b).
Asaph declared that God judges among the gods. Obviously, the use of the word *gods* is unusual, making it the subject of much discussion. Because it is the Hebrew word *elohim*, it is translated as *gods* in the NIV and a number of other Bible versions. While *elohim* usually refers to the one true God, it is sometimes used of the false gods of pagans and also of angels. Occasionally in Scripture, *elohim* is used of human judges, and that is the case here (Ex.21:6; 22:8-9). Bible teacher Warren Wiersbe explains this simply and clearly:

> *The "gods" (vv. 1, 6) are not the false gods of the heathen, for such nonexistent gods are not Jehovah's judicial representatives on earth. Nor are these "gods" the holy angels, for angels cannot die (v. 7). These "gods" (elohim) are people who have been given the awesome responsibility of representing the Lord on earth and interpreting and applying His Law (Ex. 18:13-17; 21:6; Deut. 16:18-20; 17:2-13; 19:15-20; 21:2).*[1]

---

[1]   Warren W. Wiersbe. *The Bible Exposition Commentary.* WORDsearch CROSS e-book.

As always, the final authority on Scripture and its interpretation is Jesus Christ. Quoting verse 6, Jesus made it clear that gods refers to human judges (Jn.10:34-36). The leaders of the Jews had accused Jesus of blasphemy because He referred to Himself as God (Jn.10:33). As commentator James Montgomery Boice noted,

> *"What [Jesus] was doing was replying to their specific accusation...and His point was that God had used even stronger language than this of human judges in the Old Testament. Jesus' reply shows that He regarded Psalm 82 as being about Israel's civil rulers.*[2]

Thought 1. The world's judges should know that they are not the final authorities on law and justice. They will stand before God to give an account for how they discharged their duties. God Himself is the Chief Justice of all judges, and He carefully observes every courtroom on the face of the earth.

The foundational laws of most societies are actually God's laws. Throughout the world, governments agree that certain acts, such as murder and stealing, are crimes. Missionaries have attested that, upon entering places where the Bible has never been taken, a code of laws exists that mirrors the Ten Commandments. Why is this true? Because God has written His law on the heart of every human being (Ro.2:14-15). We know within ourselves that certain actions are wrong. Accordingly, God will judge every human being as to how he or she obeyed His laws, and He will judge those who were entrusted with the sacred duty to carry them out (Ro.2:16).

> **(Indeed, when Gentiles, who do not have the law, do by nature things required by the law, they are a law for themselves, even though they do not have the law, since they show that the requirements of the law are written on their hearts, their consciences also bearing witness, and their thoughts now accusing, now even defending them.) This will take place on the day when God will judge men's secrets through Jesus Christ, as my gospel declares (Ro.2:14-16).**
>
> **To the church of the firstborn, whose names are written in heaven. You have come to God, the judge of all men, to the spirits of righteous men made perfect (He.12:23).**
>
> **To judge everyone, and to convict all the ungodly of all the ungodly acts they have done in the ungodly way, and of all the harsh words ungodly sinners have spoken against him" (Jude 15).**

> **Far be it from you to do such a thing— to kill the righteous with the wicked, treating the righteous and the wicked alike. Far be it from you! Will not the Judge of all the earth do right?" (Ge.18:25).**
>
> **Then the trees of the forest will sing, they will sing for joy before the LORD, for he comes to judge the earth (1 Chr.16:33).**
>
> **"Can anyone teach knowledge to God, since he judges even the highest? (Jb.21:22).**

2 (82:2) God charges all unjust judges (v.2).

Israel's judges had failed miserably in their responsibility to fairly apply God's laws to society. God's charge against them was straightforward: they were guilty of gross injustice. God condemned their abuse of power by asking them how long they would continue to pervert justice.

a. They rule unfairly, unethically (v.2a).
With no thought of God and no regard for justice, Israel's corrupt judges handed down unjust decisions. They likely put their personal interests before the administration of justice. Whether due to bribery, seeking favor with certain people, seeking a higher position, or some other selfish motive, these officials failed to properly carry out the law in their courtrooms. Their rulings were unfair and unethical.

b. They show bias against the upright and favor the wicked (v.2b).
Israel's crooked judges "show[ed] partiality to the wicked." That is, they accepted criminals, allowing them to get away with their unlawful deeds. The verses that follow indicate that these dishonest authorities had perverted justice by favoring the rich and powerful at the expense of the poor (vv.3-4). This partiality was a flagrant violation of God's holy laws (Le.19:15; De.1:17; 16:19).

Thought 1. In some ways, our world is no different today than it has ever been. Good and evil still exist in every society. Many judges carry out their duties with integrity and honor but, sadly, some do not. Injustice and partiality do exist. Some judges accept bribes. Others hand down decisions based on self-interests. The wealthy, the powerful, political figures, celebrities, and even physically attractive people frequently have the scales of justice tipped in their favor by partial, crooked officials. In a number of cultures, people are discriminated against because of their social or financial status, race, religion, or gender.

God has a standard for human authorities to follow. The world's judges need to know that God is keeping a record of every violation of that standard. Scripture is clear: every unrighteous act on earth is recorded in heaven (Re.20:12). Corrupt authorities may get by

---

[2] James Montgomery Boice. *An Expositional Commentary–Psalms, Volume 2: Psalms 42-106.* WORDsearch CROSS e-book.

with their evil acts on earth, but they will not get away with them in the court of the Supreme Judge. Just as He announced the charges against Israel's unjust judges, God will also indict and condemn every dishonest official in the coming day of judgment.

> I charge you, in the sight of God and Christ Jesus and the elect angels, to keep these instructions without partiality, and to do nothing out of favoritism (1 Ti.5:21).

> Suppose a man comes into your meeting wearing a gold ring and fine clothes, and a poor man in shabby clothes also comes in. If you show special attention to the man wearing fine clothes and say, "Here's a good seat for you," but say to the poor man, "You stand there" or "Sit on the floor by my feet," have you not discriminated among yourselves and become judges with evil thoughts?...But if you show favoritism, you sin and are convicted by the law as lawbreakers (Js.2:2-4, 9).

> But the wisdom that comes from heaven is first of all pure; then peace-loving, considerate, submissive, full of mercy and good fruit, impartial and sincere (Js.3:17).

> These men are grumblers and fault-finders; they follow their own evil desires; they boast about themselves and flatter others for their own advantage (Jude 16).

> The LORD takes his place in court; he rises to judge the people. The LORD enters into judgment against the elders and leaders of his people: "It is you who have ruined my vineyard; the plunder from the poor is in your houses. What do you mean by crushing my people and grinding the faces of the poor?" declares the Lord, the LORD Almighty (Is.3:13-15).

> He has showed you, O man, what is good. And what does the LORD require of you? To act justly and to love mercy and to walk humbly with your God (Mi.6:8).

3 (82:3-4) **God commands all judges.**
The corruption of Israel's judges filled God with righteous indignation. Therefore, He sharply called them back to their sacred duty: to secure justice for all.

a. **You must defend and uphold the rights of all—especially the helpless and oppressed (v.3).**
God-ordained authorities are charged by Him to defend the cause of justice and maintain the rights of all people—especially those who cannot defend themselves:

> ➤ The *weak*
> ➤ The *fatherless*
> ➤ The *poor*
> ➤ The *oppressed*

It is usually the disadvantaged of society who do not receive justice, and this was the case in Israel. However, God's law required the courts to disregard a person's social and financial status. Judges were commanded not to discriminate at all, whether against the poor or against the wealthy (Le.19:15).

b. **You must rescue the vulnerable and needy from the wicked (v.4).**
God boldly ordered Israel's authorities to deliver or rescue the weak and needy from their wicked oppressors. Judges were to be the champions of the poor and oppressed. When greedy, wicked people took advantage of them, judges were commanded to rise in their defense. They were to stop the wicked from exploiting them.

Thought 1. Judges need to recognize and embrace their sacred duty as it has been defined by God, the Supreme Judge. They are the protectors of those who do not have the means or ability to protect themselves. They are to stand for those who cannot stand for themselves. Judges are duty-bound to rescue the abused from their abusers and the exploited from those who take advantage of them. They should see themselves as God sees them—as champions of the afflicted and helpless.

> "The King will reply, 'I tell you the truth, whatever you did for one of the least of these brothers of mine, you did for me' (Mt.25:40).

> As it is written: "He has scattered abroad his gifts to the poor; his righteousness endures forever" (2 Co.9:9).

> "Do not deny justice to your poor people in their lawsuits (Ex.23:6).

> Do not show partiality in judging; hear both small and great alike. Do not be afraid of any man, for judgment belongs to God. Bring me any case too hard for you, and I will hear it (De.1:17).

> If a king judges the poor with fairness, his throne will always be secure (Pr.29:14).

> Speak up and judge fairly; defend the rights of the poor and needy" (Pr.31:9).

4 (82:5-8) **God condemns all evil judges.**
After laying out the charges against Israel's evil judges, God announced His condemnation of them. Because they willfully ignored His laws and despised their sacred responsibility, they would face His fierce judgment.

a. You are ignorant of the truth, its importance and strength (v.5ᵃ).

God stated that Israel's wicked judges did not know or understand the importance of the truth. *Know* (yada) means to know personally, to know by experience. To *understand* (biyn) is to perceive or discern. In other words, God was saying that fairness, righteousness, and justice were foreign concepts to Israel's dishonest officials. They willfully ignored how vital these virtues are to a civil society and to the citizens whose quality of life depends on them.

b. You walk in darkness and your unjust rulings shake society (v.5ᵇ).

Instead of opening their eyes to the light of God's truth and changing their ways, Israel's authorities continued to walk in the darkness of their corruption. As a result, the foundations of the earth were shaken. A peaceful and civil society is built on God's laws. When His principles are violated, chaos erupts. The unjust rulings of these crooked judges had shaken society to its very core.

c. You are God's representatives of justice but you abuse the office (v.6).

God emphatically stated that these judges' authority came directly from Him: *I said, 'You are "gods."* By referring to them as *gods* (elohim), God was not only emphasizing the power they exercised, but also that they were His representatives on earth. They had been entrusted with the awesome responsibility of executing justice on His behalf.

In addition, God addressed them as "sons of the Most High." Commentator Donald M. Williams explains that "the judges are sons by appointment, not by nature, since they are called to execute God's will and character. This concept is based on the calling in Israel of faithful sons to execute the will and character of their father."[3] Yet, they abused the office.

d. You will die like all other mortals and fall like all rulers (v.7).

In response to the judges' arrogance—an arrogance that elevated their personal desires over God's law—God jolted the perverted officials back to reality: they were mere mortals, and they were going to die like all other mortals. Every prince or ruler eventually falls, either through death or defeat. These wicked, power-abusing officials were no different.

e. You will face God's judgment and lose God's inheritance—the new earth, 2 Pe.3:10-13 (v.8).

Psalm 82 closes with an appeal to God from the psalmist. Asaph called on God to arise and judge the earth—to stop the world's corrupt judges by execut-ing justice Himself. "Thou shalt inherit all nations" points to Jesus Christ, God's Son and the Savior of mankind. He will rule over all the earth for eternity. God has decreed that the nations of the earth are His inheritance (Ps.2:7-8). When He returns, perfect justice will reign forevermore.

Fear should strike the hearts of brazen unjust judges. Without exception, all unjust judges will face God's judgment. The earth and everything in it belongs to God (Ps.24:1; 89:11). Asaph ended this psalm as he began it: God is the Supreme Judge, and He executes justice on all (v.1).

Thought 1. Those who hold important positions must be careful not to think more highly of themselves than they ought to think (Ro.12:3). The world's judges need to recognize that their power comes from an Authority who is higher than the municipalities, states, and nations that appoint them. They are God's representatives, and, ultimately, they have to answer to Him. The earth and everything in it is God's, and He will judge it. Like every other human being, corrupt judges will die and then stand before God in judgment (He.9:27). Their judgment will be severe because much—the very execution of justice itself—has been committed to them (Lu.12:48).

> **But the one who does not know and does things deserving punishment will be beaten with few blows. From everyone who has been given much, much will be demanded; and from the one who has been entrusted with much, much more will be asked (Lu.12:48).**
>
> **Everyone must submit himself to the governing authorities, for there is no authority except that which God has established. The authorities that exist have been established by God....For he is God's servant to do you good. But if you do wrong, be afraid, for he does not bear the sword for nothing. He is God's servant, an agent of wrath to bring punishment on the wrongdoer (Ro.13:1, 4).**
>
> **Not many of you should presume to be teachers, my brothers, because you know that we who teach will be judged more strictly (Js.3:1).**
>
> **And I saw the dead, great and small, standing before the throne, and books were opened. Another book was opened, which is the book of life. The dead were judged according to what they had done as recorded in the books (Re.20:12).**
>
> **For God will bring every deed into judgment, including every hidden thing, whether it is good or evil (Ec.12:14).**

---

3   Donald Williams. *Psalms 73-150*, p.93.

PSALM 83

When Evil Threatens & You Face a Severe Crisis, 83:1-18

A Song. A Psalm of Asaph.

1. Make an urgent appeal to God a. To speak up: Give you guidance b. To act: Meet your need **2. Describe the crisis to God: In Israel's case, enemies had risen up against God & His people** a. Their sly conspiracy: They devised a plot against God's people, those He cherished b. Their purpose: To exterminate God's people c. Their alliance of evil unbelievers: A ten-tribe or ten-nation alliance 1) The Edomites, Ishmaelites, Moabites, & Hagrites 2) The nations of Gebal, Ammon, Amalek, Philistia, & Tyre 3) The nation of Assyria	O God, do not keep silent; be not quiet, O God, be not still. 2 See how your enemies are astir, how your foes rear their heads. 3 With cunning they conspire against your people; they plot against those you cherish. 4 "Come," they say, "let us destroy them as a nation, that the name of Israel be remembered no more." 5 With one mind they plot together; they form an alliance against you— 6 The tents of Edom and the Ishmaelites, of Moab and the Hagrites, 7 Gebal, Ammon and Amalek, Philistia, with the people of Tyre. 8 Even Assyria has joined them to lend strength to the descendants of Lot. Selah	9 Do to them as you did to Midian, as you did to Sisera and Jabin at the river Kishon, 10 Who perished at Endor and became like refuse on the ground. 11 Make their nobles like Oreb and Zeeb, all their princes like Zebah and Zalmunna, 12 Who said, "Let us take possession of the pasturelands of God." 13 Make them like tumbleweed, O my God, like chaff before the wind. 14 As fire consumes the forest or a flame sets the mountains ablaze, 15 So pursue them with your tempest and terrify them with your storm. 16 Cover their faces with shame so that men will seek your name, O LORD. 17 May they ever be ashamed and dismayed; may they perish in disgrace. 18 Let them know that you, whose name is the LORD—that you alone are the Most High over all the earth.	**3. Pray for God's powerful deliverance** a. A deliverance such as He worked in the past 1) He used Gideon to defeat Midian & used Deborah to defeat the Canaanites (Sisera & Jabin), Jud. 4–8 2) He defeated the Midianite commanders Oreb & Zeeb & their kings Zebah & Zalmunna 3) He defeated them because of their attack against the promised land b. A deliverance needed now 1) Pray that He scatter the enemy 2) Pray that He consume & destroy the enemy 3) Pray that He overpower & terrify the enemy **4. Ask God to use the enemies' shame (their defeat) for good: To stir people to seek Him** a. That obstinate unbelievers—those who refuse to submit to God—be shamed & perish forever b. That believers—those who truly turn to the LORD—glorify His name: Honor Him alone as the Most High God

PSALM 83

When Evil Threatens and You Face a Severe Crisis, 83:1-18

(83:1-18) Introduction: "It's URGENT...!" We generally reserve this statement for pressing situations that require immediate attention. By not using the words carelessly or applying them to less weighty matters, we preserve its effectiveness for when it is truly needed.

In Psalm 83, Asaph boldly but reverently requested God's attention to an urgent matter. Ten nations had joined forces against Israel and an attack was imminent. Many scholars think the occasion that brought about the writing of this psalm was Moab and Ammon's united attack when Jehoshaphat reigned in Judah (2 Chr.20). Scripture notes that other nations joined with them in this effort (2 Chr.20:1). Scripture also records that Jehoshaphat responded to this threat by calling the nation to prayer (2 Chr.20:3-4). Clear parallels exist between Scripture's account of this situation and Psalm 83 (2 Chr.20:11 and Ps.83:12; 2 Chr.20:29 and Ps.83:16-18).[1]

Commentator Derek Kidner notes a link between Asaph and this particular event, pointing out that "it was an Asaphite who prophesied Jehoshaphat's victory, and the levitical singers who paved the way for it (2 Chr.20:14, 19, 22)."[2] If this is the occasion for the psalm, Asaph's descendants, a group of worship leaders called by his name, would have composed it.

Whatever the specific setting, Psalm 83 reminds us that Satan and the world have always opposed God's people. They will continue to do so until Christ returns to defeat God's enemies and rule the world. Assaults by unbelievers and radicals of false religions will grow ever hotter against God's people as we approach the coming of Christ and the end of this age. Psalm 83 teaches us what to do when we are threatened by evil: we are to pray. Psalm 83 is a prayer. There are no assignments to the chief musician or some other worship leader and no musical instructions as in other psalms. Psalm 83 became a song in the Hebrew hymnal, but it began as a prayer, pure and simple. This is, *When Evil Threatens and You Face a Severe Crisis,* 83:1-18.

1. Make an urgent appeal to God (v.1).
2. Describe the crisis to God: In Israel's case, enemies had risen up against God and His people (vv.2-8).

---

1 Warren W. Wiersbe. *The Bible Exposition Commentary.* WORDsearch CROSS e-book.

2 Derek Kidner. *Psalms 73-150,* p.330.

3. Pray for God's powerful deliverance (vv.9-15).
4. Ask God to use the enemies' shame (their defeat) for good: To stir people to seek Him (vv.16-18).

1 (83:1) Make an urgent appeal to God.

The psalmist and the nation were intensely shaken by the threat they were facing: a ten-nation confederacy was rising up against Israel. Even more troubling was the fact that they had seen no activity from God. The situation was critical and an attack was imminent. In light of this, Asaph urgently appealed to God.

a. That He speak up: Give guidance (v.1ª).

Asaph pressed God to speak up and give guidance to His distraught people. They needed a word from the LORD. And the king needed specific directions from God. So far, though, God had not spoken in regard to this crisis. Therefore, the psalmist pleaded with God not to keep silent or be quiet any longer. When referring to God, *be quiet* (charash) can mean to be silent, or it can mean to be deaf, not to listen to. In using this word, Asaph may have been asking God to give attention to his urgent prayer. Either way, his request is the same: the people of Israel desperately needed God to speak to their situation—to *say* something.

b. That He act: Meet your need (v.1ᵇ).

The people of Israel also desperately needed God to *do* something—to intervene in their crisis and act in their behalf. Consequently, the psalmist implored God to no longer be still or idle. The armies of ten nations—including mighty Assyria—were marching on God's chosen people. Israel's only hope was God. If the people were going to survive, God had to act.

Thought 1. At times in our lives, we may all find ourselves facing challenges that only God can meet:
➤ A life-threatening illness or injury to ourselves or a loved one
➤ A serious marriage conflict
➤ Substance abuse or addiction
➤ Bankruptcy
➤ Persecution
➤ Physical or sexual abuse
➤ Any other evil attack or threatening situation

At such times, we need to fall on our faces before God and cry out urgently for His help. When our situation seems hopeless, there is still hope. We have a God who hears and answers prayer. He loves us more than we can begin to comprehend. Again and again in Scripture, He invites and urges us—even commands us—to call on Him when we are in trouble.

Casual, half-hearted prayers will not do when our need is urgent. Severe crises call for fervent, faith-filled prayers (Js.5:16; 1:6-7). At the root of many of

our crises is a spiritual battle. Prayer is the strongest weapon we have against evil spiritual forces. The battle will be won when we fight on our knees—kneeling before the Lord and crying out to Him in prayer (Ep.6:18; 2 Co.10:3-4).

Urgent prayers are also persistent prayers. We need to pray and continue to pray until the battle is won. Do not be discouraged when God does not act immediately. Do not quit praying in the middle of the battle. Jesus taught us to keep on asking and to keep on seeking and to keep on knocking. Along with this instruction, He gave us a promise:

> **"Ask and it will be given to you; seek and you will find; knock and the door will be opened to you. For everyone who asks receives; he who seeks finds; and to him who knocks, the door will be opened (Mt.7:7-8).**

> **During the days of Jesus' life on earth, he offered up prayers and petitions with loud cries and tears to the one who could save him from death, and he was heard because of his reverent submission (He.5:7).**

> **Therefore confess your sins to each other and pray for each other so that you may be healed. The prayer of a righteous man is powerful and effective. Elijah was a man just like us. He prayed earnestly that it would not rain, and it did not rain on the land for three and a half years (Js.5:16-17).**

> **"Now therefore, O our God, the great, mighty and awesome God, who keeps his covenant of love, do not let all this hardship seem trifling in your eyes—the hardship that has come upon us, upon our kings and leaders, upon our priests and prophets, upon our fathers and all your people, from the days of the kings of Assyria until today (Ne.9:32).**

> **And call upon me in the day of trouble; I will deliver you, and you will honor me" (Ps.50:15).**

> **In the day of my trouble I will call to you, for you will answer me (Ps.86:7).**

2 (83:2-8) Describe the crisis to God: In Israel's case, enemies had risen up against God and His people.

After appealing to God to intervene, the psalmist proceeded to describe the pressing crisis. An alliance of ten nations was arrogantly rearing up its head against God and His people. Asaph's perception of the situation was right on target: these nations hated the God that the people of Israel claimed to follow (the only living and true God) as much as they hated the nation of Israel.

a. Their sly conspiracy: They devised a plot against God's people, those He cherished (v.3).

The enemies of God had conspired together against His people. "With cunning they conspire" means they had devised a shrewd plan to destroy Israel. Picture the kings of ten nations sitting down together, diabolically plotting how they could best pool their resources to gain victory. Their intended victims: the people of God whom God dearly cherished—the apple of His eye (De.32:10; La.2:18; Zec.2:8). *Those you cherish* (tsaphan) speaks of how valuable the Israelites are to God: they are His precious treasure, whom He carefully shelters and protects (Ex.2:2-3; Jos.2:4).

b. Their purpose: To exterminate God's people (v.4).

The satanically-inspired kings had set their differences and egos aside in order to accomplish a hellish purpose: they sought to erase the nation of Israel from the face of the earth. They wanted to totally eliminate God's chosen people.

c. Their alliance of evil unbelievers: A ten-tribe or ten-nation alliance (vv.5-8).

After agreeing on their objective and the military strategy they would use to accomplish it, these ten nations of evil unbelievers formed an unholy alliance against Israel (v.5). Saying they were confederate means they made an official covenant to be allies in an effort to destroy God's people. Asaph understood the significance of this: their attack was not so much against Israel as it was against God. They were going to war against God's plan and purpose for humanity, a plan that would be carried out through the Hebrew people. Through the Jews, God would send both the Savior (Messiah) and His Holy Word to the world.

Asaph proceeded to identify the ten nations or tribes involved:

➤ The Edomites (v.6)	➤ Ammon (v.7)
➤ The Ishmaelites (v.6)	➤ Amalek (v.7)
➤ The Moabites (v.6)	➤ Philistia (v.7)
➤ The Hagrites (v.6)	➤ Tyre (v.7)
➤ Gebal (v.7)	➤ Assyria or Assur (v.8)

Some of these nations were Israel's relatives. The *Edomites* were the descendants of Esau, the twin brother of Jacob. The *Ishmaelites* were the descendants of Isaac's half-brother, whom Abraham had with Hagar, Sarah's handmaiden. *Moab* and *Ammon* were the children of Lot (v.8). The confederacy was largely comprised of the nations surrounding Israel that Israel had defeated. They banded together to get their revenge, recruiting the most powerful nation of those days, Assyria, to join with them.

Thought 1. Describing our crises to God is for our benefit, not His. He is aware of what is happening in our world and in our lives. He knows our need even before we pray. As we tell God about our situation, we unload its burden from our hearts and present it to Him (Ps.55:22). Describing our troubles to God also enables us to see them from the right perspective. Asaph was able to see the spiritual battle behind the enemies' actions (Ep.6:12). Satan has always opposed God's purpose, His plan to send His Word (the Holy Bible) and His Son, Jesus Christ, to the world through the Jewish people (Jn.4:22). It is no different today. Satan continues to fight against God's will and work in our lives and in our world. Seeing our situations from the right perspective empowers us to pray more effectively and according to God's will. Prayers offered in agreement with God's will are powerful and effective. Scripture promises that they will be heard (1 Jn.5:14).

> **One of those days Jesus went out to a mountainside to pray, and spent the night praying to God (Lu.6:12).**
>
> **He said to them, "When you pray, say: "'Father, hallowed be your name, your kingdom come (Lu.11:2).**
>
> **For this reason I kneel before the Father (Ep.3:14).**
>
> **Elijah was a man just like us. He prayed earnestly that it would not rain, and it did not rain on the land for three and a half years (Js.5:17).**
>
> **This is the confidence we have in approaching God: that if we ask anything according to his will, he hears us (1 Jn.5:14).**
>
> **Give ear, O God, and hear; open your eyes and see the desolation of the city that bears your Name. We do not make requests of you because we are righteous, but because of your great mercy (Da.9:18).**

3 (83:9-15) **Pray for God's powerful deliverance.** Knowing that Israel could not fend off this powerful alliance of armies in her own strength, the psalmist turned to God for help. He fervently prayed for God to miraculously deliver His beloved people again. As commentator Warren Wiersbe aptly notes,

> *Even if Jehoshaphat's situation was not the same as that described by Asaph, his prayer would have fit the occasion: "O our God, will You not judge them? For we have no power against this great multitude that is coming against us; nor do we know what to do, but our eyes are upon you" (2 Chr.20:12, NKJV).*[3]

---

3 Warren W. Wiersbe. *The Bible Exposition Commentary.* WORDsearch CROSS e-book.

a. A deliverance such as He worked in the past (vv.9-12).

Asaph recalled how God had mightily delivered His people from their enemies in the past. He looked back on the times of the judges, when God empowered Gideon to defeat the Midianites and used Deborah to overthrow the Canaanite kings, *Sisera* and *Jabin* (v.9; Jud.4-8). *Endor* was near Taanach, where Deborah and Barak defeated the kings of Canaan (v.10; Jud.5:19).

The psalmist prayed that God would make the leaders of this alliance like *Oreb* and *Zeeb*, military leaders of the Midianites, and *Zebah* and *Zalmunna*, the kings of Midian (v.11; Jud.7:25; 8:5-21). God defeated these greedy, arrogant fools because they brashly attacked His *houses* or *pasturelands*, the promised land (v.12). In like fashion, the leaders of this confederacy were rising up against God and all that belonged to Him.

b. A deliverance needed now (vv.13-15).

God's people desperately needed His deliverance once again. Asaph prayed that God would scatter His enemies like a *tumbleweed* and like the *stubble* or chaff blown away by the wind.

Along with his appeal for deliverance, the psalmist asked God to consume His enemies just as a fire destroys the woods or forest and spreads across the mountains, setting them ablaze (v.14). He prayed that God would *pursue* (radaph, means chase, run after, persecute) them like a tempest or whirlwind. Picture a terrified man running desperately from a tornado with every ounce of energy he has, only to be overtaken by it eventually. Asaph prayed that God would overthrow and terrify His demonically-influenced enemies in the same way (v.15).

Thought 1. Spiritual powers or demonic forces are stronger than we are. This means that we cannot defeat them in our own strength or by our own devices. Only God can overpower them (1 Jn.4:4). The Lord alone can deliver us from their evil clutches. We need to understand this before we pray, and we need to pray accordingly by asking for God's powerful deliverance. Spiritual battles are won with spiritual weapons (2 Co.10:4). Our spiritual weapons are the Word of God and prayer (Ep.6:17-18). God can do anything. Nothing is too hard for Him (Ge.18:14; Je.32:27). As we pray, He will unleash His power and angelic forces to deliver us from the enemy (Dan.6:22; 10:1-21; Mt.26:53; Ac.5:18-19; 12:11).

> Then Peter came to himself and said, "Now I know without a doubt that the Lord sent his angel and rescued me from Herod's clutches and from everything the Jewish people were anticipating" (Ac.12:11).

> He has delivered us from such a deadly peril, and he will deliver us. On him we have set our hope that he will continue to deliver us (2 Co.1:10).

> The Lord will rescue me from every evil attack and will bring me safely to his heavenly kingdom. To him be glory for ever and ever. Amen (2 Ti.4:18).

> He brought me out into a spacious place; he rescued me because he delighted in me (Ps.18:19).

4 (83:16-18) Ask God to use the enemies' shame (their defeat) for good: To stir people to seek Him.

The psalmist prayed not only for his enemies' defeat but also for God's glory to prevail. He asked God to use the shame the enemies would experience in defeat for good: to stir people to seek His name. Specifically, he prayed that others would seek the LORD (Yahweh, Jehovah), the one true God who keeps His promises to His people. The psalmist then prayed that the people of all nations would see how God rescued His people and believe in Him. The verses that follow (vv.17-18) further express this request.

a. That obstinate unbelievers—those who refuse to submit to God—be shamed and perish forever (v.17).

Israel's enemies were obstinate unbelievers who refused to submit to God. Therefore, Asaph prayed for their disgrace and destruction. The second statement of this verse is a restatement of the first, emphasizing the fervency of his request. He prayed that they would be confounded or put to shame, and that they would be *troubled* or *perish* forever.

b. That believers—those who truly turn to the LORD—glorify His name: Honor Him alone as the Most High God (v.18).

Asaph elaborated on his request for people to seek the LORD for His destruction of Israel's enemies. He prayed that people would know that He—*JEHOVAH*—is the most high (Elyon) over all the earth. He further asked that they would truly turn to Him and become genuine believers who glorify and honor His name.

Thought 1. We serve a God who brings good out of evil and uses our afflictions to help others (Ge.50:20). As we seek His deliverance, we should pray for the salvation of others and for God to be glorified. We need to see the crises of life and enemy attacks against us as opportunities for God's glory to prevail. When we are suffering, we have an opportunity to let our light shine, that others may see God in us and glorify Him (Mt.5:16). We should respond to crises in such a way that the light of the glorious gospel of

Christ is able to shine through us (2 Co.4:3:12). For this to occur, we must always speak in faith, not expressing doubt nor speaking against God in the midst of our trials (2 Co.4:13-15). In all things, God's glory should be our first priority.

In the same way, let your light shine before men, that they may see your good deeds and praise your Father in heaven (Mt.5:16).

So that with one heart and mouth you may glorify the God and Father of our Lord Jesus Christ (Ro.15:6).

So whether you eat or drink or whatever you do, do it all for the glory of God (1 Co.10:31).

For we who are alive are always being given over to death for Jesus' sake, so that his life may be revealed in our mortal body. So then, death is at work in us, but life is at work in you (2 Co.4:11-12).

We pray this so that the name of our Lord Jesus may be glorified in you, and you in him, according to the grace of our God and the Lord Jesus Christ (2 Th.1:12).

Live such good lives among the pagans that, though they accuse you of doing wrong, they may see your good deeds and glorify God on the day he visits us (1 Pe.2:12).

Then Nebuchadnezzar said, "Praise be to the God of Shadrach, Meshach and Abednego, who has sent his angel and rescued his servants! They trusted in him and defied the king's command and were willing to give up their lives rather than serve or worship any god except their own God (Da.3:28).

PSALM 84

When You Yearn to Be in the Presence of God, 84:1-12

For the director of music. According to gittith. Of the Sons of Korah. A psalm.

1. Tell God that you love Him—love being in His presence	How lovely is your dwelling place, O LORD Almighty!	c. *Comfort*: A refreshed & renewed spirit—even when you pass through the valley of weeping (Baca)
a. Bc. your soul longs to worship Him: Your heart & your flesh cry out for the presence of the living God	2 My soul yearns, even faints, for the courts of the LORD; my heart and my flesh cry out for the living God.	d. *Sustaining power*: Growing stronger through life's pilgrimage until you appear before Him
b. Bc. your heart longs to live where even the sparrow & swallow have access: Near the very altar of God's presence	3 Even the sparrow has found a home, and the swallow a nest for herself, where she may have her young—a place near your altar, O LORD Almighty, my King and my God.	**3. Ask God to hear your prayer**
1) Bc. He is the LORD of hosts (heaven's armies)		
2) Bc. He is your King & God	4 Blessed are those who dwell in your house; they are ever praising you. Selah	a. That He favor & honor the anointed (Messianic) king, your protector: A picture of Christ
2. Thank God for the blessings of His presence	5 Blessed are those whose strength is in you, who have set their hearts on pilgrimage.	b. That He grant His presence
a. *Happiness*: Joy & praise		1) Bc. one day in His presence is better than a thousand anywhere else, 3-4
b. *Strength*: Given to you when you set your heart on seeking God's presence	6 As they pass through the Valley of Baca, they make it a place of springs; the autumn rains also cover it with pools.	2) Bc. humble service in His presence is better than wealth & public recognition
	7 They go from strength to strength, till each "appears before God in Zion.	3) Bc. His presence is your light or guide & protection
	8 Hear my prayer, O LORD God Almighty; listen to me, O God of Jacob. Selah	• He favors & honors you
	9 Look upon our shield, O God; look with favor on your anointed one.	• He withholds no good thing if you walk righteously
	10 Better is one day in your courts than a thousand elsewhere; I would rather be a doorkeeper in the house of my God than dwell in the tents of the wicked.	c. That He bless—give joy & happiness to—the person who trusts Him
	11 For the LORD God is a sun and shield; the LORD bestows favor and honor; no good thing does he withhold from those whose walk is blameless.	
	12 O LORD Almighty, blessed is the man who trusts in you.	

PSALM 84

When You Yearn to Be in the Presence of God, 84:1-12

(84:1-12) **Introduction:** even with the amazing means of communication we have in our modern age, nothing compares to actually being *with* someone we love. Telephone conversations, instant messaging, and video conferencing are great blessings for those who cannot be together. Even so, as helpful as they are, they cannot replace being in the presence of someone who is dear to us. Nothing is the same as actually *being together*.

Psalm 84 is the psalmist's own testimony: he loves being in the presence of God. In the psalm, he describes what it meant to abide in God's house and to make the journey of those who traveled to Jerusalem to worship at the tabernacle and later at the temple. The psalm is attributed to the *sons of Korah,* who were devoted worshippers. They served in the tabernacle as singers and musicians and were also the doorkeepers of God's house (see Introduction—Ps.42–43 for more discussion). Many scholars think one of the sons of Korah wrote Psalm 84 while away from Jerusalem for a period of time, perhaps during the Babylonian captivity. He expressed his longing to return and once again worship in God's presence, at the tabernacle. To the Jew, the tabernacle was the place where God's presence dwelled in a very special way.

The author's passion for God's presence should remind us, as believers, how privileged we are to have God's presence dwelling in us through His Holy Spirit. It should also move us to look forward to eternity, when we will dwell forevermore with the Lord in a new heaven and new earth. For the here and now, though, it should stir us to dedicate ourselves daily to living in God's presence through prayer, the study of His Word, and worship. This is, *When You Yearn to Be in the Presence of God,* 84:1-12.

1. Tell God that you love Him—love being in His presence (vv.1-3).
2. Thank God for the blessings of His presence (vv.4-7).
3. Ask God to hear your prayer (vv.8-12).

1 (84:1-3) **Tell God that you love Him—love being in His presence.**

The psalmist could not contain his love for God, his longing to be in God's presence. His delighted spirit overflowed with an exclamation of praise for the LORD's tabernacle or dwelling place, the place where God abode in a unique way. He described this holy place as *lovely* (yadid), well-loved or dearly loved (De.33:12; Is.5:1). This word is a term of affection often used in romantic poetry. It appears in the heading to Psalm 45 as a *wedding song,* or a song of loves. The psalmist's passionate love of God's presence reflected his passionate love for God.

a. Because your soul longs to worship Him: Your heart and your flesh cry out for the presence of the living God (v.2).

The soul of the psalmist ached to be in the LORD's courts, the place where people went when they wanted to experience God's glorious presence. *Courts* refers to the courtyards of the tabernacle, the areas outside of the Holy Place and Holy of Holies. The psalmist's use of a number of words expresses his intense longing to worship God. Soul, heart, and flesh describe his entire being, all that he is and all that is within him. Long, faint, and cry out speak of how desperately he needed to be in the presence of the living God. Notice that the psalmist was careful to clarify that it was not the building or structure of the tabernacle he longed for, but the living God whose presence was distinctly manifested there.

b. Because your heart longs to live where even the sparrow and swallow have access: Near the very altar of God's presence (v.3).

Speaking poetically, the psalmist declared that even the birds longed to be close to God. They built their houses and nests near His altars—likely in the eaves of the open tabernacle. The tabernacle area contained three altars (see Tabernacle illustrations at the end of Ex.25:1-2).

➤ The altar of burnt offerings in the outer courtyard where sacrifices were offered (Ex.27:1-8)

➤ The altar of incense in the inner courtyard that pictured the prayers of the people rising to heaven (Ex.30:1-10, 34-38; Ps.141:2; Re.8:3-4)

➤ The mercy seat on the ark of the covenant in the Holy of Holies. This is the altar upon which the blood of the atoning sacrifice was sprinkled annually and where God's presence was centered (Ex.25:10-32; 37:1-9)

Because sparrows and swallows were so abundant in ancient Israel, they were considered a worthless nuisance. Yet, the psalmist stated, they were welcome in the presence of God. They had found a home—a haven, a shelter, a safe place where they could lay their eggs—in God's house. Surely, these despised birds are meant to be a symbol of sinners who are welcomed into the presence of the LORD through the blood of the covenant. We are all wandering strangers flitting about in a foreign land (this world), but we find refuge and refreshment in the presence of God.

The psalmist emphasized the privilege of being in God's presence by mentioning two facts: first, God is the LORD *Almighty*, the Commander of heaven's armies. Second, he, the psalmist, had a personal relationship with the LORD. The LORD is *my King and my God.*

Thought 1. The psalmist emphasized how much he loved to be in God's presence. Under the Old Covenant, God's people were allowed to go only so far into the tabernacle itself. They could not go into the Most Holy Place (the Holy of Holies) where God's presence actually dwelled at the mercy seat.

As believers on this side of the cross, however, we can enter the very presence of God at any time. When Christ died, God supernaturally split the veil of the tabernacle (Mk.15:38). Consequently, Christ's sacrifice permanently removed the barrier between God and humanity.

We have a privilege that Old Testament saints never knew. We can enter directly into God's presence. Christ has made a way for us to go beyond the veil (He.10:19-20). Yet, how much of our lives do we actually spend in the glorious presence of God?

Psalm 84 emphasized the strenuous journey believers would make just for the privilege of spending time in God's presence. God's special presence no longer abides in a tent or a temple; rather, it abides within *us*. God dwells in believers through His Holy Spirit (Ro.8:9). Out of heartfelt love and gratitude for God, we ought to live every day in the awareness of His presence, not act as if He were not there. We should set aside time daily for the sole purpose of going before God's throne in prayer. We have this glorious privilege that has been purchased for us by the blood of Jesus Christ. We also have a standing invitation to come boldly before God's throne (He.4:16). But, sadly, many professing believers spend little, if any, time in God's presence.

The psalmist's passion for God's house was a reflection of his passion for God. Likewise, if we truly love the Lord, we will love being in His presence. Neglecting to spend time in God's presence reveals a heart that is lacking in deep devotion and love for the Lord, a heart that loves other things far more than God.

The curtain of the temple was torn in two from top to bottom (Mk.15:38).

We have this hope as an anchor for the soul, firm and secure. It enters the inner sanctuary behind the curtain, where Jesus, who went before us, has entered on our behalf. He has become a high priest forever, in the order of Melchizedek (He.6:19-20).

Therefore, brothers, since we have confidence to enter the Most Holy Place by the blood of Jesus, by a new and living way opened for us through the curtain, that is, his body, and since we have a great priest over the house of God, let us draw near to God with a sincere heart in full assurance of faith, having our hearts sprinkled to cleanse us from a guilty conscience and having our bodies washed with pure water (He.10:19-22).

I love the house where you live, O LORD, the place where your glory dwells (Ps.26:8).

One thing I ask of the LORD, this is what I seek: that I may dwell in the house of the LORD all the days of my life, to gaze upon the beauty of the LORD and to seek him in his temple (Ps.27:4).

2 (84:4-7) Thank God for the blessings of His presence.

The psalmist declared that those who are privileged to dwell in God's house, to abide in His presence, are blessed. To be *blessed* (esher) is to be happy, but it is so much more than just surface or superficial happiness. It is a joy, peace, and assurance that rises above our circumstances (see DEEPER STUDY #1—Psalm1:1 for more discussion). The psalmist proceeded to cite four blessings of living in God's presence.

a. *Happiness*: Joy and praise (v.4ᵇ).

Those who abide in God's presence experience genuine happiness. They are fulfilled, whole, content, and filled with the joy of the LORD. As a result, they praise God continually. *Praise* is an imperfect Hebrew verb, meaning that their praise is never complete or finished.

b. *Strength*: Given to you when you set your heart on seeking God's presence (v.5).

Those who are blessed to abide in God's presence find their *strength* in Him. "Who have set their hearts on pilgrimage" refers to the Jews who journeyed up to Zion to worship in God's house. *Pilgrimage* (mesillah) means highways or public roads (Jud.20:31). The hearts of those who were determined to travel to Jerusalem to worship were truly set on seeking God's presence. Their longing to worship God was so strong that they were willing to travel many miles in difficult conditions. They found their strength for the journey in the joy they would experience when they reached Zion and basked in the LORD's presence (He.12:2).

c. *Comfort*: A refreshed and renewed spirit—even when you pass through the valley of weeping (Baca) (v.6).

Many of the worshippers who traveled up to Jerusalem had to pass through the *valley of Baca*, which means weeping. Apparently, it was a dry place and the most dreaded section of the journey. *Baca* is the Hebrew word for balsam or mulberry trees (2 Sa.5:23-24; 1 Chr.14:14-15). The valley of Baca may have been an area where these trees grew abundantly.

Mentioned in the Bible only here, many scholars are not sure that Baca was an actual geographical location. Rather, they think it may have been used here poetically as a symbol of the painful experiences of our journey through life.

Whether Baca is a real or symbolic place, the message of this verse is tender and beautiful. Baca represents the trials and troubles of life, the painful experiences that cause us to weep. God's presence comforts us in this valley, refreshing and renewing our spirits in the worst times. His presence empowers us to *make it a place of springs,* that is, to turn our most trying times into experiences of spiritual refreshing and joy. When we make *pools* in life's deserts, the LORD will fill them with the heavenly *rain* of His presence.

d. *Sustaining power*: Growing stronger through life's pilgrimage—until you appear before Him (v.7).

Those who abide in God's presence are not only comforted but also sustained throughout their lives. They go from strength to strength, growing ever stronger through life's pilgrimage until they appear before God in Zion (Jb.17:9; Is.40:31). In every difficult place, they find the strength they need to persevere and continue on. As they near the end of their journey, their capacity to endure actually increases instead of decreasing the longer they travel. God's presence energizes them along the way (Jn.1:16). As preacher Charles Spurgeon said, "If we spend our strength in God's ways we shall find it increase."[1]

Thought 1. The saints' journey to Jerusalem is a picture of our journey through life. We are strangers and pilgrims in this world; it is not our true home (He.11:13; 1 Pe.2:11; Ph.3:20). We are on our way to a better country, heaven, where we will live eternally in God's presence (He.11:14-16). The journey is filled with many dangers—both temptations and trials—and is often difficult and exhausting. Nevertheless, we are blessed along the way, for the Lord's presence is always with us (He.13:5; Mt.28:20). As a result, the journey is a happy one, filled with joy and praise (Ps.16:11). We are given divine strength for every mile of every day (Is.40:31; Ph.4:13). When we have to pass through a valley of tears, God Himself comforts us, refreshing us and renewing our spirits (2 Co.1:3-5; 4:16). Though we sometimes become tired, our endurance increases as we grow in grace and Christian maturity (2 Pe.3:18; Ep.4:15; 2 Th.1:3; Jude 20). The burdens of the journey seem lighter as the glory of our destination comes into view (2 Co.4:17-18). Commentator J.J. Stewart Perowne offered this rich description of the pilgrimage:

Every spot of the familiar road, every station at which they rested, lives in their heart. The path may be dry and dusty, through a lonely and sorrowful valley, but nevertheless they love it. The pilgrim band,

---

1 Charles Spurgeon. *Treasury of David.* WORDsearch CROSS e-book.

rich in hope, forgets the trials and difficulties of the way: hope changes the rugged and stony waste into living fountains. The vale blossoms as if the sweet rain of heaven had covered it with blessings. Hope sustains them at every step; from station to station they renew their strength as they draw nearer to the end of their journey, till at last they appear before God, present themselves as His worshipers, in His sanctuary in Zion....No wonder that in all ages men have rejoiced to find in this beautiful picture an image of the Christian life.[2]

For where two or three come together in my name, there am I with them" (Mt.18:20).

And teaching them to obey everything I have commanded you. And surely I am with you always, to the very end of the age" (Mt.28:20).

Keep your lives free from the love of money and be content with what you have, because God has said, "Never will I leave you; never will I forsake you." So we say with confidence, "The Lord is my helper; I will not be afraid. What can man do to me?" (He.13:5-6).

I am with you and will watch over you wherever you go, and I will bring you back to this land. I will not leave you until I have done what I have promised you" (Ge.28:15).

The LORD replied, "My Presence will go with you, and I will give you rest" (Ex.33:14).

You have made known to me the path of life; you will fill me with joy in your presence, with eternal pleasures at your right hand (Ps.16:11).

"Fear not, for I have redeemed you; I have summoned you by name; you are mine. When you pass through the waters, I will be with you; and when you pass through the rivers, they will not sweep over you. When you walk through the fire, you will not be burned; the flames will not set you ablaze (Is.43:1ᵇ-2).

3 (84:8-12) **Ask God to hear your prayer.**
The psalmist asked God to hear his prayer and to give it His full attention. More than anything else, he longed to spend the rest of his life serving in God's house. Dwelling in God's glorious presence was more important to him than anything else in the world.

a. That He favor and honor the anointed (Messianic) king, your protector: A picture of Christ (v.9).
The psalmist's first request was for God to favor and honor the king, Israel's shield or protector. *Your anointed one* speaks not only of Israel's present king but also of the Messiah who would come from the line of David (Ps.2:2; 2 S.7:12-16). By praying for the king to be favored and blessed, the psalmist prayed for the coming of the Messiah as well. And when the Messiah came, He would thereafter be the shield and protector of His dear people as they walked through life.

b. That He grant His presence (vv.10-11).
The psalmist prayed that God would grant him the privilege of continuing to dwell in His presence. In addition to being musicians and singers, the sons of Korah were also the doorkeepers or gatekeepers of the temple. They guarded the entrance to God's House (1 Chr.6:16-33; 9:19; 26:1-19). They considered themselves greatly blessed to have the privilege of serving in God's presence, even though they served in a somewhat low-level position. To the psalmist, one day in God's presence was better than a thousand anywhere else; and having the privilege of serving in God's house—even in a low position—was better than all the wealth and recognition the world could offer (v.10; vv.3-4).

Next, the psalmist testified that the LORD God was his sun and shield (v.11). Like the sun, God's presence was the light of his life and guided him along the right path (Ps.27:1). Like a shield, it protected him from every danger and threat. These blessings, the psalmist noted, are reserved for those who walk uprightly or righteously. They alone are granted the privilege of abiding in God's presence (Ps.15:1-5; 24:3-5). God will bestow honor upon them: they will be the recipients of His grace and glory. The LORD gives them "grace for the journey and glory at the end of the journey (Ro.5:1-2; 1 Pe.5:10)."[3] He will withhold no good thing from them. Those who choose a life of holiness will enjoy *all* the blessings of God's presence and *all* the riches of His grace.

c. That He bless—give joy and happiness to—the person who trusts Him (v.12).
Having described the *blessed* man as one who dwells in God's presence and finds his strength in Him (vv.4-5), the psalmist closed by adding that the man who *trusts* in God is blessed. Because the LORD is his confidence and security, he will know a joy and happiness that nothing on this earth can supply.

Thought 1. We should pray daily for God to help us to live holy lives so that we too can enjoy the full blessings of His presence. If we have genuinely repented of

---

2   J.J. Stewart Perowne, *The Book of Psalms,* p.413.

3   Warren W. Wiersbe. *The Bible Exposition Commentary.* WORDsearch CROSS e-book.

our sin and accepted Christ, we know that we will spend eternity in God's presence. We need to remember, though, that we are not saved by our works or by holy living but by the sacrificial death of Christ on the cross. By Him, we are declared to be righteous before God (Ro.3:24; 5:1, 9).

When we have sin in our lives, however, our fellowship with God is hindered. We do not enjoy the full blessing of His presence in our lives because our sin strains our relationship with Him. The joy of the Lord vanishes. We live in our own strength rather than in His. Instead of being renewed and refreshed by spending time in God's Word and in prayer, Scripture becomes silent to us and our attempts at prayer are feeble.

We need to walk in the power of God's indwelling Spirit moment by moment, day after day. We need to ask Him to deliver us from temptation and to strengthen us to resist sin (Ga.5:16; Ro.8:4). Thank God, when we do sin, we can confess our sins and be restored to fellowship with Him immediately (1 Jn.1:9). Yet the greater way to live is to walk uprightly, choosing to obey God and resist the temptation to sin. If we do, then we can enjoy the fullness of God's presence in our lives at all times. This is possible only through God's power and through the continuous cleansing of His Word (Ep.5:26; Jn.15:3). When we trust in Him, we will be richly blessed.

If you remain in me and my words remain in you, ask whatever you wish, and it will be given you. This is to my Father's glory, that you bear much fruit, showing yourselves to be my disciples (Jn.15:7-8).

But now that you have been set free from sin and have become slaves to God, the benefit you reap leads to holiness, and the result is eternal life. For the wages of sin is death, but the gift of God is eternal life in Christ Jesus our Lord (Ro.6:22-23).

For the eyes of the Lord are on the righteous and his ears are attentive to their prayer, but the face of the Lord is against those who do evil" (1 Pe.3:12).

If my people, who are called by my name, will humble themselves and pray and seek my face and turn from their wicked ways, then will I hear from heaven and will forgive their sin and will heal their land (2 Chr.7:14).

Lord, who may dwell in your sanctuary? Who may live on your holy hill? He whose walk is blameless and who does what is righteous, who speaks the truth from his heart (Ps.15:1-2).

PSALM 85

When You Fail & Are Disciplined by God, 85:1-13

For the director of music. Of the Sons of Korah. A psalm.

1. Remember God's past mercy
a. How He blessed the land & delivered His people from slavery
b. How He forgave & covered His people's sins
c. How He withdrew His fury & turned away from His fierce wrath
2. Ask God to restore His people—to set aside His anger & judgment once again
a. Bc. He is God our Savior
b. Bc. we are desperate for relief: His anger (judgment) seems to be unending
c. Bc. we need to be revived again: We want to be filled with

You showed favor to your land, O LORD; you restored the fortunes of Jacob.
2 You forgave the iniquity of your people and covered all their sins. Selah
3 You set aside all your wrath and turned from your fierce anger.
4 Restore us again, O God our Savior, and put away your displeasure toward us.
5 Will you be angry with us forever? Will you prolong your anger through all generations?
6 Will you not revive us again, that your people may

rejoice in you?
7 Show us your unfailing love, O LORD, and grant us your salvation.
8 I will listen to what God the LORD will say; he promises peace to his people, his saints—but let them not return to folly.
9 Surely his salvation is near those who fear him, that his glory may dwell in our land.
10 Love and faithfulness meet together; righteousness and peace kiss each other.
11 Faithfulness springs forth from the earth, and righteousness looks down from heaven.
12 The LORD will indeed give what is good, and our land will yield its harvest.
13 Righteousness goes before him and prepares the way for his steps.

praise & joy in Him, Ze.4:6
d. Bc. we need His unfailing love & mercy as well as His salvation (deliverance)
3. Listen carefully to God's Word
a. God promises peace to His faithful people, His saints
b. God warns against backsliding—returning to foolish ways
c. God saves those who truly fear Him: A promise of God's gifts now & in His coming kingdom
1) To fill our land with *glory*
2) To shower His *mercy* on us, 2
3) To work His *righteousness* in our lives & give us peace
4) To stir *truth* to flourish in our hearts & throughout the earth & *righteousness* to flow down from heaven
5) To give us "every *good & perfect gift*" to meet our needs, Mt.6:30-33; Js.1:17
d. God's righteousness prepares the earth for Him & His coming kingdom: A picture of Christ

PSALM 85

When You Fail and Are Disciplined by God, 85:1-13

(85:1-13) Introduction: *Failure is never final with the Father.* Scripture says that "though a righteous man falls seven times, he rises again" (Pr.24:16). Two truths are clear in this comforting verse:

➤ As believers, we will fail at times in our walk with the Lord.
➤ When we fail, we can get up and go on in our walk with the Lord. By God's grace, we can be forgiven and restored.

The history of Israel is one of repeated spiritual failure. Under the leadership of Moses, the judges, and the kings, God's people repeatedly turned away from Him. Their cycle of rebellion, retribution, repentance, and restoration is most clearly seen in the Old Testament book of *Judges.* Again and again, God disciplined His people. Again and again, they turned away from Him.

Finally, after generations of warnings, God lifted His hand of protection from His people and they were invaded by the Babylonians. Jerusalem was destroyed, thousands were slain, and the survivors were taken captive. For seventy years, God's people lived in a foreign land. Then, just as God had promised, their oppressors released them from captivity. A remnant returned to Jerusalem to rebuild the city and the temple.

God's people had failed miserably; consequently, He had disciplined them harshly. Now, His judgment was complete, and He offered the people forgiveness and res-

toration. This is the setting for Psalm 85, and its lessons are just as relevant for believers today as they were when the psalm was written. When we sin, we can expect God to discipline us (He.12:5-11). But God's discipline is corrective in nature, not punitive. He will forgive us, and He will restore us to fellowship with Him. He will bless us and use us again—if we repent. Psalm 85 is a prayer from the godly people of Israel for those in their nation who were still living in disobedience to the LORD. It is preserved in God's Word to guide people in every generation. This is, *When You Fail and Are Disciplined by God,* 85, 1-13.

1. Remember God's past mercy (vv.1-3).
2. Ask God to restore His people—to set aside His anger and judgment once again (vv.4-7).
3. Listen carefully to God's Word (vv.8-13).

1 (85:1-3) **Remember God's past mercy.**
The psalmist reflected on the mercy God had shown His sinful people in the past. He had forgiven them and returned them to the promised land. After seventy years of judgment, He had turned from His wrath.

a. How he blessed the land and delivered His people from slavery (v.1).
The psalmist began by declaring that God had restored His blessing to His chosen people. The land God

gave them had been devastated by the Babylonians' ruthless attack. Imagine the scene the remnant returned to after seventy years of captivity. Jerusalem had been utterly destroyed and the rubbish remained. Seventy years of desolation had left both the city and the countryside untended and overgrown.

In generations long past, God had blessed the land by bringing His people out of Egyptian slavery so they could inherit and develop the land. Now, God had once again showered His favor on the land. He had delivered His people from captivity and brought them back home (Je.29:14). They would rebuild, and God would restore Israel's glory.

b. How he forgave and covered His people's sins (v.2).

By restoring His people to the promised land, God showed that He had graciously forgiven their iniquity, or sins. The word *iniquity* (avown) speaks of the people's perverseness and their guiltiness before God. *Forgave* (nasah) means that God lifted the guilt of their sin from them and carried it away. *Covered* (kasah) means that God hid their sins from view (Ps.32:1). Through His great mercy, their sins were no longer before the LORD (Ps.103:11-12).

c. How he withdrew His fury and turned away from His fierce wrath (v.3).

God's anger against His people was righteous and well-deserved. Through the prophets, He had repeatedly warned them of His impending wrath if they did not turn from their wicked ways (2 Chr.36:15-16). Still, they persisted in their sin. Without question, God was righteous in judging them as harshly as He did.

Then, when God granted His forgiveness, He withdrew His fury and turned away from His fierce wrath. No longer were His people sentenced to judgment. In lifting the guilt of their sin, the LORD lifted His chastening hand from Israel.

Thought 1. God's mercy is revealed in the way He deals with us when we sin. Because He loves us so much, He will not permit us to continue in sin. Therefore, He disciplines us. But He also forgives us when we confess our sin: He carries our sin away and conceals it from His sight. Through the blood of Christ, God cancels the debt we owe for our sin and no longer holds us responsible for it.

Sadly, many people live with guilt for sins that God has forgiven and forgotten. Satan uses guilt to rob us of the joy Christ died to give us. Christ bore the burden of our sins on the cross. When we confess and forsake our sin, God carries it away in His mercy. He remembers it no more, and neither should we. He wants us to live with the joy of being fully forgiven, not with a cloud of guilt hanging over our heads. What a wonderful, merciful God we serve!

> But because of his great love for us, God, who is rich in mercy, made us alive with Christ even when we were dead in transgressions—it is by grace you have been saved (Ep.2:4-5).

> He saved us, not because of righteous things we had done, but because of his mercy. He saved us through the washing of rebirth and renewal by the Holy Spirit (Tit.3:5).

> Let us then approach the throne of grace with confidence, so that we may receive mercy and find grace to help us in our time of need (He.4:16).

> Remember not the sins of my youth and my rebellious ways; according to your love remember me, for you are good, O LORD (Ps.25:7).

> Because of the LORD's great love we are not consumed, for his compassions never fail. They are new every morning; great is your faithfulness....Though he brings grief, he will show compassion, so great is his unfailing love (Lam.3:22-23, 32).

> Who is a God like you, who pardons sin and forgives the transgression of the remnant of his inheritance? You do not stay angry forever but delight to show mercy (Mi.7:18).

2 (84:4-7) Ask God to restore His people—to set aside His anger and judgment once again.

"The return of the people to the land was no guarantee that all of them had returned to the Lord."[1] God had forgiven the people collectively. He had lifted His judgment from the nation of Israel, and a remnant had returned to the land. Even so, the restoration of the nation did not mean that all the people had repented. The book of *Ezra* records that many people continued to live in grievous sin after returning to Israel (Ezr.9:1-2). Those whose hearts remained hardened toward God would continue to receive His painful discipline. Therefore, the godly of the remnant asked the LORD to restore His people and to set aside His judgment once again in their lives.

The effects of God's judgment lingered on the land (v.9, 12). The people prayed for a return to the way things used to be when God had protected and prospered His people. If the people would repent, God would forgive them and heal their land (2 Chr.7:14).

a. Because He is God our Savior (v.4).

The people prayed for God to *restore* (shub) them back to Him—to bring them to repentance and restore

---

1 Warren W. Wiersbe. *The Bible Exposition Commentary.* WORD*search* CROSS e-book.

them to the path of righteousness (see outline and notes—Ps.23:3 for more discussion). They appealed to God as *our Savior* or salvation. They realized that they had no hope apart from Him and His work in their hearts.

b. **Because we are desperate for relief: His anger (judgment) seems to be unending (v.5)**

The people who participated in this prayer were desperate to be relieved from God's judgment once and for all. As they surveyed the shambles of their once shining city, they surely felt that things would never be as they once were. They felt that God's anger toward them would never end. And if the people did not repent but continued in sin, they were right. God's wrath would continue on down through future generations. The righteous knew this; therefore, they were desperate for relief—desperate for God to send a sweeping revival that would affect all the people.

c. **Because we need to be revived again: We want to be filled with praise and joy in Him (v.6; see Ze.4:6).**

Israel desperately needed a touch from God that would convict sinful hearts and turn people back to Him. Knowing that, the godly of the remnant prayed for HIm to revive them again, to bring the people back from spiritual deadness and restore them to spiritual living. A blanket of gloom covered the land, not only because of what *had* happened, but also because of what was *still* happening. Even though the Israelites had lost everything and spent seventy years in captivity, many of the people continued in sin. Those who loved God wanted to be filled with praise and joy once again, but the persistent sin of the rebellious kept the fear of God's judgment aflame in their hearts.

d. **Because we need His unfailing love and mercy as well as His salvation (deliverance) (v.7).**

Those who loved God prayed that He would reveal His *unfailing, covenant love* (chesed), His mercy, by doing a mighty work in the people's hearts . They begged God to send His salvation upon the nation by reviving those who continued to walk in sin as well as those whose hearts had become lukewarm to Him.

Thought 1. No matter how dark the night seems to be in our world, in our nations, and even in our churches, we must never stop praying for revival. Those who know and love God and live for Him must be tireless in crying out for a spiritual awakening. We must plead for a fresh wind of God's Spirit to blow on our churches and set people's hearts aflame for Him. God can breathe new life into the dry bones of backslidden people. God can stir us all to live again in full commitment to Him. When the army of Christ arises, the tide of evil in our nations can be turned, and God can heal our land.

The Lord's hand was with them, and a great number of people believed and turned to the Lord (Ac.11:21).

Many of those who believed now came and openly confessed their evil deeds. A number who had practiced sorcery brought their scrolls together and burned them publicly. When they calculated the value of the scrolls, the total came to fifty thousand drachmas. In this way the word of the Lord spread widely and grew in power (Ac.19:18-20).

Yet I hold this against you: You have forsaken your first love. Remember the height from which you have fallen! Repent and do the things you did at first. If you do not repent, I will come to you and remove your lampstand from its place (Re.2:4-5).

If my people, who are called by my name, will humble themselves and pray and seek my face and turn from their wicked ways, then will I hear from heaven and will forgive their sin and will heal their land (2 Chr.7:14).

Then he said to me, "Prophesy to these bones and say to them, 'Dry bones, hear the word of the LORD! This is what the Sovereign LORD says to these bones: I will make breath enter you, and you will come to life. I will attach tendons to you and make flesh come upon you and cover you with skin; I will put breath in you, and you will come to life. Then you will know that I am the LORD" (Eze.37:4-6).

The Ninevites believed God. They declared a fast, and all of them, from the greatest to the least, put on sackcloth (Jon.3:5).

So he said to me, "This is the word of the LORD to Zerubbabel: 'Not by might nor by power, but by my Spirit,' says the LORD Almighty (Zech.4:6).

3 (85:8-13) **Listen carefully to God's Word.**
The psalmist believed the promises of God, that He would answer the people's earnest prayers. Filled with great confidence, he proclaimed that God would speak to His burdened people. Therefore, he pledged to hear, to listen carefully and obey, everything God had to say.

a. **God promises peace to His faithful people, His saints (v.8ᵃ).**
The psalmist declared that God would speak a message of *peace* (shalom) to the godly people of Israel (see outline and notes—Ps.72:3 for more discussion).

Their hearts were heavy because of God's judgment and the ongoing sin of so many people. Despite everything that had taken place, they had remained faithful to God. Thus, the psalmist was sure that God would encourage and comfort their grieving spirits (Je.29:11). They would enjoy fulfilled, abundant lives, even in the midst of their difficulties.

b. God warns against backsliding—returning to foolish ways (v.8ᵇ).

God had a word for those who had repented and come back to Him. They must not backslide, not return to their foolish, sinful ways. They could expect to experience peace as long as they walked in obedience to the LORD. "To those, and those only, peace is spoken, who turn from sin; but, if they return to it again, it is at their peril."[2]

c. God saves those who truly fear Him: A promise of God's gifts now and in His coming kingdom (vv.9-12).

The people had prayed for God to save their nation and those who still rebelled against Him. God announced that His salvation was near those who would fear Him, submit to and obey Him (v.9ᵃ). He was ready and waiting to save them, but they had to repent. He promised that when the people of the nation turned back to Him, He would bestow His gifts on Israel. He would...

- fill their land with His *glory* (v.9ᵇ)
- shower His *unfailing love* and *faithfulness* (truth) on them (v.10ᵃ)
- work His *righteousness* in their lives and give them *peace* (v.10ᵇ; Is.32:17)
- stir faithfulness to flourish in their hearts and throughout the earth, and *righteousness* to flow down from heaven (v.11)
- give them "every good and perfect gift" to meet their needs (v.12; Mt.6:30-33; Js.1:17).

d. God's righteousness prepares the earth for Him and His coming kingdom: A picture of Christ (v.13).

Finally, God declared that His righteousness goes before Him, "as if leading the way in this restoration and revival of God's people."[3] This Word from God was not just for Israel at that time but also for her future.

God's righteousness prepares the earth for Him and His coming kingdom. When Jesus Christ reigns in righteousness, the blessings God promised to Israel will fill the earth. When Christ comes again, Israel will turn to Him and be saved. His steps—the footsteps of Christ—will be the way or path for all people. They will walk on a highway of holiness, and all the earth will be filled with His glory and rejoice in Him (Is.35:1-10).

Thought 1. All who fear the LORD can experience these gifts in their lives. God's Word never changes. What He said to broken Israel remains true today. When we walk in righteousness, we will receive His peace in our hearts (Ps.29:11; Pr.3:17; Jn.14:27; Jn.16:33; Ph.4:7). We will see God's glory manifested in and through us (2 Co.3:18; 1 Pe.4:14). God will shower His mercy on us, and we will find that His faithfulness never fails (1 Co.1:9; 1 Th.5:24; He.10:23). He will give us "every good and perfect gift," providing for our every need (Mt.6:30-33; Ph.4:19: Js.1:17). When we have failed and been disciplined by God, we need to listen carefully to His Word. We can be restored, blessed, and fruitful in His service—if we repent and obey Him.

> He who has ears, let him hear (Mt. 11:15).
>
> But the one who received the seed that fell on good soil is the man who hears the word and understands it. He produces a crop, yielding a hundred, sixty or thirty times what was sown" (Mt. 13:23).
>
> We must pay more careful attention, therefore, to what we have heard, so that we do not drift away (He.2:1).
>
> He read it aloud from daybreak till noon as he faced the square before the Water Gate in the presence of the men, women and others who could understand. And all the people listened attentively to the Book of the Law (Neh.8:3).
>
> And he said to me, "Son of man, listen carefully and take to heart all the words I speak to you (Eze.3:10).

---

2 Matthew Henry. *Matthew Henry's Commentary on the Whole Bible.* WORD*search* CROSS e-book.

3 Steven Lawson and Max Anders. *Holman Old Testament Commentary—Psalms.* WORD*search* CROSS e-book.

PSALM 86

When Desperation Drives You to Continually Cry Out for God's Help, 86:1-17

A prayer of David.

1. **Turn your attention to me, O LORD; hear my prayer: Bc. I am in desperate need**
2. **Protect my life, save my soul**
   a. Bc. I am devoted to you
   b. Bc. I am your servant & I trust in you
3. **Be merciful, O LORD: Bc. I call out to you all day long**
4. **Give joy to my soul, O LORD**
   a. Bc. I am your servant: I give myself to serve you
   b. Bc. you are good, ready to forgive, & merciful to all who call on you
5. **Hear my prayer, my urgent cry, O LORD**
   a. Bc. I am in trouble & you promise to hear me
   b. Bc. you are the only living & true God: No one can do what you do
   c. Bc. one day in the future every person & every nation will submit to you & worship you, Ph.2:9-11

Hear, O LORD, and answer me, for I am poor and needy.
2 Guard my life, for I am devoted to you. You are my God; save your servant who trusts in you.
3 Have mercy on me, O Lord, for I call to you all day long.
4 Bring joy to your servant, for to you, O Lord, I lift up my soul.
5 You are forgiving and good, O Lord, abounding in love to all who call to you.
6 Hear my prayer, O LORD; listen to my cry for mercy.
7 In the day of my trouble I will call to you, for you will answer me.
8 Among the gods there is none like you, O Lord; no deeds can compare with yours.
9 All the nations you have made will come and worship before you, O Lord; they will bring glory to your name.
10 For you are great and do marvelous deeds; you alone are God.
11 Teach me your way, O LORD, and I will walk in your truth; give me an undivided heart, that I may fear your name.
12 I will praise you, O Lord my God, with all my heart; I will glorify your name forever.
13 For great is your love toward me; you have delivered me from the depths of the grave.
14 The arrogant are attacking me, O God; a band of ruthless men seeks my life—men without regard for you.
15 But you, O Lord, are a compassionate and gracious God, slow to anger, abounding in love and faithfulness.
16 Turn to me and have mercy on me; grant your strength to your servant and save the son of your maidservant.
17 Give me a sign of your goodness, that my enemies may see it and be put to shame, for you, O LORD, have helped me and comforted me.

   1) For you are great & perform wonderful deeds
   2) For you alone are God
6. **Teach me your way, O LORD, & give me a pure heart**
   a. That I may walk according to your truth & genuinely honor your name
   b. That I may praise & glorify your name forever

   1) Bc. your mercy (everlasting love) toward me is great, Ro.5:8; Ep.2:4-10
   2) Bc. you have delivered me
      • From attacks by prideful & violent men
      • From people who reject you (your salvation)
   c. That I may declare your nature
   1) Bc. you are compassionate & gracious
   2) Bc. you are patient (long-suffering), loving, & faithful
7. **Turn to me & have mercy, O LORD**
   a. Bc. I am your servant & need your strength
   b. Bc. I am your maidservant's son & need to be saved
8. **Show me a sign of your favor**
   a. Bc. my enemies need to see evidence of your existence & goodness & be shamed
   b. Bc. you have helped & comforted me

PSALM 86

When Desperation Drives You to Continually Cry Out for God's Help, 86:1-17

(86:1-17) **Introduction:** some situations in life are so threatening that we cannot get them off our minds. Our days are unproductive because of the stress and anxiety they create. We cannot sleep at night because when we close our eyes our troubles are still before us. All we can do is continually cry out for God's help.

David wrote Psalm 86 when he found himself in such a situation—this is the only psalm in the third book of *Psalms* authored by him. We do not know the specific occasion that held David in such deep distress. It may have been Saul's pursuit, Absalom's rebellion, or some other less prominent conflict with enemies. Whatever the situation, his desperation was so great and his need so urgent that he constantly cried out to God.

Health crises, family crises, financial crises, fierce persecution, and a host of other troubles can plunge us so deep into despair that we can do nothing but pray. And pray we should, for in such times nothing else can truly help. In this psalm, David teaches us how to pray when facing critical situations. This is, *When Desperation Drives You to Continually Cry Out for God's Help,* 86:1-17.

1. Turn your attention to me, O LORD; hear my prayer: Because I am in desperate need (v.1).
2. Protect my life, save my soul (v.2).
3. Be merciful, O LORD: Because I call out to you all day long (v.3).
4. Give joy to my soul, O LORD (vv.4-5).
5. Hear my prayer, my urgent cry, O LORD (vv.6-10).
6. Teach me your way, O LORD, and give me a pure heart (vv.11-15).
7. Turn to me and have mercy, O LORD (v.16).
8. Show me a sign of your favor (v.17).

1 (86:1) **Turn your attention to me, O LORD; hear my prayer: Because I am in desperate need.**
In desperate need of God's help, David cried out to the LORD. He asked God to bow down His ear, to turn His attention to him and *answer* (ana) his prayer. By referring

to himself as *poor* (ani), David was saying that he was sorely distressed. *Needy* (ebyon) means that he was helpless and in need of God's assistance. He could do nothing to change his circumstances.

Thought 1. When we are brought low by trouble, we can call on God. As we pass through life, we will face many situations that are out of our control. But even when we can do nothing to change our circumstances, we are not helpless. God is our helper, and He has promised to hear us when we cry out to Him.

> **Do not be anxious about anything, but in everything, by prayer and petition, with thanksgiving, present your requests to God (Ph.4:6).**
> **Is any one of you in trouble? He should pray. Is anyone happy? Let him sing songs of praise (Js.5:13).**
> **I call on you, O God, for you will answer me; give ear to me and hear my prayer (Ps.17:6).**
> **Yet I am poor and needy; may the Lord think of me. You are my help and my deliverer; O my God, do not delay (Ps.40:17).**
> **For he will deliver the needy who cry out, the afflicted who have no one to help (Ps.72:12).**

2 (86:2) **Protect my life, save my soul.**
David was under attack from ruthless enemies who sought his life (v.14). Unable to ensure his own safety, he asked God to preserve or guard his soul or life and to save him from his enemies.

a. **Because I am devoted to you (v.2ᵃ).**
David appealed to God for protection on the basis of his devotion to God. He humbly stated that he was *devoted* (chasid) and that the LORD was his God. When used as a noun, *chasid* is usually translated as *saint.* It speaks of those who have a covenant relationship with the LORD and who "reflect the character of God in their actions or personality."[1] Because David lived righteously and was faithful to God, he could boldly ask God to be faithful to him.

b. **Because I am your servant and I trust in you (v.2ᵇ).**
David also appealed to God for protection because he was God's servant. Like the bondservant, who chooses to stay with his master out of love, David willingly served God because he loved Him (Ex.21:5-6). And, he trusted God for protection and for the provision of his

needs in return. This was the servant-master relationship: the servant dedicated his life to his master, and the master was responsible for taking care of the servant.

Thought 1. When we are faithful to the LORD, we can expect Him to be faithful to us. Because we have placed our faith in Jesus Christ, we are God's sons and daughters (Ga.3:26). We should also be His servants, ones who freely and willingly dedicate our lives to Him. We are to present ourselves as living sacrifices to God. When we consider His mercies toward us, we are to give ourselves fully to Him. This is our reasonable service (Ro.12:1).

Even when we are unfaithful, God is still faithful (2 Ti.2:13). Yet serving God faithfully fills us with boldness to approach Him for our needs, and it gives us the confidence that He will faithfully take care of us.

> **Persecuted, but not abandoned; struck down, but not destroyed (2 Co.4:9).**
> **The Lord will rescue me from every evil attack and will bring me safely to his heavenly kingdom. To him be glory for ever and ever. Amen (2 Ti.4:18).**
> **The LORD commanded us to obey all these decrees and to fear the LORD our God, so that we might always prosper and be kept alive, as is the case today (De.6:24).**
> **Keep me safe, O God, for in you I take refuge (Ps.16:1).**
> **The LORD will protect him and preserve his life; he will bless him in the land and not surrender him to the desire of his foes (Ps.41:2).**
> **I will save you; you will not fall by the sword but will escape with your life, because you trust in me, declares the LORD " (Je.39:18).**

3 (86:3) **Be merciful, O LORD: Because I call out to you all day long.**
David pleaded with God to be merciful to Him. *Have mercy* (chanan) means to "bend or stoop in kindness to an inferior."[2] It is to be gracious toward or show pity to a person in need. David's need for God's help was so great that he cried out to God throughout the day, all day long.

Thought 1. Anything we receive from God is a result of His mercy toward us. We always need to remember that we deserve nothing from Him but judgment. Every gift we receive from God is due to His graciousness: it is His nature to help us and to do good for us. We

---

[1] Spiros Zodhiates. *AMG Complete Word Study Dictionary.* WORDsearch CROSS e-book.

[2] James Strong. *Strong's Exhaustive Concordance.*

are the blessed benefactors of a good, loving, and merciful God.

> **But because of his great love for us, God, who is rich in mercy (Ep.2:4).**
>
> **He saved us, not because of righteous things we had done, but because of his mercy. He saved us through the washing of rebirth and renewal by the Holy Spirit (Tit.3:5).**
>
> **Let us then approach the throne of grace with confidence, so that we may receive mercy and find grace to help us in our time of need (He.4:16).**
>
> **Give thanks to the LORD, for he is good; his love endures forever (1 Chr.16:34).**
>
> **And call upon me in the day of trouble; I will deliver you, and you will honor me" (Ps.50:15).**
>
> **Because of the LORD's great love we are not consumed, for his compassions never fail. They are new every morning; great is your faithfulness (Lam.3:22-23).**

4 (86:4-5) Give joy to my soul, O LORD.

David desired more than to be rescued from his enemies: he longed for the joy of the LORD to fill his soul again. Because his troubling circumstances had robbed him of his joy, he needed a special touch from God. In lifting up his soul to Him, David asked God to lift him out of the depths of despair and to fill his heart with joy. To lift up your soul to God is turn to Him with all that you are (Ps.25:1).

a. Because I am your servant: I give myself to serve you (v.4).

Once more, David emphasized the fact that he was God's servant. Having given himself fully to God, he asked the Lord to meet his desperate need for encouragement, comfort, and hope.

b. Because you are good, ready to forgive, and merciful to all who call on you (v.5).

In calling out for God's help, David claimed what he knew to be true about God, about His character and nature. Notice that David addressed God as *Lord* (Adonai), which means master. David appealed to God on the basis of his servant relationship to Him.

First, David praised God because He is always *forgiving*. Even though God is perfectly holy and righteous, He does not stand by waiting for the opportunity to judge us. Rather, as David noted, He stands ready to forgive us. As believers in Jesus Christ, we are still sinners, and yet God has no record of our sins. He has carried our sins away, casting them in the depths of the sea forever (Mi.7:19; Je.31:34; Ps.103:12). On our

very worst days, we can rejoice because we have been forgiven.

Second, David praised the Lord for being *good*. Life's severe trials do not change who God is and what He is like. On the darkest days of our lives, God is still good (1 Chr.16:34; Ps.145:9). Even though David was sorely distressed by his trouble, he did not lose sight of God's goodness.

Third, David praised the Lord because He is *abounding in love*. *Love* (chesed) is God's steadfast, covenant love (see outline and notes—Ps.5:7 for more discussion). When we call on Him, He responds according to His unfailing love for us. *Abounding* speaks of the depth and magnitude of God's love and mercy toward us as well as all that He does for us because of His great love. God's mercy is abundant—far beyond what we could ever need.

Thought 1. David realized that he could have joy in the midst of his intense trouble. Notice what he did:

➤ He asked God to give him joy.
➤ He took his eyes off of his trouble and focused instead on God's goodness, forgiveness, and mercy.

Even when we are depressed, discouraged, or in a state of desperation, God is still God. He is still good, forgiving, and merciful. He never changes. When our trouble has brought us low, we can still have the joy of the Lord in our hearts. Meditating on God—on who He is and all that He does for us—will bring gladness to our souls in our darkest hours.

> **I tell you the truth, you will weep and mourn while the world rejoices. You will grieve, but your grief will turn to joy (Jn.16:20).**
>
> **I have great confidence in you; I take great pride in you. I am greatly encouraged; in all our troubles my joy knows no bounds (2 Co.7:4).**
>
> **Being strengthened with all power according to his glorious might so that you may have great endurance and patience, and joyfully (Col.1:11).**
>
> **Though you have not seen him, you love him; and even though you do not see him now, you believe in him and are filled with an inexpressible and glorious joy (1 Pe.1:8).**
>
> **For you, O LORD, have delivered my soul from death, my eyes from tears, my feet from stumbling (Ps.116:8).**

5 (86:6-10) Hear my prayer, my urgent cry, O LORD.

David again asked God to hear his prayer and to *listen* (qashab) to his cry for mercy. In other words, he wanted

God to give his requests full attention and then to do or fulfill his requests. *Cries for mercy* (tachanun) are earnest pleas for favor from one who is helpless. David was pleading for God to bend down and show him mercy. By using this word, David conveyed the urgency of his cry.

a. Because I am in trouble and you promise to hear me (v.7).

David's petition was so urgent because his crisis was so severe. He had learned to call on God when he was in trouble, for God had promised to hear and answer his prayers. His experiences had proved God to be true to His Word, strengthening his confidence in the LORD. Therefore, he could boldly say, "You will answer me."

b. Because you are the only living and true God: No one can do what you do (v.8).

In his time of urgent need, David turned to the Lord because of his deep conviction that He is the only living and true God. He held God up against the gods of the heathen nations and declared that there was no comparison: not one of them was like his Lord—the Master he freely served. Not one of the pagan idols could do the works that God did. He alone is alive and real. He alone is God.

c. Because one day in the future every person and every nation will submit to you and worship you, Ph.2:9-11 (vv.9-10).

David prophesied that all nations will one day turn from their idols and acknowledge his Lord and Master as God (v.10). They too will submit to His Lordship and worship Him. They will bow the knee at the name of God's Son, Jesus Christ, and they will glorify Him (Ph.2:9-11). On that day, all of creation will join with God's people in de-claring that God is great and that He performs miraculous, wonderful deeds. All will confess that He alone is God (v.10).

Thought 1. We can carry our most urgent petitions to God with full confidence that He is alive and that He is the one true God. We do not pray to an object but to a living Spirit—the force of creation, the source and sustainer of all life (Jn.4:24; Ac.17:28). As believers, we can call on God with unwavering assurance that He hears us and will answer us (1 Jn.5:14-15). Furthermore, we can pray with absolute certainty that He is able to solve our greatest problems, meet our deepest needs, and deliver us from our fiercest enemies. He is God. He is omnipotent. Nothing is too hard for Him. No one can do what He can do!

> "Ask and it will be given to you; seek and you will find; knock and the door will be opened to you (Mt.7:7).

> Therefore I tell you, whatever you ask for in prayer, believe that you have received it, and it will be yours (Mk. 11:24).

> This is the confidence we have in approaching God: that if we ask anything according to his will, he hears us. And if we know that he hears us—whatever we ask—we know that we have what we asked of him (1 Jn.5:14-15).

> And call upon me in the day of trouble; I will deliver you, and you will honor me" (Ps.50:15).

> 'Call to me and I will answer you and tell you great and unsearchable things you do not know' (Je.33:3).

6 (86:11-16) Teach me your way, O LORD, and give me a pure heart.

David paused his fervent prayer for deliverance to make an unusual request of the LORD. He asked God to teach him His way and to give him a pure heart. In spite of his urgent need, David was concerned with pleasing God and living to glorify Him.

a. That I may walk according to your truth and genuinely honor your name (v.11).

As God's willing servant, David desired to obey and please the LORD in all things. He asked God to teach him His way so that he could walk according to God's truth. David believed that "faith without works is dead" (Js.2:26). He longed to have a living faith, a faith demonstrated by obedience to God's Word (Js.1:22-25). He sincerely asked God to "give me an undivided heart that I may fear your name." Simply stated, he petitioned God for a heart that was not torn between obeying God's Word and fulfilling his own desires. He longed to fear God wholeheartedly—to obey and submit to Him—that he might genuinely honor God's holy name.

b. That I may praise and glorify your name forever (vv.12-14).

David yearned not only to obey God wholeheartedly but also to praise God will all his heart (v.12). He promised God to praise and glorify His name forever. He felt this was the least he could do in return for all that God had done for him. He was the recipient of God's great mercy and unfailing love (v.13ᵃ). God had preserved his life, delivering him from the depths of the grave (death) on many occasions (v.13ᵇ). *The grave* (sheol) refers to the world of the dead. Indeed, God had delivered him time and again from his enemies. At present, David was being attacked yet again by prideful and violent men who had rejected God and were now seeking his soul or life. The words *attacking me* suggest that he was facing a revolt from within his own nation.

c. That I may declare your nature (v.15).

David responded to his enemies' threat by resting in God's nature. He declared that the Lord is compassionate and gracious. He is slow to anger, patient and longsuffering. Likewise, His mercy and truth are abundant.

Thought 1. Throughout life, even in the midst of serious crises, we should live for God's glory. Like David, we ought to ask God repeatedly to teach us His way—the way of righteousness, holiness, and godliness. We ought to pray for God to deliver us from the desires of our sinful nature, asking Him to create in us a heart that is wholly devoted to Him. These requests should not be made in an effort to seek God's favor or help but, rather, in gratitude for His abundant mercy and faithful love.

> **For the grace of God that brings salvation has appeared to all men. It teaches us to say "No" to ungodliness and worldly passions, and to live self-controlled, upright and godly lives in this present age (Tit.2:11-12).**
>
> **My dear brothers, take note of this: Everyone should be quick to listen, slow to speak and slow to become angry (Js.1:19).**
>
> **Show me your ways, O LORD, teach me your paths (Ps.25:4).**
>
> **Create in me a pure heart, O God, and renew a steadfast spirit within me (Ps.51:10).**
>
> **Teach me, O LORD, to follow your decrees; then I will keep them to the end (Ps.119:33).**

7 (86:16) Turn to me and have mercy, O LORD.

David ended his prayer with one last appeal for God's help. He asked God to turn toward him and to have mercy on him (v.3). *Turn* (panah) is the root of the Hebrew word for face. Literally, David petitioned God to "turn His face toward [him] in grace."[3]

a. Because I am your servant and need your strength (v.16ᵃ).

Again declaring himself to be God's servant, David prayed that God would give him His very own strength. He did not intend to stand by idly while his enemies fiercely threatened him; instead, he was determined to rise up and defend himself. His foes were powerful and intimidating, and David knew he could not defeat them in his own strength. In light of that, he asked God to endue him with *His* mighty power.

b. Because I am your maidservant's son and need to be saved (v.16ᵇ).

David reminded God that his mother was also His servant. This may have been an expression of humility, or David may have been asking the Lord to save him for his godly mother's sake. Some scholars see a prophetic reference to Jesus, whose mother described herself as "the handmaid of the Lord" (Lu.1:38).

Thought 1. Because Jesus Christ is our Great High Priest, we have a standing invitation to come boldly to God for grace and mercy (He.4:14-16). We need God's favor, and we need God's help. In addition, we desperately need God's strength to fight against our enemy—Satan and his evil forces (1 Pe.5:8-9). If we battle the enemy in our own strength, we will surely suffer defeat. But when we stand in the power of God's might, we will be victorious (Ep.6:10-12). We must never hesitate nor neglect to call on God for help and strength.

> **Finally, be strong in the Lord and in his mighty power (Ep.6:10).**
>
> **I can do everything through him who gives me strength (Ph.4:13).**
>
> **Be self-controlled and alert. Your enemy the devil prowls around like a roaring lion looking for someone to devour. Resist him, standing firm in the faith, because you know that your brothers throughout the world are undergoing the same kind of sufferings (1 Pe.5:8-9).**
>
> **The LORD make his face shine upon you and be gracious to you (Nu.6:25).**
>
> **You are awesome, O God, in your sanctuary; the God of Israel gives power and strength to his people. Praise be to God! (Ps.68:35).**
>
> **May your unfailing love come to me, O LORD, your salvation according to your promise (Ps.119:41).**
>
> **I have sought your face with all my heart; be gracious to me according to your promise (Ps.119:58).**

8 (86:17) Show me a sign of your favor.

David asked God to show him a token or sign that His favor was on him. Most likely, David was referring to God's delivering him from his enemies. He was not asking God to give him a sign that he would deliver him, but for God's deliverance to be the sign that proved His favor toward David.

---

3 Donald Williams. *Psalms 73-150*, p.120.

a. **Because my enemies need to see evidence of your existence and goodness and be shamed (v.17ᵃ).**
God's deliverance of David would serve as a sign to his enemies that God exists and that He is truly God. When they saw God's goodness bestowed on His servant, they would be ashamed or disgraced.

b. **Because you have helped and comforted me (v.17ᵇ).**
When God delivered David, his enemies would see that the LORD had helped and comforted him. Notice that David did not address God here as *Lord* (Adonai) but as *LORD* (Yahweh, Jehovah), God's covenant name. In the end, David wanted everyone to know that God is faithful to His people. His deliverance would serve as a strong witness that God can be trusted and that He will, without fail, stand by those who belong to Him.

Thought 1. Like David, we can expect God's favor when we serve Him faithfully and call on His name. The Lord loves us so much that He gave His only Son for us. He will not withhold His help and strength in our time of need (Ro.8:32). He promises to comfort us in all of our trials (2 Co.1:3-4). When we are in a desperate situation, we need to cry out for God's help continually, fully expecting God to show Himself strong on our behalf. And when we faithfully serve and obey Him, we can be sure that God will not ignore us in our time of need.

> But the Lord stood at my side and gave me strength, so that through me the message might be fully proclaimed and all the Gentiles might hear it. And I was delivered from the lion's mouth (2 Ti.4:17).
>
> So we say with confidence, "The Lord is my helper; I will not be afraid. What can man do to me?" (He.13:6).
>
> For surely, O LORD, you bless the righteous; you surround them with your favor as with a shield (Ps.5:12).
>
> Let me not be put to shame, O LORD, for I have cried out to you; but let the wicked be put to shame and lie silent in the grave (Ps.31:17).
>
> But you give us victory over our enemies, you put our adversaries to shame (Ps.44:7).

	PSALM 87	4 "I will record Rahab and Babylon among those who acknowledge me—Philistia too, and Tyre, along with Cush—and will say, 'This one was born in Zion.'"
		 5 Indeed, of Zion it will be said, "This one and that one were born in her, and the Most High himself will establish her."
		 6 The LORD will write in the register of the peoples: "This one was born in Zion." Selah
		 7 As they make music they will sing, "All my fountains are in you."
			2. God offers everyone the privilege of being a citizen of Jerusalem
			 a. All who truly know Him will be registered as citizens: A picture of the new birth, Lu.10:20; Ga.4:21-31; Ph.3:20-21; He.12:22-24
			   1) He will make her a global city of believers, Is.2:1-4; 26:1-4; Mic.4:1-4; Zec.8:23
			   2) He Himself will establish (bless) the city
			   3) He will register believers of all nations as citizens of Jerusalem Ps.69:28; Da.7:10; 12:102; Mal.3:16; Re.13:8
			 b. All who are citizens of Jerusalem will praise God as the source of their citizenship & blessings, Ph.3:20-21

	Jerusalem, the City of God: A Picture of the Heavenly Capital of the New Heavens & Earth, 87:1-7; Is.65: 17-25; Re.21:1–22:6 *Of the Sons of Korah. A psalm. A song.*		
1. God chose Jerusalem as the site for His temple: Christ's ministry & future rule would be there a. He loves her more than any other city: Would redeem His people there, Jn.4:22 b. He foretold glorious things about her, not yet all fulfilled	He has set his foundation on the holy mountain; 2 The LORD loves the gates of Zion more than all the dwellings of Jacob. 3 Glorious things are said of you, O city of God: Selah		

PSALM 87

Jerusalem, the City of God: A Picture of the Heavenly Capital of the New Heavens and Earth, 87:1-7

(87:1-7) **Introduction:** most nations of the world have national anthems, songs written by people who love their country, who want to proclaim their loyalty to and pride in it. Many of the world's great cities are also the subject of songs written and sung by people who love them.

Psalm 87 is one of several songs in the Hebrew hymnal written about the glories of Jerusalem (see Ps.46–48; 76; 125; 129; 137). Attributed to the sons of Korah, this psalm emphasizes the true glory of Jerusalem, that is, God's presence there and His plan for Zion.

The psalmist reminds us that Israel's capital will be the world capital during the reign of Jesus Christ. It is also a picture of the New Jerusalem, the heavenly capital of the new heaven and the new earth. As you study this psalm, ask God to grip your heart with a fervent love for this city that He loves so dearly, and commit yourself to pray for the peace of Jerusalem on a daily basis (Ps.122:6). Why? Because Jerusalem is relevant to every believer in every nation: as Holy Scripture states, she is the mother of all who believe (Ga.4:26). This is, *Jerusalem, the City of God: A Picture of the Heavenly Capital of the New Heavens and Earth,* 87:1-7.

1. God chose Jerusalem as the site for His temple: Christ's ministry and future rule would be there (vv.1-3).
2. God offers everyone the privilege of being a citizen of Jerusalem (vv.4-7).

1 (87:1-3) **God chose Jerusalem as the site for His temple: Christ's ministry and future rule would be there.**
Although the sons of Korah sang the glories of Zion in this psalm, the true focus of their praise was God. Jerusa-

lem was glorious because God had chosen it as the site for His temple—the place where a special manifestation of His presence was to be given to the world. God is omnipresent, meaning that He is everywhere. Still, God selected Jerusalem as the special place where His presence resided in an unusual way.

All the way back to Abraham's day, Jerusalem was a unique place. Long before God gave His law to Israel, it was the center of a different type of government. The mysterious Melchizedek was its king and its priest, its political and spiritual leader (Ge.14:18). Hundreds of years later, David, God's chosen king for Israel, took Jerusalem from the Jebusites and established the capital of his kingdom there (2 S.5:6-10). Subsequently, the LORD placed His temple in Jerusalem, uniting Israel's worship with her government. God's special nation was to be a theocracy, a nation ruled by God. There was no separation of church and state, so to speak. Jerusalem became known as the City of David, but, more importantly, it was "the city of the Great King"—Jehovah (Ps.48:2). It is where God set His foundation, where He founded or established His city. For this reason, the mountains of Jerusalem are holy.

a. He loves her more than any other city: Would redeem His people there, Jn.4:22 (v.2).
The LORD loves Jerusalem more than any other dwellings of Jacob or cities of Israel. The psalmist specifically stated that God loves the gates of Zion. A city's gates were where the important activities of life took place as well as where people entered and exited the city. As some commentators mention, God loved to see people coming through the gates of Jerusalem to worship Him when the feasts took place. Yet there is surely a broader significance to this statement: "The gates of Zion are

mentioned to indicate the accessibility of the city to all men; for the means of grace...are intended to bring salvation to all men."[1] God would redeem His people from Jerusalem. Salvation would come through the Jews (Jn.4:22). Christ would be crucified and buried in Jerusalem, and there He would rise again for our justification (Ro.4:25). The church would begin in Jerusalem, and minsters of the gospel would depart through its gates to carry the message of salvation to the world.

b. He foretold glorious things about her, not yet all fulfilled (v.3).

The psalmist declared that glorious things are spoken about Jerusalem. The Jews loved to celebrate the beautiful city of God, referring to it as "the joy of the whole earth" (Ps.48:2). But the people's praises of Zion are not all that is in view here. The psalmist was speaking of the prophecies concerning Jerusalem. Through the prophets, God foretold glorious things about Jerusalem. Some of these prophecies were fulfilled in Christ's first coming to earth. Many, however, remain to be fulfilled when Jesus comes again.

Thought 1. The rich history of Israel is only a shadow of the glorious things God has spoken of her future. Not only did God show His love for Jerusalem by making it the site of His temple, but He also chose it as the place where Christ's future reign will be centered. When Jesus comes again, He will rule the earth from David's throne in Jerusalem (Lu.1:32). The entire world will revolve around Jerusalem. It will be the center of both world government and world worship. The order of Melchizedek, the priestly line that never ends, will be restored (He.7:11-22). Jesus Christ, our Great High Priest, will also rule as King over the entire earth. A perfect King will preside over a perfect government, and Jerusalem will be the seat of it all.

"When the Son of Man comes in his glory, and all the angels with him, he will sit on his throne in heavenly glory (Mt.25:31).

He will be great and will be called the Son of the Most High. The Lord God will give him the throne of his father David, and he will reign over the house of Jacob forever; his kingdom will never end" (Lu.1:32-33).

In the presence of God and of Christ Jesus, who will judge the living and the dead, and in view of his appearing and his kingdom, I give you this charge (2 Ti.4:1).

'Since the day I brought my people out of Egypt, I have not chosen a city in any tribe of Israel to have a temple built for my Name to be there, nor have I chosen anyone to be the leader over my people Israel. But now I have chosen Jerusalem for my Name to be there, and I have chosen David to rule my people Israel' (2 Chr.6:5-6).

"I have installed my King on Zion, my holy hill" (Ps.2:6).

This is what Isaiah son of Amoz saw concerning Judah and Jerusalem: In the last days the mountain of the LORD's temple will be established as chief among the mountains; it will be raised above the hills, and all nations will stream to it. Many peoples will come and say, "Come, let us go up to the mountain of the LORD, to the house of the God of Jacob. He will teach us his ways, so that we may walk in his paths." The law will go out from Zion, the word of the LORD from Jerusalem. He will judge between the nations and will settle disputes for many peoples. They will beat their swords into plowshares and their spears into pruning hooks. Nation will not take up sword against nation, nor will they train for war anymore. Come, O house of Jacob, let us walk in the light of the LORD (Is.2:1-5).

For to us a child is born, to us a son is given, and the government will be on his shoulders. And he will be called Wonderful Counselor, Mighty God, Everlasting Father, Prince of Peace. Of the increase of his government and peace there will be no end. He will reign on David's throne and over his kingdom, establishing and upholding it with justice and righteousness from that time on and forever. The zeal of the LORD Almighty will accomplish this (Is.9:6-7).

See, a king will reign in righteousness and rulers will rule with justice (Is.32:1).

You who bring good tidings to Zion, go up on a high mountain. You who bring good tidings to Jerusalem, lift up your voice with a shout, lift it up, do not be afraid; say to the towns of Judah, "Here is your God!" See, the Sovereign LORD comes with power, and his arm rules for him. See, his reward is with him, and his recompense accompanies him. He tends his flock like a shepherd: He gathers the lambs in his arms and carries them close

---

1   Paul E. Kretzmann. *The Popular Commentary of the Bible*, 1924. WORD*search* CROSS e-book.

to his heart; he gently leads those that have young (Is.40:9-11).

They will live in the land I gave to my servant Jacob, the land where your fathers lived. They and their children and their children's children will live there forever, and David my servant will be their prince forever (Eze.37:25).

Then the angel who was speaking to me said, "Proclaim this word: This is what the LORD Almighty says: 'I am very jealous for Jerusalem and Zion (Zec. 1:14).

It is he who will build the temple of the LORD, and he will be clothed with majesty and will sit and rule on his throne. And he will be a priest on his throne. And there will be harmony between the two' (Zec.6:13).

2 (87:4-7) **God offers everyone the privilege of being a citizen of Jerusalem.**
The psalmist looked beyond the present population of Jerusalem to a time when the city's rolls would be enlarged to include people of all nations. The future of Zion was far greater than her past. God would offer everyone the privilege of being a citizen of Jerusalem. The City of God would become the capital of a global kingdom and the forerunner of heaven on earth.

a. **All who truly know Him will be registered as citizens: A picture of the new birth, Lu.10:20; Ga.4:21-31; Ph.3:20-21; He.12:22-24 (vv.4-6).**
The psalmist sang of a time when Jerusalem's citizens would include many others besides the Jews (v.4a). All who truly know or acknowledge God, regardless of race or nationality, will be registered as citizens of the City of God. To *acknowledge* (yada) does not mean to know of or to be acquainted with. It means to know personally and intimately. It refers to those who have a personal relationship with God. Even believers among Israel's enemies will be among those whom the LORD makes mention of or counts as the people of Zion:

➤ Rahab or Egypt (Ps.89:10; Is.51:9)
➤ Babylon
➤ Philistia
➤ Tyre
➤ Cush or Ethiopia

Along with people of all nations, these will be counted as citizens of Jerusalem, the same as those who were born in Zion (v.4b-5a). God will make Jerusalem a global city of believers. People of every earthly land will consider Jerusalem their spiritual home, and they will come there to worship (Is.2:1-4; 26:1-4;

Mi.4:1-4; Zec.8:23). God Himself will establish the city (v.5b). *Most High* (Elyon) is the name that exalts God as the highest authority. He will personally build His worldwide kingdom with Jerusalem as its capital. And He will personally register believers of all nations as citizens (v.6).

b. **All who are citizens of Jerusalem will praise God as the source of their citizenship and blessings, Ph.3:20-21 (v.7).**
The psalmist described a worship festival in Jerusalem that will far exceed any in Zion's history. The singers and instrumentalists will lead all the citizens—people of every nation, tribe, and tongue—in singing praise to God. The congregation of the redeemed will sing "all my fountains are in you," a song celebrating the LORD as the fountain of every blessing, the wellspring of overflowing joy, and the source of eternal life.

Thought 1. As the psalmist presented some of Israel's future glories, he described the reign of Christ, when people of all nations will flock to Jerusalem to worship. At the same time, he looked beyond the earthly reign of Jesus Christ to Christ's eternal kingdom. The earthly Jerusalem, God's city, is a picture of the New Jerusalem, the heavenly capital of the new heaven and the new earth (Is.65:17-25; Re.21:1-22:6).

The emphasis of this passage is on the citizens of Jerusalem. The psalmist wrote of a new order of God's people, one consisting of people of all nations, Gentiles as well as Jews. All who know God—who have a personal relationship with Him—will be citizens of the heavenly Jerusalem. Being *born in Zion* is a picture of the new birth by faith in Jesus Christ (vv.4-5; Jn.3:3-16; 1 Pe.1:23). When we repent of our sin and believe on Jesus, accept Him as Savior and Lord of our lives, we become citizens of heaven. The LORD's writing the names of those born in Zion in a registry of its citizens is a picture of God's writing believers' names in the book of life (Ps.69:28; Da.7:10; 12:1-2; Mal.3:16; Lu.10:20; Re.13:8). The citizens of the heavenly Jerusalem—Christ's eternal kingdom—are the genuine believers of all nations and all ages. The song described by the psalmist is their eternal song of praise to God (v.7).

No written or spoken word, no song sung, can say about the importance of our making the right decision regarding eternity. Will you be among the citizens of that great city of God? Is your name written in heaven? Have you been born again?

Take note of the following Scriptures:

However, do not rejoice that the spirits submit to you, but rejoice that your names are written in heaven" (Lu.10:20).

It was not through law that Abraham and his offspring received the promise that he would be heir of the world, but through the righteousness that comes by faith....Therefore, the promise comes by faith, so that it may be by grace and may be guaranteed to all Abraham's offspring—not only to those who are of the law but also to those who are of the faith of Abraham. He is the father of us all (Ro.4:13, 16).

You are all sons of God through faith in Christ Jesus, for all of you who were baptized into Christ have clothed yourselves with Christ. There is neither Jew nor Greek, slave nor free, male nor female, for you are all one in Christ Jesus. If you belong to Christ, then you are Abraham's seed, and heirs according to the promise (Ga.3:26-29).

But the Jerusalem that is above is free, and she is our mother. For it is written: "Be glad, O barren woman, who bears no children; break forth and cry aloud, you who have no labor pains; because more are the children of the desolate woman than of her who has a husband." Now you, brothers, like Isaac, are children of promise. At that time the son born in the ordinary way persecuted the son born by the power of the Spirit. It is the same now. But what does the Scripture say? "Get rid of the slave woman and her son, for the slave woman's son will never share in the inheritance with the free woman's son." Therefore, brothers, we are not children of the slave woman, but of the free woman (Ga.4:26-31).

But our citizenship is in heaven. And we eagerly await a Savior from there, the Lord Jesus Christ, who, by the power that enables him to bring everything under his control, will transform our lowly bodies so that they will be like his glorious body (Ph.3:20-21).

But you have come to Mount Zion, to the heavenly Jerusalem, the city of the living God. You have come to thousands upon thousands of angels in joyful assembly, to the church of the firstborn, whose names are written in heaven. You have come to God, the judge of all men, to the spirits of righteous men made perfect, to Jesus the mediator of a new covenant, and to the sprinkled blood that speaks a better word than the blood of Abel (He.12:22-24).

Then I saw a new heaven and a new earth, for the first heaven and the first earth had passed away, and there was no longer any sea. I saw the Holy City, the new Jerusalem, coming down out of heaven from God, prepared as a bride beautifully dressed for her husband. And I heard a loud voice from the throne saying, "Now the dwelling of God is with men, and he will live with them. They will be his people, and God himself will be with them and be their God (Re.21:1-3).

"Behold, I will create new heavens and a new earth. The former things will not be remembered, nor will they come to mind. But be glad and rejoice forever in what I will create, for I will create Jerusalem to be a delight and its people a joy. I will rejoice over Jerusalem and take delight in my people; the sound of weeping and of crying will be heard in it no more (Is.65:17-19).

PSALM 88

When You Suffer the Darkness of Despair & Your Prayers Go Unanswered, Ps.88:1-18

A song. A psalm of the Sons of Korah. For the director of music. According to mahalath leannoth. A maskil of Heman the Ezrahite.

1. Cry out day & night for God's help

a. Bc. God alone can save you

b. Bc. God alone can hear & answer prayer & you desperately need Him to listen to you

c. Bc. your life (soul) is full of adversity & suffering & you sense death is near

  1) You feel like a dead man

    • Are very weak, with no strength left

    • Are like a corpse lying in the grave

  2) You feel God has forgotten you & does not care

  3) You feel God has put you into the darkest pit of suffering & despair

d. Bc. you feel it is God's discipline (anger) overwhelming & weighing heavily on you (perhaps due to sin?)

  1) Your wretched condition makes you repulsive to your

O LORD, the God who saves me, day and night I cry out before you.
2 May my prayer come before you; turn your ear to my cry.
3 For my soul is full of trouble and my life draws near the grave.
4 I am counted among those who go down to the pit; I am like a man without strength.
5 I am set apart with the dead, like the slain who lie in the grave, whom you remember no more, who are cut off from your care.
6 You have put me in the lowest pit, in the darkest depths.
7 Your wrath lies heavily upon me; you have overwhelmed me with all your waves. Selah
8 You have taken from me my closest friends and have

made me repulsive to them. I am confined and cannot escape;
9 My eyes are dim with grief. I call to you, O LORD, every day; I spread out my hands to you.
10 Do you show your wonders to the dead? Do those who are dead rise up and praise you? Selah
11 Is your love declared in the grave, your faithfulness in Destruction?
12 Are your wonders known in the place of darkness, or your righteous deeds in the land of oblivion?
13 But I cry to you for help, O LORD; in the morning my prayer comes before you.
14 Why, O LORD, do you reject me and hide your face from me?
15 From my youth I have been afflicted and close to death; I have suffered your terrors and am in despair.
16 Your wrath has swept over me; your terrors have destroyed me.
17 All day long they surround me like a flood; they have completely engulfed me.
18 You have taken my companions and loved ones from me; the darkness is my closest friend.

    friends & they shun you

  2) Your despair confines you, makes you feel trapped

2. Cry out urgently & repeatedly for God's mercy

a. Bc. your grief is unbearable: Your tears blind your eyes

b. Bc. once you are dead, you cannot...

  1) Appreciate God's works

  2) Praise God

  3) Declare God's love or faithfulness

  4) Know God's wonderful & righteous deeds

3. Cry out again in the morning— start afresh in prayer: Never stop believing & calling out for God's help

a. Bc. you feel God has abandoned & hidden His face from you

b. Bc. you have suffered for a very long time: The psalmist had been afflicted since his youth

  1) He felt it was God's discipline (anger) overwhelming & driving him to despair

  2) He felt completely engulfed by the waters of affliction & discouragement

  3) He was forsaken by his loved ones & friends

PSALM 88

When You Suffer the Darkness of Despair and Your Prayers Go Unanswered, 88:1-18

(88:1-18) **Introduction:** thankfully, many of life's serious challenges are temporary in nature. But some are not. Some illnesses or other physical conditions are not healed. Some problems are never solved. Some difficult circumstances never change. Some troubles never go away.

Psalm 88 is the pitiful cry of a man who faced an ongoing trial. He was suffering miserably from a chronic illness that had plagued him from his childhood. Over and over again, he had cried out to God for healing, but healing never came. Apparently, his condition worsened through the years to the point that it crippled his entire life. His friends forsook him, and he felt he was at the point of death.

The heading to Psalm 88 identifies Heman the Ezrahite as its author. Heman was one of David's three chief musicians—a primary leader of worship in Israel (1 Chr.6:33; 15:17-19; 16:41-42; 25:1, 6; 2 Chr.5:12). He was respected for his wisdom and served as one of Da-

vid's chief spiritual advisors (1 K.4:31; 1 Chr.25:5). Yet, as his only psalm reveals, he suffered intensely.

Various commentators have described Psalm 88 as the saddest, gloomiest, and darkest of all the psalms. Early commentators applied it to the suffering of Christ at Gethsemane and Calvary. Even today, it is often read at Good Friday services.

Psalm 88 is different from every other psalm about suffering and trouble. In other psalms of lament, there is a transition in which the psalmist is delivered or his burden is lightened and his sorrow is transformed to joy. As in these other psalms, Heman prays diligently, earnestly calling on the LORD for help and deliverance. In his case, however, his prayers seem to go unanswered. No deliverance comes. No confidence or hope of deliverance is given. He receives no comfort or relief from his suffering. The last word of the psalm is *darkness*. At the end of the psalm, he is still suffering and in despair.

Through Heman's excruciating suffering of both body and soul, God used this wise worship leader in a wonderful way. Sixteenth century theologian John Calvin wrote,

> *God, in so sorely* [testing] *Heman, whom he had adorned with such excellent gifts to be an example to others, did not do this for the sake of his servant only. His object was to present...instruction to all his people. Carrying out this* [purpose], *Heman...testifies to the whole Church his infirmities as well as his faith and constancy.*[1]

Heman's prayer is raw and bursting with emotion. It speaks to all who experience ongoing suffering and to those who fear the experience of suffering. Any of us whose healing never comes, whose circumstances never change, and whose prayers seem to go unheard can identify with his emotions. Heman does not describe his circumstances as they actually are but as he perceives them to be—the way he sees them. For example, he feels that God has forsaken him and angrily stricken him. Still, the Holy Spirit inspired him to write his psalm this way—uncensored and unfiltered—so we can know that we are not alone in questioning God and can see that we have the liberty to express our true feelings to our Heavenly Father.

At the same time, Heman stands as a sterling example of unwavering faith. After years of his prayers for relief going unanswered, he continued to pray. Hebrews 11 recalls the great faith of heroes like Abraham, Joseph, Moses, and David. At the end of the list of those who did great deeds and won shining victories, Scripture then mentions another group:

> **Some faced jeers and flogging, while still others were chained and put in prison. They were stoned; they were sawed in two; they were put to death by the sword. They went about in sheepskins and goatskins, destitute, persecuted and mistreated—the world was not worthy of them. They wandered in deserts and mountains, and in caves and holes in the ground (He.11:36-38).**

Heman will forever remain one of the unnamed *others* who were never delivered from their trouble, yet never faltered in their faith. He may have questioned and complained to God, but he never stopped believing in God. This is, *When You Suffer the Darkness of Despair and Your Prayers Go Unanswered,* 88:1-18.

1. Cry out day and night for God's help (vv.1-8).
2. Cry out urgently and repeatedly for God's mercy (vv.9-12).

3. Cry out again in the morning—start afresh in prayer: Never stop believing and calling out for God's help (vv.13-18).

1 (88:1-8) **Cry out day and night for God's help.**
In the depths of despair and desperate for help, the suffering psalmist cried out to God day and night. He poured out his anguished heart to the LORD, freely expressing his feelings and frustrations. While he was clearly disappointed in God, he had not lost his faith, nor had he lost hope that God would respond to his pleas.

a. **Because God alone can save you (v.1).**
Heman addressed the LORD as the *God who saves me.* His illness was grave, and he had apparently suffered with it since childhood (v.15). It is reasonable to assume that he had pursued every means of help available to him throughout his life, but to no avail. Despite everything, he continued to believe that God could save him, that He could heal and deliver him from his illness.

b. **Because God alone can hear and answer prayer and you desperately need Him to listen to you (v.2).**
With God as his only hope, the psalmist pleaded with the LORD to hear and answer his prayer. Although he had cried out to God for years, relief from his suffering never came. He surely felt that his supplications were not reaching God, or that God was not listening. With that in mind, he asked that his prayers would come before God's face. He desperately needed God to listen to him. *Cry* (rinnah) usually speaks of loud shouts of joy in the Old Testament. *The Expositor's Bible Commentary* describes it here as a "deeply piercing shout," stating that it is "a loud cry for divine help. The psalmist shouts loudly to the Lord, hoping that He will hear."[2]

c. **Because your life (soul) is full of adversity and suffering and you sense death is near (vv.3-6).**
Frustrated and worn down by years of suffering, Heman emptied his soul to the LORD. He began by stating that he was full of trouble (v.3a). The Hebrew word for *full* (sabea) is used of one who has eaten to the point that he or she can eat no more. Bluntly stated, the psalmist declared that he had endured all the trouble that he could stand. His suffering was so intense that he felt he stood at the very brink of death (v.3b). *Draws near* (nagah) means to touch or make personal contact with. He sensed that he was so near death that he could actually reach out and touch *the grave* (sheol)—the place where the dead reside.

---

1 John Calvin. *Calvin's Commentaries.* WORD*search* CROSS e-book.

2 Frank E. Gaebelein, ed. *The Expositor's Bible Commentary*, p.565.

In fact, the psalmist expressed that he felt like a dead man (v.4ᵃ). Others avoided him, treating him as if he were already dead. He was very weak; he had no strength to continue fighting his affliction (v.4ᵇ). Exhausted and discouraged, he had reached the point where he felt he could go on no longer.

Not only was the psalmist shunned by others, but to Heman it also seemed that God had abandoned him (v.5). He felt as if he were a corpse lying in the grave. In spite of his unending cries for God's help, his situation never changed. It was as if he were dead, as if God had forgotten him and did not care about him.

The severity of his suffering caused the psalmist to feel that God had caused his affliction (v.6). He plainly stated that *God* had put him into the lowest pit imaginable. *God* had plunged him into the darkest depths. *God* was responsible for his agony—or so it seemed.

d. Because you feel it is God's discipline (anger) overwhelming and weighing heavily on you (perhaps due to some sin?) (vv.7-8).

The psalmist reasoned that he was suffering so intensely because of God's wrath (v.7ᵃ). He assumed that God was angry with him and was disciplining him, perhaps for some sin he had committed. He felt trapped beneath the weight of God's fury, struggling to survive the relentless waves of a fierce storm (v.7ᵇ). Before he could recover from one crippling blow, another wave struck. He was like a drowning man, unable to keep his head above water.

To make matters even worse, the psalmist was fighting his way through this alone. Repulsed by Heman's wretched condition, his friends shunned him (v.8). He was confined by his despair, trapped and unable to escape the sorrow that squeezed the very life and hope out of his soul.

Thought 1. All who persevere through prolonged suffering can identify with Heman's feelings:
➤ He felt God was not listening to his prayers, that He was ignoring him (v.1-2).
➤ He thought he could not go on any longer—that he could endure no more pain (vv.3-4).
➤ He felt nobody cared about him—that he had no true friends (v.4).
➤ He felt God had caused His suffering—that God had done this to him (vv.5-8).
➤ He felt imprisoned by his affliction—trapped with no hope of escape (v.8).

By inspiring Heman to express these feelings so candidly, the Holy Spirit wanted us to know that we, too, can freely pour out our hearts to God. Naturally, God already knows what we are feeling; our expressing our thoughts and emotions to Him merely opens the door for His Spirit to minister and speak to us. This is one of *Psalms*' greatest lessons.

Notice that, while Heman was brutally honest in his prayer, he was never irreverent or disrespectful toward God. Likewise our relationship with God provides us the liberty to communicate honestly with Him, but we should never lose sight of who God is: He is *God*, the sovereign LORD and Majesty of the universe. He is the One who loved us so much that He gave His only Son for us.

In addition to showing us that we can pray freely, Heman also taught us that we should never stop praying. We should never give up when our prayers go unanswered. Rather, we should persist in prayer (Lu.11:5-10; 18:1). Like Heman, we must never doubt that God can deliver us but, instead, should tenaciously pursue God's help and strength.

> **And being in anguish, he prayed more earnestly, and his sweat was like drops of blood falling to the ground (Lu.22:44).**
>
> **But when he asks, he must believe and not doubt, because he who doubts is like a wave of the sea, blown and tossed by the wind (Js.1:6).**
>
> **Is any one of you in trouble? He should pray. Is anyone happy? Let him sing songs of praise. Is any one of you sick? He should call the elders of the church to pray over him and anoint him with oil in the name of the Lord. And the prayer offered in faith will make the sick person well; the Lord will raise him up. If he has sinned, he will be forgiven. Therefore confess your sins to each other and pray for each other so that you may be healed. The prayer of a righteous man is powerful and effective (Js.5:13-16).**
>
> **"Hear my prayer, O LORD, listen to my cry for help; be not deaf to my weeping. For I dwell with you as an alien, a stranger, as all my fathers were (Ps.39:12).**

2 (88:9-12) **Cry out urgently and repeatedly for God's mercy.**

Once more, the psalmist urgently cried out to God for mercy. Along with expressing his grief, he pleaded with God for his very life. He longed to live so that he could continue serving and praising the LORD.

a. Because your grief is unbearable: Your tears blind your eyes (v.9).

Heman's grief was greater than be could bear. Even his eyesight was affected, being constantly blurred by a seemingly endless flow of tears. Every day, he called out to the LORD. His outstretched hands conveyed his desperation as well as the urgency of his heart-wrenching pleas.

b. Because once you are dead, you cannot... (vv.10-12). The suffering psalmist desperately wanted to live. Heman was a leader of worship in God's house. He delighted in ushering people into God's presence and directing them to sing His praise. He presented his case for continued life to the LORD through a series of questions. Obviously, the answer to each of these questions is "No!" Once Heman was dead, he could no longer...

- appreciate God's works (v.10a). The dead do not witness God's wonders or miracles.
- praise God (v.10b). The dead do not sing praise to God, much less lead others in exalting Him.
- declare God's *love* (chesed), His steadfast love and faithfulness (v.11). Testimonies of God's goodness are not offered from the grave or the place of *destruction* (abaddon), a synonym for sheol, the dwelling place of the dead (Jb.26:6; Pr.15:11; 27:20).
- know God's wonderful and righteous deeds (v.12).

Thought 1. Once again, the despondent psalmist taught us to keep on crying out to God. Persistence in prayer is the theme of this heartrending psalm. When the heavens are as brass, appearing to be closed, continue to pray. When your prayers are unanswered, continue to pray. Pray urgently, pray fervently, and pray repeatedly.

> I tell you, though he will not get up and give him the bread because he is his friend, yet because of the man's boldness he will get up and give him as much as he needs. "So I say to you: Ask and it will be given to you; seek and you will find; knock and the door will be opened to you. For everyone who asks receives; he who seeks finds; and to him who knocks, the door will be opened (Lu.11:8-10).
>
> Then Jesus told his disciples a parable to show them that they should always pray and not give up (Lu.18:1).
>
> Then the man said, "Let me go, for it is daybreak." But Jacob replied, "I will not let you go unless you bless me" (Ge.32:26).
>
> Evening, morning and noon I cry out in distress, and he hears my voice (Ps.55:17).
>
> O LORD, I call to you; come quickly to me. Hear my voice when I call to you (Ps.141:1).

3 (88:13-18) **Cry out again in the morning—start afresh in prayer: Never stop believing and calling out for God's help.**

Now, for the third time, the psalmist cried out to God for help. He started each day afresh in prayer. Every morning, Heman came before the LORD with his petitions, but day after day nothing changed in his life. In spite of God's silence, however, Heman never stopped believing and calling out to God.

a. Because you feel God has abandoned and hidden His face from you (v.14). From Heman's perspective, God had cast him off. Broken by what he viewed as God's rejection, he cried out to the LORD for understanding. He needed to know why God did not answer his prayers. God's silence only multiplied his excruciating pain. Feeling that God had abandoned him and was hiding His face from him pushed Heman into utter despair.

b. Because you have suffered for a very long time: The psalmist had been afflicted since his youth (vv.15-18). Once again, the psalmist emptied his sorrows at God's throne. He began by reminding God that he had suffered a long, long time (v.15a). He had been afflicted since his youth, and at times he had been ready to die or close to death.

For a second time, Heman cited God as the source of his suffering. He stated that he was distracted or overcome by despair because of God's terrors—the horrifying pain that he felt God had inflicted on him (v.15b). It was God's fierce wrath or severe discipline that was overwhelming him and driving him to despair (v.16). God's painful blows beat upon him like crashing flood waters (v.17). He felt completely compassed about or engulfed by affliction and discouragement (v.17).

The distraught psalmist came to the conclusion again that, because of what he felt God had done, his loved ones and friends had forsaken him (v.18). His only remaining acquaintance was the darkness that consumed his soul. Despair, depression, and impending death were his only companions.

Thought 1. Sometimes our suffering continues without relief. We pray and pray and pray, but the answer we are looking for never comes. We are never healed. Our circumstances do not change. Our conflicts go unresolved. Our trouble continues, and we can find no relief.

At such times, we need to strive to see our suffering through the looking glass of God's Word. Things are not always as we think they are, but as God's Word says they are. We may think that God has abandoned us, but His Word promises that He will never leave nor forsake us (He.13:5; Mt.28:20). We may feel that we can go on no longer, but God's Word says we can do all things through Christ, and His grace is sufficient for us (Ph.4:13; 2 Co.12:9).

When our prayers go unanswered and despair sets in, we must believe God's Word and keep crying out to Him. This is what the psalmist did: he proved his trust in God by continuing to pray. Through the power of God's indwelling Spirit, we can follow his noble example. Remember, even Paul the apostle suffered continually because of some physical infirmity that God refused to remove (see 2 Co.12:7-10 for more discussion).

> *"Abba*, Father," he said, "everything is possible for you. Take this cup from me. Yet not what I will, but what you will" (Mk.14:36).

> We are hard pressed on every side, but not crushed; perplexed, but not in despair; persecuted, but not abandoned; struck down, but not destroyed....It is written: "I believed; therefore I have spoken." With that same spirit of faith we also believe and therefore speak, be- cause we know that the one who raised the Lord Jesus from the dead will also raise us with Jesus and present us with you in his presence (2 Co.4:8-9, 13-14).

> Do not be anxious about anything, but in everything, by prayer and petition, with thanksgiving, present your requests to God. And the peace of God, which transcends all understanding, will guard your hearts and your minds in Christ Je- sus (Ph.4:6-7).

> That is why I am suffering as I am. Yet I am not ashamed, because I know whom I have believed, and am convinced that he is able to guard what I have en- trusted to him for that day (2 Ti.1:12).

> Though he slay me, yet will I hope in him; I will surely defend my ways to his face (Jb.13:15).

> For the king trusts in the LORD; through the unfailing love of the Most High he will not be shaken (Ps.21:7).

> But I call to God, and the LORD saves me (Ps.55:16).

PSALM 89

When God's Promises Seem to Fail, 89:1-52

A maskil of Ethan the Ezrahite.

1. Praise God—proclaim His unfailing love & faithfulness to young & old alike

a. Bc. He guarantees His love & mercy forever & His faithfulness is as "enduring as the heavens," (NLT)

b. Bc. He made an eternal covenant with David: A promise of the Messiah, 2 S.7:11a-17
 1) He chose David, His servant
 2) He secured David's throne forever (thru Christ, God's Son), 29, 36-37; He.1:8; 10:12; 20-21; Re.11:15

c. Bc. heaven's exalted beings praise His wonders & faithfulness: An example we, as lowly human beings, should follow
 1) They praise God's uniqueness: No heavenly being or mighty angel compares to Him
 2) They—even the highest & most majestic heavenly beings—fear & stand in awe of God's greatness
 • Bc. He is all powerful
 • Bc. He is totally faithful: He will fulfill all promises

d. Bc. He rules over nature's raging seas: He faithfully helps His people thru natural disasters

e. Bc. He crushes the mightiest enemies (Rahab or Egypt): He faithfully defeats all who oppose Him & His dear people

f. Bc. He is the Sovereign Creator & Ruler of the universe & of all that exists therein

 1) The north & the south
 2) The mighty mountains that tower above the land: Even these praise God's name

g. Bc. He possesses absolute & unlimited power: He is able to fulfill all of His promises

h. Bc. His kingdom (throne) is based on righteousness & justice, love & faithfulness

i. Bc. He blesses those who praise & worship Him: He guides & enables them to walk in the light of His presence

I will sing of the LORD's great love forever; with my mouth I will make your faithfulness known through all generations.
2 I will declare that your love stands firm forever, that you established your faithfulness in heaven itself.
3 You said, "I have made a covenant with my chosen one, I have sworn to David my servant,
4 'I will establish your line forever and make your throne firm through all generations.'" Selah
5 The heavens praise your wonders, O LORD, your faithfulness too, in the assembly of the holy ones.
6 For who in the skies above can compare with the LORD? Who is like the LORD among the heavenly beings?
7 In the council of the holy ones God is greatly feared; he is more awesome than all who surround him.
8 O LORD God Almighty, who is like you? You are mighty, O LORD, and your faithfulness surrounds you.
9 You rule over the surging sea; when its waves mount up, you still them.
10 You crushed Rahab like one of the slain; with your strong arm you scattered your enemies.
11 The heavens are yours, and yours also the earth; you founded the world and all that is in it.
12 You created the north and the south; Tabor and Hermon sing for joy at your name.
13 Your arm is endued with power; your hand is strong, your right hand exalted.
14 Righteousness and justice are the foundation of your throne; love and faithfulness go before you.
15 Blessed are those who have learned to acclaim you, who walk in the light of your presence, O LORD.

16 They rejoice in your name all day long; they exult in your righteousness.
17 For you are their glory and strength, and by your favor you exalt our horn.
18 Indeed, our shield belongs to the LORD, our king to the Holy One of Israel.
19 Once you spoke in a vision, to your faithful people you said: "I have bestowed strength on a warrior; I have exalted a young man from among the people.
20 I have found David my servant; with my sacred oil I have anointed him.
21 My hand will sustain him; surely my arm will strengthen him.
22 No enemy will subject him to tribute; no wicked man will oppress him.
23 I will crush his foes before him and strike down his adversaries.
24 My faithful love will be with him, and through my name his horn will be exalted.
25 I will set his hand over the sea, his right hand over the rivers.
26 He will call out to me, 'You are my Father, my God, the Rock my Savior.'
27 I will also appoint him my firstborn, the most exalted of the kings of the earth.
28 I will maintain my love to him forever, and my covenant with him will never fail.
29 I will establish his line forever, his throne as long as the heavens endure.
30 "If his sons forsake my law and do not follow my statutes,
31 If they violate my decrees and fail to keep my commands,
32 I will punish their sin with the rod, their iniquity with flogging;
33 But I will not take my love from him, nor will I ever betray my faithfulness.
34 I will not violate my covenant or alter what my lips have uttered.
35 Once for all, I have sworn by my holiness—and I will not lie to David—
36 That his line will continue forever and his throne

1) His name & righteousness are the basis for their rejoicing
2) His glory & strength uphold & empower them

3) His sovereign shield or protection is their security

2. Trust God to fulfill His promises

a. God's choice of David, & David's trust in Him, 1 S.16:1-13
 1) He chose David from among the common people & exalted him
 2) He anointed David to be king

b. God's promises to David
 1) He would always sustain & strengthen David, Ph.4:13
 2) He would protect David from his enemies

 3) He would make David victorious over all foes & adversaries, 1 Jn.5:4-5
 4) He would always love & be faithful to David & would use His divine authority to exalt David's power
 5) He would give David universal rule: A rule over the sea & the rivers, Ps.72:8
 6) He would stir David to trust & call on Him as Father, God, Rock, & Savior, Ro.8:16-17
 7) He would make David His first born son & the mightiest king on earth: A prophecy of Christ, Re.1:5-6
 8) He would love & keep His covenant with David: Fulfilled in Christ who will rule forever, Is.11:1-9; Re.17:14; 19:16
 • Would preserve David's line
 • Would preserve David's throne forever

c. God's warning to David's descendants

 1) They must not forsake God's law nor refuse to follow & keep His commandments
 2) They would suffer the consequences of disobedience & be punished

d. God's affirmation of His love for & faithfulness to David

 1) He would not betray His faithfulness

 2) He would not violate or alter His covenant with David

 3) He has sworn by His holiness...

• That David's line & throne would continue forever (thru Christ) • That His kingdom would be established forever (thru Christ)	endure before me like the sun; 37 it will be established forever like the moon, the faithful witness in the sky." Selah	throne to the ground. 45 You have cut short the days of his youth; you have covered him with a mantle of shame. Selah	3) Had cut short the king's rule (David's dynasty) & publically shamed them
3. Beware—know that God rejects those who reject His promises (covenant), He.4:1-2	38 But you have rejected, you have spurned, you have been very angry with your anointed one.	46 How long, O LORD? Will you hide yourself forever? How long will your wrath burn like fire?	**4. Plead with God to fulfill His promises—never give up hope**
a. God rejected Israel's rulers: From a human perspective, it seemed that God had renounced the covenant...	39 You have renounced the covenant with your servant and have defiled his crown in the dust.	47 Remember how fleeting is my life. For what futility you have created all men!	a. Cry out that you cannot go on cut off from Him
1) Had defiled the crown	40 You have broken through all his walls and reduced his strongholds to ruins.	48 What man can live and not see death, or save himself from the power of the grave? Selah	1) Bc. your life is so short & is meaningless without Him
2) Had destroyed Jerusalem & the other fortresses (cities) of Israel			2) Bc. you are incapable of escaping or saving yourself from death
3) Had allowed His people to be plundered & scorned	41 All who pass by have plundered him; he has become the scorn of his neighbors.	49 O Lord, where is your former great love, which in your faithfulness you swore to David?	
b. God exalted His people's foes: From a human perspective, it seemed that God had made His own enemies victorious...	42 You have exalted the right hand of his foes; you have made all his enemies rejoice.	50 Remember, Lord, how your servant has been mocked, how I bear in my heart the taunts of all the nations,	b. Cry out for the same great love & faithfulness He promised to David
1) It seemed that God had failed to support Israel & the king (David's dynasty) in battle	43 You have turned back the edge of his sword and have not supported him in battle.	51 The taunts with which your enemies have mocked, O LORD, with which they have mocked every step of your anointed one.	c. Cry out for God to think of the persecution you are suffering 1) The reproach & insults by so many people 2) The taunts & mockery by God's enemies 3) The mockery of God's anointed one, David's descendant: A picture of Christ's being mocked
2) Had ended the king's glory & overturned his throne	44 You have put an end to his splendor and cast his	52 Praise be to the LORD forever! Amen and Amen.	d. Cry out in praise to the LORD forever! Cry out until He answers!

PSALM 89

When God's Promises Seem to Fail, 89:1-52

(89:1-52) **Introduction:** doubtless, we have all learned through disappointing or painful experiences, that many people fail to keep their word. We usually learn this lesson at a relatively young age, and it is confirmed time and again as we proceed through life.

Thankfully, God's Word promises that we can always trust Him to keep His Word. The Bible teaches that God cannot lie (Titus 1:2; He.6:18). In contrast, we are sinners and therefore capable of failing. But God is not like us. Because He is perfect and holy, He is incapable of lying or failing to do all He has promised (Nu.23:19). His promises are sure (2 Co.1:20).

Psalm 89 is a prayer for God to keep His promise, specifically, the Davidic Covenant (2 S.7:8-17). The LORD promised David that his seed would reign forever over an everlasting kingdom. However, one of David's successors had suffered a crushing defeat, and the kingdom had been overthrown. By all appearances, God's covenant with David had been violated (vv.38-45).

We cannot be sure of the specific defeat referred to in this psalm. Many scholars feel it was the overthrow of Jerusalem by Babylonia in 586 B.C. If this is true, the Davidic line would have ended with Jehoiachin, the evil young king who ruled over Judah at that time (2 K.24:6-

16). This opinion is supported by the fact that God condemned Jehoiachin, decreeing that none of his descendants would sit on David's throne (Je.22:24-30).

However, if the Babylonian invasion and captivity were the occasion for Psalm 89, it creates a problem. The psalm is attributed to Ethan the Ezrahite, one of David's chief worship leaders (1 Chr.15:17-18; 1 K.4:31). How could Ethan have written it, seeing that he died hundreds of years before the fall of Jerusalem to Babylon? Among the various opinions that have been offered about this dilemma, three are most reasonable:

➢ Psalm 89 is a compilation of inspired material by two or more authors. Verses 1-37 were written by Ethan to celebrate God's covenant with David. Later, when Jerusalem was overthrown, another individual added to Ethan's work, addressing what appeared to be the breaking of this covenant. Bible teacher and commentator John Phillips speculates that this later author was Daniel.[1] Some think that Jeremiah wrote this section of the psalm, while still others think it was composed by Israel's captured king.

---

1 John Phillips. *Exploring Psalms, Volume 1.* WORDsearch. CROSS e-book.

> Toward the end of a long life, Ethan wrote Psalm 89 upon the division of the kingdom between Rehoboam and Jeroboam, who was not a descendant of David (1 K.12:1-24).
> Ethan wrote prophetically of a devastating event that would occur in the future.

Regardless which opinion is correct, the eighty-ninth psalm addresses a problem that can challenge the faith of even the strongest believers at one time or another. The problem is this: believing that God cannot lie, we stand firmly on the promises of God; yet, circumstances occur and situations arise in our lives or in our world that seem to contradict a promise from God.

In confronting this dilemma, Psalm 89 resounds with the theme of God's faithfulness to His Word (vv.1, 2, 5, 8, 14, 33, 49). Commentator Herbert C. Leupold offered a valuable insight to understanding it:

This is a psalm that informs us indirectly as to how deeply the Messianic hope was imbedded in the thinking of at least the faithful in Israel. For in a time of affliction it is keenly felt how sadly Israel's desolate state is at odds with the glorious hopes that God had kindled in the heart of the nation by the promises of the future greatness of the nation and its great king.[2]

The believers in Israel embraced God's promise of a glorious kingdom ruled by a glorious king. Even so, the circumstances that led to this psalm seemed to make the fulfillment of that promise impossible. In our own lives and in our world, we will face similar dilemmas. At such times, we need to cling to our faith in God's faithfulness. God's promise to David *will be fulfilled* when Jesus Christ comes again. Likewise, in God's good time and according to His divine purpose, *He will keep* every promise He has ever made to us. This is, *When God's Promises Seem to Fail*, 89:1-52.

1. Praise God—proclaim His unfailing love and faithfulness to young and old alike (vv.1-18).
2. Trust God to fulfill His promises (vv.19-37).
3. Beware—know that God rejects those who reject His promises (covenant), He.4:1-2 (vv.38-45).
4. Plead with God to fulfill His promises—never give up hope (vv.46-52).

1 (89:1-18) **Praise God—proclaim His unfailing love and faithfulness to young and old alike.**
The psalmist declared that he would forever praise God for His *great love* (chesed), His steadfast, unfailing love (v.1ª). In addition, he pledged to announce God's *faithfulness* (emunah) to every generation (v.1ᵇ).

a. Because He guarantees His love and mercy forever and His faithfulness is as "enduring as the heavens" (NLT) (v.2).
God's love is permanent (v.2ª). His love is guaranteed: it will not fail. Nothing can separate us from the love of God (Ro.8:35-39). How can we know this? Because God is faithful, and His faithfulness does not depend on our faithfulness to Him. He is faithful to love us because it is His character to be faithful. He cannot deny Himself (2 Ti.2:13).

Moreover, God has established His faithfulness in heaven itself (v.2ᵇ). *Heaven* (shamayim) may refer either to the skies (the universe) or to God's abode or dwelling place. God's faithfulness is established in both. The precise, consistent order of the universe declares that God is unchanging and faithful. With every passing hour of every day, God continually establishes that He is faithful.

Here, however, it would seem that heavens refers to God's abode, as supported by the verses that follow (vv.5-8). His faithfulness is established in heaven, "above all the elements of the world."[3] Nothing that happens on earth can affect or change the fact that God is faithful. His faithfulness is eternally fixed on higher ground.

b. Because He made an eternal covenant with David: A promise of the Messiah, 2 S.7:11ª-17 (vv.3-4).
God's faithfulness guarantees the eternal covenant He made with David (2 S.7:-11ª). The LORD chose David, His servant, to be the privileged recipient of His promise (v.3). After establishing David as Israel's king, God vowed to secure his throne forever. David's descendants would always be the heirs to Israel's throne. The ultimate fulfillment of this promise would come through the Messiah, God's Son, Jesus Christ (vv.29, 36-37; He.1:8; 10:12, 20-21; Re.11:15). In His human lineage, the Messiah would be a descendant of David (Mt.1:1; Lu.1:32).

c. Because heaven's exalted beings praise His wonders and faithfulness: An example we, as lowly human beings, should follow (vv.5-8).
The psalmist continued to emphasize God's faithfulness—an aspect of His holy character—as the guarantee of the Davidic Covenant. Referring to the beings in heaven, he stated that the heavens continually praise God's *wonders* (pele'), His miracles or marvels, deeds beyond human ability (v.5). Notice that *wonders* is parallel to *faithfulness* in the text: God's faithfulness is a *wonder*—a miraculous, supernatural thing. Only God is capable of being perfectly faithful. No other being, human or angelic, can be faithful to the degree that God is.

---

2 H.C. Leupold. *Exposition of the Psalms*, p.632.

3 John Calvin. *Calvin's Commentaries.* WORDsearch. CROSS e-book.

For this reason, heaven's exalted beings praise God unceasingly. *The assembly of the holy ones* (v.5) and *the council of the holy ones* (v.7) refer to heaven. *Holy ones* (qadosh) means saints. Here, it speaks of the holy angels of heaven who praise God for His uniqueness (v.6). No heavenly being or mighty angel compares to Him. *Heavenly beings* is another reference to angels.

The highest and most majestic heavenly beings fear God and stand in awe of His greatness (v.7). No being in heaven or earth is like Him (v.8). He is all powerful, and He is completely faithful. Without exception, He will fulfill all of His promises.

d. Because He rules over nature's raging seas: He faithfully helps His people through natural disasters (v.9).

Ethan elaborated on God's unrivalled power, a power that He exercises in behalf of His people. He rules over nature's raging seas. When the angry waves threaten destruction, He stills them—an illustration of how the LORD faithfully helps His people through natural disasters (Mt.8:24-27).

e. Because He crushes the mightiest enemies (Rahab or Egypt): He faithfully defeats all who oppose Him and His dear people (v.10).

As a second example of God's power, Ethan recalled how God miraculously overthrew the armies of Egypt. Rahab is another name for Egypt (Ps.87:4; Is.51:9). God crushes the mightiest enemies with His *strong arm*—a symbol of His undefeatable might (Je.21:5; 32:21). He faithfully overpowers all who oppose Him and His dear people.

f. Because He is the Sovereign Creator and Ruler of the universe and of all that exists therein (vv.11-12).

These two verses, as well as any in Scripture, demonstrate the magnitude of God's might and power. God is the Sovereign Creator and Ruler of the universe and everything that exists within it (v.11). The heavens and the earth and the fullness thereof (everything in them) belong to God. He created the north and the south (v.12). Even the mighty mountains that tower over the land stand as praise to His faithful, glorious name.

The north and south speak of the extremities of the earth, what we call the North Pole and the South Pole. At 1,900 feet, *Tabor* was most likely the lowest mountain in the land. *Hermon*, which seemed to touch the sky at 9,000 feet, was the highest. By referring to these opposites, the psalmist was declaring that God created these extremes as well as everything in between them.

g. Because He possesses absolute and unlimited power: He is able to fulfill all of His promises (v.13).

The arm, the hand, and the right hand were all symbols of power in Hebrew thought. By mentioning all three together, the psalmist was proclaiming that God possesses absolute and unlimited power. As the omnipotent One, nothing is impossible for Him (Ge.18:14; Je.32:17, 27; Mt.19:26; Lu.1:37). Therefore, He is able to fulfill all of His promises (2 Co.1:20; Ep.3:20).

h. Because His kingdom (throne) is based on righteousness and justice, love and faithfulness (v.14).

God is both faithful to use His power to help His people and faithful to His principles. God's throne or kingdom is based on justice and judgment or righteousness and justice. God is right and fair in everything He does. He cannot do wrong, and He cannot be unjust. Along with righteousness and justice are God's love and faithfulness, which are ever before Him. Love is God's unfailing covenant love. *Faithfulness* (emeth) refers not just to God's trustworthiness and faithfulness but also to His absolute truth as revealed in His Word. These four attributes—righteousness, justice, love, and faithfulness—are the foundation of everything God does.

i. Because He blesses those who praise and worship Him: He guides and enables them to walk in the light of His presence (vv.15-18).

The psalmist declared that those who "have learned to acclaim you" are blessed (v.15). How are faithful worshippers blessed? God will guide them and enable them to walk in the light of His countenance or presence. His presence will illuminate their path, and His favor will rest upon them.

Because they live in the light of God's presence, the blessed are able to rejoice in all circumstances (v.16). God's name—the representation of all that He is—and His righteousness are the basis for their rejoicing. His glory and strength uphold and empower them (v.17). The horn is a symbol of power. "You exalt our horn" may simply mean that God will make His people strong.

However, *our horn* may be a reference to David, Israel's king at the time Ethan wrote this part of the psalm. This understanding certainly fits the context or setting of this statement within the rest of the psalm. It introduces the verses that follow and set forth God's promises to David (vv.19-37). Therefore, "you exalt our horn" may mean that God will exalt David because of His favor on him (v.24).

Bible versions vary in their translation of verse 18. The NIV and other versions state that Israel's *shield*— her protector, the *king*—belongs to the LORD. The KJV states that the LORD is Israel's *defence* or shield and their king. Both renderings express the same truth: Israel's security is in God. Ultimately, He is their sovereign shield and their protection.

Thought 1. We need to follow the example of the holy angels of heaven who constantly praise God for His wonders and faithfulness. As we exalt Him, we should not only praise God for His faithfulness to His people throughout history but also for what He has done for us personally. Too often, we do not take the time to consider God's faithfulness in our lives. As a result, our prayers are general and unspecific, and we fail to appreciate all that God does for us on a daily basis. Meditating on God's wondrous work in our lives and the lives of those we love will stir us to stand in awe of Him.

We ought to openly proclaim God's unfailing love and faithfulness to all people, young and old alike. The world needs the Lord, and we have been commissioned by Jesus Christ Himself to witness to every creature. Things in this world are constantly changing. People can be selfish, deceptive, and hypocritical. Even the best people with the noblest intentions are not absolutely trustworthy. But God can be trusted. We can count on His Word. He will never fail us.

> **To show mercy to our fathers and to remember his holy covenant (Lu.1:72).**
>
> **For no matter how many promises God has made, they are "Yes" in Christ. And so through him the "Amen" is spoken by us to the glory of God(2 Co.1:20).**
>
> **The one who calls you is faithful and he will do it (1 Th.5:24).**
>
> **If we are faithless, he will remain faithful, for he cannot disown himself (2 Ti.2:13).**
>
> **Your love, O LORD, reaches to the heavens, your faithfulness to the skies (Ps.36:5).**
>
> **He remembers his covenant forever, the word he commanded, for a thousand generations (Ps.105:8).**
>
> **Because of the LORD's great love we are not consumed, for his compassions never fail. They are new every morning; great is your faithfulness (Lam.3:22-23).**

2 (89:19-37) **Trust God to fulfill His promises.**
The psalmist related how God chose David to be Israel's king, then he reviewed the covenant God made with David. The important fact to remember is this: even if David's descendants proved unfaithful to God, God vowed that He would keep His covenant. In their present crisis, the faithful people of Israel had to trust God to fulfill His promise.

a. God's choice of David, and David's trust in Him, 1 S.16:1-13 (vv.19-20).
Ethan recalled how God chose David from among the common people of Israel and exalted him (v.19). The LORD spoke to His *faithful people* (plural in the He-

brew text)—the prophets Samuel and Nathan—to affirm His selection of David as Israel's shepherd (1 S.16:1-13; 2 S.7:1-17). Having proven himself to be God's servant, David, a young man and a fearless warrior, was anointed as king (v.20).

b. God's promises to David (vv.21-29).
God sovereignly selected David to lead His beloved people and made a series of promises to him:
- He would always sustain and strengthen David (v.21; Ph.4:13). God's hand and arm, symbols of His power, would always be on him (v.13).
- He would protect David from his enemies (v.22). His adversaries would never defeat him nor "subject him to tribute," that is, force him to pay tribute to them.[4]
- He would make David victorious over all of his foes (v.23; 1 Jn.5:4-5).
- He would always love and be faithful to David, and He would use His divine authority to exalt David's power (v.24).
- He would give David universal rule: a rule over the sea and rivers (v.25; Ps.72:8).
- He would stir David to trust Him and to call on Him as his Father, God, Rock, and Savior (v.26). David would have a close relationship with God.
- He would make David His first born son and the mightiest king on earth (v.27). This promise is a prophecy of the Messiah, Jesus Christ (Ro.8:29: Co.1:15; Re.1:5-6).
- He would uphold His unfailing love or mercy toward David and keep His covenant with him (v.28). This also meant the LORD would preserve David's seed or kingly line and throne forever (v.29). Ultimately, this promise will be fulfilled in Christ, who will rule forever (Is.11:1-9; Re.17:14; 19:16).

c. God's warning to David's descendants (vv.30-32).
The LORD issued a stern warning to David's descendants, those of his line who would succeed him as king: they must not forsake His law nor refuse to keep His commandments (vv.30-31). If they did, they would suffer the painful consequences of their disobedience and be severely punished (v.32).

---

4 Other Bible versions translate *exact* or *subject him to tribute* (nasha) as deceive or outwit. However, the Hebrew word and its derivatives refer to forcing someone to pay a debt or high rate of interest (Ne.5:7; 10:31). The *Theological Wordbook of the Old Testament* explains: "According to the context in which the verb form occurs, a man either has a creditor or he acts as a creditor against another. He 'makes exactions' of the person indebted to him, often in the heartless manner implied in the old term 'usury,' the modern 'loan shark.' So serious a matter was this reckoned to be that in a psalm celebrating God's choice and care of David, the latter is characterized as one having divine protection against this abuse (Ps.89:22)." R. Laird Harris, ed. *Theological Wordbook of the Old Testament.* WORD*search* CROSS e-book.

d. God's affirmation of His love for and faithfulness to David (vv.33-37).

The LORD confirmed His love and faithfulness to David. Even if David's descendants forsook the LORD, He would still keep His promise to David (v.33). God cannot betray His faithfulness; He cannot allow His promise to fail (2 Ti.2:13). He absolutely would not violate or alter His covenant with David. Everything He had spoken, He would do (v.34).

God proceeded to make a strong statement: He had sworn by His holiness that David's line and throne would continue forever (vv.35-36). Likewise, his kingdom would be established forever (v.37). "The covenant with David is so important to the Lord that He swore by Himself (Is.45:23; Am.6:8)."[5] As sure as the sun and the moon appear in the skies each day, David's line and kingdom will endure eternally. These promises, of course, will be fulfilled through the eternal reign of Jesus Christ.

Thought 1. If it has not happened already, all of us will face times in the future when we feel God is not keeping His Word, His promises. Trials and troubles will arise. Difficult circumstances can shake our faith to its very core. At such times, our faith is tested. And it is then that we must, by faith, take God at His Word.

In Hebrews 11, God tells us about the Old Testament heroes of the faith. Every one of them faced a serious test to his or her faith. Yet, in spite of their trying circumstances, they believed God and acted according to His Word.

In the darkest valleys of life, we need to trust God. When our circumstances do not make sense to us, we need to place our faith in Him. When it seems God's promises are collapsing, more than ever, we need to believe Him and stand on His Word. Faith releases the power of God in our lives. When we cannot see the way, we have to trust Him to fulfill His promises.

> Yet he did not waver through unbelief regarding the promise of God, but was strengthened in his faith and gave glory to God (Ro.4:20).

> That is why I am suffering as I am. Yet I am not ashamed, because I know whom I have believed, and am convinced that he is able to guard what I have entrusted to him for that day (2 Ti.1:12).

> By faith Abraham, even though he was past age—and Sarah herself was barren—was enabled to become a father because he considered him faithful who had made the promise (He.11:11).

> Trust in the LORD and do good; dwell in the land and enjoy safe pasture. De-

light yourself in the LORD and he will give you the desires of your heart. Commit your way to the LORD; trust in him and he will do this (Ps.37:3-5).

> Trust in the LORD with all your heart and lean not on your own understanding; in all your ways acknowledge him, and he will make your paths straight (Pr.3:5-6).

> Who among you fears the LORD and obeys the word of his servant? Let him who walks in the dark, who has no light, trust in the name of the LORD and rely on his God (Is.50:10).

3 (89:38-45) **Beware—know that God rejects those who reject His promises (covenant), He.4:1-2.**
At this point, an abrupt transition takes place in the psalm. A stunning turn of events had occurred in Jerusalem. The city had been destroyed, and the king had been overthrown. By all appearances, God had broken His covenant with David. Therefore, the psalmist was perplexed. He did the only thing he could do: he confronted God about what had happened.

a. God rejected Israel's rulers: From a human perspective, it seemed that God had renounced the covenant (vv.38-41).
Contrary to what God had promised, the Davidic line appeared to have come to an end. God had rejected Israel's king (v.38). In doing so, the LORD gave the impression that He was angry with the dynasty of David, His anointed—the servant whom He had personally chosen and with whom He had made His covenant (v.20). From a human perspective, it looked as if God had renounced this covenant, that He had defiled or profaned David's crown (v.39). The psalmist's accusation against God was sharp: he stated bluntly that God had stomped David's crown into the dirt.

The psalmist's charges against the LORD continued. He declared that God had demolished David's kingdom (v.40). Jerusalem was utterly destroyed, and the other strongholds or fortified cities in Israel were reduced to ruins. God had allowed His people to be plundered by their enemies. In fact, Israel had become a reproach or scorn, an object of ridicule—to the neighboring nations (v.41).

b. God exalted His people's foes: From a human perspective, it seemed that God had made His own enemies victorious (vv.42-45).
To make matters worse, God's judgment of His unfaithful people gave the impression that He had exalted or lifted up the right hand of His people's enemies (v.42). In contrast to His promise, it appeared that God had made David's enemies victorious over his

5   Frank E. Gaebelein, ed. *The Expositor's Bible Commentary*, p.582.

descendants (vv.22-23). Outwardly, it looked like the LORD had...

- failed to support Israel's king, David's descendant, in battle (v.43)
- ended the king's, and David's, glory by overturning David's throne (v.44)
- cut short the king's rule, David's dynasty, and publically brought shame on him (v.45)

In all of these things, it appeared that God had broken His covenant with David. Note that "days of his youth" supports the opinion that Psalm 89 was written in response to the Babylonian invasion. Jehoiachin, Israel's king, was only twenty-six years old when Jerusalem was overthrown (1 K.24:8-12).

Thought 1. When God's promises seem to fail, we need to consider God's Word in its entirety. To the psalmist, it appeared that God was not keeping His covenant to bless and continue the Davidic line of kings. But the same covenant that promised an everlasting throne and kingdom included a stern warning:

> **I will be his father, and he will be my son. When he does wrong, I will punish him with the rod of men, with floggings inflicted by men (2 S.7:14).**

God's rejection of the king was actually the fulfillment of His covenant. The king and the people had rejected God's promises by disobeying Him. Therefore, God chastened His rebellious people exactly as He had promised. God also promises to chasten us when we persist in sin (Pr.3:12; 1 Co.11:30-32; He.12:5-11). When we experience God's painful discipline, it does not mean that God is breaking any of His promises to us. By considering *all* of God's promises, we learn that He not only blesses, protects and provides for us but, as a loving Father, also promises to discipline us. This was the case in Psalm 89, and it is often the case in our lives as well.

> **That is why many among you are weak and sick, and a number of you have fallen asleep. But if we judged ourselves, we would not come under judgment. When we are judged by the Lord, we are being disciplined so that we will not be condemned with the world (1 Co.11:30-32).**
>
> **And you have forgotten that word of encouragement that addresses you as sons: "My son, do not make light of the Lord's discipline, and do not lose heart when he rebukes you, because the Lord disciplines those he loves, and he pun-**

ishes everyone he accepts as a son" (He.12:5-6).

> **Those whom I love I rebuke and discipline. So be earnest, and repent (Re. 3:19).**
>
> **Know then in your heart that as a man disciplines his son, so the LORD your God disciplines you. Observe the commands of the LORD your God, walking in his ways and revering him (De.8:5-6).**
>
> **Until the LORD removed them from his presence, as he had warned through all his servants the prophets. So the people of Israel were taken from their homeland into exile in Assyria, and they are still there (2 K.17:23).**

4 (89:46-52) **Plead with God to fulfill His promises—never give up hope.**
After confronting the LORD about what appeared to be a betrayal of His Word, the psalmist pleaded with God to fulfill the promises He had made to David. He fervently cried out to the LORD, begging Him to deliver his beloved nation and to restore the Davidic king to the throne. In spite of all that had taken place, the psalmist's faith in God's faithfulness filled him with hope that God would reverse Israel's grievous circumstances.

a. Cry out that you cannot go on cut off from Him (vv.46-48).
As in the previous passage (vv.38-45), the psalmist spoke frankly to God. He asked God how long He would be angry with His people and withdraw Himself from them (v.46). The psalmist passionately longed for God to turn His face back toward Israel and restore them to His favor. They could not go on feeling cut off from God.

He implored God to remember the brevity of life (v.47). His people's time on earth was so short, and without God, it was meaningless. Surely, the psalmist reasoned, God did not create humans to live in *futility* (shav), to live empty, useless, and worthless lives (Ps.127:1; Is.1:13; Mal.3:14). And yet that is exactly what life was like without God's presence and blessing. Like every human being who ever drew a breath of air, God's people were going to die (v.48). They were incapable of delivering themselves from death. Surely, God did not want what precious little time they had left to be wasted.

b. Cry out for the same great love and faithfulness He promised to David (v.49).
Having previously addressed God as LORD (Yahweh, Jehovah), His covenant name, the psalmist now called Him *Lord* (Adonai) or Master. Addressing God by this name was a sign of humility and submission to Him. It

indicated that the psalmist grasped the truth that God had rejected Israel because of her brazen disobedience to Him. In addition, it indicated that they were returning to Him as His servants. Because of this submission, he cried out for God to show them the same great love and faithfulness He had promised to His servant, David.

c. Cry out for God to think of the persecution you are suffering (vv.50-51).

Finally, the psalmist humbly asked God to consider the persecution His servants were suffering and take pity on them. The reproach and insults from so many people were unbearable (v.50). "All the nations" is better translated as *all the many peoples* (NKJV, NASB). The psalmist stated that people from all the nations were ridiculing him. Even worse, these people were God's enemies (v.51). God was allowing His anointed to be mocked by people who hated Him.

These verses offer strong support to the opinion that Israel's king wrote the second part of this psalm (vv.38-51). The singular *I* (v.50) is parallel to *your anointed one* (v.51), the Davidic king. The mockery by his enemies is a picture of Christ—the Messiah, God's Anointed One—being mocked by those who crucified Him (Mt.27:29-31).

d. Cry out in praise to the LORD forever! Cry out until He answers! (v.52)

Each of the five books of *Psalms* concludes with a doxology, and this exclamation of praise marks the end of Book Three. The book ends with God's people in captivity and God's faithfulness in question. Still, the LORD's people are praising Him. As *The Expositor's Bible Commentary* states, it "affirms the necessity to praise the Lord as an appropriate response to all the circumstances in life."[6] The double amen—so be it, may it be true—should be our prayer.

Thought 1. When God's promises seem to fail, we should plead with God to fulfill them. We must never give up hope that God will faithfully do all He has promised. At the same time, we need to remember that many of God's promises are conditional upon our obedience. This was the case with many of His promises to Israel.

As explained in the commentary, the psalmist understood that God's deliverance of His people from their enemy was conditional upon their return to Him (v.49). Likewise, when we sin, God promises to forgive us, cleanse us, and restore us to fellowship with Him. But a condition is involved: we have to confess our sins—agree with God about them (1 Jn.1:9). True confession of sin involves turning away from it. When we genuinely repent of our sin, *then* God forgives and restores us.

We need to study God's Word diligently so we can fully understand God's promises to us. As we grow in our understanding of God and His ways, we will also grow in our obedience to Him. In doing so, we will be able to praise God in all circumstances, including when He disciplines us. We need to remember that God's discipline is according to His promises and His great love for us. He is always faithful to His Word—all of it—and He is always faithful to us.

> **We want each of you to show this same diligence to the very end, in order to make your hope sure. We do not want you to become lazy, but to imitate those who through faith and patience inherit what has been promised (He.6:11-12).**
>
> **God did this so that, by two unchangeable things in which it is impossible for God to lie, we who have fled to take hold of the hope offered to us may be greatly encouraged (He.6:18).**
>
> **I wait for you, O LORD; you will answer, O Lord my God (Ps.38:15).**
>
> **Why are you downcast, O my soul? Why so disturbed within me? Put your hope in God, for I will yet praise him my Savior and my God (Ps.42:5).**
>
> **I know, O LORD, that your laws are righteous, and in faithfulness you have afflicted me (Ps.119:75).**

---

6 Frank E. Gaebelein, ed. *The Expositor's Bible Commentary*, p.585.

BOOK IV
PSALMS 90–106

PSALM 90

When You Sense the Brevity, Frailty, & End of Human Life, 90:1-17

A prayer of Moses the man of God.

1. **Acknowledge God's love & care**
   a. He is our dwelling place: Our refuge & security in life
   b. He is the Creator, the One who gave birth to the universe: A picture of parental care

2. **Recognize the problems of human mortality**
   a. The appointment with death
   b. The brevity of life
      1) We die so quickly: If we live 1000 years, it is only like one day to God
      2) We are like fleeting dreams that come & go in the night
      3) We are like new grass that springs forth in the morning but by evening dries up & withers away
   c. The alienation between God & man
      1) God's holy anger creates a great barrier between Himself & us
      2) The cause: Our sins, both

Lord, you have been our dwelling place throughout all generations. 2 Before the mountains were born or you brought forth the earth and the world, from everlasting to everlasting you are God. 3 You turn men back to dust, saying, "Return to dust, O sons of men." 4 For a thousand years in your sight are like a day that has just gone by, or like a watch in the night. 5 You sweep men away in the sleep of death; they are like the new grass of the morning— 6 Though in the morning it springs up new, by evening it is dry and withered. 7 We are consumed by your anger and terrified by your indignation. 8 You have set our iniquities before you, our secret sins in the light of your

presence. 9 All our days pass away under your wrath; we finish our years with a moan. 10 The length of our days is seventy years—or eighty, if we have the strength; yet their span is but trouble and sorrow, for they quickly pass, and we fly away. 11 Who knows the power of your anger? For your wrath is as great as the fear that is due you. 12 Teach us to number our days aright, that we may gain a heart of wisdom. 13 Relent, O LORD! How long will it be? Have compassion on your servants. 14 Satisfy us in the morning with your unfailing love, that we may sing for joy and be glad all our days. 15 Make us glad for as many days as you have afflicted us, for as many years as we have seen trouble. 16 May your deeds be shown to your servants, your splendor to their children. 17 May the favor of the Lord our God rest upon us; establish the work of our hands for us—yes, establish the work of our hands.

open & secret sins
   d. The wretched trials & sufferings of life
      1) We die in sorrow & moaning
      2) We live about 70 to 80 years & our days are filled with trouble & suffering

   e. The power of God's anger to execute justice: He dooms all who refuse to fear (revere) Him, He.9:27; 2 Pe.2:9; Jude 14-16

3. **Appeal for God's mercy & help**
   a. That He teach us to live wisely & make the most of each day
   b. That He return to us & not delay: No longer be alienated, but instead have compassion on us
   c. That He satisfy us daily with His unfailing love (mercy)
      1) By filling us with joyful song & rejoicing in life
      2) By replacing our former years of affliction & evil with a spirt of gladness— gladness that lasts as long as our former misery
      3) By revealing His works to His people (described in Ps.111)
      4) By revealing His glory to our children
   d. That He shelter us with His favor & make us successful in life—our personal behavior as well as our work

BOOK IV: *PSALMS 90–106*

PSALM 90

When You Sense the Brevity, Frailty, and End of Human Life, 90:1-17

(90:1-17) **Introduction:** as we grow older, the brevity and frailty of life become increasingly real to us. We look back on our lives and wonder where the years have gone and how they have flown by so quickly. It seems we are hastening toward death, with the days speeding by faster than ever before. Sadly, many of us will shed bitter tears of regret over words spoken or not spoken, deeds done or not done, and days that cannot be relived.

Psalm 90 mourns the brevity, frailty, and end of human life. It is the only inspired psalm written by Moses, making it the oldest of all the psalms. Its content leads us to conclude that he wrote it during the 40-year period when the Israelites wandered in the wilderness because of their unbelief. Moses would have been between 80 and 120 years old at the time, which means he had al-

ready lived well beyond the expected lifespan (v.10). With the brevity of life and the certainty of death in clearer focus than ever before, Moses' heart was heavy for his people who would waste the rest of their days in the wilderness.

The psalms were carefully arranged by God's people into five books that correspond to the five books of the Pentateuch. Psalm 90 marks the beginning of *Book IV*, which correlates with the book of *Numbers*, the fourth book of the Pentateuch. It is appropriate that Moses' prayer is the first psalm in this book, since the faithless Israelites' failure at Kadesh Barnea and their subsequent years of wandering are recorded in *Numbers.*

If we are wise, we will adopt Moses' prayer in Psalm 90 as our own. Not only will it help us to prepare for eternity, but it will also help us to live wisely, lest, like the rebellious Israelites, we waste our brief lives in disobedience and unbelief. This is, *When You Sense the Brevity, Frailty, and End of Human Life,* 90:1-17.

1. Acknowledge God's love and care (vv.1-2).
2. Recognize the problems of human mortality (vv.3-11).
3. Appeal for God's mercy and help (vv.12-17).

1 (90:1-2) Acknowledge God's love and care.

Moses began his prayer by acknowledging God's great love and faithful care for His people. He illustrated God's boundless love for us with two endearing images, that of a loving home and that of a loving parent.

a. He is our dwelling place: Refuge, home—oasis of love and security (v.1).

As the homeless Israelites wandered through the wilderness, Moses realized how little our worldly residences matter. From the very beginning of Israel's history, when God called Abram to leave Ur of the Chaldees, they had been a nation of nomads—wanderers, travelers, people on a journey. Through every mile, however, they had been cared for and protected. Even now, as they paid the price for their unbelief, God was with them. This thought led Moses to confess that God had been their *dwelling place,* their...

- refuge
- security
- home
- habitation
- comfort
- place of rest

As the author of Hebrews noted, "they were aliens and strangers on the earth" (He.11:13). What was true for Old Testament saints is true for church-age believers as well. We are described in the New Testament as aliens and strangers (1 Pe.2:11). We are not citizens of this world but of heaven (Ph.3:20). Interestingly, when discussing our earthly needs, both Jesus and Paul mentioned food and clothing but neither mentioned shelter (Mt.6:25, 31; 1 Ti.6:8). They understood that God is our home, now and throughout eternity.

b. He is the Creator, the One who gave birth to the universe: A picture of parental care (v.2).

God, our dwelling place, is eternal. *From everlasting to everlasting,* Moses declared, He is God. Bible teacher J. Vernon McGee explained:

> *[Everlasting* (olam)] *is figurative in the Hebrew. It means "from the vanishing point to the vanishing point." God is from the vanishing point in the past and reaches to the vanishing point in eternity future.*

Just as far as you can see, from vanishing point to vanishing point, He is still God.[1]

Moses firmly stated that God is the Creator, the One who gave birth to the universe. Before the creation of the world—before there was anything else—God existed, and He brought all things into existence. *Born* (yalad) is the Hebrew word for giving birth. *Brought forth* (chuwl) is used of the labor pains that accompany childbirth (Ps.29:9; Is.26:17-18). The picture here is clear: God is the Divine Parent of the universe. Just as a mother lovingly cares for her child, God cares for His creation, especially the human race. He loves us so much that He gave His Son to redeem us (Jn.3:16; Ro.5:8; 8:32).

Thought 1. As stated, God is our home, both now and throughout eternity. Nineteenth century preacher Charles Spurgeon expressed this beautifully:

> *To the saints the Lord Jehovah, the self existent God stands instead of mansion and rooftree; he shelters, comforts, protects, preserves, and cherishes all his own. Foxes have holes and the birds of the air have nests, but the saints dwell in their God, and have always done so in all ages. Not in the tabernacle or the temple do we dwell, but in God himself; and this we have always done since there was a church in the world. We have not shifted our abode. Kings' palaces have vanished beneath the crumbling hand of time—they have been burned with fire and buried beneath mountains of ruins, but the imperial race of heaven has never lost its regal habitation...Where dwelt our fathers a hundred generations since, there dwell we still.*[2]

As our dwelling place, God is our refuge and security. He is our shelter; we abide safely and peacefully in Him. As our Creator, He did, in a sense, give birth to us. As a mother conceives and gives birth to her child, so God brought us—the entire human race—into existence. Spiritually, He is our Father. When we are born again through repentance and faith in Jesus Christ, we are born spiritually into God's family.

These endearing images remind us how much God loves us and how faithfully He cares for us. Life on earth, on the other hand, often weighs us down with trials and trouble of one sort or another. Thankfully, as believers, we have an open invitation from our Lord to abide in Him (Jn.15:4). We can return to Him at the end of each day for comfort and rest. In Him, we find protection. In Him, our needs are supplied. Though rejected by the world, we are welcomed and accepted in Him. We should always be careful to

---

1 J. Vernon McGee. *Thru the Bible with J. Vernon McGee.* WORD*search* CROSS e-book.

2 Charles Spurgeon. *Treasury of David.* WORD*search* CROSS e-book.

acknowledge God's love and care for us and to praise Him for it all of our days.

> **"Come to me, all you who are weary and burdened, and I will give you rest (Mt.11:28).**
>
> **If you remain in me and my words remain in you, ask whatever you wish, and it will be given you (Jn.15:7).**
>
> **Cast all your anxiety on him because he cares for you (1 Pe.5:7).**
>
> **Surely it is you who love the people; all the holy ones are in your hand. At your feet they all bow down, and from you receive instruction (De.33:3).**
>
> **He who dwells in the shelter of the Most High will rest in the shadow of the Almighty (Ps.91:1).**
>
> **If you make the Most High your dwelling—even the LORD, who is my refuge—then no harm will befall you, no disaster will come near your tent (Ps.91:9-10).**
>
> **The LORD appeared to us in the past, saying: "I have loved you with an everlasting love; I have drawn you with loving-kindness (Je.31:3).**

2 (90:3-11) Recognize the problems of human mortality.

Because we are sinners, we face several grave problems. Our time on earth is brief and often plagued by trouble and suffering. Then, it ends in death. Even more unsettling, though, is the fact that, as sinners, we are alienated from God. When this life is over, we will stand before God and face His certain judgment.

a. The appointment with death (v.3).

Moses acknowledged the cold reality that every one of us is going to die, stating that God turns people to dust. *Dust* (dakka) is the noun form of a Hebrew verb that means to crush or grind. The noun speaks of "an object crushed into a powder, or pulverized dust."[3] By using this specific word, Moses reinforced what God said after Adam and Eve sinned:

> **By the sweat of your brow you will eat your food until you return to the ground, since from it you were taken; for dust you are and to dust you will return" (Ge.3:19).**

The sentence of death is the just wage or payment for our sin (Ro.5:12; 6:23). Each of us has an inescap-

able appointment with death (He.9:27). However, we do not know the day or time when this appointment has been set. Therefore, we need to prepare in advance for death and the judgment that follows it.

b. The brevity of life (vv.4-6).

Moses was at least 80 years old when he wrote this psalm and, just as we often do, he bemoaned the fact of life's brevity. Moses stated that, even if we could live 1,000 years, it would only be like one day to God or like a "watch in the night" (four hours) (v.4). As we grow older, we too look back over the years of our lives and lament how quickly they passed. In comparison to eternity, our time on earth is staggeringly short and we die so quickly.

When Moses compared one day in heaven to 1,000 years on earth, he was not speaking in absolute or conclusive terms. His mention of a watch in the night proves that this is not what he was saying. He was simply illustrating how shockingly brief our lives are compared to eternity, the timeless dimension in which God dwells (Is.57:15). Our lifespan on earth is only a tiny speck on the timeline of eternity, a dot so small that it is invisible to the naked eye.

Moses compared death to being swept away in a flood suddenly and swiftly (v.5a). He described our brief lives as a sleep (v.5b). We are like fleeting dreams that come quickly and then fade into the night. Moses also likened our lives to the new grass that grew in Palestine. It sprang up in the morning, but by evening it had dried up and withered away (v.5c-6; 103:15-16; Is.40:6-8).

c. The alienation between God and man (vv.7-8).

Moses turned his prayer to a third serious problem for the human race: the alienation between God and us. God's wrath is set resolutely against all sin, and, tragically, we are all sinners. Therefore, God's holy anger toward sin creates a great barrier between Himself and us (v.7). Our sins, both open and secret, separate us from God (v.8). They are ever before Him. And in light of His omniscience—His knowledge of all things—none can be hidden from Him. Even our secret sins—the ones nobody on earth knows about—are exposed in the light of God's countenance or presence.

The original context or setting for this statement was Israel's wandering in the wilderness. Because of their unbelief, God had sentenced that generation of Israelites to die in the wilderness. The rest of their lives, Moses lamented, would be *consumed* (kalah), spent, wasted, brought to completion. They would never enter the promised land. They would never experience the indescribable blessings God had intended for them. Instead, they would spend the rest of their lives troubled or terrified by God's wrath. This sad fate illustrates a universal truth: because we are

---

3 Spiros Zodhiates. *AMG Complete Word Study Dictionary*. WORD-search CROSS e-book.

all sinners, we are all alienated from God and from the blessings He wants to bestow on us (Ro.3:23; 5:12).

d. The wretched trials and sufferings of life (vv.9-10).

We spend our lives on a planet that has been cursed by God's wrath against sin (Ge.3:17-18). All of our days pass away under God's judgment because of man's transgressions (v.9). For this reason, life on earth is filled with trials and sufferings. Consequently, we spend or finish our years on this earth in sorrow and mourning "with a moan." *Moan* (hegeh) means a low, rumbling sound (Jb.37:2). It is a sound of mourning—a sigh or groan (Eze.2:10). In other words, our time on earth is marked by sighs of grief.

Moses noted that our normal lifespan is 70 to 80 years (v.10). Sadly, the days of these years are filled with labor and sorrow, painful toil and trouble. Moses' life had exceeded this expected lifespan, and his experiences testified to the truth of this statement. Yet, in spite of life's grievous difficulties, our years fly by, and we then *fly away* to eternity.

e. The power of God's anger to execute justice: He dooms all who refuse to fear (revere) Him, He.9:27; 2 Pe.2:9; Jude 14-16 (v.11).

Moses rightly concluded that no one fully knows or understands the power of God's anger; although, those who are wise greatly fear or revere God because of it (see outline and notes—Pr.1:7 for more discussion). Moses also stated that God is deserving of man's fear because His wrath is so great (Ro.1:18). Yet, as Scripture declares, many people have no fear of God (Ro.3:18). Nevertheless, God will execute perfect, uncompromised justice against sinners according to His fierce anger against sin. All who refuse to fear Him are doomed to receive His judgment (He.9:27; 2 Pe.2:9; Jude 14-16).

Thought 1. All of these problems are the fruits of our sin. But the good news is, Christ has solved them all! Because of His atoning death and glorious resurrection...

- we need not fear death (v.3). Christ removed the sting from death and conquered the grave, removing its power over us and making it a peaceful place for our bodies to await the resurrection (1 Co.15:55). He destroyed the devil, who had power over death, and set us free from bondage to it (He.2:14-15). If Jesus returns during our lifetime, we will not even experience death. The generation living when He comes will never die (Jn.11:25-26; 1 Th.4:17)!
- we have eternal life (v.4). Our time on earth may be brief, but through Christ, we are going to live forever in a dimension unbound by time (Jn.3:16; 10:28; 1 Jn.2:25; 5:11).

- we are no longer alienated from God (vv.7-8). Christ has torn down the barrier that existed between us and God (Mt.27:51; Ep.2:11-15; He.10:19-23). Through Him, we are reconciled to God (2 Co.5:18-21). Our sins are forgiven and forgotten (Ep.1:7). They have been removed as far as the east is from the west; they have been cast into the depths of the sea (Ps.103:12; Mi.7:19).
- we are going to live eternally in a new heaven and a new earth: a place untouched and uncursed by sin, a place where trials and suffering will exist no more (vv.9-10; Re.21:4-5; 22:3).
- we need not fear God's wrath and judgment (v.11). Christ received our judgment on the cross. He paid the price for our sin (Is.53:4-5). Because we have placed our faith in Christ, we face no condemnation (Ro.8:1). We will be judged for our service to Him, but not for our sin.

Before we can receive these wonderful blessings, however, we have to come to Christ in repentance and faith. We need to fear God to the point of turning away from our sin and turning toward Him. If we do not, we will face the wrath of His judgment and eternal death—separation from God in the lake of fire (Re.20:11-15).

> *"Life is short.*
> *Death is sure.*
> *Sin the cause,*
> *Christ the cure."*
> (author unknown)

For all have sinned and fall short of the glory of God (Ro.3:23).

Therefore, just as sin entered the world through one man, and death through sin, and in this way death came to all men, because all sinned (Ro.5:12).

For the wages of sin is death, but the gift of God is eternal life in Christ Jesus our Lord (Ro.6:23).

As for you, you were dead in your transgressions and sins, in which you used to live when you followed the ways of this world and of the ruler of the kingdom of the air, the spirit who is now at work in those who are disobedient. All of us also lived among them at one time, gratifying the cravings of our sinful nature and following its desires and thoughts. Like the rest, we were by nature objects of wrath. But because of his great love for us, God, who is rich in mercy, made us alive with Christ even when we were dead in transgressions—it is by grace you have been saved. And God

raised us up with Christ and seated us with him in the heavenly realms in Christ Jesus, in order that in the coming ages he might show the incomparable riches of his grace, expressed in his kindness to us in Christ Jesus. For it is by grace you have been saved, through faith—and this not from yourselves, it is the gift of God—not by works, so that no one can boast. (Ep.2:1-9).

Just as man is destined to die once, and after that to face judgment (He.9:27).

3 (90:12-17) Appeal for God's mercy and help.

As Moses considered the generation that would perish in the wilderness and their children, he appealed to God for His mercy and help. He prayed for God to teach them to live wisely. He also asked God to have compassion on them and to turn from His wrath. Through God's unfailing love and grace, the people could live joyfully, faithfully, and successfully even in the wilderness and, eventually, in the promised land.

a. That He teach us to live wisely and make the most of each day (v.12).

Moses prayed that God would teach them to number their days, that is, help them to understand just how brief their lives were. Grasping the brevity of life should also stir us to live wisely each day.

Consider Moses' perspective when he wrote these words. The faithless Israelites had made a poor decision. Gripped by fear and unbelief, they refused to move forward into the promised land. As a result, they were forced to spend the rest of their lives wandering aimlessly in the wilderness. Their precious days on earth were wasted because of their cowardly decision and their lack of faith.

Because the future of the unbelieving Israelites was already set, Moses' prayer was surely more for our benefit than theirs. May God help us to understand how few our days on earth actually are, that we may live wisely—according to His will and Word (see outline and notes—Pr.1:2-7 for more discussion).

b. That He return to us and not delay: No longer be alienated, but instead have compassion on us (v.13).

Moses asked God how long it would be before He returned or turned again toward His people. He prayed that God would *have compassion* (nacham) or mercy on them and relent of His anger toward them. For God to relent is not an admission that He was wrong or that He made a mistake. When God relents, "He changes His dealings with men according to His sov-

ereign purposes."[4] Usually, it involves His withholding of judgment or granting relief from the painful consequences of His judgment (Jud.2:18; De.32:36; 1 Chr.21:5; Je.18:8; 26:3; Jon.3:10).

c. That He satisfy us daily with His unfailing love (mercy) (vv.14-16).

Moses prayed for God to fill or satisfy His people with His *unfailing love* (chesed), His mercy (v.14a; see outline and notes—Ps.5:7 for more discussion). *Satisfy* (sabea) means to be completely full. It is the word used of a person who has eaten to the point that he or she can eat no more (Ex.16:8). Moses prayed that God would satisfy His people daily with His unfailing love by...

➤ filling their lives with joyful song and rejoicing (v.14b).

➤ replacing their former years of affliction and evil with a spirit of gladness (v.15). He asked God to make their gladness last as long as their misery lasted—to give them a measure of joy equal to their suffering.

➤ revealing His works to His people (v.16a; Ps.111). He asked God to work in His people's lives through their time of discipline.

➤ revealing His splendor to their children (v.16b). He asked God to lead His people's children into the glory or *splendor* of the promised land.

d. That He shelter us with His favor and make us successful in life—our personal behavior as well as work (v.17).

Finally, Moses prayed for God's favor to come upon His people. *Favor* (no'am) means beauty, grace, or pleasantness. It is comparable to the Greek word for *grace* (charis) in the New Testament. With God's favor covering them, the people could still be successful in life, both in their personal behavior as well as in their work. The repeating of "establish the work of our hands" emphasized the earnestness of Moses' request and how greatly he desired God to shelter the people from future failure.

Thought 1. This passage teaches us a glorious truth: failure is not final with God. When we fail due to disobedience and unbelief, we can be restored. We can be joyful and productive again in the work of the Lord. When we confess and repent of our sin, God promises to forgive us and to cleanse us of unrighteousness (1 Jn.1:9). We may still have to live with the consequences of our sin, but at the same time, we can receive God's grace and go on for Him.

When we sin, we should appeal to God for His mercy and help. We should also pray for those who fall

---

4 R. Laird Harris, ed. *Theological Wordbook of the Old Testament.* WORD*search* CROSS e-book.

into sin, that God will have compassion on them and bring them back to Him.

But because of his great love for us, God, who is rich in mercy (Ep.2:4).

Let us then approach the throne of grace with confidence, so that we may receive mercy and find grace to help us in our time of need (He.4:16).

As you know, we consider blessed those who have persevered. You have heard of Job's perseverance and have seen what the Lord finally brought about. The Lord is full of compassion and mercy (Js.5:11).

Know therefore that the LORD your God is God; he is the faithful God, keeping his covenant of love to a thousand generations of those who love him and keep his commands (De.7:9).

The Lord our God is merciful and forgiving, even though we have rebelled against him (Da.9:9).

Who is a God like you, who pardons sin and forgives the transgression of the remnant of his inheritance? You do not stay angry forever but delight to show mercy (Mi.7:18).

PSALM 91

When You Feel Insecure and Need God's Presence, 91:1-16

1. Draw near—live in God's presence
  a. Bc. of who He is
    1) The Most High (Elyon)
    2) The Almighty (Shaddai)
    3) The LORD (Yahweh)
    4) Your God (Elohim)
  b. Bc. He is your security in all things: Your refuge & fortress
2. Believe God—trust Him to help you
  a. He will save you from the foe's trap & from the fatal plague
  b. He will cover & protect you under His wings of care
    1) He will be a refuge for you
    2) He will give you the armor of His faithful promise
  c. He will reassure you through all fearful situations
    1) In times of terror or attack
    2) In times of disease & destruction
    3) In times of inescapable danger

He who dwells in the shelter of the Most High will rest in the shadow of the Almighty.
2 I will say of the LORD, "He is my refuge and my fortress, my God, in whom I trust."
3 Surely he will save you from the fowler's snare and from the deadly pestilence.
4 He will cover you with his feathers, and under his wings you will find refuge; his faithfulness will be your shield and rampart.
5 You will not fear the terror of night, nor the arrow that flies by day,
6 Nor the pestilence that stalks in the darkness, nor the plague that destroys at midday.
7 A thousand may fall at your side, ten thousand at your right hand, but it will not come near you.
8 You will only observe with your eyes and see the punishment of the wicked.
9 If you make the Most High your dwelling—even the LORD, who is my refuge—
10 Then no harm will befall you, no disaster will come near your tent.
11 For he will command his angels concerning you to guard you in all your ways;
12 They will lift you up in their hands, so that you will not strike your foot against a stone.
13 You will tread upon the lion and the cobra; you will trample the great lion and the serpent.
14 "Because he loves me," says the LORD, "I will rescue him; I will protect him, for he acknowledges my name.
15 He will call upon me, and I will answer him; I will be with him in trouble, I will deliver him and honor him.
16 With long life will I satisfy him and show him my salvation."

  d. He will make sure *you* escape & witness the punishment of the wicked
3. Be aware—God's protection is conditional: You must live in His presence & take refuge in Him
  a. Then His presence will be with you when facing evil threats or plagues
  b. Then He will charge His angels to guard you day by day
    1) They will *protect* you
    2) They will lift you up & *guide* you
  c. Then He will make you victorious over the lion & the serpent: images of Satan, 1 Pe.5:8; Re. 12:9; 20:2; Ge.3:1-24; 2 Co.11:3

4. Cling to the LORD
  a. Love & acknowledge Him: He will deliver, protect, & exalt you
  b. Call upon Him & He will answer you
    1) Be with you in trouble
    2) Deliver & honor you
    3) Reward you with long life
    4) Give you His salvation

PSALM 91

When You Feel Insecure and Need God's Presence, 91:1-16

(91:1-16) **Introduction:** our sinful world is full of danger. Diseases, injuries, and disasters are risks of everyday life. We never know when we might contract a serious illness, be involved in an accident, or find ourselves in the midst of a disaster. Over and above these perils, the greatest threat in our world is the evil perpetrated by wicked people who pose a very real threat to all who truly follow Christ. Scripture warns us that as we grow nearer to the return of Christ, the wickedness of people will increase and we will find ourselves living in perilous times (2 Ti.3:1-5).

The dangers of life and its ongoing threats can leave us feeling insecure. In spite of our best efforts to protect ourselves, we know that we cannot totally shield ourselves from harm. For generations, God's people have turned to Psalm 91 for comfort and courage. Written by an unknown author, it reminds us that God is our security.

Psalm 91 appears to promise that those who live close to God will be exempt from harm, disaster, and disease. This impression presents a problem: many people who faithfully abide in Christ *do* experience harm. They *do* encounter and sometimes perish in disasters. They *do* contract serious diseases. What about the persecuted?

What about the martyrs? The experience of God's people does not agree with the supposed promises of this psalm.

The answer to this dilemma is found in correctly understanding *to whom* these promises were made. Psalm 91 celebrates the specific promises of God's covenant with Israel. Two specific perils are prominent in this psalm: the peril of enemy attack and the peril of pestilence or plague (vv.3-7). Notice how these specific perils stand out in God's covenant conditions and promises in the book of Deuteronomy:

If you pay attention to these laws and are careful to follow them, then the LORD your God will keep his covenant of love with you, as he swore to your forefathers. He will love you and bless you and increase your numbers. He will bless the fruit of your womb, the crops of your land—your grain, new wine and oil—the calves of your herds and the lambs of your flocks in the land that he swore to your forefathers to give you. You will be blessed more than any other people;

none of your men or women will be childless, nor any of your livestock without young. The LORD will keep you free from every disease. He will not inflict on you the horrible diseases you knew in Egypt, but he will inflict them on all who hate you. You must destroy all the peoples the LORD your God gives over to you. Do not look on them with pity and do not serve their gods, for that will be a snare to you. You may say to yourselves, "These nations are stronger than we are. How can we drive them out?" But do not be afraid of them; remember well what the LORD your God did to Pharaoh and to all Egypt. You saw with your own eyes the great trials, the miraculous signs and wonders, the mighty hand and outstretched arm, with which the LORD your God brought you out. The LORD your God will do the same to all the peoples you now fear. Moreover, the LORD your God will send the hornet among them until even the survivors who hide from you have perished. Do not be terrified by them, for the LORD your God, who is among you, is a great and awesome God. The LORD your God will drive out those nations before you, little by little. You will not be allowed to eliminate them all at once, or the wild animals will multiply around you. But the LORD your God will deliver them over to you, throwing them into great confusion until they are destroyed. He will give their kings into your hand, and you will wipe out their names from under heaven. No one will be able to stand up against you; you will destroy them (De.7:12-24).

The connection between this Deuteronomy passage and Psalm 91 is clear. These promises were made to Israel as a part of the old covenant, and they were conditional on Israel's faithfulness to God. They are about God's disciplinary judgment on those who are unfaithful to Him. As long as Israel remained faithful to God—made Him their dwelling or refuge—He would protect them from their enemies and from deadly diseases. If they turned from God and broke His covenant, He would lift His hand of protection. Throughout Israel's history, this has proven to be true.

These promises were not made to the church. In fact, Jesus promised His followers exactly the opposite: They *would* face harm. They *would* be persecuted. If the promises of Psalm 91 were to the church, then they were broken in the very first generation of Christ-followers. The apostles were beaten and imprisoned. History records that all but one died as martyrs. Paul spoke openly of the many perils he encountered:

> Three times I was beaten with rods, once I was stoned, three times I was shipwrecked, I spent a night and a day in the open sea, I have been constantly on the move. I have been in danger from rivers, in danger from bandits, in danger from my own countrymen, in danger from Gentiles; in danger in the city, in danger in the country, in danger at sea; and in danger from false brothers. I have labored and toiled and have often gone without sleep; I have known hunger and thirst and have often gone without food; I have been cold and naked (2 Co.11:25-27).

How, then, does Psalm 91 apply to us? First, we should study it in light of John 15 and Jesus' teaching on abiding in Him. John 15 is to New Testament believers what Psalm 91 was to God's people under the old covenant.

Second, we should study Psalm 91 in light of the promises God has made to us, the believers of the new covenant. God has not promised us total protection from peril, but He has promised His presence in and through all things. He will be with us, and He will help us.

> Keep your lives free from the love of money and be content with what you have, because God has said, "Never will I leave you; never will I forsake you." So we say with confidence, "The Lord is my helper; I will not be afraid. What can man do to me?" (He.13:5-6).

While the specific promises of Psalm 91 are not to the church, its principles are:
- God is to us today everything He has always been to His people.
- God is our refuge.
- We need not live in fear of danger or threats, for God is always with us.
- If we faithfully abide in Christ, we need not fear God's discipline or judgment.
- God's angels continue to guard His children.
- God is our security in these perilous times of the last days (2 Ti.3:1).

Scripture says that the new covenant is established on better promises than the old (He.8:6). Whereas Israel was promised God's conditional protection, we are promised God's unconditional presence. Under the old covenant, the people had to dwell in God. Under the new covenant, God dwells in us. There is no comparison. This is, *When You Feel Insecure and Need God's Presence*, 91:1-16.

1. Draw near—live in God's presence (vv.1-2).
2. Believe God—trust Him to help you (vv.3-8).
3. Be aware—God's protection is conditional: You must live in His presence and take refuge in Him (vv.9-13).
4. Cling to the LORD (vv.14-16).

1 (91:1-2) Draw near—live in God's presence.

The promises of this psalm apply exclusively to those who draw near to God and live in His holy presence (v.1). There is a *shelter* (sether)—a hiding place, a place where we can be concealed and covered—where we can be secure (Ps.17:8; 27:5;31:20). The psalmist identifies this shelter as under God's wings (v.4). This image not only speaks of protection and shelter but also of closeness and intimacy. Before we can rest in the security of God, we must continually draw near to Him, live in close communion with Him.

a. Because of who He is (vv.1-2).

One of the ways God has revealed Himself to us is through His names. A prominent feature of Hebrew poetry is the restating of a thought using synonyms—different words that mean the same thing. However, this is not the case here. The psalmist's repeated reference to God using different names is for a distinct purpose: each name reveals who God is to His people. He is...

- *The Most High* (Elyon)—He is the Highest, the Supreme Being and owner of the universe. As such, He is all-powerful and cannot be overthrown. This name "cuts every threat down to size."[1]
- *The Almighty* (Shaddai)—He is sufficient for everything we need. By His inherent power, He sustains us, protects us, and provides for us.
- *The LORD* (Yahweh, Jehovah)—He is the faithful God who makes a covenant with us and keeps His covenant without fail. He keeps all of His promises always.
- *My God* (Elohim)—*Elohim* emphasizes the fullness and exceeding greatness of God's power. The possessive pronoun *my* declares that we can have a personal, intimate relationship with Him. He knows us, communes with us, and cares for us individually and personally.

b. Because He is your security in all things: Your refuge and fortress (v.2).

Because the psalmist understood who God is to His people, he was able to say with confidence that the LORD was his personal security, his refuge and fortress. A refuge is a shelter from trouble or danger (Is.4:6; Ps.104:18). A fortress is a safe, secure place that is inaccessible to the enemy. Therefore, the

psalmist declared that he would continually trust in the LORD. He would fully depend on Him for protection and security, and he would faithfully run to Him when threatened by danger or trouble.

Thought 1. Once again, God is to us what He has always been to His people. He is the same God now that He has always been. He is our...

- all-powerful One
- all-sufficient One
- faithful One
- God
- refuge and fortress

All that God is—His character and divine attributes—is even more available to us today, in the church age, than it was to God's people when this psalm was written. Why? Because He dwells *in* us. His power does not merely work *for* us but also works *in* and *through* us by His indwelling Spirit (Ep.3:20; Ro.8:11). In light of that, we need to draw near to God and to live in the fullness of His presence in every aspect of our lives. Simply stated, we need to abide in Christ (Jn.15:1-17). We have open access into God's presence—a great privilege secured for us by the blood of Christ. But before we can abide in His presence, we have to be clean. We need to allow God's Word to purify our hearts and our lives, so we can live in His holy presence at all times (He.10:19-22; Jn.15:3; Js.4:8).

> **Remain in me, and I will remain in you. No branch can bear fruit by itself; it must remain in the vine. Neither can you bear fruit unless you remain in me. "I am the vine; you are the branches. If a man remains in me and I in him, he will bear much fruit; apart from me you can do nothing. If anyone does not remain in me, he is like a branch that is thrown away and withers; such branches are picked up, thrown into the fire and burned. If you remain in me and my words remain in you, ask whatever you wish, and it will be given you (Jn.15:4-7).**

> **(For the law made nothing perfect), and a better hope is introduced, by which we draw near to God (He.7:19).**

> **Therefore, brothers, since we have confidence to enter the Most Holy Place by the blood of Jesus, by a new and living way opened for us through the curtain, that is, his body, and since we have a great priest over the house of God, let us draw near to God with a sincere heart in full assurance of faith, having our hearts sprinkled to cleanse us from a**

---

1 Derek Kidner. *Psalms 73-150*, p.364.

guilty conscience and having our bodies washed with pure water (He.10:19-22).

Come near to God and he will come near to you. Wash your hands, you sinners, and purify your hearts, you double-minded (Js.4:8).

And now, dear children, continue in him, so that when he appears we may be confident and unashamed before him at his coming (1 Jn.2:28).

2 (91:3-8) **Believe God—trust Him to help you.** God protects those who draw near to Him. In every dangerous situation of life, we need to believe God and trust Him to help us rather than living in a state of fear.

a. He will save you from the foe's trap and from the fatal plague (v.3).
God will deliver us from or through the enemy's trap and the fatal plague. The *fowler's snare* and the *noisome* or *deadly pestilence* represent all of the dangers we face in life. A fowler was a hunter of birds and symbolizes those who seek to harm or destroy us. A pestilence was a dreaded, deadly disease or epidemic.

b. He will cover and protect you under His wings of care (v.4).
God is omnipotent, all-powerful. He will cover and protect us under His wings of care when we stay close to Him. The psalmist compared God's care for His people to a bird gathering her young under her wings in order to protect them. This is a common picture throughout the Old Testament (Ru.2:12; Ps.17:8; 57:1; 61:4). It is also the image used by Jesus to describe His great love for the Jews and His desire to save them (Mt.23:37). The LORD will be our refuge, covering and protecting us in the dangers of life.

The *faithfulness* of God will be our shield and rampart. The *shield* (tsinnah) was a large rectangular piece of armor that a soldier would hide behind and be completely covered (1 S.17:7, 41). In the New Testament, God has given us His faithful promises to use as our armor for life's battles (Ep.6:11-17). We are protected by His faithfulness to His Word. Knowing that, we can have complete confidence that He will fulfill His promises to us.

c. He will reassure you through all fearful situations (vv.5-7).
God's powerful and protective presence reassures us in the fearful situations of life. And although the world is swarming with violent, wicked people, we need not fear terror or attacks (v.5). Likewise, perils abound in our sin-cursed world, but we have no reason to be frightened or panicked in times of disease or destruction due to life-threatening disasters (v.6). God will ei-

ther protect or deliver us through times of inescapable danger, even when thousands of others are doomed (v.7).

The mention of *night, day, darkness,* and *midday* reinforces the great truth that God never sleeps or slumbers (Ps.121:4). He protects us at all times, around the clock. We can work and sleep in peace, for God is on guard.

d. He will make sure *you* escape and witness the punishment of the wicked (v.8).
The psalmist declared confidently that those who live in God's presence will escape and witness the reward or punishment of the wicked. God's judgment is in view here. At the time of His choosing, He will punish the wicked, but the righteous will escape. The righteous will only observe God's judgment, not be included in it (Ro.1:18; 8:1).

Thought 1. In perilous times, we need to trust God to help us. When we abide in Him and live in the fullness of His Spirit, we can face every situation of life without fear. Satan's fury against God, His Word, and His people is becoming more savage every day. More and more believers are paying a price for their faith in Jesus Christ. Radical religious fanatics as well as governments are brutally attacking and, in some cases, slaughtering followers of Christ. People who love sin and hate God's Holy Word are viciously lashing out at those who stand for God's truth.

Through it all, however, God is our helper and He is always with us (He.13:5-6). We are not alone as we bear the banner of the cross. Our Savior has promised to be with us to the end (Mt.28:20). Like the faithful young Hebrew men of old, we may find ourselves in the fire, but the fourth man in their furnace—the Son of God Himself—will be in ours as well (Da.3:25). Think of faithful Stephen, the first to lay down his life for Christ. As he was being viciously attacked, Scripture says he looked up and saw Jesus (Ac.7:55-56). In that moment, he rejoiced in the experience of suffering for Christ. No experience with Christ can compare to the fellowship of His sufferings (Ph.3:10).

Whatever difficulties or dangers we may face, our Lord will be with us. The shadow of the Almighty will cover us through them all (v.1). He will preserve us until His purpose for our lives is complete. Then, He will take us to His heavenly kingdom (2 Ti.4:18). In most of us, Christ will magnify Himself through our lives. In others, however, He will choose to magnify Himself through our deaths (Ph.1:20). Yet we can take great comfort in knowing that if we have to walk through the valley of the shadow of death, we will not walk alone. Instead, we will walk under the comforting shelter of God's shadow. We can face death without any fear whatsoever, for He will be with us (Ps.23:4).

I eagerly expect and hope that I will in no way be ashamed, but will have sufficient courage so that now as always Christ will be exalted in my body, whether by life or by death (Ph.1:20).

The Lord will rescue me from every evil attack and will bring me safely to his heavenly kingdom. To him be glory for ever and ever. Amen (2 Ti.4:18).

Even though I walk through the valley of the shadow of death, I will fear no evil, for you are with me; your rod and your staff, they comfort me (Ps.23:4).

So do not fear, for I am with you; do not be dismayed, for I am your God. I will strengthen you and help you; I will uphold you with my righteous right hand (Is.41:10).

"Fear not, for I have redeemed you; I have summoned you by name; you are mine. When you pass through the waters, I will be with you; and when you pass through the rivers, they will not sweep over you. When you walk through the fire, you will not be burned; the flames will not set you ablaze (Is.43:1b-2).

3 (91:9-13) **Be aware—God's protection is conditional.**

The psalmist emphasized that God's protection is afforded only to those who live in His presence and take refuge in Him. In other words, it is conditional. The faithful are guarded by God's angels, who protect them from both physical and spiritual danger.

a. Then His presence will be with you when facing evil threats or plagues (v.10).

The psalmist continued to emphasize God's protective care over those who abide in His shelter, under the shadow of the Almighty. His presence is with them when they face evil threats or plagues. They are secure in the LORD. Their lives and homes (tents) are under His constant watch.

b. Then He will charge His angels to guard you day by day (vv.11-12).

Those who live in God's presence are protected by His holy angels. God gives His angels a special charge to guard us day by day. "In all your ways" means that they watch over us as we go about our daily lives. They lift us up, protecting us and guiding us away from danger.

From time to time, we may narrowly miss incidents where physical injury or death was a certainty. Somehow, though, we escaped. At other times, our plans do not work out, or we are delayed, or we are strangely led to travel a different route than planned. We should always remember that these occurrences may be the result of angels' working on God's behalf to protect and preserve our lives (He.1:14).

These verses should also remind us that Satan knows the Scripture, and he twists it in his efforts to accomplish his evil purpose in our lives. He used this very passage when he tempted the Lord, challenging Him to prove its truth by jumping off the temple (Mt.4:6). Jesus then disarmed the devil by referring to a Scripture that commands us not to foolishly test God (De.6:16). The lesson is clear: we should not abuse the promises of God by making foolish decisions or committing foolish deeds with the expectation that He will protect us.

"If you are the Son of God," he said, "throw yourself down. For it is written: "'He will command his angels concerning you, and they will lift you up in their hands, so that you will not strike your foot against a stone'" (Mt.4:6).

Do not test the LORD your God as you did at Massah (De.6:16).

c. Then He will make you victorious over the lion and the serpent: Images of Satan; 1 Pe.5:8; Re.12:9; 20:2; Ge.3:1-24; 2 Co.11:3 (v.13).

This verse is an example of two related statements where the second restates the first. The word *serpent* corresponds with *cobra* (Ex.7:9-12). Travelers in Old Testament times faced deadly creatures, lions and serpents, along their way. In Scripture, Satan is depicted as both a lion and a serpent. Here, they represent Satan and his demonic forces who seek our destruction on a daily basis.

Thought 1. As explained in the Introduction to this psalm, its promises of complete protection were to the Israelites under the old covenant. Today, when we encounter evil threats, plagues, physical harm, or disaster, God promises that His presence will be us throughout the trial.

The New Testament warns that we are in an ongoing war with Satan and his demonic forces. We need to be aware at all times of the spiritual battles that take place over and around us (Ep.6:12). God's angels are always at war with demonic forces, protecting us and preventing Satan's destructive forces from accomplishing their purposes in our lives. God has clothed us with His armor and power so that we can be victorious over our fierce enemy (Ep.6:10-17; 1 Jn.4:4; 2 Co.2:14). This means that Satan and his demons are defeated foes, having been conquered by Christ through His death and resurrection (Ge.3:15; Co.2:15).

If we are genuine believers, God's presence, His indwelling Spirit, is always with us. However, His power and protection in our lives are conditional, just as they were for Old Testament believers. Scripture warns, if we refuse to repent of grievous sins, God may discipline us. He may move us from the realm of His protection to Satan's sphere where we might be physically destroyed (see outline and notes—1 Co.5:3-5 for more discussion). The branches (a picture of believers) who do not abide in Christ and are unfruitful are *cut off* (see outline and notes—Jn.15:2 for more discussion). Those who fail to control the sinful desires of their flesh are disqualified from running the Christian race (see outline and notes—1 Co.9:24-27 for more discussion).

Abiding in Christ is the secret to gaining victory over our spiritual enemies—the world, the flesh, and the devil. It is also the secret to receiving the fullness of God's blessings in our lives.

> **If you remain in me and my words remain in you, ask whatever you wish, and it will be given you (Jn.15:7).**
>
> **If you obey my commands, you will remain in my love, just as I have obeyed my Father's commands and remain in his love (Jn.15:10).**
>
> **Greater love has no one than this, that he lay down his life for his friends (Jn.15:13).**
>
> **And now, dear children, continue in him, so that when he appears we may be confident and unashamed before him at his coming (1 Jn.2:28).**
>
> **No one who lives in him keeps on sinning. No one who continues to sin has either seen him or known him (1 Jn.3:6).**
>
> **And receive from him anything we ask, because we obey his commands and do what pleases him (1 Jn.3:22).**

4 (91:14-16) **Cling to the LORD.**
Psalm 91 closes with a message from the LORD Himself. He affirms the promises of His covenant. He personally assures that He will honor and reward the faithful person who sets his love on Him. *He loves* (chashaq) is not the usual Hebrew word for love. It is seldom used in the Old Testament, and it means to cling to, be attached to, or be devoted to.

a. Love and acknowledge Him: He will deliver, protect, and exalt you (v.14).
The LORD promised to faithfully care for the person who is devoted to Him and *acknowledges* (yada) His name, that is, who has a genuine, personal relationship with Him. He pledged to deliver him from danger and set him on high. The Hebrew word for *protect* (sagab) can mean either to put in a secure, inaccessible place or to exalt.

b. Call upon Him and He will answer you (vv.15-16).
Special blessings are promised to those who cling to the LORD. When we call on God, He promises to answer us (v.15). He will be with us in times of trouble and will deliver and honor us. Long life was one of the most coveted blessings in Old Testament times. God promised to reward those who cling to Him not only with this gift but also with a satisfying and fulfilling life (v.16; De.30:20). Then, when the believer's time on earth comes to an end, the LORD promises to show him His salvation. Thus, the believer will see and enjoy the most precious promise of all: eternal life in God's presence.

Thought 1. God is good to all people, even those who do not know Him (Mt.5:45). For instance, the good and the evil alike enjoy the blessings and the benefits of the sun and the rain. But for all who truly follow Him, He is a loving Father and He delights in giving them good things (Lu.11:9-13). Yet His richest blessings are reserved for those who love Him most, those who know Him best and cling to Him. With that in mind, we should love the Lord with our entire being— all of our heart, soul, mind, and strength (Mk.12:30). How can we grow in our love for God? First, by simply asking Him to help us understand His love, just how much He loves us:

> **We love because he first loved us (1 Jn.4:19).**
>
> **So that Christ may dwell in your hearts through faith. And I pray that you, being rooted and established in love, may have power, together with all the saints, to grasp how wide and long and high and deep is the love of Christ, and to know this love that surpasses knowledge—that you may be filled to the measure of all the fullness of God (Ep.3:17-19).**

Second, we should ask God to help us understand His gift of forgiveness. Once we grasp the greatness of our sin, we can fully appreciate Christ's sacrifice and the forgiveness we have received through Him. Jesus said that the woman who poured the precious oil on His feet *loved Him much* because she had been *forgiven much.* We will grow in our devotion to the Lord when we realize the full measure of our sinfulness as depraved human beings and the full measure of God's love in forgiving us.

Third, we should study God's Word diligently and meditate on it that we might know Him better

(Jn.17:3; Ph.3:10; 2 Pe.3:18). The better we know the Lord, the more we will love Him.

Love the Lord your God with all your heart and with all your soul and with all your mind and with all your strength' (Mk.12:30).

However, as it is written: "No eye has seen, no ear has heard, no mind has conceived what God has prepared for those who love him" (1 Co.2:9).

But the man who loves God is known by God (1 Co.8:3).

If you carefully observe all these commands I am giving you to follow—to love the Lord your God, to walk in all his ways and to hold fast to him—then the Lord will drive out all these nations be-fore you, and you will dispossess nations larger and stronger than you (De.11:22-23).

And that you may love the Lord your God, listen to his voice, and hold fast to him. For the Lord is your life, and he will give you many years in the land he swore to give to your fathers, Abraham, Isaac and Jacob (De.30:20).

But be very careful to keep the commandment and the law that Moses the servant of the Lord gave you: to love the Lord your God, to walk in all his ways, to obey his commands, to hold fast to him and to serve him with all your heart and all your soul" (Jos.22:5).

The Lord watches over all who love him, but all the wicked he will destroy (Ps.145:20).

PSALM 92

When You Need to Be Encouraged, Praise the LORD! 92:1-15

A psalm. A song. For the Sabbath day.

1. Praise & give thanks to the LORD, the Most High

a. By proclaiming God's unfailing love every morning & His faithfulness every night

b. By singing & playing musical instruments

c. By thanking God joyfully (singing) for all He has done for you

d. By acknowledging the superiority of God's works & thoughts, Ro.11:33-36

2. Realize that unbelievers are ignorant: They do not know or understand the truth...

a. About life: That they may flourish (like grass) & pros-

It is good to praise the LORD and make music to your name, O Most High,
2 To proclaim your love in the morning and your faithfulness at night,
3 To the music of the ten-stringed lyre and the melody of the harp.
4 For you make me glad by your deeds, O LORD; I sing for joy at the works of your hands.
5 How great are your works, O LORD, how profound your thoughts!
6 The senseless man does not know, fools do not understand,
7 That though the wicked spring up like grass and all

evildoers flourish, they will be forever destroyed.
8 But you, O LORD, are exalted forever.
9 For surely your enemies, O LORD, surely your enemies will perish; all evildoers will be scattered.
10 You have exalted my horn like that of a wild ox; fine oils have been poured upon me.
11 My eyes have seen the defeat of my adversaries; my ears have heard the rout of my wicked foes.
12 The righteous will flourish like a palm tree, they will grow like a cedar of Lebanon;
13 Planted in the house of the LORD, they will flourish in the courts of our God.
14 They will still bear fruit in old age, they will stay fresh and green,
15 Proclaiming, "The LORD is upright; he is my Rock, and there is no wickedness in him."

per now but will ultimately be destroyed forever

b. About God: That He is the sovereign Judge who will rule forever

c. About God's coming judgment: That they are enemies of God, evildoers who will perish

3. Give strong testimony to God's work in your life

a. That He empowers you & pours His blessings (oil) on you

b. That He gives you victory over your adversaries & all wickedness, both human & spiritual, Ep.6:10-13

c. That he causes you to flourish & grow strong

1) Flourish in life: Like a towering palm or cedar tree

2) Flourish in God's house: Because you are planted (faithfully) in the church

3) Flourish in old age, bearing fruit & proclaiming that...

- God is upright & just
- God is your security
- God has no wickedness, no evil in Him

PSALM 92

When You Need to Be Encouraged, Praise the LORD! 92:1-15

(92:1-15) Introduction: after God spent six days creating the earth and setting it in order, He rested on the seventh day. Why did God do so? What was His purpose for taking a day to rest? He is omnipotent (all-powerful), so surely He was not tired.

God's purpose for the day was to set an example for human beings. He set apart the seventh day—the sabbath—for rest and worship (see outline and notes—Ge.2:1-3 for more information). This practice was so important that God instituted it permanently as one of His Ten Commandments (Ex.20:9-11). When the church began, God's people changed the day of rest and worship from the seventh day of the week, Saturday, to the first day of the week, Sunday (Ac.20:7; 1 Co.16:2). They made this change to celebrate Christ's resurrection, which was on the first day of the week, and called it the Lord's Day (Mk.16:2; Re.1:10).

God's plan for the human race was that we should work six days of the week and rest on the seventh. In His infinite wisdom and love for humanity, God knew that we needed to rest our bodies and minds. He also knew that we needed to refresh our spirits through worshipping Him and fellowshipping with one another. Jesus clarified God's purpose for this day of rest and worship, stating that "the sabbath was made for man, not man for the sabbath" (Mk.2:27).

The heading to Psalm 92 indicates that it is a *song for the sabbath day.* It is the only psalm with this designation. Since the five psalms that follow it have no heading whatsoever, a number of scholars believe that Psalms 92-97 comprise a group of songs to be used in corporate (congregational) worship. In obedience to God's commandment, His people came together on the sabbath to worship Him (Le.23:3). God's people continue this practice today, although most meet on the Lord's Day instead of on the sabbath. We will do well to study this psalm and incorporate its themes into our worship. This is, *When You Need to Be Encouraged, Praise the LORD!* 92:1-15.

1. Praise and give thanks to the LORD, the Most High (vv.1-5).
2. Realize that unbelievers are ignorant: They do not know or understand the truth... (vv.6-9).
3. Give strong testimony to God's work in your life (vv.10-15).

1 (92:1-5) **Praise and give thanks to the LORD, the Most High.**

When we gather for worship, we should joyfully praise God and give Him thanks. The names used for God here in verse one convey the basis for our praise:

> *LORD* (Yahweh, Jehovah) is God's covenant name to His people. Through His covenant, we have a personal relationship with the LORD. He is faithful to His people and to His promises.

> *Most High* (Elyon) means that He is the Supreme One; He is above every other being in the entire universe.

a. By proclaiming God's unfailing love every morning and His faithfulness every night (v.2).

Of all God's attributes—the unique characteristics that He alone possesses—two are especially precious to His people: His lovingkindness or *unfailing love* (chesed) and His faithfulness. These qualities express God's commitment to us, and they should be the theme of our praise. The mention of morning and night, the beginning and end of the day, includes the hours in between as well. It is a poetic way of saying that we should praise God for His love and faithfulness all day long.

b. By singing and playing musical instruments (v.3).

One of the ways we should worship God is through music. In fact, Scripture indicates that the worship in heaven includes singing (Re.5:9; 14:3). *Psalms* was the hymnal of the Hebrews. When they gathered for worship, their music included singing and playing instruments.

c. By thanking God joyfully (singing) for all He has done for you (v.4).

Praise and worship include giving thanks to the LORD. We should thank God joyfully for His work in our lives. All of the wonderful things God does for us should make us glad and cause us to *sing for joy* (ranan), that is, sing loudly or shout for joy. We should never overlook praising and thanking God for everything He does for us.

d. By acknowledging the superiority of God's works and thoughts, Ro.11:33-36 (v.5).

The LORD's works are great and should be magnified in our praise. Likewise, His thoughts are very deep or profound. *Thoughts* (machashabah) speaks of God's plans and purposes. It comes from a root word that means to braid or weave together. Romans 8:28, a verse dear to many believers, explains the truth of this concept: God works all of the circumstances of our lives together to accomplish His purpose for us.

The words *great* and *profound* express the superiority of God's works and thoughts. Thus, to say that He excels in power and wisdom is a vast understatement. His ways are infinitely above our ability to understand (Is.55:9). Knowing that, our worship should include an acknowledgement of God's great work of bringing about His purpose in our lives.

Thought 1. The psalmist stated that it is good to praise and give thanks to the LORD. It is good because it is the right thing to do and because God is worthy to be praised (Ps.18:3; 145:3). Then again, it it is good for *us*. When we praise God and give Him thanks, our spirits are refreshed and renewed. When we contemplate God's unfailing love and faithfulness, we are encouraged to face our trials. We find hope and strength for our difficulties when we focus on the sufficiency of God for all our needs. Thanking Him for His work in our lives requires us to reflect on the wonderful things He does for us on a daily basis. In addition, praising and thanking God reminds us just how dependent we are on Him, for all the good things in our lives are gifts from Him. Truly, it is good for us to praise and give thanks to God when we gather with His people for worship.

> He says, "I will declare your name to my brothers; in the presence of the congregation I will sing your praises" (He.2:12).
> Through Jesus, therefore, let us continually offer to God a sacrifice of praise—the fruit of lips that confess his name (He.13:15).
> But you are a chosen people, a royal priesthood, a holy nation, a people belonging to God, that you may declare the praises of him who called you out of darkness into his wonderful light (1 Pe.2:9).
> He is your praise; he is your God, who performed for you those great and awesome wonders you saw with your own eyes (De.10:21).
> Give thanks to the LORD, for he is good; his love endures forever (1 Chr.16:34).
> Praise our God, O peoples, let the sound of his praise be heard (Ps.66:8).

2 (92:6-9) **Realize that evildoers are ignorant: They do not know or understand the truth...**

Senseless people and fools do not know or understand God and His truth. To be *senseless* (ba'ar) means to be like an animal: stupid, ignorant, and brutish (Ps.73:22; Pr.30:2-3). It refers to those who do not grasp the truth about God and therefore do not fear Him. A *fool* (kesil) is one who makes a conscious choice to reject God and His truth (Pr.1:22). Bible teacher Warren Wiersbe notes that the psalmist is referring to "the enemies of the Lord who make life difficult for God's people."[1] In this passage, they are referred to as the wicked, the workers of iniquity,

---

1 Warren W. Wiersbe. *The Bible Exposition Commentary.* WORD*search* CROSS e-book.

and God's enemies. The psalmist explains that some enemies oppose God's people because they do not know Him and His truth. Others have the knowledge, but they intentionally reject God and His wisdom.

a. About life: That they may flourish (like grass) and prosper now but will ultimately be destroyed forever (v.7).

The wicked do not understand the truth about their own lives. They do not see their end or destiny. When they quickly spring up or flourish like the grass, they feel indestructible. They prosper now, falsely assuming that they will continue on forever. But they are blind to the sobering truth that, like the grass, they will suddenly be cut down (Ps.37:2). Ultimately, they will be destroyed forever.

b. About God: That He is the sovereign Judge who will rule forever (v.8).

The wicked also do not understand the truth about God. Either they cannot see or else they stubbornly refuse to acknowledge that God is the Supreme One who does great things (vv.1, 5). As *exalted* (marowm), the LORD is most high or lifted up above all. From His high and holy throne, He will sovereignly judge all people and rule forever.

c. About God's coming judgment: That they are enemies of God, evildoers who will perish (v.9).

Most tragically, the wicked do not grasp the reality and fierceness of God's coming judgment. They are God's enemies, and He will one day unleash the full measure of His terrifying wrath on them. On that day, they will perish and be scattered forever, eternally separated from God and other people.

Thought 1. God's enemies continue to vehemently oppose His work, His Word, and His people. Nevertheless, Jesus taught us to love and pray for them (Mt.5:44; Lu.6:35). While on one hand we have to stand up firmly for God and His truth, on the other hand we have to remain obedient to Christ. We should display God's love to those who oppose us and Him. This is not easy, but Scripture gives us guidance that will help us with this difficult task.

First, we need to remember that God loves us all, even His enemies, and that Christ died for all. God desires that all people be saved (2 Ti.2:1-4).

Second, we need to remember that our battle is not with our human enemies but with Satan's spiritual forces. Satan influences people's actions and uses them to accomplish his own evil purposes (Ep.6:12).

Third, we need to follow the selfless example of our Savior. If Christ could pray for His enemies while hanging on the cross, we can pray for those who hate us and persecute us (Lu.23:34; 1 Pe.2:21-23).

As the psalmist stated, wicked people are blind to the truth about themselves, God, and His judgment. We need to pray for them, asking God to open their eyes to the light of the gospel, that they might be forgiven and saved (2 Co.4:3-4). Even though people may hate us and our message, God has chosen us to be the vessels through whom they hear the truth. By His power, we can love them, pray for them, and give them the gospel (2 Co.4:5-7).

> **For this people's heart has become calloused; they hardly hear with their ears, and they have closed their eyes. Otherwise they might see with their eyes, hear with their ears, understand with their hearts and turn, and I would heal them' (Mt.13:15).**

> **And even if our gospel is veiled, it is veiled to those who are perishing. The god of this age has blinded the minds of unbelievers, so that they cannot see the light of the gospel of the glory of Christ, who is the image of God. For we do not preach ourselves, but Jesus Christ as Lord, and ourselves as your servants for Jesus' sake. For God, who said, "Let light shine out of darkness," made his light shine in our hearts to give us the light of the knowledge of the glory of God in the face of Christ. But we have this treasure in jars of clay to show that this all-surpassing power is from God and not from us (2 Co.4:3-7).**

> **Who wants all men to be saved and to come to a knowledge of the truth (1 Ti.2:4).**

> **But these men blaspheme in matters they do not understand. They are like brute beasts, creatures of instinct, born only to be caught and destroyed, and like beasts they too will perish (2 Pe.2:12).**

> **Evil men do not understand justice, but those who seek the LORD understand it fully (Pr.28:5).**

> **But they do not know the thoughts of the LORD; they do not understand his plan, he who gathers them like sheaves to the threshing floor (Mi.4:12).**

3 (92:10-15) **Give strong testimony to God's work in your life.**

As the congregation assembled on the sabbath day, they testified of God's work in their lives. They celebrated God's power and victory over their enemies. And as they received a fresh anointing of God's Spirit, they were bountifully blessed and filled with joy. Because they were faithful to God and to His house, they flourished and bore abundant fruit for the LORD.

a. That He empowers you and pours His blessings (oil) on you (v.10).

The psalmist testified of God's power and blessings on his life. He proclaimed that the LORD had exalted his horn, meaning that God had empowered him to be victorious over his enemies. The *horn* was a symbol of power. The wild ox was regarded as an exceptionally powerful beast (Nu.24:8; Jb.39:9; Ps.29:6).

The psalmist went on to declare that God had poured fine oil upon him. Anointing with oil was an act of consecration to the Lord's service (Ps.89:20). It symbolized the power of the Holy Spirit (1 S.16:13) and also symbolized the joy and gladness that come from God's abundant blessings (Ps.45:7; Is.61:3). Therefore, fine oil represents a fresh...

- anointing from God
- infilling of God's Spirit
- enduement or transfusion of power
- bestowal of blessings and joy

b. That He gives you victory over your adversaries and all wickedness, both human and spiritual, Ep.6:10-13 (v.11).

The psalmist further testified that God had given him victory over his adversaries. He had seen God's judgment fall on his foes, vindicating him and establishing his righteousness. His enemies may have prospered for a season, but God in His justice had cut them down (v.7).

c. That He causes you to flourish and grow strong (vv.12-15).

Finally, the psalmist declared that the righteous will flourish and grow strong. The wicked are like grass (v.7), but the righteous are like the towering palm tree and the mighty cedar in Lebanon (v.12). They flourish because they are planted in the house of the LORD— they dwell in God's presence (v.13). The vivid image pictures the righteous as trees planted in the courts or courtyard of the temple. Worshipping and serving the LORD is the heart or center of their lives. Everything they do flows from their devotion to God.

Instead of springing up quickly and then immediately being cut down like the grass, these trees—the righteous—are planted firm and strong. They flourish throughout their lives (Ps.1:3-4). Even in old age, they are fat and flourishing: green, fertile, and full of sap (v.14). They do not dry out and die, but rather continue bearing fruit, proclaiming that God is upright and just, that He is their rock or security, and that He has

no wickedness in Him whatsoever (v.15). All the days of their lives, they will sing the glorious praises of God.

Thought 1. Believers, even mature believers, need a fresh provision or renewing of God's power on a regular basis. We also need a fresh anointing of His Holy Spirit (v.10). Why? Because God's power gives us victory over our enemies (v.11). Remember, as long as we are alive and living for the Lord, we will have enemies. Scripture says that our battles are spiritual battles and that our enemies are spiritual forces—not human (2 Co.10:4; Ep.6:12). We cannot defeat these spiritual forces in our own strength. Through God's power, however, the power that works in and through us, we can be victorious over our adversaries (Ep.6:10-17; 2 Co.10:4; Ep.3:20; 1 Jn.4:4). We can live fruitful, productive lives for the Lord and His kingdom (vv.13-15). Christ has chosen and ordained us to bear fruit for Him (Jn.15:16). This means we can flourish and continue to grow stronger in the Lord even in old age.

Being planted in God's house—faithful in the church—is one of the most vital keys to these blessings (v.13). Certainly, personal worship is important. We cannot expect to be victorious, fruitful, and blessed if we do not spend time in God's presence daily. But neither can we expect these blessings if do not worship faithfully with God's people, if we refuse or neglect to be faithfully involved in a local church. When we are planted in God's house, the testimony of the psalmist will become our testimony as well. We will have a strong testimony to share with others, a witness of God's wonderful work in our lives.

For we cannot help speaking about what we have seen and heard" (Ac.4:20).

So do not be ashamed to testify about our Lord, or ashamed of me his prisoner. But join with me in suffering for the gospel, by the power of God (2 Ti.1:8).

But in your hearts set apart Christ as Lord. Always be prepared to give an answer to everyone who asks you to give the reason for the hope that you have. But do this with gentleness and respect (1 Pe.3:15).

Come and listen, all you who fear God; let me tell you what he has done for me (Ps.66:16).

I will speak of your statutes before kings and will not be put to shame (Ps.119:46).

PSALM 93

When Evil Forces Seem to Win, Remember Who Reigns, 93:1-5

1. Acknowledge God's supremacy
a. He is LORD over all: Our holy, majestic, & glorious ruler
b. He is almighty, omnipotent: Our strength, whose creation cannot be shaken or moved
 	
c. He is eternal: Our Creator, whose throne & reign cannot
	PSALM 93
	
	When Evil Forces Seem to Win, Remember Who Reigns, 93:1-5
	
	The LORD reigns, he is robed in majesty; the LORD is robed in majesty and is armed with strength. The world is firmly established; it cannot be moved.
	2 Your throne was established long ago; you are
		from all eternity.
		3 The seas have lifted up, O LORD, the seas have lifted up their voice; the seas have lifted up their pounding waves.
		4 Mightier than the thunder of the great waters, mightier than the breakers of the sea—the LORD on high is mighty.
		5 Your statutes stand firm; holiness adorns your house for endless days, O LORD.
			be removed from His control
			2. Celebrate God's mighty power
			a. The raging waters represent...
			  1) The forces we fear in nature
			  2) The forces we fear in people, Is.17:12-13; Je.47:2
			b. The LORD is mightier than the destructive forces of both nature & people
			
			3. Thank God for His faithfulness
			a. His laws (His Word) stand firm
			b. His presence (house) & reign are holy & eternal

PSALM 93

When Evil Forces Seem to Win, Remember Who Reigns, 93:1-5

(93:1-5) Introduction: by all appearances, our world is spinning out of control. Wars, terrorism, violence, hatred, gross immorality, and the persecution of believers—these all prompt us to question whether our lawless planet has slipped out of God's fingers and past the point of redemption.

Yet Psalm 93 reminds us that God is still in control. The psalm's unnamed author celebrates God's sovereignty. In spite of everything happening in our world, the LORD still reigns (v.1). He is still on His throne. His Word is sure, and His holy kingdom will endure forever.

The ninety-third psalm is the first in a series of what are referred to as *theocratic* or *enthronement* psalms (Ps.93-100). Israel was a theocracy: God was her king. These psalms rejoice in that relationship. Not only do they exalt God as reigning over Israel, but also over all the earth. They are prophetic in that they point to the coming kingdom of Christ.

As believers scattered all over the world, we live under different forms of government. Regardless of the nation in which we make our earthly home, we need to remember that we are citizens of another country, and that country is a theocracy (Ph.3:20). We are merely strangers and pilgrims in this world, ambassadors on a mission for our Heavenly King (1 Pe.2:11; 2 Co.5:20). We represent His kingdom here on earth, and we will one day reign with Him in it (Re.20:6). We are also soldiers in His army, battling against the evil forces of Satan (2 Co.10:3-4; Ep.6:10-18; 2 Ti.2:3-4). Although we may lose some battles, this psalm reminds us that our Lord will win the war (Re.19:11-21). This is, *When Evil Forces Seem to Win, Remember Who Reigns,* 93:1-5.

1. Acknowledge God's supremacy (vv.1-2).
2. Celebrate God's mighty power (vv.3-4).
3. Thank God for His faithfulness (v.5).

1 (93:1-2) **Acknowledge God's supremacy.**
Psalm 93 begins with a radiant description of God. Depicting Him as a glorious king, the psalmist acknowledged God's supremacy. The LORD (Yahweh, Jehovah)—Israel's covenant-keeping God—reigns over His entire creation.

a. He is LORD over all: Our holy, majestic, and glorious ruler (v.1ᵃ).
The LORD reigns! With these joyous words, the psalmist proclaimed Israel's—and the world's—sovereign ruler. First, he described the LORD as wearing the regal garments of a great king. The LORD of all is clothed in the majesty of His holiness, righteousness, lovingkindness, and glory (Ps.104:1). No other king compares to Him.

b. He is almighty, omnipotent: Our strength, whose creation cannot be shaken or moved (v.1ᵇ).
Second, the psalmist described our sovereign God as *armed with strength.* He is almighty and omnipotent. Despite the best efforts of the world's most powerful people, God's creation cannot be shaken or moved. At times, it may seem that our world is falling apart, but God has firmly established it. He holds it together by His powerful Word (He.1:3).

Ancient kings were mighty warriors who led their armies into battle. The psalmist announced that God has armed Himself with His strength. *Armed* (azar) depicts the LORD as preparing for battle by putting on His armor and tying up his garment around His waist.

c. He is eternal: Our Creator, whose throne and reign cannot be removed from His control (v.2).
Third, the psalmist declared that our sovereign God is eternal: His throne was *established long ago.* He is from eternity past, everlasting. His reign has no beginning. He was King long before men existed to proclaim Him King. He rules by His own power and authority, as opposed to authority that has been granted to Him. Whether people acknowledge Him or not, He is still King. His throne and reign cannot be removed from His control.

Thought 1. We live in perilous times, and we can expect conditions to worsen as we draw ever closer to the return of Jesus Christ (2 Ti.3:1-5, 12-13). Nevertheless, we can take hope in the truth that God is supreme, and He is still on His throne.

These verses point to the second coming of Christ. He will return to earth in great majesty and glory, and He will come as a mighty warrior. When He comes, He will destroy His enemies with the Word of His mouth, the same Word with which He created the world and holds it together (Re.19:15, 21; Ps.33:6; He.1:3).

The throne of Jesus Christ was established by the Father long ago. He has foreordained His Son to be the Eternal King, and we can be absolutely sure that He will reign forever and ever (Ps.2:6-11; Lu.1:33; Re.11:15).

> **And lead us not into temptation, but deliver us from the evil one' (Mt.6:13).**
>
> **"The God who made the world and everything in it is the Lord of heaven and earth and does not live in temples built by hands (Ac.17:24).**
>
> **The seventh angel sounded his trumpet, and there were loud voices in heaven, which said: "The kingdom of the world has become the kingdom of our Lord and of his Christ, and he will reign for ever and ever" (Re.11:15).**
>
> **I will proclaim the decree of the LORD: He said to me, "You are my Son; today I have become your Father (Ps.2:7).**
>
> **For dominion belongs to the LORD and he rules over the nations (Ps.22:28).**
>
> **Who is this King of glory? The LORD strong and mighty, the LORD mighty in battle (Ps.24:8).**

2 (93:3-4) Celebrate God's mighty power.
The psalmist praised God's mighty power over all that strikes fear in our hearts. Without question, life in our sin-cursed world is filled with danger, and we are powerless over most of it. But God is on His throne, and we are protected by His all-surpassing power. Our King is a mighty King, and we can rest secure in Him.

a. The raging waters represent... (v.3).
The psalmist pointed to the world's raging waters as an example of the powerful, terrifying forces we face in this life. The raging seas represent, first, the forces of nature. We are powerless against the pounding current of a flooded river and the crashing waves of the angry sea. Mighty, unstoppable waters are just one example of the fierce elements of nature that threaten—and often claim—human lives.

Second, the raging waters represent the forces we fear in people. Scripture repeatedly uses the image of roaring waters to describe rulers, nations, armies, and people in an uproar (Is.8:7-8; 17:12-13; Je.47:2).

b. The LORD is mightier than the destructive forces of both nature and people (v.4).
While the destructive forces of nature and people may be mighty, the LORD is mightier by far. The most furious of earth's elements and the most savage evildoers are no match for Him. The LORD can calm the raging seas, and He can overpower the vilest of humanity.

Thought 1. The perils of this world such as catastrophic natural disasters, tyrannical governments, terrorist, violent gangs, deadly diseases, and many, many more are all very real: Yet, God has commanded us not to live in fear of these and other dangers. Instead, we are to be controlled by a spirit that trusts in God's power and love for us (2 Ti.1:7). God never promises us that we will be exempt from the perils of this world, but He does promise that He will be with us when we face them (Jos.1:9; Is.43:2). Because He is our helper, we need not fear (He.13:5-6). Through His power, we can endure all things (Ph.4:13).

> **He replied, "You of little faith, why are you so afraid?" Then he got up and rebuked the winds and the waves, and it was completely calm. The men were amazed and asked, "What kind of man is this? Even the winds and the waves obey him!" (Mt.8:26-27).**
>
> **Now to him who is able to do immeasurably more than all we ask or imagine, according to his power that is at work within us (Ep.3:20).**
>
> **I can do everything through him who gives me strength (Ph.4:13).**
>
> **For God did not give us a spirit of timidity, but a spirit of power, of love and of self-discipline (2 Ti.1:7).**
>
> **Keep your lives free from the love of money and be content with what you have, because God has said, "Never will I leave you; never will I forsake you." So we say with confidence, "The Lord is my helper; I will not be afraid. What can man do to me?" (He.13:5-6).**
>
> **Then I heard what sounded like a great multitude, like the roar of rushing waters and like loud peals of thunder, shouting: "Hallelujah! For our Lord God Almighty reigns (Re.19:6).**
>
> **Surely the nations are like a drop in a bucket; they are regarded as dust on the**

scales; he weighs the islands as though they were fine dust (Is.40:15).

All the peoples of the earth are regarded as nothing. He does as he pleases with the powers of heaven and the peoples of the earth. No one can hold back his hand or say to him: "What have you done?" (Da.4:35).

3 (93:5) Thank God for His faithfulness.

The character and integrity of God are the foundations of His reign. God is unchangeable, and God is holy. His Word is eternal and unquestionably trustworthy. The psalmist concluded Psalm 93 by praising the faithfulness of our sovereign God.

a. His laws (His Word) stand firm (v.5ᵃ).

God's statutes are the laws and commandments of His Holy Word. The psalmist bore witness that God's Word is very sure, exceedingly trustworthy. Furthermore, it is established eternally in heaven, and it will endure long after this world has passed away (Mt.24:35; Ps.119:89; Is.40:8; 1 Pe.1:25). God's Word, like God Himself, is faithful and unchangeable, and God is faithful to His Word. It stands firm throughout the ages, inviting us to stand firmly upon it.

b. His presence (house) and reign are holy and eternal (v.5ᵇ).

Finally, the psalmist declared that God's house will be adorned forever by His absolute holiness. God's house is where His presence abides. Scripture instructs us to worship the Lord in the splendor of holiness (Ps.29:2; 96:9). This means we can only dwell in God's presence when we too are living holy, righteous, and morally pure lives (He.12:14). Like God's Word, God's holiness is eternal. He cannot and will not fail. His faithfulness to His holy character will endure forevermore.

Thought 1. We cannot predict what tomorrow will hold for our constantly-changing world. War may break out, governments may fall, terrorists may strike, or we may be persecuted for our faith. Friends and family may forsake us. We may contract a disease or be crippled in an accident. We may lose our jobs or our businesses. Without question, life is uncertain.

But God is unchanging. He is ever faithful, and His promises are sure. His Word stands firm in our perilous times. When trouble finds us, we have to trust the Lord and stand firm on His Word. Everyone and everything else may fail us, but God and His Holy Word will not. He will be with us, He will help us, and He will work out everything that happens to us for our good (Ro.8:28; Je.29:11). He will preserve us until His purpose for us on earth is accomplished, and then He will transport us to His heavenly kingdom (2 Ti.4:18). We need not fear persecution or death. If we are called upon to lay down our lives for our Lord, we know that we will be immediately transferred into His glorious presence (2 Co.5:8). He has given us this great promise, and it will be so.

Heaven and earth will pass away, but my words will never pass away (Mt.24:35).

God, who has called you into fellowship with his Son Jesus Christ our Lord, is faithful (1 Co.1:9).

But the word of the Lord stands forever." And this is the word that was preached to you (1 Pe.1:25).

Know therefore that the Lord your God is God; he is the faithful God, keeping his covenant of love to a thousand generations of those who love him and keep his commands (De.7:9).

Your faithfulness continues through all generations; you established the earth, and it endures (Ps.119:90).

O Lord, you are my God; I will exalt you and praise your name, for in perfect faithfulness you have done marvelous things, things planned long ago (Is.25:1).

PSALM 94

When Wickedness Prevails Within Society & Its Leaders, 94:1-23

1. Ask God to execute justice now
  a. Bc. He is the God who avenges
  b. Bc. He is the Judge of all the earth: He will carry out perfect justice—give the wicked exactly what they deserve
  c. Bc. the wicked are shameful
    1) They revel in their sin, 52:3; 2 Th.2:12; Pr.2:14; Je.14:10
    2) They are full of arrogance & boasting
    3) They persecute God's people: Crush & oppress those who truly follow Him
    4) They kill the vulnerable: Widows, foreigners, & orphans, Is.1:17; Js.1:27
    5) They dismiss God: Do not think He knows or cares about their wicked behavior
2. Warn the wicked
  a. Bc. they are not wise: They act like brute beasts & senseless, unthinking fools
  b. Bc. God—the very Creator of all human senses—is aware of every evil act
  c. Bc. God punishes the wicked, both nations & individuals
    1) He who teaches people knows everything
    2) He even knows people's worthless & foolish thoughts
3. Welcome God's discipline
  a. Bc. He uses His Word to in-

O LORD, the God who avenges, O God who avenges, shine forth.
2 Rise up, O Judge of the earth; pay back to the proud what they deserve.
3 How long will the wicked, O LORD, how long will the wicked be jubilant?
4 They pour out arrogant words; all the evildoers are full of boasting.
5 They crush your people, O LORD; they oppress your inheritance.
6 They slay the widow and the alien; they murder the fatherless.
7 They say, "The LORD does not see; the God of Jacob pays no heed."
8 Take heed, you senseless ones among the people; you fools, when will you become wise?
9 Does he who implanted the ear not hear? Does he who formed the eye not see?
10 Does he who disciplines nations not punish? Does he who teaches man lack knowledge?
11 The LORD knows the thoughts of man; he knows that they are futile.
12 Blessed is the man you discipline, O LORD, the man

you teach from your law;
13 You grant him relief from days of trouble, till a pit is dug for the wicked.
14 For the LORD will not reject his people; he will never forsake his inheritance.
15 Judgment will again be founded on righteousness, and all the upright in heart will follow it.
16 Who will rise up for me against the wicked? Who will take a stand for me against evildoers?
17 Unless the LORD had given me help, I would soon have dwelt in the silence of death.
18 When I said, "My foot is slipping," your love, O LORD, supported me.
19 When anxiety was great within me, your consolation brought joy to my soul.
20 Can a corrupt throne be allied with you—one that brings on misery by its decrees?
21 They band together against the righteous and condemn the innocent to death.
22 But the LORD has become my fortress, and my God the rock in whom I take refuge.
23 He will repay them for their sins and destroy them for their wickedness; the LORD our God will destroy them.

  struct & mature you
  b. Bc. He protects & gives relief thru life's trouble: He will do so until the wicked are judged
  c. Bc. He never rejects or forsakes His people: You are His inheritance, His very special possession
  d. Bc. He promises a day when justice will prevail (based on righteousness): A picture of the upright living in God's kingdom
4. Trust the LORD's love & help
  a. He alone has the power to rise up & take a stand for you against evildoers
  b. He alone can help you—even as He did the psalmist
    1) Deliver you from death
    2) Keep you from slipping & hold you up when He hears your cry for help
    3) Help you thru anxiety & doubt by comforting your soul & renewing your hope
5. Be certain of God's coming judgment
  a. God will not tolerate corrupt leaders or officials
    1) Bc. they use the law for their own ends to damage others
    2) Bc. they target the righteous & condemn the innocent
  b. God is your fortress & rock: You can take refuge in Him
  c. God will execute perfect justice on the wicked
    1) He will repay them exactly as they deserve
    2) He will destroy them

PSALM 94

When Wickedness Prevails Within Society and Its Leaders, 94:1-23

(94:1-23) **Introduction:** one of the most startling warnings Jesus ever gave was directed to His followers. He told them clearly that they would face persecution (Mt.23:34; Jn.15:20). History bears this out repeatedly and is indelibly stained with the blood of those who have been beaten, tortured, and slain because of their faith in Christ. And, sadly, the wrath of evil individuals, religious fanatics, and oppressive governments continues to burn hot against Christian believers. Today, in fact, hardly a day passes without a report about another group of believers who have been attacked. For every act of violence against Christians that is reported, hundreds of other offenses ranging from discrimination to murder go unnoticed. Even in the United States—which stood as the model for Christian liberty for over two hundred years—

public persecution of believers has begun. The demands of society and government to accept and even legalize reprehensible sins—consider the gross immorality, lawlessness, and wickedness—have already resulted in the persecution of those who stand up for God's truth.

Along with what is happening in America, oppression is running rampant throughout the world. Evil people and the corrupt governments who ignore them often inflict terror and suffering on the innocent. In far too many places, civil officials sworn to uphold the laws and execute justice are themselves dishonest and abuse their power.

Psalm 94 was originally written to a society where wickedness prevailed. Its author and occasion are unknown, but some scholars believe it was written during the reign of one of Israel's ungodly kings (v.20). It is a prayer for judgment on those who persecute and oppress God's people. It is also an encouragement to the oppressed who find refuge in God. The psalmist assures them that the judge of the earth will execute justice on all evildoers (v.2, 23).

The ninety-fourth psalm has a distinctly prophetic flavor, pointing to the suffering of God's people during the period known as the great tribulation and the return of Jesus Christ to earth (Mt.24:21). Indeed, the promises of this psalm will ultimately be fulfilled in God's Son. When Christ comes to earth again, He will execute justice on all evildoers and will reign in uncompromised righteousness. This is, *When Wickedness Prevails Within Society and Its Leaders*, 94:1-23.

1. Ask God to execute justice now (vv.1-7).
2. Warn the wicked (vv.8-11).
3. Welcome God's discipline (vv.12-15).
4. Trust the LORD's love and help (vv.16-19).
5. Be certain of God's coming judgment (vv.20-23).

1 (94:1-7) Ask God to execute justice now.

The psalmist prayed for God to rise up and to execute justice on His people's oppressors immediately. By praying for the LORD to show Himself or to shine forth, he was asking God to appear in all His righteousness and glory by openly judging the wicked.

a. Because He is the God who avenges (v.1).

The psalmist addressed the LORD as the God who avenges. *Avenges* (neqamah) means the execution of justice. It is not revenge or vindictiveness but rather the upholding of the law by "[giving] justice to those who have been wronged."[1] God clearly said that the execution of justice is a responsibility that belongs exclusively to Him (De.32:35). However, He does delegate the administering of earthly justice to civil authorities. When human law enforcement and court officials perform their duties, they are acting under God's authority and on His behalf (Ro.13:1-6; Ps.82:6). But God is the author of justice and, as such, He is the only one capable of delivering it perfectly.

b. Because He is the Judge of all the earth (v.2).

The psalmist further emphasized God's responsibility to execute justice by addressing Him as the judge of the earth (Ge.18:25). He called on God to carry out perfect justice—to give the proud evildoers exactly what they deserved. To render a reward is to fully pay a person everything he or she has earned, whether it be good or bad, punishment or prize.

c. Because the wicked are shameful (vv.3-7).

It seemed to the psalmist that God was failing in His duty to administer justice by allowing the wicked to continue oppressing the saints. The psalmist asked God how long He was going to let them carry on with their shameful persecution of the righteous (v.3). Watching the wicked triumph or revel in their sin was more than he could bear (Ps.52:3; 2 Th.2:12; Pr.2:14; Je.14:10). He could tolerate no more of the arrogant words (hard things) and boasting that constantly poured out of the evildoers' mouths (v.4).

The wicked were persecuting God's people, completely crushing those who truly followed Him (v.5). God's people are His heritage or inheritance, and it seemed unjust that He would allow the wicked to so brutally afflict them. These vicious evildoers preyed on the vulnerable, killing widows, foreigners, and orphans (v.6; Is.1:17; Js.1:27). In shameless arrogance, they totally dismissed God, thinking that the LORD neither knew nor cared about their wicked behavior (v.7).

Thought 1. Psalm 94 teaches us how to respond to the persecution and oppression of believers. First, we need to pray without ceasing for God to bring judgment on those who are persecuting our brothers and sisters in Christ. We have a holy obligation to uphold the persecuted before God's throne. Pastors should lead the way in this endeavor, informing their congregations of what is taking place across the globe and setting aside time in services for prayer for the oppressed.

Second, we need to understand that God has delegated the execution of justice for evildoers to civil governments. Wherever possible, we should make every effort to urge our leaders to act in behalf of the persecuted. Locally, nationally, and internationally, the forces of right must stand up against oppression (Pr.24:11-12). In many places of the world, believers do not have the freedom to speak out, but where they do, they need to do everything they can to stir their leaders to action.

> **Do not take revenge, my friends, but leave room for God's wrath, for it is written: "It is mine to avenge; I will repay," says the Lord (Ro.12:19).**
>
> **For we know him who said, "It is mine to avenge; I will repay," and again, "The Lord will judge his people" (He.10:30).**
>
> **When he opened the fifth seal, I saw under the altar the souls of those who had been slain because of the word of God and the testimony they had maintained. They called out in a loud voice, "How long, Sovereign Lord, holy and true, until you judge the inhabitants of the earth and avenge our blood?" (Re.6:9-10).**

---

1 Warren W. Wiersbe. *The Bible Exposition Commentary.* WORD*search* CROSS e-book.

Rejoice, O nations, with his people, for he will avenge the blood of his servants; he will take vengeance on his enemies and make atonement for his land and people (De.32:43).

Say to those with fearful hearts, "Be strong, do not fear; your God will come, he will come with vengeance; with divine retribution he will come to save you" (Is.35:4).

2 (94:8-11) Warn the wicked.

The psalmist turned his attention to the evildoers who were brazenly persecuting God's people, warning them of their wicked ways. Because the psalmist spoke inspired truth, his fearless words were God's words to these black-hearted fools.

a. Because they are not wise: They act like brute beasts and senseless, unthinking fools (v.8).

The psalmist boldly informed the wicked that they were not wise. He called them senseless, like brutish animals, and fools who had chosen to reject God's truth (Ps.92:6). He commanded the senseless ones to *take heed* (biyn), to understand or discern, the truth about God. Then, he derided the fools for their folly, asking when they would become wise and live in obedience to God's commands.

b. Because God—the very Creator of all human senses—is aware of every evil act (v.9).

Rebuking their foolish assumptions about God, the psalmist warned the wicked that the LORD was fully aware of every evil act they performed. As the Creator of all human senses, God made the ear and formed the eye. Thus, to think that He did not hear their boastful words nor see their evil deeds was utterly absurd. He knew all about their senseless reasoning and their rejection of Him.

c. Because God punishes the wicked, both nations and individuals (vv.10-11).

Using a series of questions, the psalmist sternly warned the wicked that God punishes both nations and individuals who reject Him and His righteous commands (v.10ᵃ). It is the LORD who teaches people the truth. How could they possibly think He did not know what they were doing? He knows everything (v.10ᵇ). He even knows every worthless and foolish thought that proceeds from the defiled human heart (v.11).

Thought 1. God's people have a holy responsibility to warn the wicked about God's judgment. This is not easy to do. Many who speak up and boldly declare the truth will undoubtedly face persecution. Others will be prosecuted. Some may even be slain. We ought to pray fervently and frequently that God will raise up a generation of fearless witnesses who, like the prophets of old, will warn the world about God's coming judgment.

So be on your guard! Remember that for three years I never stopped warning each of you night and day with tears (Ac.20:31).

We proclaim him, admonishing and teaching everyone with all wisdom, so that we may present everyone perfect in Christ (Col.1:28).

See to it that you do not refuse him who speaks. If they did not escape when they refused him who warned them on earth, how much less will we, if we turn away from him who warns us from heaven? (He.12:25).

"Now prophesy all these words against them and say to them: "'The LORD will roar from on high; he will thunder from his holy dwelling and roar mightily against his land. He will shout like those who tread the grapes, shout against all who live on the earth (Je.25:30).

When I say to a wicked man, 'You will surely die,' and you do not warn him or speak out to dissuade him from his evil ways in order to save his life, that wicked man will die for his sin, and I will hold you accountable for his blood (Eze.3:18).

"Go to the great city of Nineveh and preach against it, because its wickedness has come up before me" (Jon.1:2).

3 (94:12-15) Welcome God's discipline.

After addressing the wicked oppressors of God's people, the psalmist had an inspired word for the wise and righteous who feared God and kept His commandments. He exhorted them to welcome God's discipline because His correction keeps them away from many of life's potential dangers. In addition, he encouraged them to realize how special they were to God, and to trust Him to do right in executing justice on all evildoers.

a. Because He uses His Word to instruct and mature you (v.12).

The psalmist declared that the person whom God chastens or disciplines is blessed (see Deeper Study #1— Ps.1:1 for more discussion). God's discipline in the lives of His sons and daughters is not punitive in nature but corrective. Its purpose is not to punish but to teach us to follow His *law* (torah), His holy commandments. While God's discipline is sometimes painful, it is always for our good. Through our trials and hardships, God instructs us in His Word. He also uses His Word to mature us and make us holy (He.12:10-11).

b. Because He protects and gives relief through life's trouble: He will do so until the wicked are judged (v.13).

When we respond to God's discipline by repenting of our disobedience, correcting our behavior, and conforming our lives to His Word, we are thereby protected and given relief from the adversity or trouble. Although we may still bear the consequences of our sinful behavior, the LORD will strengthen and give us peace as we walk through the adversity.

The psalmist assured the righteous that a pit is being dug for the wicked—the day of their judgment will come. Until then, the LORD will continue to protect His people through life's troubles.

c. Because He never rejects or forsakes His people: You are His inheritance, His very special possession (v.14).

The psalmist again assured God's people that God's precious promises would uphold them as they awaited His day of justice and endured persecution by the wicked. The LORD has promised never to reject or cast off His people. Remember, the righteous are His inheritance, His very special possession. Because we are so dear to God, He will never forsake us. The presence of trouble in our lives does not mean God has turned His back on us. To the contrary, He has promised to be with us through all of life's difficulties (Jos.1:9; Is.43:2; He.13:5).

d. Because He promises a day when justice will prevail (based on righteousness): A picture of the upright living in God's kingdom (v.15).

Apparently, Psalm 94 was written during a time when Israel's judges were corrupt (Ps.82:1-8). Speaking on God's behalf, the psalmist promised the believers who were being persecuted that judgment would be righteous again one day. Justice would prevail, and God's righteousness in avenging the oppressed would be fully seen. The upright in heart would embrace this return to righteous judgment in the land.

God's people will one day live in a kingdom of uncompromised righteousness. When Jesus returns to earth, He will establish and preside over a perfect government. The promise of this verse points to the upright living in that kingdom.

Thought 1. Out of His unfailing love for us, our Heavenly Father disciplines us when we sin. Scripture repeatedly teaches that we are to welcome God's discipline. God does not want to see us, His beloved sons and daughters, suffer the painful consequences of sin.

Like every loving parent, He desires that we live life to the fullest. He wants us to be blessed, successful, and fulfilled. In turn, we ought to submit freely to God's loving but firm hand, knowing that He is only trying to protect us. He does not want us suffering the tragic consequences of disobedience to His commands.

> **When we are judged by the Lord, we are being disciplined so that we will not be condemned with the world (1 Co.11:32).**
>
> **And you have forgotten that word of encouragement that addresses you as sons: "My son, do not make light of the Lord's discipline, and do not lose heart when he rebukes you, because the Lord disciplines those he loves, and he punishes everyone he accepts as a son." Endure hardship as discipline; God is treating you as sons. For what son is not disciplined by his father? If you are not disciplined (and everyone undergoes discipline), then you are illegitimate children and not true sons. Moreover, we have all had human fathers who disciplined us and we respected them for it. How much more should we submit to the Father of our spirits and live! Our fathers disciplined us for a little while as they thought best; but God disciplines us for our good, that we may share in his holiness. No discipline seems pleasant at the time, but painful. Later on, however, it produces a harvest of righteousness and peace for those who have been trained by it (He.12:5-11).**
>
> **Those whom I love I rebuke and discipline. So be earnest, and repent (Re.3:19).**
>
> **Know then in your heart that as a man disciplines his son, so the LORD your God disciplines you (De.8:5).**
>
> **My son, do not despise the LORD's discipline and do not resent his rebuke, because the LORD disciplines those he loves, as a father the son he delights in (Pr.3:11-12).**

4 (94:16-19) **Trust the LORD's love and help.**

The psalmist gave his own personal testimony here in an attempt to assure the hurting hearts of God's persecuted people. From his own encouraged heart, he shared how the LORD had brought him through a period of intense persecution. By testifying of God's strength and comfort, he encouraged the oppressed to trust the LORD's love and help.

a. **He alone has the power to rise up and take a stand for you against evildoers (v.16).**

The psalmist asked who would help and defend him against wicked oppressors, implying that no man was strong enough to deliver him from them. Only the LORD has the power to rise up and stand against evildoers.

b. **He alone can help you—even as He did the psalmist (vv.17-19).**

The psalmist proceeded to answer his own question: the LORD had helped him in a powerful way. The LORD had delivered him from death at the hands of his oppressors (v.17). God had proven faithful again in his life. When his foot slipped—when he thought he could stand no more and was at the point of death—he cried out to the LORD for help (v.18). And the LORD's unfailing love and mercy upheld and empowered him to persevere though his life-threatening trouble.

The psalmist's season of persecution had placed him under great stress. *Anxiety was great within me* speaks of the overwhelming fear and doubt that had nearly strangled the life out of him. But God had faithfully comforted him, bringing joy to his heart in the deepest, darkest valley he had ever walked through (v.19).

Thought 1. The evildoers who oppressed God's people are pictures of our spiritual enemies—Satan and his demonic forces. It is vital for us to remember that we cannot overcome them in our own strength. Only by clothing ourselves in the armor of God—His truth and salvation—and standing in the power of His might can we withstand their attacks (Ep.6:10-17). God's Spirit within us is greater than our enemies in this world (1 Jn.4:4). Through God's unfailing love, we can conquer every power that comes against us (Ro.8:35-39). We will be victorious, if we wholly trust the LORD's love and help.

> Who shall separate us from the love of Christ? Shall trouble or hardship or persecution or famine or nakedness or danger or sword? As it is written: "For your sake we face death all day long; we are considered as sheep to be slaughtered." No, in all these things we are more than conquerors through him who loved us. For I am convinced that neither death nor life, neither angels nor demons, neither the present nor the future, nor any powers, neither height nor depth, nor anything else in all creation, will be able to separate us from the love of God that is in Christ Jesus our Lord (Ro.8:35-39).

> I have been crucified with Christ and I no longer live, but Christ lives in me. The life I live in the body, I live by faith in the Son of God, who loved me and gave himself for me (Ga.2:20).

> His intent was that now, through the church, the manifold wisdom of God should be made known to the rulers and authorities in the heavenly realms (Ep.3:10).

> So we say with confidence, "The Lord is my helper; I will not be afraid. What can man do to me?" (He.13:6).

> So do not fear, for I am with you; do not be dismayed, for I am your God. I will strengthen you and help you; I will uphold you with my righteous right hand (Is.41:10).

> In all their distress he too was distressed, and the angel of his presence saved them. In his love and mercy he redeemed them; he lifted them up and carried them all the days of old (Is.63:9).

5 (94:20-23) **Be certain of God's coming judgment.** The psalmist ended this psalm by assuring the oppressed that their persecutors would not escape punishment for their evil deeds. God's coming judgment is certain. His righteous wrath *will* fall on the wicked. Justice *will* be served.

a. **God will not tolerate corrupt leaders or officials (vv.20-21).**

Once again the psalmist used a question to make his point. "Can a corrupt throne be allied with you—one that brings on misery by its decrees?" He addressed the LORD, asking if corrupt officials could possibly be in fellowship with Him (v.20a). His use of the word *throne* suggests that Israel's king was corrupt, and that he turned his head while evildoers oppressed God's people.

The obvious answer to the psalmist's question is *no*: God will have no fellowship with unrighteousness. Corrupt leaders damage others by using the law for their own evil purposes (v.20b). They target the righteous as their victims, working together with other corrupt officials or citizens to condemn innocent people. The persecuted could rest assured that God would not tolerate corrupt officials.

b. **God is your fortress and rock: You can take refuge in Him (v.22).**

The psalmist encouraged the people to cling to the LORD. He testified that God was his defense or fortress and his rock of refuge. We do not have to endure our troubles alone or in our own strength. We can find shelter and strength in Him.

c. God will execute perfect justice on the wicked (v.23).

Psalm 94 ends exactly where it began: with the assurance that God is the avenger of the righteous. He will execute perfect justice on the wicked and bring upon them their own iniquity—repay them exactly as they deserve. Since they have viciously destroyed others, God—the judge of all the earth—will destroy them.

Thought 1. Repeatedly in Scripture, God encourages us not to fret over evildoers but instead to rest in Him. In His time, He will judge the wicked and will bring them down (Ps.37:1-8; Pr.23:17-18; 24:19-20). We may suffer at the hands of evil people, but we can be certain of God's coming judgment. He will repay the wicked for all that they do against us and those we love. Until then, we have to take refuge in Him, persevering through persecution and patiently waiting for the day of His judgment.

The wrath of God is being revealed from heaven against all the godlessness and wickedness of men who suppress the truth by their wickedness (Ro.1:18).

When they hurled their insults at him, he did not retaliate; when he suffered, he made no threats. Instead, he entrusted himself to him who judges justly (1 Pe.2:23).

To judge everyone, and to convict all the ungodly of all the ungodly acts they have done in the ungodly way, and of all the harsh words ungodly sinners have spoken against him" (Jude 15).

And I saw the dead, great and small, standing before the throne, and books were opened. Another book was opened, which is the book of life. The dead were judged according to what they had done as recorded in the books (Re.20:12).

Let them sing before the LORD, for he comes to judge the earth. He will judge the world in righteousness and the peoples with equity (Ps.98:9).

For God will bring every deed into judgment, including every hidden thing, whether it is good or evil (Ec.12:14).

	PSALM 95	in worship, let us kneel before the LORD our Maker;	**themselves: Bow before God**

	When You Come Together for Worship, 95:1-11	7 For he is our God and we are the people of his pasture, the flock under his care. Today, if you hear his voice,	a. Bc. He is our Maker, our Creator
			b. Bc. He is our God, our Shepherd
			  1) He leads us & cares for us
			  2) We are to follow Him

1. Invite everyone to enter God's presence: Praise & sing to Him
  a. Bc. He is the Rock of salvation
  b. Bc. He is worthy of thanksgiving & worship—praising Him through music & psalms
  c. Bc. He alone is the LORD, the great King & true God
    1) He is above all false gods
    2) He alone is the Creator & Sustainer of the earth
      • Its depths & mountain peaks
      • Its seas & dry land
	Come, let us sing for joy to the LORD; let us shout aloud to the Rock of our salvation.
	2 Let us come before him with thanksgiving and extol him with music and song.
	3 For the LORD is the great God, the great King above all gods.
	4 In his hand are the depths of the earth, and the mountain peaks belong to him.
	5 The sea is his, for he made it, and his hands formed the dry land.
		8 Do not harden your hearts as you did at Meribah, as you did that day at Massah in the desert,
		9 Where your fathers tested and tried me, though they had seen what I did.
		10 For forty years I was angry with that generation; I said, "They are a people whose hearts go astray, and they have not known my ways."
		11 So I declared on oath in my anger, "They shall never enter my rest."
			3. Warn everyone to listen to God's voice & to obey His Word TODAY
			  a. Consider Israel's rebellion
			    1) They tried God's patience
			    2) They refused to obey God despite His miraculous works
			  b. Consider the tragic results of Israel's disobedience
			    1) They bore God's anger for 40 years: Never knew His peace or rest—the security of His care & destiny
			    2) They were never allowed to enter the promised land: A picture of heaven

2. Invite everyone to humble	6 Come, let us bow down		

PSALM 95

When You Come Together for Worship, 95:1-11

(95:1-11) **Introduction:** church services today often begin with a call to worship—a song, a reading from Scripture, or a personal word inviting the congregation into the LORD's presence. It may also exhort or instruct the people about how to participate or respond in the service.

The ninety-fifth psalm is a call to worship. Inspired by the Holy Spirit, the unknown author celebrated God as our King (v.3), our Creator (v.5), and our Shepherd (v.7). The LORD had a message for the people who were gathered in His name, and the psalmist delivered that message (vv.7-11).

Psalm 95 teaches us how to worship, demonstrating that worship is praising God, worship is submitting to God, and worship is obeying God. This is, *When You Come Together for Worship*, 95:1-11.

1. Invite everyone to enter God's presence: Praise and sing to Him (vv.1-5).
2. Invite everyone to humble themselves: Bow and submit to God (vv.6-7b).
3. Warn everyone to listen to God's voice and to obey His Word TODAY (vv.7c-11).

1 (95:1-5) **Invite everyone to enter God's presence: Praise and sing to Him.**
The psalmist invited the people to come or gather together in God's presence. The word *come* appears three times in the first six verses of this psalm; each time, it is the translation of a different Hebrew word. Here in verse one, it means to walk or travel or make a journey. The people were encouraged to come from wherever they were to God's house to worship Him through praise and song.

a. Because He is the Rock of salvation (v.1).
The psalmist urged the congregation to praise God jubilantly. To *shout aloud* (ruah) is to shout joyfully and victoriously. "The full-throated cries urged in the verbs of verses 1 and 2 suggest an acclamation fit for a king who is the savior of his people."[1] Indeed, the LORD is the *rock of our salvation...*

- our refuge and fortress
- the one from whom the water of life flows (Ex.17:1-7)
- our defender
- our strength
- our deliverer
- our security

b. Because He is worthy of thanksgiving and worship—praising Him through music and psalms (v.2).
In this verse, *come before* (qadam) means to meet or appear in front of. The psalmist instructed the people to enter into God's presence with *thanksgiving* (todah), an offering or sacrifice of thanks.[2] For New Testament believers, this sacrifice is the praise from our lips (He.13:15). Because every blessing and good thing in our lives comes from the LORD, He is worthy of our most heartfelt thanksgiving and worship. For this reason, the psalmist again exhorts us to make a joyful noise, to praise the LORD loudly and enthusiastically through music and psalms.

---

1 Derek Kidner. *Psalms 73-150*, p.376.
2 Spiros Zodhiates. *AMG Complete Word Study Dictionary*. WORD-search CROSS e-book.

c. Because He alone is the LORD, the great King and true God (vv.3-5).

The psalmist then encouraged the people to shout to the LORD because He is the great God and the great King (v.3ᵃ). He is above all gods—a statement declaring that He alone is God (v.3ᵇ). Every other so-called god is false. The LORD (Yahweh, Jehovah) our God, the God with whom we have a covenant, is the only living and true God.

As King, the LORD rules over the entire universe by right of creation. He alone is the Creator and Sustainer of the earth (v.4). From the depths of the earth to the highest mountain peak, it all belongs to Him. The entire earth—the sea and the dry land—are His because He made and formed it all. *Formed* (yatsar) is the word used of a potter fashioning the clay. Just imagine the LORD's shaping the continents with His skillful and mighty hands!

Thought 1. While Old Testament believers gathered at the temple to worship God, they were not allowed to enter into the area where God's actual presence resided, the Holy of Holies. That privilege was reserved for the High Priests alone. However, we have a standing invitation to enter into God's presence once we accept Jesus Christ as our Savior through His shed blood on the cross. So, while we can and should worship privately, the same passage of Scripture that invites us to boldly "enter the Most Holy Place" instructs us to faithfully assemble with God's people for worship (He.10:19-25).

Worship is praise. When we come together for worship, we should offer the sacrifice of praise to God (He.13:15). Our praise should begin with giving thanks to God. We are instructed to enter His presence with thanksgiving (v.2). As we make our way into God's house, the church, our hearts should be filled with gratitude for all He has done for us (Ps.100:4).

Our praise ought to be exuberant—the full expression of our grateful hearts to God (vv.1-2). With that in mind, we should sing enthusiastically and loudly, for the LORD deserves the very best we have to offer Him (vv.4-6). We should hold nothing back in exalting His glorious name.

> **Through Jesus, therefore, let us continually offer to God a sacrifice of praise—the fruit of lips that confess his name (He.13:15).**
>
> **May the peoples praise you, O God; may all the peoples praise you (Ps.67:3).**
>
> **Praise the LORD, all you nations; extol him, all you peoples. For great is his love toward us, and the faithfulness of the LORD endures forever. Praise the LORD (Ps.117:1-2)**

> **Let them give glory to the LORD and proclaim his praise in the islands (Is.42:12).**

2 (95:6-7ᵇ) **Invite everyone to humble themselves: Bow before God.**

The second invitation from the psalmist was for the people to humble themselves before God by bowing and submitting to Him (v.6ᵃ). Notice that we are instructed to bow down—literally, bend the knee—and kneel before the LORD. Assuming this posture is a token of our humility and subjection to God. Although we might not kneel physically every time we worship, we should always bow before the LORD in our hearts. Still, it is good for us to kneel physically before Him at times. This gesture not only honors and blesses the LORD but also keeps us humble, reminding us of who we are and who He is.

a. Because He is our Maker, our Creator (v.6ᵇ).

God is, first, our Maker, our Creator. He made us for a purpose: to fellowship with and glorify Him. When we kneel before Him, we need to remember this purpose. Far too often, our motivation in life is doing whatever makes us happy, whatever gives us personal fulfillment. God desires for all of us, His children, to be happy and fulfilled, but He wants us to find that inner joy and satisfaction in Him and in His purpose for us, not in our own selfish pursuits. Therefore, we should rededicate ourselves to fulfilling God's purpose for creating us.

b. Because He is our God, our Shepherd (v.7).

Second, the LORD is *our* God and *our* Shepherd. We can say this because we know Him and have a personal relationship with Him. We are the sheep of His hand; that is, we are under *His care* (see outline and notes—Ps.23:1-6 for more discussion). As our shepherd, God...

- leads us
- feeds us
- meets our every need
- refreshes us
- causes us to rest
- protects us
- keeps us close to Him
- corrects us when we stray
- is with us in every danger, through all the trials of life
- dwells with us

Thought 1. *Worship is submission.* True worship is not just lifting our hands and shouting out to God in praise but also bowing before Him in adoration and submission. "Our singing must give way to silence as we bow before the Lord."³ When we bow before the LORD, we acknowledge Him as our God, our Creator, and our Shepherd. We present ourselves to Him as *living sacrifices*, pledging to strive for holiness so that we might be acceptable to Him (Ro.12:1). Praise that is

---

3   Warren W. Wiersbe. *The Bible Exposition Commentary.* WORDsearch CROSS e-book.

not offered from a submissive heart means little to God.

> **Therefore, I urge you, brothers, in view of God's mercy, to offer your bodies as living sacrifices, holy and pleasing to God—this is your spiritual act of worship (Ro.12:1).**
>
> **Submit yourselves, then, to God. Resist the devil, and he will flee from you (Js.4:7).**
>
> **Humble yourselves before the Lord, and he will lift you up (Js.4:10).**
>
> **Humility and the fear of the LORD bring wealth and honor and life (Pr.22:4).**
>
> **For this is what the high and lofty One says—he who lives forever, whose name is holy: "I live in a high and holy place, but also with him who is contrite and lowly in spirit, to revive the spirit of the lowly and to revive the heart of the contrite (Is.57:15).**

3 (95:7c-11) **Warn everyone to listen to God's voice and to obey His Word TODAY.**
When the people came together to praise and worship God, the LORD spoke to them. He delivered a critical message through the psalmist: do not follow the faithless, disobedient example of your ancestors. The psalmist exhorted the congregation to *hear* (shama) God's voice, to hearken to Him and to give Him their full attention. In addition, the psalmist pressed them to obey God immediately when He spoke, to listen to and obey Him at once (today) (v.7c).

Note that the author of Hebrews applied this passage to the church (see outline and notes—He.3:7-4:19 for more discussion).

a. Consider Israel's rebellion (vv.8-9).
The psalmist faithfully delivered God's message to His people, instructing them to consider Israel's rebellion in the wilderness. *Meribah* and *Massah* were the names given to the place where the Israelites sorely tried or tested God's patience (v.8):

> **And he called the place Massah and Meribah because the Israelites quarreled and because they tested the LORD saying, "Is the LORD among us or not?" (Ex.17:7).**

Meribah means provocation or strife. *Massah* means a temptation or test. The KJV and NKJV use the definitions of these terms in verse eight, while other translations, including the NIV, use the names themselves. At Meribah and Massah, the people strove with God by refusing to trust and obey Him, despite His mi-

raculous works in their behalf (v.9). Their disobedience was also a test to see if God would judge them.

b. Consider the tragic results of Israel's disobedience (vv.10-11).
The LORD also told the people to consider the tragic results of their ancestors' disobedience. Because of their rebellion and unbelief, they bore God's anger for forty years (v.10). God disciplined them by not allowing them to enter the promised land of Canaan, the place where they could have lived in His perfect peace and rest. Instead, they never knew these wonderful blessings—the security of God's care and the destiny He had planned for them (v.11). Canaan is a picture of heaven, the place of eternal rest for all who genuinely believe in the LORD.

Thought 1. *Worship is obedience.* When we come together for worship, we need to listen to what God says to us through His Word and through His Holy Spirit who lives within us. And as the Lord speaks to us, it is our duty to respond in obedience to Him at once. We should not delay, or walk away intending to think about what God has said. Instead, we are to obey what the Lord is commanding us to do right away.

God desires our obedience more than He desires our praise. He delights in our obedience more than He delights in our sacrifices (1 S.15:22-23). In fact, the LORD rejects our *sacrifice of praise* unless we are also walking in obedience to His Holy Word.

> **He replied, "My mother and brothers are those who hear God's word and put it into practice" (Lu.8:21).**
>
> **For he says, "In the time of my favor I heard you, and in the day of salvation I helped you." I tell you, now is the time of God's favor, now is the day of salvation (2 Co.6:2).**
>
> **As obedient children, do not conform to the evil desires you had when you lived in ignorance (1 Pe.1:14).**
>
> **Do not let this Book of the Law depart from your mouth; meditate on it day and night, so that you may be careful to do everything written in it. Then you will be prosperous and successful (Jos.1:8).**
>
> **But Samuel replied: "Does the LORD delight in burnt offerings and sacrifices as much as in obeying the voice of the LORD? To obey is better than sacrifice, and to heed is better than the fat of rams. For rebellion is like the sin of divination, and arrogance like the evil of idolatry. Because you have rejected the word of the LORD, he has rejected you as king" (1 S.15:22-23).**

Sacrifice and offering you did not desire, but my ears you have pierced; burnt offerings and sin offerings you did not require. Then I said, "Here I am, I have come—it is written about me in the scroll. I desire to do your will, O my God; your law is within my heart" (Ps.40:6-8).

Outline

1. Call on all people of the earth to worship the LORD

a. To sing a *new song* to Him

b. To praise Him—all He is

c. To proclaim daily the good news that He saves us

d. To make God's glory & His amazing works known among all people & nations

e. To declare how great & worthy of praise He is

1) Bc. He alone is to be feared, not other *so-called* gods
- Manmade gods are mere idols, false gods
- God alone is LORD, Creator of the universe

2) Bc. He is the exalted LORD: His royal presence radiates...
- Honor & majesty
- Strength & beauty

2. Call on all nations of the earth to acknowledge the LORD

PSALM 96

A Call to Bear Witness to All Peoples & Nations of the Earth, 96:1-13

Sing to the LORD a new song; sing to the LORD, all the earth.
2 Sing to the LORD, praise his name; proclaim his salvation day after day.
3 Declare his glory among the nations, his marvelous deeds among all peoples.
4 For great is the LORD and most worthy of praise; he is to be feared above all gods.
5 For all the gods of the nations are idols, but the LORD made the heavens.
6 Splendor and majesty are before him; strength and glory are in his sanctuary.
7 Ascribe to the LORD, O families of nations, ascribe to the LORD glory and strength.
8 Ascribe to the LORD the glory due his name; bring an offering and come into his courts.
9 Worship the LORD in the splendor of his holiness; tremble before him, all the earth.
10 Say among the nations, "The LORD reigns." The world is firmly established, it cannot be moved; he will judge the peoples with equity.
11 Let the heavens rejoice, let the earth be glad; let the sea resound, and all that is in it;
12 Let the fields be jubilant, and everything in them. Then all the trees of the forest will sing for joy;
13 They will sing before the LORD, for he comes, he comes to judge the earth. He will judge the world in righteousness and the peoples in his truth.

---

a. Recognize how glorious & strong He is

b. Give all glory to the LORD

c. Bring an offering in tribute to the LORD when you enter His presence

d. Worship the LORD
1) Bc. of His awesome holiness
2) Bc. everyone should fear & tremble before Him

3. Call on everyone to prepare for the LORD's coming

a. Bc. the LORD reigns: He will perfect His creation, 2 Pe.3:10-13

b. Bc. He will execute true justice

c. Bc. all creation will rejoice when the LORD comes
1) The heavens, the earth, & the sea will rejoice
2) The fields & the trees—all that grows on the earth—will sing for joy

d. Bc. the LORD's return is sure
1) He will restore true justice
2) He will judge in truth
- Take vengeance on the wicked
- Deliver the godly

PSALM 96

A Call to Bear Witness to All Peoples and Nations of the Earth, 96:1-13

(96:1-13) **Introduction:** just before Jesus ascended to heaven, He gave His followers their primary mission:

> **But you will receive power when the Holy Spirit comes on you; and you will be my witnesses in Jerusalem, and in all Judea and Samaria, and to the ends of the earth" (Ac.1:8).**

The primary mission of the church—as defined by Christ Himself—is to bear witness about Him in every corner of the earth. Christ commanded His followers to proclaim the gospel to every person (Mk.16:15). The church's Great Commission is to make disciples or followers of Christ who will, in turn, reach out to others and make disciples of them as well (Mt.28:18-20; 2 Ti.2:2). Through this method of multiplication, the gospel will be preached in all the earth.

Many churches today are involved in numerous programs, and they offer an array of activities to their church members. The majority of these endeavors are probably worthwhile causes. Sadly, though, too many churches have lost sight of their true calling: to make disciples and thereby participate in evangelizing the world.

Psalm 96 calls God's people to the task of bearing witness to all peoples and nations of the earth. It is a song about global worship. A compilation of previous psalms, it is prophetic in nature, pointing to the day when Christ returns and reigns over all the earth.

It is no coincidence that Ps.96:11 is at the exact center of the Bible. The very heart of God's Word points to that day when all of creation rejoices in the Lordship of Jesus Christ. Scripture declares that, on that day, every created being in every dimension of the universe will bow and confess that Jesus Christ is Lord (Ph.2:10-11). Even those in hell will acknowledge Jesus—God's sinless, crucified, risen Son—as Lord of all.

Even so, God loves all people, and He passionately desires that every individual freely receive Jesus Christ as Lord and Savior in *this* lifetime. God wants every person to live with Him eternally, where they can join the throng that sings praises to the Lamb forever. For this reason, Christ sent His followers into the world. This is, *A Call to Bear Witness to All Peoples and Nations of the Earth,* 96:1-13.

1. Call on all people of the earth to worship the LORD (vv.1-6).
2. Call on all nations of the earth to acknowledge the LORD (vv.7-9).
3. Call on everyone to prepare for the LORD's coming (vv.10-13).

1 (96:1-6) Call on all people of the earth to worship the LORD.

The psalmist invited all the peoples of the earth to worship the LORD. Israel was special to God, but the chosen nation understood that God loves the people of all nations. They also knew that the LORD was the only living and true God. This universal call to worship urged the Gentiles to turn from their lifeless idols to acknowledge the God of Abraham, Isaac, and Jacob as the only living God.

a. To sing a *new song* to Him (v.1).

The psalmist invited all the earth's inhabitants to join Israel in singing a new song to the LORD. A *new song* does not necessarily refer to a new composition, that is, a song that has been recently written or never sung before. Rather, it speaks of a fresh song, a song sung with new fervor, enthusiasm, and passion (see outline and notes—Ps.33:3 for more discussion). It is "a response that will match the freshness of [God's] mercies, which are 'new every morning.'"[1] This command reminds us that we must never allow our praise to become stale or heartless.

b. To praise Him—all He is (v.2ᵃ).

The psalmist invited the earth to bless His name. God's name is the representation of all that He is—His character, nature, attributes, and acts. Specifically, he called on the earth to praise the name of the *LORD* (Yahweh, Jehovah). This is God's personal name by which He revealed Himself to His people and made a covenant with them. Clearly, the invitation was to acknowledge the LORD, the God of Israel as God and to come into a relationship with Him.

c. To proclaim daily the good news that He saves us (v.2ᵇ).

The LORD is the God of salvation. He alone can save people from their sins. He loves people so much that He made a way for us to be forgiven and reconciled to Him. Those who have received God's salvation are commanded to proclaim daily the good news of salvation to others. As many commentators note, in the Septuagint (the ancient Greek translation of the Old Testament), *proclaim* is the word used for preaching the gospel. Accordingly, the psalmist not only invited the peoples of the earth to receive God's salvation but also to join Israel in making His salvation known to the world.

d. To make God's glory and His amazing works known among all people and nations (v.3).

One way God reveals Himself to humanity is through His works. Truly, we can see God's glory in the wonders of creation in countless ways every day (Ps.19:1-6). God had revealed Himself to the Gentile nations through His creation, but they were also aware of His wonders—the miraculous deeds He had performed in Israel's behalf. These amazing works should convince all the people of the earth that the LORD is God. For that reason, the psalmist invited them to acknowledge this and to join Israel in making God's glory known among all people and nations.

e. To declare how great and worthy of praise He is (vv.4-6).

The LORD's wondrous works establish His greatness over all other gods. Because the LORD is so great, He is worthy of all praise. Declaring that He is *most worthy of praise* means that He deserves the highest, most exalted praise. He alone is to be feared, not the other so-called gods worshipped by the pagan nations (v.4). The psalmist boldly declared that manmade gods are mere idols, false gods incapable of performing any deed whatsoever. In contrast to their total lack of amazing works, *the LORD made the heavens* (v.5). He alone is the Creator of the universe. He alone is the exalted LORD. His royal presence radiates honor and majesty. His sanctuary is filled with strength and beauty (v.6).

Thought 1. It is God's will that He be glorified by people of every nation, tribe, and language. Scripture is clear: God does not want any person to perish. It is His will that every individual be saved, that all repent and come to knowledge of the truth (2 Pe.3:9; 1 Ti.2:4). The Lord Jesus Christ has assigned *us* the responsibility of taking the gospel to the ends of the earth (Mt.28:18-20; Mk.16:15; Ac.1:8; 2 Co.5:18-20). As His ambassadors, we are to call all people of all nations to worship the LORD, and to join us in proclaiming that He is the God of salvation. We have the sacred task of taking the gospel to every person on earth so that they, too, might have the opportunity to be a part of that heavenly choir that will one day sing a *new song* to the Lamb of God (v.1; Re.5:9)!

> **And they sang a new song: "You are worthy to take the scroll and to open its seals, because you were slain, and with your blood you purchased men for God from every tribe and language and people and nation (Re.5:9).**
>
> **Who will not fear you, O Lord, and bring glory to your name? For you alone are holy. All nations will come and worship before you, for your righteous acts have been revealed" (Re.15:4).**
>
> **Sing to him a new song; play skillfully, and shout for joy (Ps.33:3).**

---

1 Derek Kidner. *Psalms 73-150*, p.379.

Praise the Lord. Sing to the Lord a new song, his praise in the assembly of the saints (Ps.149:1).

2 (96:7-9) Call on all nations of the earth to acknowledge the Lord.

The psalmist continued calling for universal worship of the Lord. The phrase "families of nations" speaks of all the tribes of the earth—every family in every group of people in every pocket of every nation. This call is an exhortation to turn from idols and to acknowledge the Lord as God (v.5).

a. Recognize how glorious and strong He is (v.7).

Only the Lord is glorious and strong. False gods can do nothing. They are lifeless objects made out of wood, stone, metal, or mere figments of people's imagination. The psalmist called on all people of the earth to recognize this truth and to ascribe all glory and strength to the Lord.

b. Give all glory to the Lord (v.8ᵃ).

Sadly, people gave their false gods the glory and worship that was due the Lord. Instead of worshipping the God who created them, they created gods within their own minds and credited their imaginary deities with the marvelous deeds performed by the Lord. The psalmist called on the people to stop robbing the Lord of the honor *He* deserved and give Him the glory due His great name (v.2).

c. Bring an offering in tribute to the Lord when you enter His presence (v.8ᵇ).

"In days of old every major act of worship found expression in a sacrifice."[2] This practice was followed by the false worshippers as well as by the people of God, who sacrificed in obedience to the Lord's commands. In accordance with this practice, the psalmist called on the families of the earth to bring an offering to the Lord when they entered His presence.

All of the sacrifices commanded under the law were fulfilled by the offering of Jesus Christ at Calvary. As believers under the New Covenant, we are commanded to offer spiritual sacrifices to the Lord (1 Pe.2:5). The spiritual sacrifices include...
- presenting our lives to Christ for His service (Ro.12:1)
- praise (He.13:15)
- winning souls to Christ (Ro.15:16)
- giving our financial and material resources to His work (Ph.4:18)
- helping and sharing with others (He.13:16)
- laying down our lives for the Lord if so required, dying because of our faith in Him (2 Ti.4:6)

d. Worship the Lord (v.9).

The psalmist called for all people to worship the Lord instead of their false gods. By definition, *worship* (shachah) includes the physical act of bowing down to the Lord, whether by bowing the head (Ge.24:26), kneeling (Ps.95:6), or falling on one's face and lying prostrate (Ge.48:12; Nu.22:31). Bowing was a gesture of respect and submission.

All humanity should bow down and worship the Lord because of His awesome holiness. When we grasp the beauty or splendor of God's holiness, we will see ourselves as we truly are—dark and filthy sinners in need of His cleansing (Is.6:1-7). When a person truly grasps the magnitude of the Lord's holiness, he or she will be stricken with fear and tremble before Him.

Thought 1. Sadly, people across the earth continue to give the Lord's glory to false gods. In fact, there is an ever-growing movement across the world insisting that all religions worship the same *so-called* god, and that he has revealed himself through many different religions. Christians especially are under increasing pressure to accept this false teaching. But the opinion that all religions worship the same god is a lie from Satan, and the pressure mounted against Christians to accept this is satanic.

Scripture clearly establishes that the one true God, the God who created all things, is the Lord. His name is *Yahweh* or *Jehovah.* The only way to enter into a relationship with Him is through His Son, Jesus Christ, who laid down His life as the sacrifice for our sin (Jn.14:6). As genuine believers, we must stand lovingly, but firmly, on this truth. We cannot be silent while others teach that there are many roads to heaven and that all religions worship the same God. The love of Christ constrains us to tell people the truth (2 Co.14-15). As we grow closer and closer to the return of Christ, persecution against those who stand faithfully on the gospel of Jesus Christ will grow more and more intense. Even so, we must not let anyone or anything stop us from calling on all people of all nations to acknowledge the Lord as the only living and true God. Nor can we allow any pressure—no matter how strong—to keep us from telling them that the only way to God is through His Son, Jesus Christ (Ac.4:12). We must be willing to follow the example of early believers and faithful martyrs down through the centuries who died with the name of Jesus on their lips, proclaiming that He alone is Lord and Savior.

Jesus answered, "I am the way and the truth and the life. No one comes to the Father except through me (Jn.14:6).
Salvation is found in no one else, for there is no other name under heaven given to men by which we must be saved" (Ac.4:12).

---

2 H.C. Leupold. *Exposition of the Psalms*, p.684.

For I tell you that Christ has become a servant of the Jews on behalf of God's truth, to confirm the promises made to the patriarchs so that the Gentiles may glorify God for his mercy, as it is written: "Therefore I will praise you among the Gentiles; I will sing hymns to your name." Again, it says, "Rejoice, O Gentiles, with his people." And again, "Praise the Lord, all you Gentiles, and sing praises to him, all you peoples." And again, Isaiah says, "The Root of Jesse will spring up, one who will arise to rule over the nations; the Gentiles will hope in him" (Ro.15:8-12).

From one New Moon to another and from one Sabbath to another, all mankind will come and bow down before me," says the LORD (Is.66:23).

My name will be great among the nations, from the rising to the setting of the sun. In every place incense and pure offerings will be brought to my name, because my name will be great among the nations," says the LORD Almighty (Mal.1:11).

3 (96:10-13) **Call on everyone to prepare for the LORD's coming.**

The psalmist concluded by calling on all the peoples of the earth to prepare for the LORD's coming. He prophesied of that future day when Christ will return to reign in righteousness. Emphasizing that this day would definitely come to pass, he warned all unbelievers that they would face the fierce judgment of the LORD.

a. **Because the LORD reigns: He will perfect His creation, 2 Pe.3:10-13 (v.10ᵃ).**

The phrase, "the LORD reigns" is more than a statement of God's sovereignty over the earth. It refers to the time when God's kingdom will be established on earth. With the complete revelation of God's Word before us, we know that God's kingdom will come when Jesus Christ returns to earth. As King of kings and Lord of lords, He will establish a perfect world order—a system of government that is firm and that cannot be moved or overthrown. After Christ reigns for a thousand years on this earth, God will destroy the current heavens and earth and create them anew in perfection (2 Pe.3:10-13). Throughout eternity, Jesus will reign over a new heaven and new earth in perfect righteousness.

b. **Because He will execute true justice (v.10ᵇ).**

As King of kings and Lord of lords, Christ will judge the people righteously. From east to west and north to south, true justice will be flawlessly executed in every corner of the earth. Christ's perfect justice will begin in His millennial reign, and it will continue throughout eternity in the new heaven and new earth.

c. **Because all creation will rejoice when the LORD comes (vv.11-12).**

When the LORD comes, all of creation—the heavens, the earth, the sea, and everything in them—will rejoice (v.11). The fields and the trees and everything that grows on the earth will sing for joy (v.12).

Scripture also says that all creation is anticipating this glorious day. Like a mother in labor, it is groaning in pain to give birth to that which is to come (Ro.8:19-22). When the LORD perfects His creation—a world cursed by man's sin—the elements of God's handiwork themselves will rejoice.

d. **Because the LORD's return is sure (v.13).**

The psalmist finished his compelling statements by announcing that the LORD's return is sure; it is an absolute certainty. This declaration serves as an encouragement to believers and a warning to the unbelievers of the world. Although skeptics have always scoffed at the promise of Christ's return (2 Pe.3:3-4), God's Word stands sure. The LORD is coming to judge the earth (2 Pe.3:5-7; Jude 14-15). And when He comes, Christ will not only restore true justice to the world, but He will also take vengeance on the wicked and deliver the godly from them.

Thought 1. We are responsible to challenge every person to prepare for the coming of the LORD. Jesus is coming again, and with every passing day, we are one day closer to His return. Scoffers continue to doubt God's Word, but their claims cannot change the truth that the day of the Lord will come (2 Pe.3:10). We have been called to sound the alarm and to warn the world of impending judgment. As watchmen of peoples' souls, we are not responsible for their response to the truth, but we are responsible to warn them (Eze.33:7-9). Furthermore, we will be held accountable by Him for our obedience or disobedience in bearing witness to the world.

He commanded us to preach to the people and to testify that he is the one whom God appointed as judge of the living and the dead (Ac.10:42).

First of all, you must understand that in the last days scoffers will come, scoffing and following their own evil desires. They will say, "Where is this 'coming' he promised? Ever since our fathers died, everything goes on as it has since the beginning of creation." But they deliberately forget that long ago by God's word the heavens existed and the earth was formed out of water and by water. By these waters also the world of that time was deluged and destroyed. By the same word the present heavens and earth are reserved for fire, being kept for the day of judgment and destruction of ungodly men. But do not forget this one thing, dear friends: With the Lord a day is like a thousand years, and a thousand years are like a day. The Lord is not slow in keeping his promise, as some understand slowness. He is patient with you, not wanting anyone to perish, but everyone to come to repentance. But the day of the Lord will come like a thief. The heavens will disappear with a roar; the elements will be destroyed by fire, and the earth and everything in it will be laid bare (2 Pe.3:3-10).

Enoch, the seventh from Adam, prophesied about these men: "See, the Lord is coming with thousands upon thousands of his holy ones to judge everyone, and to convict all the ungodly of all the ungodly acts they have done in the ungodly way, and of all the harsh words ungodly sinners have spoken against him." (Jude 14-15).

And I saw the dead, great and small, standing before the throne, and books were opened. Another book was opened, which is the book of life. The dead were judged according to what they had done as recorded in the books (Re.20:12).

The LORD reigns forever; he has established his throne for judgment (Ps.9:7).

He will judge between the nations and will settle disputes for many peoples. They will beat their swords into plowshares and their spears into pruning hooks. Nation will not take up sword against nation, nor will they train for war anymore (Is.2:4).

	PSALM 97	7 All who worship images are put to shame, those who boast in idols—worship him, all you gods!	2. Warn all who trust in worthless idols: They will be shamed
1. Proclaim the truth to all the earth: The LORD reigns! Rejoice!	**When People Have a Distorted View of God, 97:1-12**	8 Zion hears and rejoices and the villages of Judah are glad because of your judgments, O LORD.	a. Bc. all will eventually bow to the LORD, Ph.3:9-11
a. He is awe-inspiring, veiled in clouds far above human sight & understanding	The LORD reigns, let the earth be glad; let the distant shores rejoice.	9 For you, O LORD, are the Most High over all the earth; you are exalted far above all gods.	b. Bc. God's people will rejoice when God executes justice on earth: They will be vindicated
b. He rules in righteousness & justice	2 Clouds and thick darkness surround him; righteousness and justice are the foundation of his throne.	10 Let those who love the LORD hate evil, for he guards the lives of his faithful ones and delivers them from the hand of the wicked.	c. Bc. God is the Most High: He is exalted far above all so-called (false) gods
c. He consumes His enemies with fiery holiness—all who reject & rebel against Him	3 Fire goes before him and consumes his foes on every side.		**3. Encourage true believers—all who love the LORD—to hate evil**
d. He bears witness of Himself	4 His lightning lights up the world; the earth sees and trembles.	11 Light is shed upon the righteous and joy on the upright in heart.	a. Bc. God protects you & delivers you from the wicked
1) Thru the forces of nature • Lightning • Earthquakes & volcanic eruptions	5 The mountains melt like wax before the LORD, before the Lord of all the earth.	12 Rejoice in the LORD, you who are righteous, and praise his holy name.	b. Bc. God's light guides you & His joy floods your heart
2) Thru the heavens: They declare His rgt. & glory, that His rule is good & orderly	6 The heavens proclaim his righteousness, and all the peoples see his glory.		c. Bc. all you who are righteous should walk rejoicing in Him & praising His holy name

PSALM 97

When People Have a Distorted View of God, 97:1-12

(97:1-12) **Introduction:** without a doubt, we are living in a day and age when the bulk of humanity does not understand who God really is and what He is like. Although God has clearly revealed Himself to the human race through nature, many people reject this knowledge. They also reject the revelation of God's inspired Word, the Holy Bible. Instead, they choose to believe a particular secular theory or some other fabricated proposal as the origin of the universe and life (Ro.1:19-23). By rejecting the knowledge of God, they remove themselves from accountability for their actions—or so they think. If there is no God, they reason, there is no judgment.

Other people believe there is a God, but they view Him according to their own ideas rather than holding to the truth of Scripture. They deny God's holiness, declaring evil to be good and good to be evil (Is.5:20). In reality, they create their own god: a god who agrees with them and condones their sinful behavior, a god who designs people to be the way they are, that is, who programs into them their sinful desires, desires that contradict the truth of God's Holy Word.

Still others see God exclusively as a God of love, not a God of holiness and judgment. They brazenly deny the truth of judgment as revealed in Scripture, that God will judge all unrighteousness and ungodliness in men (Ro.1:18; 2:2, 5-6, 16). A loving God, after all, would never condemn anyone—or so they think.

Across the globe, countless people are trapped in false religions. They worship human beings, animals, perversions of God, and false deities. They see God through the teachings of their cults and man-conceived doctrines.

Psalm 97 continues a series of psalms proclaiming and celebrating the LORD as King. They shout out the truth that the LORD reigns, regardless of what people believe and profess. God's holiness cannot be compromised, and His judgment on all sin is sure. Ultimately, these psalms will find their fulfillment in the reign of Christ over all the earth.

The ninety-seventh psalm also encourages those who truly follow God, who live in the midst of a world that rejects the truth about Him. It exhorts us to stand firm on the truth of God and to rejoice in the glory that is to come. This is, *When People Have a Distorted View of God,* 97:1-12.

1. Proclaim the truth to all the earth: The LORD reigns! Rejoice! (vv.1-6).
2. Warn all who trust in worthless idols: They will be shamed (vv.7-9).
3. Encourage true believers—all who love the LORD—to hate evil (vv.10-12).

1 (97:1-6) **Proclaim the truth to all the earth: The LORD reigns! Rejoice!**

The psalmist began by proclaiming the truth that the LORD reigns, calling on creation itself to rejoice in His kingship (v.1; 96:11-13). The *earth* refers to the continents, the large masses of land. In contrast, the *distant shores* are the small islands that dot the sea. The inhabitants of all these places are included in the call. All are to celebrate the righteous reign of God over the earth.

a. He is awe-inspiring, veiled in clouds far above human sight and understanding (vv.1-2ᵃ).

The psalmist described God's awe-inspiring and intimidating throne with God sitting in sovereign judgment over the entire universe. The throne is veiled in clouds and darkness, symbolizing that God reigns far above human sight and understanding. The clouds and darkness also serve as a shroud that conceals humanity from the radiant glory of God's holiness. "On Sinai when God came down, there were 'thunderings and lightnings, and a thick cloud' (Ex.19:16). Not even Moses could see His face and live (Ex.33:20)."[1]

b. He rules in righteousness and justice (v.2ᵇ).

From His holy throne, the LORD reigns in righteousness and justice, or judgment. These holy attributes are the habitation or foundation of His reign. God is the Judge of the earth, and He always does what is right (Ge.18:25; Ps.94:2). His rule is built on righteousness and the fair execution of justice on all who fall short of His absolute holiness.

c. He consumes His enemies with fiery holiness—all who reject and rebel against Him (v.3).

Because of the LORD's holy and righteous judgment, He is to be greatly feared. The psalmist described fire—a symbol of God's judgment—shooting forth from His presence and consuming His enemies (Ps.21:9; Is.29:6; 2 Th.1:8; He.10:27; 12:29). All who reject and rebel against Him must face the fiery judgment demanded by His uncompromised holiness.

d. He bears witness of Himself (vv.4-6).

The LORD bears witness of His holiness and justice through the forces of nature. When flashes of lightning illuminate the night sky, we are reminded of God's terrifying power (v.4ᵃ). Earthquakes are described as the earth's trembling in fear of Him (v.4ᵇ). Volcanic eruptions are depicted as the mountains' melting like wax at His presence (v.5; Mi.1:4). This image may also be a prophetic picture of the day of the LORD, when "the elements will be destroyed by fire," and the earth and everything in it will be burned up (2 Pe.3:10).

God also bears witness of His holiness and justice through the heavens—the skies and the sun, the moon and the stars (v.6). They majestically declare His righteousness and glory, testifying by their orderliness that everything God does is good and perfect (Ps.19:1-6).

Thought 1. We are to proclaim the truth that the LORD reigns. Regardless of...
- what the world may say, the LORD reigns
- what is going on around us, the LORD reigns

- the unbelief and lawlessness that grip our society, the LORD reigns
- whatever we may be forced to endure, the LORD reigns

The LORD—Yahweh, Jehovah—is God, and He will forever reign in righteousness and holiness. This means that His judgment of all unbelievers is sure. Knowing that, we need to proclaim the truth about God's holiness, about His righteousness and judgment. We need to point people to the God of the Bible: a God who loves humanity so much that He gave His only Son for our sins but who is also just—a consuming fire. All who reject Him will suffer the full measure of His fierce wrath.

> **And give relief to you who are troubled, and to us as well. This will happen when the Lord Jesus is revealed from heaven in blazing fire with his powerful angels. He will punish those who do not know God and do not obey the gospel of our Lord Jesus. They will be punished with everlasting destruction and shut out from the presence of the Lord and from the majesty of his power (2 Th.1:7-9).**
>
> **Now to the King eternal, immortal, invisible, the only God, be honor and glory for ever and ever. Amen (1 Ti.1:17).**
>
> **But only a fearful expectation of judgment and of raging fire that will consume the enemies of God (He.10:27).**
>
> **The LORD will reign for ever and ever" (Ex.15:18).**
>
> **Let the heavens rejoice, let the earth be glad; let them say among the nations, "The LORD reigns!" (1 Chr.16:31).**
>
> **But the LORD is the true God; he is the living God, the eternal King. When he is angry, the earth trembles; the nations cannot endure his wrath (Je.10:10).**

2 (97:7-9) Warn all who trust in worthless idols: They will be shamed.

The psalmist next addressed those who trust in worthless idols. He issued a serious warning: those who serve and boast in idols will be shamed or confounded. Idol worshippers will sink in disgrace on that day when their gods are proven to be nothing but lifeless objects and the satanically-inspired creations of human imagination (Is.45:15-17).

a. Because all will eventually bow to the LORD, Ph.3:9-11 (v.7).

As if the pagans' false gods had life and were actually capable of doing so, the psalmist commanded them to

---

1 Donald Williams. *Psalms 73-150*, p.193.

bow down and worship the LORD. Some commentators feel that *gods* refers to demons, as they are the powers behind idol worship. Commentator J.J. Stewart Perowne, however, sees a reference to the Philistine idol Dagon falling down before the ark of God (1 S.5:1-5). "As all the worshipers are confounded," Perowne wrote, "so must all the objects of their worship be overthrown...all must yield before Him who is the Lord of the whole earth."[2] Indeed, every being in every dimension will one day bow down and confess that Jesus Christ is Lord (Ph.3:9-11).

b. **Because God's people will rejoice when God executes justice on earth: They will be vindicated (v.8).**

In addition to the termination of all idol worship, the prophesied day of the LORD will bring God's judgment on all evildoers. When God executes justice on earth, Zion and the villages of Judah will greatly rejoice. *Zion* and the *villages of Judah* refer literally to Jerusalem and the Jewish people, whom Christ will deliver when He returns to earth. In effect, they represent all of God's people who will be vindicated and see their enemies avenged on that great and terrible day.

c. **Because God is the Most High: He is exalted far above all so-called (false) gods (v.9).**

The psalmist concluded this warning by firmly declaring that the LORD is *the Most High* [Elyon], high above all the earth. The entire universe and everything in it is His (Ge.14:19). This means, of course, that the LORD is above all false gods, above all who worship them, and above all who persecute His people. Each and everyone should cringe in fear before Him (Ps.96:4-5).

Thought 1. Like the psalmist, we need to boldly warn those who worship other gods, or no god at all, that they will suffer eternal shame if they do not turn to the LORD. Scripture is clear: every knee *will* bow to the LORD. Every tongue *will* confess that Jesus Christ is Lord—willingly or unwillingly. Jesus *will* reign, and those of every age in every dimension *will* acknowledge Him.

As followers of Christ, we are commissioned to be His witnesses. We have to stand firm against the world's pressure to silence us. At the same time, when we point people to the truth, we are not trying to force our beliefs on anyone. Rather, we are simply following our Lord's example to love people enough to share the good news of the gospel with them so they can escape the coming day of justice and judgment and live eternally with God.

Warning others about the truth can cost us a great deal: our families, our friends, our liberty, and, in many places, our lives. Still, we must be faithful to the command of the One who called us to be His witnesses throughout the earth.

It is written: "'As surely as I live,' says the Lord, 'every knee will bow before me; every tongue will confess to God'" (Ro.14:11).

Therefore God exalted him to the highest place and gave him the name that is above every name, that at the name of Jesus every knee should bow, in heaven and on earth and under the earth, and every tongue confess that Jesus Christ is Lord, to the glory of God the Father (Ph.2:9-11).

Then I heard every creature in heaven and on earth and under the earth and on the sea, and all that is in them, singing: "To him who sits on the throne and to the Lamb be praise and honor and glory and power, for ever and ever!" (Re.5:13).

But those who trust in idols, who say to images, 'You are our gods,' will be turned back in utter shame. (Is.42:17).

"Turn to me and be saved, all you ends of the earth; for I am God, and there is no other. By myself I have sworn, my mouth has uttered in all integrity a word that will not be revoked: Before me every knee will bow; by me every tongue will swear. They will say of me, 'In the LORD alone are righteousness and strength.'" All who have raged against him will come to him and be put to shame (Is.45:22-24).

He was given authority, glory and sovereign power; all peoples, nations and men of every language worshiped him. His dominion is an everlasting dominion that will not pass away, and his kingdom is one that will never be destroyed (Da.7:14).

3 (97:10-12) **Encourage true believers—all who love the LORD—to hate evil.**

The psalmist then encouraged true believers—all who genuinely love the LORD—to hate evil (Pr.8:13; Ro.12:9). But we must always remember that we can stand against evil only in the power of God's strength (Ep.6:10-17). Therefore, we need to constantly cling to God and His truth lest we be conformed to the wickedness of this world (Ro.12:2). When we walk in God's light, we know that He will judge all evil, and His righteousness will reign throughout eternity. Consequently, we can rejoice in Him knowing that He will always be victorious.

---

2 J.J. Stewart Perowne, *The Book of Psalms*, p.473.

a. Because God protects you and delivers you from the wicked (v.10).

When we hate evil and stand against it, we can expect the ungodly to rise up against us. However, we need not take matters into our own hands against those who do evil toward us. Instead, we can trust God to protect us and to deliver us from the wicked. God is the Most High; therefore, He is in control of our lives (Ro.12:17-21). Because we love Him, He has promised to work all things together for our good and to accomplish His purpose for us (Ro.8:28).

b. Because God's light guides you and His joy floods your heart (v.11).

We who love the LORD are given His light and His joy. God's light is the guidance He gives us through His Word and His indwelling Spirit (Ps.119:105; Ro.8:14). Light also represents the dawning of a new day—the day of righteousness that will emerge when Christ returns to earth to establish His kingdom. The seeds of this light, this glorious day, have been sown in our hearts through the prophetic promises in God's Word. In addition, gladness will flood the hearts of the upright when evildoers are judged and righteousness reigns (Ps.119:130; Is.60:1-5).

c. Because all you who are righteous should walk rejoicing in Him and praising His holy name (v.12).

Because we know and believe God's Word, these seeds of light and joy should also gladden our hearts now. We understand that...

- the LORD will judge evildoers and vindicate us (v.8)
- the LORD is the Most High (v.9)
- the LORD protects and delivers us (v.10)
- the LORD is coming again and will reign in righteousness (vv.1, 6, 11)

Keeping all of this in mind, we who are righteous should rejoice in the LORD, giving thanks and praising His holy name even in the midst of the darkness that characterizes our present age.

Thought 1. As stated in the Introduction, we are living in a time when the majority of people around the world have a distorted view of God. In our lifetime, the truth of God's Word is being rejected as never before. People refuse to acknowledge God as their Creator and Judge. Instead of worshipping Him, they worship the idols of pleasure, possessions, and power. As a result, persecution of believers is rapidly spreading across the globe.

If we truly love the LORD, we will hate the evil of our God-rejecting world. We will not allow ourselves to be conformed to the warped thinking and values of this permissive society. We will stand firm on God's truth, refusing to bow beneath the pressure to accept sinful abominations as normal and honorable. We will refuse to bow down to governments and terrorists who demand that we deny our faith in Jesus Christ. Regardless of the cost, we will stand fast—if we genuinely love the LORD.

In spite of the spreading darkness, we who love the LORD should not be discouraged. God is the Most High, and He is in control. We need to entrust ourselves into His care, always looking toward the day of Christ's return to deliver us from this evil world (Tit.2:13). As commentator Derek Kidner wrote, "Encouragement to hold on till daylight and victory come is the note on which the psalm ends."[3] We have every reason to be encouraged and to be overflowing with hope. May God help us to walk in His truth, always rejoicing in the glory that is to come (1 Pe.4:12-13)!

> **"Do not let your hearts be troubled. Trust in God; trust also in me. In my Father's house are many rooms; if it were not so, I would have told you. I am going there to prepare a place for you. And if I go and prepare a place for you, I will come back and take you to be with me that you also may be where I am (Jn.14:1-3)**
>
> **Love must be sincere. Hate what is evil; cling to what is good (Ro.12:9).**
>
> **Avoid every kind of evil (1 Th.5:22).**
>
> **It teaches us to say "No" to ungodliness and worldly passions, and to live self-controlled, upright and godly lives in this present age, while we wait for the blessed hope—the glorious appearing of our great God and Savior, Jesus Christ (Tit.2:12-13)**
>
> **Dear friend, do not imitate what is evil but what is good. Anyone who does what is good is from God. Anyone who does what is evil has not seen God (3 Jn.11).**
>
> **I have kept my feet from every evil path so that I might obey your word (Ps.119:101).**
>
> **Do not be wise in your own eyes; fear the LORD and shun evil (Pr.3:7).**
>
> **To fear the LORD is to hate evil; I hate pride and arrogance, evil behavior and perverse speech (Pr.8:13).**

---

3   Derek Kidner. *Psalms 73-150*, p.383.

PSALM 98

A Celebration of God's Victory Over the World, 98:1-9

A Psalm.

1. Praise the Lord for His salvation

a. Bc. through His power (right hand & holy arm) He gained the victory & saved you

b. Bc. He uses your deliverance to bear strong witness to unbelievers—a witness of His salvation & righteousness

c. Bc. He remembers His promises
1) That He will love & be faithful to you (all His people)
2) That the ends of the world will witness His salvation

Sing to the LORD a new song, for he has done marvelous things; his right hand and his holy arm have worked salvation for him.
2 The LORD has made his salvation known and revealed his righteousness to the nations.
3 He has remembered his love and his faithfulness to the house of Israel; all the ends of the earth have seen the salvation of our God.

4 Shout for joy to the LORD, all the earth, burst into jubilant song with music;
5 Make music to the LORD with the harp, with the harp and the sound of singing,
6 With trumpets and the blast of the ram's horn—shout for joy before the LORD, the King.
7 Let the sea resound, and everything in it, the world, and all who live in it.
8 Let the rivers clap their hands, let the mountains sing together for joy;
9 Let them sing before the LORD, for he comes to judge the earth. He will judge the world in righteousness and the peoples with equity.

2. Worship the LORD, the King of all

a. Invite everyone—all the earth—to break into joyful song & praise
1) Playing musical instruments
2) Blowing the trumpet & ram's horn
3) Making a joyful noise

b. Summon all of nature to praise Him
1) The sea & its creatures
2) The world & its people, 7
3) The rivers & the mountains

3. Call on all creation to celebrate the LORD's coming

a. He is coming to judge the earth
b. He will execute justice righteously & fairly

PSALM 98

A Celebration of God's Victory Over the World, 98:1-9

(98:1-9) **Introduction:** a universal war has been in motion ever since Lucifer rebelled against God and was cast out of heaven (Is.14:12-14; see DEEPER STUDY #1, *Satan*—Re.12:9 for more discussion). Often called *the battle between good and evil*, it is the war Satan and his demonic forces are waging against God. In Satan's quest to hurt and cut the heart of God, he continually opposes God's works, His purposes, and His people. Satan is seeking revenge, seeking to get back at God by destroying people's lives. Why? Because in the ancient past, God executed justice and judgment upon him.

Throughout history, Satan has won many battles, beginning with the very first human beings on earth. He successfully tempted Adam and Eve to sin in the Garden of Eden. On every level—from individual hearts to world events—Satan has known a measure of success, for sinners are always available to do his bidding. However, Scripture reveals how this war will end: God will prevail, and Satan will be cast into the lake of fire for all eternity (Re.20:10).

Psalm 98 is a celebration of God's victory over the world. Many scholars think the occasion for its writing was God's deliverance of His people from the Babylonian captivity. As the psalm progresses, the focus shifts from this particular victory to God's ultimate victory when He comes to judge and rule the world in righteousness.

These are dark days we are living in, and we can only expect the world's condition to worsen as we approach the return of Christ (2 Ti.3:1, 13). Why? Because Satan will fight more viciously than ever as he senses his reign is nearing its end (Re.12:12). At times, it may seem that there is no hope for humanity or for this sin-cursed world. It is then that we should turn to this song and lift our hearts up to the LORD. This is, *A Celebration of God's Victory Over the World*, 98:1-9.

1. Praise the Lord for His salvation (vv.1-3).
2. Worship the LORD, the King of all (vv.4-8).
3. Call on all creation to celebrate the LORD's coming (v.9).

1 (98:1-3) **Praise the Lord for His salvation.**
The psalmist called for a *new song* to celebrate God's salvation of His people. God had done a wonderful work on their behalf by victoriously delivering them. His fresh blessings deserved a fresh expression of their praise.

a. Because through His power (right hand and holy arm) He gained the victory and saved you (v.1).
Through His incomparable power, God gained the victory for His people and saved them. God's *right hand* and His *arm* are both symbols of His mighty power. The description of His arm as *holy* emphasizes that He used His great power to perform an act of righteousness. If the occasion for this psalm was the people's return from Babylonian captivity, *holy* would speak of God's righteousness in fulfilling His promise to deliver His people after seventy years (Je.25:9-12; 29:10).

b. Because He uses your deliverance to bear strong witness to unbelievers (v.2).
God's deliverance of His people was a compelling witness to unbelievers of His salvation and righteousness. The Gentile nations observed God's righteousness in that He did not overlook His people's disobedience. But they also saw His salvation in that He came to their aid and rescued them from their oppressors.

c. **Because He remembers His promises (v.3).**

The psalmist called for fresh praise to the LORD because of His unfailing love and faithfulness. *Unfailing love* (chesed) is God's covenant love. *Faithfulness* (emunah) is His truth. The LORD had remembered His covenant promises to Israel and graciously delivered the people from captivity, proving that He will love and be faithful to His people. As a result, His salvation was witnessed to the ends of the earth—all throughout the world.

Thought 1. God's deliverance of His people is a picture of the eternal salvation He offers to all humanity. All of us are sinners; therefore, because God is righteous, He simply cannot overlook our sin. He has to judge us because of our sin. But He rescued us from the bondage of sin by sending His Son, Jesus Christ, to bear our judgment on the cross. By His mighty power, He defeated Satan and death. Thus, we can be delivered from sin—both its penalty and its power over us—if we will genuinely repent and believe in Him.

We who have received God's great salvation should praise Him every day of our lives. And, through our transformed lives and the witness of our words, we should make God's glorious salvation known to unbelievers. God wants His salvation to be seen throughout the world, and we have been commissioned to carry it to the ends of the earth.

> "For God so loved the world that he gave his one and only Son, that whoever believes in him shall not perish but have eternal life. For God did not send his Son into the world to condemn the world, but to save the world through him (Jn.3:16-17).
>
> That God was reconciling the world to himself in Christ, not counting men's sins against them. And he has committed to us the message of reconciliation. We are therefore Christ's ambassadors, as though God were making his appeal through us. We implore you on Christ's behalf: Be reconciled to God (2 Co.5:19-20).
>
> Who gave himself for our sins to rescue us from the present evil age, according to the will of our God and Father (Ga.1:4).
>
> And, once made perfect, he became the source of eternal salvation for all who obey him (He.5:9).
>
> But I trust in your unfailing love; my heart rejoices in your salvation (Ps.13:5).
>
> Then my soul will rejoice in the LORD and delight in his salvation (Ps.35:9).
>
> Surely God is my salvation; I will trust and not be afraid. The LORD, the

> LORD, is my strength and my song; he has become my salvation" (Is.12:2).

2 (98:4-8) **Worship the LORD, the King of all.**

The psalmist again called for a loud shout or joyful noise to be raised to the LORD. This time, he invited all the people of the earth to participate, as well as the elements of nature. Every segment of creation should worship the LORD, the King of all.

a. **Invite everyone—all the earth—to break into joyful song and praise (vv.4-6).**

The psalmist implored everyone on earth to break into a song of praise to the LORD (v.4). *Shout for joy* (ruah) means to shout loudly and triumphantly for joy. The people's singing was to be accompanied by the playing of musical instruments (v.5), the blowing of trumpets (v.6ᵃ), and the blast of the shophar, that is, the cornet or ram's horn (v.6ᵇ). The shophar held a special significance for the Jews. It announced the beginning of the festival season as well as the Year of Jubilee (Le.23:24; Ps.81:3; Le.25:8-9). This occasion of God's salvation deserved the full measure of celebration reserved for those special times. Likewise, it was worthy of the people's most energetic and enthusiastic praise, prompting the psalmist to repeat the command to shout for joy (v.6ᶜ).

b. **Summon all of nature to praise Him (vv.7-8).**

Next, the psalmist summoned all of nature to join the song of praise to the LORD for His great victory and salvation:

➤ The sea and everything—all the creatures—in it (v.7ᵃ)
➤ The world and all of its people (v.7ᵇ)
➤ The rivers and mountains (v.8)

Thought 1. When man sinned, the entire universe was affected. Ever since then, all of creation has suffered under the curse of sin (Ge.3:17). In addition, creation has suffered abuse at the hands of sinful humans beings who are selfish, indifferent, and corrupt, recklessly damaging and polluting the earth's environment.

Through Christ's death on the cross, He redeemed everything that was lost because of sin. This includes creation itself. Scripture teaches that the created world anticipates the coming of Christ and its deliverance from the corruption of sin (Ro.8:19-22). Even nature is depicted in Scripture as joining humanity in praising God for His great salvation. In fact, nature itself will be saved from sin's corruption along with human beings. Then all the redeemed will worship the LORD, the King of the universe, for His unfailing love and faithfulness.

That at the name of Jesus every knee should bow, in heaven and on earth and under the earth, and every tongue confess that Jesus Christ is Lord, to the glory of God the Father (Ph.2:10-11).

Then I heard every creature in heaven and on earth and under the earth and on the sea, and all that is in them, singing: "To him who sits on the throne and to the Lamb be praise and honor and glory and power, for ever and ever!" (Re.5:13).

Let the heavens rejoice, let the earth be glad; let them say among the nations, "The LORD reigns!" (1 Chr.16:31).

All the ends of the earth will remember and turn to the LORD, and all the families of the nations will bow down before him, for dominion belongs to the LORD and he rules over the nations (Ps.22:27-28).

All the earth bows down to you; they sing praise to you, they sing praise to your name." Selah (Ps.66:4).

You will go out in joy and be led forth in peace; the mountains and hills will burst into song before you, and all the trees of the field will clap their hands. Instead of the thornbush will grow the pine tree, and instead of briers the myrtle will grow. This will be for the LORD's renown, for an everlasting sign, which will not be destroyed" (Is.55:12-13).

3 (98:9) **Call on all creation to celebrate the LORD's coming.**

The call for unreserved praise now shifts from the LORD's present victory in delivering His people to His future triumph over the world. The psalmist called on all creation to celebrate His coming. The LORD is coming in power and great glory to judge the earth. At that moment in time, for the first time since Adam sinned, perfect justice will reign on the earth. The LORD will execute justice righteously and fairly throughout the world. Although righteousness and justice have suffered many defeats through the ages, in the end, God will be victorious. His righteousness will reign throughout eternity.

Thought 1. The call for a universal celebration of the LORD's coming is a call to praise God's Son, Jesus Christ. It is He who is coming to earth to rule and reign in righteousness. It is He who will judge the

world (Jn.5:22; Ac.17:31). Scripture reveals that when He returns, He will conquer this present earth and rule over it for one thousand years (see DEEPER STUDY #2, *Jesus Christ, Millennial Reign*—Re.20:4-6 for more discussion). He will also immediately judge all existing ungodliness and evildoers. At the end of the millennium (His one thousand year reign), the unbelieving dead of every age will stand before Him at the Great White Throne Judgment (Re.20:11-15). There, they will be judged for their works—every sinful thought, word, and deed of their lives—and be cast into the lake of fire for eternity. Following that final judgment, the present heavens and earth will be destroyed, a new heaven and new earth will be created, and Christ will reign as King of kings and Lord of lords throughout eternity (2 Pe.3:10:13).

Beginning at the Garden of Eden, Satan has won many battles throughout world history. But ultimately, God will win the war. He will be victorious over the world, and all of creation will exalt His Son, Jesus Christ, as Lord. Until that glorious day comes, we are to lift up His name in the highest praise for the great salvation He has promised.

"At that time men will see the Son of Man coming in clouds with great power and glory (Mk.13:26).

"Men of Galilee," they said, "why do you stand here looking into the sky? This same Jesus, who has been taken from you into heaven, will come back in the same way you have seen him go into heaven" (Ac.1:11).

Enoch, the seventh from Adam, prophesied about these men: "See, the Lord is coming with thousands upon thousands of his holy ones to judge everyone, and to convict all the ungodly of all the ungodly acts they have done in the ungodly way, and of all the harsh words ungodly sinners have spoken against him." (Jude 14-15).

Then I saw a great white throne and him who was seated on it. Earth and sky fled from his presence, and there was no place for them (Re.20:11).

"In my vision at night I looked, and there before me was one like a son of man, coming with the clouds of heaven. He approached the Ancient of Days and was led into his presence (Da.7:13).

	PSALM 99	and worship at his foot-stool; he is holy.	**Exalt Him & worship at His feet**
	When People Need a Renewed Vision of God, 99:1-9	6 Moses and Aaron were among his priests, Samuel was among those who called on his name; they called on the LORD and he answered them.	a. Bc. He is holy
1. Summon the people & the earth itself to tremble before the LORD	The LORD reigns, let the nations tremble; he sits enthroned between the cherubim, let the earth shake.		b. Bc. He answers & helps all who call on Him (He.4:14-16): The example of Moses, Aaron, & Samuel leading Israel
a. Bc. He is so awesome: He reigns between the cherubim			1) They called on Him
b. Bc. He is great: He works out all things for His people (Zion) & is exalted above all nations	2 Great is the LORD in Zion; he is exalted over all the nations.	7 He spoke to them from the pillar of cloud; they kept his statutes and the decrees he gave them.	2) He spoke & guided them by a pillar of cloud
c. Bc. He is holy: His great & awesome name is to be praised by all people & nations	3 Let them praise your great and awesome name—he is holy.		3) They obeyed His Word
d. Bc. He is mighty: He is the King who loves perfect justice	4 The King is mighty, he loves justice—you have established equity; in Jacob you have done what is just and right.	8 O LORD our God, you answered them; you were to Israel a forgiving God, though you punished their misdeeds.	4) He forgave their sins when they asked for forgiveness, but He disciplined them when they went astray
1) He establishes equity: Fair treatment			c. Bc. He deserves your exaltation, reverence, & worship
2) He does what is just & right		9 Exalt the LORD our God and worship at his holy mountain, for the LORD our God is holy.	1) Due to His helping you, 6-8
2. Submit yourself to the LORD:	5 Exalt the LORD our God		2) Due to His holiness

PSALM 99

When People Need a Renewed Vision of God, 99:1-9

(99:1-9) **Introduction:** one of the ways we can know and appreciate God more fully is to study His attributes. God's attributes are the unique characteristics and qualities that He alone possesses. As humans, we may exhibit these qualities to some degree, but only God demonstrates them fully—perfectly and without fail. God alone is completely...

- holy
- good
- loving
- merciful
- wise
- true
- faithful
- righteous
- just
- eternal
- unchangeable
- all-powerful (omnipotent)
- all-knowing (omniscient)
- present everywhere (omnipresent)

Psalm 99 emphasizes one of these attributes in particular: God's holiness. One-third of the psalm's verses state the fundamental truth that *God is holy* (vv.3, 5, 9). It stands apart from the other enthronement psalms in this section (93–100), calling for a spirit of reverence rather than celebration.

Of all God's attributes, His holiness may be the most ignored in the church today as well as in the world. Pastor and commentator Donald M. Williams accurately and effectively states the attitude of our world and churches toward God's holiness:

> *That God is holy receives little pulpit or pew attention today. In this anxious age, we want a God who makes us feel secure...who accepts us...who will build our self-esteem and forgive our sins. But we would rather avoid holiness with its themes of moral absolutes.* [1]

Our world today is the fulfillment of what Paul described in Romans 1:18-32. It is a world that has lost sight of who God is and what He is like, a world to whom God has revealed Himself but that refuses to glorify Him as God. To many people, God is nothing more than the product of their vain imaginations (Ro.1:21). They view God as they wish to see Him, not as He has revealed Himself in His Word and in His son, the Lord Jesus Christ. As a result, sin and wickedness run rampant throughout the world (Ro.1:28-31). Integrity and moral values have all but disappeared. People even take pleasure in violating God's laws, totally ignoring or overlooking the fact that God is watching and that they one day face His righteous judgment (Ro.1:32).

The world desperately needs to see God as He really is. As Dr. Williams went on to say, "Whether we like it or not, God is holy and ultimately we will have to deal with Him as He is." [2] This is, *When People Need a Renewed Vision of God*, 99:1-9.

1. Summon the people and the earth itself to tremble before the LORD (vv.1-4).
2. Submit yourself to the LORD: Exalt Him and worship at His feet (vv.5-9).

1 (99:1-4) **Summon the people and the earth itself to tremble before the LORD.**

As in previous psalms, Psalm 98 begins with the proclamation that the LORD reigns over all (v.1; 93:1; 97:1). With that in mind, the psalmist summoned the people and the earth itself to tremble before Him. Four of God's attributes should stir the universe to fear Him.

---

1 Donald Williams. *Psalms 73-150*, p.201.

2 Ibid, p.201.

a. Because He is so awesome: He reigns between the cherubim (v.1).

The earth should tremble before the LORD because He is awesome. The psalmist emphasized how magnificent and fearsome the LORD's presence is by focusing attention on His holy throne where He reigns between the cherubim (Nu.7:89; 1 S.4:4; Is.37:16). The mercy seat in the temple—the earthly center of God's presence—was overshadowed by two golden cherubim. These figures were a representation of God's heavenly throne, which is surrounded by angels that protect and proclaim God's holiness (Is.6:1-3; He.9:24).

b. Because He is great: He works out all things for His people (Zion) and is exalted above all nations (v.2).

Second, the psalmist emphasized the LORD's greatness. *Great* (gadol), as used here, means large, magnified, important, and highly valued. The LORD was great in Zion (Jerusalem) because of how He had worked out all things for His people.

The LORD is exalted over all nations; He reigns over the entire earth. Whether or not people acknowledge Him does not change the truth of His sovereign power. But His greatness was especially magnified among His covenant people, for whom He had done marvelous and miraculous things.

c. Because He is holy: His great and awesome name is to be praised by all people and nations (v.3).

Third, the psalmist emphasized God's holiness, the theme of this song. The earth should tremble before the LORD because He is holy. All people should praise His great and awesome name. Note the following definitions and descriptions of God's holiness:

➢ "He is pure and righteous...He cannot look upon sin but with abhorrence."[3]
➢ "He is holy, set apart from His creation, separated, transcendent, high and lifted up, above and beyond His creation, utterly distinct and different from it."[4]
➢ "In Him is no flaw or fault, excess or deficiency, error or iniquity. He is wholly excellent, and is therefore called holy. In His words, thoughts, acts, and revelations as well as in Himself, He is perfection itself."[5]
➢ "Because God is holy, He is free from the moral imperfections and frailties common to man (Hos.11:9) and can be counted on to be faithful to His promises (Ps.22:3-5)."[6]

➢ "*Holy* is a word to emphasize the distance between God and man: not only morally, as between the pure and the polluted, but in the realm of being, between the eternal and the creaturely."[7]
➢ "He is removed from and far above all those limitations and imperfections that mark man."[8]

d. Because He is mighty: He is the King who loves perfect justice (v.4).

Fourth, the psalmist emphasized the LORD's power. The earth should tremble before Him because He is mighty. With all of His strength, the King of the earth loves perfect justice (judgment). Indeed, the LORD is the author of justice. In His absolute holiness and righteousness, He established a perfect standard of *equity* (mesharim), fair treatment and justice. And in all of His dealings with Israel (Jacob), the LORD had done that which was just and right. Thus, the psalmist testified that God had always acted consistently, in perfect accord with His covenant and His law.

Thought 1. "There is no fear of God before their eyes" (Ro.3:18). With this condemning statement, Paul described sinful humanity. Sadly, this charge is also true of many who profess Christ. They continue on in their sin, living for themselves and their own desires rather than for God.

Simply stated, we need both an accurate and a complete vision of the LORD. We need to understand God as He truly is. Preachers have a duty to proclaim *all* the attributes of God, not just the ones that make people feel warm and comfortable. Yes, people need to know that God is loving and merciful, but they also need to know that He is mighty, holy, righteous, and just. When we see God as He truly is, then we will see ourselves as we truly are. This should drive us to fall down trembling before Him in a spirit of humility, brokenness, and repentance.

> Do not be afraid of those who kill the body but cannot kill the soul. Rather, be afraid of the One who can destroy both soul and body in hell (Mt.10:28).
> Since, then, we know what it is to fear the Lord, we try to persuade men. What we are is plain to God, and I hope it is also plain to your conscience (2 Co.5:11).
> He said in a loud voice, "Fear God and give him glory, because the hour of his judgment has come. Worship him who made the heavens, the earth, the sea and the springs of water" (Re.14:7).
> Moses said to the people, "Do not be afraid. God has come to test you, so that

3 Albert Barnes. *Barnes Notes on the Old Testament.* WORD*search* CROSS e-book.
4 Steven Lawson and Max Anders. *Holman Old Testament Commentary—Psalms.* WORD*search* CROSS e-book.
5 Charles Spurgeon. *Treasury of David.* WORD*search* CROSS e-book.
6 R. Laird Harris, ed. *Theological Wordbook of the Old Testament.* WORD*search* CROSS e-book.
7 Derek Kidner. *Psalms 73-150,* p.387.
8 H.C. Leupold. *Exposition of the Psalms,* p.696.

the fear of God will be with you to keep you from sinning" (Ex.20:20).

So that they will fear you and walk in your ways all the time they live in the land you gave our fathers (2 Chr.6:31).

Let all the earth fear the LORD; let all the people of the world revere him (Ps.33:8).

Through love and faithfulness sin is atoned for; through the fear of the LORD a man avoids evil (Pr.16:6).

2 (99:5-9) **Submit yourself to the LORD: Exalt Him and worship at His feet.**

Underscoring both God's holiness and His forgiveness, the psalmist called for the people to exalt the LORD and to worship at His feet (v.5). When we fully grasp God's faithfulness to His character—His holiness and righteousness—along with His love for people, we will want to submit ourselves wholly to Him. We will bow before Him in gratitude and worship.

a. Because He is holy (v.5).

The psalmist reemphasized God's holiness as the basis for fearing Him. In other words, we should exalt the LORD and worship at His footstool because He is holy. Sometimes, God's footstool is a symbol of His power and authority (Ps.110:1). Here, however, it is a symbol of His presence and the place where He rests (Is.66:1). *The Expositor's Bible Commentary* explains that "the ark of the covenant...became known as His 'footstool' (Ps.132:7-8; 1 Chr.28:2). By extension the 'footstool' also referred to the temple (Is.60:13) and Jerusalem (see Lam.2:1)."[9] The picture is of God's people bowing at His feet in submission to Him at the unique place that signified His presence on earth. Today, through the sacrifice of Christ, we have open access to God's heavenly throne. Therefore, we should bow humbly before the LORD on a regular basis, worshipping and presenting ourselves to Him for His service.

b. Because He answers and helps all who call on Him (He:4:14-16): The example of Moses, Aaron, and Samuel leading Israel (vv.6-8).

We should also exalt and bow before the LORD because of His love and faithfulness to us. He hears and answers our prayers and helps us when we call on Him. The psalmist cited Moses, Aaron, and Samuel as examples. As God's priests, Moses and Aaron represented the people before the LORD. Samuel, a prophet, spoke to the people on God's behalf. Also a Levite, Samuel performed priestly duties as well (1 Chr.6:16-28; 1 S.7:9). These godly men all called on the LORD for the people's sake, and God answered them (v.6). He spoke to and guided Moses and Aaron by the pillar of cloud (v.7; Ex.13:21-22; Nu.12:5). The LORD also spoke through His Word—the testimonies and ordinance that He gave them—which they obeyed. When the people disobeyed the LORD and these priests asked God to forgive them, God forgave their sins. Still, He disciplined them when they went astray, because He loved them and wanted them to learn to walk in obedience to Him (v.8). When He punished their sinful, fleshly deeds, He proved Himself to be faithful both to His holiness and to His love for His people.

c. Because He deserves your exaltation, reverence, and worship (v.8).

Such a God—a God who is uncompromisingly holy, yet loving and gracious—deserves the fullest measure of our devotion. We should exalt Him, reverence Him, and worship at His holy hill, that is, in His presence. The LORD never betrays His holiness, which means that He never overlooks our sin. At the same time, He never fails to help us gain victory over our sinful tendencies. When we fail Him and sincerely seek His face, He will forgive us and teach us to obey. This is the LORD our God: He is ever faithful to His perfect holiness and also to His imperfect people who repeatedly violate it.

Thought 1. God's love and mercy can only be truly understood in the light of His holiness. Likewise, we will never fully appreciate God's faithful love for us until we grasp the concept of His absolute holiness. When we do, we can have only one response: to bow down before Him in submission and worship. We will give ourselves over completely to Him, offering our lives as the only reasonable sacrifice for His love and mercies (Ro.12:1).

God is spirit, and his worshipers must worship in spirit and in truth" (Jn.4:24).

Therefore, I urge you, brothers, in view of God's mercy, to offer your bodies as living sacrifices, holy and pleasing to God—this is your spiritual act of worship (Ro.12:1).

And he died for all, that those who live should no longer live for themselves but for him who died for them and was raised again (2 Co.5:15).

Look, he is coming with the clouds, and every eye will see him, even those who pierced him; and all the peoples of the earth will mourn because of him. So shall it be! Amen (Re.1:7).

Ascribe to the LORD the glory due his name. Bring an offering and come before him; worship the LORD in the splendor of his holiness (1 Chr.16:29).

Then I heard the voice of the Lord saying, "Whom shall I send? And who will go for us?" And I said, "Here am I. Send me!" (Is.6:8).

---

9 Frank E. Gaebelein, ed. *The Expositor's Bible Commentary*, pp.635-36.

	PSALM 100 **A Summons to All the Earth: Acknowledge & Receive the LORD, 100:1-5** *A Psalm. For giving thanks.*	3 Know that the LORD is God. It is he who made us, and we are his; we are his people, the sheep of his pasture.	**2. Receive the LORD: Confess (know) that He is the only true God** a. He is our Creator: We are His b. He is our Shepherd: He guides & cares for us as His sheep
1. Acknowledge the LORD (Yahweh, Jehovah): Praise Him alone a. Serve Him with a glad heart b. Approach Him with joyful songs	Shout for joy to the LORD, all the earth. 2 Worship the LORD with gladness; come before him with joyful songs.	4 Enter his gates with thanksgiving and his courts with praise; give thanks to him and praise his name. 5 For the LORD is good and his love endures forever; his faithfulness continues through all generations.	**3. Enter the LORD's presence, His temple, with a thankful heart** a. Bc. He is worthy of praise b. Bc. He is good & loving: His love never fails c. Bc. He is faithful & true to every generation

PSALM 100

A Summons to All the Earth: Acknowledge and Receive the LORD, 100:1-5

(100:1-5) Introduction: every Sunday, a beautiful thing happens all around the world: millions and millions of people gather in churches to worship and praise the LORD. Whether in structures great or small, magnificent or simple, extravagant or beautifully plain, out in the open or in secret, people from all walks of life gather in God's holy name.

On the other hand, millions and millions of people do not follow this pattern. Millions worship false gods or no god at all. Their eyes are blinded to the truth. They cannot or do not see that the LORD is their Creator and God (2 Co.4:4).

Psalm 100 is the last in a series of psalms that emphasize the LORD as King (93–100). It describes God's people going into His house to worship Him, and it spells out what their attitude should be as they go. It also calls out to all the people of the earth, urging them to recognize that the LORD is God and inviting them to receive Him.

In a very practical sense, this psalm teaches us the actual purpose of the church: to joyfully express praise and thanksgiving to God, to present ourselves for God's service, and to urge all people of the earth to come into a relationship with God through His Son. This is, *A Summons to All the Earth: Acknowledge and Receive the LORD*, 100:1-5.

1. Acknowledge the LORD (Yahweh, Jehvovah): Praise Him alone (vv.1-2).
2. Receive the LORD: Confess (know) that He is the only true God (v.3).
3. Enter the LORD's presence, His temple, with a thankful heart (vv.4-5).

1 (100:1-2) **Acknowledge the LORD (Yahweh, Jehovah): Praise Him alone.**
Psalm 100 begins with a summons to all the lands to *shout for joy* (ruah), shout loudly and exuberantly, to the LORD. German commentator Franz Delitzsch (1813–1890) described this call as "a blowing of the trumpets"[1]

for the earth's population to come together to worship the LORD. It is an exhortation to the Gentile nations to turn from their false gods and to acknowledge that the LORD, the God of Israel, is the only true and living God. All the people of all the lands should praise the LORD and Him alone.

a. Serve Him with a glad heart (v.2ᵃ).
A vital part of worship is presenting ourselves to the LORD for His service. The New Testament instructs us to offer ourselves as living sacrifices to Him (Ro.12:1). "Worship leads to service, and true service is worship."[2] We should not serve the LORD out of duty or obligation but out of the gladness of our hearts. Because of God's great love and mercies, we should serve Him willingly and with joy. We should also remember what a tremendous privilege it is to be the servants of such a great King!

b. Approach Him with joyful songs (v.2ᵇ).
We should come before the LORD with songs of joy on our lips. This command is directed to our demeanor or attitude when we come to God's house for worship. We are to approach Him reverently, yes, but also with joyful hearts and joyful songs. The LORD's presence was centered in the temple in the Old Testament. Now, both the church and our bodies are designated as the house of God (1 Ti.3:15).

Thought 1. Since our bodies are the temple of God's Holy Spirit, we should worship the LORD as we walk throughout each day (1 Co.6:19-20). But we should also acknowledge the LORD by gathering with His people for worship every week. Just as the psalmist extended the call to worship here, so churches across the world extend the call to come and worship the Lord with them. Sadly, many professing believers do not answer this call. Many simply disobey God's command to

---

1 Franz Delitzsch. *Commentary on the Old Testament.* WORDsearch CROSS e-book.

2 Warren W. Wiersbe. *The Bible Exposition Commentary.* WORDsearch CROSS e-book.

assemble with other believers (He.10:25). Others go to church, but they do so grudgingly or half-heartedly, out of duty or obligation.

Our attitude about going to church should be one of anticipation and joy. Never should we say, "I *have* to go to church today." To the contrary, serving the Lord and going to His house is a high privilege and ought to be among the greatest joys in our lives (Ps.122:1). We should serve the Lord cheerfully and worship Him wholeheartedly. Anything less is unworthy of God and His great love for us.

> **Speak to one another with psalms, hymns and spiritual songs. Sing and make music in your heart to the Lord (Ep.5:19).**
>
> **Let us not give up meeting together, as some are in the habit of doing, but let us encourage one another—and all the more as you see the Day approaching (He.10:25).**
>
> **But you are a chosen people, a royal priesthood, a holy nation, a people belonging to God, that you may declare the praises of him who called you out of darkness into his wonderful light (1 Pe.2:9).**
>
> **Then will I go to the altar of God, to God, my joy and my delight. I will praise you with the harp, O God, my God (Ps.43:4).**
>
> **I rejoiced with those who said to me, "Let us go to the house of the LORD" (Ps.122:1).**

2 (100:3) Receive the LORD: Confess (know) that He is the only true God.

The psalmist invited all the people of the earth to receive the LORD. The LORD (Yahweh, Jehovah) is the name by which God revealed Himself to His people. It is the name by which He swore when He made His covenant with us. His name guarantees that He will keep His promises at all costs. To *know* (yada) means to know personally, intimately, and by experience. Essentially, the psalmist was inviting all people to come into a personal relationship with God, to experience God and see for themselves that He keeps His covenant (promises). He is the only true and living God.

a. He is our Creator: We are His (v.3a).

The psalmist appealed to the people of the earth, first, on the basis of creation. God is our Creator. He made us; therefore, we are His. He formed our bodies and our souls (Ps.139:14-16). He crafted our spirits and blew His breath—the only source of life—into us (Ge.2:7). We live, breathe, and exist because of Him

(Ac.17:28). We are not self-made; we are made by God, who personally and individually created us for fellowship with Him, to enjoy the fullness of the glory of His presence forever and ever (1 Jn.1:3; Ep.2:4-7. Accordingly, He is our rightful owner. "He has an incontestable right to, and property in, us and all things. His we are, to be actuated [used] by His power, disposed of by His will, and devoted to His honor and glory."[3]

b. He is our Shepherd: He guides and cares for us as His sheep (v.3b).

Second, the psalmist appealed to the people of the earth on the basis of God's guidance and care for them. He is our Shepherd, and we are His sheep (Ps.95:7). His pasture is the earth, which He so wisely created to provide for us and to meet all of our needs.

The LORD is a shepherd who deeply loves and cares for His sheep (see outline and notes—Ps.23:1-6 for more discussion). He loves us so much that He was willing to sacrifice His one and only Son to lay down His life for us (Jn.10:11, 15). Through His creation, His Word, and the circumstances of our lives, He seeks to guide us into a relationship with Him.

Thought 1. Many people do not know that the Lord is God. Like sheep, they have gone astray and are wandering far from Him (Is.53:6). It is our responsibility as believers to invite them to come into a relationship with God. We know that the Lord is God. We know that He created us for a relationship with Him. We know that He gave His Son for us, and that by repenting and believing Him, we can be one of His sheep. Christ has commissioned us to point the world to Him, showing people that He is the only way into the LORD's fold (Jn.10:7-11; 14:6). God wants every individual to know Him and to come into a relationship with Him. Thus, we are responsible to take the gospel into all the earth (Ac.1:8).

> **But you will receive power when the Holy Spirit comes on you; and you will be my witnesses in Jerusalem, and in all Judea and Samaria, and to the ends of the earth" (Ac.1:8)**
>
> **When they heard this, they raised their voices together in prayer to God. "Sovereign Lord," they said, "you made the heaven and the earth and the sea, and everything in them (Ac.4:24).**
>
> **For as I walked around and looked carefully at your objects of worship, I even found an altar with this inscription: TO AN UNKNOWN GOD. Now what you worship as something unknown I am**

---

3 Matthew Henry. *Matthew Henry's Commentary on the Whole Bible.* WORD*search* CROSS e-book.

going to proclaim to you. "The God who made the world and everything in it is the Lord of heaven and earth and does not live in temples built by hands. And he is not served by human hands, as if he needed anything, because he himself gives all men life and breath and everything else. From one man he made every nation of men, that they should inhabit the whole earth; and he determined the times set for them and the exact places where they should live. God did this so that men would seek him and perhaps reach out for him and find him, though he is not far from each one of us. 'For in him we live and move and have our being.' As some of your own poets have said, 'We are his offspring' (Ac.17:23-28).

For God, who said, "Let light shine out of darkness," made his light shine in our hearts to give us the light of the knowledge of the glory of God in the face of Christ (2 Co.4:6).

When all the people saw this, they fell prostrate and cried, "The LORD—he is God! The LORD —he is God!" (1 K.18:39).

"Be still, and know that I am God; I will be exalted among the nations, I will be exalted in the earth" (Ps.46:10).

Come, let us bow down in worship, let us kneel before the LORD our Maker; for he is our God and we are the people of his pasture, the flock under his care. Today, if you hear his voice (Ps.95:6-7).

3 (100:4-5) Enter the LORD's presence, His temple, with a thankful heart.

The psalmist addressed the people ascending Mount Zion to worship the LORD at the temple, the place where His presence resided in a special way. As they entered through the gates into the courts or courtyard of the temple, they were to offer their thanksgiving and praise to the LORD. The message is clear: God wants us to come into His presence with thankful hearts. Gratitude to Him is at the heart of worship.

a. Because He is worthy of praise (v.4).

As our Creator and Shepherd, the LORD is worthy of praise. He made us, and He guides and cares for us throughout our lives. More than that, however, He is our Savior. When we—the most special objects of His creation—strayed from Him by sinning, He made a way back for us. He provided for our salvation by offering His Son as the sacrifice for our sin. Without question, God's power in creating us and His faithfulness in caring for us merit our unending praise. But

His love for us as demonstrated at Calvary exceeds every other reason for offering our thanks and praise to Him.

b. Because He is good and loving: His love never fails (v.5ᵃ).

We should enter God's presence with thankful hearts because He is good and loving. Every day, the LORD displays His goodness to us. He is even good to those who do not know Him (Mt.5:45; Ro.2:4). He especially delights in giving good gifts to His children, though (Mt.7:11). Every good thing in our lives is a gift from Him (Js.1:17).

Additionally, we should give thanks to God for His unfailing, covenant *love* (chesed). God's love for us never fails; it *endures forever*. We may fail Him, but He never fails us. Nothing can overcome His love for us (Ro.8:35-39).

c. Because He is faithful and true to every generation (v.5ᵇ).

Finally, we should enter God's presence with thanksgiving for His *faithfulness* (emunah) or truth. The LORD is faithful and true to every generation. We can count on God and we can count on His truth. He and His Word can be trusted. From generation to generation, He is always the same (Js.1:17; He.1:12; 13:8).

Thought 1. Psalm 100 teaches us what our attitude should be when we go to God's house. Not only should we come before the LORD with gladness and joy (v.2), but we should enter His presence with thanksgiving and praise. God is good to us every day. He is ever faithful to us, and His love never fails. As we walk or ride to church, we should prepare our hearts to give thanks by reflecting on all He has done for us in the past week. As we walk through the doors, our hearts should be filled with praise. When we enter the sanctuary, and the service begins, we should lift our voices and wholeheartedly sing the praises of our good, loving, and faithful God.

Under God's law, His people expressed their gratitude to God by offering a sacrifice (Le.7:11-34). As New Testament believers, we too are instructed to offer a sacrifice of thanksgiving:

Through Jesus, therefore, let us continually offer to God a sacrifice of praise—the fruit of lips that confess his name (He.13:15).

Always giving thanks to God the Father for everything, in the name of our Lord Jesus Christ (Ep.5:20).

And whatever you do, whether in word or deed, do it all in the name of the Lord Jesus, giving thanks to God the Father through him (Col.3:17).

Give thanks in all circumstances, for this is God's will for you in Christ Jesus (1 Th.5:18).

I will praise God's name in song and glorify him with thanksgiving (Ps.69:30).

Let them sacrifice thank offerings and tell of his works with songs of joy (Ps.107:22).

The sounds of joy and gladness, the voices of bride and bridegroom, and the voices of those who bring thank offerings to the house of the LORD, saying, "Give thanks to the LORD Almighty, for the LORD is good; his love endures forever." For I will restore the fortunes of the land as they were before,' says the LORD (Je.33:11).

	PSALM 101 **When You Make a Commitment & Declare Your Loyalty to the LORD, 101:1-8** *Of David. A Psalm.*	have nothing to do with evil. 5 Whoever slanders his neighbor in secret, him will I put to silence; whoever has haughty eyes and a proud heart, him will I not endure.	4) Silence the slanderer & reject the prideful

1. Praise & bear witness for the LORD
  a. He is merciful & loving
  b. His judgments are just
2. Live a blameless life
  a. Essential private behavior
    1) Seek God's presence
    2) Walk in integrity at home, in private
  b. Essential public behavior
    1) Guard your eyes, 1 Jn.2:15-16
    2) Hate the backslider's sins: Let no sin cling to you
    3) Reject the perverse: Stay away from all evil
	I will sing of your love and justice; to you, O LORD, I will sing praise.
	2 I will be careful to lead a blameless life—when will you come to me? I will walk in my house with blameless heart.
	3 I will set before my eyes no vile thing. The deeds of faithless men I hate; they will not cling to me.
	4 Men of perverse heart shall be far from me; I will
		6 My eyes will be on the faithful in the land, that they may dwell with me; he whose walk is blameless will minister to me.
		7 No one who practices deceit will dwell in my house; no one who speaks falsely will stand in my presence.
		8 Every morning I will put to silence all the wicked in the land; I will cut off every evildoer from the city of the LORD.
			3. Seek the right companions for fellowship, counsel, & service
			  a. Choose those who are trustworthy, who walk blamelessly
			  b. Reject those who are deceitful, who lie: Do not let them...
			    1) Live in your house
			    2) Stay in your presence
			4. Recommit yourself daily to uphold righteousness & justice
			  a. Silence the wicked
			  b. Remove all lawless evildoers from society

PSALM 101

When You Make a Commitment and Declare Your Loyalty to the LORD, 101:1-8

(101:1-8) Introduction: living a holy and godly life is not something that we do casually or automatically. Holiness and godliness are contrary to human nature, contrary to the desires of our flesh. To make our efforts that much more difficult, every day presents new temptations to hinder godly living. Therefore, walking in holiness and godliness requires commitment, discipline, and diligence. Young Daniel did not defile himself in Babylon not because he was not tempted to do so but because he purposed, or determined, in his heart not to do so (Da.1:8). Likewise, if we are going to be holy in our corrupt and sin-infected world, we too have to purpose in our hearts to be holy. We have to make a commitment to godliness.

In Psalm 101, David made a series of commitments to the LORD, pledging to be holy and godly. David most likely wrote this psalm upon assuming the throne of Israel. He wanted to be a man of integrity, a man who was faithful to God's laws and righteousness. With its repeated *I will* statements, it is a prayer of commitment to the LORD.

David was not a perfect man and, as God's Word tells us, he failed at times to live up to these commitments. Nevertheless, he strived to keep these goals, repenting and rededicating himself to them each time he failed. To this day, he stands as Israel's godliest and greatest king. With this psalm, he set an example for all who genuinely long to be holy and godly. This is, *When You Make a Commitment and Declare Your Loyalty to the LORD*, 101:1-8.

1. Praise and bear witness for the LORD (v.1).
2. Live a blameless life (vv.2-5).
3. Seek the right companions for fellowship, counsel, and service (vv.6-7).
4. Recommit yourself daily to uphold righteousness and justice (v.8).

1 (101:1) **Praise and bear witness for the LORD.** David began by exalting the righteous character of God. He declared that he would sing God's praise and bear witness of the LORD's mercy and justice. The LORD was Israel's true king, and David desired to lead God's people in a way that honored and glorified Him.

a. He is merciful and loving (v.1a).

David exalted God for His *unfailing, covenant love* (chesed), His mercy. God's relationship with His people was based on His covenant with them, and the LORD had proven Himself to be faithful to His word. He had never failed His people. His loyalty and steadfastness toward them were sure.

b. His judgments are just (v.1b).

David also exalted God because of His judgment, His perfect justice. In all of His ways, God is absolutely just. He is the author of justice, establishing a flawless standard of fairness and righteousness. David was determined to make God's holy law the basis for all judgments in the nation.

Thought 1. Regardless of what happens in our lives or in our world, the LORD is faithful, and the LORD is just. Nothing can separate us from His unfailing love (Ro.8:35-39). The presence of trouble and trials in our lives does not mean that God has failed us or that He no longer loves us. To the contrary, God works our trials together for good, using them to accomplish His purpose for us (Ro.8:28).

Furthermore, God is just in all of His ways. He always does what is right. When others persecute us or sin against us, we should not agonize over the situation nor should we seek vengeance. Instead, we should rest in the LORD, knowing that in His good time and in His right way, He will judge our enemies and vindicate us.

It is easy to praise the LORD when things are going smoothly, but it is not so easy when we are in the midst of painful or trying times. For this reason, we need to make a commitment to praise Him in all things, regardless of our circumstances. In our darkest hours, our song bears the strongest witness to others of God's love and faithfulness (Ac.16:25).

> **About midnight Paul and Silas were praying and singing hymns to God, and the other prisoners were listening to them (Ac.16:25).**
>
> **So that the Gentiles may glorify God for his mercy, as it is written: "Therefore I will praise you among the Gentiles; I will sing hymns to your name" (Ro.15:9).**
>
> **Through Jesus, therefore, let us continually offer to God a sacrifice of praise—the fruit of lips that confess his name (He.13:15).**
>
> **With praise and thanksgiving they sang to the LORD: "He is good; his love to Israel endures forever." And all the people gave a great shout of praise to the LORD, because the foundation of the house of the LORD was laid (Ezr.3:11).**
>
> **Therefore I will praise you among the nations, O LORD; I will sing praises to your name (Ps.18:49).**
>
> **I will tell of the kindnesses of the LORD, the deeds for which he is to be praised, according to all the LORD has done for us—yes, the many good things he has done for the house of Israel, according to his compassion and many kindnesses (Is.63:7).**

2 (101:2-5) Live a blameless life.

As the leader of God's chosen people, David grasped the seriousness of his position. He had a holy obligation to God and to God's people. He had to be a vessel whom God could use and bless, walking in full obedience to His commands. Then, he had to provide a proper example for the people, earning their confidence and assuring them that they would be treated righteously and justly. With a firm understanding of his holy duty as king, David pledged to live a blameless life, both privately and publicly.

a. Essential private behavior (v.2).

David desired to be holy in every area of his life. He longed to please the LORD in his personal life as well as

in his administration of the kingdom. Accordingly, he made a commitment to walk in a *blameless* (tamim) way and *with blameless* (tom) *heart.* These Hebrew words come from a root word that means to be complete or whole. They refer to living with integrity, with being…

- consistently pure
- wholly righteous
- honest through and through
- the same inwardly and outwardly
- pure in motive as well as in word and deed

David knew that living with integrity would require God's help. Temptation would be everywhere, especially in his position, and relying on human wisdom could lead him to rationalize and make wrong decisions. Therefore, he sought God's presence and invited Him into his life. He even asked the LORD when He would come to him. David wanted God's presence and needed His power to help him behave wisely.

In his commitment to integrity, David asked God to help him be the same man in his personal life as he presented himself to be in his public life. The palaces of kings were "usually places where passion, lust, and excess were given full reign."[1] Even so, David pledged to walk in integrity within his house—at home and in private. Realizing his responsibility to his family and his servants, he determined to model God's love and righteousness before them.

b. Essential public behavior (vv.3-5).

David then turned his attention to his public behavior, making a commitment to protect himself from evil things and wicked people. Desiring to live above reproach, he determined to guard his eyes from anything that was *vile* (beliya'al'), anything defiling, wicked, morally corrupt, or worthless (v.3ᵃ). He would not look at anything that would tempt him to have or to do what God had forbidden (Lu.11:34; 1 Jn.2:15-16). In addition, he pledged to hate the deeds of those who turn aside from God and His law, backsliders who drift away from God and into sin (v.3ᵇ). He refused to allow them or their sinful ways to cling to him.

Determined to have no dishonest officials in his administration, David promised to reject those with *perverse* hearts, people who were morally crooked and corrupt (v.4). He resolved to stay away from all evil, declaring that he would not become personally involved with any wickedness.

David also made a commitment to *put to silence* (tsamath) those who secretly slandered others (v.5). He would not tolerate prideful, self-important people who sought to further themselves at the expense of others. For that reason, He vowed to reject them for positions in his administration.

---

1 John Phillips. *Exploring Psalms, Volume 1.* WORD*search* CROSS e-book.

Thought 1. Like David, each of us should make a commitment to live a blameless life—a life of integrity that is above reproach. Certainly, before we can shine as lights in the world and point people to Christ, we have to strive to live blamelessly (Ph.2:15). This is why those who serve in the Biblical offices of pastor and deacon are required to be blameless (1 Ti.3:2, 10; Tit.1:6-7).

If we truly walk in integrity, we will be the same in private as we are in public. We will not behave one way around our co-workers or fellow church members and another way around our families. We will be as godly at home as we are outside of the home. Even more telling of our character, the true test of integrity is how we behave when no one else is around. Do we change our behavior or do we remain the same?

Walking consistently in integrity is not easy in a world contaminated by sin. It requires commitment to stay away from everything and everyone who might tempt us to fall away from godliness. We have to guard our eyes, realizing that what we see affects our hearts (La.3:51). Further, we need to separate ourselves from those who are unfaithful to the Lord, lest they influence us to backslide. Along with these, we need to stay away from all wickedness, avoiding even that which has the appearance of being evil (1 Th.5:22). If we are going to be people of true integrity, we ought to make David's commitments our own.

> So that you may become blameless and pure, children of God without fault in a crooked and depraved generation, in which you shine like stars in the universe (Ph.2:15).
>
> We put no stumbling block in anyone's path, so that our ministry will not be discredited (2 Co.6:3).
>
> "Therefore come out from them and be separate, says the Lord. Touch no unclean thing, and I will receive you." "I will be a Father to you, and you will be my sons and daughters, says the Lord Almighty" (2 Co.6:17-18).
>
> For he chose us in him before the creation of the world to be holy and blameless in his sight. In love (Ep.1:4).
>
> You are witnesses, and so is God, of how holy, righteous and blameless we were among you who believed (1 Th.2:10).
>
> So then, dear friends, since you are looking forward to this, make every effort to be found spotless, blameless and at peace with him (2 Pe.3:14).
>
> Do not love the world or anything in the world. If anyone loves the world, the love of the Father is not in him. For everything in the world—the cravings of sinful man, the lust of his eyes and the boasting of what he has and does—comes not from the Father but from the world (1 Jn.2:15-16).

3 (101:6-7) **Seek the right companions for fellowship, counsel, and service.**
David wisely understood the importance of seeking the right companions for fellowship, counsel, and service. After describing the kinds of people he would reject, David identified the types of individuals he would select to assist him in governing God's people.

a. **Choose those who are trustworthy, who walk blamelessly (v.6).**
David promised to select faithful people to be his associates. *Faithful* (aman) describes those who...
  * are trustworthy and dependable
  * are constant and stable
  * are loyal and dedicated
  * are proven and can be counted on to do what is right
  * are honorable and have solid reputations and backgrounds

The young king saw the importance of surrounding himself with the right kind of people—people whose way is blameless (v.2). "Only by surrounding himself with the best and most capable men who will advance the interests of God can the king rest assured that the kingdom of God is strengthened."[2] Taking everything into consideration, David pledged to choose only men of integrity to serve under him. He would seek only those who had a record of walking blamelessly and above reproach.

b. **Reject those who are deceitful, who lie (v.7).**
Not stopping with whom he *would* select as companions, David proceeded to state whom he *would not* select. In fact, he strongly declared that he would reject any who were deceitful or who had lied. He would not allow them to dwell in his house, nor would he let them stay in his presence. In using these phrases, David was speaking of his inner circle of associates, his closest advisors who would work directly with him. He was determined not to "walk in the counsel of the wicked" nor to "stand in the way of sinners" (Ps.1:1). If any of his officials ever deceived or lied to him or any spoke falsely about others, he would promptly remove them from their positions.

Thought 1. Scripture repeatedly warns about the power and influence other people can have over us. We will be impacted either for good or for evil by the

---

2 Frank E. Gaebelein, ed. *The Expositor's Bible Commentary*, p.643.

people with whom we associate. Our attitudes, mannerisms, speech patterns, opinions, and philosophies are all affected by our companions. Therefore, if we want to live holy and godly lives and we want to walk with integrity, we have to surround ourselves with godly people. At the same time, we have to avoid close associations with those who are ungodly. We need to be vigilant in our daily lives, always on guard for those who might be a bad influence on us. This is not to say that we should not reach out in love to those who do not know Christ. However, we must be careful not to fall under their influence. To protect ourselves and our families, we need to walk closely with the Lord and always be sensitive to the leading of the Holy Spirit.

> I have written you in my letter not to associate with sexually immoral people (1 Co.5:9).
>
> Do not be misled: "Bad company corrupts good character" (1 Co.15:33).
>
> Do not be yoked together with unbelievers. For what do righteousness and wickedness have in common? Or what fellowship can light have with darkness? (2 Co.6:14).
>
> Do not let them live in your land, or they will cause you to sin against me, because the worship of their gods will certainly be a snare to you" (Ex.23:33).
>
> In the LORD I take refuge. How then can you say to me: "Flee like a bird to your mountain (Ps.11:1).
>
> He who walks with the wise grows wise, but a companion of fools suffers harm (Pr.13:20).

4 (101:8) **Recommit yourself daily to uphold righteousness and justice.**
David closed by recommitting himself to uphold righteousness and justice among God's people. One of the king's most important duties was to hear the people's cases and execute justice. David promised to make this a priority of his administration, giving it his first attention every day. "Every morning I will" is literally translated morning by morning.

a. **Silence the wicked (v.8ᵃ).**
David promised to be fearless and just in all of his verdicts. He would *silence* (tsamath) or destroy the wicked—cut off their opportunity to do evil.

b. **Remove all lawless evildoers from society (v.8ᵇ).**
David also promised to remove all lawless evildoers from society. *Cut off* (karath) may mean that he would expel them from Jerusalem, or it may mean that he would execute them according to the law.

Thought 1. Holy and godly living requires daily effort. It requires walking in integrity every day. Just as David recommitted himself daily to the duty of upholding righteousness and justice, we need to recommit ourselves daily to our duties as believers. Remember, we have to purpose or determine to do right before we will do right. We have to purpose to be holy before we will be holy. The world, the flesh, and the devil will never tire of trying to steer us away from obedience to God's commands. We can be sure that we will face these enemies every day. Therefore, we need to dedicate ourselves anew every morning to holiness and godliness, clothing ourselves in the armor of God and arming ourselves with God's powerful Word (Ep.6:10-17).

> I put this in human terms because you are weak in your natural selves. Just as you used to offer the parts of your body in slavery to impurity and to ever-increasing wickedness, so now offer them in slavery to righteousness leading to holiness (Ro.6:19).
>
> Therefore, I urge you, brothers, in view of God's mercy, to offer your bodies as living sacrifices, holy and pleasing to God—this is your spiritual act of worship (Ro.12:1).
>
> And to put on the new self, created to be like God in true righteousness and holiness (Ep.4:24).
>
> Then Moses said, "You have been set apart to the LORD today, for you were against your own sons and brothers, and he has blessed you this day" (Ex.32:29).
>
> "'Consecrate yourselves and be holy, because I am the LORD your God (Le.20:7).

PSALM 102

When You are Overwhelmed by Suffering & Sense That Death Is Near, 102:1-23

A prayer of an afflicted man. When he is faint and pours out his lament before the LORD.

1. Cry out for the LORD's help
  a. Ask Him to hear & to accept your prayer
    1) That He not ignore your distress, not hide His face from you
    2) That He turn & listen to you & answer you quickly
  b. Describe your anguish to Him
    1) Your days are wasting away bc. of your burning pain
    2) You are so heartsick that you have no appetite to live, even to eat or drink
    3) You groan in pain constantly & thus are reduced to skin & bones
    4) You feel alone, isolated in the ruins of your life
    5) You cannot sleep, & like a solitary bird on a roof, you watch the world go by
    6) You feel rejected, even despised, being mocked, taunted, & cursed by enemies
    7) You are utterly miserable, as though eating ashes & drinking tears
    8) You feel cast aside by God, alienated from Him, that He is disciplining you for some sin in your life
    9) You feel your days are quickly fading away, like evening shadows

2. Trust in God's promises
  a. He reigns forever: His promises & mercies never fail & are proclaimed by all generations
  b. He fulfills His promises to His people (as foretold, He was to deliver them from Babylon after 70 yrs., Je.25:11-14; 29:10): Pointed to God's

Hear my prayer, O LORD; let my cry for help come to you.
2 Do not hide your face from me when I am in distress. Turn your ear to me; when I call, answer me quickly.
3 For my days vanish like smoke; my bones burn like glowing embers.
4 My heart is blighted and withered like grass; I forget to eat my food.
5 Because of my loud groaning I am reduced to skin and bones.
6 I am like a desert owl, like an owl among the ruins.
7 I lie awake; I have become like a bird alone on a roof.
8 All day long my enemies taunt me; those who rail against me use my name as a curse.
9 For I eat ashes as my food and mingle my drink with tears
10 Because of your great wrath, for you have taken me up and thrown me aside.
11 My days are like the evening shadow; I wither away like grass.
12 But you, O LORD, sit enthroned forever; your renown endures through all generations.
13 You will arise and have compassion on Zion, for it is time to show favor to her; the appointed time has come.

14 For her stones are dear to your servants; her very dust moves them to pity.
15 The nations will fear the name of the LORD, all the kings of the earth will revere your glory.
16 For the LORD will rebuild Zion and appear in his glory.
17 He will respond to the prayer of the destitute; he will not despise their plea.
18 Let this be written for a future generation, that a people not yet created may praise the LORD:
19 "The LORD looked down from his sanctuary on high, from heaven he viewed the earth,
20 To hear the groans of the prisoners and release those condemned to death."
21 So the name of the LORD will be declared in Zion and his praise in Jerusalem
22 When the peoples and the kingdoms assemble to worship the LORD.
23 In the course of my life he broke my strength; he cut short my days.
24 So I said: "Do not take me away, O my God, in the midst of my days; your years go on through all generations.
25 In the beginning you laid the foundations of the earth, and the heavens are the work of your hands.
26 They will perish, but you remain; they will all wear out like a garment. Like clothing you will change them and they will be discarded.
27 But you remain the same, and your years will never end.
28 The children of your servants will live in your presence; their descendants will be established before you."

coming kingdom
    1) Bc. God's people love Jerusalem
    2) Bc. the nations will be stirred to fear & revere the LORD

      • When He rebuilds Jerusalem
      • When He appears in glory
  c. He hears the prayers of the truly needy & never rejects their pleas for help
  d. He had His great promise written in His Holy Word to stir future generations to praise Him
    1) The fact that He reigns from His heavenly sanctuary & keeps watch over the earth
    2) The fact that He hears the people's groans: A picture of Christ releasing us from sin & death, Lu.4:18-19
    3) The fact that He delivers His people for one purpose
      • So they will praise His name
      • So all peoples & nations will worship Him

3. Ask God to heal you & to spare your life
  a. Bc. your situation is desperate: You are weak & about to die in midlife
  b. Bc. He (God) is eternal: He has the power to heal & extend life
    1) He existed in the beginning, prior to the universe
    2) He created both the earth & the heavens
    3) He will still exist, still be living, when the universe perishes
    4) He will transform the universe—make a new heavens & earth, 2 Pe.3:10-13
    5) He is unchanging, unchangeable, & eternal—always the same
  c. Bc. He will be the God of all generations to come: He will keep the descendants of the godly in His presence

PSALM 102

When You Are Overwhelmed by Suffering and Sense That Death Is Near, 102:1-28

(102:1-28) **Introduction:** few people will pass through life without experiencing seasons of suffering. Tragically, many will suffer extensively and for long periods of time. Some will suffer the rest of their lives due to handicaps, injuries, or incurable illnesses. Multitudes live with the knowledge that their condition is never going to improve. Others must deal with the reality that, unless God miraculously intervenes, their affliction is going to result in an early death. Such suffering can, at times, be so overwhelming—so life-shattering, so frightening, or so excruciating—that it is simply more than those afflicted can bear.

The heading to Psalm 102 clearly states its purpose: it is a prayer for those who are overwhelmed by their troubles or afflictions. It was written by a man who had suffered long with a condition that, by all appearances, was going to claim his life prematurely. To add to his grief, the Babylonian captivity of Israel had forced him to live in a foreign land because of God's judgment on his unfaithful nation. His weakened heart mourned for his now fractured nation of Israel; yet he longed for home nonetheless.

Psalm 102's author is not identified. Perhaps the Holy Spirit chose to leave it anonymous so that each dear believer who faces extended anguish or affliction can claim it as his or her own. This is, *When You Are Overwhelmed by Suffering and Sense That Death Is Near,* 102:1-28.

1. Cry out for the LORD's help (vv.1-11).
2. Trust in God's promises (vv.12-22).
3. Ask God to heal you and to spare your life (vv.23-28).

1 (102:1-11) Cry out for the LORD's help.

Overcome by pain, the psalmist cried out desperately for the LORD's help. He poured out his complaint before the LORD, describing his suffering at length and relating how it had affected his life.

a. Ask Him to hear and to accept your prayer (vv.1-2).

Feeling that God was oblivious to his suffering and not paying attention to his repeated requests, the ailing psalmist asked the LORD to hear and to accept his prayer (v.1). He pleaded with God not to ignore his distress (v.2). His pain was slowly strangling the life out of him, so he called on God not to hide His face from him in his trouble any longer. Desperate for help, he begged God to listen and to answer him quickly by giving him relief.

b. Describe your anguish to Him (vv.3-11).

In heartbreaking detail, the psalmist described his anguish to the LORD. His life was drifting away like smoke slowly rising and vanishing into the sky (v.3). His days were *vanishing* (kalah), wasted by the burning pain that raged deep in his frail body. "My bones are burned" may describe the intensity of his pain or it may speak of a high fever that tormented him constantly.

The psalmist's unbearable suffering had affected him in every way imaginable. Not surprisingly, his physical pain was compounded by emotional and mental stress. He was so heartsick that he had no appetite for life, not even for food or drink (v.4). He compared his anguished heart to grass that had dried up due to a drought or disease. His unrelenting pain had taken over his mind, consumed him to the point that he could not even remember to eat. This lack of nourishment along with the physical stress of constant pain had reduced him to mere skin and bones (v.5).

As he lay suffering in his house or his bed, this pitiable man felt all alone. He compared himself to the birds that lived in the wilderness and the desert—desolate places, ruins (v.6). *Desert ruins* "almost always refers to an area ruined by the judgment of God" (Is.51:3; 52:9; Je.25:11; Mal.1:4).[1] The psalmist may have been thinking of the fowls that roosted in the rubble of his beloved Jerusalem. Like them, he felt totally isolated in the ruins of his shattered life.

Writhing in pain of both body and soul, the afflicted psalmist could not sleep (v.7). He lay awake watching, like a solitary bird on a roof merely observing the world go by. *Lie awake* (shaqad) is sometimes used of the watchmen who stayed awake at night to guard the city (Ps.127:1). It refers here to the psalmist's sleeplessness.

Rejection by other people added to the psalmist's sorrows (v.8). His enemies gloated over his condition, mocking, taunting, and cursing him all day long. He was utterly miserable. He saw his food as ashes and his drink as being mixed with weeping or tears (v.9). Ashes were a symbol of mourning. People in mourning placed ashes on their heads as a sign of their grief. By stating that ashes and tears were his food and drink, the psalmist was saying poetically that he was totally consumed with grief.

In all this, the psalmist reasoned that his suffering was the result of God's indignation, His fury or wrath (v.10). He felt alienated and cast aside by God, whom he assumed was disciplining him for some sin in his life. Overwhelmed by his physical, emotional, and spiritual pain, he felt that his days were quickly fading away like the evening shadows (v.11). He concluded his complaint by stating again that he was withering away like dying grass (v.4).

Thought 1. Psalm 102 reemphasizes one of this book's greatest lessons: we can freely pour out our hearts to God when we are hurting. We can be honest with God. The afflicted psalmist withheld nothing from God, teaching us that we can tell our Heavenly Father exactly how we feel. When we release our suffering to Him, we open the door for His grace to flood into our own hurting hearts.

The LORD longs to help us through our trials. He has promised His presence in life's deepest valleys and darkest nights (Is.43:2; He.13:5-6). We do not have to bear life's heavy burdens on our own. God invites us to cast our burdens on Him with the promise that He will sustain us (Ps.55:22). When we are overwhelmed with problems or suffering, we should never hesitate to cry out to the LORD for help.

---

1 Spiros Zodhiates. *AMG Complete Word Study Dictionary.* WORD-search CROSS e-book.

"Come to me, all you who are weary and burdened, and I will give you rest. Take my yoke upon you and learn from me, for I am gentle and humble in heart, and you will find rest for your souls (Mt.11:28-29).

Let us then approach the throne of grace with confidence, so that we may receive mercy and find grace to help us in our time of need (He.4:16).

During the days of Jesus' life on earth, he offered up prayers and petitions with loud cries and tears to the one who could save him from death, and he was heard because of his reverent submission (He.5:7).

Then we cried out to the LORD, the God of our fathers, and the LORD heard our voice and saw our misery, toil and oppression (De.26:7).

In my distress I called to the LORD; I cried to my God for help. From his temple he heard my voice; my cry came before him, into his ears (Ps.18:6).

2 (102:12-22) Trust in God's promises.

The psalmist lived and suffered during the Jews' captivity in Babylon. Yet, in spite of his overwhelming personal affliction, he was filled with hope, for the time had come for God to deliver His people and to return them to Jerusalem. He trusted in God's promises, fully believing that God would keep His Word.

a. He reigns forever: His promises and mercies never fail and are proclaimed by all generations (v.12).

The psalmist declared that, unlike himself, the LORD is enthroned forever. In addition, God's remembrance—the memory of all the wonderful works He has done—would continue forever. God's promises and mercies never fail, and they will be proclaimed by all generations. "As long as His rule lasts, His fame will be told and retold."[2] The psalmist made this statement in anticipation of the glorious work he believed God would soon do on His chosen people's behalf.

b. He fulfills His promises to His people: Pointed to God's coming kingdom (vv.13-16).

The psalmist rejoiced in the fulfillment of God's promises to His people. Specifically, he was referring to God's promise to deliver the Jews from Babylon after seventy years of captivity (Je.25:11-14; 29:10). Those seventy years had passed, and the set time had come for God to have mercy on His people and once again show His favor to them. Therefore, he believed that

they would be released soon. What astounding faith! The psalmist truly believed that God would free the Jews from their captivity. And God did—soon thereafter.

The psalmist continued confessing his confidence in the LORD, reminding God how His people loved Jerusalem (v.14). They held dear the very stones with which the city was constructed, and their hearts broke at the thought of the Holy City being reduced to dust.

God's restoration of His people to their land would stir the pagan nations to fear and be in awe of the LORD (v.15). When He rebuilt Jerusalem and His glory appeared there once again, even the kings of the world would bow down to Him (v.16). The psalmist was referring here to the word of the prophets, which will find its fulfillment in the coming kingdom of Jesus Christ (Is.40:2-4; 61:1-4; Zec.1:12-17). He spoke of these future events in the Hebrew perfect tense—as if they were already done—showing his absolute confidence in God to keep His Word.

c. He hears the prayers of the truly needy and never rejects their pleas for help (v.17).

The psalmist further praised God for His mercy and compassion toward His people. He not only hears the prayers of the destitute—those who have been stripped of everything they have and are truly needy—but His heart is also tender toward any of His people who are suffering. He never despises or rejects their desperate pleas for help.

In the present, the psalmist was speaking of the Jews who had lost everything in the Babylonian invasion. Prophetically, he was speaking of the Jews living during the great tribulation, who will be persecuted then as never before (Mt.24:15-22).

d. He had His great promise written in His Holy Word to stir future generations to praise Him (vv.18-22).

The LORD recorded His great promise of deliverance in His Word to stir future generations to praise Him (v.18). They would read how God watches over the earth from His heavenly sanctuary, a display of His love and concern for people (v.19). As the Jews were held captive in Babylon, He heard their groaning, their crying out to Him for relief (v.20). Just as He had promised to do, God set them free to return to Jerusalem so they would not die in Babylon.

The LORD delivered His people for a special purpose: so they would declare and praise His great name (v.21). The LORD (Yahweh, Jehovah) is the name by which God made His covenant with His people. It speaks of His relationship with them and His faithfulness to them. God's people would forever praise Him as they bore witness of His faithfulness to His promises.

---

2 Frank E. Gaebelein, ed. *The Expositor's Bible Commentary*, p.647.

The release of the Jews from Babylonian captivity is a picture of Christ's releasing us from the bondage of sin and death (Lu.4:18-19; Ro.6:23; 8:2). It points prophetically to the salvation of the Gentiles and Christ's kingdom of all the redeemed. One day, when all the peoples and nations of the world are gathered together in Christ's eternal kingdom, they will worship Him for His great redemption.

Thought 1. In the midst of our trials and afflictions, we need to cling tightly to God's promises. Although the psalmist's life was quickly fading, he found hope in God's faithfulness to His people. Likewise, God has given us—His people living today—some precious promises:

➤ He is with us at all times; we do not face our suffering alone (He.13:5-6).

➤ He is working out all things—including our suffering—for our good and to accomplish His purpose in our lives (Ro.8:28-29).

➤ His grace will be sufficient for our suffering, making us strong through our weakness (2 Co.12:9-12).

➤ He is coming again for His people—the blessed hope of the church (Tit.2:13; John 14:3).

➤ We have eternal life (Tit.1:2; 1 Jn.2:25).

➤ We have nothing to fear in death (Ps.23:4; He. 2:15).

➤ We will be transported immediately into His presence at death (Lu.23:43; Ph.1:23; 2 Co.5:8).

➤ He is preparing a place for us to dwell with Him eternally (Jn.14:2).

➤ We will receive a special reward for enduring suffering faithfully (Js.1:12; Re.2:10).

Along with all these promises, God has promised that He cannot lie (Nu.23:19; Tit.1:2; He.6:18). In our lowest moments, when all else seems hopeless, we can trust Him to do everything He has promised. His promises are our hope, anchoring our souls and serving as a comforting refuge for us during our most difficult times (He.6:11-20).

> **Being fully persuaded that God had power to do what he had promised (Ro.4:21).**
>
> **For no matter how many promises God has made, they are "Yes" in Christ. And so through him the "Amen" is spoken by us to the glory of God (2 Co.1:20).**
>
> **A faith and knowledge resting on the hope of eternal life, which God, who does not lie, promised before the beginning of time (Tit.1:2).**
>
> **Through these he has given us his very great and precious promises, so that through them you may participate in the**

divine nature and escape the corruption in the world caused by evil desires (2 Pe.1:4).

But in keeping with his promise we are looking forward to a new heaven and a new earth, the home of righteousness (2 Pe.3:13).

And this is what he promised us—even eternal life (1 Jn.2:25).

3 (102:23-28) Ask God to heal you and to spare your life.

The suffering psalmist longed to see the fulfillment of God's promises to His people, yet he feared that his life was racing toward its end. He longed to take part in God's great deliverance of His people, so he called on God to heal him and to spare His life. He declared his faith in God's eternal power and unchanging nature.

a. Because your situation is desperate: You are weak and about to die in midlife (v.23).

The psalmist shared his desperate situation: in the way or course of his life, in midlife, he had suffered a serious, disabling affliction. Because of it, he did not expect to live to a full age. It had so weakened him that he felt he could die at any time.

b. Because He (God) is eternal: He has the power to heal and extend life (vv.24-27).

The psalmist's condition was grim, but he refused to accept the sentence of death. Firmly believing that God had the power to heal him and extend his life, he begged God to spare him from an early death (v.24a). He declared his faith in God, confessing that He is eternal (v.24b). God existed in the beginning, prior to the creation of the universe (v.25). He created both the earth and the heavens. From the prophecy of Isaiah, the psalmist knew that the universe would one day perish (Is.51:6) but that God would *remain* (amad) or continue to exist forever (v.26a). Isaiah also prophesied, along with Peter and others, that God would make a new heaven and new earth (2 Pe.3:10-13). Like a person throwing away dirty, worn out clothes and replacing them with sparkling new ones, God will one day destroy this sin-stained universe and transform it into one that is completely new and undefiled (v.26b). The author of *Hebrews* confirmed that this prophecy would find its fulfillment in the eternal kingdom of Jesus Christ in a new heaven and new earth (He.1:8-13).

Although the psalmist's strength was quickly fading, his faith remained strong. No matter what changes life or time might bring—even the destruction of the universe—God remains the same (v.27). He is unchanging, unchangeable, and eternal.

c. Because He will be the God of all generations to come: He will keep the descendants of the godly in His presence (v.28).

Even though he might not live to see it, the psalmist declared that God would fulfill His promise to His people. The children of God's servants—the descendants of the current generation of Jews—would *live* (shakhan) or dwell in the land God had promised to Abraham. They would be established before God in Zion, where His presence would once again be manifested among His people in a very special way.

Thought 1. Multitudes of people live with physical conditions that, barring a miracle, will never change. Many have incurable diseases that steal the quality from whatever time remains. Others, according to doctors, have only a short time to live. Apparently, this was the case with the psalmist. Yet, he continued to pray for God to heal him and to extend his life, and so should we. God can do what doctors and medicine cannot; He has the power to heal us miraculously. King Hezekiah of old was sick with a terminal disease. Still, he prayed fervently and God extended his life an additional fifteen years (2 K.20:1-6).

At the same time, all who suffer from devastating or terminal illnesses or injuries should remember this: God may choose to glorify Himself through their suffering or through their deaths rather than through their lives (Ph.1:20). If God wills to heal us by trans-porting us to His heavenly kingdom, we should remain strong in our faith. Just as this psalmist did, we too should believe and declare that God is true to His promises, and that His work will continue in and through those who come behind us.

> **Going a little farther, he fell with his face to the ground and prayed, "My Father, if it is possible, may this cup be taken from me. Yet not as I will, but as you will" (Mt.26:39).**
>
> **"So I say to you: Ask and it will be given to you; seek and you will find; knock and the door will be opened to you (Lu.11:9).**
>
> **During the days of Jesus' life on earth, he offered up prayers and petitions with loud cries and tears to the one who could save him from death, and he was heard because of his reverent submission (He.5:7).**
>
> **"Remember, O LORD, how I have walked before you faithfully and with wholehearted devotion and have done what is good in your eyes." And Hezekiah wept bitterly (2 K.20:3).**
>
> **Look away from me, that I may rejoice again before I depart and am no more" (Ps.39:13).**

1. Praise the LORD with your whole being	PSALM 103 **When You Become Deeply Aware of God's Mercy & Goodness, 103:1-22** *Of David.*	great is his love for those who fear him; 12 As far as the east is from the west, so far has he removed our transgressions from us.	Him that soars above the highest heavens • He forgives & removes our sins from us, casting them afar forevermore

1. Praise the LORD with your whole being
  a. Praise His holy name
  b. Praise Him for all His goodness

  1) Forgiveness
  2) Healing

  3) Redemption
  4) Love
  5) Compassion

  6) Satisfaction
  7) Physical & spiritual renewal

2. Acknowledge the LORD's works
  a. He provides justice for His people & punishes their oppressors
  b. He revealed Himself—His ways & works—to the world: Revealed thru Moses & Israel
  1) He is a merciful judge: Understanding, slow to anger, overflowing with love
  • He does not constantly accuse us nor harbor anger when we do wrong
  • He does not punish nor repay us as much as our sins deserve
  • He has a love for all who truly fear & reverence

Praise the LORD, O my soul; all my inmost being, praise his holy name.
2 Praise the LORD, O my soul, and forget not all his benefits—
3 Who forgives all your sins and heals all your diseases,
4 Who redeems your life from the pit and crowns you with love and compassion,
5 Who satisfies your desires with good things so that your youth is renewed like the eagle's.
6 The LORD works righteousness and justice for all the oppressed.
7 He made known his ways to Moses, his deeds to the people of Israel:
8 The LORD is compassionate and gracious, slow to anger, abounding in love.
9 He will not always accuse, nor will he harbor his anger forever;
10 He does not treat us as our sins deserve or repay us according to our iniquities.
11 For as high as the heavens are above the earth, so

12 As far as the east is from the west, so far has he removed our transgressions from us.
13 As a father has compassion on his children, so the LORD has compassion on those who fear him;
14 For he knows how we are formed, he remembers that we are dust.
15 As for man, his days are like grass, he flourishes like a flower of the field;
16 The wind blows over it and it is gone, and its place remembers it no more.
17 But from everlasting to everlasting the LORD's love is with those who fear him, and his righteousness with their children's children—
18 With those who keep his covenant and remember to obey his precepts.
19 The LORD has established his throne in heaven, and his kingdom rules over all.
20 Praise the LORD, you his angels, you mighty ones who do his bidding, who obey his word.
21 Praise the LORD, all his heavenly hosts, you his servants who do his will.
22 Praise the LORD, all his works everywhere in his dominion. Praise the LORD, O my soul.

Him that soars above the highest heavens
• He forgives & removes our sins from us, casting them afar forevermore

2) He is like a compassionate father: Tender, loving, & caring toward all who genuinely fear & revere Him
3) He is our Creator & knows our exact nature...
• That we are mere dust
• That we are as frail as grass & flowers: Subject to nature, disease, & death with only a brief lifespan on earth

c. He showers His eternal love & righteousness on all who fear Him
1) Showers His love on their families for generations
2) Showers His love on all who are faithful & obedient

3. Call for universal praise to the LORD
  a. Bc. He has established His kingdom throughout the heavens & He rules over all
  b. Bc. He is worthy of all worship
  1) By His mighty angels who serve Him in the celestial court
  2) By all the heavenly hosts
  3) By everything He has created, all His works
  4) By every one of us, every single individual

PSALM 103

When You Become Deeply Aware of God's Mercy and Goodness, 103:1-22

(103:1-22) **Introduction:** the simplest but, perhaps most profound definition of God's mercy and grace is this: grace is God's giving us what we do *not* deserve, and mercy is God's *not* giving us what we *do* deserve. Truly, we sinners do not deserve God's salvation and all the blessings that accompany it. We do deserve God's judgment and punishment for our sins. Nevertheless, God, in His great mercy, judged and punished His Son in our place. So when we repent and genuinely believe in Christ, our sins are forgiven and we stand *justified* before God. Or, as has often been said, God views us "just as if we had never sinned."

God's mercy is the theme of Psalm 103. In this psalm, David expresses a deep awareness of God's great mercy in his life. He had committed terrible sin—adultery and murder—and although he had suffered the devastating

consequences of his sin, God had forgiven and restored him. In previous psalms, David talked about the inescapable guilt that gripped his soul because of his despicable sins. But nowhere in this psalm does he mention that guilt. God, in His boundless mercy and goodness, had not only forgiven David, but He had also healed him of the self-inflicted wounds on his own spirit (v.12).

Before we can fully appreciate God's mercy, we first have to understand how serious and contemptible our sin is in God's eyes (1 Ti.1:15-17). When we do, then the greatness and the extent of God's mercy become clear to us. And when we clearly see God's mercy, we will praise Him with everything that is within us (v.1). This is, *When You Become Deeply Aware of God's Mercy and Goodness*, 103:1-22.

1. Praise the LORD with your whole being (vv.1-5).

2. Acknowledge the LORD's works (vv.6-18).
3. Call for universal praise to the LORD (vv.19-22).

1 (103:1-5) Praise the LORD with your whole being.

David began with an eruption of praise to the LORD. To *praise the LORD* is to express love and gratitude for all that God is and all that He does. With all that was within him—his whole being, the depths of his innermost self—David praised God for who He is and for His unlimited goodness to His people.

a. Praise His holy name (v.1).

First, David praised and exalted the holy name of the LORD. *Yahweh* or *Jehovah* is God's personal name. More than any of His other names, it reveals His heart and what He is like. It is the name by which He revealed Himself to His people and established His covenant with them (Ex.6:2-8). As the LORD, He is the God who makes and keeps His covenant (His promises) with His people, pledging to them His unfailing love and faithfulness.

God's name is holy—sacred, hallowed, consecrated. It is to be so revered, so honored, that God commanded His people never to take His name in vain—never to use it commonly, casually, or insincerely (Ex.20:7). We are to set God's name apart, never daring to use it in any way that demeans or takes away from its sacredness.

b. Praise Him for all His goodness (vv.2-5).

Second, David praised the LORD for His goodness to His people. He admonished himself never to forget God's *benefits* (gemul)—all of the blessings God bestows in His dealings with us (Ps.13:6). David listed seven benefits that God, in His lavish goodness, freely gives us:

➢ Forgiveness of our sins (v.3a)
➢ Healing of our diseases (v.3b)
➢ Redemption of our lives from destruction, death, or the pit—a picture of our enslaving sin and its deadly consequences (v.4a)
➢ *Love* (chesed)—His steadfast, unfailing love (v.4b)
➢ Compassion or tender mercies—excessive acts of love with which the LORD crowns us because we are His royal sons and daughters (v.4c)
➢ Satisfaction of our desires, especially our spiritual longings (v.5a; Ps.107:9; Mt.5:6; Jn.6:35)
➢ Physical and spiritual renewal, like the restored strength the eagle receives when it sheds its old feathers in the molting process (v.5b; Is.40:31)

Thought 1. A lack of thankfulness and praise to God is the result of taking His blessings for granted. All too often, we can only see the difficult circumstances facing us or the things that we do not have, completely overlooking all that we have in Christ. On our very worst days—if we have genuinely trusted Christ—we are forgiven and redeemed. We are sons and daughters of God, recipients of His unfailing love and tender mercies. We have a peace and inner satisfaction that this world cannot offer.

The challenges of life are merely temporary, but the benefits of God's goodness and mercy are eternal (2 Co.4:17). We need to take our eyes off of the things we can see—the afflictions and difficulties of this life—and focus on those things we cannot see: the eternal blessings God has so mercifully given us (2 Co.4:18). When we do, like David, we will overflow with praise to the LORD.

> **Praise be to the God and Father of our Lord Jesus Christ, the Father of compassion and the God of all comfort (2 Co.1:3).**
>
> **Praise be to the God and Father of our Lord Jesus Christ, who has blessed us in the heavenly realms with every spiritual blessing in Christ (Ep.1:3).**
>
> **Praise be to the God and Father of our Lord Jesus Christ! In his great mercy he has given us new birth into a living hope through the resurrection of Jesus Christ from the dead (1 Pe.1:3).**
>
> **I will extol the LORD at all times; his praise will always be on my lips (Ps.34:1).**
>
> **I will exalt you, my God the King; I will praise your name for ever and ever (Ps.145:1).**

2 (103:6-18) Acknowledge the LORD's works.

David reflected on the great things God had done for him personally and for His people, the nation of Israel. He acknowledged the LORD's wonderful works, praising Him for His righteousness, mercy, and love.

a. He provides justice for His people and punishes their oppressors (v.6).

David testified that God is faithful to His people and that He works in their behalf against those who persecute and oppress them. In His righteousness, God provides justice for them by carrying out judgment against their oppressors. God had faithfully demonstrated this throughout the years of David's life. He had delivered David many times, beginning with the giant Philistine, Goliath, who mocked the LORD and His people. Again and again, David had witnessed God's judging those who oppressed him, including the jealous Saul, and, tragically, his rebellious son Absalom.

God had also proven Himself to be just in His dealings with His people. The greatest example of this is God's deliverance of Israel from Egyptian bondage.

When they were oppressed by Pharaoh, God miraculously set them free, judging Egypt's proud king, his nation, and his armies.

b. He revealed Himself—His ways and works—to the world: Revealed through Moses and Israel (vv.7-16).
Having been forgiven much, David exalted the LORD for His loving and merciful ways. God had revealed Himself—His ways and works—through Moses and His people, Israel (v.7). David referred back to a specific episode in Israel's history. Out of a burning desire to know and understand the LORD, Moses humbly asked God to reveal His ways to Him. God graciously promised to grant his request (Ex.33:12-23). The next morning, Moses ascended Mount Sinai and the LORD passed by, revealing Himself to Israel's leader (Ex.34:1-9). Then, the LORD made a promise to Moses and the people of Israel: He pledged to do marvelous works in their behalf, miracles never before seen in all the world (Ex.34:10-27).

David recalled that God had revealed Himself to Moses as a merciful judge. He quoted what God had proclaimed about Himself to Moses: He is compassionate, understanding, gracious, slow to anger, and overflowing with mercy (v.8; Ex.34:6).

Continuing to exalt God's mercy, David declared that the LORD does not constantly accuse us nor does He harbor anger when we do wrong (v.9). Certainly, He does not punish or repay us as much as our sins deserve (v.10). His love for all who truly fear Him—who reverence, submit to, and obey Him—soars above the highest heavens (v.11). He completely forgives our sins and removes them from us, casting them far away forevermore (v.12).

Note that the LORD does not remove our sins as far as the north is from the south but *as far as the east is from the west*. Why is this significant? Because the north and the south eventually meet. You can travel north only so far—to the North Pole of the earth—and then you will begin travelling south. A person travelling east, however, can travel east infinitely. He could circle the earth again and again, all the while heading east. Just as east and west never meet, we who are forgiven by God's grace will never again meet with our sins. What amazing grace!

David described God as a compassionate father who knows His children and understands their weaknesses. He is ever tender, loving, and caring toward all who genuinely fear and revere Him (v.13). As our Creator, God knows our exact nature. He understands that we are mere dust (v.14). Like the grass and flowers of the field, we are subject to the laws and limitations of nature. We flourish for a time, but only for a brief time. Disease and age strike rapidly, and then our brief lives on earth come to an end (vv.15-16).

c. He showers His eternal love and righteousness on all who fear Him (vv.17-18).
Thankfully, God's love extends beyond the fleeting moments of our short lives. His mercy or unfailing love knows no bounds. His love is the essence of who God is and what He is like. Therefore, like God, His love is from everlasting to everlasting—infinite, unlimited, and eternal (v.17). The LORD showers His eternal love and righteousness on all who fear Him, proving Himself faithful to their families for generations.

David further explained that God showers His unfailing love on all who are faithful to His covenant and obedient to His commandments (v.18). While God's love is unconditional, many of His blessings are conditional depending on our obedience. This was the case regarding God's covenant with Israel. His love and faithfulness to His chosen people is unchanging and eternal. However, some of the promises of the covenant were directly tied to the people's faithfulness and obedience to Him.

Thought 1. Everything that we are and have is attributable to God's mercy and goodness toward us (1 Co.15:10). Where would we be were it not for God's wonderful work in our lives? Where would we be without His mercy and unfailing love?

God's works are the fruit of His ways. The LORD wants us to understand what He is like. He is merciful, compassionate, and forgiving. His love for us is beyond our comprehension (Ep.3:17-19). God is not an angry tyrant but rather a kind, understanding father. He knows what we are like; He understands our weaknesses. Just as significant, His Son became one of us in order to identify with us as frail human beings. Because Christ lived facing the trials and temptations of life, He is able to help us when we are tempted and tried (He.2:16-18; 4:15-16).

In countless ways, God is good to us, blessing us in spite of our unworthiness. In addition, as a loving Father, God also delights in rewarding us when we are obedient to Him. The full measure of His blessings is reserved for those who fear Him: those who reverence Him and submit to His Word. This promise should stir us to wholly dedicate ourselves to Him and to walk in complete obedience to His commandments.

> **Oh, the depth of the riches of the wisdom and knowledge of God! How unsearchable his judgments, and his paths beyond tracing out! (Ro.11:33).**
> **And sang the song of Moses the servant of God and the song of the Lamb: "Great and marvelous are your deeds, Lord God Almighty. Just and true are your ways, King of the ages (Re.15:3).**

Then hear from heaven, your dwelling place. Forgive and act; deal with each man according to all he does, since you know his heart (for you alone know the hearts of all men), so that they will fear you all the time they live in the land you gave our fathers (1 K.8:39-40).

Let them give thanks to the LORD for his unfailing love and his wonderful deeds for men (Ps.107:8).

Because of the LORD's great love we are not consumed, for his compassions never fail (La.3:22).

3 (103:19-22) Call for universal praise to the LORD.

David concluded his celebration of God's mercy and goodness with a call for universal praise to the LORD. He summoned God's angels and everything God created to join him in blessing the holy name of the LORD.

a. Because He has established His kingdom throughout the heavens and He rules over all (v.19).

David directed our praise to God's throne in heaven, where He reigns over the entire universe. We should praise Him because He is LORD of all: He has made His kingdom in the heavens and, in His sovereignty, He rules there over His entire creation.

b. Because He is worthy of all worship (vv.20-22).

As the eternal, sovereign, merciful God, the LORD is worthy of all worship. David called upon God's mighty angels who serve Him in His celestial court to bless the LORD (vv.20-21). All the heavenly hosts should worship Him.

Scripture tells us relatively little about what angels are like. In three parallel statements, the Holy Spirit used David to give us a significant portion of what the Bible reveals about them:

➢ Angels excel in strength (v.20a); they are exceedingly mighty, the most powerful of all God's created beings.

➢ Angels do what God commands them to do; they obey His word (v.20b).

➢ Angels are God's heavenly *hosts* (tsabah), His heavenly army that wars against Satan's demonic forces (v.21a).

➢ Angels are God's ministers or servants (v.21b).

➢ Angels do God's will—what pleases Him. They labor to accomplish God's will on earth (v.21c).

In addition to the angels, David called upon all God's works—everything that God created—to praise and worship Him (v.22a). "Everywhere in his dominion" means every place that God rules. In other words, it speaks of the entire universe.

David ended Psalm 103 exactly as he began it: by charging his own soul to bless the LORD (v.22b). Every one of us, every single individual, should join David in praising and worshipping the LORD.

Thought 1. Everything that God made He created for His glory. David understood this and called for all of God's works—angels included—to give Him praise. David's call is a call to us, most undeserving of His grace. It is through us sinful human beings that God chose to most vividly display His glory. We are His workmanship, His masterpieces (Ep.2:8-10). As great as God's work in creation is, His work in salvation is even greater. All of His works will praise His name, but we whose lives have been redeemed and transformed by His goodness and mercy should proclaim His glory the loudest.

In order that we, who were the first to hope in Christ, might be for the praise of his glory (Ep.1:12).

To him be glory in the church and in Christ Jesus throughout all generations, for ever and ever! Amen (Ep.3:21).

Then I heard every creature in heaven and on earth and under the earth and on the sea, and all that is in them, singing: "To him who sits on the throne and to the Lamb be praise and honor and glory and power, for ever and ever!" (Re.5:13).

Yours, O LORD, is the greatness and the power and the glory and the majesty and the splendor, for everything in heaven and earth is yours. Yours, O LORD, is the kingdom; you are exalted as head over all (1 Chr.29:11).

Let heaven and earth praise him, the seas and all that move in them (Ps.69:34).

All you have made will praise you, O LORD; your saints will extol you (Ps.145:10).

PSALM 104

When You Consider God's Astounding Creation & Provision, Stand Amazed! 104:1-35

1. Worship the LORD for His greatness—glorify Him for creation
a. He is clothed in royal splendor & wraps Himself in light (holiness), 1 Jn.1:5; 1 Ti.6:16
b. He is all powerful
  1) He stretched out the heavens like a tent over earth
  2) He has put His heavenly home above the skies (firmament)
  3) He uses the clouds & winds for His own purposes
  4) He uses angels (winds) to do His bidding[DS1]
  5) He hung the earth in space on a firm foundation so it can never be moved
    • Covered it with a flood of water that rose above the mountains
    • Dispersed the waters by His command, sending them to the valleys where they were assigned
    • Set a boundary for the waters so they would never again cover the earth

2. Praise God for His provision
a. His provision of water
  1) Water for people (springs of water)
  2) Water for all animals
    • The example of donkeys
    • The example of birds
  3) Water for the vegetation of the mountains & the earth
b. His provision of vegetation & food
  1) Grass for cattle
  2) Plants for people to cultivate & produce...
    • Wine for pleasure
    • Oil for beauty
    • Bread for food
c. His provision of shelter
  1) The trees to house animals (& to provide lumber for people)
    • The birds

Praise the LORD, O my soul. O LORD my God, you are very great; you are clothed with splendor and majesty.
2 He wraps himself in light as with a garment; he stretches out the heavens like a tent
3 And lays the beams of his upper chambers on their waters. He makes the clouds his chariot and rides on the wings of the wind.
4 He makes winds his messengers, flames of fire his servants.
5 He set the earth on its foundations; it can never be moved.
6 You covered it with the deep as with a garment; the waters stood above the mountains.
7 But at your rebuke the waters fled, at the sound of your thunder they took to flight;
8 They flowed over the mountains, they went down into the valleys, to the place you assigned for them.
9 You set a boundary they cannot cross; never again will they cover the earth.
10 He makes springs pour water into the ravines; it flows between the mountains.
11 They give water to all the beasts of the field; the wild donkeys quench their thirst.
12 The birds of the air nest by the waters; they sing among the branches.
13 He waters the mountains from his upper chambers; the earth is satisfied by the fruit of his work.
14 He makes grass grow for the cattle, and plants for man to cultivate—bringing forth food from the earth:
15 Wine that gladdens the heart of man, oil to make his face shine, and bread that sustains his heart.
16 The trees of the LORD are well watered, the cedars of Lebanon that he planted.
17 There the birds make their nests; the stork has its

home in the pine trees.
18 The high mountains belong to the wild goats; the crags are a refuge for the coneys.
19 The moon marks off the seasons, and the sun knows when to go down.
20 You bring darkness, it becomes night, and all the beasts of the forest prowl.
21 The lions roar for their prey and seek their food from God.
22 The sun rises, and they steal away; they return and lie down in their dens.
23 Then man goes out to his work, to his labor until evening.
24 How many are your works, O LORD! In wisdom you made them all; the earth is full of your creatures.
25 There is the sea, vast and spacious, teeming with creatures beyond number—living things both large and small.
26 There the ships go to and fro, and the leviathan, which you formed to frolic there.
27 These all look to you to give them their food at the proper time.
28 When you give it to them, they gather it up; when you open your hand, they are satisfied with good things.
29 When you hide your face, they are terrified; when you take away their breath, they die and return to the dust.
30 When you send your Spirit, they are created, and you renew the face of the earth.
31 May the glory of the LORD endure forever; may the LORD rejoice in his works—
32 He who looks at the earth, and it trembles, who touches the mountains, and they smoke.
33 I will sing to the LORD all my life; I will sing praise to my God as long as I live.
34 May my meditation be pleasing to him, as I rejoice in the LORD.
35 But may sinners vanish from the earth and the wicked be no more. Praise the LORD, O my soul. Praise the LORD.

• The stork
  2) The high mountains to provide refuge for wild goats & coneys

d. His provision of orderliness in nature
  1) The seasons
  2) The night: Allows animals to prowl & seek their food

  3) The day
    • Allows nocturnal animals to rest
    • Allows people to arise & work

3. Declare God's wisdom
a. His wisdom in creating & filling the earth with such diversity
  1) The earth with all of His creatures & possessions
  2) The vast ocean with its...
    • Innumerable life species, both large & small, swarming throughout
    • Merchant ships sailing around the world
    • Huge leviathan (large sea animal) frolicking about
b. His wisdom in meeting all needs in both life & death
  1) In providing our necessities—food
  2) In providing good things that satisfy our desires
  3) In taking away our lives: Death
  4) In replenishing the earth with new life by His Spirit

4. Pray for God's glory to endure forever
a. Pray that God continue to sustain & rejoice in His creation
  1) Bc. He is the One who controls the universe
  2) Bc. you are committed to singing to Him & praising Him as long as you live
  3) Bc. your desire is to please Him in all that you think (meditate on) & do
b. Pray that God remove the wicked from the earth: That His glory alone be seen without any corruption of sin, Mt.6:9-10; 2 Pe.3:10-13

PSALM 104

When You Consider God's Astounding Creation and Provision, Stand Amazed! 104:1-35

(104:1-35) **Introduction:** where do we begin to describe the stunning beauty of nature? How can we begin to grasp the mindboggling processes of the natural world? Without question, humans have accomplished many spectacular things in this world. But they all pale in comparison to the glory and beauty of nature—the things God has made.

Psalm 104 is one of the most beautiful in the Hebrew hymnal. In poetic language and simple, yet majestic, images, it describes God's glory in creation in a way that rouses the soul to worship Him. The psalmist walks us through the six days of creation, providing a scenic example of God's wonderful works. The seventh day—the day of rest and worship—fills the entire psalm as it stirs us to rest in God's power and wisdom while lifting up our hearts and voices to worship Him.

Some scholars think Psalm 104 is a continuation of Psalm 103, making David its author. If the author is indeed David, we can easily imagine him writing this psalm while he tended his father's sheep. Picture the young man after God's own heart reclining against a rock while the sheep grazed in green pastures, describing the beautiful natural surroundings that stretched out before him. Imagine him meditating—with the opening chapters of the Torah in mind—on the wonderful works of the LORD, comparing the days of creation with what he had seen of heaven and earth.

Whoever the author is, his attention to God's handiwork and his awe of the One who made it all should lift our spirits to new levels of worship. This is, *When You Consider God's Astounding Creation and Provision, Stand Amazed!*, 104:1-35.

1. Worship the LORD for His greatness—glorify Him for creation (vv.1-9).
2. Praise God for His provision (vv.10-23).
3. Declare God's wisdom (vv.24-30).
4. Pray for God's glory to endure forever (vv.31-35).

1 (104:1-9) **Worship the LORD for His greatness—glorify Him for creation.**
The psalmist began by arousing his soul to worship the LORD for His greatness. As he proceeded, he glorified God specifically for His amazing creation. Such a marvelous, complex universe requires a Creator who is greater than the creation itself. Hence, the psalmist declared that the LORD is very great—exceedingly great, greater than anyone or anything else that exists.

a. He is clothed in royal splendor and wraps Himself in light (holiness), 1 Jn.1:5; 1 Ti.6:16 (v.1-2ª).
In awe of God's divine glory, the psalmist depicted Him as a stunningly majestic king. He is clothed in royal splendor, and He wraps Himself in light. The honor or splendor in which God is clothed is His magnificent creation. On the first day of creation, God created light (Ge.1:3-5). Speaking poetically, the psalmist described God as covered with light, like a king who arrays himself in a radiant robe.

When Moses asked to see God's glory, the LORD warned him that no man could look upon Him and live. Therefore, when God passed by Moses, He covered him with His hand (Ex.33:18-23). When Moses returned to the people after being in God's presence, his face glowed with the light of God's radiant glory. It was so bright that he had to cover his face with a veil (Ex.34:32-35). Scripture says that the New Jerusalem (the capital of the new heavens and earth) will not need the light of the sun or the moon; it will be brilliantly illuminated by the light of God's glory (Re.21:23).

Light is a symbol of God's holiness (1 Jn.5:1; 1 Ti.6:16), and His holiness shields Him from all defilement. At the same time, it exposes the sin and darkness of this world while illuminating the way of eternal life. Theologian John Calvin noted that, through this light (Jesus Christ), the invisible God "appears in a manner visible to us."[1]

b. He is all powerful (vv.2ᵇ-9).
Describing the creation of the universe's foundational elements, the psalmist emphasized God's supreme power. He is the all-powerful Creator and Controller of the mighty forces of nature. On the second day of creation, God stretched out the heavens like a curtain, with the starry skies forming a tent or canopy over the earth (v.2ᵇ). He then divided the waters above from the waters below, calling the space between them the sky or firmament. Next, he laid the beams of His heavenly home on the waters above the skies (v.3ª; Ge.1:6-8). God uses the elements of nature for His own purposes, making the *clouds* and the *winds* carry out His will (v.3ᵇ).

The LORD also made angels (winds) to do His bidding (v.4; 103:20-21). Interestingly, God created the angels sometime prior to creating the universe, for Scripture reveals that they shouted for joy when God laid the foundation of the earth (Jb.38:4-7). Here, Scripture teaches us that angels (not winds) are spirits. Elsewhere, they are called God's ministers or servants, as stated in the previous psalm (103:21; He.1:14).

Flames of fire as His servants may be a reference to lightning, with the psalmist describing the angels darting swiftly through the skies like lightning

---

1 John Calvin. *Calvin's Commentaries.* WORDsearch CROSS e-book.

(Da.9:21). Or, it may be a symbol of God's judgment, as fire often is in Scripture. God sometimes uses angels to carry out His judgment, as He will in the tribulation period (Re.8:1-11:19; 16:1-17). A third possibility is that it refers to the angels who surround God's throne like a flaming fire (Da.7:9-10).

Some scholars offer a completely different understanding of verse 4, translating *winds* as *spirits.* The *New King James Version*, for example, interprets the verse as referring to angles' being God's servants rather than wind (see DEEPER STUDY #1–PS.104:4 for more discussion).

The psalmist continued his poetic account of creation, describing the events of day three. God hung the earth in space on a firm foundation so it could never be moved (v.5). He covered the planet with a flood of water that rose above the mountains (v.6). Then, He dispersed the waters by His command, sending them to their assigned locations in the valleys (vv.7-8). To bar the waters from ever covering the earth again, the LORD set firm boundaries for them—the beaches and coastlines (v.9; Jb.26:10; Je.5:22).

DEEPER STUDY #1

(104:4) A number of scholars offer a different understanding of Psalm 104:4, translating *winds* (ruach) as *spirits.* Note the translation of this verse in the *New King James Version:*

> **"Who makes His angels spirits, His ministers a flame of fire" (Ps.104:4 NKJV).**

The arguments for the NIV and other similar translations are reasonable, but this is a case where Scripture interprets *Scripture.* The author of *Hebrews* quoted this verse from Psalms 104:4, saying,

> **"And of the angels he saith, Who maketh his angels spirits, and his ministers a flame of fire" (He.1:7, KJV).**

Clearly, the *context* or setting in which it is quoted in Hebrews 1 is speaking of angels. In fact, the entire passage is about Christ's superiority over the angels (He.1:4-14). This clarifies the meaning of Psalm 104:4.

Perplexingly, the translators of the NIV and other versions that interpret Psalm 104:4 as speaking of wind and fire rather than angels *acknowledge* that their translation of Hebrews 1:7, which is quoting Ps.104:4, is speaking of angels. Note the NIV:

> **"In speaking of the angels he says, 'He makes his angels winds, his servants flames of fire'" (He.1:7 NIV).**

The Divine inspiration of all Scripture decides the issue (2 Ti.3:16). The fact that God's Spirit moved the author of *Hebrews* to quote Psalm 104:4 as referring to *angels* proves that angels are the intended subject of the verse. Obviously, the Holy Spirit—the *Spirit of truth* (Jn.16:13)—would not have inspired the author of *Hebrews* to misquote or incorrectly apply another verse of Scripture. While the NIV and similar translations of Psalm 104:4 state a truth—God uses wind and fire to accomplish His purposes—Hebrews 1:7 establishes that it is not the truth intended in the verse.

Thought 1. Under Satan's influence, the world—through false teachings and other foolish ideas of the human imagination—has robbed God of the glory due Him for His creation (Ro.1:19-24). More and more, those who hold to God's creation of the universe are being ridiculed.

As believers, we need to stand firm on the truth, pointing people to God through the greatness of His creation. His very first means of revealing Himself to humans is His creation. For that reason, the beginning of faith is realizing that the universe was made by a higher power. When we have personally acknowledged this, then we can point people to the Bible, where God—*the* Higher Power—has more fully revealed Himself through His Word.

Like the psalmist, we should take time to observe the beauty and wonder all around us. Doing so will fill us with a sense of awe for God's glory and power, stirring us to fall down before Him in worship.

> **"And why do you worry about clothes? See how the lilies of the field grow. They do not labor or spin. Yet I tell you that not even Solomon in all his splendor was dressed like one of these (Mt.6:28-29).**
>
> **Yet he has not left himself without testimony: He has shown kindness by giving you rain from heaven and crops in their seasons; he provides you with plenty of food and fills your hearts with joy" (Ac.14:17).**
>
> **Since what may be known about God is plain to them, because God has made it plain to them. For since the creation of the world God's invisible qualities—his eternal power and divine nature—have been clearly seen, being understood from what has been made, so that men are without excuse (Ro.1:19-20).**
>
> **The heavens declare the glory of God; the skies proclaim the work of his hands (Ps.19:1).**

The heavens proclaim his righteousness, and all the peoples see his glory (Ps.97:6).

Do you not know? Have you not heard? Has it not been told you from the beginning? Have you not understood since the earth was founded? (Is.40:21).

2 (104:10-23) Praise God for His provision.

As the psalmist moved through the glories of God's creation, he emphasized how God provided for humanity through the things He made. The LORD's wonderful work reveals not only His brilliant wisdom but also His genuine love and concern for human beings, the summit of His creation. Realizing how God so carefully provided for us in creation should stir us to wholeheartedly praise His great name.

a. His provision of water (vv.10-13).

God's creatures, including humans, cannot survive without water. The LORD lovingly provided for this crucial need on the third day of creation, making the springs that run through the valleys and hills (v.10). These refreshing fountains of life provide water for both people and animals. The psalmist specifically cited donkeys and birds as examples (vv.11-12). In doing so, he depicted a vivid image of God's beautiful creation: wild donkeys sipping from a bubbling brook while the birds cheerfully sing from their nests in the branches of nearby trees (vv.11-12).

God provides water for the vegetation of the earth also. From His chambers—the heavens—the LORD waters the mountains with refreshing rains (v.13). As the showers from the sky soak into the soil, the thirsty earth is satisfied by this invigorating gift from God's gracious hand.

b. His provision of vegetation and food (vv.14-15).

On the third day of creation, God also set in motion the process by which everything He created would be nurtured and fed. He caused the earth's vegetation to provide food and other life-enriching products. The grass feeds the cattle, and other plants grown through human service or labor produce necessary foods. The psalmist was speaking of our fruits, vegetables, and grains, all of which require us to cultivate the earth (v.14; Ge.1:11-12). In addition to supplying us with necessary bread or food, these blessings furnish other items that contribute to our enjoyment of life, such as wine and oils that beautify our skin (v.15).

c. His provision of shelter (vv.16-18).

The trees God created provide shelter for many of His creatures (v.16). Animals such as birds and the stork make their homes in tree branches (v.17). Humans use their lumber to build houses as well as shelters for livestock. The mountains provide refuge or shelter for goats, while the conies or badgers live in mountainous rocky cliffs (v.18).

d. His provision of orderliness in nature (vv.19-23).

Moving on to the fourth day of creation, the psalmist pointed out that God established nature's orderliness through the sun and the moon (Ge.1:14-19). These heavenly bodies operate according to God's marvelous design, precisely regulating the seasons, the days, and the years (v.19; Ge.1:14).

The psalmist then praised God for the darkness of night. While people are resting, nocturnal animals prowl and seek their food (vv.20-21). He carefully noted that their food comes from God. Everything God made has a purpose; for instance, some creatures were created for the benefit of other creatures— another example of God's orderliness in design.

When the sun rises, these night-loving animals return to their dens to rest. Meanwhile, people are awakening to begin another day of work (v.22-23). It is a wonderful, painstakingly precise system, one that could only have been designed—and is continuously sustained—by an all-wise, all-powerful God.

Thought 1. How wonderful to think of God's care for His creation! Every creature He made is important to Him, and He has provided for each one through His works. As humans, we are most important to God, and He gave us authority over the rest of His creation (Ge.1:26-27). Believers in Jesus Christ are the special objects of His care, for we are God's sons and daughters. He is our Heavenly Father, a Father who promises to provide for His children. If God said in His Word that those who do not provide for their families are worse than infidels, think how much more He will provide for His children's needs (1 Ti.5:8)! We may face difficulties and times when we have little. Unemployment, famine, persecution, economic recessions, and other trials may leave us in need. At the other extreme, many have far more than they need. In either case, we should depend on God and not on ourselves, trusting Him to provide for us.

"Therefore I tell you, do not worry about your life, what you will eat or drink; or about your body, what you will wear. Is not life more important than food, and the body more important than clothes? Look at the birds of the air; they do not sow or reap or store away in barns, and yet your heavenly Father feeds them. Are you not much more valuable than they? Who of you by worrying can add a single hour to his life? "And why do you worry about clothes? See how the lilies of the field grow. They do not labor or spin. Yet I tell you that not even Solomon in all his splendor was dressed like one of these. If that is how God clothes the grass of the field, which is here today and tomorrow is thrown into the fire, will he not much more clothe you, O you of little faith? So do not worry, saying, 'What shall we eat?' or 'What shall we drink?' or 'What shall we wear?' For the pagans run after all these things, and your heavenly Father knows that you need them. But seek first his kingdom and his righteousness, and all these things will be given to you as well (Mt.6:25-33).

And God is able to make all grace abound to you, so that in all things at all times, having all that you need, you will abound in every good work. As it is written: "He has scattered abroad his gifts to the poor; his righteousness endures forever." Now he who supplies seed to the sower and bread for food will also supply and increase your store of seed and will enlarge the harvest of your righteousness (2 Co.9:8-10).

And my God will meet all your needs according to his glorious riches in Christ Jesus (Ph.4:19).

Command those who are rich in this present world not to be arrogant nor to put their hope in wealth, which is so uncertain, but to put their hope in God, who richly provides us with everything for our enjoyment (1 Ti.6:17).

He gave you manna to eat in the desert, something your fathers had never known, to humble and to test you so that in the end it might go well with you. You may say to yourself, "My power and the strength of my hands have produced this wealth for me." But remember the LORD your God, for it is he who gives you the ability to produce wealth, and so confirms his covenant, which he swore to your forefathers, as it is today (De.8:16-18).

I was young and now I am old, yet I have never seen the righteous forsaken or their children begging bread (Ps.37:25).

3 (104:24-30) Declare God's wisdom.

The wonders of creation declare the infinite wisdom of our great God (Ps.136:5; Pr.3:19-20; Jer.10:2). God created a fascinating system consisting of a wide diversity of creatures. Each has a purpose, and they all contribute in some way to the sustaining of life on earth. God brilliantly designed the meeting of His creatures' needs into creation itself, with His Spirit as the force behind it all.

a. His wisdom in creating and filling the earth with such diversity (vv.24-26).

The psalmist declared God's wisdom in creating and filling the earth with such a variety of creatures (v.24). *Creatures* (qinyan) is literally possessions, the things acquired through work. The earth and everything in it belong to God; it is His by right of creation (Ps.24:1; 89:11). The psalmist praised the LORD for the animal kingdom, which God made on the fifth day of creation (Ge.1:20-23). Specifically, He praised God for the ocean with its innumerable species of creatures large and small that swarm through its seemingly endless expanse (v.25).

As he meditated on the wonders of the sea, the psalmist's mind went to the commercial ships that sailed around the world (v.26). The wisdom to create such vessels was given by God. He also thought of the leviathan—a giant creature that frolicked in the sea but that struck fear in people's hearts. While we do not know what the leviathan actually was, God's description of it in His discourse to Job suggests that it may have been a huge crocodile (Jb.41:1-34).

b. His wisdom in meeting all needs in both life and death (vv.27-30).

On the sixth day of creation, God instructed man as to how he would receive his food (Ge.1:29-31). All of God's creatures—especially humans—depend on Him for their food. God, in His incomparable wisdom, meets all of their needs in due season or at the appropriate time (v.27). People gather their food as the LORD faithfully provides it (v.28ᵃ). In addition, He opens His hand—a picture of God's overflowing generosity—and out of His never-ending grace, the LORD satisfies our desire for good things (v.28ᵇ).

The psalmist next turned his attention to God's provision at death (v.29). Commentator Alexander Kirkpatrick provides an excellent explanation of this verse:

> All creatures depend upon God for life as well as food. The breath or spirit of God is the source of the life-breath of His creatures. The psalmist probably had Job 34:14-15 in his mind (Acts 17:25; Col.1:17). The 'hiding' of God's face is usually the symbol of His wrath; but here it denotes rather the withdrawal of His (life) sustaining power (Ps.30:7).[2]

"You hide your face" and "you take away their breath" are parallel statements, both referring to death. To God alone belongs the power of life and death (Nu.16:22; 27:16; He.12:9). He determines the

---

2 A.F. Kirkpatrick. *The Book of Psalms*. WORDsearch CROSS e-book.

length of our lives (Jb.14:5). *Breath* (ruach) is also the Hebrew word for spirit. God takes away the life of His creatures at death, and they return to dust—a reference to the process of decomposition (Ge.3:19; Ec.12:7).

But death does not mark the end of God's creation. In His infinite wisdom, He designed His creatures with the marvelous ability to reproduce (v.30; Ge.1:24-25). Through the reproduction process, God's Spirit continually creates new life that replenishes the earth. As Kirkpatrick said, "Life not death rules in Nature. A new generation takes the place of the old. Creation continues, for God is perpetually sending forth His Spirit and renewing the face of the earth with fresh life."[3] This verse clearly teaches that all life is given through the work of God's Spirit.

Thought 1. God's wisdom in His works is truly astonishing. As man's knowledge of nature—God's creation—increases as never before, we are continually amazed by the wisdom of God in His works and in His ways.

God's powerful wisdom is available to us, for He has revealed it to us through His Word. We can live wisely when we fear the LORD, when we revere and submit to Him and walk in obedience to His Word (Ps.111:10; 119:99). Scripture reveals that all the treasures of God's wisdom are hidden in Jesus Christ (Col.2:3). Therefore, when we receive Christ as Savior, and His Spirit comes to dwell within us, we then have the wisdom of God available to us. When we yield to the Holy Spirit and follow His leadership, we will be led by God's wisdom—the same wisdom by which He wondrously made the universe.

> **Oh, the depth of the riches of the wisdom and knowledge of God! How unsearchable his judgments, and his paths beyond tracing out! (Ro.11:33).**
>
> **But to those whom God has called, both Jews and Greeks, Christ the power of God and the wisdom of God. For the foolishness of God is wiser than man's wisdom, and the weakness of God is stronger than man's strength (1 Co.1:24-25).**
>
> **It is because of him that you are in Christ Jesus, who has become for us wisdom from God—that is, our righteousness, holiness and redemption (1 Co.1:30).**
>
> **When you were dead in your sins and in the uncircumcision of your sinful nature, God made you alive with Christ. He forgave us all our sins (Col.2:13).**
>
> **Blessed is the man who finds wisdom, the man who gains understanding, for she is more profitable than silver and yields better returns than gold. She is more precious than rubies; nothing you desire can compare with her. Long life is in her right hand; in her left hand are riches and honor. Her ways are pleasant ways, and all her paths are peace. She is a tree of life to those who embrace her; those who lay hold of her will be blessed. By wisdom the LORD laid the earth's foundations, by understanding he set the heavens in place; by his knowledge the deeps were divided, and the clouds let drop the dew (Pr.3:13-20).**
>
> **"Tell them this: 'These gods, who did not make the heavens and the earth, will perish from the earth and from under the heavens.'" But God made the earth by his power; he founded the world by his wisdom and stretched out the heavens by his understanding (Je.10:11-12).**
>
> **And said: "Praise be to the name of God for ever and ever; wisdom and power are his (Da.2:20).**

4 (104:31-35) **Pray for God's glory to endure forever.** After rejoicing in God's marvelous creation, the psalmist prayed for God's glory to endure forever. He asked that God would rejoice in His own works. Then, he prayed for the glory of God to be seen in His creation—a glory compromised by sin, but to be fully restored to the earth when Christ returns.

a. Pray that God continue to sustain and rejoice in His creation (vv.31-34).

As the psalmist delighted in God's wonderful works, he prayed that the LORD Himself would always rejoice in His creation (v.31). The glory of the LORD suggests God's empowering, life-giving presence among what He has made. "His handiwork will flourish as long as He sustains it."[4] He is the One who controls the universe. For example, earthquakes and volcanos are caused by His touch (v.32). The psalmist was praying for God to always take pleasure in His beautiful creation and continue to uphold it by His power (Col.1:17; He.1:3).

After reflecting on the marvels of God's works, the psalmist made a commitment to sing praises to the LORD as long as he lived (v.33). He further prayed that his *meditation* (siyach)—what he thought and said about God—would always be sweet or pleasing to the LORD (v.34). Simply put, he asked the LORD to help him always display a grateful spirit. To that end, he made a commitment to be glad in the LORD. God had created him and allowed him to live on His beautiful earth,

---

3 Ibid.

4 Frank E. Gaebelein, ed. *The Expositor's Bible Commentary*, p.664.

giving him the opportunity to enjoy so many good things (v.28). Therefore, the psalmist was determined to rejoice and not complain, regardless of his circumstances.

b. **Pray that God remove the wicked from the earth: That His glory alone be seen without any corruption of sin, Mt.6:9-10; 2 Pe.3:10-13 (v.35).**
The psalmist deeply longed for the LORD's glory to be seen without the corruption of sin. With that in mind, he prayed for God to remove the wicked from the earth. Looking forward to that day when God will once again reign throughout His creation, he praised the LORD for the glory of what is, and for the greater glory of what is to come (Mt.6:9-10; 2 Pe.3:10-13; Re.21:1).

Thought 1. Jesus taught us to pray for God's will to be done and for His kingdom to be established on earth (Mt.6:9-10). In essence, this was the psalmist's prayer. Today, we can pray with the firm assurance that our prayers will be answered: Christ will return to establish His kingdom on earth, just as Scripture promises. Since a special reward is promised to those who love His appearing, we should long for Christ's return and pray for Him to come quickly (2 Ti.4:8; Re.22:20). Even creation itself groans to be delivered from the corruption of sin (Je.12:4; Ro.8:21-22). Ultimately, this deliverance will come when the Lord creates a new heaven and new earth, a new universe that will forever be untouched by sin (2 Pe.3:10-13; Re.22:3-5; Re.22:1-8).

> Now to the King eternal, immortal, invisible, the only God, be honor and glory for ever and ever. Amen (1 Ti.1:17).

And the God of all grace, who called you to his eternal glory in Christ, after you have suffered a little while, will himself restore you and make you strong, firm and steadfast (1 Pe.5:10).

But the day of the Lord will come like a thief. The heavens will disappear with a roar; the elements will be destroyed by fire, and the earth and everything in it will be laid bare. Since everything will be destroyed in this way, what kind of people ought you to be? You ought to live holy and godly lives as you look forward to the day of God and speed its coming. That day will bring about the destruction of the heavens by fire, and the elements will melt in the heat. But in keeping with his promise we are looking forward to a new heaven and a new earth, the home of righteousness (2 Pe.3:10-13).

Have mercy on me, O God, have mercy on me, for in you my soul takes refuge. I will take refuge in the shadow of your wings until the disaster has passed (Ps.57:1).

Praise be to his glorious name forever; may the whole earth be filled with his glory. Amen and Amen (Ps.72:19).

"And I, because of their actions and their imaginations, am about to come and gather all nations and tongues, and they will come and see my glory (Is.66:18).

PSALM 105

When You Are Struggling & Need God's Encouragement, 105:1-45

1. Remember God's marvelous works & faithfully praise Him
a. Call on His name & tell others what He has done
   1) Through songs of praise & testimony that tell of His wonderful deeds
   2) Through glorifying & rejoicing in His holy name
b. Look to the LORD for strength & seek His presence (face) always
c. Call to mind His former miracles & the judgments He pronounced on the disobedient
   1) Bc. you are a descendant of Abraham—chosen by God, Ro.4:9-17, esp.16-17
   2) Bc. He is the LORD our God
   3) Bc. He executes justice throughout the earth

2. Remember God's great promise (covenant)—the promise He gave to a thousand generations
a. The promise was given to Abraham & his descendants, the descendants of faith, Ge.12:1-4; Ro.4:9-25
b. The promise, which was eternal, was the inheritance of Canaan, the promised land of God (a picture of heaven)

3. Remember God's strong protection
a. He protected Abraham & his followers as they began to seek the promised land
   1) They were few in number
   2) They journeyed from nation to nation in their search
b. He protected them from all oppressors & even kings: Bc. they were His chosen people & His prophets (messengers)

4. Remember God's wonderful care for His people
a. God sent famine on the land: Bc. of the people's sin, Ge.34:37, 38
b. God sent a man, Joseph, to prepare a way to deliver them
   1) He was sold as a slave
   2) He was jailed by his Egyptian master, falsely accused of sexual assault, Ge.39
   3) He helped other prisoners by interpreting their dreams:

Give thanks to the LORD, call on his name; make known among the nations what he has done.
2 Sing to him, sing praise to him; tell of all his wonderful acts.
3 Glory in his holy name; let the hearts of those who seek the LORD rejoice.
4 Look to the LORD and his strength; seek his face always.
5 Remember the wonders he has done, his miracles, and the judgments he pronounced,
6 O descendants of Abraham his servant, O sons of Jacob, his chosen ones.
7 He is the LORD our God; his judgments are in all the earth.
8 He remembers his covenant forever, the word he commanded, for a thousand generations,
9 The covenant he made with Abraham, the oath he swore to Isaac.
10 He confirmed it to Jacob as a decree, to Israel as an everlasting covenant:
11 "To you I will give the land of Canaan as the portion you will inherit."
12 When they were but few in number, few indeed, and strangers in it,
13 They wandered from nation to nation, from one kingdom to another.
14 He allowed no one to oppress them; for their sake he rebuked kings:
15 "Do not touch my anointed ones; do my prophets no harm."
16 He called down famine on the land and destroyed all their supplies of food;
17 And he sent a man before them—Joseph, sold as a slave.
18 They bruised his feet with shackles, his neck was put in irons,
19 Till what he foretold came to pass, till the word of the LORD proved him

true.
20 The king sent and released him, the ruler of peoples set him free.
21 He made him master of his household, ruler over all he possessed,
22 To instruct his princes as he pleased and teach his elders wisdom.
23 Then Israel entered Egypt; Jacob lived as an alien in the land of Ham.
24 The LORD made his people very fruitful; he made them too numerous for their foes,
25 Whose hearts he turned to hate his people, to conspire against his servants.
26 He sent Moses his servant, and Aaron, whom he had chosen.
27 They performed his miraculous signs among them, his wonders in the land of Ham.
28 He sent darkness and made the land dark—for had they not rebelled against his words?
29 He turned their waters into blood, causing their fish to die.
30 Their land teemed with frogs, which went up into the bedrooms of their rulers.
31 He spoke, and there came swarms of flies, and gnats throughout their country.
32 He turned their rain into hail, with lightning throughout their land;
33 He struck down their vines and fig trees and shattered the trees of their country.
34 He spoke, and the locusts came, grasshoppers without number;
35 They ate up every green thing in their land, ate up the produce of their soil.
36 Then he struck down all the firstborn in their land, the firstfruits of all their manhood.
37 He brought out Israel, laden with silver and gold, and from among their tribes no one faltered.
38 Egypt was glad when they left, because dread of Israel had fallen on them.
39 He spread out a cloud as a covering, and a fire to give

All came true, Ge.40
   4) He was brought to the king's attention, who freed him to rule over the nation, Ge.41
      • He was to protect the king's possessions against the coming famine
      • He was to oversee the nation's leaders as they tried to preserve the economy
c. God stirred Israel (70 persons) to move to Egypt bc. of the famine, Ge.46
   1) They lived there as foreigners for 400 years & grew so numerous they became a threat
   2) They were hated by the Egyptians who eventually enslaved them, Ex.1

5. Remember God's judgments
a. The executioners of God's judgment: Moses & Aaron
b. The judgments: They were miraculous but terrifying warnings to all the wicked & disobedient of the earth
   1) A frightening darkness: Due to Egypt's rebellion against God's Word (to set His people free)
   2) A pollution of all waters & the destruction of the fishing industry
   3) An infestation of frogs that overran Egypt's land & households

   4) A plague of maddening flies & gnats that swarmed throughout the land

   5) A season of destructive hail & frightening storms
      • Ruined the fruit industry
      • Ruined the forests & lumber industry

   6) An invasion of locusts & grasshoppers
      • Ate all green vegetation
      • Destroyed the farming industry & food

   7) A striking down of the eldest son: The tragic consequences of Egypt's rebellion against God

6. Remember God's redemption
a. He saved & set His people free
   1) Led Egypt to pay restitution
   2) Strengthened His people
   3) Struck enough fear in Egypt to make them willing & glad to release His people
b. He led & protected His people both day & night

	light at night.	43 He brought out his	a. He brought His people out of
c. He provided nourishment for His people	40 They asked, and he brought them quail and sat-	people with rejoicing, his chosen ones with shouts of	the wilderness (after 40 years) & filled them with joy
1) Fresh meat & bread	isfied them with the bread of heaven.	joy; 44 He gave them the lands	& rejoicing b. He gave His people their
2) Fresh water	41 He opened the rock, and water gushed out; like a	of the nations, and they fell heir to what others had	promised inheritance: Lands that pagans had owned &
	river it flowed in the desert.	toiled for—	toiled for
7. Remember God's faithfulness in keeping His sacred promise	42 For he remembered his holy promise given to his	45 That they might keep his precepts and observe	c. He did everything for one reason: So His people would
	servant Abraham.	his laws. Praise the LORD.	obey His laws & praise Him

PSALM 105

When You Are Struggling and Need God's Encouragement, 105:1-45

(105:1-45) **Introduction:** Psalm 105 was written to a group of people living in extremely challenging times. Just who was this group? It was the remnant who returned to Jerusalem after the 70-year Babylonian captivity. They came home to a heart-sickening mess, facing the overwhelming task of rebuilding the city and society God had judged. As they struggled and desperately needed encouragement, an unnamed psalmist was moved by God's Spirit to write a song reminding them of God's faithfulness. In it, he covers the highlights of Israel's history from Abraham to Canaan, emphasizing God's demonstration of His unfailing love to the people of His covenant.

Psalm 105 speaks to a broad range of people, but it is especially helpful to those living in difficult times. It is for those overwhelmed and exhausted from building and battling for God's kingdom. It is for those who fight for the souls of their loved ones to no avail. It is for the weary and discouraged laborers in the Lord's vineyard who see little fruit for their tireless efforts. It is for those who feel they can go on no longer. It is for those who have been beaten up by the world. It is for those who cannot find the strength to face another day. It is for the persecuted. It is for those who are left to pick up the pieces of their unfaithful nation once God has passed judgment on their beloved land. It is for those who question whether God has forsaken them. It is for those who are ready to quit.

God's people have always faced challenging times, and believers living today are no different. Those living in the time just before Christ's return will face unparalleled challenges and persecution. As the spiritual descendants of Abraham, we can claim this psalm personally, making its themes our very own. This is, *When You Are Struggling and Need God's Encouragement,* 105:1-45.

1. Remember God's marvelous works and faithfully praise Him (vv.1-7).
2. Remember God's great promise (covenant)—the promise He gave to a thousand generations (vv.8-11).
3. Remember God's strong protection (vv.12-15).
4. Remember God's wonderful care for His people (vv.16-25).
5. Remember God's judgments (vv.26-36).
6. Remember God's redemption (vv.37-41).
7. Remember God's faithfulness in keeping His sacred promise (vv.42-45).

1 (105:1-7) **Remember God's marvelous works and faithfully praise Him.**

The history of Israel is nothing short of miraculous. It is the story of God's amazing works in behalf of a people He chose to be His own. The psalmist called on these people to give thanks to the LORD and to faithfully praise Him for all He had done for their nation. Notice the emphasis of this passage on God's...

- *deeds* (v.1)
- *wonderful acts* (v.2)
- *marvelous works* (v.3)

a. **Call on His name and tell others what He has done (vv.1-3).**

The centuries-long record of faithfulness that God had with Israel was an encouragement for His people to call on Him for whatever they needed. Because of the LORD's faithfulness, the people were to proclaim what He had done for them to the other people or nations of the world (v.1). The psalmist instructed them to bear witness about the LORD through songs of praise and testimony that told of His wonderful acts (v.2). Through their rejoicing in the LORD, those who did not know Him would learn of His faithful love (v.3).

b. **Look to the LORD for strength and seek His presence (face) always (v.4).**

The remnant that returned to Jerusalem after the Babylonian captivity must have battled constant discouragement. The city was little more than a pile of rubble, having been abandoned and neglected for seventy years after its total destruction by Babylon. The elderly who had been dragged from Jerusalem seven decades earlier would surely have been brokenhearted if they had lived to see the shambles of the place where God had once dwelled with them. The young people who were taken as well as those who had been born in Babylon were no doubt overwhelmed by the work that lay ahead.

Keeping all these factors in mind, the psalmist exhorted the people to seek the LORD and His strength. Time and again, He had proven Himself strong in His people's behalf. When those charged with rebuilding Jerusalem grew weary in the work, the face or presence of the LORD would renew their tired spirits to labor on.

c. **Call to mind His former miracles and the judgments He pronounced on the disobedient (vv.5-7).** The psalmist further counseled the disheartened people to recall the miracles God had performed for Israel as well as the judgments He had pronounced on the disobedient (v.5). Their faithless ancestors had perished in the wilderness without ever seeing the promised land. Those wasted years were filled with incidents where God judged the rebellious in their midst. Even in their own lifetime, they had endured God's judgment—the Babylonian invasion and captivity—because of a prevailing spirit of unfaithfulness to God in their nation.

The psalmist reminded the remnant of three reassuring truths. First, they were the descendents of Abraham—people of the covenant and heirs to exciting, exclusive promises (v.6). They were God's chosen ones, specially favored by Him for a glorious purpose: to bless all the earth by bringing the Messiah into the world (Ge.22:18).

Second, he reminded them that *the LORD* (Yahweh, Jehovah) was their God (v.7ª). He had made His covenant with them and repeatedly proven Himself faithful to His Word. Their God was the LORD, the One who worked miracles to keep His covenant with His people.

Third, he reminded them that the LORD executes judgment or justice throughout the earth (v.7ᵇ). "These judgments are the decisive, dynamic deeds of God, saving His people and destroying His enemies."[1]

This returning remnant could not lose sight of these glorious truths. And they could not forget their history, both good and bad. God had brought them back to the land and longed to do great and mighty things for them again. How tragic it would be if, like so many of their ancestors, they too failed in their faith.

Thought 1. Without exception, each of us will battle discouragement in our walk with the LORD at some point. Trouble and trials are an inevitable part of life.

In addition to the natural consequences of living in a sin-cursed world, genuine believers also face Satan's fierce opposition. Yet Scripture encourages us not to become weary in serving the Lord. To accomplish this, we need to constantly be on guard and renew our spirits (Ga.6:9; 2 Co.4:16).

Several scholars point out that there are ten commandments in this passage (vv.1-7). We might accurately title them "The Ten Commandments for Fighting Discouragement:"
(1) Give thanks to God (v.1ª).
(2) Call on God's name for everything you need (v.1ᵇ).
(3) Make God's great works known to the lost (v.1ᶜ).
(4) Sing praises to God at all times (v.2ª).
(5) Testify of the wonderful things God has done for you (v.2ᵇ).
(6) Glory in God's holy name (v.3ª).
(7) Rejoice in the LORD always (v.3ᵇ).
(8) Look to the LORD for strength (v.4ª).
(9) Seek and enter the LORD's presence through prayer and worship (v.4ᵇ).
(10) Remember the LORD's miracles and judgments in His people's behalf throughout history (v.5).

We must not allow Satan to defeat us through discouragement. When we follow these commandments faithfully—even when we do not feel like it—God will lift us up, restore our joy, and strengthen us to labor on for Him. Remembering God's marvelous works and faithfully praising Him will lead us to victory.

> **About midnight Paul and Silas were praying and singing hymns to God, and the other prisoners were listening to them (Ac.16:25).**
>
> **Speak to one another with psalms, hymns and spiritual songs. Sing and make music in your heart to the Lord, always giving thanks to God the Father for everything, in the name of our Lord Jesus Christ (Ep.5:19-20).**
>
> **He says, "I will declare your name to my brothers; in the presence of the congregation I will sing your praises" (He.2:12).**
>
> **And sang the song of Moses the servant of God and the song of the Lamb: "Great and marvelous are your deeds, Lord God Almighty. Just and true are your ways, King of the ages (Re.15:3).**
>
> **I will remember the deeds of the LORD; yes, I will remember your miracles of long ago. I will meditate on all your works and consider all your mighty deeds (Ps.77:11-12).**
>
> **Sing to the LORD, for he has done glorious things; let this be known to all the**

---

1 Steven Lawson and Max Anders. *Holman Old Testament Commentary—Psalms.* WORD*search* CROSS e-book.

world. Shout aloud and sing for joy, people of Zion, for great is the Holy One of Israel among you" (Is.12:5-6).

2 (105:8-11) **Remember God's great promise (covenant)—the promise He gave to a thousand generations.**
The psalmist again encouraged the remnant by reminding them of the LORD's covenant with Israel. *The word which He commanded* "puts the stress on God's initiative and authority in the [making of the covenant], which means that this bond with men is by grace."[2] He further assured them that God would remember or be faithful to His great promise to His people, even for a thousand generations, that is to say, forever and ever.

a. **The promise was given to Abraham and his descendants, the descendants of faith, Ge.12:1-4; Ro.4:9-25 (vv.9-10).**
The LORD originally gave His covenant to Abraham, the great man of faith who left his homeland to follow God wherever He led (v.9ᵃ; Ge.12:1-4). God confirmed the covenant with Abraham's miraculously-conceived son, Isaac, and then with Isaac's son, Jacob (vv.9ᵇ-10ᵃ; Ge.26:1-5; 28:13-15).

God's promise is an everlasting covenant, given to Abraham's descendants, the nation of Israel (v.10ᵇ). But the New Testament reveals that all those whose faith is in the LORD are descendants of Abraham, regardless of race or nationality. Abraham has a physical seed—the Jews—but he also has a spiritual seed—all who trust the Lord for righteousness (Ro.4:9-25; Ga.3:6-9, 29).

b. **The promise, which was eternal, was the inheritance of Canaan, the promised land of God (a picture of heaven) (v.11).**
To Abraham's physical seed, God's eternal promise was the inheritance of Canaan, the promised land of God. Or put another way, Canaan was the land God promised to His people. Canaan is also a picture of heaven, the eternal inheritance of Abraham's spiritual seed (He.9:15; 1 Pe.1:4).

Thought 1. When we are struggling or discouraged, we need to remember God's precious promises to us (2 Pe.1:4). True believers are promised an inheritance like no other—eternal life and an eternal reward in heaven with the Lord. If we have genuinely repented of our sin and trusted Christ as Savior, we can trust God to keep His promise to us. Lest we doubt God's Word, He has guaranteed this promise with His Holy Spirit who dwells within us as down payment on our inheritance (Ep.1:11-14).

Remembering God's great promise gives us hope. Like a firm anchor, it will hold us steady in the storms of life (He.6:11-20). When we are discouraged and feel we can go on no longer, we need to keep our eyes fixed on heaven and the joy that awaits us there. This is what Abraham, our spiritual father, did, and it helped keep his faith strong when he was severely tested (He.11:14-19). Likewise, this is what our Savior did: He endured the cross by focusing on the joy that He would later know in heaven (He.12:1-3).

> **Being fully persuaded that God had power to do what he had promised (Ro.4:21).**
>
> **For no matter how many promises God has made, they are "Yes" in Christ. And so through him the "Amen" is spoken by us to the glory of God (2 Co.1:20).**
>
> **Because God wanted to make the unchanging nature of his purpose very clear to the heirs of what was promised, he confirmed it with an oath. God did this so that, by two unchangeable things in which it is impossible for God to lie, we who have fled to take hold of the hope offered to us may be greatly encouraged. We have this hope as an anchor for the soul, firm and secure. It enters the inner sanctuary behind the curtain (He.6:17-19).**
>
> **Let us hold unswervingly to the hope we profess, for he who promised is faithful (He.10:23).**
>
> **Therefore, since we are surrounded by such a great cloud of witnesses, let us throw off everything that hinders and the sin that so easily entangles, and let us run with perseverance the race marked out for us. Let us fix our eyes on Jesus, the author and perfecter of our faith, who for the joy set before him endured the cross, scorning its shame, and sat down at the right hand of the throne of God. Consider him who endured such opposition from sinful men, so that you will not grow weary and lose heart (He.12:1-3).**
>
> **"Praise be to the LORD, who has given rest to his people Israel just as he promised. Not one word has failed of all the good promises he gave through his servant Moses (1 K.8:56).**

3 (105:12-15) **Remember God's strong protection.**
Abraham and his family faced many potential dangers as they journeyed in search of the promised land. All the while, though, God protected them, keeping the people of

---

2 Derek Kidner. *Psalms 73-150*, p.408.

other nations from doing them harm. Similarly, the remnant that returned to Jerusalem after the Babylonian captivity feared enemy attack. The psalmist encouraged them by reminding them of God's strong protection of their ancestors.

a. He protected Abraham and his followers as they began to seek the promised land (vv.12ᵇ-13).

Abraham and his followers were also few in number, but God protected them as they began to seek the promised land (v.12). Keep in mind that neither Abraham nor his followers knew their destination, but they believed and trusted the LORD. So, as they followed God's leading, they journeyed from nation to nation (v.13). Being strangers or foreigners and few in number as well, they were extremely vulnerable.

b. He protected them from all oppressors and even kings: Because they were His chosen people and His prophets (messengers) (vv.14-15).

God protected Abraham's group from all who would oppress them and do them wrong. To *oppress them* (ashaq) can mean to deceive, defraud, or exploit; to forcibly rob; or to commit violence against. God even rebuked kings who could have harmed them, even when Abraham was less than completely honest with them (v.14). Pharaoh and Abimelech, king of Gerar, are examples of this (Ge.12:14-20; 20:1-7). These faith-filled pilgrims were God's anointed or chosen people; and Abraham, their leader, was a prophet of God (v.15; 20:7). Therefore, God would not allow the kings or any others who dwelled in the land to *touch* (nagah) them, lay a hand on them, strike them, or sexually assault them.

Thought 1. Like Abraham and his followers, we too face potential dangers as we journey toward heaven, dangers such as...

- being injured or killed while travelling—car wrecks, plane crashes, etc.
- being robbed
- being violently attacked
- being physically or sexually abused
- being exploited or taken advantage of financially
- being injured or killed in war or in a war-torn country
- being persecuted or even slain for our faith

The list of potential dangers is endless. Realistically, danger can occur in nearly every area of life, from the forces of nature to the forces of evil, from an innocent accident to the wicked deeds of the heart, and so on. As we grow ever closer to our Lord's return, Scripture warns that people will become increasingly fierce, and we will live in the midst of perilous times (2 Ti.3:1-5). We must not, however, allow fear to control us or fall into its strangling grip. Instead, we need

to trust in God's love and power to protect us and to see us through whatever danger threatens us. We also need to make every effort to be ruled by a sound mind and not by irrational, fear-filled thinking (2 Ti.1:7). Being filled with God's Spirit will give us peace in perilous times (Ga.5:22). We can rest in the knowledge that God will fulfill His purpose for our lives, and He will protect us according to His will for us (2 Ti.4:18). Like Paul, we need to surrender to whatever will glorify God the most, realizing that the Lord might be magnified more through our suffering or dying than through our living (Ph.1:20).

> **That is why I am suffering as I am. Yet I am not ashamed, because I know whom I have believed, and am convinced that he is able to guard what I have entrusted to him for that day (2 Ti.1:12).**
>
> **The Lord will rescue me from every evil attack and will bring me safely to his heavenly kingdom. To him be glory for ever and ever. Amen (2 Ti.4:18).**
>
> **Who through faith conquered kingdoms, administered justice, and gained what was promised; who shut the mouths of lions, quenched the fury of the flames, and escaped the edge of the sword; whose weakness was turned to strength; and who became powerful in battle and routed foreign armies (He.11:33-34).**
>
> **It was the LORD our God himself who brought us and our fathers up out of Egypt, from that land of slavery, and performed those great signs before our eyes. He protected us on our entire journey and among all the nations through which we traveled (Jos.24:17).**
>
> **On the twelfth day of the first month we set out from the Ahava Canal to go to Jerusalem. The hand of our God was on us, and he protected us from enemies and bandits along the way (Ezr.8:31).**
>
> **O LORD, you will keep us safe and protect us from such people forever (Ps.12:7).**
>
> **The LORD will keep you from all harm—he will watch over your life (Ps.121:7).**

4 (105:16-25) **Remember God's wonderful care for His people.**

As the psalmist encouraged God's people by recalling the LORD's wonderful works throughout their history, he moved to the story of Joseph (Ge.37-50). God raised Joseph up for a crucial time—a time of deadly famine.

Through Joseph, God demonstrated His wonderful care for His people. God also used Joseph's life to give a clear prophetic picture of Christ: Joseph suffered so that the people might ultimately be saved.

a. God sent famine on the land: Because of the people's sin (v.16).

Pharaoh had a dream in which God warned him that He was going to strike Egypt's food sources for seven long years (Ge.41). And later God did that very thing! He sent a severe famine on the land of Egypt in judgment for the people's sin.

b. God sent a man, Joseph, to prepare a way to deliver them (vv.17-22).

In His providential care, God prepared a way to deliver His people by sending Joseph to Egypt years before the famine struck (v.17). However, Joseph's course to Egypt was not an easy one: he was sold as a slave by his jealous brothers (Ge.37). But God was with him in an unusual way, and he found favor with his Egyptian master, Potiphar. Then, Potiphar's lustful wife tried to seduce Joseph, and the godly young man resisted her advances. Scorned and seeking revenge, Potiphar's wife falsely accused Joseph of sexually assaulting her. As a result, Joseph was jailed by his master (v.18; Ge.39).

While in prison, Joseph helped other prisoners by interpreting their dreams. Joseph's interpretations all came true, proving that God had spoken to and through him (Ge.40). Through a series of providential circumstances, Joseph was brought to the king's attention. After he correctly interpreted Pharaoh's dreams, Egypt's king freed Joseph from prison and placed him directly under him as ruler of the nation (vv.19-21; Ge.41).

Pharaoh set Joseph over everything he had, charging him to protect his possessions and the kingdom from the coming famine (v.21). In addition, Joseph was to oversee the nation's leaders as they tried to preserve Egypt's economy through the famine (v.22). Through Joseph's God-given wisdom, both Egypt and Israel survived the seven-year crisis.

c. God stirred Israel (70 persons) to move to Egypt because of the famine, Ge.46 (vv.23-25).

God continued to work to preserve His people, stirring Israel (Jacob) to move his family to Egypt (the land of Ham) because of the famine (v.23; Ge.46). *The land of Ham* is another name for Egypt. God blessed the Israelites in an unusual way, causing them to multiply quickly. Eventually, Jacob's family of seventy people grew so numerous that Pharaoh perceived them as a threat to Egypt (v.24). The insecure king turned his nation against the Israelites; consequently, the Egyptians treated them as slaves and forced them to do brutal manual labor in the scorching sun (Ex.1:1-14).

Thought 1. The story of Joseph perfectly illustrates God's wonderful care for His people. God was ahead of the famine, and He prepared for the preservation of His people before the famine struck. From the pit to the prison to the palace, God's hand is evident in Joseph's life every step of the way—as is Satan's. The wicked things that happened to Joseph were not caused by God; they were a part of Satan's attempt to destroy God's people and ultimately prevent Christ from ever being born. But God brought good out of the evil intended against Joseph and the Hebrew nation (Ge.50:20). God worked through Joseph's ongoing persecution to position him to save the world—including God's people. Satan's efforts through evil people could not stop God's purposes from being accomplished.

In like fashion, God takes care of us. Although we cannot always see Him, God is always a step ahead of us, preparing the way for our preservation and the accomplishment of His will. We need to remember that God is always present in the circumstances of our lives, as painful and perplexing as they may be. We can be encouraged in difficult times by knowing that He is there, silently working all things together for our good. He loves us so much that He did not spare His own Son from the cross. With this in mind, we can be absolutely sure that He will care for us in the valleys and the dark times of our lives. Nothing can separate us from His conquering love (Ro.8:28-39).

> **If that is how God clothes the grass of the field, which is here today and tomorrow is thrown into the fire, will he not much more clothe you, O you of little faith? So do not worry, saying, 'What shall we eat?' or 'What shall we drink?' or 'What shall we wear?' For the pagans run after all these things, and your heavenly Father knows that you need them. But seek first his kingdom and his righteousness, and all these things will be given to you as well (Mt.6:30-33).**

> **And we know that in all things God works for the good of those who love him, who have been called according to his purpose (Ro.8:28).**

> **Who shall separate us from the love of Christ? Shall trouble or hardship or persecution or famine or nakedness or danger or sword? As it is written: "For your sake we face death all day long; we are considered as sheep to be slaughtered." No, in all these things we are more than conquerors through him who loved us. For I am convinced that neither death nor life, neither angels nor demons, neither the present nor the future,**

nor any powers, neither height nor depth, nor anything else in all creation, will be able to separate us from the love of God that is in Christ Jesus our Lord (Ro.8:35-39).

Cast all your anxiety on him because he cares for you (1 Pe.5:7).

But God sent me ahead of you to preserve for you a remnant on earth and to save your lives by a great deliverance (Ge.45:7).

Yet I am poor and needy; may the Lord think of me. You are my help and my deliverer; O my God, do not delay (Ps.40:17).

5 (105:26-36) Remember God's judgments.

The LORD saw His dear people as they labored under the oppressive Egyptian bondage. They cried out in distress, and the LORD heard their cries (Ex.2:23-25). He remembered His covenant with Abraham, Isaac, and Jacob, and He sent them a deliverer. God set His people free, and in the process, He sharply judged their oppressors.

a. The executioners of God's judgment: Moses and Aaron (v.26).

The LORD sent Moses to deliver the Israelites and called his brother, Aaron, to help him (Ex.3-4). Not only would they lead God's people out of bondage, but they would also be the executioners of God's judgment on the Egyptians. They were the human agents through whom God carried out His wrath on the nation that had so long tortured His chosen people.

b. The judgments: They were miraculous but terrifying warnings to all the wicked and disobedient of the earth (vv.27-36).

Moses and Aaron obediently performed God's signs and wonders before Pharaoh and the land of Egypt (v.27). These signs were the ten plagues that God inflicted on the Egyptian oppressors (Ex.7-12). The plagues were miraculous, but they were also terrifying and, in the end, deadly. God's fierce judgment on Egypt should serve as a warning to all the wicked and disobedient of the earth: there is danger in opposing God's plan and in oppressing His people. The psalmist recited the dreadful plagues through which God judged Egypt:

➢ A frightening darkness due to Egypt's rebellion against God's command to set His people free (v.28; Ex.10:21-23). This was actually the ninth plague, but the psalmist mentioned it first.

➢ A pollution of all the waters and the destruction of the fishing industry (v.29; Ex.7:17-25).

➢ An infestation of frogs that overran Egypt's land and households (v.30; Ex.8:1-11).

➢ A plague of maddening flies and lice or gnats that swarmed throughout the land (v.31; Ex.8:16-24).

➢ A season of destructive hail and frightening storms that ruined the fruit industry along with the forests and lumber industry (vv.32-33; Ex.9:18-26).

➢ An invasion of locusts and grasshoppers that ate all the green vegetation, destroying Egypt's farming industry and food supply (vv.34-35; Ex.10:4-15).

➢ The striking down of the eldest son of every family (v.36; Ex.11:1-11; 12:29-30). God had given Egypt nine previous opportunities to obey Him before sending this drastic judgment. It was the tragic consequence of their continued rebellion against God and His command.

Thought 1. Persecution is advancing against believers throughout our world at an alarming rate. Oppressive governments and religious fanatics are leading the charge against those who serve Jesus Christ. This should not surprise us: our Lord warned us that we would face persecution. It will only worsen as we approach the return of Christ and the end of this age. In his vision of things to come, John foresaw a great host who will be slain for the Word of God and their testimony of faith (Re.6:9-11). May the steadfast faith of the martyred apostles, the early Christians, and the millions who have laid down their lives for Christ through the centuries inspire us to be faithful until death as well!

John saw this martyred host in heaven crying out for God to judge their persecutors and avenge their blood (Re.6:10). Every persecuted believer can be encouraged by God's judgment on the Egyptians. God will righteously judge every single individual who oppresses His people. Jesus promised that God will avenge His people in His time, challenging us to be faithful until He comes (Lu.18:7-8).

Furthermore, all who dare rise up against Israel should be warned by God's judgment on Egypt. God promised Abraham that He would curse those who curse him and his descendants (He.12:3). Throughout history, the LORD has proven Himself true to His Word, eventually bringing down those who oppressed His chosen people. Those who are alive now or yet to be born who oppress God's people can be certain of this: they too will stand before God in judgment in His time.

And will not God bring about justice for his chosen ones, who cry out to him day and night? Will he keep putting them off? (Lu.18:7).

When they hurled their insults at him, he did not retaliate; when he suffered, he made no threats. Instead, he entrusted himself to him who judges justly (1 Pe.2:23).

And give relief to you who are troubled, and to us as well. This will happen when the Lord Jesus is revealed from heaven in blazing fire with his powerful angels. He will punish those who do not know God and do not obey the gospel of our Lord Jesus (2 Th.1:7-8).

And I saw the dead, great and small, standing before the throne, and books were opened. Another book was opened, which is the book of life. The dead were judged according to what they had done as recorded in the books (Re.20:12).

Far be it from you to do such a thing—to kill the righteous with the wicked, treating the righteous and the wicked alike. Far be it from you! Will not the Judge of all the earth do right?" (Ge.18:25).

Those who oppose the LORD will be shattered. He will thunder against them from heaven; the LORD will judge the ends of the earth. "He will give strength to his king and exalt the horn of his anointed" (1 S.2:10).

6 (105:37-41) Remember God's redemption.

The psalmist reminded the remnant that God had successfully delivered His people from Egypt. And He had protected and provided for them all along their journey. Remembering God's redemption would strengthen them for the trying times in which they lived.

a. He saved and set His people free (vv.37-38).

The LORD faithfully saved His chosen people and set them free from Egyptian bondage. When God's full judgment fell upon the terrified Egyptians, they quickly sent the Israelites on their way. They even gave the Israelites provisions for their journey along with silver and gold because of their oppression down through the years—a form of restitution (v.37a; Ex.3:21-22; 11:1-3; 12:29-36). As the enslaved people hastily fled from their taskmasters, the LORD continuously strengthened them for their rigorous journey. Not one of the Israelites grew weak or faltered along the way (v.37b).

God's purpose for His people had been accomplished: His intense judgments had at last struck enough fear in the Egyptians to make them willing, and even glad, to release the Israelites (v.38). But at what a price! Their stubborn rebellion against God had cost them nearly everything they had—most tragically, their firstborn sons.

b. He led and protected His people both day and night (v.39).

As the Israelites embarked on their journey, God led and protected them along the way (v.39). His cloud went before them during the day, and His fire lit their way at night. The cloud and the fire were symbols of God's glorious presence with His people. Not only did they serve to guide God's people in their journey, but they also protected them from the Egyptians who pursued them (Ex.13:21-22; 14:19-20; Ps.78:14).

c. He provided nourishment for His people (vv.40-41).

As God's people traveled toward the promised land, the LORD provided their nourishment (Ex.13:1-16). When they asked for food, He directed quail to fly their way (v.40a; Ps.78:26-29). Every morning, He faithfully sent the bread of heaven, a fresh supply of sweet manna that was more than enough to satisfy their hunger (v.40b; Ps.78:24-25). He also provided life-giving water for them in the dry places along the way, causing water to miraculously gush out of a rock (v.41; Ps.78:15-16; Ex.17:1-7). The water was so abundant that it flowed like a river.

Thought 1. When we are struggling or discouraged, we need to remember God's great work of redemption in our lives. Through the riches of His grace and the blood of His Son, the Lord Jesus Christ, we have been saved and set free from the bondage of sin (Ep.1:7; Ro.6:22-23). Like the children of Israel, He has set us on a journey to the land that He has promised—heaven itself. And, like their journey, ours is not always easy.

Thankfully, we do not travel alone: God has promised that His presence will be with us every step of the way (He.13:5-6). He will lead, protect, and provide for us daily. We need not be afraid, and we need not worry. Our Lord has instructed us to focus on God's kingdom. When we live for Him, He will care for our every need until He takes us to our heavenly home (Mt.6:25-33; Ph.4:19).

"Praise be to the Lord, the God of Israel, because he has come and has redeemed his people (Lu.1:68).

In him we have redemption through his blood, the forgiveness of sins, in accordance with the riches of God's grace (Ep.1:7).

Who gave himself for us to redeem us from all wickedness and to purify for himself a people that are his very own, eager to do what is good (Tit.2:14).

"In your unfailing love you will lead the people you have redeemed. In your strength you will guide them to your holy dwelling (Ex.15:13).

And who is like your people Israel—the one nation on earth that God went out to redeem as a people for himself, and to make a name for himself, and to perform great and awesome wonders by driving out nations and their gods from before your people, whom you redeemed from Egypt? (2 S.7:23).

He provided redemption for his people; he ordained his covenant forever—holy and awesome is his name (Ps.111:9).

7 (105:42-45) **Remember God's faithfulness in keeping His sacred promise.**

As he neared the end of this divinely-inspired song, the psalmist revealed his purpose for taking God's struggling people on a journey through their past: to remind them of God's faithfulness in keeping His sacred promise (v.42). The LORD made a covenant with Abraham, and He had never forgotten His vow to the man who trusted Him enough to leave everything behind and follow Him by faith (Ro.4:20-21).

a. He brought His people out of the wilderness (after 40 years) and filled them with joy and rejoicing (v.43).

The psalmist reminded the discouraged remnant that God had always remained faithful to their forefathers in spite of their failures. After all that God had done for them in miraculously delivering them from Egypt, the Israelites did not trust Him enough to enter the promised land. Therefore, God disciplined them by requiring them to wander in the wilderness for forty years. But after these forty years had ended, God brought His people out of the wilderness, filling them with joy and rejoicing. This example surely resonated with the faithful remnant, for God had brought them out of Babylon at the end of seventy years of His discipline on their unfaithful nation.

b. He gave His people their promised inheritance: Lands that pagans had owned and toiled for (v.44).

God kept His Word by giving His people the inheritance He had promised them: the land of Canaan. Lands that pagans had owned and toiled for became theirs, all in fulfillment of the LORD's promise to Abraham. In like manner, God had returned the present generation of faithful Israelites back to Jerusalem, just as He had promised.

c. He did everything for one reason: So His people would obey His laws and praise Him (v.45).

God had a special reason behind everything He did for the Israelites: He wanted a people who would sincere-

ly trust, worship, and serve Him and obey His laws. Of all the peoples of the earth, God selected the descendants of faithful Abraham to be His peculiar treasure, His unique, special people (Ex.19:5; Ps.135:4). All of His wonderful works in their behalf were performed to win the full devotion of their hearts: to stir them to love Him enough to follow and obey His Word.

Realizing God's favor on Israel and remembering all He had done for them led the psalmist to call for the only appropriate response from His people: *Praise the LORD!*

Thought 1. As Abraham's spiritual seed, we can be assured that the LORD will keep His promises to us, just as He has been faithful to His covenant with Abraham's physical seed, the Jews. Like them, we can expect to suffer affliction as we walk through life. We will also face trials and temptations. And when we disobey God, He will discipline us as our loving Father. Others of us will be persecuted because of our faith in Christ. And all of us will have to make difficult choices whether or not to obey God, choices that may require us to make great sacrifices. Some will have to choose between Christ and their families. Others will have to choose between Christ and their homes and possessions. Still others will have to choose between Christ and their jobs, businesses, or careers. Sadly, some will have to choose between Christ and their lives, actually facing martyrdom.

When we are struggling or discouraged, we need to hold fast to God's faithfulness to His people. He will not fail us, even when we fail Him (2 Ti.2:13). When we accepted His offer of salvation through faith in His Son, we entered into a covenant with Him. He is the LORD—*Yahweh, Jehovah*—the God who keeps His covenant. He will never forsake us. His love for us is steadfast and unfailing. We are the recipients of His favor, mercy, and grace. We are His peculiar people, a chosen generation, a holy nation (1 Pe.2:9; Tit.2:14). God will do all that He has promised. He will preserve us in life and ultimately transport us to His heavenly kingdom, where we will live with Him eternally (2 Ti.4:18). *Praise the LORD!*

God, who has called you into fellowship with his Son Jesus Christ our Lord, is faithful (1 Co.1:9).

Being confident of this, that he who began a good work in you will carry it on to completion until the day of Christ Jesus (Ph.1:6).

Let us hold unswervingly to the hope we profess, for he who promised is faithful (He.10:23).

So then, those who suffer according to God's will should commit themselves to their faithful Creator and continue to do good (1 Pe.4:19).

"Now I am about to go the way of all the earth. You know with all your heart and soul that not one of all the good promises the LORD your God gave you has failed. Every promise has been fulfilled; not one has failed (Jos.23:14).

"Praise be to the LORD, who has given rest to his people Israel just as he promised. Not one word has failed of all the good promises he gave through his servant Moses (1 K.8:56).

"'The days are coming,' declares the LORD, 'when I will fulfill the gracious promise I made to the house of Israel and to the house of Judah (Je.33:14).

PSALM 106

When You Are Guilty of Forgetting God & Backsliding into Sin, 106:1-48

1. Praise & give thanks to the LORD
   a. Bc. He is good
      1) His love for you will never end
      2) His mighty acts & the praise due Him can never be fully understood or declared
   b. Bc. all who treat others justly & live righteously will be blessed

2. Ask God not to forget you when He delivers His people
   a. Bc. you need His help: You need to be rescued as well
   b. Bc. you want to be one of His followers: You want to share in His people's prosperity & joy (His inheritance) & praise Him with them

3. Confess your sins: Humbly acknowledge that you are guilty even as your forefathers (the Israelites) were, guilty of…
   a. Rebellion—ignoring & forgetting God, Ex.14:10-31
      1) Israel's sin: When fleeing Egypt & facing the Red Sea, they feared the pursuing army, forgot God, & rebelled against Moses (God's servant)
      2) God's deliverance: He heard their cry & rescued them, to demonstrate His mighty power
         • He rolled back the Red Sea & led His people through the dried path
         • He saved His people from the pursuing army by letting the water loose, drowning the soldiers in the sea
      3) Israel's renewed belief in God's promises: They praised Him
   b. Impatience & uncontrolled desires, Ex.15:22-27; ch.16; Nu. 11:4-15, 31-35
      1) Israel's sin: In the wilderness, they murmured & craved former pleasures, putting God to the test
      2) God's judgment: He gave them their desires but sent a plague among them
   c. Jealousy & stirring up trouble among God's people
      1) Israel's sin: Some were envious of Moses & Aaron

Praise the LORD. Give thanks to the LORD, for he is good; his love endures forever.
2 Who can proclaim the mighty acts of the LORD or fully declare his praise?
3 Blessed are they who maintain justice, who constantly do what is right.
4 Remember me, O LORD, when you show favor to your people, come to my aid when you save them,
5 That I may enjoy the prosperity of your chosen ones, that I may share in the joy of your nation and join your inheritance in giving praise.
6 We have sinned, even as our fathers did; we have done wrong and acted wickedly.
7 When our fathers were in Egypt, they gave no thought to your miracles; they did not remember your many kindnesses, and they rebelled by the sea, the Red Sea.
8 Yet he saved them for his name's sake, to make his mighty power known.
9 He rebuked the Red Sea, and it dried up; he led them through the depths as through a desert.
10 He saved them from the hand of the foe; from the hand of the enemy he redeemed them.
11 The waters covered their adversaries; not one of them survived.
12 Then they believed his promises and sang his praise.
13 But they soon forgot what he had done and did not wait for his counsel.
14 In the desert they gave in to their craving; in the wasteland they put God to the test.
15 So he gave them what they asked for, but sent a wasting disease upon them.
16 In the camp they grew envious of Moses and of Aaron, who was consecrated to the LORD.

17 The earth opened up and swallowed Dathan; it buried the company of Abiram.
18 Fire blazed among their followers; a flame consumed the wicked.
19 At Horeb they made a calf and worshiped an idol cast from metal.
20 They exchanged their Glory for an image of a bull, which eats grass.
21 They forgot the God who saved them, who had done great things in Egypt,
22 Miracles in the land of Ham and awesome deeds by the Red Sea.
23 So he said he would destroy them—had not Moses, his chosen one, stood in the breach before him to keep his wrath from destroying them.
24 Then they despised the pleasant land; they did not believe his promise.
25 They grumbled in their tents and did not obey the LORD.
26 So he swore to them with uplifted hand that he would make them fall in the desert,
27 Make their descendants fall among the nations and scatter them throughout the lands.
28 They yoked themselves to the Baal of Peor and ate sacrifices offered to lifeless gods;
29 They provoked the LORD to anger by their wicked deeds, and a plague broke out among them.
30 But Phinehas stood up and intervened, and the plague was checked.
31 This was credited to him as righteousness for endless generations to come.
32 By the waters of Meribah they angered the LORD, and trouble came to Moses because of them;
33 For they rebelled against the Spirit of God, and rash words came from Moses' lips.
34 They did not destroy the peoples as the LORD had commanded them,
35 But they mingled with the nations and adopted their customs.
36 They worshiped their

2) God's judgment, Nu.16–17
   • An earthquake swallowed the rebel leaders

   • Fire consumed their followers

d. Idolatry—worshipping the world's so-called gods instead of the only living & true God
   1) Israel's sin, Ex.32
      • They traded the glorious God for an image of an ox
      • They forgot that God was their Savior, that He had miraculously delivered them from Egyptian slavery & led them across the Red Sea
   2) God's judgment
      • He was ready to destroy the people but Moses interceded, Ex.32
      • He had mercy: A picture of Christ's intercession, He.7:25
e. Unbelief, grumbling, & disobedience
   1) Israel's sin, Nu.13–14
      • Did not trust God's word
      • Grumbled over hardship
      • Disobeyed God's charge to enter the promised land
   2) God's judgment
      • He would destroy them in the wilderness

      • He would scatter & exile succeeding generations throughout the nations

f. Evil associations & immorality
   1) Israel's sin: They participated in the false worship & sinful lifestyle of unbelievers
   2) God's judgment: He sent a deadly plague to strike them, Nu.25; see Nu.22–24

   3) Phinehas' faith & stand against Israel's wickedness
      • God stopped the plague
      • God assured him that he & his descendants would be accepted by God
g. Rebellion—caused others to sin
   1) Israel's sin, Nu.20:1-13
      • Grumbled bc. of no water
      • Provoked Moses to sin
      • Rebelled against God
   2) Moses' disobedience: Angrily struck the rock instead of speaking to it
h. Defiance & sinful compromise
   1) Israel's sin, Nu.33:50-56
      • Did not destroy or drive out all enemies as ordered
      • Chose to mingle with them

• Adopted their evil ways • Worshipped their false gods, leading to their great fall, Ex.20:3-6 • Sacrificed their children to demons: They murdered their own sons & daughters for Canaan's lifeless idols & desecrated the land with their blood • Defiled themselves: Were guilty of spiritual adultery by turning away from the LORD to false gods 2) God's judgment • He was so angered by His people's adultery that He detested them • He abandoned them: Allowed their enemies to oppress & rule over them	idols, which became a snare to them. 37 They sacrificed their sons and their daughters to demons. 38 They shed innocent blood, the blood of their sons and daughters, whom they sacrificed to the idols of Canaan, and the land was desecrated by their blood. 39 They defiled themselves by what they did; by their deeds they prostituted themselves. 40 Therefore the LORD was angry with his people and abhorred his inheritance. 41 He handed them over to the nations, and their foes ruled over them. 42 Their enemies oppressed them and subjected them to their power.	43 Many times he delivered them, but they were bent on rebellion and they wasted away in their sin. 44 But he took note of their distress when he heard their cry; 45 For their sake he remembered his covenant and out of his great love he relented. 46 He caused them to be pitied by all who held them captive. 47 Save us, O LORD our God, and gather us from the nations, that we may give thanks to your holy name and glory in your praise. 48 Praise be to the LORD, the God of Israel, from everlasting to everlasting. Let all the people say, "Amen!" Praise the LORD.	**4. Grasp God's great love & salvation: He repeatedly delivers His people** a. He saved Israel time & again despite her constant failure 1) He saw His people's distress & heard their cries for help 2) He remembered His covenant concerning the promised land & restrained His judgment bc. of His love b. He caused Israel's enslavers & oppressors to pity His people c. He is the "LORD our God" to whom we should all call 1) The Psalmist cried out for the LORD's deliverance, that Israel might praise Him 2) The Psalmist called upon all people to praise the LORD—to praise Him who lives from everlasting to everlasting

PSALM 106

When You Are Guilty of Forgetting God and Backsliding into Sin, 106:1-48

(106:1-48) **Introduction:** it is encouraging to remember that God has recorded His people's failures in His Word along with their victories. For we, too, fail God far too often. In the Old Testament, David is probably the most prominent example of a believer who sorely failed the LORD due to sin. In the New Testament, Peter stands out. We are helped by their stories when we come short, disobey, and fail the LORD.

The history of Israel in the Old Testament is a story of repeated failure. Those failures are summarized in Psalm 106. Psalm 105 and 106 are similar in a number of ways. Both are history lessons. Both are written to the returning remnant from the Babylonian captivity. But they are also different. Psalm 105 addresses the remnant after they returned to the promised land; Psalm 106 addresses them while they are still in Babylon.

The key difference between the psalms is the perspective from which they examine Israel's history:

➤ Psalm 105 reviews Israel's history with a view to God's faithfulness to Israel.
➤ Psalm 106 reviews Israel's history with a view to Israel's unfaithfulness to God.

At its core, however, the theme of Psalm 106 is God's faithfulness to His people. It proclaims the encouraging truth that God's unfailing love overcomes our failures. Both a psalm of encouragement and a psalm of instruction, this is, *When You Are Guilty of Forgetting God and Backsliding into Sin, 106:1-48.*

1. Praise and give thanks to the LORD (vv.1-3).
2. Ask God not to forget you when He delivers His people (vv.4-5).

3. Confess your sins: Humbly acknowledge that you are guilty even as your forefathers (the Israelites) were, guilty of... (vv.6-42).
4. Grasp God's great love and salvation: He repeatedly delivers His people (vv.43-48).

1 (106:1-3) **Praise and give thanks to the LORD.**
As the psalmist prepared to point out the sins of his nation throughout her history, he stated his purpose for writing the psalm: he was writing to praise and thank the LORD for His everlasting mercy toward His people. Time and again, Israel had been unfaithful to God. Yet in spite of her many failures, God had always been faithful to His chosen people.

a. Because He is good (vv.1-2).
The psalmist declared the goodness of God toward humanity. Our sins and failures do not change God's nature. He is good even to those who reject Him, even seeking to bring them to repentance (Ro.2:4; Mt.5:44-45).

God's goodness to His people is seen through His faithful, *unfailing love* (chesed), His mercy (v.1). In addition, His love for us will never end. In His righteousness, God judged His unfaithful people by allowing their enemies to invade them and take them captive. But in His unfailing, covenant love, He brought them home again. His everlasting mercy prevailed over His nation's sin.

Throughout Israel's history, God had also demonstrated His goodness through His mighty acts (v.2). The extent of the LORD's powerful deeds in His people's behalf could never be fully conveyed or understood, nor could His people ever praise Him enough for the great things He had done for them.

b. Because all who treat others justly and live righteously will be blessed (v.3).

Because God is perfectly just and righteous, He is the champion of the oppressed. In His time, He judges all who abuse, persecute, or mistreat others. On the other hand, He blesses all who keep or honor justice (judgment) and who live righteously, according to God's commands. "If Israel had done this, she would have never gone into exile."[1] As the remnant rebuilt their society, they needed to keep this truth ever before them.

Thought 1. Psalm 106 begins with the word that is the same in every language: *Praise* (halal) *the* LORD (Yah)—Hallelujah! We should praise the LORD daily and give thanks for His...

- *goodness* (v.1). Every day of our lives, God showers His blessings on us. He does many good things for us as a routine part of our lives. Too often, we are all guilty of failing to recognize and acknowledge His faithful acts of lovingkindness.
- *unfailing love* (v.1). No matter how many times we may fail Him, the LORD never gives up on us. Every morning, His mercies are new (Lam.3:22-23). Nothing can separate us from His conquering love (Ro.8:35-39).
- *mighty acts* (v.2). In addition to God's everyday blessings, occasionally He does something unusual for us, something out of the ordinary, something spectacular and, at times, miraculous. God can do far beyond what our finite minds can imagine, so on occasion, He releases His mighty power for our benefit (Ep.3:20).
- *blessing* (v.3). He rewards us when we live righteously. Because the LORD is just, He will not forget our efforts to love others and obey His commandments (He.6:10).

> And again, "Praise the Lord, all you Gentiles, and sing praises to him, all you peoples" (Ro.15:11).
>
> Through Jesus, therefore, let us continually offer to God a sacrifice of praise—the fruit of lips that confess his name (He.13:15).
>
> Let them give thanks to the LORD for his unfailing love and his wonderful deeds for men (Ps.107:8).
>
> They will celebrate your abundant goodness and joyfully sing of your righteousness (Ps.145:7).

> I will tell of the kindnesses of the LORD, the deeds for which he is to be praised, according to all the LORD has done for us—yes, the many good things he has done for the house of Israel, according to his compassion and many kindnesses (Is.63:7).

2 (106:4-5) Ask God not to forget you when He delivers His people.

The psalmist believed God's wonderful promise, that He would release His people from captivity after seventy years (Je.25:11; 29:10). With a deep longing for his homeland, the psalmist asked God not to forget him when He delivered His people.

a. Because you need His help: You need to be rescued as well (v.4).

Knowing that he would never leave Babylon without God's help, the psalmist expressed his longing to be rescued with the people of God. He needed God's help, for he did not want to die in Babylon. Therefore, he prayed that God would let him live long enough and keep him healthy enough to return to the promised land. Sadly, relatively few of the Israelites shared His desire, as only a remnant returned.

b. Because you want to be one of His followers: You want to share in His people's prosperity and joy (His inheritance) and praise Him with them (v.5).

Having spent his life as a stranger in a foreign land, the psalmist dreamed of what it would be like when God's people returned home. He passionately wanted to be among those who followed God back to Jerusalem. He longed to see God's goodness and prosperity fall on His chosen people once again. His homesick heart ached to share in the joy of the faithful—God's inheritance—when they jubilantly glorified God for bringing them back home.

Thought 1. The psalmist yearned to receive every promise that God had given His people. He deeply desired to receive the full measure of God's favor. What a strong example for us to follow! We, too, should have that earnest desire to receive as many of God's blessing or promises as possible.

We need to remember that many of God's promises are conditional; they depend on whether or not we are faithful. Since we cannot be faithful without God's help, we ought to ask for God's help daily, lest we become unfaithful to Him and miss His blessings.

First, we should ask God to help make us holy. God's richest blessings are promised to those who separate themselves from sin and walk in righteousness (2 Co.6:16-18; He.12:14). Then, we ought to ask God to help us become strong in faith and patient in

---

1 Donald Williams. *Psalms 73-150*, p.254.

trials. It is through faith and patience that we inherit God's promises (He.6:11-12).

Christ came to give us abundant life (Jn.10:10). As we walk in Him, we can have the fullness of His joy and blessings, all of which are promised to those who faithfully follow Him.

> Therefore, since the promise of entering his rest still stands, let us be careful that none of you be found to have fallen short of it (He.4:1).
>
> God is not unjust; he will not forget your work and the love you have shown him as you have helped his people and continue to help them. We want each of you to show this same diligence to the very end, in order to make your hope sure. We do not want you to become lazy, but to imitate those who through faith and patience inherit what has been promised (He.6:10-12).
>
> So do not throw away your confidence; it will be richly rewarded. You need to persevere so that when you have done the will of God, you will receive what he has promised. For in just a very little while, "He who is coming will come and will not delay. But my righteous one will live by faith. And if he shrinks back, I will not be pleased with him" (He.10:35-38).
>
> Cry out, "Save us, O God our Savior; gather us and deliver us from the nations, that we may give thanks to your holy name, that we may glory in your praise" (1 Chr.16:35).
>
> Though I am lowly and despised, I do not forget your precepts (Ps.119:141).
>
> O LORD, be gracious to us; we long for you. Be our strength every morning, our salvation in time of distress (Is.33:2).

3 (106:6-42) **Confess your sins: Humbly acknowledge that you are guilty even as your forefathers (the Israelites) were, guilty of...**

From Babylon, the psalmist reflected on the sins of his people through the centuries. As he traced the failures of his forefathers, he confessed the sins of his generation, humbly acknowledging that they too were guilty, just as their ancestors had been (v.6).

a. Rebellion—ignoring and forgetting God, Ex.14:10-31 (vv.7-12).

Even as the LORD was delivering the Israelites from Egypt, their rebellious hearts were exposed. When fleeing Egypt and facing the Red Sea, the people feared Pharaoh's pursuing army and rebelled against Moses,

God's chosen servant (v.7; Ex.14:9-12). They ignored the wondrous work God was doing for them, and they forgot His multitude of mercies, the abundant acts of grace He was showering on them out of His unfailing, covenant love.

Still, the LORD delivered His people. In spite of their faithless murmuring, He heard their fearful cry and rescued them, demonstrating His mighty power (v.8). The psalmist noted that the LORD saved them for His name's sake—to prove Himself faithful to His covenant.

In one of the greatest miracles of the Old Testament, God spectacularly rolled back the Red Sea and led His people across on a dried path (v.9). "He rebuked the Red Sea" suggests that God parted the mighty waters by the power of His Word, calling forth a strong wind that blew back the billows and dried the sea bed (Ex.14:21). "Through the depths" describes the walls of water that towered on either side of the people as they safely crossed on dry ground (Ex.14:22). When Pharaoh's army pursued them, the LORD caused these walls to collapse, letting the waters loose and drowning the soldiers in the sea. As the psalmist noted, not one of them survived (vv.10-11).

The LORD's mighty miracle renewed Israel's belief in God's promises (v.12). With fresh faith they sang the LORD's praises, declaring that He was their strength and their salvation (Ex.15).

b. Impatience and uncontrolled desires, Ex.15:22-27; ch.16; Nu.11:4-15, 31-35 (vv.13-15).

Sadly, the Israelites' confidence in the LORD was short-lived. Just three days after the miracle at the Rea Sea, their faithless hearts emerged again when they could not find water in the wilderness (Ex.15:22-27). How quickly they forgot what God had done for them! As they plodded on through the wilderness, they repeatedly complained, bluntly stating that they should never have left Egypt. Impatient and unable to control their desires, the Hebrews murmured and craved the pleasures they had enjoyed there, putting the LORD to the test (vv.13-14; Ex.16; Nu.11:4-15).

The LORD responded by giving the Israelites what they wanted, but not without consequence. He judged them for their impatience and unbelief by sending a deadly plague that claimed many lives (Nu.11:31-35).

c. Jealousy and stirring up trouble among God's people (vv.16-18).

As he journeyed on through Israel's sinful history, the psalmist mentioned the people's jealousy and divisiveness. Some of them stirred up trouble in the camp because they were envious of Moses and also of Aaron, as the saint of the LORD—a reference to his role as a consecrated priest (v.16; Nu.16:1-3). But God judged these people swiftly for their sin. Immediately thereafter, the earth opened up—perhaps due to an earthquake—and swallowed the leaders of the rebellion (v.17; Nu.16:32-34). Then, God sent a fire that consumed two hundred and fifty of their followers (v.18; Nu.16:35).

d. Idolatry—worshipping the world's so-called gods instead of the only living and true God (vv.19-23).
Shockingly, the Israelites' unbelief and discontent only worsened, progressing to idolatry. They worshipped the so-called gods of the world instead of the only living and true God. The psalmist recalled how they made themselves a golden calf to worship, trading the glorious God for the image of an ox or bull (vv.19-20; Ex.32). Tragically, they forgot that God was their Savior. They completely overlooked his amazing works in the land of Ham and how He had miraculously delivered them from Egyptian slavery, leading them across the Red Sea. The land of Ham is another name for Egypt. (vv.21-22).

After everything the LORD had done for them, the people's idolatry ignited His fury. He was ready to destroy them, but Moses interceded. Instead, God had mercy on them and changed His mind (Ex.32:7-14). Moses' appeal to God on behalf of the sinful people is a picture of Christ's intercessory work for us. Because of His sacrifice at Calvary, God's wrath toward our sin is appeased (He.7:25-27).

e. Unbelief, grumbling, and disobedience (vv.24-27).
The Israelites refused to be satisfied with God's presence and provision, so they persisted in their unbelief, grumbling, and disobedience. And because they did not trust God's Word, they would not listen to His voice (v.24). They complained about the hardships they faced and disobeyed God's charge to enter the promised land (v.25).

Once again, God judged His people for their disobedience and unbelief. The LORD lifted up His hand or made an oath, signifying that His judgment was final. He would not change His mind (Ps.95:11; He.3:11). Because they did not trust Him enough to obey, the rebellious generation of Jews would perish in the wilderness. They would never enter the promised land (v.26; Nu.13, 14). If future generations followed their unbelieving ways, they would be scattered and exiled throughout the nations (v.27; De.28:63-64; Le.26:33).

f. Evil associations and immorality (vv.28-31).
Continuing through the list of Israel's failures, the psalmist came to their evil associations and immorality. The people sinned grievously by participating in the false worship and sinful lifestyle of unbelievers, committing fornication with the women of Moab (v.28; Nu.25:1-3; Ho.9:10). *Baal of Peor* was "a Moabite deity worshipped on the summit of Mt. Peor with immoral rites."[2]

As expected, the Israelites' wickedness provoked God's fierce wrath (v.29). He judged them by sending a deadly plague that ultimately struck 24,000 Jews. But Phinehas, a priest, took a stand against this wickedness. One of the vulgar men of Israel brazenly brought a woman from Midian to the tabernacle—directly before Moses and the congregation of Israel as they mourned over God's judgment! Out of zeal for God's holiness, Phinehas himself slayed the blasphemous man and the pagan, immoral woman. As a result, God's wrath was appeased and He stopped the plague (v.30; Nu.25:4-9).

Because of Phinehas' fearless stand, the LORD richly blessed him and his descendants. The godly priest's bold faith was counted to him for righteousness, leaving a shining testimony for all future generations (v.31). In addition, God made him the next High Priest, and for generations to come, the High Priest would come from Phineas' descendants (Nu.25:10-13).

g. Rebellion—caused others to sin (vv.32-33).
The faithless Israelites' ongoing rebellion provoked others to sin. After years of repeated failures in the wilderness, the people continued to complain to Moses and blamed him for bringing them out of Egypt. In Meribah, where God had previously brought forth water out of the rock, they grumbled again because of no water. Their never-ending rebellion against God angered the LORD and provoked Moses to sin (v.32). Out of sheer frustration, Moses spoke rashly and disobeyed the LORD. Instead of speaking to the rock as God had commanded, he angrily struck the rock, bringing God's judgment upon himself (Nu.20:1-13).

h. Defiance and sinful compromise (vv.34-42).
Lastly, the psalmist noted Israel's defiance towards God's commands. They compromised by refusing to drive out all enemies from the land as the LORD had ordered (v.34; Jud.1:21-36). Instead, they chose to mingle with the sinful heathen. Then, the mingling led to their adopting the heathens' evil ways (v.35; Jud.2, 3). This compromise resulted in their violating God's first commandment: they actually worshiped the pagan gods of their foreign friends (v.36; Ex.20:3-6). The pagan idols became a snare to them, leading to their great fall.

Eventually, the idolatrous Israelites followed all of the pagans' customs, including sacrificing their own children to devils or demons. Out of the depravity of their hearts, they murdered their own sons and daughters for Canaan's lifeless idols, thereby desecrating the land with their innocent blood (vv.37-38; De.32:17; Le.18:24-28).

In worshipping these worthless idols, the Israelites grossly defiled themselves. Even worse, by turning away from the LORD to the false gods, they were guilty of spiritual adultery (v.39; Ho.2:2-20).

---

2   Merrill F. Unger, R.K. Harrison, ed. *The New Unger's Bible Dictionary.* WORD*search* CROSS e-book.

God was so angered by His people's idolatry—their adultery against Him—that He detested them (v.40). He gave them over to the heathen, allowing their enemies to oppress and rule over them (vv.41-42; Jud.2). For over one hundred years, the Israelites were the servants of their enemies in their own land, as recorded throughout the book of *Judges*.

Thought 1. The New Testament teaches that Israel's sinful failures are preserved in God's inspired Word as an example for us—an example of what *not* to do (1 Co.10:1-13). In other words, we are to learn from Israel's mistakes so we will not follow in their unfaithful footsteps. Like Israel, we are subject to fail God at any time. We need to recognize our tendency and capacity to sin, clearly identifying the specific sins that tempt us so easily (He.12:1). We need to stay close to the LORD at all times and avoid everything that could possibly tempt us to disobey Him.

To some degree, we all have a tendency to see others' sins and to overlook our own. Nevertheless, like the psalmist, we need to readily acknowledge our own sinfulness and freely confess our sins to the LORD. If we sincerely confess, God will have mercy and forgive us (Pr.28:13; 1 Jn.1:9). Therefore, we should ask God daily to search us through and through so we might become aware of anything in our lives that displeases Him (Ps.139:23-24). And when His Spirit convicts us of sin, we need to confess it immediately and seek God's strength to overcome it.

> **Come near to God and he will come near to you. Wash your hands, you sinners, and purify your hearts, you double-minded. Grieve, mourn and wail. Change your laughter to mourning and your joy to gloom. Humble yourselves before the Lord, and he will lift you up (Js.4:8-10).**
>
> **If we confess our sins, he is faithful and just and will forgive us our sins and purify us from all unrighteousness (1 Jn.1:9).**
>
> **"But if they will confess their sins and the sins of their fathers—their treachery against me and their hostility toward me, which made me hostile toward them so that I sent them into the land of their enemies—then when their uncircumcised hearts are humbled and they pay for their sin, I will remember my covenant with Jacob and my covenant with Isaac and my covenant with Abraham, and I will remember the land (Le.26:40-42).**
>
> **He who conceals his sins does not prosper, but whoever confesses and renounces them finds mercy (Pr.28:13).**

> **Only acknowledge your guilt—you have rebelled against the LORD your God, you have scattered your favors to foreign gods under every spreading tree, and have not obeyed me,'" declares the LORD (Je.3:13).**

4 (106:43-48) **Grasp God's great love and salvation: He repeatedly delivers His people.**
The book of *Judges* is a record of the never-ending failure of God's people. The sin cycle repeats itself throughout the book (Jud.2:11-23):
- ➢ Israel rebels against the LORD.
- ➢ The LORD allows Israel to be overtaken by her enemies.
- ➢ Israel cries out to the LORD and repents.
- ➢ The LORD delivers Israel and restores her to His favor.

The psalmist pointed the captive Israelites back to *Judges* to remind them that God repeatedly delivers His people. He wanted them to be filled with hope that their time in Babylon would soon end. God would keep His promise to deliver them, and they would return to the promised land.

a. He saved Israel time and again despite her constant failure (vv.43-45).
Despite the nation's constant failure, the LORD saved Israel time and again (v.43). When the people cried out to the LORD, He saw their distress and heard their cries for help (v.44; Jud.3:9; 4:3; 6:7; 10:10). He remembered His covenant with them and restrained His judgment because of His abundant mercies (v.45).

b. He caused Israel's enslavers and oppressors to pity His people (v.46).
To accomplish His purpose, the LORD changed the hearts of Israel's oppressors toward His people. Whereas they had been filled with aggression and hatred for the Jews, God caused them to feel pity toward His repentant nation.

c. He is the "LORD our God" to whom we should all call (vv.47-48).
Through reviewing Israel's sin-stained history, the psalmist had established God's faithful love for His people. Professing the LORD—the One who keeps His covenant—as His people's God, he concluded by calling for the LORD's deliverance once again (v.47). He asked God to gather the scattered Jews just as He had promised, that they might exalt His holy name and glory in His praise.

Like each of the other four books of *Psalms, Book IV* ends with a doxology—an outburst of praise to God. The psalmist called upon all people to bless the LORD, Israel's merciful, faithful God. He declared that the

LORD lives from everlasting to everlasting, leading the people to voice their agreement by exclaiming, *Amen*—it is true, let it be so. Filled with thankfulness and hope, the psalmist closed with a shout to the LORD:

Praise (halal) *the* LORD (Yah)—Hallelujah!

Thought 1. The LORD faithfully keeps us, in spite of ourselves. We are not kept by our own goodness, but by the power of God (1 Pe.1:5; Jude 24). When we genuinely repent and trust Christ for salvation, we enter into a covenant with God. Just as God faithfully kept His covenant with Israel—in spite of their repeated failures—He will keep His covenant with us.

God's unfailing love is greater than our sin. His grace abounds over our sin (Ro.5:20-21). This does not mean that we can freely continue to sin. Genuine believers cannot live in habitual sin without facing God's severe discipline (Ro.6; He.12:5-11; 1 Co.11:30-33). The seal of God's Holy Spirit on a genuine believer causes him or her to seek to overcome sin (2 Ti.2:19; 1 Jn.3:9-10).

Until we are wholly transformed into the image of Christ, we will battle our sin nature. At times, we will fail the LORD. When we fail, we need to grasp the full measure of God's boundless love. We need to know without any doubt whatsoever that, when we repent, He will forgive and restore us to fellowship with Him (Ep.3:17-19; 1 Jn.1:9).

> **Who shall separate us from the love of Christ? Shall trouble or hardship or persecution or famine or nakedness or danger or sword? As it is written: "For your sake we face death all day long; we are considered as sheep to be slaughtered." No, in all these things we are more than conquerors through him who loved us. For I am convinced that neither death nor life, neither angels nor demons, neither the present nor the future, nor any powers, neither height nor depth, nor anything else in all creation, will be able to separate us from the love of God that is in Christ Jesus our Lord. (Ro.8:35-39).**

> **But because of his great love for us, God, who is rich in mercy (Ep.2:4).**

> **So that Christ may dwell in your hearts through faith. And I pray that you, being rooted and established in love, may have power, together with all the saints, to grasp how wide and long and high and deep is the love of Christ, and to know this love that surpasses knowledge—that you may be filled to the measure of all the fullness of God (Ep.3:17-19).**

> **For the sake of his great name the LORD will not reject his people, because the LORD was pleased to make you his own (1 S.12:22).**

> **The LORD appeared to us in the past, saying: "I have loved you with an everlasting love; I have drawn you with loving-kindness (Je.31:3).**

PSALMS II
OUTLINE & SUBJECT INDEX

REMEMBER: When you look up a subject and turn to the Scripture reference, you have not just the Scripture but also an outline and a discussion (commentary) of the Scripture and subject.

This is one of the GREAT FEATURES of *The Preacher's Outline & Sermon Bible®*. Once you have all the volumes, you will have not only what all other Bible indexes give you, that is, a list of all the subjects and their Scripture references, but in addition you will have...

- an outline of every Scripture and subject in the Bible
- a discussion (commentary) on every Scripture and subject
- every subject supported by other Scripture, already written out or cross referenced

DISCOVER THE UNIQUE VALUE for yourself. Quickly glance below to the following subject of the Index:

> **ANGER** (See **JUDGMENT**; **WRATH**)
> God's
>   Against Egypt. 78:49-50
>   Because of sin. 79:5
>   He is slow to **a.** 103:8
>   No one can stand against God's **a.** 76:7
>   Powerful beyond human understanding. 90:11

Turn to the first reference. Glance at the Scripture and the outline, then read the commentary. You will immediately see the TREMENDOUS BENEFIT of the INDEX of *The Preacher's Outline & Sermon Bible®*.

OUTLINE AND SUBJECT INDEX

ABANDONED (See **FORSAKE**)

ABHOR (See **HATE**)

ABUNDANCE
Provided in the land. 68:10

ADULTERY, ADULTERERS
Wicked participate in **a.** 50:18

ADVERSARY (See **ENEMY**)

ADVERSITY (SEE **GRIEF**; **SORROW**; **TRIALS**; **TROUBLE**)

ADVICE (See **COUNSEL**)

AFFLICT, AFFLICTION, AFFLICTED (See **POOR**; **SUFFERING**; **TROUBLE**)
As a youth. 88:15
Confessed to God. 69:29; 70:5
Described. Like a flood. 88:17
Encouragement of the **a.** By praise to God. 69:32
Prayers of the **a.** Heard by God. 69:33

AGE, OLD (See **OLD AGE**)

AGONY, ANGUISH (See **AFFLICTION**; **SUFFERING**)
Causes.
    Betrayal by friend. 55:1-23
    Disgrace and shame. 44:15-16
    Fear of enemies. 44:16; 55:1-5
    Rejection by others. 44:14
    Reproach of neighbors. 44:13
What to do. Share **a.** with God. 77:3-6; 102:3-12

ALIEN (See **STRANGER**)

ALONE (See **LONELY**)

ANGELS
Described.
    Are like a flaming fire. 104:4
    Are spirits. 104:4
    Cannot compare to God. 89:6
    Commanded to praise God. 103:20-21
    Exceptionally strong. 103:20
    Fear God. 89:7
Duties.
    Do God's bidding. 103:20-21; 104:4
    Protect and guide God's people. 68:17; 91:11-12

ANGER (See **JUDGMENT**; **WRATH**)
God's
    Against Egypt. 78:49-50
    Because of sin. 79:5
    He is slow to **a.** 103:8
    No one can stand against God's **a.** 76:7
    Powerful beyond human understanding. 90:11
    Rises like smoke. 74:1
    Turned away in mercy. 78:38

ANIMALS
All **a.** belong to God. 50:9-13
Needs provided by God. 104:11-12, 14, 17-22, 27
People die like **a.** 49:12
People without understanding are like **a.** 49:20

ANOINT, ANOINTED
God **a.** us with fresh oil. 92:10
The King (Christ) **a.** with joy. 45:7

ARM
Symbol of God's power. 77:15; 44:3; 89:10, 13, 21; 98:1

ARROGANT (See **PROUD**)

ASCENSION
Christ's **a.** Pictured. 68:18
God's to Mt. Zion. 68:18

ASHAMED (See **SHAME**)

ASSOCIATIONS
Whom to avoid.
    Slanderers. 101:5
    The deceitful. 101:7
    The perverse. 101:4.
Whom to seek or chose.
    The blameless. 101:6
    The trustworthy. 101:6

ASSURANCE (See **CONFIDENT**)

ATHEIST, ATHEISM
God's appraisal of. 53:1

ATONE, ATONEMENT (See **FORGIVENESS**)
Praise for **a.** 65:3
Prayer for **a.** 79:9

AUTHORITY (**GOD'S**)
Over Israel. 59:13

AVENGE (See **VENGEANCE**)

AWESOME
God is **a.** 47:2

BACKSLIDE, BACKSLIDING, BACKSLIDDEN
Warning against **b.** 85:8
When you are **b.** into sin. 106:1-48

INDEX

BANNER
Given by God to those who fear Him. 60:4
Of the wicked. Set up in the sanctuary. 74:4

BEASTS (See **ANIMALS**)

BEHAVIOR
Commit to wise **b.** 101:2

BETRAY, BETRAYAL
When friends **b.** you. 55:1-23

BIRDS
Find a home in God's presence. 84:3
Provided for by God. 104:12, 17

BITTER, BITTERNESS
Toward God. Because of the prosperity of the wicked. 73:21

BLAMELESS, BLAMELESSLY (See **INTEGRITY**; **RIGHTEOUS**)
Commit to live a **b.** life. 101:2

BLASPHEME, BLASPHEMY
Of God's name. 74:10, 18

BLESSED
Who or what.
    Christ as King. 45:2
    Righteous rulers. 72:15-19
    The earth to bring forth a harvest. 67:6
    The king. 45:2; 72:15-19
    Those who live in God's presence. 84:4-7
    Those who live righteously. 106:3
    Those who praise/worship God. 89:15
    Those who treat others justly. 106:3
    Those who trust in God. 84:12
    Those whom God disciplines. 94:12-13
    Those whose strength is in God. 84:5

BLESSING
Received.
    By living in God's presence. 65:4; 84:4-7
    Through praise and worship of God. 67:5-7

BLOODY, BLOODTHIRSTY (See **VIOLENT**)

BOAST
B. in God alone. 44:8

BOLD, BOLDNESS
In prayer. 61:6

BOW (See **WEAPONS**)

BRIDE
Of Christ. Depicted. 45:10-15

BRIDEGROOM
Christ as **b.** 45:10-17

BRUTISH (See **STUPID**)

BROKEN, BROKENNESS
Causes
    Defeat by enemies. 44:194
    God's chastening. 51:8
Of spirit. Desired by God (repentance). 51:17

BUCKLER (See **SHIELD**)

BURDEN
Borne by the LORD. 68:19
Cast your **b.** on the LORD. 55:22

CAPTIVITY
Of Babylon.
    Prayer for deliverance. 106:4-5, 47
    Return from.85:1; 102:13, 19-23

CARE, CARES (See **BURDEN**)

CHALLENGE, CHALLENGES
How to face life's **c.** 71:1-24

CHARIOT, CHARIOTS
God's.
    Number in the tens of thousands. 68:17
    The clouds are God's **c.** 104:3

CHASTEN, CHASTENING (See **DISCIPLINE**)
Brings brokenness. 51:8

CHILD, CHILDREN
Israel's. Sacrificed to idols. 106:37-38
Of God's servants. Continue before them. 102:28
To be taught lessons of the past. 78:4-8

CHRIST
As a victorious Warrior. 45:3-5
As Israel's Savior. 80:17-19
As King. 45:1-17; 68:24-28; 80:17-19
As Ruler.
    Proclaimed. 45:6-9
    Pictured. 72:1-20
As shepherd. Pictured. 78:70-72
As the Anointed One. 84:9
As the exalted Bridegroom. 45:10-17
As the fulfillment of Davidic Covenant. 89:3-4
As the ideal Man. 45:1-2
His mockery. Pictured. 89:51
Kingdom of. 45:6-7; 67:3-7; 68:18
Pictured. By David. 78:70-72
Prophecies.
    Given gall and vinegar on the cross. 69:21
    His ascension. 47:5
    Will bring peace to the nations. 65:7
Second coming.
    Pictured. 68:24-28
    Prophesied. 98:9

CLEAVE, CLING
To God. 63:8

CLEAN, CLEANSE (See **FORGIVE**; **PURE**)
Only God can **c.** 51:7

CLOUDS
Used by God.
    As His chariot. 104:3
    To guide Israel. 99:7; 105:39
    To protect Israel. 105:39

COMFORT (See **ENCOURAGEMENT**; **STRENGTH**)
In anxiety. 94:19
In life's troubles. 71:21
Sought but not found. 69:20; 77:2
Source.
    God's help. 86:17
    God's presence. 84:6
When you need **c.** 91:1-16

COMMANDMENTS
Keep God's **c.** 78:7

COMMIT, COMMITMENT (See **VOWS**)
Renewal of **c.** to God. 51:13-15
To choose the right companions. 101:4-7
To guard your eyes from evil. 101:3
To live wisely and blamelessly. 101:2
To praise God. 61:8; 101:1
To uphold righteousness and justice. 101:8
To walk in integrity at home. 101:2
To worship and obey God. 66:13-20
When you make a **c.** to the LORD. 101:1-8

COMPANIONS (See **ASSOCIATIONS**; **FRIENDSHIP**)

COMPASSION (See **LOVINGKINDNESS**; **MERCY**)
God's
    Declared. 86:15
    Grants forgiveness. 78:38
    Turns away His anger. 78:38

COMPLAIN (See **MURMUR**)

COMPROMISE
Of Israel. In associating with sinful nations. 106:28-40

CONDEMNATION (See **JUDGMENT**)

CONDUCT (See **BEHAVIOR**)

CONFESS, CONFESSION
Of foolishness and ignorance. 73:22
Of lack of understanding. 73:2-16
Of sin. 51:1-19
Of struggles. 73:2-16
Of the LORD as God. 100:3

CONFIDENT, CONFIDENCE (See **FAITH**; **HOPE**; **SECURITY**; **TRUST**)
In God.
    As judge. 59:8; 54:5; 55:19-23
    Declared. 44:4-8; 65:5; 71:5
    To help and deliver from enemies. 54:4-5; 56:9

INDEX

DOG
Enemies compared to **d.** 59:6, 14-15

DOMINION (See **AUTHORITY**)

DOWNCAST (See **DEPRESSION**; **DESPAIR**)

DOVE
Symbol of God's beloved people. 74:19

DRAGON
Symbol of Egypt. 74:13

DUTY
Regarding public worship. 81:1-16

DWELLING PLACE
The LORD is our **d.** 90:1

EAGLE
God renews our youth like the **e.** 103:5

EARTH (See **LAND**)
Belongs to God. 50:12; 89:11
Called to judgment. 50:1
Created and controlled by God. 74:16-17; 102:25
Established firmly by God. 93:1; 96:10; 104:5
Fears God's judgment. 76:8
Filled with God's glory. 72:19
Filled with violence. 74:20
God exalted in **e.** 46:10; 57:5, 11
God exalted above all the **e.**97:9
God judge of all the **e.** 94:2; 105:7
God's judgment a witness to the **e.** 59:13
Jerusalem is the joy of the **e.**48:2
Made desolate by God. 46:8
New **e.**
Declared. 102:26
Pictured. 72:10
Peace on **e.** In the last days. 46:9
Replenished by God's wisdom. 104:30
Satisfied by God's works. 104:13
Summoned to worship the Lord. 100:1-5
Will rejoice when the Lord comes. 96:11
Will worship God. 66:4

EARTHQUAKE
God's rejection compared to **e.** 60:2

EGYPT
God's deliverance of Israel from **E.**
Commemorated by feasts. 81:5
Declared. 74:13-15; 77:16-20; 78:42-51; 80:8; 81:10; 89:10
Described. 81:6-7; 105:24-38; 106:8-11
Forgotten. 106:13
Marvelous. 78:12-16
God sent Joseph to **e.**105:16-17
Plagues upon. 78:43-50; 105:27-36
Referred to as land of Ham. 105:23, 27; 106:22
Referred to as Raha**b.** 89:10
Smiting of the firstborn. 78:51; 105:36

ENCOURAGE, ENCOURAGEMENT (See **COMFORT**; **STRENGTH**)
Of the afflicted. By praise to God. 69:32
When you need **e.** 91:1-16; 92:1-15; 105:1-45

END (See **DESTINY**)

ENDURE, ENDURANCE (See **STEADFAST**)

ENEMY, ENEMIES
Attack, abuse from **e.** 55:3; 56:2-6; 59:3-4; 62:3-4; 83:2-8; 86:14
Caught in their own traps. 57:6; 69:22
Compared.
To dogs. 59:6, 14-15
To lions. 57:4
Deeds.
Hate you without a cause. 69:4
May defeat and plunder you. 44:9-15
Mock you. 79:4; 80:6; 102:8
Oppress the righteous. 42:9-10
Seek to destroy you. 69:4; 86:14
Slander you. 71:10-11
Defeated by God. 44:2-8; 59:10; 60:8, 12; 64:7-8; 76:3; 81:13-15
Deliverance from. 55:18; 57:2-6; 59:1-7; 78:42; 83:9-18; 86:16-17
Destroyed. 63:9-10; 68:23
Fear of **e.**44:16; 55:1-5
God is our refuge against **e.** 61:3
God's.
Blaspheme His name. 74:10, 18
Defeated by Him. 78:65-66; 89:10
Destroyed by Him. 97:3
Destroyed the sanctuary. 74:7-8
Hate Him. 83:2
Join together against Him. 83:5-8
Seek to destroy His people. 83:4
Will be judged by Him. 68:21-23; 74:22-23
Will perish. 92:9
Will submit to Him. 66:3
Israel's. Exalted by God in His judgment on Israel. 89:47
Justly rewarded by God. 54:5
Known by God. 69:19
Persecution by **e.**69:1-36; 83:4
Prayer.
For judgment/justice on **e.**55:9-15; 56:7-9; 59:11-13; 69:22-28; 83:13-18
To be ashamed. 70:2-3; 71:13, 24; 83:16-18
To be scattered. 68:1-2
Protection from **e.**62:3-4; 64:1-6; 91:3
Victory over **e.**44:4-5; 54:7; 59:10; 60:8-12; 64:7-8; 68:21-23; 76:1-13; 92:11
When you feel defeated by **e.** 74:1-23

ENVY, ENVIOUS
Of the wicked. Confessed. 73:3-5

EPHRAIM, TRIBE OF
Example of disobedience to God. 78:9-11
Rejected by God. 78:67

ETERNAL
Life.
Cannot be purchased. 49:7-9
Prayer for. 61:4, 7
Who or what.
God Himself. 90:1-2; 93:2; 102:12; 102:25-27
God's covenant with David. 89:3-4
God's faithfulness. 89:2
God's glory. 104:31
God's judgment of the wicked. 52:5
God's kingdom. 45:6
God's mercy. 89:2
God's rule. 92:8

EVIL (See **WICKED**)
Command. Stay away from all **e.**101:4
Hatred of. By those who love God. 97:10
Love of. 52:3
When **e.** forces seem to win. 93:1-5

EVILDOERS (See **WICKED**)
Deliverance from. 59:2
Despised by God. 53:5
Fear God's judgment. 53:5
Have no knowledge (never learn). 53:4
Persecute God's people. 53:4
Will not call on God. 53:4

EXALT (See **PRAISE**)

EXHAUST, EXHAUSTION
Cause. Crying out for help. 69:3

EXTORTION
Stems from trusting in wealth. 62:10

EYES
Guard your **e.** from evil. 101:3

FACE (See **COUNTENANCE**; **PRESENCE**)
God's.
Hidden. 44:24; 51:9
Symbol of His favor. 80:3, 7, 19

FAIL, FAILURE
When you **f.** 85:1-13

FAITH
When your **f.** is challenged. 62:1-12

FAITHFUL, FAITHFULNESS (See **TRUTH**)
Choose **f.** companions. 101:6
God's.
Declared. 89:8; 98:3
Delivers us from enemies. 57:3
Is eternal. 89:2; 100:5
Protects His people. 61:7
Reaches the skies. 57:10
To be praised. 71:22; 92:2
To His people. 105:8-45
To justice. 54:5
To reward us according to our works. 62:12
In suffering. 44:22
Rewards of the **f.** Showered by God's love. 103:17-18

FAMILY (See CHILDREN; FATHER; HOUSE)
May forsake you. 88:8, 15
May turn against you because of your devotion to God. 69:8-9
Of the righteous. Showered by God's love. 103:17

FAMINE
God's provision for His people in f. 105:16-17

FASTING
May bring reproach. 69:10

FATE (See DESTINY)

FATHER (See FAMILY)
God as F. Pities His children. 103:13-14

FATHERLESS (See ORPHANS)

FAVOR (See GRACE)
God's.
Deliverance from enemies a sign of f. 86:17
In giving the promised land. 44:3
On His land/people. 85:1; 106:4
Prayer for. 67:1-2; 80;3, 7, 19; 90:17

FEAR
Command. Do not f. 91:5-7
Of death. 55:4
Of enemies. 44:16; 55:1-5; 64:1
Of God.
Brings a great heritage. 61:5
Brings great mercy. 103:11
Brings His blessing/gifts. 85:9-12
By the nations. 102:15-17
Commanded. 76:7, 11; 96:4, 9
Prayer to f. God wholeheartedly. 86:11
Through His awesome works. 65:8
Through His blessings. 67:7
Wicked do not f. God. 55:19
Of righteous rulers. 72:5
Of the wealthy. 49:16
Of trouble from the wicked. 49:5
Victory over.
By trusting God. 56:3-4
Through God's strength. 46:2

FEASTS, FESTIVALS
Purpose. To commemorate God's deliverance from Egypt. 81:3-5

FIRE
Symbol.
Of God's anger. 78:21
Of God's judgment. 80:16; 83:14
Used by God.
In judgment. 78:63
To destroy His enemies. 97:3
To guide Israel. 78:14; 105:39
To protect Israel. 105:39

FLATTER, FLATTERY
From deceitful enemies. 62:4
Sign of insecurity. 78:36

FLEE
Desire to f. expressed. 55:6-8

FOLLOW
God. By clinging to Him. 63:8

FOOLS, FOOLISH, FOOLISHNESS
Confessed to God. 73:22
Described. Do not understand God's truth. 92:6
Known by God. 69:5
Warned by God. 75:4-5; 94:8-11
Who or what.
Atheists. 53:1
Blasphemers. 74:18

FOREIGNER (See STRANGER)

FORGET, FORGETTING, FORGOTTEN
Command. Do not f. God's benefits. 103:2
God. Warning. 50:22
God's deliverance. 78:41-51
God's works. 78:7, 11; 106:7, 13
When you feel f. by God. 88:5

FORGIVE, FORGIVEN, FORGIVENESS
Declared. 103:3
God is ready to f. 86:5
Granted.
Because of God's compassion. 78:38
Because of God's mercy. 85:2
Of Israel. Declared. 99:8
Praise for. 65:3
Prayer for. 51:1-19; 79:9

FORSAKE, FORSAKEN
By friends or loved ones. 88:8, 15
God will not f. His people. 94:14
Prayer. That God not f. you in old age. 71:9, 18
When you feel f. by God. 42:9; 74:1-23; 88:5, 14; 102:10

FORTRESS (See PROTECTION; REFUGE)

FRIEND, FRIENDS, FRIENDSHIP
Forsaken by f. 88:8, 15
When you are betrayed by f. 55:1-23

FRUITFUL, FRUITFULNESS
Of God's people in Egypt. 105:2
Of the righteous in old age. 92:14-15

GENERATION, GENERATIONS
Former g. Sins of. 79:8
God's covenant extends to 1000 g. 105:8
God's mercies proclaimed by all g. 106:12
Testimony preserved for many g. 61:6
Witness to future g.
Of God's faithfulness. 89:1
Of God's power. 71:18; 78:4
Of God's praises. 78:4; 79:13
Of God's protection. 48:12-13
Of God's works. 78:4

GIFT, GIFTS
From God. To those who fear Him. 85:8-12

GLAD, GLADNESS (See JOY)

GLORIFY
God.
For defeating enemies. 83:18
For deliverance from trouble. 50:15
For His great power. 66:2-3
For His judgment of the wicked. 64:10
Through praise. 50:23; 105:3

GLORY
Given by God. 84:11
Of the king (Christ). 45:3
The eternal destination of God's people. 73:24
To be given to God. 96:7-8

GLORY, OF GOD
Dwells in the promised land. 85:9
Empowers His people. 89:17
Fills the earth. 72:19
Is eternal. 104:31
Is more majestic than the mountains. 76:4
Needed by His people. 80:1
Revealed.
Through the heavens. 97:6
Through worship. 63:2
Shamed. By the sin of His people. 79:9-12
To be declared among the nations. 96:3

GOD MOST HIGH
57:2; 92:1, 8

GOD OF HOSTS
59:5; 80:4,7, 14, 19; 84:1, 3, 8, 12; 89:8; 69:6

GOD OF JACOB
46:7; 94:7; 75:9; 76:6; 81:1,4; 84:8

GODLY, GODLINESS (See RIGHTEOUS)

GOLD
Of Ophir. 45:9

GOOD, GOODNESS
Who or what. God's name. 52:9; 54:6
God's.
Crowns the year. 65:11
Declared. 86:5; 100:5
Gratitude for. 65:1-13
Provides for the poor. 68:10
Seven benefits. 103:2-5

GOSSIP (See LIES; SLANDER)

GRACE, GRACIOUS (See FAVOR)
Given by God. 84:11
God's. Declared. 86:15; 103:8
Of the king's (Christ's) speech. 45:2

INDEX

GRASS
Given by God to provide for cattle. 104:14
Symbol.
Of declining health. 102:4, 11
Of life's brevity. 90:5-6; 103:15-16
Wicked compared to **g.** 92:7

GRATEFUL, GRATITUDE
For God's goodness. What you should do. 65:1-13

GRAVE (See **DEATH**)

GREAT, GREATNESS
God's.
Beyond compare. 77:13-14
Declared. 48:1; 77:13; 86:10; 95:3; 96:4; 99:2; 104:1
Seen in His creation. 104:1-9
Who or what.
God as King. 47:2; 48:2; 95:3
God's mercy. 57:10; 86:13; 103:11
God's name. 99:3
God's works. 71:19; 92:5; 106:21

GRIEF
Described. Unbearable. 88:9
God's. Over His people's rebellion. 78:40

GUIDE, GUIDANCE
David's **g.** as king.
Skillful. 78:72
With integrity. 78:72
God's.
By His counsel (Word) 73:24
Continues until death. 48:14
Given through His light. 97:11
Goes before His people. 68:7-18
In bringing His people out of Egypt. 78:14, 52-54
Of Israel's leaders. 99:7
Prayer for **g.** 43:3

GUILT, GUILTY
Of sin.
Acknowledge **g.** before God. 105:6-7
Deliverance from. 51:14
Is overwhelming. 51:3; 65:3

HAND (See **RIGHT HAND**)
Command.
Clap in praise to God. 47:1
Lift in praise to God. 62:4
God's.
Controls the earth. 95:4-5
Gives victory. 98:1
Is filled with righteousness. 48:10
Provides good things of life. 104:28
Upholds us. 63:8

HAPPY (See **BLESSED**)

HATE, HATRED
Enemies **h.** you without a cause. 69:4
Of evil. By all who love God. 97:10
Of God. By His enemies. 83:2

HEAL, HEALING
God's. Declared. 103:3

HEART
Broken.
By reproach. 69:20
By suffering. 102:4
Clean.
Created by God. 51:10
Receives God's goodness. 72:1
Grieved. By the prosperity of the wicked. 73:21
Of rejoicing. In God's name. 105:3
Of the faithful. Is steadfast in troubles. 57:7
Of the wicked.
Corrupt. Loves evil. 51:3
Cunning and completely evil. 64:6
Perfect. 101:2
Pour your **h.** out to God. 62:8
Pure. Will fear God. 86:11
Repentant. Desired by God. 51:17
Secrets of. Known by God. 44:21
Warning. Do not harden your **h.** 95:8-11

HEATHEN (See **NATIONS**)

HEAVEN, HEAVENS
Belong to God. 89:11
Created by God. 102:25
Declare God's righteousness and glory. 97:6
God sends help from **h.** 57:3
God's presence is **h.** 73:25
H. praise God. 89:5-6
Judgment from h.76:8
New **h.**
Declared. 102:26
Pictured. 72:16
Pictured. 71:21
By Jerusalem. 48:1-14
By the Promised Land. 47:4; 60:6; 69:35-36
Stretched out by God. 104:2
Will rejoice when the Lord comes. 96:11

HELP, HELPER
God is our **h.** 54:4; 60:11; 63:7; 70:5
God's.
Cry out for. 77:1; 88:13
Needed quickly. 70:1, 5; 71:12
Sent from heaven. 57:3
Supplied. 86:17; 94:17-19
When you need God's **h.** 54:1-7
When you receive God's **h.** 66:1-20
Of man. Is worthless. 60:11

HERITAGE (See **DESCENDENTS; INHERITANCE**)
Promised. To all who fear God. 61:6

HISTORY
Learn and pass on truths from **h.** 78:1-72

HOLY, HOLINESS (OF GOD)
Declared. 99:5, 9
God speaks in **h.** 60:6
Of God's name. 99:3; 103:1; 105:3

Seen.
In His house (reign). 93:5
In His throne. 47:8
In Jerusalem. 48:1
Worship in God's **h.** 96:9

HOLY ONE (See **CHRIST**)

HOME (See **HOUSE**)

HONEST, HONESTY (See **INTEGRITY**)

HONOR
Comes from God. 62:7

HOPE (See **FAITH; TRUST; WAIT**)
God is our **h.** 65:5; 71:5
In God.
When you are depressed. 42:5, 11; 43:5
For rest and security. 62:5
For salvation. 62:1, 6
When attacked by enemies. 71:14

HORN
Symbol.
Of power. 92:10
Of pride and rebellion. 75:4-5, 10

HOUSE (See **FAMILY**)
Walk with integrity in your **h.** 101:2

HOUSE, GOD'S (See **PRESENCE, GOD'S; SANCTUARY; TABERNACLE; TEMPLE**)
Approach with praise. 42:4
Described.
Eternal. 93:5
Holy. 93:5
Devotion to. 69:9
Longed for. 42:4; 84:1-12
Service in. Better than wealth and recognition. 84:10
Those faithful to God's **h.** will flourish. 92:12-15

HUMAN, HUMANS, HUMANITY (See **MAN**)
H. nature. Known by God. 103:14-16

HUMBLE, HUMILITY
In confession of sin. 106:6-7

IDOLS, IDOLATRY
Described.
All man-made gods are **i.** 96:5
I. cannot do great works like God. 86:8
Will worship God. 97:7
God is exalted above all **i.** 97:9
Of Israel.
Declared. 78:58; 106:19-22, 36-39
Judged. 78:59-64; 106:23
Warning against. 81:9
Worshippers.
Known by God. 44:20-21
Will be shamed. 97:7

IMMORAL, IMMORALITY
Of Israel. 106:28-31

INDEX

INHERIT, INHERITANCE
God's.
His people. 68:9; 74:2; 78:62, 71; 79:1; 94:14; 106:5, 40
The nations. 82:8
Of God's people. Chosen by God. 47:4

INIQUITY (See **SIN**)

INJUSTICE
Cause. Corrupt rulers. 57:2

INNOCENT
Unjustly attacked by enemies. 59:3-4

INSTRUCT, INSTRUCTION (See **TEACH**)
Hated by the wicked. 50:17
Refused by corrupt rulers. 58:5

INSTRUMENTS
Harp. 43:4; 71:22; 98:5
Trumpet. 98:6
Used in worship/praise. 43:4; 68:25; 71:22; 81:2; 92:3; 98:5-6

INTEGRITY
At home. 101:2
Of David. 78:72

ISRAEL (See **PEOPLE, GOD'S**)

JEALOUS, JEALOUSY
God's.
Against His people's sin. 79:5
Because of idolatry. 78:58

JERUSALEM
Citizens of J. (heaven)
All who know God. 87:4-5
From other nations. 87:4-5
Love Jerusalem. 106:14
Registered by God. 87:6
Rejoice in God's judgment. 97:8
Will praise God. 87:6
Described.
Beautiful. 48:2
City of God. 46:4; 48:1,8; 87:3
Loved by God. 87:2
Specially chosen by God. 78:68-69; 82:1
The envy of other nations. 68:16
The joy of the whole earth. 48:2
Destroyed by enemies. 79:1, 7
Exalts God's greatness. 99:2
Glorious things spoken of J. 87:3-4
God is praised in J. 65:1; 102:21
God's presence in J.
Gives protection. 46:4-5; 48:3-8
Location of His tabernacle. 76:2
Makes J. holy. 48:1
Where God dwells. 74:2
Kings will give tribute to God in J. 68:29
Picture of heavenly capital of new heaven and earth. 87:1-7
Prayer for. Prosperity and protection. 51:18
Salvation comes out of J. 53:6
Will be saved by God. 69:35

JOY, JOYFUL
Command.
Praise God with **j.** 62:5; 66:1; 81:1; 95:1-2
Make a **j.** noise. 95:1-2; 98:4; 100:1; 66:1; 81:1
Serve God with **j.** 100:2
Of Israel. When corrupt rulers are judged. 58:10
Of the earth. Jerusalem. 48:2
Of the righteous. Declared. 97:11
Oil of **j.** 45:7
Restored. By forgiveness. 51:8; 12
Source.
God. 43:4
God's justice. 67:4
God's unfailing love. 90:14-15
God's works. 92:5

JUDAH, TRIBE OF
As the lawgiver: seat of authority. 60:7
Chosen.
For God's sanctuary. 78:69
To bring salvation to the world. 78:68

JUDGE, JUDGES (See **RULERS**)
Corrupt.
Because of partiality. 82:2
Condemned. 82:5-8
Described. God's representatives. 82:6
God as **j.** 67:4; 68:5; 72:2,4; 50:6; 75:7; 82:1,8; 94:2; 96:10, 13; 98:9
What **j.** should know. 82:1-8

JUDGMENT
God's.
A witness to the world. 59:13; 83:18
At His appointed time. 75:2
Delayed. 74:10-11
Escaped by the righteous. 90:8
For the oppressed. 103:6
Is just and righteous. 51:4; 96:10, 13; 98:9
Makes the earth desolate. 42:8
Of enemies. 55:15; 56:7; 69:22-28; 70:2-3; 79:6, 12; 83:13-18
Of Israel in the wilderness. 78:21-22, 31-34; 106:15-33
Of Israel's idolatry. 78:59-64
Of Israel's rejection of His covenant. 89:38-45
Of Israel's sins. 79:5; 80:12-13
Of the nations. 59:5, 8
Of the wicked. 55:23; 64:7-10; 91:8; 94:10, 11
Prepare for coming **j.** 50:1-23
Promised. 50:21
Provokes fear. 76:8
Reason for praise. 75:9-10; 76:10
Reason for rejoicing. 48:11; 97:8
Stirs people to repent. 78:34-35
Three purposes. 76:9-10
To be remembered. 105:5
Your focus in light of **j.** 75:1-10
Symbols.
Fire. 80:16; 83:14; 89:46
Storm. 85:15

JUST (See **RIGHTEOUS; UPRIGHT**)
Who or what.
Christ as King. 72:1-2
God's judgment. 51:4; 96:10; 99:4

JUSTICE
Commanded. 82:3-4
Corrupted.
By partial judges. 82:2
By wicked rulers. 58:2
God's.
Against the wicked. 94:23
Declared. 99:4
Give thanks for. 75:1
Is executed throughout the earth. 105:7
Is righteous and just. 98:9; 96:10
On corrupt rulers. 58:6-9; 94:23
On enemies. 54:5; 55:9-15; 56:7-9; 59:11-13; 64:8; 68:21-23; 69:22-28; 79:12
Over the nations. 67:4
To be praised. 101:1
Prayer for **j.** 94:1-4
Will one day reign throughout the earth. 94:15; 96:10

KING, KINGS (See **REIGN, OF GOD; RULERS**)
Christ. 45:1-17
Pictured. 68:24-28; 72:1-20
David.
Chosen by God. 89:19-20
God's promises to. 89:21-37
Earthly.
Belong to God and exalt Him. 47:9
Compassionate. 72:12-14
Defeated by God when they come against Jerusalem. 48:4-8
Prayer for. 72:1-20
Righteous. 72:1-7
Will bow to Christ. 72:8-11
Will give tribute to God. 68:29
God.
Gives victory. 44:4
Is great. 95:3; 47:2; 48:2
Israel's **k.** 89:18
Nations will give Him tribute. 68:18, 29
Over all the earth. 72:1-20
Over the nations. 47:8
The eternal **k.** 74:12
Will come in victory. 68:24
Israel's. Rejected God's covenant and brought on His judgment. 89:39-45
Solomon. Prayer for. 72:1-20

KINGDOM
Christ's.
Eternal. 45:6; 89:3-4
Pictured. 67:3-7; 68:18
Righteous. 45:7
David's. Eternal through Christ. 89:3-4, 29, 36-37
God's. Foundations of. 89:14
Rules over all. 103:19

KNOWLEDGE
That the LORD is God. 100:3

INDEX

LABOR (See **WORK**)
Fills all our days. 90:10

LAND, PROMISED (See **EARTH**)
A picture of heaven. 69:35-36
Faithless generation forbidden to enter. 95:11
Favored by God. 85:1
Filled with glory. 85:9
Filled with the violence of the enemy. 74:20
God guided His people to the l. 78:54; 105:39
God provides through the l. 85:12
God settled His people in the l. 68:10-14; 78:55; 80:8
Possession of the l. secured by God. 44:2-3; 69:35; 105:44
Prepared for God's people. 80:9
Promised in God's covenant. 105:9-11
The inheritance of God's people. 47:4; 56:6-7; 69:36; 78:55

LAUGH, LAUGHTER
God's. At those who think He does not hear their evil speech. 59:8

LAW, GOD'S (See **WORD, GOD'S**)
Disobeyed. 78:10
Established in Israel. 78:5
Given at Mt. Sinai 68:8
To be obeyed. 105:45
To worship at appointed times. 81:3-5

LEAD (See **GUIDE**)

LEADERS (See **RULERS**)
When l. are wicked. 94:1-23

LEVIATHAN
104:26; 74:14

LIES, LYING, LIARS
Command. Reject l. 101:6
Of enemies. 62:4
Will be stopped by God. 63:11

LIFE
Brevity of. 90:1-17
70 to 80 years expected. 90:10
Compared to grass. 90:5-6; 103:15-16
Declared. 90:4
Realization of. Gives wisdom. 90:12
To be remembered. 89:47
Described.
Consumed by suffering. 102:3, 11
Filled with labor and trouble. 90:10
Meaningless without God. 84:47
Eternal. Cannot be purchased. 49:7-9
Given by God's Spirit. 104:30
God's guidance promised throughout l. 48:14
God's love is better than l. 63:3
Long l.
Benefit of loving God. 91:16
Prayer for. 102:24
Of the poor. Precious to a righteous ruler. 72:14

Of the saints. Preserved by God. 97:10
Shortened due to illness. 102:23
Success in l. From God's favor. 90:17
Sustained by God through nature. 65:9-13

LIGHT
God is clothed in l. 104:2
Of God. Never seen by the self-sufficient. 49:19
Of God's countenance. 44:3
Of life. 56:13
Prayer for l. 43:3
Received by the righteous. 97:11

LION
Corrupt rulers compared to l. 58:6
Enemies compared to l. 57:4
Provided for by God. 104:21-22
Satan compared to l. 91:13

LONELY, LONELINESS
Cause. Suffering. 106:6-7

LONGSUFFERING (See **PATIENT**)
God's. Declared. 86:15; 103:8-9

LORD OF HOSTS
46:7, 11; 48:8; 84:1, 3, 12

LORD MOST HIGH
47:2

LOVE (See **LOVINGKINDNESS; MERCY**)
For God.
Benefits. 91:14-16
Results in hatred of evil. 97:10
God's
Better than life. 63:3
Declared. 103:8
For Israel. 47:4; 44:3

LOVE, STEADFAST (See **LOVINGKINDNESS; MERCY**)

LOVE, UNFAILING (See **LOVINGKINDNESS; MERCY**)

LOVINGKINDNESS, GOD'S
Basis for forgiveness. 51:2
Declared. 103:4
Described.
Better than life. 63:3
Constant. 42:8
Good. 69:16
Remembered. 48:9
To be proclaimed. 92:2

LOYAL, LOYALTY
To God and His covenant. 44:18

MAJESTY
God's.
Described. 93:1
God is clothed with m. 104:1
Declared. 96:6
The king's. 45:3-4

MAN, MANKIND (See **HUMAN**)
All are sinful and corrupt. 53:3
God observes and examines m. 53:2

MANNA
Provided to God's people. 78:24-25

MEDITATE, MEDITATION (See **THINK, THOUGHTS**)
M. on God at night. 62:6
M. on God is sweet. 104:34
M. on God's works. 77:12

MERCY, GOD'S (See **FAVOR; LOVE; LOVINGKINDNESS,**)
Declared. 103:4, 8
Demonstrated. In repeatedly delivering Israel. 106:43-45
Described.
Eternal. 89:2; 100:5; 103:17; 106:1
Goes before (precedes, leads) us. 59:10
In relation to our sins. 103:8-14
Is abundant. 69:13, 16; 86:5, 15
Is great. 86:13
Not withheld from the righteous. 66:20
Protects His people. 61:7
Reaches to the heavens. 57:10
Sent by God. 57:3; 62:11
Upholds us. 94:18
Prayer for m. 51:1-19; 56:1-13; 57:1-11; 79:8; 85:7; 86:3, 16
Proclaimed. 89:1-2; 101:1
Promised. 85:10; 98:3
Remembered. 85:1-3
Result.
Rejoicing. 90:15
Satisfaction. 90:14
Trust in God's m. 52:8
When you become deeply aware of God's m. 103:1-22

MESSIAH (See **CHRIST**)

MIGHT (See **POWER**)

MILITARY
Of nations. Destroyed by God. 46:9; 76:6

MIRACLES (See **WORKS, OF GOD**)

MOCK, MOCKED, MOCKING (See **PERSECUTE; REPROACH; SCORN**)
By enemies. 79:4; 80:6; 102:8
Of God. By His enemies. 74:10, 18

MONEY (See **WEALTH**)

MORNING
A time for prayer. 55:17; 88:13
A time for worship and praise. 57:8; 59:16

MOUNTAIN, MOUNTAINS
Envy Mt. Zion, where God abides. 68:16
Established by God's power. 65:6

When you feel overwhelmed. 61:1-8
When you sense the brevity and frailty of life. 90:1-17
When you suffer despair. 88:1-18

PRESENCE, GOD'S (See **HOUSE**; **SANCTUARY**; **TABERNACLE**; **TEMPLE**)
Command.
Bring an offering when entering God's **p.** 96:8
Come before God's **p.** with thanksgiving. 95:2
Enter God's **p.** with thanksgiving and praise. 100:4
Seek God's **p.** 105:4
Described.
Dooms the rebellious. 76:5
Feared by creation. 77:16-18
Guides and protects. 84:11
Holy and eternal. 93:5
Radiates honor and majesty. 96:6
Radiates strength and beauty. 96:6
Veiled by clouds. 97:2
In fire and storm. 50:3
In Jerusalem. 46:4; 48:1-3; 74:2; 76:2; 86:1
In perfection and beauty. 50:2
In the time of trouble. 46:1, 7, 11; 91:15
Is near His people. 75:1
Living in God's **p.**
A reward for praising Him. 89:15
Brings great blessings. 65:4; 84:4-7
Brings satisfaction. 65:4
Brings understanding. 73:17-28
Desired. 61:4
Gives encouragement and strength. 91:1
Gives protection. 91:2-14
Is heaven. 73:25
Needed by His people. 80:1
When you seek God's **p.** 63:1-11
When you yearn for God's **p.** 84:8-11

PRESERVE (See **PROTECT**)

PRISONERS (See **OPPRESSED**)
Prayer for. 79:11

PROCLAIM (See **WITNESS**)

PROMISE, PROMISES
God's.
Israel's failure to believe God's **p.** 106:24
Remembered by Him. 98:3; 105:42-45
To David as king. 89:21-37
To deliver Israel from Babylon. 102:13, 19-23
To give Israel the land. 105:9-11
When God's **p.** seem to fail. 89:1-52
To God. (See **VOWS**)

PROMISED LAND (See **LAND**)

PROPHECIES OF CHRIST (See **CHRIST**)

PROSPER, PROSPERITY, PROSPEROUS
Brought by righteous rulers. 72:3, 7, 16
In Christ's kingdom. 72:3, 7, 16
Of God's people. In the land. 80:9-11
Of the wicked. 73:1-28

PROTECT, PROTECTION, GOD'S (See **SECURE**; **SHIELD**; **REFUGE**)
A reward for obedience. 81:13-15
Causes rejoicing. 63:7
Declared. 97:10
From enemies. 62:3-4; 69:29; 91:3
Provided by righteous rulers. 72:4, 13-14
Reason for praise. 61:8; 66:8-9
Since conception and birth. 71:6
Through angels. 68:17; 91:11-12
Through God's mercy and truth. 61:7
Through God's presence.
As a shield. 84:11
In Jerusalem. 46:5; 48:3-8
In shadow of His wings. 57:1
Under His shadow. 91:1-14
Through Joseph. 105:16-23

PROUD, PRIDE
Command. Reject the **p.** 101:5
The wicked are clothed in **p.** 73:6
Warned by God. 75:4-8
Who or what. Enemies. 86:14

PROVIDE, PROVISION, GOD'S
A reward for obedience. 81:16
For His creation.
Orderliness. 104:19-22
Shelter. 104:16-18
Vegetation and food. 104:14-15, 27-28
Water. 104:10-13
For the poor. 68:10
In the famine. Through Joseph. 105:16-24
In the promised land. 68:10
In the wilderness. 68:9; 74:15; 78:15-16, 23-29
Is bountiful. 65:11
Of all of our soul's needs. 63:5
Promised. 81:10
Through nature. 65:9-13
Through the land. 85:12
To those who fear Him. 85:12

PURE, PURIFY, PURIFICATION
A purpose of trials. 66:10
P. heart.
Created by God. 51:10
Receives God's goodness. 73:1

PURPOSE, OF GOD
For your life. Fulfilled by Him. 57:2
In trials. Purification. 66:10

QUESTION, QUESTIONING
Of God. When in trouble. 77:7-9

REBELLION, REBELLIOUS
Doomed by God's presence. 76:5
Grieves God. 78:40

Of Israel against God. 106:7-12, 43; 78:8; 81:11-12; 95:8-11
Warned by God. 75:4-8

REBUKE (See **DISCIPLINE**)

RED SEA
Parting.
An example of God's power. 66:6; 77:16; 106:8
Declared. 78:13, 53
Turned to dry land. 66:6; 106:9

REDEEM, REDEEMED, REDEMPTION (See **SALVATION**)
By God's power. 77:15
Declared. 103:4
From sin. 65:3
Of God's people. 74:2; 105:37-41
Of the soul. Not by wealth. 49:7-8
Praise for **r.** 71:23

REFRESH, REFRESHMENT
In overwhelming trouble. 46:4
Who or what. Righteous rulers. 72:6

REFUGE (See **PROTECTION**)
God is our **r.**
Against corrupt leaders. 94:22
Declared. 56:1,,7,11; 59:9, 16-17; 61:3; 62:2, 7-8; 71:3; 73:28; 90:1; 91:2
In facing life's challenges. 71:6
In the shadow of His wings. 57:1; 61:4
Jerusalem's **r.** 48:3

REIGN, OF GOD
Command. Proclaim to the nations. 96:10
Declared. 93:1-2; 97:1; 99:1
Described.
Eternal. 93:5
Holy. 93:5
Righteous and just. 97:2

REJECT, REJECTED, REJECTION (See **FORSAKE**)
By God.
Described. 60:2-3
What to do. 144:1-26
When you feel **r.** 60:1-12; 77:7-9

REJOICE, REJOICING (See **JOY**)
Causes of.
God's astounding works. 104:34
God's help and protection. 63:7
God's judgment of the wicked. 64:10; 70:4
God's judgments. 48:11
God's name. 89:16
God's righteousness. 89:16
God's victory. 68:2-3
God's wondrous creation. 65:8
Commanded. 94:12; 98:4
Creation will **r.** when the LORD comes. 96:11-13

REMEMBER, REMEMBERED, REMEMBRANCE
By God.
His covenant. 105:8-11, 42; 106:45
Our tears and sorrow. 56:8

INDEX

SECURE, SECURITY (See **PROTECTION**; **REFUGE**; **ROCK**)
Found in God. 62:2, 6-7; 91:2

SEED (See **DESCENDANTS**)

SEEK, SEEKING, SOUGHT
God looks to see who **s.** Him. 53:2
Of God.
    Comes from longing for Him. 63:1
    His strength. 105:4
    In times of trouble. 77:2
    Rejoice in His judgment. 70:4

SELAH
44:8; 46:3, 7, 11; 47:4; 48:8; 49:13, 15;
50:6; 52:3, 5; 54:3; 55:7, 19; 57:3, 6;
59:5, 13; 60:4; 61:4; 62:4, 8; 66:7,
15; 67:1, 4; 68:7, 19, 32; 75:3; 76:3,
9; 77:3, 9, 15; 81:7; 82:2; 83:8; 84:4,
8; 85:2; 87:3, 6; 88:7, 10; 89:4, 37,
45, 48

SELF-SUFFICIENT
Destiny of. 49:13-14, 17-19

SENIOR CITIZENS (See **OLD AGE**)

SENSELESS (See **STUPID**)

SERPENT
Corrupt rulers compared to. 58:4-5
Satan compared to. 91:13

SERVE, SERVANT, SERVICE
David was God's **s.** 78:70; 89:20
Of God.
    Basis for asking for joy. 86:4
    Basis for asking for strength. 86:16
    Basis for asking, for protection.
    86:2
S. God with gladness. 100:2

SHADOW
God's. Place of protection. 57:1; 91:1;
    63:7
Of death. 44:19

SHAME, ASHAMED
Cause.
    Defeat by enemies. 43:10-15; 79:4,
    11; 80:6
    Persecution. 69:7
    Rejection by God. 44:9-15
    Sins of other believers. 69:6
Prayer for enemies to be **a.** 70:2-3;
    71:13, 24; 83:16-18; 86:17

SHEEP
God's people are His **s.** 77:20; 78:52;
    79:13; 80:1; 95:7; 100:3

SHEPHERD
David as Israel's **s.** 78:70-72
God as **s.** 77:20; 78:52; 79:13; 80:1;
    95:7; 100:3

SHELTER (See **PROTECTION**; **REFUGE**)

SHIELD (See **PROTECTION**; **REFUGE**)
God is our **s.** 59:11; 84:9, 11; 89:18

SHIPS OF TARSHISH.
48:7

SIGN
Prayer for a **s.** of God's favor. 86:17

SIN, SINFUL, SINFULNESS
All **s.** is against God. 51:4
Confession of. 51:1-19
Dealt with mercifully by God. 103:8-14
Forgiveness of. 85:2-3; 103:3
Guilt of.
    Deliverance from. 51:14
    Haunts the guilty. 51:3
    Is overwhelming. 51:3; 65:3
Known by God. 69:5; 90:8
Man is **s.** by nature. 51:5; 53:3
Of Israel.
    Confessed. 106:6-39
    Seven sins. 106:7-39
Removed as far as east from west.
    103:12
The wicked participate in **s.** 50:18
Unconfessed. Hinders prayers. 66:18

SING, SINGING, SONG
A new song. 96:1; 98:1
God's praises. 92:1; 95:1-2; 96:2; 98:5-
    6; 104:33
In the midst of danger. 57:7
Of God's glory. 66:2
Of God's justice. 101:1
Of God's mercy. 59:16; 101:1
Of God's power. 59:16; 81:1
Of God's redemption. 71:23
Of God's righteousness. 51:14
Of thanksgiving. 69:30-32
To God among the nations. 57:9;
    105:2

SINNERS
Conversion of. Through teaching.
    51:13
Deserve judgment. 51:4
Haunted by guilt. 51:3
Judgment of. 68:21-23; 104:35

SKY (See **CREATION**; **NATURE**)

SLANDER, SLANDERERS (See **LIES**; **WORDS**)
By enemies. 71:10-11
By the wicked. 50:20
Command. Silence **s.** 101:5
When people **s.** you. 56:1-13

SLEEP
Symbol of death. 90:5

SLEEPLESSNESS
Cause.
    Overwhelming trouble. 77:4
    Suffering. 102:7

SMOKE
A picture of God's anger. 74:1; 68:2

SNAKE (See **SERPENT**)

SNARE (See **TRAP**)

SNOW
Symbol of cleansing of sin. 51:7

SOLOMON
Prayer for **s.** as king. 72:1-20

SORROW (See **AFFLICTION**; **DESPAIR**)
Confessed to God. 69:29
Fills all of our days. 90:10
Remembered by God. 56:8

SOUL (See **LIFE**)
Downcast. 42:6-11; 43:5
Lift up your **s.** to God. 86:4
Plagued by troubles. 88:3
Satisfied by God. 62:5
Thirsts for God. 42:1-2; 62:1

SOVEREIGN, SOVEREIGNTY, GOD'S (See **POWER**)

SPEAK, SPEECH (See **WORDS**)

SPIRIT, GOD'S
Is the source of life. 104:30

SPIRIT, MAN'S
Of obedience to God. 51:12
Of rulers. Broken by God. 76:12
Overwhelmed by trouble. 77:3
Renewed by God. 51:10

STABLE, STABILITY (See **SECURE**)

STATUTES (See **LAW, GOD'S**; **WORD, GOD'S**)

STEADFAST, STEADFASTNESS
In troubles. 57:7

STEAL, STEALING (See **THIEF**)
Stems from trusting in wealth. 62:10

STORM
Symbol of God's judgment. 85:15

STRESS
Cause. The prosperity of the wicked.
    73:14

STRANGER, STRANGERS
God's people were **s.** in the land.
    105:12-13
Oppressed by the wicked. 94:6
To family. Bc. of your devotion to God.
    67:8-9

STRONG, STRENGTH (See **ROCK**)
God's
    Declared. 77:14; 89:17
    Of His presence. 96:6
    Parted the Red Sea. 74:13
    Seek God's **s.** 105:4
Man's.
    Found in God's presence. 84:5
    God's is our **s.** 43:2; 46:1; 59:9, 17;
    71:16; 73:26

INDEX

WISE, WISDOM
Commit to **w.** behavior. 101:2
Concerning wealth and deeds 49:120
Source. Realizing the brevity of life.
90:12
Taught by God. 51:6

WITNESS
Bear **w.** to all the earth. 96:1-13
God's judgment is a **w.** to the world.
59:13
Of God's protection to future genera-
tions. 48:12-13
Of God's works. 73:22; 77:12
Of what God has done for you. 66:16-20
To make God known throughout the
earth. 66:2; 67:2
To sinners. 51:13

WONDERS (See **WORKS, OF GOD**)

WORD, GOD'S (See **LAW, GOD'S**)
Command. Listen to. 85:8
Described.
Brings blessing. 94:12
Given by God. 68:11
Gives guidance. 73:24
Protects from trouble. 94:13
Stands firm. 93:5
Worthy of praise. 56:10
Rejected by the wicked. 50:17

WORDS (See **LIES; SLANDER**)
Evil.
Bring judgment. 59:11-13
By enemies. 59:7
By the wicked. 50:19-20; 52:2-4
Of the wicked.
Destructive. 55:11
Smooth and deceitful. 55:21
Used as weapons. 57:4; 64:3

WORK, WORKS
Of God.
Great. 92:15
Awesome. 65:5; 66:3, 5
Be a witness of. 73:28; 77:12
Bring gladness and joy. 92:4
Cannot by fully declared. 106:2
Cause Him to rejoice. 104:31
Cause people to fear and praise
Him. 65:8
Commanded to praise Him. 103;22
Declare His wisdom. 104:24-30
Declared. 77:14
Forgotten by Israel. 78:7, 11, 42-43;
106:7, 13
In delivering His people. 74:12-15
Incomparable. 86:8
Make the earth desolate. 46:8
Not seen by the dead. 88:10
Performed by Moses and Aaron in
Egypt. 105:27
Reason for giving thanks. 75:1
Remember God's **w.** 77:11-12;
105:5
Revealed to the world. 103:7
Satisfy His creation. 104:13
To be acknowledged. 103:6-17
To be proclaimed. 71:16-17; 96:3;
105:2
To be taught to future generations.
78:4
Witnessed by God's people. 90:16
Wondrous. 72:18; 74:14; 78:4;
86:10; 88:10; 105:5
Of man.
A part of God's orderliness. 104:23
Established by God. 90:17

WORLD (See **CREATION; EARTH**)

WORSHIP
Approved by God. 50:8

Commanded. 95:6; 96:9; 99:5, 9;
100:1-5
Of idols. Forbidden. 81:9
Reveals God's power and glory. 63:2
Universal. 66:4; 86:9
When you gather to **w.** 92:1-15; 95:1-11
Your duty regarding public **w.** 81:1-16
When to **w.**
At scheduled times. 81:3-5
Early in the morning. 57:8; 63:1
When you seek God's presence. 63:2

WORTHLESS
Who or what. Man's help. 60:11

WRATH, GOD'S/CHRIST'S (See **ANGER;**
JUDGMENT; DISCIPLINE)
Against those who forget Him. 50:22
Against your enemies. 56:7; 59:13;
69:24; 79:6-7
Against Israel.
Because of idolatry. 78:59-64
In the wilderness. 78:21-22, 31-34;
95:10-11
Prayer for **w.** to cease. 85:4-5
Withdrawn. 85:3
As discipline. Is overwhelming. 88:7, 15
Described.
Like fire. 89:46
Troubles our lives. 90:7
Stirs the righteous to praise. 76:10
Warning to all people. 75:8

YOUNG, YOUTH
Afflicted as a **y.** 88:15
God teaches us from our **y.** 71:17
Renewed by God. 103:5
Trust God in your **y.** 71:5

ZEAL
For God. Brings persecution. 69:9

ZION (See **JERUSALEM**)

OUTLINE BIBLE RESOURCES

This material, like similar works, has come from imperfect man and is thus susceptible to human error. We are nevertheless grateful to God for both calling us and empowering us through His Holy Spirit to undertake this task. Because of His goodness and grace, *The Preacher's Outline & Sermon Bible*® New Testament and the Old Testament volumes are now complete.

The Minister's Personal Handbook, The Believer's Personal Handbook, and other helpful **Outline Bible Resources** are available in printed form as well as releasing electronically on various software programs.

God has given the strength and stamina to bring us this far. Our confidence is that as we keep our eyes on Him and remain grounded in the undeniable truths of the Word, we will continue to produce other helpful Outline Bible Resources for God's dear servants to use in their Bible Study and discipleship.

We offer this material, first, to Him in whose name we labor and serve and for whose glory it has been produced and, second, to everyone everywhere who studies, preaches, and teaches the Word.

Our daily prayer is that each volume will lead thousands, millions, yes even billions, into a better understanding of the Holy Scriptures and a fuller knowledge of Jesus Christ the Incarnate Word, of whom the Scriptures so faithfully testify.

You will be pleased to know that Leadership Ministries Worldwide partners with Christian organizations, printers, and mission groups around the world to make Outline Bible Resources available and affordable in many countries and foreign languages. It is our goal that *every* leader around the world, both clergy and lay, will be able to understand God's Holy Word and present God's message with more clarity, authority, and understanding—all beyond his or her own power.

LEADERSHIP MINISTRIES WORLDWIDE
P.O. Box 21310 • Chattanooga, TN 37424-0310
(423) 855-2181 FAX (423) 855-8616
info@outlinebible.org
www.outlinebible.org – FREE download materials

LEADERSHIP MINISTRIES WORLDWIDE

Publishers of Outline Bible Resources

- **THE PREACHER'S OUTLINE & SERMON BIBLE® (POSB)** • **KJV – NIV**

NEW TESTAMENT

Matthew 1 (chapters 1–15)
Matthew 2 (chapters 16–28)
Mark
Luke
John
Acts
Romans

1 & 2 Corinthians
Galatians, Ephesians, Philippians, Colossians
1 & 2 Thessalonians, 1 & 2 Timothy, Titus, Philemon
Hebrews, James
1 & 2 Peter, 1, 2, & 3 John, Jude
Revelation
Master Outline & Subject Index

OLD TESTAMENT

Genesis 1 (chapters 1–11)
Genesis 2 (chapters 12–50)
Exodus 1 (chapters 1–18)
Exodus 2 (chapters 19–40)
Leviticus
Numbers
Deuteronomy
Joshua
Judges, Ruth
1 Samuel
2 Samuel

1 Kings
2 Kings
1 Chronicles
2 Chronicles
Ezra, Nehemiah, Esther
Job
Psalms 1 (chapters 1-41)
Psalms 2 (chapters 42-106)
Psalms 3 (chapters 107-150)
Proverbs
Ecclesiastes, Song of Solomon

Isaiah 1 (chapters 1-35)
Isaiah 2 (chapters 36-66)
Jeremiah 1 (chapters 1-29)
Jeremiah 2 (chapters 30-52),
  Lamentations
Ezekiel
Daniel, Hosea
Joel, Amos, Obadiah, Jonah,
  Micah, Nahum
Habakkuk, Zephaniah, Haggai,
  Zechariah, Malachi

Print versions of all Outline Bible Resources are available in various forms.

- **The Preacher's Outline & Sermon Bible New Testament** — **3 Vol. Hardcover** • **KJV – NIV**
- *What the Bible Says to the Believer* — **The Believer's Personal Handbook**
  11 Chs. – Over 500 Subjects, 300 Promises, & 400 Verses Expounded - Italian Imitation Leather or Paperback
- *What the Bible Says to the Minister* — **The Minister's Personal Handbook**
  12 Chs. - 127 Subjects - 400 Verses Expounded - Italian Imitation Leather or Paperback
- **Practical Word Studies In the New Testament** — 2 Vol. Hardcover Set
- **The Teacher's Outline & Study Bible™ - Various New Testament Books**
  Complete 30 - 45 minute lessons – with illustrations and discussion questions
- **Practical Illustrations** — **Companion to the POSB**
  Arranged by topic and Scripture reference
- **What the Bible Says About Series – Various Subjects**
- **OBR on various digital platforms**
  See current digital providers on our website at www.outlinebible.org
- **Non-English Translations of various books**
  See our website for more information or contact our office

— Contact LMW for quantity orders and information —

LEADERSHIP MINISTRIES WORLDWIDE or Your Local Christian Bookstore
PO Box 21310   • Chattanooga, TN 37424-0310
(423) 855-2181 (9am – 5pm Eastern) • FAX (423) 855-8616
E-mail - info@outlinebible.org • Order online at www.outlinebible.org

PURPOSE STATEMENT

LEADERSHIP MINISTRIES WORLDWIDE

exists to equip ministers, teachers, and laymen in their understanding, preaching, and teaching of God's Word by publishing and distributing worldwide *The Preacher's Outline & Sermon Bible*® and related **Outline Bible Resources**; to reach & disciple men, women, boys and girls for Jesus Christ.

MISSION STATEMENT

1. To make the Bible so understandable – its truth so clear and plain – that men and women everywhere, whether teacher or student, preacher or hearer, can grasp its message and receive Jesus Christ as Savior, and...

2. To place the Bible in the hands of all who will preach and teach God's Holy Word, verse by verse, precept by precept, regardless of the individual's ability to purchase it.

The **Outline Bible Resources** have been given to LMW for printing and distribution worldwide at/below cost, by those who remain anonymous. One fact, however, is as true today as it was in the time of Christ:

THE GOSPEL IS FREE, BUT THE COST OF TAKING IT IS NOT

LMW depends on the generous gifts of believers with a heart for Him and a love for the lost. They help pay for the printing, translating, and distributing of **Outline Bible Resources** into the hands of God's servants worldwide, who will present the Gospel message with clarity, authority, and understanding beyond their own.

LMW was incorporated in the state of Tennessee in July 1992 and received IRS 501 (c)(3) non-profit status in March 1994. LMW is an international, nondenominational mission organization. All proceeds from USA sales, along with donations from donor partners, go directly to underwrite translation and distribution projects of **Outline Bible Resources** to preachers, church and lay leaders, and Bible students around the world.